T0281518

# Lecture Notes in Computer Science    13498

## Formal Methods

Subline of Lectures Notes in Computer Science

More information about this series at https://link.springer.com/bookseries/558

Thao Dang · Volker Stolz (Eds.)

# Runtime Verification

22nd International Conference, RV 2022
Tbilisi, Georgia, September 28–30, 2022
Proceedings

*Editors*
Thao Dang ⓘ
CNRS/Verimag
Saint Martin d'Hères, France

Volker Stolz ⓘ
Høgskulen på Vestlandet
Bergen, Norway

ISSN 0302-9743         ISSN 1611-3349   (electronic)
Lecture Notes in Computer Science
ISBN 978-3-031-17195-6         ISBN 978-3-031-17196-3   (eBook)
https://doi.org/10.1007/978-3-031-17196-3

This Springer imprint is published by the registered company Springer Nature Switzerland AG
The registered company address is: Gewerbestrasse 11, 6330 Cham, Switzerland

# Preface

This volume contains the peer-reviewed proceedings of the 22nd International Conference on Runtime Verification (RV 2022), a hybrid event held during September 28–30, 2022. The conference was part of the Computational Logic Autumn Summit (CLAS 2022), running during September 19–30, 2022, on the campus of the Ivane Javakhishvili Tbilisi State University in Tbilisi, Georgia.

The RV series is a sequence of annual meetings that brings together scientists from both academia and industry interested in investigating novel lightweight formal methods to monitor, analyze, and guide the runtime behavior of software and hardware systems. Runtime verification techniques are crucial for system correctness, reliability, and robustness; they provide an additional level of rigor and effectiveness compared to conventional testing, and are generally more practical than exhaustive formal verification. Runtime verification can be used prior to deployment, for testing, verification, and debugging purposes, and after deployment for ensuring reliability, safety, and security, for providing fault containment and recovery, and for online system repair.

RV started in 2001 as an annual workshop and turned into a conference in 2010. The workshops were organized as satellite events of established forums, including the Conference on Computer-Aided Verification and ETAPS. The proceedings of RV from 2001 to 2005 were published in Electronic Notes in Theoretical Computer Science. The RV proceedings have been published in Springer's Lecture Notes in Computer Science since 2006. Previous RV conferences took place in Istanbul, Turkey (2012); Rennes, France (2013); Toronto, Canada (2014); Vienna, Austria (2015); Madrid, Spain (2016); Seattle, USA (2017); Limassol, Cyprus (2018); and Porto, Portugal (2019). The conferences in 2020 and 2021 were held virtually due to the ongoing COVID-19 pandemic.

This year we received 40 submissions, 33 as regular contributions and seven as short or tool papers. Each of these submissions went through a rigorous single-blind review process as a result of which all papers except for a desk-reject received at least three review reports. The Program Committee selected 12 regular and five short/tool papers for presentation during the conference and inclusion in these proceedings. At the suggestion of the reviewers, the authors of five regular contributions that were not initially selected for publication were invited to provide short papers summarizing their ideas and providing pointers to their tools, and these have been included in the proceedings after a final short review. The evaluation and selection process involved thorough discussions among the members of the Program Committee and external reviewers through the EasyChair conference manager, before reaching a consensus on the final decisions.

The conference featured two keynote speakers:

- Serdar Tasiran, Amazon Web Services, USA
- Michal Valko, DeepMind and Inria, France

We are grateful for the support provided by the many people who contributed to RV 2022, including the Steering Committee members. We also thank the members of the Program Committee and their sub-reviewers for their timely and high-quality reviews as well as their contributions to the discussions. The conference organization was partially supported through sponsorship from Runtime Verification Inc., Amazon Web Services, and Springer.

Besik Dundua as local organizing chair assured the smooth organization and running of RV and the other affiliated events at CLAS. Finally, we appreciate the support and assistance provided by the team at Springer, as well as Ana Cavalcanti's and Marie-Claude Gaudel's confidence for including these proceedings into the Formal Methods subline. Volker Stolz is supported by the Norwegian Research Council through grant 309527 – COEMS Training Network.

Thao Dang is supported by the French-Japanese ANR-JST CyphAI project and the UGA DAMon project.

August 2022

Thao Dang
Volker Stolz

# Organization

## Program Committee Chairs

Thao Dang — CNRS/Verimag and Université Grenoble Alpes, France
Volker Stolz — Western Norway University of Applied Sciences, Norway

## Steering Committee

Howard Barringer — University of Manchester, UK
Ezio Bartocci — Technical University of Vienna, Austria
Saddek Bensalem (Co-chair) — Verimag and Université Grenoble Alpes, France
Yliès Falcone — Université Grenoble Alpes and Inria Grenoble, France
Klaus Havelund — NASA's Jet Propulsion Laboratory, USA
Insup Lee — University of Pennsylvania, USA
Martin Leucker — University of Lübeck, Germany
Giles Reger — University of Manchester, UK
Grigore Rosu — University of Illinois Urbana-Champaign, USA
Oleg Sokolsky (Co-chair) — University of Pennsylvania, USA

## Program Committee

Benoît Barbot — LACL, Université Paris-Est Créteil, France
Domenico Bianculli — University of Luxembourg, Luxembourg
Borzoo Bonakdarpour — Michigan State University, USA
Chih-Hong Cheng — Fraunhofer IKS, Germany
Jyotirmoy Deshmukh — University of Southern California, USA
Alexandre Donzé — Decyphir SAS, France
Yliès Falcone — Université Grenoble Alpes and Inria Grenoble, France
Chuchu Fan — MIT, USA
Lu Feng — University of Virginia, USA
Dana Fisman — Ben-Gurion University of the Negev, Israel
Bernd Finkbeiner — CISPA, Germany
Adrian Francalanza — University of Malta, Malta
Sylvain Hallé — Université du Québec à Chicoutimi, Canada
Klaus Havelund — NASA's Jet Propulsion Laboratory, USA
Bettina Könighofer — TU Graz, Austria
Insup Lee — University of Pennsylvania, USA
Martin Leucker — University of Lübeck, Germany
Anna Lukina — TU Delft, The Netherlands
Laura Nenzi — University of Trieste, Italy

| Dejan Ničković | AIT, Austria |
| Gordon Pace | University of Malta, Malta |
| Nicola Paoletti | Royal Holloway, University of London, UK |
| Doron Peled | Bar-Ilan University, Israel |
| Giles Reger | University of Manchester, UK |
| José I. R. Jarabo | Universidad Complutense de Madrid, Spain |
| Indranil Saha | IIT Kanpur, India |
| César Sánchez | IMDEA, Spain |
| Gerardo Schneider | Chalmers University of Technology, Sweden |
| Julien Signoles | CEA, France |
| Oleg Sokolsky | University of Pennsylvania, USA |
| Hazem Torfah | University of California, Berkeley, USA |
| Dmitriy Traytel | University of Copenhagen, Denmark |
| Stavros Tripakis | Northeastern University, USA |
| Masaki Waga | Kyoto University, Japan |
| Wenhua Yang | Nanjing University of Aeronautics and Astronautics, China |

## Additional Reviewers

Shaun Azzopardi
Maryam Bagheri
Jan Baumeister
Allan Blanchard
Martin Ceresa
Filip Cano Córdoba
Hongkai Chen
Luis Miguel Danielsson
Souradeep Dutta
Kunal Garg
Jonathan Huerta Y. Munive
Hannes Kallwies
Karam Kharraz

Tom Kuipers
Josephine Lamp
Adrien Le Coent
Yannan Li
Vivian Lin
Yue Meng
Anik Momtaz
Victor Roussanaly
Joshua Schneider
Julian Siber
Chukri Soueidi
Daniele Varacca
Songyuan Zhang

# Learning by Bootstrapping of Latents (Abstract)

Michal Valko[1,2]

[1] DeepMind, Paris, France
[2] Inria, Lille, France

**Abstract.** We will discuss self-supervised representation learning and a new paradigm for it based on bootstrapping of latents. We first present BYOL ("Bootstrap Your Own Latent") for images, which relies on two neural networks, referred to as *online* and *target*, that interact and learn from each other: From an augmented view of an image, we train the online network to predict the target network representation of the same image under a different augmented view. At the same time, we update the target network with a slow-moving average of the online network. While prior methods had intrinsically relied on negative pairs, BYOL achieved a new state of the art without them. We will also describe follow-ups of BYOL that we have explored within DeepMind, BGRL for graphs, MYOW for new uncharted domains such as neural readings, and BraVe for videos. We finally apply the paradigm to reinforcement learning and discuss curiosity-driven exploration when the rewards are sparse or absent. For this setting, we give a brand new algorithm BYOL-Explore that jointly learns a world representation, the world dynamics, and an exploration policy.

# Contents

## Short and Tool Papers

# Full Papers

# Randomized First-Order Monitoring
# with Hashing

Joshua Schneider[(✉)] [iD]

Institute of Information Security, Department of Computer Science, ETH Zürich,
Zürich, Switzerland
`joshua.schneider@inf.ethz.ch`

**Abstract.** Online monitors for first-order specifications may need to
store many domain values in their state, requiring significant memory. We propose an approach that compresses the monitor's state using
randomized hash functions. Unlike input sampling, our approach does
not require the knowledge of distributions over traces to achieve low
error probability. We develop algorithms that insert hash functions into
temporal–relational algebra specifications and compute upper bounds
on the resulting error probability. We employ a special hashing scheme
that allows us to merge values across attributes, which further reduces
memory usage. We evaluated our implementation and achieved memory
reductions up to 33% when monitoring traces with large domain values,
with error probability less than two in a million.

**Keywords:** Online monitoring · Temporal–relational algebra ·
Hashing

## 1  Introduction

Online monitors must run in diverse environments that possibly offer limited
computing resources. For instance, the monitoring of operating system ker-
nels [37] competes with the user's applications, embedded hardware is often
underpowered and not easily extendable (e.g., in unmanned aerial systems [43]),
and so forth. However, online monitors for first-order specification languages
may use a significant amount of memory, which hampers their applicability in
such environments. One reason is that they store domain values from the trace
in their internal state. These values can be large in some applications (consider
events that are parametrized by natural language texts or URLs).

To address this problem, we develop a monitoring algorithm that compresses
the domain values using randomized hash functions. Large values such as strings
are replaced by hash values which have more compact in-memory representations. Hashing may incur a loss of accuracy: because of collisions, the algorithm's

© The Author(s), under exclusive license to Springer Nature Switzerland AG 2022
T. Dang and V. Stolz (Eds.): RV 2022, LNCS 13498, pp. 3–24, 2022.
https://doi.org/10.1007/978-3-031-17196-3_1

output may be incorrect with non-zero probability. Our monitor therefore satisfies a probabilistic correctness property. Thanks to the randomization, collisions are independent of the domain values in the trace. Crucially, we demonstrate how to compute an *a priori* upper bound on the error probability for any given specification from the hash functions' collision probability.

Simple specification languages permit very efficient monitors, e.g., every past-time LTL specification can be monitored in constant space [24]. Some applications demand more complex specifications. We focus on a temporal–relational algebra (TRA, see Sect. 2), which corresponds to a fragment of metric first-order temporal logic monitorable using finite relations. First-order languages such as TRA are more concise and, assuming an infinite domain of event parameters, more expressive than propositional languages such as LTL. However, monitoring a fixed TRA specification requires space polynomial in the size of the trace [6]. Specifically, the space usage depends linearly on the size of the domain values' representation. We show that hashing removes this dependency for a nontrivial fragment of TRA and traces whose rate is bounded by a constant.

Randomization and hashing are well-established in algorithm design. Previous research has mostly focused on simpler problems, such as approximate set membership [9,35,40]. First-order monitors often operate on *structured* sets, which cannot be easily encoded using the existing space-optimal data structures. We present compact data structures that provide the operations needed by monitors for expressive languages, but we do not aim at optimality. Moreover, hashing has been used successfully in model checkers to reduce space [13,27]. In that domain, the error analysis generally depends on the number of reachable states, whereas in our case the specification's structure is significant.

*Core Ideas.* Let us illustrate our approach on the example specification, "every $a(x, y)$ event must be preceded by a corresponding $b(x, y)$ event not more than 10 time units ago." We assume that simultaneous events are possible. We represent, at every point in time recorded in the trace, the $a$ events at that time by a relation that stores tuples $(x, y)$ with the events' parameters; the $b$ events are handled similarly. To evaluate the specification, our monitor maintains in its memory another relation $R$ that is equal to the union of all $b$ relations from the past 10 time units, relative to the trace position that the monitor is currently processing. The set difference of the current $a$ relation and $R$ yields $(x, y)$ tuples that witness violations of the specification.

We reduce a specific factor of the memory usage: the representation of domain values in the monitor's state (for our example, in the $R$ relation). This representation usually adds a factor linear in the binary size of the largest value. The basic idea is to replace the domain values $x$ with their images $h(x)$ under a hash function $h$, which is sampled randomly from a suitable collection at the start of monitoring. As an additional optimization, we merge multiple attributes (tuple elements) into a single hash value whenever the attributes are used consistently as a group. Merged hashes over disjoint attribute sets can be combined in an order-independent way. This hashing scheme repurposes a well-known construction that extends the domain of universal hash functions [49]. To the best of our knowledge, the construction's merging property has not been used before to compress relations.

Hashing is possible because many of the TRA's operators continue to give correct results up to $h$. For instance, hashing the domain values in a relation commutes with the union operation. However, some operations may randomly introduce errors with a small probability, which manifest themselves as added or missing tuples. Such errors occur whenever hashes $h(x)$ are compared for equality, e.g., in an intersection. It is important to bound the error probability; otherwise, the monitor would be of little use. Therefore, we develop an algorithm that computes upper bounds for these probabilities by taking the TRA expression's structure and information about the trace into account. Specifically, the algorithm expects as inputs upper bounds on the cardinalities of the relations consumed and computed by the monitor. For the above example and a hash size of 63 bits, the error probability is computed to be at most $3.3 \cdot 10^{-19} \cdot n_a \cdot 10 n_b$ per time-point (position) in the trace, where $n_a$ and $n_b$ are the maximum number of $a$ and $b$ events per time unit. This is the only information we require about the trace; in particular, we do not assume a probabilistic model explaining the trace distribution. Our approach and the error analysis are independent of implementation details, such as the data structure used to implement the 10 time unit sliding window.

Some operators are incompatible with hashing, specifically order comparisons. We handle them on a best-effort basis: values are not hashed if they are used by the problematic operators. However, we still demonstrate an overall reduction of memory usage on relevant traces empirically. For TRA expressions with bounded intervals, no functions, no aggregations except for counting, and no order comparisons, we show that the linear factor can indeed be eliminated if the number of events per time unit is bounded by a constant.

*Summary.* We make the following contributions.

- Our space-efficient monitor (Sect. 3) relies on the key observation that many temporal–relational operations can be computed on relations containing hashed values, with low error probability. As an additional space optimization, we provide a hashing scheme that merges hashes from different attributes within a relation.
- We analyze the error probabilities of TRA expressions with hashing operators (Sect. 4). Our analysis is compositional and yields upper bounds. One can thus estimate the error probability for every hash size by observing or estimating these cardinalities, or alternatively, minimize the error given a space constraint.
- We implement our space-efficient monitor as an extension of MonPoly (Sect. 5). The extended tool automatically inserts hash operators into user-provided specifications and it outputs error bounds for individual input traces. We discuss the specifications most amenable to our optimization and evaluate the memory usage and accuracy of our tool. In a case study with real data, we could reduce the memory usage by 33% with an error probability

below $2 \cdot 10^{-6}$. Our evaluation demonstrates that the technique is particularly effective for traces with large domain values, such as long strings.

This paper is accompanied by an artifact that consists of the monitor implementation and the evaluation scripts. The artifact is available at https://bitbucket.org/jshs/hashmon. Our extended report [42] provides the proofs for all lemmas and theorems.

## 2  Temporal–Relational Algebra

Our monitoring algorithm extends MonPoly's, which has been designed for specifications expressed in metric first-order temporal logic (MFOTL) with aggregations [5,6]. MonPoly translates MFOTL to a temporal–relational algebra (TRA), which it then evaluates using finite relations over an infinite domain. To simplify the presentation, we focus on the TRA, as our algorithms work directly with its operators, which do not map one-to-one to MFOTL's operators. We note that other variants of TRA exist in the literature [38,46].

We assume a countably infinite set $\mathcal{A}$ of attributes and a domain $\mathcal{D}$ of constants totally ordered by $\leq$. A tuple $u$ over a finite set $U \subset \mathcal{A}$ of attributes is a mapping from $U$ to $\mathcal{D}$. We write $att(u)$ for $u$'s attributes $U$, and $u(a)$ for $u$'s value at $a \in att(u)$. A relation $R$ over $U$ is a finite set of tuples over $U$; overloading notation, we define $att(R) = U$. A schema $S$ is a collection of relation names $r$ with associated attribute sets $att_S(r)$. A database $D$ over $S$ is a mapping from $r \in S$ to relations $D(r)$ over $att_S(r)$.

The following grammar defines the expressions $e$ of TRA. We write $\bar{z}$ for a list of elements derived from nonterminal $z$. The nonterminals $a$ and $a'$ range over attributes; $c$ is a constant in $\mathcal{D}$; and $I$ and $I^\infty$ are finite and infinite intervals over $\mathbb{N}$, respectively.[1]

$$t ::= a \mid c \mid f(\bar{t}) \qquad \circ ::= = \mid \neq \mid \leq \mid < \qquad \omega ::= \mathsf{COUNT} \mid \mathsf{SUM} \mid \mathsf{MIN} \mid \mathsf{MAX}$$
$$e ::= R \mid r \mid \pi(\bar{a})e \mid \varrho(\overline{a \leftarrow a'})e \mid \sigma(t_1 \circ t_2)e \mid \eta(a \mapsto t)e$$
$$\mid e_1 \bowtie e_2 \mid e_1 \rhd e_2 \mid e_1 \cup e_2 \mid \mathbf{Y}_I \infty e \mid e_1\, \mathbf{S}_{I\infty}^m\, e_2 \mid \mathbf{X}_I \infty e \mid e_1\, \mathbf{U}_I^m\, e_2 \mid \omega(a' \mapsto t; \bar{a})e$$

Terms $t$ are either attributes, constants, or function applications; we do not further specify the available function symbols $f$. An expression can be a constant relation $R$, a relation name $r \in S$, or a compound expression. We sometimes write $r(\bar{a})$ to indicate that $att_S(r) = \bar{a}$. The projection operator $\pi(\bar{a})$ preserves only the attributes $\bar{a}$ and removes all other attributes. The renaming operator $\varrho(\overline{a \leftarrow a'})$ replaces the attributes in the list $\overline{a'}$ simultaneously by the corresponding attributes in $\bar{a}$. The selection operator $\sigma(t_1 \circ t_2)$ filters tuples according to the condition $t_1 \circ t_2$. The assignment operator $\eta(a \mapsto t)$ computes a new attribute $a$ from the term $t$. The natural join $e_1 \bowtie e_2$ contains exactly those tuples that are in $e_1$ and $e_2$ when restricted to $e_1$'s and $e_2$'s attributes, respectively. The anti-join $e_1 \rhd e_2$ is similar, except that the restrictions to $e_2$'s attributes must not be in $e_2$.

---

[1] The meta-variable $I$ will later be used for both types of intervals.

**Table 1.** Syntax, well-formedness, attributes, and semantics of TRA expressions

| $e$ | $e$ is well-formed iff | $att(e)$ | $\forall u,i.\ u \in [\![e]\!]_i$ iff $att(u) = att(e)$ and |
|---|---|---|---|
| $R$ | no restriction | $att(R)$ | $u \in R$ |
| $r$ | $r \in S$ | $att_S(r)$ | $u \in \xi_i(r)$ |
| $\pi(\overline{a})e_1$ | $\overline{a} \subseteq att(e_1)$ | $\overline{a}$ | $\exists u' \in [\![e_1]\!]_i.\ u = u'|_{\overline{a}}$ |
| $\varrho(\overline{a} \leftarrow \overline{a'})e_1$ | $\overline{a'} = att(e_1)$ | $\overline{a}$ | $\exists u' \in [\![e_1]\!]_i.\ \bigwedge_k u(a_k) = u'(a'_k)$ |
| $\sigma(t_1 \circ t_2)e_1$ | $att(t_1) \subseteq att(e_1),\ att(t_2) \subseteq att(e_1)$ | $att(e_1)$ | $u \in [\![e_1]\!]_i$ and $t_1(u) \circ t_2(u)$ |
| $\eta(a \mapsto t)e_1$ | $att(t) \subseteq att(e_1)$ | $att(e_1) \cup \{a\}$ | $\exists u' \in [\![e_1]\!]_i.\ u = u'[a \mapsto t(u')]$ |
| $e_1 \bowtie e_2$ | no restriction | $att(e_1) \cup att(e_2)$ | $u|_{att(e_1)} \in [\![e_1]\!]_i$ and $u|_{att(e_2)} \in [\![e_2]\!]_i$ |
| $e_1 \rhd e_2$ | $att(e_1) \supseteq att(e_2)$ | $att(e_1)$ | $u \in [\![e_1]\!]_i$ and $u|_{att(e_2)} \notin [\![e_2]\!]_i$ |
| $e_1 \cup e_2$ | $att(e_1) = att(e_2)$ | $att(e_1)$ | $u \in [\![e_1]\!]_i \cup [\![e_2]\!]_i$ |
| $\mathbf{Y}_I e_1$ | no restriction | $att(e_1)$ | $i > 0$ and $\tau_i - \tau_{i-1} \in I$ and $u \in [\![e_1]\!]_{i-1}$ |
| $e_1\, \mathbf{S}_I^m\, e_2$ | $att(e_1) \subseteq att(e_2)$ | $att(e_2)$ | $\exists j \le i.\ \tau_i - \tau_j \in I$ and $u \in [\![e_2]\!]_j$ and $\forall k.\ j < k \le i \Rightarrow u|_{att(e_1)} \in_m [\![e_1]\!]_k$ |
| $\mathbf{X}_I e_1$ | no restriction | $att(e_1)$ | $\tau_{i+1} - \tau_i \in I$ and $u \in [\![e_1]\!]_{i+1}$ |
| $e_1\, \mathbf{U}_I^m\, e_2$ | $att(e_1) \subseteq att(e_2)$ | $att(e_2)$ | $\exists j \ge i.\ \tau_j - \tau_i \in I$ and $u \in [\![e_2]\!]_j$ and $\forall k.\ j > k \ge i \Rightarrow u|_{att(e_1)} \in_m [\![e_1]\!]_k$ |
| $\omega(a' \mapsto t; \overline{a})e_1$ | $att(t) \subseteq att(e_1),\ \overline{a} \subseteq att(e_1),\ a' \notin \overline{a}$ | $\overline{a} \cup \{a'\}$ | $M \ne \{\!\|\!\}$ and $u(a') = \omega(M)$, where $M = \{\!\|t(u') \mid u' \in [\![e_1]\!]_i, u|_{\overline{a}} = u'|_{\overline{a}}\|\!\}$ |

The metric *previously* ($\mathbf{Y}$) and *since* ($\mathbf{S}$) operators are as in MTL [29]. We write $[l,u]$ for the interval $\{x \in \mathbb{N} \mid l \le x \le u\}$. The superscript $m \in \{\lhd, \bowtie\}$ indicates whether $\mathbf{S}$'s left operand is negated or not. We also support the future counterparts *next* ($\mathbf{X}$) and *until* ($\mathbf{U}$) with finite intervals. The derived connective $\mathbf{O}_{I\infty} e$ abbreviates $\{()\}\mathbf{S}_{I\infty}^{\bowtie} e$, where () is the unique tuple with an empty domain. Finally, $\omega(a' \mapsto t; \overline{a})$ is an aggregation of type $\omega$ over $t$ with grouping attributes $\overline{a}$ and result in $a'$. For SUM aggregations, we assume that $\mathcal{D}$ is equipped with an associative and commutative addition operator. We usually omit the term $t$ in COUNT aggregations as it is not used.

Table 1 defines the well-formedness, attributes, and semantics of expressions. The semantics, which implicitly depends on the trace $\xi$, assigns to every well-formed expression $e$ an infinite sequence of relations $[\![e]\!]_i$, where $i \in \mathbb{N}$. A trace is an infinite sequence of time-stamped databases over the schema associated with $e$. We model time-stamps as natural numbers and make the standard assumption that the time-stamps are non-strictly increasing and always eventually increasing. The attributes $att(e)$ of $e$ coincide with $att([\![e]\!]_i)$ for all $i$. The following notation is used in Table 1: We write $\xi_i$ for the $i$th database in the trace, which additionally carries the time-stamp $\tau_i \in \mathbb{N}$. We write $u|_U$ for the tuple $u$ restricted to the attributes $U$. Terms $t$ are interpreted as mappings $t(u)$ from tuples $u$ over supersets of $att(t)$, the attributes occurring in $t$, to $\mathcal{D}$. By $x \in_m A$ we mean $x \in A$ if $m = \bowtie$ and $x \notin A$ if $m = \lhd$. The notation $\{\!\|\ldots\|\!\}$ denotes a multiset. The aggregation operators COUNT and SUM account for multiplicities of tuples.

*Example 1.* Suppose that the trace $\xi$ describes product reviews submitted by customers to a webshop, with time-stamps expressed in days. The trace is over the schema $S = \{p, r\}$, where $att(p) = \{pid, b\}$ and $att(r) = \{rid, pid, rating\}$. The relations $p$ contain products with identifier $pid$ and brand $b$ whenever they are first added to the webshop. The relations $r$ contain the reviews of product $pid$ by a reviewer $rid$ with the given $rating$. We want to detect review spam campaigns that target specific brands. The expression $e_{rb} \equiv r \bowtie (\mathbf{O}_{\mathbb{N}} p)$ augments each review with the brand, using the $\mathbf{O}_{\mathbb{N}}$ operator as the reviewed product must have been added before the review; we have $att(e_{rb}) = \{rid, pid, rating, b\}$. The expression $e_{ex} \equiv \pi(b)\sigma(n_1 \geq 3n_2)\big((\mathsf{COUNT}(n_1; b)\mathbf{O}_{[0,6]}e_{rb}) \bowtie (\mathsf{COUNT}(n_2; b)\mathbf{O}_{[7,27]}e_{rb})\big)$ obtains the set of brands that received at least three times as many reviews in the previous week than in all of the three weeks before. These brands are possible targets of spam.

The evaluation of individual TRA operators is described elsewhere [6]. We reuse their implementation from MonPoly and briefly explain the evaluation of $e_1 \, \mathbf{S}_I^{\bowtie} \, e_2$. For this operator, the algorithm stores a list containing pairs of time-stamps and relations. This list is continuously updated so that at time-point $i$, $[\![e_1 \, \mathbf{S}_I^{\bowtie} \, e_2]\!]_i$ is equal to the union of the relations in the list whose time-stamp difference to the current time-stamp $\tau_i$ is in the interval $I$. For every new time-point $j$, the algorithm first intersects all relations in the list with $[\![e_1]\!]_j$ and then adds $(\tau_j, [\![e_2]\!]_j)$ to it. Elements that are too old with respect to $I$ are removed. We note that there exists a faster algorithm [4], but we believe that it has little or no advantage in terms of space as it stores more (redundant) information to obtain a better time complexity. Confirming this intuition empirically is left as future work.

# 3   Algorithmic Details

Our monitoring algorithm has two phases. In the initialization phase, the monitor randomly chooses a hash function, and it rewrites the TRA expression to introduce explicit hashing operators. The rewriting will be explained in Sect. 3.2. In the main phase, the rewritten expression is evaluated over the incoming trace. The main phase is mostly the same as MonPoly's algorithm and we will only discuss how our modifications affect it.

## 3.1   Hash Abstractions

We begin by describing the hashing operators that we added to the TRA and how they are evaluated. We first focus on the simpler case where attributes are hashed individually before we generalize to merged attributes. Our monitoring algorithm is parametrized by a family $\mathcal{H}$ of hash functions from $\mathcal{D}$ to $2^k$, where $k \in \mathbb{N}$ is the hash size in bits. The monitor samples a single function $h \in \mathcal{H}$ uniformly at random in the initialization phase. We assume a set $\mathcal{A}_{\#}$ denoting hashed attributes, disjoint from $\mathcal{A}$. The set contains an attribute named $\#a$ for every $a \in \mathcal{A}$. Let $u$ be a tuple and $X \subseteq att(u) - \mathcal{A}_{\#}$. We define $h_X(u)$ as the tuple over $(att(u) - X) \cup \{\#v \mid v \in X\}$ satisfying

$$h_X(u)(a) = \mathbf{if}\, a = \#b \text{ for } b \in X \,\mathbf{then}\, h(u(b)) \,\mathbf{else}\, u(a).$$

For a relation $R$ and $X \subseteq att(R) - \mathcal{A}_{\#}$, let $h_X(R)$ be the image of $R$ under $h_X$. We call $h_X(u)$ and $h_X(R)$ *hash abstractions*, as many different tuples and relations map to the same value. We could now add $h_X$ as a new operator to TRA, with the semantics just described. All other operators would be extended to attributes from the set $\mathcal{A} \cup \mathcal{A}_{\#}$.

Consider the example $p(a,b) \, \mathbf{S}_{[0,9]}^{\bowtie} \left( (\mathbf{O}_{[0,9]}q(a)) \bowtie (\mathbf{O}_{[0,9]}r(b)) \right)$. Intuitively, all atomic expressions should be hashed, as the temporal operators $\mathbf{O}$ and $\mathbf{S}$ store their results for some time. Therefore, we would monitor $h_{\{a,b\}}p(a,b) \, \mathbf{S}_{[0,9]}^{\bowtie}$ $\left( (\mathbf{O}_{[0,9]}h_{\{a\}}q(a)) \bowtie (\mathbf{O}_{[0,9]}h_{\{b\}}r(b)) \right)$. Observe that both arguments to the top-level $\mathbf{S}$ operator have attributes $\{\#a, \#b\}$. The operator compares the equality of tuples over these attributes, i.e., it always compares the values of both $\#a$ and $\#b$ simultaneously. If we hashed these values again into a single $k$-bit hash, we would only need half the number of bits to store a tuple in $\mathbf{S}$'s state while still being able to correctly test equality with high probability. However, the following example shows that generalizing this idea is not straightforward.

*Example 2.* In the expression

$$\left( p(a) \bowtie \mathbf{O}_{\mathbb{N}}q(b,c) \right) \mathbf{S}_{[0,9]}^{\bowtie} \left( (\varrho(c \leftarrow a)p(a)) \bowtie \mathbf{O}_{\mathbb{N}}\varrho(a \leftarrow b, b \leftarrow c)q(b,c) \right),$$

it is impossible to hash every atomic expression into a single attribute *and* to do the same with the relations going into the $\mathbf{S}$ operator. The reason is that the left operand's values would have the shape $h(a, h(b, c))$ whereas for the right operand it is $h(c, h(a, b))$.

We solve this problem by employing special hash functions on tuples. Functions from this family have the property that the hash of a tuple $u$ over $U$ can be computed even if for some disjoint subsets $U' \subseteq U$ only the hashes of $u|_{U'}$ are available. Specifically, it is possible to merge hashes of tuples over disjoint attribute sets such that the result is independent of the merging order. The construction works in two steps: First, a single hash function as above compresses the values of each attribute to $k$ bits. Second, we combine these "pre-hashes" using a linear form over the finite field $GF(2^k)$, whose elements are in a bijection with $k$-bit strings. The coefficients of the linear form, one for every attribute, are chosen uniformly at random in the initialization phase.

The second (combining) step is a well-known method [34] for extending the domain of universal hash functions that was proposed by Wegman and Carter [49]. Accordingly, we assume that the "pre-hash" family $\mathcal{H}$ is $\epsilon'$-almost universal:

**Definition 1** [45]. *A finite family $\mathcal{H}$ of functions $\mathcal{D} \to 2^k$ is $\epsilon'$-almost universal iff $|\{h \in \mathcal{H} \mid h(x) = h(y)\}|/|\mathcal{H}| \leq \epsilon'$ for all distinct $x, y \in \mathcal{D}$.*

We generalize the combining step to tuples over any subset of attributes. The resulting hashes for different attribute sets are not related in a meaningful way. This is not an issue: the monitoring algorithm always compares hashes over the same attributes. To merge hashes for disjoint attribute sets, we simply add them in $GF(2^k)$. As a further modification, pre-hashes are not multiplied with their coefficients until they are about to be merged for the first time. Thus, the hash values for different *nonmerged* attributes remain comparable. This allows us to evaluate a selection operator that compares two different hashed attributes, for example. We arrive at the following definition for our hash family derived from $\mathcal{H}$. Fix a finite set of attributes $\mathcal{A}_e \subset \mathcal{A}$, which will be instantiated with the set of all attributes that occur in the monitored expression $e$.

**Definition 2.** *The distribution $\mathcal{H}^*$ is obtained by sampling $h \in \mathcal{H}$ and $f \in \mathcal{A}_e \to GF(2^k)$ uniformly and independently at random, then mapping $(h, f)$ to the function*

$$h^*(u) = \textbf{if } att(u) = \{a\} \text{ for some } a \textbf{ then } h(u(a)) \textbf{ else } \sum_{a \in att(u)} f(a) \cdot h(u(a))$$

*defined on tuples $u$ over subsets of $\mathcal{A}_e$. All arithmetic is over $GF(2^k)$.*

**Lemma 1.** *Suppose that $\mathcal{H}$ is $\epsilon'$-almost universal. Define $\epsilon = \epsilon' + 2^{-k}$. For all tuples $u_1 \neq u_2$ over the same attributes in $\mathcal{A}_e$, $\Pr_{h^* \in \mathcal{H}^*}[h^*(u_1) = h^*(u_2)] \leq \epsilon$.*

As before, we would like to control which attributes are hashed and also how they are merged. We generalize $\mathcal{A}_\#$ to attributes of the form $\#X$, where $X$ is a finite, nonempty subset of $\mathcal{A}$. A *hash specifier* $Y$ is a set of disjoint and nonempty subsets of $\mathcal{A}_e \subset \mathcal{A}$. We then generalize hash abstractions as follows, where $u$ is a tuple with $\bigcup Y \subseteq att(u)$:

$$h^*_Y(u)(a) = \textbf{if } a = \#X \text{ for } X \in Y \textbf{ then } h^*(u|_X) \textbf{ else } u(a).$$

The bound on the collision probability from Lemma 1 carries over to hash abstractions: $h^*_Y(u_1)$ is equal to $h^*_Y(u_2)$ for two distinct tuples $u_1$ and $u_2$ with probability at most $\epsilon$.

The next lemma is a key property of $\mathcal{H}^*$. It allows us to extend the domain of $h^*_Y$ to tuples that already contain hashed values, as long as they are compatible with $Y$. This restriction is captured by the relation $Y_1 \sqsubseteq Y_2$ defined by $\forall X_1 \in Y_1. \exists X_2 \in Y_2. X_1 \subseteq X_2$.

**Lemma 2.** *Let $Y_1 \sqsubseteq Y_2$ be hash specifiers. Then $h^*_{Y_2}(u)$ can be computed from $h^*_{Y_1}(u)$.*

We conclude with a summary of the augmented TRA. We add the hashing operator $h^*_Y e$ to the syntax introduced in Sect. 2. It is well-formed iff $Y$ is a hash specifier satisfying $hsp(e) \sqsubseteq Y$, where $hsp(e) = \{X \mid \#X \in att(e)\}$ is the unique hash specifier induced by $e$'s attributes. We have $att(h^*_Y e) = (att(e) - \mathcal{A}_\# - \bigcup Y) \cup \{\#X \mid X \in Y\}$. There are new well-formedness requirements for the other operators: Hashed attributes may be renamed only if they have not been merged. If a hashed attribute occurs in a selection or assignment operator, it must be nonmerged and both terms must consist of a single hashed attribute or a constant; the selection must be of type $=$ or $\neq$. Hashed attributes must not occur in an aggregation's term. For binary operators, the operands' induced hash specifiers must be equal on the operands' common attributes. The semantics $[\![h^*_Y e]\!]_i$ is obtained by applying the computation from Lemma 2 to each tuple in the input relation $[\![e]\!]_i$, which is interpreted as a hash abstraction over $hsp(e)$. The hash function $h^*$ used in these computations is sampled from the distribution $\mathcal{H}^*$ during the monitor's initialization phase.

## 3.2 Expression Rewriting

We now describe how the hash operators are inserted in the initialization phase. Ideally, this transformation should result in a space-optimal evaluation while keeping the worst-case error probability below a used-defined threshold (or vice versa). Achieving this objective is a hard optimization problem. For example, it might not be optimal to hash a temporal operator's operand that always evaluates to a small relation. The error incurred by later operators may be comparatively large and it would be more effective to spend the error budget elsewhere. It is impossible to compute exact bounds on the relations' sizes because the satisfiability of relational algebra queries is already undecidable [1]. Therefore, one must relax the optimization, and it is not clear how to do that in a principled manner. We defer the analysis of this problem to future work and instead rely on a heuristic to rewrite the expression. The heuristic is based on the following principles:

- The expression's structure does not change except that hash operators are inserted.
- Every attribute is hashed greedily in the operands of temporal connectives, as these connectives contribute the most to the monitor's state. Operands of the other binary connectives may be hashed so that they have the same hashed attributes. An attribute cannot be hashed if any operator on the path to the expression's root performs an operation other than equality testing with the attribute's value. The equality test may be implicit, e.g., as part of a join. The reason is that other operations, such as orderings, cannot be evaluated on hashed values (which incidentally hampers the expressiveness of BDD-based monitors [21,22]). Order-preserving perfect hash functions are not suited for our purpose because of their superlinear space lower bound [17].
- Any set of hashed attributes is merged greedily whenever it is used homogeneously by all operators on the path to the root, i.e., all attributes' values are always compared together. For instance, $a$ and $b$ cannot be merged in the join's operands in $p(a, b) \bowtie q(a)$ because $a$'s but not $b$'s values are compared.
- In general, the greedy approach assumes that it is better to hash and merge than not. Other objectives may be more appropriate in specific applications. For example, if specification violations must always be detected but false alerts are acceptable, a different heuristic taking the predicted error (Sect. 4.1) into account should be used.

---

**Algorithm 1.** Expression rewriting

---

let addHash$((e, Y), Y') = $ if $Y' = Y$ then $e$ else $h^*_{Y'} e$

let rec rw$(apx, Y, e) = $ match $e$ with
| $\pi(\overline{a})e_1$ ⇒ let $(\tilde{e}_1, Y_1) = $ rw$(apx, Y \cup \{att(e_1) - \overline{a}\}, e_1)$ in
         let $\overline{a'} = \{$if $a \in \bigcup Y_1$ then $\#X$ for unique $X \in Y_1$ s.t. $a \in X$ else $a \mid a \in \overline{a}\}$ in
         $(\pi(\overline{a'})\tilde{e}_1, \{X \cap \overline{a} \mid X \in Y_1\})$
| $e_1 \, \mathbf{S}^m_I \, e_2$ ⇒ let $K = att(e_1)$, $apx' = apx \wedge (|I| < \infty)$ in
         let $Y' = (\{X - K \mid X \in Y\} \cup ($if $apx'$ then $\{X \cap K \mid X \in Y\}$ else $\emptyset))$ in
         (addHash(rw$(apx', Y', e_1), Y'$) $\mathbf{S}^m_I$ addHash(rw$(apx', Y', e_2), Y'$), $Y'$)
| ...

---

We implemented the heuristic as a bottom-up rewriting procedure (Algorithm 1). We only show the $\pi$ and $\mathbf{S}$ cases due to space constraints; see the extended report [42] for the full algorithm. The projection case illustrates how the connectives' parameters are adjusted, and $\mathbf{S}$ imposes the most interesting constraints on its operands.

The main function rw$(apx, Y, e)$ transforms the expression $e$. Its result is a pair $(\tilde{e}, Y')$, where $\tilde{e}$ is the rewritten expression and $Y' = hsp(\tilde{e})$ is the hash specifier induced by $\tilde{e}$. The constraints $apx$ and $Y$ represent the restrictions imposed by the operations on the path from the root to the current expression $e$. The boolean $apx$ indicates whether $\tilde{e}$ may introduce errors. There can be hash operators in $\tilde{e}$ even if errors are disallowed, but the hashed attributes must not be tested for equality. The hash specifier $Y$ partitions the sub-expression's attributes. Attributes not in $\bigcup Y$ are excluded from hashing, and the partitioning in $Y$ indicates which attributes may be merged. For the root expression, we set $apx$ to true, and the specifier $Y$ is the empty set: as the relations computed for the root are output to the user, there should not be any hashed values in that output.

For projections $\pi(\overline{a})e_1$, the sub-expression $e_1$ is rewritten using the same constraints, except that the removed attributes $att(e_1) - \overline{a}$ can be hashed and merged (but not with other attributes). The rewriting function computes a new list $\overline{a'}$ of projected attributes to account for the new names of the hashed attributes. The order of this list does not matter, hence we define it using set notation. Note that the heuristic is not greedy for projections: no hash abstraction is inserted if $\{X \cap \overline{a} \mid X \in Y_1\}$ differs from the constraint $Y$.

For $e_1 \, \mathbf{S}^m_I \, e_2$, the key $K$ consists of the attributes $att(e_1)$ that the connective tests for equality internally. The operands are rewritten recursively. The $apx$ flag is propagated unless $I$ is unbounded. In this case, it could be possible to force an error at a sufficiently large time-point if the operands are not exact. The specifier $Y'$ is derived from $Y$: If errors are allowed, the sets in $Y$ are split into key and non-key attributes. Otherwise, all key attributes are removed, as the equality test on hashed keys might introduce errors. Finally, the rewritten operands are wrapped in hashing operations so that both operands have compatible hashed attributes (namely $Y'$).

*Example 3.* The expressions from Example 1 are rewritten to $\tilde{e}_{rb} \equiv h^*_{Y_2}((h^*_{Y_1} r) \bowtie (\mathbf{O}_{\mathbb{N}} h^*_{Y_1} p))$ and $\tilde{e}_{ex} \equiv \pi(b)\sigma(n_1 \geq 3n_2)((\mathsf{COUNT}(n_1; b)\mathbf{O}_{[0,6]}\tilde{e}_{rb}) \bowtie (\mathsf{COUNT}(n_2; b)\mathbf{O}_{[7,27]}\tilde{e}_{rb}))$. The attribute $b$ representing the brand is never hashed because it is part of the monitor's output, which evaluates $\tilde{e}_{ex}$. At first only $Y_1 = \{pid\}$ is hashed, as $pid$ is the only attribute apart from $b$ exposed to a temporal connective in $\tilde{e}_{rb}$. After the join in $\tilde{e}_{rb}$, $Y_2 = \{pid, rid, rating\}$ can be merged, as all three attributes are discarded by the aggregations.

## 4   Analysis of the Algorithm

In this section, we analyze the error probability of our monitor and comment on its space complexity. Our analysis relates the error probability to the size of the hash values, which affects the algorithm's space complexity. Specifically, we show how to compute an upper bound on the error probability for a given expression. This results in a symbolic expression whose variables refer to the collision probability $\epsilon$, the maximum number of time-points per unit of time, and the maximum relation sizes that may occur during the expression's evaluation. Based on this information, the user can adjust the hash size to achieve the desired level of accuracy. Additionally, we show that a concrete error bound can be computed by the monitor for a particular trace. This may provide a more precise error estimate.

### 4.1   Error Bounds

We first establish a formal framework in which we carry out our analysis. To this end, we introduce the notion of randomized monitoring, which allows us to quantify the monitor's accuracy in terms of its worst-case error probability. A *randomized monitor* $M$ is modeled as a mapping from finite trace prefixes to discrete probability distributions over finite sequences of relations. We assume that $M$ satisfies the following completeness property. For every (infinite) trace $\xi$ there exists a look-ahead function $\ell_\xi$, which maps any desired length of the monitor's output to a sufficient length of the monitor's input. More precisely, the length of the sequences in the support[2] of $M(x)$ is at least $n$ for every prefix $x$ of $\xi$ with length $|x| \geq \ell_\xi(n)$. In other words, outputs may be delayed, but the monitor must always eventually compute a verdict. Our monitor inherits its look-ahead function from MonPoly; it depends only on the upper bounds of the future operator's intervals and on the time-stamps in $\xi$.

We parametrize the monitoring problem by a nonempty, possibly infinite set $X$ of traces, which represents the application-specific knowledge about the possible inputs to the monitor. We also fix a TRA expression $e$ and perform the following random experiment: for any trace $\xi \in X$ and time-point $i \in \mathbb{N}$, the monitor is run on a sufficiently long prefix of $\xi$ using fresh randomness. We are interested in the worst-case probability (over the choice of $\xi$ and $i$) of the $i$th output deviating from the correct relation. Let $x \ll \xi$ denote that $x$ is a finite prefix of $\xi$, and let $x_i$ denote the $i$th element in the sequence $x$. We make the

---

[2] The support of a discrete probability distribution is the set of values with nonzero probability.

semantics' dependency on the trace explicit: from now on, we write $[\![e]\!]_i^\xi$ instead of $[\![e]\!]_i$, where $\xi$ is the trace.

**Definition 3.** *The* error probability *of $M$ on $X$ is*

$$err_X(M) = \sup_{\xi \in X, i \in \mathbb{N}, x \ll \xi, |x| \ge \ell_\xi(i)} Pr_M[M(x)_i \ne [\![e]\!]_i^\xi].$$

*Similarly, the* false-positive probability *$fp_X(M)$ and the* false-negative probability *$fn_X(M)$ are defined by*

$$fp_X(M) = \sup_{\xi \in X, i \in \mathbb{N}, x \ll \xi, |x| \ge \ell_\xi(i)} Pr_M[M(x)_i \not\subseteq [\![e]\!]_i^\xi]$$

$$fn_X(M) = \sup_{\xi \in X, i \in \mathbb{N}, x \ll \xi, |x| \ge \ell_\xi(i)} Pr_M[M(x)_i \not\supseteq [\![e]\!]_i^\xi].$$

**Lemma 3.** $\max\{fp_X(M), fn_X(M)\} \le err_X(M) \le fp_X(M) + fn_X(M).$

The error probability is our measure of the monitor's accuracy. The false-positive and false-negative probabilities provide more information about the nature of the errors. In some applications it may be more tolerable to have errors of the one kind than of the other. No probability distribution is associated with $X$; the probabilities are taken solely with respect to the internal coin flips of the algorithm implementing $M$.

According to Definition 3, the trace $\xi$ cannot depend on the randomness of $M$. Such a dependency would be incompatible with our hashing approach, as one could construct an adversarial input that causes an error with certainty at sufficiently large time-points (by trying different values until a hash collision is found). However, the probability of an error at *some* time-point can be 1 even if $err_X(M) < 1$, as for many specifications it is unavoidable that a collision occurs somewhere in an infinite trace if the domain is large enough. Therefore, we consider the probability for each time-point in isolation in Definition 3.

The following design decisions guide our error analysis: (1) It should be compositional so that the bounds can be computed by recursion over the expression's structure. (2) The set of traces is parameterized by the maximum rate and the maximum relation sizes for each sub-expression, as defined below. We need to bound these quantities because the worst-case error probability would otherwise be 1 for most expressions. Moreover, relying on concrete numeric upper bounds makes the analysis more precise. (3) We analyze the false-positive and false-negative probabilities separately; by Lemma 3, this allows us to approximate the overall error probability within a factor of 2.

The first step is to adapt the notions of false-positive and false-negative probabilities to rewritten expressions $\tilde{e}$. To this end, we recover the original, exact expression $e$ from $\tilde{e}$ by removing all hash operators. We perform the analysis on $\tilde{e}$ instead of $e$ to decouple it from the heuristic used by Algorithm 1.

**Definition 4.** *Let $X$ be a set of traces. Suppose that $e$ is the unique expression obtained by removing all hash operators from $\tilde{e}$ and flattening attributes of the form $\#X$ into an enumeration of $X$ (see the extended report [42] for details).*

**Table 2.** Upper bounds on false-positive and false-negative error probabilities, per time-point

| $\tilde{e}$ | $fp(\tilde{e}) \leq \ldots$ | $fn(\tilde{e}) \leq \ldots$ | |
|---|---|---|---|
| $R$, $r$ | 0 | 0 | |
| $h_Y^* \tilde{e}_1$, $\pi(\_)\tilde{e}_1$, $\varrho(\_)\tilde{e}_1$, $\eta(\_)\tilde{e}_1$, $\sigma(t_1 \circ t_2)\tilde{e}_1$, $\mathbf{Y}_I \tilde{e}_1$, $\mathbf{X}_I \tilde{e}_1$ | $fp(\tilde{e}_1)$ | $fn(\tilde{e}_1)$ | (1) |
| $\sigma(\#\{a\} = t)\tilde{e}_1$ | $fp(\tilde{e}_1) + \epsilon|e_1|$ | $fn(\tilde{e}_1)$ | |
| $\sigma(\#\{a\} \neq t)\tilde{e}_1$ | $fp(\tilde{e}_1)$ | $fn(\tilde{e}_1) + \epsilon|e_1|$ | |
| $\tilde{e}_1 \bowtie \tilde{e}_2$ | $fp(\tilde{e}_1) + fp(\tilde{e}_2) + \epsilon|e_1||e_2|$ | $fn(\tilde{e}_1) + fn(\tilde{e}_2)$ | (2) |
| $\tilde{e}_1 \triangleright \tilde{e}_2$ | $fp(\tilde{e}_1) + fn(\tilde{e}_2)$ | $fn(\tilde{e}_1) + fp(\tilde{e}_2) + \epsilon|e_1||e_2|$ | (2) |
| $\tilde{e}_1 \cup \tilde{e}_2$ | $fp(\tilde{e}_1) + fp(\tilde{e}_2)$ | $fn(\tilde{e}_1) + fn(\tilde{e}_2)$ | (2) |
| $\tilde{e}_1 \, \mathbf{S}_I^{\bowtie} \, \tilde{e}_2$, $\tilde{e}_1 \, \mathbf{U}_I^{\bowtie} \, \tilde{e}_2$ | $a_I \cdot fp(\tilde{e}_1) + b_I \cdot fp(\tilde{e}_2) + \epsilon \cdot b_I|e_1||e_2|$ | $a_I \cdot fn(\tilde{e}_1) + b_I \cdot fn(\tilde{e}_2)$ | (2) |
| $\tilde{e}_1 \, \mathbf{S}_I^{\triangleleft} \, \tilde{e}_2$, $\tilde{e}_1 \, \mathbf{U}_I^{\triangleleft} \, \tilde{e}_2$ | $a_I \cdot fn(\tilde{e}_1) + b_I \cdot fp(\tilde{e}_2)$ | $a_I \cdot fp(\tilde{e}_1) + b_I \cdot fn(\tilde{e}_2) + \epsilon \cdot c_I|e_1||e_2|$ | (2) |
| $\omega(a' \mapsto t; \overline{a})\tilde{e}_1$ | $fp(\tilde{e}_1) + fn(\tilde{e}_1) + \epsilon(|e_1|^2 - |e_1|)/2$ | $fp(\tilde{e}_1) + fn(\tilde{e}_1) + \epsilon(|e_1|^2 - |e_1|)/2$ | (3) |

$a_I = (maxRate \cdot u) - 1$ and $b_I = maxRate \cdot (u - l)$ and $c_I = b_I \cdot (maxRate \cdot l + (b_I + 1)/2)$ for any half-open interval $I = \{x \in \mathbb{N} \mid l \leq x < u\}$. Set $a_I = b_I = c_I = \infty$ if $I$ is unbounded.
Side conditions and remarks: (1) no hashed attribute in $t_1$ nor in $t_2$; (2) replace $\epsilon$ by 0 if there is no hashed attribute in $att(\tilde{e}_1) \cap att(\tilde{e}_2)$; (3) replace $\epsilon$ by 0 if: $\omega \in \{\mathsf{MIN}, \mathsf{MAX}\}$ and no hashed attribute in $\overline{a}$, or $\omega \in \{\mathsf{COUNT}, \mathsf{SUM}\}$ and no hashed attribute in $e_1$.

*Writing $h_Y^*(R)$ for the image of $R$ under $h_Y^*$, the false-positive and false-negative probabilities of $\tilde{e}$ are*

$$fp(\tilde{e}) = \sup_{\xi \in X, i \in \mathbb{N}} \Pr[\llbracket \tilde{e} \rrbracket_i^\xi \not\subseteq h_{hsp(\tilde{e})}^*(\llbracket e \rrbracket_i^\xi)], \quad fn(\tilde{e}) = \sup_{\xi \in X, i \in \mathbb{N}} \Pr[h_{hsp(\tilde{e})}^*(\llbracket e \rrbracket_i^\xi) \not\subseteq \llbracket \tilde{e} \rrbracket_i^\xi].$$

The applications of $h_{hsp(\tilde{e})}^*$ ensure that the relations are over the same attributes. It may be surprising that a hash collision in $\llbracket e \rrbracket_i^\xi$ (i.e., two tuples $u, v \in \llbracket e \rrbracket_i^\xi$ such that $h_Y^*(u) = h_Y^*(v)$) does *not* count as an error. Definition 4 is nonetheless useful as $hsp(\tilde{e})$ is forced to be $\emptyset$ at the monitored expression's root. Our main result follows.

**Theorem 1.** *Suppose that $\mathcal{H}$ is an $\epsilon'$-almost universal hash family with $k$ bits. Then the bounds in Table 2 follow, where $\epsilon = \epsilon' + 2^{-k}$, $|e| = \sup_{\xi \in X, i \in \mathbb{N}} |\llbracket e \rrbracket_i^\xi|$ is the maximum size of the relations computed for $e$, and $maxRate = \sup_{\xi \in X, x \in \mathbb{N}} |\{i \mid \tau_i = x\}|$ is the traces' maximum rate per time unit. If upper bounds on $maxRate$ and on $|e|$ for every sub-expression $e$ of $e_0$ are given, one can compute constants $c$ and $c'$ in polynomial time such that $fp_X(\tilde{M}) \leq \epsilon \cdot c$ and $fn_X(\tilde{M}) \leq \epsilon \cdot c'$, where $\tilde{M}$ is our monitor for $e_0$ and $\mathcal{H}$.*

The factors $a_I$, $b_I$, and $c_I$ in Table 2 are estimates of the number of time-points or pair of time-points that may be the source of errors of a particular kind. The derivation of the factors is explained in the extended report [42]. The asymmetry between $fp(\tilde{e}_1 \, \mathbf{S}_I^{\bowtie} \, \tilde{e}_2)$ and $fn(\tilde{e}_1 \, \mathbf{S}_I^{\triangleleft} \, \tilde{e}_2)$ and similarly for $\mathbf{U}$ is noteworthy. It is possible to construct examples that show that the false-negative probability of the $\triangleleft$ operators may exceed the tighter bound that uses $b_I$ instead of $c_I$.

Table 2 can be used to calculate error bounds given $\epsilon$, or to calculate the largest $\epsilon$ such that the error is below a given threshold. The collision probability $\epsilon$ is a proxy for the hash values' size, and thereby a factor of the randomized monitor's space complexity. Although the bounds in Table 2 are not tight, our empirical evaluation (Sect. 5) shows that they are useful. Moreover, as the size of the hash values is logarithmically related to $\epsilon$, achieving a tight bound is not critical in practice.

*Example 4.* For $e_{ex}$ from Example 1, we compute using Table 2 that $fp(\tilde{e}_{ex}), fn(\tilde{e}_{ex}) \leq \epsilon \cdot (28 \cdot maxRate \cdot |r| \cdot |\mathbf{O}_\mathbb{N}p| + (|\mathbf{O}_{[0,6]}e_{rb}|^2 + |\mathbf{O}_{[7,27]}e_{rb}|^2 - |\mathbf{O}_{[0,6]}e_{rb}| - |\mathbf{O}_{[7,27]}e_{rb}|)/2)$. Our implementation (Sect. 5) achieves a collision probability of $\epsilon \approx 2^{-61}$ with 63-bit hashes. Now assume that there are $10^6$ products in total $(|\mathbf{O}_\mathbb{N}p| = 10^6)$, and at most $10^5$ reviews are received per day $(maxRate \cdot |r| \leq 10^5, |\mathbf{O}_{[0,6]}e_{rb}| \leq 7 \cdot 10^5$, etc.). This yields an upper bound of around $2.3 \cdot 10^{-6}$ for each error type, or $4.6 \cdot 10^{-6}$ for the probability of any error occurring, per time-point. Conversely, we can compute that $\epsilon \leq 9.6 \cdot 10^{-17}$, which roughly corresponds to 55 hash bits, is sufficient to achieve an error rate below 0.1%.

The size bounds $|e|$ referred to by Theorem 1 are for the original, non-rewritten sub-expressions. Nonetheless, extensive domain knowledge might be necessary to obtain such bounds prior to monitoring, e.g., to choose the hash size appropriately. There is an alternative use of Table 2: The monitor may compute estimates of $fp(e_0)$ and $fn(e_0)$ for the specific trace it monitors. These can be more precise than the *a priori* estimates using Theorem 1. Our implementation computes trace-specific error bounds and presents them to the user. This can aid the user in judging the reliability of these verdicts. However, one challenge is that the observed relation sizes may be smaller than the bounds $|e|$, namely if there are false negatives, or hash collisions such that $|h_Y^*(\llbracket e \rrbracket_i^\xi)| < |\llbracket e \rrbracket_i^\xi|$. Calculating with observed sizes could result in estimates that are too small. (Larger observed sizes do not affect correctness because all our error bounds are monotonic.) We circumvent this by falling back to conservative upper bounds (e.g., the sum of the operands' sizes for a union) for those sub-expressions with hashed attributes and/or possible false negatives.

## 4.2   Space Complexity

We focus on data complexity [47] and characterize a subset of expressions on which our approach works best, in that the monitor state contains only hashed values. An expression $e$ is called *simple* if it is closed (i.e., $att(e) = \emptyset$), all intervals are finite, no functions appear in terms, all selections have the form $\sigma(t_1 = t_2)$ or $\sigma(t_1 \neq t_2)$, and all aggregations have type COUNT. Then the temporal connectives in the rewritten expression involve only hashed (not necessarily merged) attributes, which eliminates the influence of the domain value's encoding as follows. Let $X_{m,n}$ be the class of traces for which $maxRate \leq m, |r| \leq m$ for every relation name $r \in S$, and all domain values are represented by at most $n$ bits. It is known that $e$ can be monitored over prefixes of $X_{m,n}$ using polynomially many (in $m$) relations [6]. These relations have polynomially bounded cardinality as every interval in $e$ is finite. A typical monitor for $e$ would store all domain values that occur in the relations, and therefore the space complexity is multiplied by $n$. In contrast, our monitor works exclusively with relations over $k$-bit hashes. The polynomial bound on the number and cardinality of these relations persists, but it suffices to choose $k$ on the order of $\log(\text{poly}(m)) - \log x = O(\log m - \log x)$ to achieve an error probability below $x$. This follows from Theorem 1 and the fact that every sub-expression of $e$ has polynomially bounded size. Therefore, $k$ is independent of $n$.

**Theorem 2.** *Simple expressions can be monitored over traces in $X_{m,n}$ in $O(\text{poly}(m) + n)$ space (with a fixed error bound).*

## 5   Implementation and Evaluation

We implemented our randomized monitor as an extension of the MonPoly tool [6], written in OCaml. The extension is transparent to the user: hashing can be enabled by setting a single command-line option. We performed experiments, using both Amazon review data [36] and randomly generated data, to answer the following questions: (Q1) Are there non-trivial specifications and data for which monitoring benefits from our approach? (Q2) How much does it reduce the monitor's peak memory usage in practice? (Q3) How do our theoretical error bounds compare to the empirically observed error probability?

We added a module to MonPoly that implements the rewriting algorithm described in Sect. 3.2. Merging of attributes can be disabled to study its impact. For $\mathcal{H}$ we use the CLHASH family [32] truncated to $k = 63$ bits, the size of native integers in OCaml. Truncated CLHASH is $\epsilon'$-almost universal with $\epsilon' = 2.004/2^{63}$ for strings up to $2^{64}$ bytes [32, Lemmas 1 and 9], requiring only around 1 KiB to represent an element of $\mathcal{H}$. We modified MonPoly's relation data type to keep track of the error and size bounds as described in Sect. 4. OCaml programs rely on a garbage collector (GC), which makes it difficult to measure peak memory usage in a meaningful way. However, we found OCaml's GC to be conservative. Measured differences above a few MB were generally robust.

Our experiments were performed on two groups of expressions and data. The first group focused on a realistic use case, specifically the detection of fraudulent customer reviews. We used review data from Amazon spanning a period of over 20 years [36]. We restricted our attention to the "gift cards" category, which had the smallest number of products (1548) and a moderate number of reviews (147 194). We monitored Example 1 (adjusted to ignore additional attributes) and a formalization $e_{frd}$ of the first stage of Heydari et al.'s fake review detection system [25], shown in the extended report [42]. The latter detects weeks and product brands with suspicious review counts. (The second stage would require some natural language processing, which is outside of our scope.) We modified the fake detection example to use a one-year sliding window for the review average per brand, whereas the original uses a global average, which would require offline monitoring.

The second group was based on the expressions $e_1 \equiv \pi()(p(a) \bowtie \mathbf{O}_{[0,9]} q(a))$, $e_2 \equiv \pi()(p(a)\, \mathbf{S}^{\lhd}_{[0,9]}\, q(a))$, $e_3 \equiv \pi()((p(a)\, \mathbf{U}^{\bowtie}_{[0,9]}\, q(a,b)) \rhd q(a,b))$, and the one from Example 2 with all attributes projected away as $e_4$. In $e_3$, the hash abstraction of $q$ is computed twice: once for each of $q$'s occurrences. The expression $e_3'$ is a modification of $e_3$ in which the hash abstraction is shared by both occurrences. We generated pseudorandom trace prefixes with consecutive, non-repeating time-stamps over 100 time units with 20 000 tuples each, which were assigned randomly and uniformly to the relation names in the expression. For $e_4$, we generated only 50 tuples per time-point because the formula computes a Cartesian product, resulting in a large blow-up. The domain values were random alphanumeric strings with exactly 100 characters. The second group's purpose was to determine the impact of the expressions' structure on the memory usage. It is clear that hashing is less effective for smaller values, so we did not perform further experiments with such values.

We performed additional experiments with data suitable for the DejaVu tool [21,22]. DejaVu is a monitor for first-order past LTL with time constraints, implemented using binary decision diagrams (BDDs) instead of finite relations. DejaVu is the only other tool handling a large subset of TRA that we are aware of. Of our expressions, only $e_1$, $e_2$, and $e_4$ are supported by DejaVu because it lacks aggregation and future operators. It also cannot process simultaneous events. Therefore, we generated a separate set of traces (the "thin" set) with 2 000 time-points per time-stamp (50 for $e_4$), each consisting of a single tuple.

**Table 3.** Performance evaluation ($B$ = baseline, $Hm$ = merged hashes; percentages relative to $B$)

| | Memory (MiB) | | | | Runtime (s) | | Max. error bound | |
|---|---|---|---|---|---|---|---|---|
| | $B$ | $ID$ | $H$ | $Hm$ | $B$ | $Hm$ | $fp$ | $fn$ |
| $e_{ex}$ | 13.7 | 13.7 (−0%) | 12.9 (−6%) | 12.0 (−12%) | 20.5 | 17.2 (−16%) | $1 \cdot 10^{-5}$ | $1 \cdot 10^{-5}$ |
| $e_{frd}$ | 35.4 | 39.6 (+12%) | 28.8 (−19%) | 23.9 (−33%) | 22.7 | 22.2 (−2%) | $2 \cdot 10^{-10}$ | $2 \cdot 10^{-10}$ |
| $e_1$ | 81.0 | 74.7 (−8%) | 63.1 (−22%) | 63.3 (−22%) | 12.5 | 14.3 (+14%) | $3 \cdot 10^{-10}$ | 0 |
| $e_2$ | 56.0 | 56.0 (+0%) | 44.5 (−21%) | 44.6 (−20%) | 28.9 | 26.1 (−9%) | 0 | $1 \cdot 10^{-9}$ |
| $e_3$ | 80.9 | 104.2 (+29%) | 81.0 (+0%) | 81.1 (+0%) | 9.3 | 15.9 (+70%) | $1 \cdot 10^{-9}$ | $3 \cdot 10^{-10}$ |
| $e_3'$ | 80.8 | 81.0 (+0%) | 56.1 (−31%) | 56.4 (−30%) | 9.3 | 12.7 (+31%) | $1 \cdot 10^{-9}$ | $3 \cdot 10^{-10}$ |
| $e_4$ | 30.3 | 47.3 (+56%) | 50.0 (+65%) | 37.7 (+24%) | 12.0 | 14.3 (+19%) | $2 \cdot 10^{-9}$ | 0 |

*Memory Usage and Runtime.* We measured the peak memory usage and runtime using MonPoly's original algorithm ($B$), a special mode ($ID$) where the hash function is replaced by identity, and nonmerged ($H$) and merged ($Hm$) hashing. The purpose of $ID$ was to determine whether our expression rewriting, the added operators, and the error tracking code had any effect on their own. Measurements were obtained on a laptop with an Intel i5-7200U CPU (2.5 GHz, Turbo Boost disabled) and 8 GB RAM (no swap) under Linux 5.15.13. MonPoly was compiled with OCaml 4.12.0 and default GC settings. We used the UNIX time command to measure elapsed real time ("runtime") and the maximum resident set size ("memory"). We computed the arithmetic mean over 3 repetitions. We compared against DejaVu revision 1e1f4eb0, running under OpenJDK 11.0.13 with an initial heap size of 8 MB. The BDD size was set to 15 bits based on the expected number of distinct domain values within the expressions' intervals.

Table 3 shows the results. The percentages are relative to the baseline $B$. Hashing reduced the amount of memory needed for all formulas except $e_3$ and $e_4$, and merging reduced it further for the Amazon examples. The effect was small for $e_{ex}$ because there the relevant domain values were fairly short (at most 14 bytes each). The memory for $e_3$ increased under $ID$ because the added hashing operators prevent the sharing of nodes in the immutable AVL trees that MonPoly uses to represent relations. Under $B$, the two occurrences of $q$ share these trees. They are hashed twice in $e_3$, resulting in independent copies, but not in $e_3'$, where memory improved. This sensitivity to the expression structure demonstrates the complexity of the optimization problem from Sect. 3.2. We conjecture that the generally bad behavior of $e_4$ is also due to the loss of sharing, specifically in the O operators.

We could not draw definite conclusions about the impact on runtime. Computing hashes and transforming the relations obviously incurs some overhead, whereas comparing hash values in the search tree implementation might be faster than comparing long strings. The last two columns of Table 3 show the largest error bound output by the monitor (maximum across time-points and repetitions). For our test data, we find that the accuracy loss is very small and errors are highly unlikely. For example, the error bounds for the $e_{frd}$ experiment correspond to a probability of less than $2 \cdot 10^{-6}$ for an error occurring anywhere in the trace prefix, which consisted of 2 889 time-points.

DejaVu generally used much more memory than MonPoly on the "thin" traces: 984 MiB for $e_1$ (MonPoly $Hm$: 26.2 MiB) and 972 MiB for $e_2$ ($Hm$: 12.1 MiB). Memory usage exceeded 2 GiB for $e_4$, hence we decided to exclude this expression from the experiments. Further research is necessary to determine whether the large memory footprint is due to the implementation or a fundamental consequence of using BDDs. We note that the runtimes of DejaVu and MonPoly are highly incomparable, the latter being more than 6 times faster on $e_1$ but 81 times slower on $e_2$. Hashing is ineffective on the "thin" traces, resulting in an increase by 1% over $B$ for $e_1$ and a decrease by 8% for $e_2$, which are likely just noise. However, these traces are one order of magnitude smaller than those used for Table 3, so factors that are independent of the domain values dominate.

*Error Probabilities and Bounds.* We artificially truncated hash values to simulate the impact of their size. The left plot in Fig. 1 shows the error probability observed over 100 repetitions with different hash function seeds. We computed the midpoint of a Wilson score interval [50] at 95% confidence for every time-point, and took the maximum over all time-points. The right plot in Fig. 1 shows the corresponding error bounds output by the monitor (*fp* and *fn* added together, mean across all repetitions, then the maximum over time-points). The error bounds are almost tight for $e_1$: as true positives are extremely unlikely for our pseudorandom traces, every collision in $e_1$'s join is observed as a false

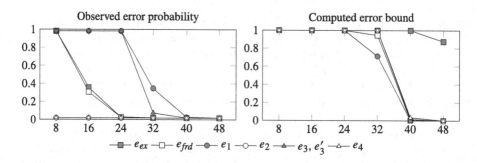

**Fig. 1.** Error probabilities and bounds for truncated hashes ($x =$ number of bits)

positive. For $e_{ex}$, the bounds overestimate the observed error by a large margin. This partially due to the projection operator, which hides deviations in the count aggregations as long as they do not affect the selection, and the fact that our worst-case analysis for aggregations holds for one large group, whereas the Amazon data has many groups. For $e_2$ and $e_4$, we never observed any error because uniformly random traces are not the worst case for these expressions. For example, we can trigger errors for $e_2$ by generating much fewer $q$ than $p$ tuples.

## 6   Related Work

Approaches for monitoring parametrized events can be classified into several categories [23]. We focus on the bottom-up evaluation of specifications using finite relations [10,20], which has been implemented in the MonPoly tool [6] for a fragment of metric first-order temporal logic (MFOTL) formulas. Our temporal–relational algebra (TRA) described in Sect. 2 is a direct encoding of that fragment. The principle of hashing event parameters could be applied to some of the other monitoring approaches as well, e.g., parametric trace slicing [41] and automatic structures [22]. Our error probability analysis is specific to TRA.

Some specifications can be monitored in constant space even on streams with parametrized events and unbounded rate [12,16,33]. Hashing allows us to reduce the memory needed for a class of specifications that falls outside of the constant-space fragment. Alternatively, monitoring performance can be improved by sampling from the input trace and interpolating over the gaps [3,28]; a hidden Markov model represents the prior knowledge about the monitored system and it plays an important role for achieving high accuracy. Unlike our approach, sampling usually reduces the time overhead of monitoring. Grigore and Kiefer [18] studied optimal event sampling strategies for systems modeled as Markov chains. In contrast to these works that rely on sampling, we do not require any prior knowledge about the monitored system. Only for bounding the error probability we assume that certain trace statistics are available.

Statistical model checking [31,44] is concerned with the verification of stochastic systems. The checked properties are quantitative: they express constraints on probabilities. Statistical model checking uses randomized simulations and thus yields approximate results. It is different from the randomized monitoring we consider, as our monitor checks individual traces, not system models, for safety properties with nonprobabilistic semantics.

There exists an extensive body of research on randomized algorithms and lower bounds related to data storage and retrieval. The standard example is the Bloom filter [8], which approximately answers set membership queries for static sets. There are variants supporting deletion [15] and dynamic resizing [2]. Set membership queries on dynamic sets can be reduced to the monitoring problem for sufficiently expressive specifications, but the latter is clearly more general. Intersections [19] and Cartesian products [48] of Bloom filters do not scale well to complex queries over relations with varying attributes, which frequently occur in first-order monitoring.

Bloom filters have been used successfully to save space in model checking algorithms, e.g., in the bitstate method [13,27], where the filters are used to track visited states. The only operation performed on the filter is a membership test, whereas first-order monitors apply complex transformations to their state. Therefore, we cannot hash the relations in the state as a whole, and the error analysis becomes more intricate. A different line of work in the model checking domain uses lossless compression schemes for states [7,26,30]. To our knowledge, such schemes have not yet been applied to monitoring, with the exception of BDDs [22]. Some of the ideas could prove fruitful, e.g., the work by Laarman et al. [30], which enforces sharing in a systematic way.

Another family of probabilistic data structures [14,39] represents the elements of a finite set using compact hash values. The work by Naor and Yogev [35] on membership queries over sliding windows is perhaps the closest to monitoring. Unlike them, we do not aim at achieving close-to-optimal memory usage, but rather we consider more richly structured sets (relations). Probabilistic data structures have been analyzed in adversarial environments [11], which can be relevant in the context of monitoring security policies. We do not consider an adversary model in this paper. Instead, we assume that there is no feedback from the monitor's output to a possible adversary who could influence the trace adaptively.

## 7   Conclusion

We presented a randomized monitoring algorithm that compresses domain values using hash functions. We analysed its error probability and showed that useful upper bounds can be obtained in practice. Based on the evaluation results, we believe that hashing is a useful optimization in space-constrained applications where a small error probability can be tolerated. There are three main limitations: First, the focus on domain values means that the approach is ineffective for traces with small domain values. Second, the current implementation within MonPoly is not optimized for memory usage, and its immutable data structures sometimes exhibit unpredictable behavior. We plan to reimplement and optimize the monitor using imperative data structures. Third, the structure of the specification may prevent hashing of some or all attributes, e.g., if functions are computed over the attributes. Open questions include: Can expressions be rewritten to allow more hashing, and how could this optimization problem be solved? What are space lower bounds for the operations relevant to first-order monitoring, going beyond basic set membership and sliding windows?

**Acknowledgement.** The author thanks David Basin, Srđan Krstić, Dmitriy Traytel, and the anonymous reviewers for their helpful comments and suggestions. This research was supported by the US Air Force grant "Monitoring at Any Cost" (FA9550-17-1-0306).

# References

1. Abiteboul, S., Hull, R., Vianu, V.: Foundations of Databases. Addison-Wesley, Boston (1995)
2. Almeida, P.S., Baquero, C., Preguiça, N.M., Hutchison, D.: Scalable Bloom filters. Inf. Process. Lett. **101**(6), 255–261 (2007)
3. Bartocci, E., Grosu, R., Karmarkar, A., Smolka, S.A., Stoller, S.D., Zadok, E., Seyster, J.: Adaptive runtime verification. In: Qadeer, S., Tasiran, S. (eds.) RV 2012. LNCS, vol. 7687, pp. 168–182. Springer, Heidelberg (2013). https://doi.org/10.1007/978-3-642-35632-2_18
4. Basin, D., Dardinier, T., Heimes, L., Krstić, S., Raszyk, M., Schneider, J., Traytel, D.: A formally verified, optimized monitor for metric first-order dynamic logic. In: Peltier, N., Sofronie-Stokkermans, V. (eds.) IJCAR 2020. LNCS (LNAI), vol. 12166, pp. 432–453. Springer, Cham (2020). https://doi.org/10.1007/978-3-030-51074-9_25
5. Basin, D., Klaedtke, F., Marinovic, S., Zălinescu, E.: Monitoring of temporal first-order properties with aggregations. Formal Methods Syst. Des. **46**(3), 262–285 (2015). https://doi.org/10.1007/s10703-015-0222-7
6. Basin, D., Klaedtke, F., Müller, S., Zălinescu, E.: Monitoring metric first-order temporal properties. J. ACM **62**(2), 15:1–15:45 (2015)
7. Berg, F.I.: Recursive variable-length state compression for multi-core software model checking. In: Dutle, A., Moscato, M.M., Titolo, L., Muñoz, C.A., Perez, I. (eds.) NFM 2021. LNCS, vol. 12673, pp. 340–357. Springer, Cham (2021). https://doi.org/10.1007/978-3-030-76384-8_21
8. Bloom, B.H.: Space/time trade-offs in hash coding with allowable errors. Commun. ACM **13**(7), 422–426 (1970)
9. Carter, L., Floyd, R.W., Gill, J., Markowsky, G., Wegman, M.N.: Exact and approximate membership testers. In: STOC 1978, pp. 59–65. ACM (1978)
10. Chomicki, J.: Efficient checking of temporal integrity constraints using bounded history encoding. ACM Trans. Database Syst. **20**(2), 149–186 (1995)
11. Clayton, D., Patton, C., Shrimpton, T.: Probabilistic data structures in adversarial environments. In: CCS 2019, pp. 1317–1334. ACM (2019)
12. D'Angelo, B., et al.: LOLA: runtime monitoring of synchronous systems. In: TIME 2005, pp. 166–174. IEEE Computer Society (2005)
13. Dillinger, P.C., Manolios, P.: Bloom filters in probabilistic verification. In: Hu, A.J., Martin, A.K. (eds.) FMCAD 2004. LNCS, vol. 3312, pp. 367–381. Springer, Heidelberg (2004). https://doi.org/10.1007/978-3-540-30494-4_26

14. Fan, B., Andersen, D.G., Kaminsky, M., Mitzenmacher, M.: Cuckoo filter: practically better than bloom. In: CoNEXT 2014, pp. 75–88. ACM (2014)
15. Fan, L., Cao, P., Almeida, J.M., Broder, A.Z.: Summary cache: a scalable wide-area web cache sharing protocol. IEEE/ACM Trans. Netw. $8(3)$, 281–293 (2000)
16. Faymonville, P., Finkbeiner, B., Schledjewski, M., Schwenger, M., Stenger, M., Tentrup, L., Torfah, H.: StreamLAB: stream-based monitoring of cyber-physical systems. In: Dillig, I., Tasiran, S. (eds.) CAV 2019. LNCS, vol. 11561, pp. 421–431. Springer, Cham (2019). https://doi.org/10.1007/978-3-030-25540-4_24
17. Fox, E.A., Chen, Q.F., Daoud, A.M., Heath, L.S.: Order-preserving minimal perfect hash functions and information retrieval. ACM Trans. Inf. Syst. $9(3)$, 281–308 (1991)
18. Grigore, R., Kiefer, S.: Selective monitoring. In: CONCUR 2018. LIPIcs, vol. 118, pp. 20:1–20:16. Schloss Dagstuhl - Leibniz-Zentrum für Informatik (2018)
19. Guo, D., Wu, J., Chen, H., Yuan, Y., Luo, X.: The dynamic bloom filters. IEEE Trans. Knowl. Data Eng. $22(1)$, 120–133 (2010)
20. Havelund, K.: Rule-based runtime verification revisited. Int. J. Softw. Tools Technol. Transf. $17(2)$, 143–170 (2014). https://doi.org/10.1007/s10009-014-0309-2
21. Havelund, K., Peled, D.: First-order timed runtime verification using BDDs. In: Hung, D.V., Sokolsky, O. (eds.) ATVA 2020. LNCS, vol. 12302, pp. 3–24. Springer, Cham (2020). https://doi.org/10.1007/978-3-030-59152-6_1
22. Havelund, K., Peled, D., Ulus, D.: First-order temporal logic monitoring with BDDs. Formal Methods Syst. Des. $56(1)$, 1–21 (2020)
23. Havelund, K., Reger, G., Thoma, D., Zălinescu, E.: Monitoring events that carry data. In: Bartocci, E., Falcone, Y. (eds.) Lectures on Runtime Verification. LNCS, vol. 10457, pp. 61–102. Springer, Cham (2018). https://doi.org/10.1007/978-3-319-75632-5_3
24. Havelund, K., Roşu, G.: Synthesizing monitors for safety properties. In: Katoen, J.-P., Stevens, P. (eds.) TACAS 2002. LNCS, vol. 2280, pp. 342–356. Springer, Heidelberg (2002). https://doi.org/10.1007/3-540-46002-0_24
25. Heydari, A., Ali Tavakoli, M., Salim, N.: Detection of fake opinions using time series. Expert Syst. Appl. $58$, 83–92 (2016)
26. Holzmann, G.J.: State compression in SPIN: recursive indexing and compression training runs. In: SPIN Workshop 1997 (1997)
27. Holzmann, G.J.: An analysis of bitstate hashing. Formal Methods Syst. Des. $13(3)$, 289–307 (1998)
28. Kalajdzic, K., Bartocci, E., Smolka, S.A., Stoller, S.D., Grosu, R.: Runtime verification with particle filtering. In: Legay, A., Bensalem, S. (eds.) RV 2013. LNCS, vol. 8174, pp. 149–166. Springer, Heidelberg (2013). https://doi.org/10.1007/978-3-642-40787-1_9
29. Koymans, R.: Specifying real-time properties with metric temporal logic. Real Time Syst. $2(4)$, 255–299 (1990)
30. Laarman, A., van de Pol, J., Weber, M.: Parallel recursive state compression for free. In: Groce, A., Musuvathi, M. (eds.) SPIN 2011. LNCS, vol. 6823, pp. 38–56. Springer, Heidelberg (2011). https://doi.org/10.1007/978-3-642-22306-8_4
31. Legay, A., Delahaye, B., Bensalem, S.: Statistical model checking: an overview. In: Barringer, H., et al. (eds.) RV 2010. LNCS, vol. 6418, pp. 122–135. Springer, Heidelberg (2010). https://doi.org/10.1007/978-3-642-16612-9_11
32. Lemire, D., Kaser, O.: Faster 64-bit universal hashing using carry-less multiplications. J. Cryptogr. Eng. $6(3)$, 171–185 (2015). https://doi.org/10.1007/s13389-015-0110-5

33. Mamouras, K., Raghothaman, M., Alur, R., Ives, Z.G., Khanna, S.: StreamQRE: modular specification and efficient evaluation of quantitative queries over streaming data. In: PLDI 2017, pp. 693–708. ACM (2017)
34. Mitzenmacher, M., Upfal, E.: Probability and Computing: Randomization and Probabilistic Techniques in Algorithms and Data Analysis, 2nd edn. Cambridge University Press, Cambridge (2017)
35. Naor, M., Yogev, E.: Tight bounds for sliding bloom filters. Algorithmica **73**(4), 652–672 (2015)
36. Ni, J., Li, J., McAuley, J.J.: Justifying recommendations using distantly-labeled reviews and fine-grained aspects. In: EMNLP 2019, pp. 188–197. Association for Computational Linguistics (2019). Dataset: https://nijianmo.github.io/amazon/index.html
37. de Oliveira, D.B., Cucinotta, T., de Oliveira, R.S.: Efficient formal verification for the Linux kernel. In: Ölveczky, P.C., Salaün, G. (eds.) SEFM 2019. LNCS, vol. 11724, pp. 315–332. Springer, Cham (2019). https://doi.org/10.1007/978-3-030-30446-1_17
38. Orgun, M.A., Wadge, W.W.: A relational algebra as a query language for temporal DATALOG. In: Tjoa, A., Ramos, I. (eds.) DEXA 1992, pp. 276–281. Springer, Vienna (1992). https://doi.org/10.1007/978-3-7091-7557-6_48
39. Pagh, A., Pagh, R., Rao, S.S.: An optimal Bloom filter replacement. In: SODA 2005, pp. 823–829. SIAM (2005)
40. Pagh, R., Segev, G., Wieder, U.: How to approximate a set without knowing its size in advance. In: FOCS 2013, pp. 80–89. IEEE Computer Society (2013)
41. Roşu, G., Chen, F.: Semantics and algorithms for parametric monitoring. Log. Methods Comput. Sci. **8**(1) (2012)
42. Schneider, J.: Randomized first-order monitoring with hashing (extended report) (2022). https://ethz.ch/content/dam/ethz/special-interest/infk/inst-infsec/information-security-group-dam/research/publications/pub2022/rv22-extended.pdf
43. Schumann, J., Rozier, K.Y., Reinbacher, T., Mengshoel, O.J., Mbaya, T., Ippolito, C.: Towards real-time, on-board, hardware-supported sensor and software health management for unmanned aerial systems. Int. J. Progn. Health Manag. **6**(1), 1–27 (2015)
44. Sen, K., Viswanathan, M., Agha, G.: Statistical model checking of black-box probabilistic systems. In: Alur, R., Peled, D.A. (eds.) CAV 2004. LNCS, vol. 3114, pp. 202–215. Springer, Heidelberg (2004). https://doi.org/10.1007/978-3-540-27813-9_16
45. Stinson, D.R.: Universal hashing and authentication codes. Des. Codes Cryptogr. **4**(4), 369–380 (1994)
46. Tuzhilin, A., Clifford, J.: A temporal relational algebra as basis for temporal relational completeness. In: VLDB Conference 1990, pp. 13–23. Morgan Kaufmann (1990)
47. Vardi, M.Y.: The complexity of relational query languages (extended abstract). In: STOC 1982, pp. 137–146. ACM (1982)
48. Wang, Z., Luo, T., Xu, G., Wang, X.: The application of cartesian-join of Bloom filters to supporting membership query of multidimensional data. In: 2014 IEEE International Congress on Big Data, pp. 288–295. IEEE Computer Society (2014)
49. Wegman, M.N., Carter, L.: New hash functions and their use in authentication and set equality. J. Comput. Syst. Sci. **22**(3), 265–279 (1981)
50. Wilson, E.B.: Probable inference, the law of succession, and statistical inference. J. Am. Stat. Assoc. **22**(158), 209–212 (1927)

# Automated Surgical Procedure Assistance Framework Using Deep Learning and Formal Runtime Monitoring

Gaurav Gupta$^{(\boxtimes)}$, Saumya Shankar$^{(\boxtimes)}$, and Srinivas Pinisetty$^{(\boxtimes)}$

Indian Institute of Technology Bhubaneswar, Bhubaneswar, India
{gg13,ss117,spinisetty}@iitbbs.ac.in

**Abstract.** There have been tremendous developments in minimally invasive approaches for various surgical treatments due to the benefits for patients such as less pain and faster recovery. However, surgeons face a number of obstacles while performing these surgeries, including inadequate depth perception, limited range of motion, and difficulty gauging the force to be delivered in the tissue. As a result, improved support for these surgeries is needed to provide surgeons with automated assistance, reducing complications and needless patient damage.

In this work, we propose an approach, leveraging deep learning and formal methods, to develop an automated surgical procedure assistance framework. To the best of our knowledge, our framework is the first to develop an automated surgical procedure assistant using deep learning and formal methods. We use Faster R-CNN to identify the surgical instruments/tools used to perform the surgical procedure. Based on the high-level description of the crucial guidelines that should be obeyed during a good surgical procedure, we obtain the monitoring code that identifies a bad behaviour in a surgical procedure using formal monitor synthesis techniques. For example, any violation in the tools' usage during the surgical procedure can alert the surgeons to take immediate corrective measures. To illustrate the practical applicability of the proposed approach, we consider the case of cholecystectomy (laparoscopic) surgery and illustrate how our framework can assist a surgeon during a laparoscopic surgical procedure. We implemented the proposed framework, and validated its technical feasibility using (offline) video samples of the surgical procedure from the modified Cholec80 dataset.

**Keywords:** Deep learning · Faster R-CNN · Formal methods · Laparoscopic surgery · Surgical tool detection

## 1 Introduction

In the surgical field, nowadays people not only care about the treatment results, but also the comfort and minimal invasion during the treatment, which has given

---

This work has been partially supported by IIT Bhubaneswar Seed Grant (SP093).

T. Dang and V. Stolz (Eds.): RV 2022, LNCS 13498, pp. 25–44, 2022.
https://doi.org/10.1007/978-3-031-17196-3_2

rise to the new era of Minimally Invasive Surgeries (MISs). MIS emerged in the 1980s, which include surgical techniques that limit the size of incisions needed. Here, surgeons make tiny cuts in the skin, and insert small tools, cameras, and lights to operate the patient. In the last 20 years, many surgeons have come to prefer MIS over the traditional (open) surgeries since, it requires smaller incisions and cause less pain, scarring, and damage to healthy tissue. Thus, the patient will have a faster recovery and shorter hospital stays (up to 50% reductions for some procedures [17]).

There have been constant innovations to improve MIS that include technological innovations in instruments used (such as laparoscopic instruments), novel clinical measurements, and MIS-associated technologies (such as surgical robotics, image guidance systems, and advanced signal processing methods). However, MIS is accompanied with many visualization and control challenges (images from the camera are from unnatural positions with unintuitive scale). There are problems like inadequate depth perception, limited range of motion, and difficulty gauging the force to be delivered in the tissue. These are often time taking and have risks of complications due to anesthesia, bleeding and infections.

MIS require surgeons to have a particular skill set to gain excellence and optimized outcomes. Experience and assistance (manual or automated) during surgeries reduces operative time and complications, especially in complex surgeries. Thus, giving high confidence to the surgeons. The assistance provided during surgeries mainly includes, experts giving immediate feedback on the ongoing surgery performed by surgeons. According to a study report[1], there is a critical shortage of expert surgeons (as supervisors), and unavailability of considerable time from them to observe and provide feedback on the surgeries performed by the trainee surgeons. Thus, there is a need to adopt the automated way of providing feedback to the surgeons during the surgery.

The automated assistance through observation and feedback, may include various Artificial Intelligence (AI) techniques to analyze a surgical procedure. For example, Machine Learning (ML) models can be trained on surgical procedure videos, which can detect various patterns and forecast health risks/illness as well as treatments, to ease the overall process for surgeons. In the last decade, we have seen tremendous improvements in the field of AI/ML. These ML techniques have been applied in robot-assisted surgeries [22] for better performances. For example, ML techniques have successfully performed detection of the surgical tools, so that we can analyse the movement of each tool during a complex surgery and can generate feedback for the surgeons [23]. This kind of rich analysis using Deep Learning (DL) [19] can help upgrade the surgical procedure. These ML approaches combined with techniques providing rigorous correctness guarantees, such as formal methods, help in building robust and reliable systems.

Designing and developing critical systems require the use of formal methods and model-driven developments. Since formal specification languages have a

---

[1] The Complexities of Physician Supply and Demand: Projections From 2018 to 2033, Prepared for the AAMC by IHS Markit Ltd., June 2020, https://www.aamc.org/media/45976/download?attachment.

precise syntax and semantics, formally defining policies will make them clearer. It will eliminate ambiguities and inconsistencies, and make them more easily amenable to automatic processing and code synthesis with certain correctness guarantees.

Although there are few frameworks [3,38], with absolute guarantees of correctness, but these do not provide specific automated feedback to the surgeons during a surgery. Thus, we propose a framework for providing automated surgical procedure assistance, using DL and formal runtime monitoring approaches. We use Faster R-CNN [41], a region-based Convolutional Neural Network (CNN) to identify/detect the surgical instruments/tools that appear during a surgery. The critical policies that should be followed in a good surgical procedure are formally defined (expressed as Valued Discrete Timed Automata, see Sect. 4). Based on the monitor synthesis approaches proposed in [29,37], the runtime monitors are generated directly from these policies. These monitors will take the array of identified tools from CNN and detect any violation of the critical policies during the surgical procedure and alert the surgeons about it. This ensures inappropriate behaviour (deviations from policies) during a surgical procedure are identified.

To demonstrate the adaptable use of the proposed approach, we consider the case of cholecystectomy (laparoscopic) surgeries. Cholecystectomy is a type of laparoscopic surgery performed in the gall bladder, with the aid of a laparoscope (video camera). We illustrate how our framework can assist a surgeon during a laparoscopic surgical procedure, by identifying bad behaviours and alerting the surgeons about it. We implemented the proposed framework[2], and the technical feasibility of the approach is validated using (offline) video samples of the surgical procedure from the modified Cholec80 dataset [46].

## 2  Overview of the Proposed System

As discussed in Sect. 1, we work on automated surgical procedure assistance framework in a (real-time) surgery using DL and formal runtime monitoring approaches. We do so by providing feedback to the surgeons during a surgery, so that it can be carried out effectively even without the expert's supervision. Here is an overview of our work: we employ DL approaches to detect tools that are used during a surgical procedure. Based on the knowledge of the clinical guidelines from the domain expert surgeons, the key policies to be followed for safe surgical procedure can be understood. From that understanding, we formally specify the policies from which a monitor is synthesized. It will identify any bad behaviour during a surgical procedure by looking at the sequence, time of tools' occurance, etc. and intimate the surgeons about it. In this section, we give the architecture (shown in Fig. 1) of the work which comprises of two modules: tool identification module and monitoring module. We describe each module and discuss this framework for a laparoscopic surgery.

---

[2] The framework is available at *https://doi.org/10.5281/zenodo.6899355*.

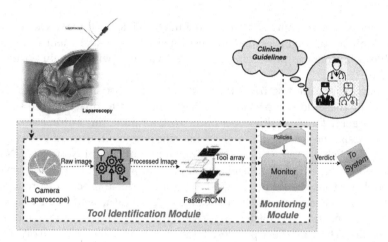

**Fig. 1.** Architecture of the proposed system

*Software Architecture:* The first module is the tool identification module. It consists of an input source (video camera) which captures frames/images in real time and processes it (processing may involve various transformations, such as image enhancement, scaling, etc.) to make it suitable to be fed to the Deep Neural Network (DNN) model. The DNN model is trained on the surgery dataset which takes the processed frame and identifies/detects the surgical instruments used in the frame (if any). It returns an array having a boolean entry for each tool's presence or absence. This array is forwarded to the monitoring module which will analyze the tool's occurrence against some policies.

The clinical guidelines for a safe surgical procedure, from domain expert surgeons can be formally defined as policies. In the monitoring module, the monitor is synthesized directly from these policies, which will take the tool occurrence array and will keep track of the specified policies being obeyed by the received arrays. It will report violations of the policies, if any. At last, the violation message is sent to the system which will convey it to the surgeon to take the corrective action.

The above architecture generalizes well to many surgeries having an annotated dataset to train the model. In order to use the proposed architecture to a specific surgery, the appropriate transformations have to be applied to the captured frames. Then, these frames have to be fed to the DNN model that has been trained on the corresponding surgery's dataset. Also, relevant policies have to be understood from the experts and specified formally, which covers "good" practices during a surgery (or resp. "bad" practices that may happen in a surgery) to synthesize a monitor.

As stated in Sect. 1, we consider laparoscopic surgeries, which are MIS, performed in the abdomen (gall bladder), with the aid of a laparoscope. A laparoscope is a lean slender shaped tool with tiny video camera and light on the tip. With few millimeters small incisions, the surgeon inserts different instruments, including the laparoscope through the abdominal wall, and performs the surgery while visualizing it on a video screen. One can even generate a diverse multitude of realistically looking synthetic images, by image-to-image translation method, from a simple laparoscopy simulation, to gather ample data [30]. We take modified Cholec80 dataset [46] of cholecystectomy (laparoscopic) surgery, for training the DNN model of the tool identification module. For illustrating our approach, we consider the following set of example policies for the laparoscopic surgeries (specifying a good surgical behaviour):

*Example 1 (Example policies).* Consider simple policies $P_1$ and $P_2$, defined below, which analyzes tool usage patterns and are used to validate a surgical procedure:

- $P_1$: "Tool $T_2$ (e.g. Irrigator) should not be used after tool $T_3$ (e.g. Specimen Bag)";
- $P_2$: "Tool $T_1$ (e.g. Bipolar) should not be used for more than 20 t.u. continuously".

One can also include other policies, for example, a policy which keeps a count on the usage of tool in the complete surgery, etc.

In the following sections, we will see further details of each of the modules presented in the architecture (shown in Fig. 1).

## 3   Surgical Tool Detection

One of the most complex challenges in computer vision is object detection. Researchers have been developing various algorithms for improvements and have achieved remarkable results. Traditional object detection methods like the Viola-Jones detector (2001) [47], HOG (2006) [8] and DPM (2008) [12] have performed quite well. These methods have their limitations in dealing with images and videos because of their complex features.

Since the last decade, we have seen tremendous improvements in ML and DL techniques. When DL is used for object detection, it has shown to achieve state-of-the-art results. DL-based object detector solves object detection in two steps: 1) finds an arbitrary number of objects in the frame, 2) classify every object and estimate its size with a bounding box. One can divide these tasks into stages (like Fast-RCNN [15]) to make the process easier to achieve better results. Some methods, like YOLO [40], combine both tasks into one step to achieve better performance but at the cost of accuracy. We have used Faster-RCNN for tool detection, a two-stage object detection algorithm which gave high precision and accuracy.

### 3.1   Faster-RCNN

Faster R-CNN Fig. 2 is a region-based CNN technique mainly developed for object detection. The approach is inclined towards real-time object detection. Faster R-CNN introduced Region Proposal Network (RPN), which increased its performance over Fast R-CNN [15]. RPN takes an image as input and gives a set of proposed regions where objects can be found, as output. We are using a pre-trained CNN model of VGG-16 with 13 sharable layers. It is connected to two fully connected layers- a box regression layer (reg) and a box classification layer (cls). We are using a $3 \times 3$ spatial window size on this input image to generate region proposals.

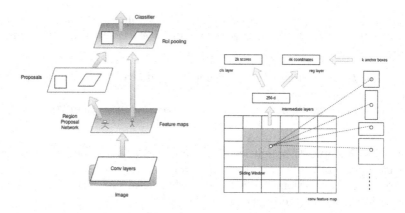

**Fig. 2.** Architecture of Faster R-CNN [41]

Faster R-CNN also uses the concept of anchors Fig. 2, which are fixed-sized boxes generated, having their centre at the sliding window. Anchors uses scales and aspects ratios; we have used three scales and three aspect ratios in our model, resulting in a total of 9 anchor boxes at each sliding window position. Faster R-CNN assigns a binary objectness label to each anchor, indicating the presence of an object in it. To the anchors with positive objectness label, it further assigns positive or negative labels depending on their Intersection over Union (IoU) with any ground truth box. Positive labels are assigned to anchors with IoU greater than 0.7, and negative labels are assigned to anchors with IoU less than 0.3. Only positive and negative labelled anchors are used for the training of RPN.

Now, we define our multi-task (classification and regression) loss function [41] as:

$$L\left(\{p_i\}, \{t_i\}\right) = \frac{1}{N_{cls}} \sum_i L_{cls}\left(p_i, p_i^*\right) + \lambda \frac{1}{N_{reg}} \sum_i p_i^* L_{reg}\left(t_i, t_i^*\right)$$

where:

- $i$: index of the anchor
- $p_i$: predicted probability of anchor $i$ being an object
- $p_i^*$: label for ground truth anchor {1: positive , 0: negative}
- $t_i$: vector for 4 parametrised coordinates giving the position of the positive anchor

- $t_i^*$: ground truth box coordinates associated with a positive anchor.
- $N_{cls}$: normalising factor for classification loss.
- $N_{reg}$: normalising factor for regression loss.
- $\lambda$: balancing factor
- $L_{cls}$: log loss over two classes (object or not)
- $L_{reg}$ : robust loss (smooth L1 loss)

We also parametrise each coordinate of bounding box regression as:

$$t_x = \frac{(x - x_a)}{w_a}; t_y = \frac{(y - y_a)}{h_a}$$

$$t_w = \log\left(\frac{w}{w_a}\right); t_h = \log\left(\frac{h}{h_a}\right)$$

$$t_x^* = \frac{(x^* - x_a)}{w_a}; t_y^* = \frac{(y^* - y_a)}{h_a}$$

$$t_w^* = \log\left(\frac{w^*}{w_a}\right); t_h^* = \log\left(\frac{h^*}{h_a}\right)$$

where:

- $x, y$ are box centre coordinates
- $w, h$ are width and height of the box
- $x, x^*, x_a$ are for predicted box, anchor box and ground truth box respectively.

*Note:* We are calculating regression loss only for positively labelled anchors, that's why $p_i^* L_{reg}$.

## 3.2   Dataset

In 2016, M2CAI[3] had launched two open online challenges- M2CAI tool presence detection challenge and M2CAI workflow (phase) detection challenge. Cholec80 provided a dataset having 80 videos with phase and tool annotations for these challenges. Fifteen videos were used in the M2CAI tool presence detection challenge (10 for training and validation, 5 for testing). These released videos are 30 to 70 min long, having 25 frames per second (fps) but later sampled to 1 fps to obtain around 23000 total frames. These frames had been binary classified for presence or absence of 7 tools - Grasper, Hook, Scissors, Specimen bag, Bipolar, Clipper and Irrigator (shown in the Fig. 3).

We have used a modified version of this dataset, released by Stanford University [19], since we want to do both tool detection and localisation in a frame. It contains 2811 frames having spatial bounding boxes annotations around the tools done by experts. Out of these 2811 frames, 2248 and 563 are used for training and validation respectively. These frames contain at most three tools being used simultaneously. Table 1 shows number of annotated images for each tool in this dataset.

---

[3] Workshop and challenges on modeling and monitoring of computer assisted interventions, http://camma.u-strasbg.fr/m2cai2016/index.php/program-challenge/.

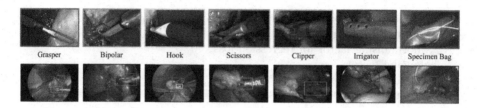

**Fig. 3.** Showing all 7 tools used in our dataset. (Source [19])

**Table 1.** Annotated images for each tool in our dataset

| Tools | Number of annotated images |
|---|---|
| Bipolar | 450 |
| Clipper | 400 |
| Grasper | 1422 |
| Hook | 308 |
| Irrigator | 485 |
| Scissors | 388 |
| Specimen Bag | 476 |

### 3.3 Implementation

RPNs are trained by backpropagation using Stochastic Gradient Descent (SGD). In this strategy, we use $N(= 256)$ randomly sampled positive and negative anchors. This mini-batch is selected so that the ratio of positive to negative anchors is close to 1:1, ensuring the model to be unbiased. We use transfer learning for initializing weights in our RPN. Since we use VGG-16, we initialise our first 13 layers with the weights of the model pre-trained on ImageNet classification, through which it learns to detect basic features. We fine-tune our network by training it with our dataset. In the training part, we set our learning rate to 0.001 and use ReduceLRonPlateau (built-in function of Keras) to decrease it by a factor of 10, if it remains constant for five epochs. Thus, we made our model's learning rate adaptable which improved precision and accuracy. We implemented this Faster R-CNN in our surgical tool detection. Since, the size of the image in our dataset is $334 \times 596$, thus we keep our image resizing to 450 to ensure that our trained model also works well for tool detection in surgical videos with a frame size of $460 \times 680$.

Anchors have different scales and aspect ratios. We have used anchors with box areas of $128^2$, $256^2$ and $512^2$ pixels and with aspect ratios of 1:1, 1:2 and 2:1. These anchor boxes per sliding window were found sufficient to cover most objects.

The usage of Non-Maximal Suppression (NMS), which helps in predicting the correct box around the tools was required. We have used NMS on the proposal regions based on classification scores. Since tool localisation does not involve a complete tool, we have set the NMS to 0.05. This means that if there are two predicted boxes for the same tool with more than 5% common area, NMS will remove one with lesser probability.

### 3.4  Model Performance

We evaluate our model performance on test images and videos (of different lengths varying from 30 to 70 min). We used 563 annotated surgical images and 5 videos to test our model (testing was done by comparing the boolean vector indicating the presence or absence of tools for each frame, with the given ground truth boolean vectors). Figure 4 shows 1 to 3 tools detected in various frames by our framework.

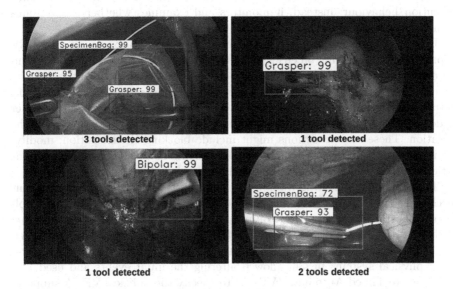

**Fig. 4.** Surgical tools in frames having 1 to 3 tools detected by our framework

Our model processed around 5 fps and provided an average precision and accuracy of 88.21% and 95.82% for video level detection (see Table 2).

## 4  Formal Runtime Monitoring

Runtime Verification (RV) [2,10] techniques allow one to check if a run of a system under observation complies with (or violates) a specified policy/property. Because the focus is on verifying the current execution/trace of the system being monitored, a formal model of the system is not required (system being monitored is usually considered as a black-box). As a result, RV techniques are lightweight, and issues like state explosion are avoided because always one (current) execution

Table 2. Model's performance on test videos

| Videos | Accuracy | Precision |
|---|---|---|
| Video 1 | 96.11 | 90.56 |
| Video 2 | 94.93 | 82.84 |
| Video 3 | 97.60 | 92.73 |
| Video 4 | 95.77 | 86.14 |
| Video 5 | 94.67 | 88.79 |
| Average | 95.82 | 88.21 |

of the system is monitored/verified. An RV monitor does not change the system's execution/behaviour; instead, it monitors and examines whether the system's actual execution is meeting the specified properties.

Runtime Enforcement (RE) [31,32] approaches are an extension of the RV approachs, concentrating on ensuring that the executions of systems being monitored are consistent with some desired policy. An enforcement monitor converts an (untrustworthy) input execution (series of events) into a policy-compliant output sequence of events (e.g., defining a desired safety requirement). In order to do so, an enforcement monitor performs certain evasive actions to prevent the violation. These evasive actions might include blocking the execution, modifying input sequence by suppressing and/or inserting actions, and buffering input actions until a future time when it could be forwarded.

The different monitoring frameworks differ on the power of the enforcement mechanism (i.e. the different evasive actions it can take) and the supported policy specification language. For example, monitors in [11,33] allowed buffering of the input events and used automata to specify the policies ([33] used timed automata [1] to specify real-time policies); whereas monitors for reactive and cyber-physical systems in [36] allowed altering the input events and used Valued Discrete Timed Automata (VDTA) to specify the policies. VDTA supports valued signals, internal variables, and complex guard conditions, ensuring compatibility with real-world cyber-physical and industrial systems.

In this work, we employ formal runtime monitoring approaches for "assessing" a surgical procedure and thus providing assistance to the surgeon, in the form of feedback during the surgeries. We write policies and synthesize "verification" monitor out of it. We use approaches proposed in [29,37] to synthesize the monitor, as these approaches synthesize the monitoring code directly from the specified policies. The generated monitor also ensures correctness and safe behaviour in safety-critical systems. These approaches use VDTA to specify policies which is an automaton with a finite set of locations, a finite set of discrete clocks used to represent time evolution, and external input-output channels which represents system data. They also have internal variables that are used for internal computations.

We mainly use the monitor synthesis mechanism to realize some of the requirements or a component, in the overall system automatically. As illustrated in Fig. 5, (verification and enforcement) monitors are seen as modules outside a (black-box) system, which take as input a stream of events (output of the system being monitored) and verify or correct this stream according to the policy. In this work, we mainly utilize the monitor synthesis approaches to realize a component (the monitoring module of the proposed system as shown in Fig. 5) that deals with providing feedback to the surgeons during a surgery. Instead of implementing that component, we rely on synthesis of the component from high-level policies using formal monitor synthesis approaches, so that the component is correct-by-construction.

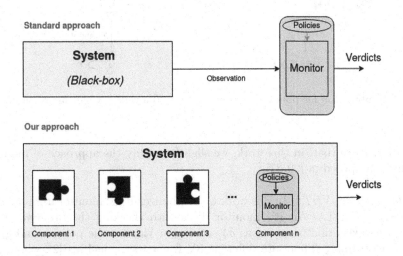

**Fig. 5.** Formal RV monitoring context: usual Vs. our system

*Example 2.* Let us define policies $P_1$ and $P_2$ of Example 1, via VDTA. Let $I = \{T_1, T_2, T_3, T_4, T_5, T_6, T_7\}$ be the external boolean input channels and the set of clock variables $V = \{v\}$[4] The alphabet $\Sigma = 2^I = \{0000000, 0000001, \cdots, 1111111\}$, where each event will be denoted as a bit-vector. For example, $\{T_1\} \subseteq I$ is denoted as $1000000 \in \Sigma$, and $\{T_1, T_4\} \subseteq I$ is denoted as $1001000 \in \Sigma$. Figure 6 shows policies $P_1$ and $P_2$ where, $L = \{l_0, l_1, l_2\}$ is the set of locations, with $l_0$ as the initial location and $\{l_0, l_1\}$ as the accepting locations in both the automata. According to policy $P_2$, from initial state $l_0$, upon input event $!T_1$[5] (indicating absence of tool $T_1$ in the captured frame), the system remains in same state (self-loop on $l_0$). The transition from location $l_0$ to

---

[4] VDTA can handle more expressive policies. Its entire potential (e.g., the output channels, the internal variables) has not been realised here.

[5] $!T_1$ denotes set of all the events in $\Sigma$, where tool $T_1$ is absent (bit corresponding to $T_1$ is 0 and other bits can be 0/1), e.g., $(0000000), (00000001), \cdots, (0111111)$. Similarly, $T_1$ denotes set of all the events in $\Sigma$, where tool $T_1$ is present (bit corresponding to $T_1$ is 1), e.g., $(1000000), (1000001), \cdots, (1111111)$.

$l_1$ is taken upon input event $T_1$ (indicating presence of tool $T_1$ in the captured frame), with clock $v$ reset to 0. From location $l_1$, if the input event is $!T_1$, then the system again goes back to location $l_0$, otherwise remains at $l_1$ till the value of the clock $v$ is $< 20$. With input event $T_1$, when $v$ is $\geq 20$, it goes to dead location[6] $l_2$, thus ensuring adherence to the policy. Policy $P_1$ can be similarly expressed as a VDTA as illustrated in Fig. 6.

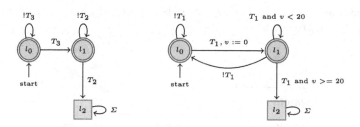

**Fig. 6.** Automaton for policy $P_1$ (on left) and $P_2$ (on right) (Color figure online)

*Remark 1.* Note that, in this work, we slightly modify the approach of monitor synthesis, proposed in [29,37].[7].

*RV Monitor from VDTA:* In this work we synthesize an RV monitor from policies expressed as VDTA. An RV monitor deals with checking the observation of the current execution (denoted as $\sigma$) satisfies or violates the policies and gives verdict accordingly. There are different RV frameworks, such as [2], where the verdicts provided are $\{$ *True, False, ?* $\}$. Verdict *True* means every continuation of $\sigma$ satisfies the policy, verdict *False* means there is no continuation of $\sigma$ which satisfies the policy and verdict "*?*" means unknown (no conclusive verdict can be provided). There are other frameworks, such as [34], which refines the unknown verdicts into *Currently true* and *Currently false*. Verdict *Currently true* indicates that the current observation of the execution satisfies the policy but not every continuation of it satisfies the policy and similarly, *Currently false* indicates that the current observation of the execution violates the policy but not every continuation of it violates the policy.

In this work, we define and implement our RV monitoring framework for VDTAs, where a monitor for a policy defined as a VDTA takes a stream of events over $\Sigma$ as input (current observation), and emits a verdict in $\{$ *True, False, Currently true, Currently false* $\}$.

---

[6] A dead location (denoted by red squares throughout the paper) is a location in the automaton, from where there is no path in the automaton from that location, to reach an accepting location.

[7] We synthesize a verification monitor instead of an enforcement monitor. Thus, our model will give verdicts in the form of feedback when it detects a violation and will not exercise its power of correcting faulty inputs i.e., editing erroneous inputs/outputs using edit functions as proposed in the followed paper.

# 5   Experimentation

To evaluate the performance of our proposed framework, we implemented the architecture, given in Fig. 1. This section shows the experimentation of the implemented architecture. We build the module for tool identication (following Sect. 3.1), take the dataset (discussed in Sect. 3.2) and evaluate the framework against some simple policies (given in Example 1).

The captured and processed frame is supplied to the tool identification module (built using the approaches discussed in Sect. 3), which identifies the tools present in the current frame. It yields an array of boolean variables showing presence or absence of each tool. The obtained array is then passed to the monitoring module (built using the approaches discussed in Sect. 4). It contains monitors synthesized from the specified policies. For experimentation, we consider policies $P_1$ and $P_2$ defined in Example 1 of Sect. 2 with $I = \{T_1, T_2, T_3, T_4, T_5, T_6, T_7\}$ (the boolean tool array) and the set of clock variables $V = \{v\}$. These policies are defined in the intended format as illustrated in 1.1 and as automata illustrated in Fig. 6. The policies are combined using standard product construction [37] as $P_1 \cap P_2$ which corresponds to the conjunction of both policies $P_1$ and $P_2$. The monitor is directly synthesized for the policy defining $P_1 \cap P_2$.

The monitor (C code synthesized from high-level policies) integrated with the system takes the tool array and checks if the policies are obeyed or not. It will raise an alert if the surgical procedure is not carried out according to the specified policies.

```
interface of tool_detection {
  in bool T1, T2, T3, T4, T5, T6, T7;
  out int16_t res; }


policy p1 of tool_detection {
  states {
    s0 {
      -> s0 on !T3;
      -> s1 on T3;}
    s1 {
      -> s1 on !T2;
      -> violation on (T2) recover res := 1;}}}


policy p2 of tool_detection {
  internals {
    dtimer_t v;}
  states {
    s0 {
      -> s1 on T1 : v:=0;
      -> s0 on !T1;}
    s1 {
      -> s1 on (T1 and v<20);
```

```
      -> s0 on !T1;
      -> violation on (T1 and v>=20) recover res := 2;}}}
```
**Listing 1.1.** Policies in the intended format

For example, consider policy $P_1$ and received input trace $\sigma = (0000110) \cdot (0010010) \cdot (0100000)$. From initial location $l_0$, upon input event "0000110", the automaton remains in $l_0$; from $l_0$, upon input event "0010010", the automaton makes a transition to $l_1$, (the bit corresponding to tool $T_3$ is 1, indicating presence of tool $T_3$); and from $l_1$, upon input event "0100000", the automaton goes to dead location $l_2$, (the bit corresponding to tool $T_2$ is 1, indicating presence of tool $T_2$), since it violated the policy (Policy $P_1$ abstained the use of a tool $T_2$ after tool $T_3$, which may signify carelessness that should be avoided). Thus, in this case the monitor will give verdict as *False* and will reset itself and continue with the next event.

Upon reception of a *False* verdict, the system will raise an alert that the surgery is not being performed as per the specified policies.

Similarly, when a surgeon uses tool $T_1$ for a longer (than usual) period of time (which may point to rough handling of tissue resulting in tissue damage), then it will violate policy $P_2$ and the monitor will raise a similar alert.

These alerts will give instant feedback to the surgeon, and he can be more careful during the surgical procedure; thus providing assistance to the surgeon. One can set different types of alerts depending on the type of policies. For example, for some critical policies, where violating the policies can have severe consequences, alerts can be sending notifications to the senior surgeons; whereas, for the other soft policies, the alerts can be allocating resources (likely to be used in future) to avoid preoperative delays.

*Performance Discussion:* Our proposed system spends considerable time in tool identification only, since it employs DL, whose execution time is more dependent on the processing power of the available architecture. Our architecture/machine (Intel(R) Core(TM) i7-9700K CPU @ 3.60GHz with Quadro RTX 4000 and 8GB Graphics RAM/GPU) can process around 5 fps. Thus, the overall architecture ensures real-time feedback to the surgeons with the considered policies.

Moreover, our proposed architecture can utilize state-of-the-art trained model benefits and further enhance its overall performance. In one recent published work on surgical tool detection using cascading of CNN [48], researchers were able to detect tools in around 0.023 s. Use of this model in our tool identification module will further bring down frame processing time. Thus, it can process more than 40 fps.

The framework is implemented and is available for download at *https://doi.org/10.5281/zenodo.6899355*.

## 6   Related Work

Several object detection and formal runtime monitoring approaches are related to the one used in this paper. We give a comparison with approaches for these in Sect. 6.1 and Sect. 6.2 respectively.

## 6.1  Object Detection

Object detection has received a lot of research attention in recent years because of its tight association with the well known video analysis and image processing techniques. Object detection tasks can be broken down into two stages - object localization (location of objects in the image) and object classification (category of each object present).

Handcrafted features and shallow trainable structures are the foundations of traditional object identification systems. Feature extraction in these traditional methods uses SIFT [26], HOG [8] and Haar-like [25]. Classification of objects is done using traditional classifiers like Supported Vector Machine (SVM) [7], AdaBoost [13], Deformable Part-based Model (DPM) [12] etc. These methods have their limitation e.g. it cannot obtain complex features in images or videos.

With the advent of DL [24], image classification improved significantly. Because of the deep architecture of DNN and R-CNN [16], these were able to easily learn the complex features. Also, large datasets and robust training methods got rid of the need of manual feature extraction. Many improvements in the R-CNN models have been proposed. Fast R-CNN [15] further optimizes classification and bounding box regression tasks. Faster R-CNN [41] generates region proposals using an additional subnetwork. YOLO [40] uses a fixed-grid regression to detect objects. These models have made real-time object detection feasible with improved accuracy.

Robot-assisted surgeries will be widely used in the future and surgical tool detection is the first step towards it. DL approaches have shown excellent results in improving its performance. The M2CAI tool detection challenge[8] helped to achieve new benchmarks in surgical tools detection. There are several studies done to address tool detection in videos and obtain a richer analysis of surgeries. Sarikya et al. [43] used multi-modal CNN for localization and fast detection of tools in Robot-assisted surgeries. In 2019, Zhao et al. [49] proposed a method using two CNNs designed for detecting coarse and fine locations of surgical tools. Jin et al. [19] used a two-stage framework of Faster R-CNN to localize and detect tools in a frame, which was later used for surgical skill assessment in a surgical video. Chao et al. [5] proposed a one stage framework using a modified YOLO [40] architecture, which increased the detection speed of surgical tools to 48.9 fps. Nwoye et al. [28] used CNN + Convolutional LSTM (ConvLSTM) to model temporal dependencies in the motion of surgical tools, which resulted in multiple tools tracking and detection simultaneously.

## 6.2  Formal Runtime Monitoring

Formal verification is the process of checking whether a design satisfies the specified requirements/policies. The policies can be expressed using high-level formalisms such as automata [29, 33, 35–37, 44] or as temporal logic [2].

---

[8] Tool presence detection challenge results, Workshop and Challenges on Modeling and Monitoring of Computer Assisted Interventions, http://camma.u-strasbg.fr/ m2cai2016/index.php/tool-presence-detection-challenge-results/.

Model checking [6] is an automated static formal verification approach to check if the policies are satisfied by an abstract formal model of the system or not. RV [2,10] and RE [31,32] approaches do not require a formal model of the system since only a single execution of the system is considered. RV (RE) approaches checks at runtime if a run of a system under scrutiny satisfies a given correctness policy or not (enforces them in the latter case).

DL is increasingly used in domains like autonomous driving [18], healthcare [14], cybersecurity [27], etc. Designing these learning based systems that have strong, provable, assurances of correctness w.r.t. the policies is always a focal point. This has increased the discussions on verified artificial intelligence [42,45]. The very first attempt to formally verify a neural network was done by Pulina and Tacchella [39]. They came up with techniques to verify that the output of a fully-connected neural network with sigmoid activations is always within specified safety bounds. Later, [9,20,21], proposed approach for the verification of neural networks employing specific activation functions.

The adoption of DL in medical and health-care systems to facilitate a procedure has increased complexity of the system and made it more susceptible to errors. Use of formal methods, along with advanced design, control and deployment paradigms, is often recommended to guarantee the correctness and safety of these medical systems. In the attempt, Bresolin et al. [3] discussed the applications of formal methods to verify the properties of control systems built for autonomous robotic systems that performed surgeries. They demonstrated the automatic execution of simple tasks like puncturing. Brunese et al. [4] represented patient magnetic resonances as formal models and predicted the prostate cancer Gleason score. Pore et al. [38] proposed a safe deep reinforcement learning framework that guarantees safety criteria for automated surgical tasks.

The works in [3,38] deals with autonomous robot-assisted surgeries safeguarded by formal methods. But performing fully automated surgeries is quite complex and less reliable. Upskilling of the existing surgeons by providing assistance to them during complex surgeries can be really helpful. To the best of our knowledge, our framework is the first to develop an automated surgical procedure assistant using DL and formal methods. Thus, reducing complications and needless patient damage during MIS.

## 7  Conclusion and Future Work

This paper presents a complete framework using DL and runtime monitoring for developing an automated surgical procedure assistant. In this approach, we use Faster R-CNN to identify the surgical tools used to perform the surgical procedure. Then, we specify some policies on tools' usage pattern that should be obeyed during a good surgical procedure. We obtain a monitoring code out of the policies. It will identify a bad behaviour in a surgical procedure. This way, we can catch any violation in the tool's usage during the surgical procedure and can alert surgeons to take immediate corrective measures.

To illustrate the practical applicability of the proposed framework, we consider the case of cholecystectomy (laparoscopic) surgery. We have implemented the framework and have evaluated its technical feasibility using some example properties on (offline) video samples of the surgical procedure from the modified Cholec80 dataset.

In the future, we plan to enrich this framework with diverse policies to cover a large number of safe behaviours and then use this framework for robot assisted surgeries.

**Acknowledgment.** Gaurav expresses gratitude to Prof. Neelam Sinha for her invaluable guidance during the summer research internship at International Institute of Information Technology, Bangalore organised by Indian Academy of Sciences. The work done there has helped to generate new ideas for this paper.

# References

1. Alur, R., Dill, D.L.: A theory of timed automata. Theor. Comput. Sci. **126**(2), 183–235 (1994). https://doi.org/10.1016/0304-3975(94)90010-8, https://www.sciencedirect.com/science/article/pii/0304397594900108
2. Bauer, A., Leucker, M., Schallhart, C.: Runtime verification for LTL and TLTL. ACM Trans. Softw. Eng. Methodol. **20**, 14 (2011). https://doi.org/10.1145/2000799.2000800
3. Bresolin, D., Geretti, L., Muradore, R., Fiorini, P., Villa, T.: Formal verification of robotic surgery tasks by reachability analysis. Microprocess. Microsyst. **39** (2015). https://doi.org/10.1016/j.micpro.2015.10.006
4. Brunese, L., Mercaldo, F., Reginelli, A., Santone, A.: Formal methods for prostate cancer gleason score and treatment prediction using radiomic biomarkers. Magn. Resonan. Imaging **66**, 165–175 (2020). https://doi.org/10.1016/j.mri.2019.08.030, https://www.sciencedirect.com/science/article/pii/S0730725X19302437
5. Choi, B., Jo, K., Choi, S., Choi, J.: Surgical-tools detection based on convolutional neural network in laparoscopic robot-assisted surgery, vol. 2017, pp. 1756–1759 (2017). https://doi.org/10.1109/EMBC.2017.8037183
6. Clarke, E.M., Henzinger, T.A., Veith, H.: Introduction to Model Checking. In: Handbook of Model Checking, pp. 1–26. Springer, Cham (2018). https://doi.org/10.1007/978-3-319-10575-8_1
7. Cortes, C., Vapnik, V.: Support-vector networks. Mach. Learn. **20**(3), 273–297 (1995). https://doi.org/10.1023/A:1022627411411
8. Dalal, N., Triggs, B.: Histograms of oriented gradients for human detection. In: CVPR 2005, vol. 1, pp. 886–893 (2005). https://doi.org/10.1109/CVPR.2005.177
9. Ehlers, R.: Formal verification of piece-wise linear feed-forward neural networks. In: D'Souza, D., Narayan Kumar, K. (eds.) ATVA 2017. LNCS, vol. 10482, pp. 269–286. Springer, Cham (2017). https://doi.org/10.1007/978-3-319-68167-2_19
10. Falcone, Y., Fernandez, J.-C., Mounier, L.: Runtime verification of safety-progress properties. In: Bensalem, S., Peled, D.A. (eds.) RV 2009. LNCS, vol. 5779, pp. 40–59. Springer, Heidelberg (2009). https://doi.org/10.1007/978-3-642-04694-0_4
11. Falcone, Y., Mounier, L., Fernandez, J.C., Richier, J.L.: Runtime enforcement monitors: composition, synthesis, and enforcement abilities. Formal Meth. Syst. Des. **38** (2011). https://doi.org/10.1007/s10703-011-0114-4
12. Felzenszwalb, P.F., Girshick, R.B., McAllester, D., Ramanan, D.: Object detection with discriminatively trained part-based models. IEEE Trans. Pattern Anal. Mach. Intell. **32**(9), 1627–1645 (2010). https://doi.org/10.1109/TPAMI.2009.167

13. Freund, Y., Schapire, R.E.: A decision-theoretic generalization of on-line learning and an application to boosting. J. Comput. Syst. Sci. **55**(1), 119–139 (1997). https://doi.org/10.1006/jcss.1997.1504, https://www.sciencedirect.com/science/article/pii/S002200009791504X

14. Ghassemi, M., Naumann, T., Schulam, P., Beam, A., Chen, I., Ranganath, R.: A review of challenges and opportunities in machine learning for health, May 2020

15. Girshick, R.: Fast r-cnn (2015). https://doi.org/10.1109/ICCV.2015.169

16. Girshick, R., Donahue, J., Darrell, T., Malik, J.: Rich feature hierarchies for accurate object detection and semantic segmentation, November 2013. https://doi.org/10.1109/CVPR.2014.81

17. Grunstad, J.: Two new studies reveal benefits of laparoscopic surgery for uterine cancer, March 2006

18. Huang, Y., Chen, Y.: Autonomous driving with deep learning: a survey of state-of-art technologies (2020)

19. Jin, A., et al.: Tool detection and operative skill assessment in surgical videos using region-based convolutional neural networks, March 2018. https://doi.org/10.1109/WACV.2018.00081

20. Katz, G., Barrett, C., Dill, D.L., Julian, K., Kochenderfer, M.J.: Reluplex: an efficient SMT solver for verifying deep neural networks. In: Majumdar, R., Kunčak, V. (eds.) CAV 2017. LNCS, vol. 10426, pp. 97–117. Springer, Cham (2017). https://doi.org/10.1007/978-3-319-63387-9_5

21. Khedr, H., Ferlez, J., Shoukry, Y.: Effective formal verification of neural networks using the geometry of linear regions. CoRR abs/2006.10864 (2020). https://arxiv.org/abs/2006.10864

22. Klodmann, J., et al.: An introduction to robotically assisted surgical systems: current developments and focus areas of research. Current Robot. Rep. **2**(3), 321–332 (2021). https://doi.org/10.1007/s43154-021-00064-3

23. Lavanchy, J., et al.: Automation of surgical skill assessment using a three-stage machine learning algorithm. Sci. Rep. **11** (2021). https://doi.org/10.1038/s41598-021-84295-6

24. LeCun, Y., Bengio, Y., Hinton, G.: Deep learning. Nature **521**, 436–444 (2015). https://doi.org/10.1038/nature14539

25. Lienhart, R., Maydt, J.: An extended set of haar-like features for rapid object detection. In: Proceedings of the International Conference on Image Processing, vol. 1, p. I (2002). https://doi.org/10.1109/ICIP.2002.1038171

26. Lowe, D.G.: Distinctive image features from scale-invariant keypoints. Int. J. Comput. Vision **60**(2), 91–110 (2004). https://doi.org/10.1023/B:VISI.0000029664.99615.94

27. Macas, M., Wu, C.: Review: Deep learning methods for cybersecurity and intrusion detection systems (2020)

28. Nwoye, C.I., Mutter, D., Marescaux, J., Padoy, N.: Weakly supervised convolutional LSTM approach for tool tracking in laparoscopic videos. Int. J. Comput. Assist. Radiol. Surg. **14**(6), 1059–1067 (2019). https://doi.org/10.1007/s11548-019-01958-6

29. Pearce, H., Pinisetty, S., Roop, P.S., Kuo, M.M.Y., Ukil, A.: Smart I/O modules for mitigating cyber-physical attacks on industrial control systems. IEEE Trans. Industr. Inf. **16**(7), 4659–4669 (2020). https://doi.org/10.1109/TII.2019.2945520

30. Pfeiffer, M., et al.: Generating large labeled data sets for laparoscopic image processing tasks using unpaired image-to-image translation. In: Shen, D., et al. (eds.) MICCAI 2019. LNCS, vol. 11768, pp. 119–127. Springer, Cham (2019). https://doi.org/10.1007/978-3-030-32254-0_14

31. Pinisetty, S., Falcone, Y., Jéron, T., Marchand, H.: Runtime enforcement of regular timed properties. In: Proceedings of the 29th Annual ACM Symposium on Applied Computing, pp. 1279–1286. SAC 2014, Association for Computing Machinery, New York, NY, USA (2014). https://doi.org/10.1145/2554850.2554967

32. Pinisetty, S., Falcone, Y., Jéron, T., Marchand, H., Rollet, A., Nguena Timo, O.L.: Runtime enforcement of timed properties. In: Qadeer, S., Tasiran, S. (eds.) RV 2012. LNCS, vol. 7687, pp. 229–244. Springer, Heidelberg (2013). https://doi.org/10.1007/978-3-642-35632-2_23

33. Pinisetty, S., Falcone, Y., Jéron, T., Marchand, H., Rollet, A., Timo, O.N.: Runtime enforcement of timed properties revisited. Formal Meth. Syst. Des. **45**(3), 381–422 (2014). https://doi.org/10.1007/s10703-014-0215-y

34. Pinisetty, S., Jéron, T., Tripakis, S., Falcone, Y., Marchand, H., Preoteasa, V.: Predictive runtime verification of timed properties. J. Syst. Softw. **132**, 353–365 (2017). https://doi.org/10.1016/j.jss.2017.06.060, https://www.sciencedirect.com/science/article/pii/S0164121217301310

35. Pinisetty, S., Preoteasa, V., Tripakis, S., Jéron, T., Falcone, Y., Marchand, H.: Predictive runtime enforcement. Formal Meth. Syst. Des. **51**(1), 154–199 (2017). https://doi.org/10.1007/s10703-017-0271-1

36. Pinisetty, S., Roop, P., Smyth, S., Tripakis, S., von Hanxleden, R.: Runtime enforcement of reactive systems using synchronous enforcers, November 2016

37. Pinisetty, S., Roop, P.S., Smyth, S., Allen, N., Tripakis, S., Hanxleden, R.V.: Runtime enforcement of cyber-physical systems. ACM Trans. Embed. Comput. Syst. **16**(5s) (2017). https://doi.org/10.1145/3126500

38. Pore, A., et al.: Safe reinforcement learning using formal verification for tissue retraction in autonomous robotic-assisted surgery. In: 2021 IEEE/RSJ International Conference on IROS, pp. 4025–4031 (2021). https://doi.org/10.1109/IROS51168.2021.9636175

39. Pulina, L., Tacchella, A.: An abstraction-refinement approach to verification of artificial neural networks. In: Touili, T., Cook, B., Jackson, P. (eds.) CAV 2010. LNCS, vol. 6174, pp. 243–257. Springer, Heidelberg (2010). https://doi.org/10.1007/978-3-642-14295-6_24

40. Redmon, J., Divvala, S., Girshick, R., Farhadi, A.: You only look once: unified, real-time object detection, June 2016. https://doi.org/10.1109/CVPR.2016.91

41. Ren, S., He, K., Girshick, R., Sun, J.: Faster R-CNN: towards real-time object detection with region proposal networks. In: Proceedings of the 28th International Conference on Neural Information Processing Systems, vol. 1, pp. 91–99. NIPS 2015. MIT Press, Cambridge, MA, USA (2015)

42. Russell, S., et al.: Letter to the editor: research priorities for robust and beneficial artificial intelligence: an open letter. AI Mag. **36**, 3 (2015). https://doi.org/10.1609/aimag.v36i4.2621

43. Sarikaya, D., Corso, J., Guru, K.: Detection and localization of robotic tools in robot-assisted surgery videos using deep neural networks for region proposal and detection. IEEE Trans. Med. Imaging 1 (2017). https://doi.org/10.1109/TMI.2017.2665671

44. Schneider, F.B.: Enforceable security policies. ACM Trans. Inf. Syst. Secur. **3**(1), 30–50 (2000). https://doi.org/10.1145/353323.353382

45. Seshia, S.A., Sadigh, D., Sastry, S.S.: Towards verified artificial intelligence (2020)

46. Twinanda, A., Shehata, S., Mutter, D., Marescaux, J., De Mathelin, M., Padoy, N.: EndoNet: a deep architecture for recognition tasks on laparoscopic videos, February 2016. https://doi.org/10.1109/TMI.2016.2593957

47. Viola, P., Jones, M.: Rapid object detection using a boosted cascade of simple features. In: Proceedings of the 2001 IEEE Computer Society Conference on CVPR 2001, vol. 1, p. I (2001). https://doi.org/10.1109/CVPR.2001.990517
48. Zhao, Z., Cai, T., Chang, F., Chen, X.: Real-time surgical instrument detection in robot-assisted surgery using a convolutional neural network cascade. Healthc. Technol. Lett. **6** (2019). https://doi.org/10.1049/htl.2019.0064
49. Zhao, Z., Voros, S., Chen, Z., Cheng, X.: Surgical tool tracking based on two CNNs: from coarse to fine. J. Eng. 2019 (2019). https://doi.org/10.1049/joe.2018.9401

# Relaxing Safety for Metric First-Order Temporal Logic via Dynamic Free Variables

Jonathan Julián Huerta y Munive$^{(\boxtimes)}$ ⓘ

Department of Computer Science, University of Copenhagen, Copenhagen, Denmark
jonathan.munive@di.ku.dk

**Abstract.** We define a fragment of metric first-order temporal logic formulas that guarantees the finiteness of their table-representations. We extend our fragment's definition to cover the temporal dual operators *trigger* and *release* and show that our fragment is strictly larger than those previously used in the literature. We integrate these additions into an existing runtime verification tool and formally verify in Isabelle/HOL that the tool correctly outputs the table of constants that satisfy the monitored formula. Finally, we provide some example specifications that are now monitorable thanks to our contributions.

**Keywords:** Runtime verification · Relational algebra · Safety relaxation

## 1  Introduction

Runtime verification (RV) complements other techniques for system quality-assurance such as testing or model checking [16]. It allows monitoring properties during a system's execution by indicating when they are violated. Metric first-order temporal logic (MFOTL) is among the most expressive temporal and declarative specification languages for RV [7]. It adds intervals to the logic's temporal operators to model quantitative descriptions of time [5,14]. For these reasons, it is often used in monitor implementations [4,11,19].

Besides being expressive, monitors should also be efficient and trustworthy. Efficiency allows them to be deployed more invasively by course-correcting the evolution of a system [12], while trustworthiness makes them reliable in safety-critical applications. Recently, Verimon, an MFOTL-based RV-algorithm, has achieved high expressivity [22] and efficiency [3] while staying trustworthy because of its formally verified implementation in the Isabelle/HOL proof assistant [19]. It uses finite relations to represent the set of valuations that make a specification true which contributes to its efficiency. Nevertheless, this feature also makes it inherit well-known issues from relational databases [8] forcing it to operate inside a fragment whose formula-evaluation guarantees finite outputs. This fragment is defined inductively on the structure of the formula via a

ⓒ The Author(s), under exclusive license to Springer Nature Switzerland AG 2022
T. Dang and V. Stolz (Eds.): RV 2022, LNCS 13498, pp. 45–66, 2022.
https://doi.org/10.1007/978-3-031-17196-3_3

predicate *safe-formula* which should not be confused with the notion of safety property from model checking [15]. The set of *safe* formulas that Verimon admits is rather restrictive. The fact that well-known temporal operators such as *historically* are immediately dubbed unsafe if they have free variables, is evidence of this. Here, we address this particular issue.

Our main contribution consists of the definition (Sect. 3) of a larger fragment of MFOTL-safe formulas, its formalisation in the Isabelle/HOL proof assistant, and its integration into Verimon's first implementation. This generalisation of safety enables us to monitor a wider variety of future and past operators including *globally* and historically. To address safety of formulas involving these operators in conjunction with other connectives, we introduce the set of *dynamic free variables* ($\mathrm{dfv}_i\ \alpha$) of a formula $\alpha$ at time-point $i$. It approximates the set of those free variables that contribute to the satisfiability of a formula at a specific point of a system's execution. Safety is then decided by computing a set of allowed sets of dynamic free variables and checking its nonemptiness. Essentially, we define a set of *safe sets of free variables* (ssfv) in such a way that whenever this set is nonempty, meaning that $\alpha$ is safe, $\mathrm{dfv}_i\ \alpha \in \mathrm{ssfv}\ \alpha$.

Furthermore, with the view of integrating our generalisation into the latest optimised version of Verimon [22], we explicitly add conjunctions to the syntax of our implementation. This involves defining safety for specific cases where one of the conjuncts is an equality, a constraint, or the negation of a safe formula. To go beyond the developments in the optimised version, we also (Sect. 4) add since and until's dual operators, *trigger* and *release* respectively, to Verimon's syntax. We therefore also extend Verimon's monitoring algorithm with functions to evaluate these operators and prove them correct.

Our formalisation and proof of correctness (Sect. 6) of the extended monitoring algorithm is also a major contribution of this work. It involves redefining proof-invariants to accommodate dynamic free variables which largely reverberates in the proofs of correctness for each connective. The formalisation and proofs are available online, and corresponding definitions are linked throughout the paper and indicated with the (clickable) Isabelle-logo 🐞.[1] We add to the relevance of our safety relaxation by providing examples (Sect. 5) that can be monitored due to our additions. We discuss future work and our conclusions in Sect. 7.

*Related Work.* In terms of expressivity of other monitors, our work directly extends the oldest Verimon version [19] by the above-mentioned additions. However, our generalisation has not been applied to the latest Verimon+ [22] as we do not deal with aggregators, recursive rules, or regular expressions. We foresee no issues to adapt our approach to these other extensions. Verimon+ does not have an explicit version of dual operators and deems historically and globally unsafe. A recent extension [10], adds the dual operators and describes lengthy encodings to monitor historically and globally. Yet, our work is complementary because of our larger safety fragment. Another past-only, first-order monitor is DejaVu [11]. It uses

---

[1] Readers wishing to download and see the files in Isabelle, must ensure they download commit $b4b63034eca0ccd5783085dececddb6c47cf6f52$ of branch ssfvs.

binary decision diagrams which can model infinite relations and thus, does not require a notion of safety. In contrast, our work supports both past and bounded future operators and, in general, it is hard to compare performance between both RV-approaches [11, 22].

Safety has been well studied for relational databases [1,6,8,13,21]. Kifer [13] organises and relates various definitions of safety, and Avron and Hirshfeld [2] complement his work by answering some of Kifer's conjectures at the end of his paper. More recently, evaluation of queries that are relatively safe has been explored [18]. Thereby, there is an approach to translate any relational calculus query into a pair of safe queries where, if the second holds, then the original is unsafe (produces an infinite output). Otherwise, the original query's output is the same as the output of the first one. A recent extension to the temporal setting [17] remains to be formally verified and integrated into Verimon+. Arguably, using it as black boxes for the monitoring algorithm would be less efficient than the direct integration we provide.

## 2  Metric First-Order Temporal Logic

In this section, we briefly describe syntax and semantics of MFOTL for the Verimon implementation and introduce the problem of finite representations given an MFOTL-formula. Following Isabelle/HOL conventions, we use $x :: \text{'}a$ to state that variable $x$ is of type $\text{'}a$. The type of lists and the type of sets over $\text{'}a$ are $\text{'}a\ list$ and $\text{'}a\ set$ respectively. We implicitly use "$s$" to indicate a list of terms of some type, for instance, if $x :: \text{'}a$, then $xs :: \text{'}a\ list$. The standard operations on lists that apply a function $f$ to each element (map $f\ xs$), get the $n$th element ($xs\ !\ n$), output the list's length (length $xs$) or add an element to the left ($x\ \#\ xs$) also appear throughout the paper. The expression $f\ \text{'}\ X$ denotes the set-image of $X$ under $f$. We freely use binary operations inside parenthesis as functions, that is we can write $x + y$ or $(+)\ x\ y$. Finally, the natural numbers have type $\mathbb{N}$.

The type of terms $\text{'}a\ trm$ simply consists of variables $\mathbf{v}\ x$ and constants $\mathbf{c}\ a$ with $x :: \mathbb{N}$ and $a :: \text{'}a$. The syntax of MFOTL formulas $\text{'}a\ frm$ that we use is

$$\alpha ::= p \dagger ts \mid t =_F t \mid \neg_F \alpha \mid \alpha \wedge_F \alpha \mid \alpha \vee_F \alpha \mid \exists_F \alpha \mid$$
$$Y_I\,\alpha \mid X_I\,\alpha \mid \alpha\,S_I\,\alpha \mid \alpha\,U_I\,\alpha \mid \alpha\,T_I\,\alpha \mid \alpha\,R_I\,\alpha,$$

where $p :: string$, $t :: \text{'}a\ trm$, $ts :: \text{'}a\ trm\ list$ and $I$ is a non-empty interval of natural numbers. We distinguish MFOTL connectives and quantifiers from meta-statements via the subscript $F$ and freely use well-known interval notation, e.g. $[a, b) = \{n \mid a \le n < b\}$ or $[a, b] = \{n \mid a \le n \le b\}$. Furthermore, we also write $m > I + n$ (and similar abbreviations) to state that $m$ is greater than $n$ plus any other element in $I$. Finally, the above syntax implies usage of De Bruijn indices, that is, $\exists_F\ p \dagger [\mathbf{v}\ 1, \mathbf{v}\ 0]$ represents the formula $\exists y.\ p\,x\,y$.

Verimon encodes valuations as lists of natural numbers, $v :: \mathbb{N}\ list$ where the $x$th element of the list is the value of $\mathbf{v}\ x$. That is, the evaluation of terms ($!_t$) is given by $v!_t(\mathbf{c}\ a) = a$ and $v!_t(\mathbf{v}\ x) = v!x$. For the semantics, a trace $\sigma$, meaning an infinite time-stamped sequence of sets, models the input from the monitored system. The function $\tau\,\sigma\,i :: \mathbb{N}$ outputs the time-stamp at time-point $i :: \mathbb{N}$, whereas

$\Gamma\,\sigma\,i$ outputs the corresponding set. When clear from context we use their abbreviated forms $\tau_i$ and $\Gamma_i$ respectively. The time-stamps are monotone $\forall i \leq j.\ \tau_i \leq \tau_j$ and eventually increasing $\forall n.\ \exists i.\ n \leq \tau_i$. The sets $\Gamma_i$ contain pairs $(p, xs)$ where $p$ is a name for a predicate $p :: string$ and $xs$ is a list of values "satisfying" $p$. Formally, the semantics are

$$\langle \sigma, v, i \rangle \models p \dagger ts \Leftrightarrow (p, \text{map}\,((!_t)\,v)\,ts) \in \Gamma_i, \quad \langle \sigma, v, i \rangle \models \exists_F \alpha \Leftrightarrow \exists a :: {}'a.\ \langle \sigma, a \,\#\, v, i \rangle \models \alpha$$

$$\langle \sigma, v, i \rangle \models \alpha \wedge_F \beta \Leftrightarrow \langle \sigma, v, i \rangle \models \alpha \wedge \langle \sigma, v, i \rangle \models \beta, \quad \langle \sigma, v, i \rangle \models t_1 =_F t_2 \Leftrightarrow v\,!_t\,t_1 = v\,!_t\,t_2$$

$$\langle \sigma, v, i \rangle \models \alpha \vee_F \beta \Leftrightarrow \langle \sigma, v, i \rangle \models \alpha \vee \langle \sigma, v, i \rangle \models \beta, \quad\quad \langle \sigma, v, i \rangle \models \neg \alpha \Leftrightarrow \langle \sigma, v, i \rangle \not\models \alpha$$

$$\langle \sigma, v, i \rangle \models X_I\,\alpha \Leftrightarrow \langle \sigma, v, i+1 \rangle \models \alpha \wedge (\tau_{i+1} - \tau_i) \in I$$

$$\langle \sigma, v, i \rangle \models Y_I\,\alpha \Leftrightarrow \ if\,i = 0\ then\ \text{false}\ else\ \langle \sigma, v, i - 1 \rangle \models \alpha \wedge (\tau_i - \tau_{i-1}) \in I$$

$$\langle \sigma, v, i \rangle \models \alpha\,S_I\,\beta \Leftrightarrow \exists j \leq i.\ (\tau_i - \tau_j) \in I \wedge \langle \sigma, v, j \rangle \models \beta \wedge (\forall k \in (j, i].\ \langle \sigma, v, i \rangle \models \alpha)$$

$$\langle \sigma, v, i \rangle \models \alpha\,U_I\,\beta \Leftrightarrow \exists j \geq i.\ (\tau_j - \tau_i) \in I \wedge \langle \sigma, v, j \rangle \models \beta \wedge (\forall k \in [i, j).\ \langle \sigma, v, i \rangle \models \alpha)$$

$$\langle \sigma, v, i \rangle \models \alpha\,T_I\,\beta \Leftrightarrow \forall j \leq i.\ (\tau_i - \tau_j) \in I \Rightarrow \langle \sigma, v, j \rangle \models \beta \vee (\exists k \in (j, i].\ \langle \sigma, v, i \rangle \models \alpha)$$

$$\langle \sigma, v, i \rangle \models \alpha\,R_I\,\beta \Leftrightarrow \forall j \geq i.\ (\tau_j - \tau_i) \in I \Rightarrow \langle \sigma, v, j \rangle \models \beta \vee (\exists k \in [i, j).\ \langle \sigma, v, i \rangle \models \alpha).$$

Other operators can be encoded, e.g. *true* ($\top \equiv \mathbf{c}\,a =_F \mathbf{c}\,a$), *eventually* ($F_I \alpha \equiv \top\,U_I\,\alpha$), or *historically* ($H_I \alpha \equiv \neg_F F_I \neg_F \alpha$). Moreover, trigger and release satisfy their dualities with since and until, that is, $\langle \sigma, v, i \rangle \models \alpha\,T_I\,\beta \Leftrightarrow \langle \sigma, v, i \rangle \models \neg_F ((\neg_F \alpha)\,S_I\,(\neg_F \beta))$ and $\langle \sigma, v, i \rangle \models \alpha\,R_I\,\beta \Leftrightarrow \langle \sigma, v, i \rangle \models \neg_F ((\neg_F \alpha)\,U_I\,(\neg_F \beta))$. We do not encode them because it leads to hard-to-follow case distinctions in Isabelle proofs.

Intuitively, for the formula $\alpha$, a monitor outputs the set $[\![\alpha]\!]_i = \{v \mid \langle \sigma, v, i \rangle \models \alpha\}$ at time-point $i :: \mathbb{N}$. However, these sets are redundant and infinite, e.g. $v_1 = [4, 5]$, $v_2 = [4, 5, 1]$ and $v_3 = [4, 5, 2, 7]$ are all elements of $[\![p \dagger [\mathbf{v}\,0, \mathbf{v}\,1]]\!]_i$ if $\Gamma\,\sigma\,i = \{(p, [4, 5])\}$. For these reasons, Verimon makes valuations map variables $x :: \mathbb{N}$ that are not in the set of *free variables* of $\alpha$, $x \notin \text{fv}\,\alpha$, to *None* values of type ${}'a\ option$. To address redundancy, Verimon also focuses on valuations with fixed length equal to $\text{nfv}\,\alpha = \max(\{0\} \cup ((+1)\,{}'\,\text{fv}\,\alpha))$, that is, the least number $n$ such that if $x \in \text{fv}\,\alpha$, then $x < n = \text{nfv}\,\alpha$. For example, $v_4 = [4, 5, None]$ satisfies $p \dagger [\mathbf{v}\,0, \mathbf{v}\,1]$ at $i$ if it is a subformula of $\alpha$ with $\text{nfv}\,\alpha = 4$. Formally, the predicate *wf-tuple* $n\,X\,v$ holds if length $v = n$ and $\forall i < n.\ v\,!\,i = None \Leftrightarrow i \notin X$. Thus, the monitor outputs

$$[\![\alpha]\!]_{i,n}^X = \{v :: {}'a\ option\ list \mid \langle \sigma, v, i \rangle \models_M \alpha \wedge \textit{wf-tuple}\,n\,X\,v\},$$

where $\langle \sigma, v, i \rangle \models_M \alpha$ abbreviates $\langle \sigma, \text{map}\,the\,v, i \rangle \models \alpha$ and *the* is the standard function mapping optional values *Some* $x :: {}'a\ option$ to their concrete counterparts $x :: {}'a$ and *None* to an unspecified value of type ${}'a$.

Outputs $[\![\alpha]\!]_{i,n}^X$ are relations or, from a database perspective, tables of values satisfying $\alpha$. For each subformula $\beta$ of the monitored formula $\alpha$, Verimon obtains the tables $[\![\beta]\!]_{i,\text{nfv}\,\alpha}^{\text{fv}\,\beta}$ and uses them to compute $[\![\alpha]\!]_{i,\text{nfv}\,\alpha}^{\text{fv}\,\alpha}$. For this, it includes common relational algebra operations like the (natural) join ($\bowtie$), antijoin ($\triangleright$) and union ($\cup$) of tables. However, these outputs can quickly become infinite if not treated carefully, e.g. for datatypes with infinite carrier sets, $[\![\neg_F \alpha]\!]_{i,n}^X$ is infinite when $[\![\alpha]\!]_{i,n}^X$ is finite. Verimon uses the function *safe-formula* to define a fragment of MFOTL-formulas where finite outputs are guaranteed. For instance, tables for disjunctions $[\![\alpha \vee_F \beta]\!]_{i,n}^{(\text{fv}\,\alpha) \cup (\text{fv}\,\beta)}$ can only be computed as $[\![\alpha]\!]_{i,n}^{\text{fv}\,\alpha} \cup [\![\beta]\!]_{i,n}^{\text{fv}\,\beta}$ when they are *union-compatible*, that is, they both have the same *attributes* (columns) which *safe-formula* requires as $\text{fv}\,\alpha = \text{fv}\,\beta$. Similarly, negations are only allowed inside conjunctions $[\![\alpha \wedge_F \neg \beta]\!]_{i,n}^{\mathrm{fv}\,\alpha}$ with fv $\beta \subseteq$ fv $\alpha$ to safely compute anti-joins.

This is why H$_I \alpha$ as encoded above is not generally considered safe by itself. Extending MFOTL's syntax to include trigger and release, encoding H$_I\alpha \equiv (\neg_F \top)\,\mathrm{T}_I\,\alpha$, and defining *safe-formula* for these cases [10] is still unsatisfactory. Following the semantics above, formulas $\alpha\,\mathrm{T}_I\,\beta$ remain unsafe when $0 \notin I$ because they could be vacuously true, i.e. if all $j \leq i$ satisfy $\tau_i - \tau_j \notin I$. Yet, crucially for our purposes, older Verimon versions deem some trivially true formulas like $\mathbf{c}\,a =_F \mathbf{c}\,a$ safe. They evaluate to *unit tables* $\mathbf{1}_n$, where $\mathbf{1}_n = \{\langle\rangle_n\}$ and $\langle\rangle_n ::$ 'a option list only has *None* repeated $n$ times. In fact, $\langle\rangle_n$ is the only valuation $v$ that satisfies *wf-tuple* $n\,\emptyset\,v$. In the next section, we take advantage of this and define a notion of safety that allows an encoding of H$_I\,\alpha$ with $0 \notin I$ to be safe.

The formalisation of syntax and semantics of the dual-operators is a technical contribution from our work. It involves routine extensions of definitions such as fv $\alpha$ but it also requires adding properties about satisfiability of both operators. We add more than 400 lines of code to Verimon's formalisation of syntax and semantics [19, 20].

# 3   Relaxation of Safety

Here, we generalise Verimon's fragment of safe formulas by introducing the *dynamic free variables* dfv $\sigma\,i\,\alpha$ of $\alpha$ at $i$ 🌀 and its set of *safe sets of free variables* ssfv $\alpha$ 🌀. If $\alpha\,\mathrm{T}_I\,\beta$ is vacuously true at $i$, then Verimon's output is correct if it is equal to $[\![\alpha\,\mathrm{T}_I\,\beta]\!]_{i,n}^{\emptyset} = \mathbf{1}_n$. However, in its current implementation, this would only be provable for formulas such that fv$(\alpha\,\mathrm{T}_I\,\beta) = \emptyset$. Therefore, to define a larger fragment of evaluable formulas, it is convenient to choose the correct set of attributes at time-point $i$. The function dfv $\sigma\,i\,\alpha$ approximates the set of free variables that influence the satisfiability of $\alpha$ at $i$ in the trace $\sigma$. As with other trace-functions $\Gamma$ and $\tau$, we often use its abbreviated form dfv$_i\,\alpha$. It is a semantic concept and we only need it to prove the algorithm's correctness: outputs are exactly the sets $[\![\alpha]\!]_{i,\mathrm{nfv}\,\alpha}^{\mathrm{dfv}_i\,\alpha}$ for the monitored formula $\alpha$ at each $i$. The function ssfv $\alpha$ approximates all the possible combinations of attributes that tables for $\alpha$ might have at different time-points. It is recursively defined so that we can decide $\alpha$'s safety by checking ssfv $\alpha \neq \emptyset$, that is, we define *is-safe* $\alpha \Leftrightarrow$ ssfv $\alpha \neq \emptyset$. We describe our reasoning behind the definition for each connective below and enforce various properties with our definitions: on one hand, as they are sets of free variables, $(i)$ dfv $\sigma\,i\,\alpha \subseteq$ fv $\alpha$ and $(ii)$ $\bigcup$ ssfv $\alpha \subseteq$ fv $\alpha$. On the other hand, to prove correctness, if the formula is safe ssfv $\alpha \neq \emptyset$, then our set of attributes should be a witness for it: $(iii)$ dfv $\sigma\,i\,\alpha \in$ ssfv $\alpha$. For the full formal definitions see also our Appendix A.

*Atomic Formulas.* All atoms $p\dagger ts$ are safe and their attributes do not change over time. Thus, we define ssfv$(p\dagger ts) = \{\mathrm{fv}(p\dagger ts)\}$ and dfv$_i\,(p\dagger ts) = \mathrm{fv}(p\dagger ts)$. Following Verimon, we do not make $\mathbf{v}\,x =_F \mathbf{v}\,x$ safe as it is not practically relevant for us. Therefore, ssfv maps equalities $\alpha \in \{\mathbf{v}\,x =_F t,\ t =_F \mathbf{v}\,x,\ t_1 =_F t_2\}$ to $\{\mathrm{fv}\,\alpha\}$ whenever fv $t = \emptyset$ (resp. fv $t_1 = $ fv $t_2 = \emptyset$), and to $\emptyset$ otherwise. Similarly, we define dfv$_i\,(t_1 =_F t_2) = \mathrm{fv}(t_1 =_F t_2)$ for all $t_1, t_2 ::$ 'a trm and $i :: \mathbb{N}$.

*Conjunctions.* If safe, each conjunct may have many combinations of attributes. Moreover, a join ($\bowtie$) outputs a table with all the attributes from its operands. Thus, if ssfv $\alpha \neq \emptyset$ and ssfv $\beta \neq \emptyset$, then ssfv$(\alpha \wedge_F \beta) = $ ssfv $\alpha \uplus$ ssfv $\beta$ where ($\uplus$) is the pairwise union $A \uplus B = \{a \cup b \mid a \in A \wedge b \in B\}$ 🌀. We follow Verimon+ and define safety for cases when only the left conjunct $\alpha$ is safe.[2] If $\beta$ is an equality $t_1 =_F t_2$ with fv $t_1 \subseteq X$ or fv $t_2 \subseteq X$ for each $X \in$ ssfv $\alpha$, then we can safely add any single variable on the other side of the equation, possibly not in fv $\alpha$, to the elements of ssfv $\alpha$. Therefore, in this case ssfv$(\alpha \wedge_F \beta) = ((\cup)\,(\text{fv}\,\beta))\,'\,(\text{ssfv}\,\alpha)$. Finally, if $\beta$ is a negation $\neg_F \beta'$ of a safe formula $\beta'$ and every $Y \in$ ssfv $\beta'$ satisfies $Y \subseteq X$ for each $X \in$ ssfv $\alpha$ then we can compute antijoins, and thus ssfv$(\alpha \wedge_F \beta) =$ ssfv $\alpha$. If neither of these cases holds, then ssfv$(\alpha \wedge_F \beta) = \emptyset$. Given the behaviour of join on columns, the dynamic free variables are simply dfv$_i\,(\alpha \wedge_F \beta) =$ dfv$_i\,\alpha \cup$ dfv$_i\,\beta$.

*Disjunctions.* Due to union-compatibility, we can only take unions of tables with the same attributes. Yet, we can generalise for cases when formulas might be vacuously true at some time-points. To evaluate disjunctions we use the function *eval-or* $n\,R_1\,R_2$ that outputs $\mathbf{1}_n$ if either $R_1 = \mathbf{1}_n$ or $R_2 = \mathbf{1}_n$, and $R_1 \cup R_2$ otherwise. Similarly, to ensure *wf-tuple* $n$ (dfv$_i\,(\alpha \vee_F \beta))\,\langle\rangle_n$, we state that there are no "relevant" variables (dfv$_i\,(\alpha \vee_F \beta) = \emptyset$) for the satisfiability of $\alpha \vee_F \beta$ when either $\alpha$ or $\beta$ are logically valid at $i$. If the variables of $\alpha$ are "irrelevant" (dfv$_i\,\alpha = \emptyset$) because $\alpha$ is unsatisfiable at $i$ ($[\![\alpha]\!]_i = \emptyset$), then we just need the variables of $\beta$: dfv$_i\,(\alpha \vee_F \beta) =$ dfv$_i\,\beta$. The symmetric case also holds. If both disjuncts are relevant (dfv$_i\,\alpha \neq \emptyset \neq$ dfv$_i\,\beta$), we need both sets of variables: dfv$_i\,(\alpha \vee_F \beta) =$ dfv$_i\,\alpha \cup$ dfv$_i\,\beta$.

The behaviour of dfv on disjunctions means that if $\emptyset \in$ ssfv $\alpha$ or $\emptyset \in$ ssfv $\beta$, then $\emptyset$ should also be an element of ssfv$(\alpha \vee_F \beta)$. This may happen in various ways. First, if fv $\alpha = \emptyset$ or fv $\beta = \emptyset$, then by $(ii)$ above, we know that ssfv $\alpha = \{\emptyset\}$ or ssfv $\beta = \{\emptyset\}$. In this case, we can define ssfv$(\alpha \vee_F \beta) =$ ssfv $\alpha \cup$ ssfv $\beta$ assuming both $\alpha$ and $\beta$ satisfy *is-safe*. Next, notice that if we allow attributes $X_\alpha \in$ ssfv $\alpha$ and $X_\beta \in$ ssfv $\beta$ such that $\emptyset \neq X_\alpha \neq X_\beta \neq \emptyset$, the corresponding table for $\alpha \vee_F \beta$ would need to have infinite values. Therefore, at most we may allow ssfv $\alpha \subseteq \{\emptyset, \text{fv}\,\alpha\}$, ssfv $\beta \subseteq \{\emptyset, \text{fv}\,\beta\}$ and fv $\alpha =$ fv $\beta$ with both $\alpha$ and $\beta$ having non-empty ssfvs. In this case, if $\emptyset \in$ ssfv $\alpha$ or $\emptyset \in$ ssfv $\beta$ then ssfv$(\alpha \vee_F \beta) = \{\emptyset\} \cup (\text{ssfv}\,\alpha \uplus \text{ssfv}\,\beta)$, otherwise ssfv$(\alpha \vee_F \beta) = \{\text{fv}\,\alpha\}$.

*Negations.* If $\alpha$ is safe and closed (ssfv$(\alpha) = \{\emptyset\}$ by $(ii)$), then we can safely evaluate its negation ssfv$(\neg_F \alpha) = \{\emptyset\}$. We also allow ssfv$(\neg_F\,(t =_F t)) = \{\text{fv}(t =_F t)\}$ for arbitrary term $t$ to encode the constantly false formula. Otherwise negations are unsafe ssfv$(\neg_F \alpha) = \emptyset$. For dynamic free variables, we define dfv$_i(\neg_F \alpha) =$ dfv$_i\,\alpha$.

*Quantifiers.* When interpreting De Bruijn indices, quantifiers remove 0 from fv $\alpha$ and subtract 1 to all its elements. Thus, we define dfv$_i\,(\exists_F \alpha) = (\lambda x.\,x - 1)\,'\,(\text{dfv}_i\,\alpha - \{0\})$ and $(\lambda x.\,x - 1)\,'\,(X - \{0\}) \in$ ssfv$(\exists_F \alpha)$ for each $X \in$ ssfv $\alpha$.

*Previous and Next.* The definition of the dynamic free variables for one-step temporal operators follows that of their semantics: dfv$_i\,(\mathsf{X}_I\,\alpha) =$ dfv$_{i+1}\,\alpha$ while dfv$_i\,(\mathsf{Y}_I\,\alpha) =$ dfv$_{i-1}\,\alpha$ if $i > 0$ and dfv$_i\,(\mathsf{Y}_I\,\alpha) =$ fv $\alpha$ if $i = 0$. For safety, all combinations of attributes of $\alpha$ might be used in its one-step temporal versions ssfv $(\mathsf{X}_I\,\alpha) =$ ssfv $\alpha =$ ssfv $(\mathsf{Y}_I\,\alpha)$.

*Since and Until.* Let us follow the semantics for since and until to define their dfvs at $i$. The definition for one operator emerges by dualising the time-point order and flipping subtractions of time-stamps in the other's definition, hence we omit the description

---

[2] Adding the symmetric case increases the number of proofs in the formalisation. It is easier to assume a formula rewriter can commute conjuncts if necessary.

for until. We must collect all the dynamic free variables $\text{dfv}_k \, \alpha$ and $\text{dfv}_j \, \beta$ that influence the satisfiability of $\alpha \, S_I \, \beta$. Start by defining $\downarrow_I i = \{j \mid j \leq i \wedge (\tau_i - \tau_j) \in I\}$ to identify the indices $j$ for $\beta$, and the predicate $\textit{satisf-at } j = \exists v. \, \langle \sigma, v, j \rangle \models \beta \wedge (\forall k \in (j, i]. \, \langle \sigma, v, i \rangle \models \alpha)$ so that $\alpha \, S_I \, \beta$ is unsatisfiable at $i$ if $\forall j \in \downarrow_I i. \, \neg \textit{satisf-at } j$. When this happens we let $\text{dfv}_i(\alpha \, S_I \, \beta) = \text{fv}(\alpha \, S_I \, \beta)$. Otherwise, the indices $j$ for $\beta$ are $\mathcal{J} = \{j \in \downarrow_I i \mid \textit{satisf-at } j\}$ while those $k$ for $\alpha$ are $\mathcal{K} = \bigcup_{j \in \mathcal{J}} (j, i]$. Having identified the indices, we obtain $\text{dfv}_i(\alpha \, S_I \, \beta) = \left( \bigcup_{k \in \mathcal{K}} \text{dfv}_k \, \alpha \right) \cup \left( \bigcup_{j \in \mathcal{J}} \text{dfv}_j \, \beta \right)$.

As we have seen for disjunctions, our definitions of safety depend on the operations in the formula-evaluation. In particular, to define ssfvs for since, it is convenient to understand Verimon's [19] implementation roughly represented with the equations:

$$[\![\alpha S_I \beta]\!]_i = \bigcup_{j \in \downarrow_I i} [\![\alpha S_{\{\tau_i - \tau_j\}} \beta]\!]_i \text{ and } [\![\alpha S_{\{\tau_i - \tau_j\}} \beta]\!]_i = \bigcup_{k \in \downarrow_{\{\tau_i - \tau_j\}} i} [\![\beta]\!]_k \cap \left( \bigcap_{l \in (k, i]} [\![\alpha]\!]_l \right). \quad (1)$$

That is, the algorithm obtains the valuations in $[\![\alpha S_I \beta]\!]_i$ by iteratively updating those in $[\![\alpha S_{\{\tau_i - \tau_j\}} \beta]\!]_i$ until it has visited all time-points $j \in \downarrow_I i$, when it outputs their union. In the implementation, intersections are replaced with (anti)joins and sets $[\![\varphi]\!]_l$, with tables $[\![\varphi]\!]_{l,n}^{X_l}$ having attributes $X_l$ at index $l$ for safe $\varphi$. If $0 \in I$, one of the tables involved in the output union is $[\![\beta]\!]_{i,n}^{\text{fv} \, \beta}$. Hence, by union-compatibility, all the other table-operands (represented by $[\![\alpha S_{\{\tau_i - \tau_j\}} \beta]\!]_j$) must have the same attributes. To ensure this, we require $\text{ssfv}(\alpha S_I \beta)$ to be non-empty only when $\text{ssfv} \, \beta = \{\text{fv} \, \beta\}$. Then, we define $\text{ssfv}(\alpha S_I \beta) = \{\text{fv} \, \beta\}$ if fv $\alpha \subseteq$ fv $\beta$ with $\textit{ssfv}\alpha \neq \emptyset$ because the joins in the construction of the tables represented by $[\![\alpha S_{\{\tau_i - \tau_j\}} \beta]\!]_i$ would always be guarded by the attributes fv $\beta$ of $[\![\beta]\!]_{k,n}^{\text{fv} \, \beta}$. Similarly, $\text{ssfv}(\alpha S_I \beta) = \{\text{fv} \, \beta\}$ for $\alpha = \neg \alpha'$ with $\text{ssfv} \, \alpha' \neq \emptyset$ and fv $\alpha \subseteq$ fv $\beta$ because of the corresponding antijoins.

The Verimon implementation for until is different and intuitively corresponds to

$$[\![\alpha \, U_I \, \beta]\!]_i = \bigcup_{j \in \uparrow_I i} [\![\beta]\!]_j \cap \left( \bigcap_{k \in [i, j)} [\![\alpha]\!]_k \right).$$

As before, one of the operands may be $[\![\beta]\!]_{i,n}^{\text{fv} \, \beta}$, therefore we require $\text{ssfv} \, \beta = \{\text{fv} \, \beta\}$. If fv $\alpha \subseteq$ fv $\beta$ with $\text{ssfv} \, \alpha \neq \emptyset$, then $\text{ssfv}(\alpha S_I \beta) = \{\text{fv} \, \beta\}$. But for $\alpha = \neg \alpha'$, the tables for $\alpha'$ are united separately and antijoined to each table for $\beta$ at $j$. Thus, we need to take union-compatibility into account when $\alpha = \neg \alpha'$. Hence, in this case, we define $\text{ssfv}(\alpha S_I \beta) = \{\text{fv} \, \beta\}$ if $\text{ssfv} \, \beta = \{\text{fv} \, \beta\}$ and $\text{ssfv} \, \alpha' = \{\text{fv} \, \alpha'\}$.

*Trigger and Release.* Our definition of dfvs for these dual operators is very similar to that of since and until. Assume $D \in \{T, R\}$ and let $idx = \downarrow_I i$ and $ivl \, i \, j = (j, i]$ if $D = T$; otherwise, if $D = R$, then $idx = \uparrow_I i$ and $ivl \, i \, j = [i, j)$. The key difference in the definition of dfvs for $D$ is that if $idx = \emptyset$, then $\alpha \, D_I \, \beta$ is vacuously true. Hence, we define $\text{dfv}_i(\alpha \, D_I \, \beta) = \emptyset$ because $\alpha \, D_I \, \beta$ will evaluate to the unit table. As before, we also define a predicate $\textit{satisf-at } v \, j$ that makes the formula unsatisfiable whenever $\forall v. \, \exists j \in idx. \, \neg \textit{satisf-at } v \, j$. In this case, $\text{dfv}_i(\alpha \, D_I \, \beta) = \text{fv}(\alpha \, D_I \, \beta)$. The predicate $\textit{satisf-at}$ also allows us to define sets of indices $\mathcal{K}$ and $\mathcal{J}$ to collect dfvs over time for the remaining cases: $\text{dfv}_i(\alpha \, D_I \, \beta) = \left( \bigcup_{k \in \mathcal{K}} \text{dfv}_k \, \alpha \right) \cup \left( \bigcup_{j \in \mathcal{J}} \text{dfv}_j \, \beta \right)$.

Our definition of safety for dual operators is intuitively understood by observing

$$[\![\alpha \, D_I \, \beta]\!]_i = \bigcap_{j \in idx_I i} [\![\beta]\!]_j \cup \left( \bigcup_{k \in ivl \, i \, j} rel_k \cap [\![\alpha]\!]_k \right), \quad (2)$$

where $rel_k = [\![\beta]\!]_k$ if $0 \in I$, and $rel_k = [\![\alpha]\!]_k$ otherwise. As before, whenever $0 \in I$, we define $\mathrm{ssfv}(\alpha \, D_I \, \beta) = \{\mathrm{fv}\,\beta\}$ assuming $\mathrm{ssfv}\,\beta = \{\mathrm{fv}\,\beta\}$ and $\mathrm{fv}\,\alpha \subseteq \mathrm{fv}\,\beta$, both if $\mathrm{ssfv}\,\alpha \neq \emptyset$ or if $\mathrm{ssfv}\,\alpha = \emptyset$ but $\alpha = \neg\,\alpha'$ with $\mathrm{ssfv}\,\alpha' \neq \emptyset$. When $0 \notin I$, $\alpha \, D_I \, \beta$ might be vacuously true and union-compatibility is relevant. Therefore, we define $\mathrm{ssfv}(\alpha \, D_I \, \beta) = \{\emptyset, \mathrm{fv}\,\alpha\}$ whenever $\mathrm{ssfv}\,\alpha = \{\mathrm{fv}\,\alpha\}$, $\mathrm{ssfv}\,\beta = \{\mathrm{fv}\,\beta\}$ and $\mathrm{fv}\,\alpha = \mathrm{fv}\,\beta$. Otherwise $\mathrm{ssfv}(\alpha \, D_I \, \beta) = \emptyset$.

We formalise all cases above together with the definition $is\text{-}safe\,\alpha \Leftrightarrow \mathrm{ssfv}\,\alpha \neq \emptyset$ in Isabelle/HOL. Next, by induction on the definition of ssfvs, we derive properties $(i)$ ✹, $(ii)$ ✹ and $(iii)$ ✹ above. Additionally, we also prove that for any formula $\alpha$, $is\text{-}safe\,\alpha \Leftrightarrow \mathrm{fv}\,\alpha \in \mathrm{ssfv}\,\alpha$.

In classical logic, an important property for syntactic substitutions of terms and formulas states that if two valuations $v$ and $v'$ coincide in $\mathrm{fv}\,\alpha$, then the value of $\alpha$ is the same under both valuations. Similarly, we have that if $v\,!\,x = v'\,!\,x$ for all $x \in \mathrm{dfv}\,\sigma\,i\,\alpha$, then $\langle\sigma,v,i\rangle \models \alpha \Leftrightarrow \langle\sigma,v',i\rangle \models \alpha$. This is useful for us because it ratifies that if $\langle\sigma,\langle\rangle_n,i\rangle \models_M \alpha$ for $\alpha$ with $\mathrm{dfv}_i\,\alpha = \emptyset$, then $\alpha$ is logically valid at $i$.

Let us compare our definition of safety with previous ones. To do this directly, we combine $safe\text{-}formula$ predicates from Verimon [19] and Verimon+ [10,22], restrict them to the syntax in Sect. 2 and add them to our Appendix A. Structurally, our definition of safety for conjunctions, negations, existential quantifiers, previous, next and until operators resembles that of Verimon+ [22] which is already more general than that of Verimon. However, in combination with other operators our definition deems more formulas safe (see Sect. 5). We discuss in Sect. 7 possible generalisations for these cases that involve dfvs and ssfvs. For equalities, ssfv generalises $safe\text{-}formula$ even when incorporating Verimon+'s more expressive term language that includes some arithmetic operations. By using $eval\text{-}or$, our definition of safety for disjunctions differs from $safe\text{-}formula$ by admitting vacuously true formulas satisfying $is\text{-}safe$ in either disjunct. Additionally, $is\text{-}safe\,(\alpha \, S_I \, \beta)$ allows $\alpha$ to have many ssfvs which generalises $safe\text{-}formula\,(\alpha \, S_I \, \beta)$. Dual operators are only safe in an unintegrated extension [10] of Verimon+; but we also generalise this work by making them safe when $0 \notin I$, even when they are not part of a conjunction with a safe formula. In general, we show that $is\text{-}safe$ generalises previous monitoring fragments: on one hand we prove that $is\text{-}safe\,\alpha$ if $safe\text{-}formula\,\alpha$ for any $\alpha$ ✹. On the other hand, the formula $\alpha \equiv \neg_F(\mathbf{v}\,x =_F \mathbf{v}\,x)\,T_{[1,2]}\,(p \dagger [\mathbf{v}\,x])$, which is equivalent to $H_{[1,2]}p \dagger [\mathbf{v}\,x]$, satisfies $is\text{-}safe\,\alpha$ but also $\neg\,safe\text{-}formula\,\alpha$.

The definition and formalisation of safety for MFOTL-formulas is a major contribution of this work. It involves defining ssfvs, dfvs, pairwise unions and proving their corresponding properties. The developments on this section add more than 1600 lines of code to the Verimon formalisation [19, 20].

## 4    Implementation of Dual Operators

In this section, we explain our additions of dual operators to Verimon's formalisation. Intuitively, the monitoring algorithm takes as inputs a safe MFOTL-formula $\alpha$ and an event trace $\sigma$ and outputs the table of satisfactions $[\![\alpha]\!]_{i,n}^{\mathrm{dfv}_i}\,\alpha$ at each time-point $i$. Concretely, Verimon provides two functions $minit$ and $mstep$ to initialise and update the monitor's state respectively. The model for this monitor's $state$ at $i$ is a three-part record $\langle\rho_i^\alpha,\alpha_M^i,n\rangle$. Here, $n = \mathrm{nfv}\,\alpha$ and $\rho_i^\alpha :: nat$ is the $progress$ or the earliest time-point for which satisfactions of $\alpha$ cannot yet be evaluated for lack or information. Finally, $\alpha_M^i :: {}'a\ mformula$ is a recursively defined structure associated with $\alpha$ to store all the information needed to compute $[\![\alpha]\!]_{i,n}^{\mathrm{dfv}_i}\,\alpha$. We describe our extensions to all these functions and structures in order to monitor dual operators trigger and release. In the sequel, we use $A_i = [\![\alpha]\!]_{i,n}^{\mathrm{dfv}_i}\,\alpha$, $B_i = [\![\beta]\!]_{i,n}^{\mathrm{dfv}_i}\,\beta$ and $C_i = [\![\gamma]\!]_{i,n}^{\mathrm{dfv}_i}\,\gamma$ to simplify notation.

The function $minit$ is just a wrapper calling $minit0$ to set the initial monitor's state to $\langle 0, \alpha_M^0, \mathrm{nfv}\,\alpha\rangle$. Accordingly, $minit0$ takes a safe MFOTL-formula $\alpha :: \,'a\;frm$ and transforms it into $\alpha_M^0 :: \,'a\;mformula$. The datatype $mformula$ describes the information needed at each $i$ to compute $A_i$. For instance, if $\alpha$'s main connective is a binary operator with direct subformulas $\beta$ and $\gamma$, the set of satisfactions for either of them are only available up to $\rho_i^\beta$ and $\rho_i^\gamma$ respectively at $i$. This is why, $\alpha_M^i$ includes a $buffer\;buf::\,'a\;mbuf2$ to store yet, unused tables $B_j$ (resp. $C_j$) such that $j \in [\rho_i^\gamma, \rho_i^\beta)$ (resp. $j \in [\rho_i^\beta, \rho_i^\gamma)$). Whenever both $B_j$ and $C_j$ are in the buffer, the algorithm operates them and either outputs the result or stores it in an $auxiliary\;state$ for future processing. To help the algorithm know whether to do joins or antijoins, $\alpha_M^i$ may also include a boolean indicating whether one of its direct sub-formulas is not negated. More specifically, the state-representations of $\alpha\,D_I\,\beta$ with $D \in \{T, R\}$ include their sub-mformulas $\alpha_M$ and $\beta_M$, a boolean indicating if $\alpha$ is not negated, the interval $I :: \mathcal{I}$, the $buffer\;buf$, a corresponding list of unused time-stamps $\tau s$, and its auxiliary state. Formally, we add the last two lines below to the definition of the $mformula$ datatype:

**datatype** $'a\;mformula = MRel\;'a\;option\;list\;set \mid \ldots$
$\mid MTrigger\;bool\;'a\;mformula\;bool\;\mathcal{I}\;'a\;mformula\;'a\;mbuf2\;\mathbb{N}\;list\;'a\;mtaux$
$\mid MRelease\;bool\;'a\;mformula\;bool\;\mathcal{I}\;'a\;mformula\;'a\;mbuf2\;\mathbb{N}\;list\;'a\;mraux$

where the second boolean indicates whether $0 \in I$, and $'a\;mtaux$ and $'a\;mraux$ are the type-abbreviations we use for trigger and release's auxiliary states respectively. Let us describe these in detail next.

Our implementation of the auxiliary state for trigger $Ts :: \,'a\;mtaux$ resembles Verimon's [19] auxiliary state for since. That is, it combines the intuitions in Eqs. (1) and (2): at time-point $i$, it is a list of time-stamped tables $\langle \tau_j, T_{\tau_j}^i \rangle$ that the monitor joins after it has passed all $j \in \downarrow_I i$. Abbreviating $\iota = (\min \rho_i^\alpha\,\rho_i^\beta) - 1$ and using $\bowtie^*$ to denote a join with non-negated subformula $\alpha$ and an antijoin with $\alpha$ for the direct subformula $\neg_F\,\alpha$, we intend

$$T_{\tau_j}^i = \bigotimes_{k \in \downarrow_{\{\tau_\iota - \tau_j\}}\iota} B_k \cup \left( \bigcup_{l \in (k, \iota]} B_l \bowtie^* A_l \right), \qquad \text{if } 0 \in I \text{ and} \qquad (3)$$

$$T_{\tau_j}^i = [\![\alpha\;\mathrm{T}_{\{\tau_\iota - \tau_j\}}\;\beta]\!]_{i,n}^{\mathrm{fv}\,\beta}, \qquad \text{if } 0 \notin I. \qquad (4)$$

The tables described by Eq. (3) would coincide with the tables for $\alpha\,\mathrm{T}_{\{\tau_\iota - \tau_j\}}\,\beta$ as in Eq. (4) if we remove the $B_l$s inside the union, but we use them to simplify our definition of safety as discussed after Eq. (2).

Likewise, following the intuition provided by Eq. (2), the auxiliary state for release $Rs :: \,'a\;mtaux$ at $i$ is a list of ternary tuples $\langle \tau_j, R_{\mathcal{L}}^{j,i}, R_{\mathcal{R}}^j \rangle$ such that

$$R_{\mathcal{L}}^{i,j} = if\;0 \in I\;then\;\bigcup_{k \in [j, \iota]} B_k \bowtie^* A_k\;else\;\bigcup_{k \in [j, \iota]} A_k\;\text{and} \qquad (5)$$

$$R_{\mathcal{R}}^{i,j} = \begin{cases} if\;0 \in I\;then\;B_j\;else\;\mathbf{1}_n, & \text{if } \tau_\iota < \tau_j + I, \\ [\![\alpha\;\mathrm{R}_I\;\beta]\!]_{j,n}^{\mathrm{dfv}_j(\alpha\mathrm{R}_I\beta)}, & \text{if } \tau_\iota > \tau_j + I, \\ \bigotimes_{k \in [0, \iota] \cap \uparrow_I j} B_k \cup R_{\mathcal{L}}^{k,i-1}, & \text{if } (\tau_\iota - \tau_j) \in I. \end{cases} \qquad (6)$$

The function that transforms $\alpha :: {}'a\ frm$ to $\alpha_M :: {}'a\ mformula$ is $minit0$. Our additions for this function on trigger and release follow our definition of safety. That is, $minit0$ maps $\alpha\ D_I\ \beta$ with $D \in \{T, R\}$ to

$$MDual\ (\alpha \neq \neg_F \alpha')\ (minit0\ n\ \alpha)\ (0 \in I)\ I\ (minit0\ n\ \beta)\ ([], [])\ []\ []$$

for some $\alpha'$ and $MDual \in \{MTrigger, MRelease\}$ accordingly.                                    🜂

When the monitor processes the $i$th time-point, the function $mstep$ outputs the new state $\langle \rho_i^\alpha, \alpha_M^i, n \rangle$. However, it is also a wrapper for the function $meval$ in charge of updating $\alpha_M^i :: {}'a\ mformula$. Intuitively, $meval$ takes $\alpha_M^{i-1}$ and the trace information $\Gamma\ \sigma\ i$ and $\tau\ \sigma\ i$ and outputs the updated mformula $\alpha_M^i$ and the evaluated tables $A_j$ from $j = \rho_\alpha^{i-1} - 1$ to $j = \rho_\alpha^i - 1$. We describe its behaviour on auxiliary states below.         🜂

Assuming $meval$ has produced tables $A_\iota$ and $B_\iota$, it uses the function $update\text{-}trigger$ to update the auxiliary state $Ts :: {}'a\ mtaux$ and to possibly output $[\![\alpha\ T_I\ \beta]\!]_{\iota,n}^{\mathrm{fv}\ \beta}$. This function first filters $Ts$ by removing all elements whose time-stamps $\tau_j$ are not relevant for future time-points, i.e. $\tau_j < \tau_\iota - I$. Then, following Eqs. (3) and (4), it takes the union of the latest $B_\iota \bowtie^* A_\iota$ or $A_\iota$ with all elements in $Ts$, depending on whether $0 \in I$ or not respectively. Next, it adds $B_\iota$ either as a new element $\langle \tau_\iota, B_\iota \rangle\ \#\ Ts$ if this is the first time $\tau_\iota$ is seen, or by joining it with the table in $Ts$ time-stamped with $\tau_{\iota-1} = \tau_\iota$, to obtain $T_{\tau_\iota}^i$. Finally, it joins all the tables $T_{\tau_j}^i$ in $Ts$ such that $j \in\ \downarrow_I \iota$.                    🜂

The function $update\text{-}release$ takes the union of the latest $B_\iota \bowtie^* A_\iota$ or $A_\iota$ with each $R_{\mathcal{L}}^{j,i-1}$ in $Rs :: {}'a\ mraux$, depending on whether $0 \in I$ (see Eqs. (5) and (6)). On the third entries $R_{\mathcal{R}}^{i,j}$, it joins $B_\iota \cup R_{\mathcal{L}}^{i-1,j}$ if $(\tau_i - \tau_j) \in I$, otherwise, it leaves $R_{\mathcal{R}}^{i,j}$ as it is. Finally, it adds at the end of $Rs$ the tuple $\langle \tau_\iota, B_\iota \bowtie^* A_\iota, B_\iota \rangle$ if $0 \in I$, or $\langle \tau_\iota, A_\iota, \mathbf{1}_n \rangle$ if $0 \notin I$. To output the final results $[\![\alpha\ R_I\ \beta]\!]_{j,n}^{\mathrm{dfv}_j\ \alpha R_I \beta}$, $meval$ calls the function $eval\text{-}future$ which traverses $Rs$ and outputs all $R_{\mathcal{R}}^{i,j}$ with $\tau_j + I < \tau_i$ and removes them from $Rs$.         🜂

The only other modification we do on $meval$ for the remaining logical connectives is in the disjunction case, where we have replaced every instance of the traditional union ($\cup$) with our function $eval\text{-}or$. This is the only place where we perform this substitution.

For our purposes, this concludes the description of the monitoring algorithm. It mainly consists of the initialisation function $minit$ and the single-step function $mstep$. Together, they form Verimon's online interface with the monitored system. Our additions in this regard are mostly conceptual since we only implement the evaluation of trigger and release as functions $update\text{-}trigger$ and $update\text{-}release$.

## 5   Monitoring Examples

Here, we describe various formulas that are safe according to our ssfvs definition but that are not safe in previous Verimon implementations. We present them through case-studies. Our examples occur not only in monitoring but also in relational databases.

*Quality Assessment (Operations on Globally).* A company passes its products through sequential processes $p_1$, $p_2$ and $p_3$. Every item passes through all processes. Every minute, the company logs the time $\tau$ and the identification number ID of each item in process $p_i$. It uses an online monitor to classify its products according to their quality. The best ones are those that pass through process $p_i$ for exactly $n_i$ minutes and that move to $p_{i+1}$ immediately afterwards. The second-best ones are those that pass through at least one process $p_i$ in at least $n_i$ minutes. The remaining items need to be corrected after production. To identify the best ones, the company uses the following specification

$$best \equiv \left( G_{[0,n_1)}\ p_1 \dagger [\mathbf{v}\ x] \right)\ \wedge_F \left( G_{[n_1,n_2')}\ p_2 \dagger [\mathbf{v}\ x] \right)\ \wedge_F \left( G_{[n_2',n_3')}\ p_3 \dagger [\mathbf{v}\ x] \right),$$

where $n'_2 = n_1 + n_2$ and $n'_3 = n_1 + n_2 + n_3$. Similarly, to identify those products with just good quality, they use the specification

$$good \equiv \left( G_{[0,n_1)} \, p_1 \dagger [\mathbf{v}\, x] \right) \vee_F \left( G_{[n_1,n'_2)} \, p_2 \dagger [\mathbf{v}\, x] \right) \vee_F \left( G_{[n'_2,n'_3)} \, p_3 \dagger [\mathbf{v}\, x] \right).$$

Our relaxation of safety, makes both formulas monitorable by encoding $G_I\,(p_i \dagger [\mathbf{v}\, x])$ as $\neg_F(\mathbf{v}\, x =_F \mathbf{v}\, x)\, R_I\,(p_i \dagger [\mathbf{v}\, x])$. Specifically, the safe sets of free variables are ssfv($best$) = $\{\{x\}\} \neq \emptyset$ and ssfv($good$) = $\{\emptyset, \{x\}\} \neq \emptyset$. We use the functions $minit$ and $mstep$ to monitor $best$ through a manually made trace. We assume four products with IDs $0, 1, 2$ and $3$ and fix $n_1 = n_2 = n_3 = 2$. The table below represents said trace and shows the monitor's output at each time-point.

| Time | product_id 0 | product_id 1 | product_id 2 | product_id 3 | output for $best$ |
|------|------|------|------|------|------|
| 0 | $p_1$ | $p_1$ | $p_1$ | $p_1$ | $\emptyset$ |
| 1 | $p_1$ | $p_1$ | $p_1$ | $p_1$ | $\emptyset$ |
| 2 | $p_2$ | $p_2$ | $p_1$ | $p_2$ | $\emptyset$ |
| 3 | $p_2$ | $p_2$ | $p_2$ | $p_2$ | $\emptyset$ |
| 4 | $p_3$ | $p_2$ | $p_2$ | $p_3$ | $\emptyset$ |
| 5 | $p_3$ | $p_3$ | $p_2$ | $p_3$ | $\emptyset$ |
| 6 | $-$ | $p_3$ | $p_3$ | $-$ | $\{[0],[3]\}$ @$\tau = 0$ |

The monitor correctly classifies the products with IDs 0 and 3 as the best ones after the first 6 min have passed. Before that, it outputs the empty set indicating that no product was one of the best yet. Our Appendix A includes the formalisation of this trace and a simplified version of the monitor's printed output. These encodings for $best$ and $good$ are not safe in any previous implementation. The equivalence [10]

$$G_{[a,b)} \, \alpha \equiv (F_{[a,b)} \, \alpha) \wedge_F \neg_F (F_{[a,b)}((P_{[0,b)} \, \alpha) \vee_F (F_{[0,b)} \, \alpha)) \wedge_F \neg_F \alpha)$$

also produces encodings of $best$ and $good$ that satisfy $safe$-$formula$ assuming $0 < a < b$ but these are clearly longer than simply using release $R_I$ as above. Shorter inputs require less runtime computations. Notice that eventually (F) and pastly (P) are already abbreviations making the above encoding for globally (G) have 13 connectives. Our encoding instead requires only 3. This compounds quickly, $best$ and $good$ would have in total 53 connectives instead of 14 as in our case.

*Vaccine Refrigeration Times (Conjunction of Negated Historically).* A company that manufactures dry-ice thermal shipping containers has just reported a loss of their refrigeration effectiveness after $m$ hours. This means that some vaccines transported in those containers are not effective because the vaccines are very sensitive to thermal conditions. Vaccination centres need to know which vaccines they can apply. They ask for help from the shipping company in charge of transporting the vaccines. This company needs to take into account its unpacking time that consistently requires $n > 0$ minutes. Fortunately, the shipping company has a log, that among other things, registers "@$\tau$ (travelling, $id$)" if package with ID-number $id$ is travelling at time $\tau$, and annotates "@$\tau$ (arrived, $id$)" when the package identified with $id$ arrives at a centre at time $\tau$. The company can deploy a monitor of the following specification over their log to know which packages contain vaccines that are safe to use:

$$(\text{arrived} \dagger [\mathbf{v}\, x]) \wedge_F \neg_F \, H_{[n,m_\epsilon]} (\text{travelling} \dagger [\mathbf{v}\, x]),$$

where $m_\epsilon$ is $m$ in minutes plus some margin of error $\epsilon$, and $H_I$ (travelling † [v $x$]) $\equiv$ $\neg_F(\mathbf{v}\,x =_F \mathbf{v}\,x)$ $T_I$ (travelling † [v $x$]). Previous work on Verimon+ could tackle an equivalent specification, but it would require the less straightforward encoding [10]:

$$H_{[a,b)}\,\alpha \equiv (P_{[a,b)}\,\alpha) \wedge_F \neg_F (P_{[a,b)}((P_{[0,b)}\,\alpha) \vee_F (F_{[0,b)}\,\alpha)) \wedge_F \neg_F\,\alpha), \text{ with } 0 < a < b.$$

Thus, monitoring our encoding is arguably more efficient as outlined before.

*Financial Crime Investigation (Historically with Many Variables).* Data scientists suspect a vulnerability in the security system of their employer, a new online bank. They notice the following pattern: various failed payment attempts of the same amount from one account to another for 5 consecutive minutes. Then, 30 min later, a successful payment of the same amount between the same accounts. One of the queries to the database that the scientists can issue to confirm their suspicions is

$$(\text{approved\_trans\_from\_paid\_to } \dagger\,[\mathbf{v}\,0, \mathbf{v}\,1, \mathbf{v}\,2, \mathbf{v}\,3])$$
$$\wedge_F\,H_{[30,34]}\,(\exists_F\,(\text{failed\_trans\_from\_paid\_to } \dagger\,[\mathbf{v}\,0, \mathbf{v}\,1, \mathbf{v}\,2, \mathbf{v}\,3]))\,.$$

In both predicates, $\mathbf{v}\,0$ represents the transaction ID, $\mathbf{v}\,1$ is the account that pays, $\mathbf{v}\,2$ corresponds to the amount of money transferred, and $\mathbf{v}\,3$ denotes the receiving account. The query itself finds all transactions that were successful between two accounts $\mathbf{v}\,1$ and $\mathbf{v}\,3$ at a given time-point but that were attempted for 5 consecutive minutes, 30 min earlier. This not only provides all suspicious receivers, but also all possible victims and the amount of money they lost per transaction.

We can codify $H_I\,\alpha \equiv (\bot_F\,\alpha)\,T_I\,\alpha$, where the expression $\bot_F\,\alpha$ denotes the formula $\neg_F(\mathbf{v}\,0 =_F \mathbf{v}\,0) \wedge_F \cdots \wedge_F \neg_F(\mathbf{v}\,n =_F \mathbf{v}\,n)$ and $n = \text{nfv}\,\alpha - 1$. Monitoring such a simple encoding of historically (with $0 \notin I$) is possible due to the integration of our safety relaxation into the algorithm. Simplifying this further to $\bot_F\,\alpha \equiv \neg_F(\mathbf{c}\,0 =_F \mathbf{c}\,0)$ produces an unsafe formula because the free variables on both sides of $T_I$ do not coincide. We discuss generalisations involving ssfvs and dfvs to achieve this simplification in Sect. 7.

*Monitoring Piracy (Release Operator).* To deal with a recent increase in piracy, a shipping company integrates a monitor into its tanker tracking system. By standard, their vessels constantly broadcast a signal with their location through their automatic identification system, which in good conditions arrives every minute, but in adverse ones, can take more than 14 h to update. This signalling system is one of the first turned off by pirates because it allows them to sell the tanker's contents in nearby unofficial ports. Thus, the company regularly registers the ID numbers of all moving ships whose signal is not being received via logs "@$\tau$ (no_sign, $id$)" and those who are not in the correct course as "@$\tau$ (off_route, $id$)", where $id$ is the ID of a ship satisfying the respective status. The company decides it should monitor their tankers as

$$pirated \equiv \text{off\_route } \dagger\,[\mathbf{v}\,x]\,R_{[0,n)}\,\text{no\_sign } \dagger\,[\mathbf{v}\,x].$$

The monitor would send the company a warning after $n$ minutes if it observes either of two behaviours: not receiving a signal from the ship for the entire $n$ minutes, or not receiving a signal and suddenly receiving a position outside of its planned route. This lets the company collaborate with local authorities and try to locate their vessels through alternative means. Due to our explicit implementation of the bounded release operator, the specification above is now straightforwardly monitorable. There is no previous direct implementation of the release operator in Verimon, which means that the above formula would not be monitorable. However, recent developments show [10] that 27-connectives-long encodings would be.

Running the monitor through a manual trace illustrated in the table below and assuming for simplicity $n = 2$ correctly identifies ships with IDs 1 and 2 as those possibly pirated. The formalisation of the trace and the printed monitor's output are available in our Appendix A.

| Time | ship_id 1 | ship_id 2 | ship_id 3 | output for *best* |
| --- | --- | --- | --- | --- |
| 0 | no_sign | no_sign | sign | $\emptyset$ |
| 1 | no_sign | no_sign | sign | $\emptyset$ |
| 2 | no_sign | no_sign | sign | $\emptyset$ |
| 3 | off_route | no_sign | sign | $\{[1], [2]\}$ @$\tau = 0$ |
| 4 | off_route | no_sign | sign | $\{[2]\}$ @$\tau = 1$ |

In summary, recent work [10] implies that our work's safe formulas using historically, globally, trigger or release can be encoded as previous versions safe formulas and monitored. However, the resulting encodings are longer, which impairs the runtime monitoring efficiency. Therefore, the examples above show that our relaxation of safety aids in efficiently monitoring commonly used specifications. Combining optimised implementations [3,10] of temporal operators with our contributions would augment any MFOTL-based monitor's efficiency.

# 6   Correctness

In this section, we show that the integration of our relaxation of safety into Verimon's monitoring algorithm is correct. We focus specifically on describing the proof of correctness for our implementation of dual operators. That is, we show that the algorithm described in previous sections outputs exactly the tables $[\![\alpha]\!]_{i,\mathrm{nfv}\,\alpha}^{\mathrm{dfv}_i\,\alpha}$ at time-point $i$ for safe $\alpha$. We also comment on the overall additions and adaptations required in the proof of Verimon's correctness to accommodate our definition of safety.

First, an Isabelle predicate to describe that a given set of valuations $R$ is a proper table with $n$ attributes in $X$ is $table\,n\,X\,R \Leftrightarrow (\forall v \in R.\ wf\text{-}tuple\,n\,X\,R)$. The formalisation of Verimon [20], uses the predicate $qtable\,n\,X\,P\,Q\,R$ to state correctness of outputs, where $n :: \mathbb{N}$, $X :: \mathbb{N}\ set$, $P$ and $Q$ are predicates on valuations, and $R$ is a table. It is characterised by

$$qtable\,n\,X\,P\,Q\,R \Leftrightarrow (table\,n\,X\,R) \wedge (\forall v.\ P\,v \Rightarrow (v \in R \leftrightarrow Q\,v \wedge wf\text{-}tuple\,n\,X\,v)).$$

In our case, it is typically evaluated to $qtable\,n\,(\mathrm{dfv}_i\,\alpha)\,P\,(\lambda v.\langle\sigma, v, i\rangle \models_M \alpha)\,R$ with $n \geq \mathrm{nfv}\,\alpha$. If $R$ is Verimon's output for $\alpha$ at $i$, it roughly states that $R = [\![\alpha]\!]_{i,\mathrm{nfv}\,\alpha}^{\mathrm{dfv}_i\,\alpha}$ modulo $P$ and that $table(\mathrm{nfv}\,\alpha)\,(\mathrm{dfv}_i\,\alpha)\,R$. In Verimon's and our proof of correctness, $P$ is instantiated to a trivially true statement. We do not omit $P$ here because our general results require assumptions about it.

Given our use of empty dfvs for vacuously true formulas, the behaviour of $qtable$ on empty sets of variables is relevant for us. The only tables that satisfy $qtable\,n\,\emptyset\,P\,Q\,R$ are $R = \mathbf{1}_n$ and $R = \emptyset$ so that, assuming $P\,\langle\rangle_n$, if $Q\,\langle\rangle_n$ then $R = \mathbf{1}_n$; otherwise, if $\neg\,(Q\,\langle\rangle_n)$

then $R = \emptyset$. In fact, the only way that $table\,n\,X\,\mathbf{1}_n$ holds is if $X \subseteq \{x \mid x \geq n\}$. Given that we only use sets $X$ such that $X \subseteq \{x \mid x < n\}$, only $X = \emptyset$ fits $table\,n\,X\,\mathbf{1}_n$.

Since we must join all the tables in the auxiliary states for trigger and release, we also relate *qtable* and joins ($\bowtie$). Provided dfv $\sigma\,i\,\alpha \subseteq X$ and dfv $\sigma\,i\,\beta \subseteq Y$:

$$[\![\alpha \wedge_F \beta]\!]_{i,n}^{X \cup Y} = [\![\alpha]\!]_{i,n}^{X} \bowtie [\![\beta]\!]_{i,n}^{Y}, \text{ and}$$

$$[\![\alpha \wedge_F \neg_F \beta]\!]_{i,n}^{X \cup Y} = [\![\alpha]\!]_{i,n}^{X} \triangleright [\![\beta]\!]_{i,n}^{Y}, \text{ assuming } Y \subseteq X.$$

More general results in terms of *qtable* are also available. For instance, if $\pi_X$ is the projection $\pi_X\,v = \mathrm{map}\,(\lambda i.\ if\ i \in X\ then\ v\,!\,i\ else\ None)\,[0,\dots,\mathrm{length}\,v - 1]$, then it holds that $qtable\,n\,Z\,P\,Q\,(R_1 \bowtie R_2)$ if $qtable\,n\,X\,P\,Q_1\,R_1$, $qtable\,n\,Y\,P\,Q_2\,R_2$, $Z = X \cup Y$ and $\forall v.\ wf\text{-}tuple\,n\,Z\,v \wedge P\,v \Rightarrow (Q\,v \Leftrightarrow Q_1\,(\pi_X\,v) \wedge Q_2\,(\pi_Y\,v))$. A similar statement is true for antijoins. Moreover, the join of two tables with the same attributes is simply their intersection. By our definition of ssfvs, our $n$-ary join on the auxiliary states is made on tables with the same attributes, thus we use the following fact: for a finite non-empty set of indices $\mathcal{I}$, $qtable\,n\,X\,P\,Q\,\left(\bigcap_{i \in \mathcal{I}} R_i\right)$ holds if $qtable\,n\,X\,P\,Q_i\,R_i$ and $\forall v.\ wf\text{-}tuple\,n\,X\,v \wedge P\,v \Rightarrow (Q\,v \Leftrightarrow (\forall i \in \mathcal{I}.\ Q_i\,v))$.

The relationship between *eval-or* and *qtable* is also relevant for our correctness proof due to our modifications to the algorithm. We state here the specific statement: if $qtable\,n\,(\mathrm{dfv}_i\,\alpha)\,P\,(\lambda v.\ \langle\sigma, v, i\rangle \models_M \alpha)\,R_1$ and $qtable\,n\,(\mathrm{dfv}_i\,\beta)\,P\,(\lambda v.\ \langle\sigma, v, i\rangle \models_M \beta)\,R_2$ then $qtable\,n\,(\mathrm{dfv}_i(\alpha \vee_F \beta))\,P\,(\lambda v.\ \langle\sigma, v, i\rangle \models_M \alpha \vee_F \beta)\,(eval\text{-}or\,n\,R_1\,R_2)$, provided $P\,\langle\rangle_n$ and $\mathrm{dfv}_i\,\alpha = \emptyset$, $\mathrm{dfv}_i\,\beta = \emptyset$ or $\mathrm{dfv}_i\,\alpha = \mathrm{dfv}_i\,\beta$. See more results in the Isabelle code.

To state the correctness of the algorithm, Verimon defines an inductive predicate $wf\text{-}mformula\,\sigma\,i\,n\,U\,\alpha_M\,\alpha$ where $i, n :: \mathbb{N}$, $\alpha_M :: {'a}\ mformula$, $\alpha :: {'a}\ frm$ and $U$ is a set of valuations. The set $U$ is always instantiated to the universal set $UNIV$, or the set of all terms of a given type. In fact, $P$ in *qtable* just checks for membership in $U = UNIV$. The predicate $wf\text{-}mformula$ is an invariant that holds after initialisation with *minit* and that remains true after each application of *mstep*. It carries all the information to prove correctness of outputs $R$ at $i$ via the predicate $qtable\,n\,(\mathrm{dfv}_i\,\alpha)\,P\,(\lambda v.\langle\sigma, v, i\rangle \models_M \alpha)\,R$. We describe here only our additions for dual operators.

**inductive** *wf-mformula* **where** ...

  | *Trigger*: $wf\text{-}mformula\,\sigma\,i\,n\,U\,\alpha_m\,\alpha \Longrightarrow wf\text{-}mformula\,\sigma\,i\,n\,U\,\beta_m\,\beta$
    $\Longrightarrow \alpha' = (pos \triangleright_+ \alpha) \triangleleft mem0 \triangleright \alpha \Longrightarrow mem0 \leftrightarrow 0 \in I$
    $\Longrightarrow is\text{-}safe\,(\alpha'\,\mathrm{T}_I\,\beta) \Longrightarrow wf\text{-}mbuf2'\,\sigma\,i\,n\,U\,\alpha\,\beta\,buf \Longrightarrow wf\text{-}ts\,\sigma\,i\,\alpha\,\beta\,nts$
    $\Longrightarrow wf\text{-}trigger\text{-}aux\,\sigma\,n\,U\,pos\,\alpha\,mem0\,I\,\beta\,aux\,(progress\,\sigma\,(\alpha'\,\mathrm{T}_I\,\beta)\,i)$
    $\Longrightarrow wf\text{-}mformula\,\sigma\,i\,n\,U\,(MTrigger\,pos\,\alpha_M\,mem0\,I\,\beta_M\,buf\,nts\,aux)\,(\alpha'\,\mathrm{T}_I\,\beta)$
  | *Release*: $wf\text{-}mformula\,\sigma\,i\,n\,U\,\alpha_m\,\alpha \Longrightarrow wf\text{-}mformula\,\sigma\,i\,n\,U\,\beta_m\,\beta$
    $\Longrightarrow \alpha' = (pos \triangleright_+ \alpha) \triangleleft mem0 \triangleright \alpha \Longrightarrow mem0 \leftrightarrow 0 \in I$
    $\Longrightarrow is\text{-}safe\,(\alpha'\,\mathrm{R}_I\,\beta) \Longrightarrow wf\text{-}mbuf2'\,\sigma\,i\,n\,U\,\alpha\,\beta\,buf \Longrightarrow wf\text{-}ts\,\sigma\,i\,\alpha\,\beta\,nts$
    $\Longrightarrow wf\text{-}release\text{-}aux\,\sigma\,n\,U\,pos\,\alpha\,mem0\,I\,\beta\,aux\,(progress\,\sigma\,(\alpha'\,\mathrm{T}_I\,\beta)\,i)$
    $\Longrightarrow progress\,\sigma\,(\alpha'\,\mathrm{R}_I\,\beta)\,i + length\,aux = min\,(progress\,\sigma\,\alpha\,i)\,(progress\,\sigma\,\beta\,i)$
    $\Longrightarrow wf\text{-}mformula\,\sigma\,i\,n\,U\,(MRelease\,pos\,\alpha_M\,mem0\,I\,\beta_M\,buf\,nts\,aux)\,(\alpha'\,\mathrm{R}_I\,\beta)$

The code above states that if all of the conditions before the last arrow ($\Longrightarrow$) are satisfied, then we can assert *wf-mformula* for trigger or release respectively. The function $progress\,\sigma\,\alpha\,i$ is $\rho_i^\alpha$, while $pos \triangleright_+ \alpha$ is our Isabelle abbreviation to state that $\alpha$ is not-negated according to the boolean $pos$. Similarly, $\alpha \triangleleft test \triangleright \beta$ is just $\alpha$ if $test$ is true, otherwise it is $\beta$. The predicates *wf-mbuf2'* and *wf-ts* check that the buffer and the corresponding list of time-stamps are well-formed in the sense that the buffer has every visited but yet unused table for $\alpha$ and $\beta$ while $nts$ has all the corresponding time-stamps $\tau_j$ with $(\min \rho_i^\alpha \, \rho_i^\beta) \leq j < (\max \rho_i^\alpha \, \rho_i^\beta)$. Additionally, we describe below the corresponding invariants $wf\text{-}trigger\text{-}aux$ and $wf\text{-}release\text{-}aux$ for the auxiliary states.

Recall from Eqs. (3) and (4) that trigger's auxiliary state $Ts$ at time-point $i$ is a list of pairs $\langle \tau_j, T_{\tau_j}^i \rangle$. In the formalisation (see also Appendix A), we split our definition of its invariant $wf\text{-}trigger\text{-}aux$ into two parts. First, we state the properties of the time-stamps $\tau_j$: they are strictly ordered, less than the latest $\tau_\iota$ and satisfy that $\tau_j \in \tau_\iota - I$ or $\tau_j > \tau_\iota - I$ for $\iota = (\min \rho_i^\alpha \, \rho_i^\beta) - 1$. Conversely, it also affirms that every time-stamp satisfying these properties appears in $Ts$. The second part asserts correctness. That is, $qtable \, n \, (\text{fv } \beta) \, P \, Q_{\tau_j}^i \, T_{\tau_j}^i$ where $Q_{\tau_j}^i \, v \Leftrightarrow \langle \sigma, v, \iota \rangle \models_M \alpha \, \mathrm{T}_{\{\tau_\iota - \tau_j\}} \beta$ if $0 \notin I$, and $Q_{\tau_j}^i \, v \Leftrightarrow (\forall k \leq \iota. \, \tau_k = \tau_j \Rightarrow \langle \sigma, v, k \rangle \models_M \beta \vee (\exists l \in (k, \iota]. \, \langle \sigma, v, l \rangle \models_M))$ if $0 \in I$.    ♣

The invariant $wf\text{-}release\text{-}aux$ for release's auxiliary state $Rs$ is more verbose. Assuming $0 \in I$, it asserts $qtable \, n \, (\text{fv } \beta) \, P \, Q_{\mathcal{L},0 \in I}^{i,j} \, R_{\mathcal{L}}^{i,j}$ and $qtable \, n \, (\text{fv } \beta) \, P \, Q_{\mathcal{R},0 \in I}^{i,j} \, R_{\mathcal{R}}^{i,j}$ where $Q_{\mathcal{L},0 \in I}^{i,j}$ and $Q_{\mathcal{R},0 \in I}^{i,j}$ describe the first parts of eqs. (5) and (6). That is,

$$Q_{\mathcal{L},0 \in I}^{i,j} \, v \Leftrightarrow (\exists k \in [j, \iota). \, \langle \sigma, v, k \rangle \models_M \beta \wedge \langle \sigma, v, k \rangle \models_M \alpha) \text{ and}$$
$$Q_{\mathcal{R},0 \in I}^{i,j} \, v \Leftrightarrow (\forall k \in [j, \iota). \, (\tau_k - \tau_j) \in I \Rightarrow \langle \sigma, v, k \rangle \models_M \beta \vee Q_{\mathcal{L},0 \in I}^{i,k} \, v).$$

However, when $0 \notin I$, the invariant asserts $qtable \, n \, (\text{fv } \beta) \, P \, Q_{\mathcal{L},0 \notin I}^{i,j} \, R_{\mathcal{L}}^{i,j}$ where

$$Q_{\mathcal{L},0 \notin I}^{i,j} \, v \Leftrightarrow (\exists k \in [j, \iota). \, \langle \sigma, v, k \rangle \models_M \alpha).$$

For the right table, if $\tau_\iota < \tau_j + I$, it simply asserts $R_{\mathcal{R}}^{i,j} = \mathbf{1}_n$. However, if $(\tau_\iota - \tau_j) \in I$, the invariant states that $qtable \, n \, (\text{fv } \beta) \, P \, Q_{\mathcal{R},0 \notin I}^{i,j} \, R_{\mathcal{R}}^{i,j}$ where

$$Q_{\mathcal{R},0 \notin I}^{i,j} \, v \Leftrightarrow (\forall k \in [j, \iota). \, (\tau_k - \tau_j) \in I \Rightarrow \langle \sigma, v, k \rangle \models_M \beta \vee Q_{\mathcal{L},0 \notin I}^{i,k} \, v).$$

Finally, the case when $\tau_j + I < \tau_i$ asserts $qtable \, n \, (\text{dfv}_j(\alpha \, \mathrm{R}_I \, \beta)) \, P \, Q_{\mathcal{R},0 \notin I}^{i,j} \, R_{\mathcal{R}}^{i,j}$.    ♣

We then adapt Verimon's proof of correctness [19] for the monitored formula $\alpha$. It consists of two facts: ($a$) after initialisation, $\alpha_M^0$ satisfies $wf\text{-}mformula$, and ($b$) whenever $\alpha_M^{i-1}$ satisfies $wf\text{-}mformula$, then after an execution of $meval$, the new $\alpha_M^i$ also satisfies $wf\text{-}mformula$ and all the outputs of $meval$ are correct.

At initialisation ($a$), our relaxation of safety allows us to replace $safe\text{-}formula$ with $is\text{-}safe$. Also, due to the condition $P \, \langle \rangle_n$ in our results about $qtable$ and $eval\text{-}or$, we need to assume $\langle \rangle_n \in U$ where $U$ is the set referred in $wf\text{-}mformula$. Formally, our correctness of initialisation states that if $is\text{-}safe \, \alpha$, $\langle \rangle_n$ is an element of the set $U$, and the free variables of $\alpha$ are all less than $n$, then $wf\text{-}mformula \, \sigma \, 0 \, n \, U \, (minit0 \, n \, \alpha) \, \alpha$. The proof is a typical application of inductive reasoning but not fully automatic since we need case distinctions for negations, conjunctions and dual operators.    ♣

The addition of dfvs and ssfvs produces more changes in Verimon's invariant preservation proof ($b$) than in the initialisation proof ($a$). In many preliminary definitions and lemmas, including that of $wf\text{-}mbuf2'$, we replace the argument fv $\alpha$ with $\text{dfv}_i \, \alpha$. In others, a less straightforward substitution is necessary. For instance, in the auxiliary state for until, we do not simply use $\text{dfv}_i \, \alpha$ but the union of various dfvs. This reverberates in the proof of correctness of the auxiliary state which quintuples its size from 28 to 140 lines of code due to the various cases generated by both dfvs and ssfvs.    ♣

Our proof of correctness for trigger's auxiliary state consists of a step-wise decomposition of $update\text{-}trigger$ and stating, at each step, what the tables in the auxiliary state satisfy in terms of *qtable*. It is 440 lines of code long, double the size of the proof for since due to the case distinctions $0 \in I$ and $0 \notin I$. 🐝 These also appear in the corresponding proof of correctness for release and dictate its main structure. On one hand, the case $0 \in I$ for release is further split into whether the auxiliary state was previously an empty list or not. On the other hand, the assumption $0 \notin I$ requires analysing the different cases $\tau_\iota < \tau_j + I$, $(\tau_\iota - \tau_j) \in I$ and $\tau_j + I < \tau_i$ as above. Each of these also considers the emptiness of the auxiliary state at the previous time-point.                            🐚

Finally, the theorem that uses all of these correctness results and modifications is the invariant preservation proof (*b*) above. In more detail, it states that if we start with $\alpha_M$ such that *wf-mformula* $\sigma\, i\, n\, U\, \alpha_M\, \alpha$ and *meval* $n\, \tau_i\, \Gamma_i\, \alpha_M = (outputs, \alpha_{M'})$, then *wf-mformula* $\sigma\,(i+1)\,n\,U\,\alpha_{M'}\,\alpha$ and *qtable* $n\,(\mathrm{dfv}_j\,\alpha)\,P\,(\lambda v.\ \langle\sigma, v, j\rangle \models_M \alpha)\,R_j$ for each $R_j \in outputs$ with $j \in [\rho_i^\alpha, \rho_{i+1}^\alpha)$. We do its proof over the structure of $\alpha_M :: {}'a$ *mformula*. The base step for equalities and inequalities requires some case distinctions and our results about *qtable* and $\mathbf{1}_n$. The inductive steps require mostly the same argument: from *wf-mformula* we know most of the information to prove *qtable*, we supply it to our preliminary lemmas like the correctness of auxiliary states and buffers, finally we use these results and the inductive definition of *wf-mformula* to obtain our desired conclusion. Our separation of preliminary lemmas from the main body of the proof of (*b*) highly increases readability of this long argument.                            🐚

This concludes our description of the correctness argument from definitions to explanations on the proof structure. Their formalisation is one of our major contributions. Our additions on properties about *qtable* and dfvs consists of approximately 350 lines of code, while those to the proof of correctness are more than 1500. This still does not take into account the additions on other already existing results, like the modifications to the proof of correctness of until's auxiliary state. In total, the correctness argument changed from approximately 1000 lines of code to more than 3000.

# 7   Conclusion

We defined a fragment of MFOTL-formulas guaranteeing their relational-algebra representations to be computed through well-known table operations. For this, we introduced the set of safe sets of free variables (ssfv) of a formula which collects all possible allowed attributes of the formula's table-representations over time. The fragment required this set to be non-empty. We argued that this *safe* fragment is larger than others from previous work on temporal properties and pointed to our Isabelle/HOL proof of this fact. We integrated our relaxation of safety into a monitoring algorithm. The formal verification of this integration was possible due to our newly introduced concept of dynamic free variables (dfv) of the monitored specification. We also extended the algorithm with concrete syntax and functions to monitor MFOTL dual operators *trigger* and *release*. The combination of ssfvs, dfvs and dual operators enabled the algorithm to monitor more specifications in a simpler manner, we illustrated this via examples. Overall, our contribution allows monitorability of shorter encodings of frequently used formulas. This, in turn, generates less monitoring computations at runtime. Given that general RV tools should be efficient, our above-described methods could be generally applied and benefit various MFOTL-based tools.

*Future Work.* Our relaxation of safety can be generalised in various ways. The simplest of these add cases to our definition of ssfvs. For instance, asserting ssfv($t =_F t$) = $\{\emptyset\}$

is possible since we can map it to $\mathbf{1}_n$. However, doing this has unintended consequences that forces us to rethink other cases, e.g. the conjunction $\mathbf{v}\,x =_F \mathbf{v}\,x \wedge_F \mathbf{v}\,x =_F \mathbf{v}\,y$ would become safe under the current definition. Furthermore, we lose some "nice" properties like *is-safe* $\alpha \Leftrightarrow$ fv $\alpha \in$ ssfv $\alpha$. It is also unsatisfactory that safety for $(\neg_F \alpha)\,\mathrm{S}_I\,\beta$ only requires ssfv $\beta = \{\beta\}$ and fv $\alpha \subseteq$ fv $\beta$ while that for $(\neg_F \alpha)\,\mathrm{U}_I\,\beta$ needs the stronger condition ssfv $\beta = \{\beta\}$ and ssfv $\alpha = \{\mathrm{fv}\,\alpha\}$. A reimplementation of the monitoring functions for until would alleviate this situation.

An orthogonal development replaces every instance of union, $(\cup)$ or $(\bigcup)$, in the implementation with our generalised *eval-or*. This would allow us to change our definition of safety so that more attributes are available for the right-hand-side formula in temporal operators (i.e. ssfv $\beta \subseteq \{\emptyset, \mathrm{fv}\,\beta\}$). Consequently, this would allow us to write combinations of them, e.g. $\mathrm{P}_I\,(p \dagger xs \wedge_F \mathrm{H}_J q \dagger ys)$, where $\mathrm{P}_I\alpha \equiv \top\,\mathrm{S}_I\,\alpha$.

A different avenue of research follows the standard approach in logic and the database community and defines a series of transformations that determine if a formula is equivalent to a safe one [1,8,17,18]. If such a transformation is obtained, formally verified and implemented, its integration into Verimon would mean that many more future-bounded formulas would be monitorable.

With the long-term view of developing a more trustworthy, expressive and efficient monitor than other non-verified tools, we intend to integrate our relaxation of safety into Verimon+ [22]. This requires adding more complex terms inside equalities and inequalities that contain additions, multiplications, divisions and type castings. Additionally, safety would need to be defined for aggregations like sum or average, dynamic operators from metric first-order dynamic logic, and recursive let operations. A first attempt and its not-yet complete integration into an old Verimon+ version [3] are available online. 🐞

**Acknowledgements.** I would like to thank Dmitriy Traytel and Joshua Schneider for discussions and pointers. Martin Raszyk came up with the idea of using a set of sets representing tables' attributes to define safety and coined the term "dynamic free variables", I highly appreciate his feedback throughout the implementation of this project. I also thank Leonardo Lima, Rafael Castro G. Silva and Phebe L. Bonilla Prado for their comments on drafts of the paper. I highly appreciate the helpful feedback and recommendations from the anonymous reviewers. The work itself is funded by a Novo Nordisk Fonden Start Package Grant (NNF20OC0063462).

# A    Appendix: Formal Definitions

We supply our Isabelle/HOL definitions of dynamic free variables, safe sets of free variables, a combination of Verimon's *safe-formula* predicates [10,19,22], and trigger and release's invariants for auxiliary states. We also provide the formalisation of the traces in Sect. 5 to showcase the working monitoring algorithm.

*Dynamic Free Variables.* In the code below, the notation *mem I 0* represents $0 \in I$, for interval $I$. Also, *Suc* is the successor function on natural numbers. The first two definitions correspond to the sets $\downarrow_I i$ and $\uparrow_I i$ of Sect. 3 respectively.

**definition** *down-cl-ivl* $\sigma\ I\ i \equiv \{j \mid j.\ j \leq i \wedge mem\ I\ ((\tau\ \sigma\ i - \tau\ \sigma\ j))\}$

**definition** *up-cl-ivl* $\sigma\ I\ i \equiv \{j \mid j.\ i \leq j \wedge mem\ I\ ((\tau\ \sigma\ j - \tau\ \sigma\ i))\}$

**fun** *dfv* :: $(char\ list \times\ 'a\ list)\ set\ trace \Rightarrow nat \Rightarrow\ 'a\ MFOTL\text{-}Formula.formula \Rightarrow nat\ set$

**where** $dfv\ \sigma\ i\ (p\ \dagger\ ts) = FV\ (p\ \dagger\ ts)$
| $dfv\ \sigma\ i\ (t1 =_F t2) = FV\ (t1 =_F t2)$
| $dfv\ \sigma\ i\ (\neg_F\ \alpha) = dfv\ \sigma\ i\ \alpha$
| $dfv\ \sigma\ i\ (\alpha \wedge_F \beta) = dfv\ \sigma\ i\ \alpha \cup dfv\ \sigma\ i\ \beta$
| $dfv\ \sigma\ i\ (\alpha \vee_F \beta) = (if\ dfv\ \sigma\ i\ \alpha = \{\}$
  $then\ if\ \{v.\ \langle\sigma, v, i\rangle \models \alpha\} = \{\}\ then\ dfv\ \sigma\ i\ \beta\ else\ \{\}$
  $else\ if\ dfv\ \sigma\ i\ \beta = \{\}\ then\ if\ \{v.\ \langle\sigma, v, i\rangle \models \beta\} = \{\}\ then\ dfv\ \sigma\ i\ \alpha\ else\ \{\}$
  $else\ dfv\ \sigma\ i\ \alpha \cup dfv\ \sigma\ i\ \beta)$
| $dfv\ \sigma\ i\ (\exists_F\ \alpha) = (\lambda x::nat.\ x - 1)\ `\ ((dfv\ \sigma\ i\ \alpha) - \{0\})$
| $dfv\ \sigma\ i\ (\mathbf{Y}\ I\ \alpha) = (if\ i=0\ then\ FV\ \alpha\ else\ dfv\ \sigma\ (i-1)\ \alpha)$
| $dfv\ \sigma\ i\ (\mathbf{X}\ I\ \alpha) = dfv\ \sigma\ (Suc\ i)\ \alpha$
| $dfv\ \sigma\ i\ (\alpha\ \mathbf{S}\ I\ \beta) =$
  $(let\ satisf\text{-}at = \lambda j.\ \exists v.\ \langle\sigma, v, j\rangle \models \beta \wedge (\forall k \in \{j<..i\}.\ \langle\sigma, v, k\rangle \models \alpha)\ in$
  $(if\ (\forall j \in down\text{-}cl\text{-}ivl\ \sigma\ I\ i.\ \neg\ satisf\text{-}at\ j)\ then\ FV\ (\alpha\ \mathbf{S}\ I\ \beta)$
    $else\ (let\ J = \{j \in down\text{-}cl\text{-}ivl\ \sigma\ I\ i.\ satisf\text{-}at\ j\};\ K = \bigcup\{\{j<..i\}|j.\ j \in J\}\ in$
    $(\bigcup\{(dfv\ \sigma\ k\ \alpha)|k.\ k \in K\}) \cup (\bigcup\{(dfv\ \sigma\ j\ \beta)|j.\ j \in J\}))))$
| $dfv\ \sigma\ i\ (\alpha\ \mathbf{U}\ I\ \beta) =$
  $(let\ satisf\text{-}at = \lambda j.\exists v.\ \langle\sigma, v, j\rangle \models \beta \wedge (\forall k \in \{i..<j\}.\ \langle\sigma, v, k\rangle \models \alpha)\ in$
  $(if\ (\forall j \in up\text{-}cl\text{-}ivl\ \sigma\ I\ i.\ \neg\ satisf\text{-}at\ j)\ then\ FV\ (\alpha\ \mathbf{U}\ I\ \beta)$
    $else\ (let\ J = \{j \in up\text{-}cl\text{-}ivl\ \sigma\ I\ i.\ satisf\text{-}at\ j\};\ K = \bigcup\{\{i..<j\}|j.\ j \in J\}\ in$
    $(\bigcup\{(dfv\ \sigma\ k\ \alpha)|k.\ k \in K\}) \cup (\bigcup\{(dfv\ \sigma\ j\ \beta)|j.\ j \in J\}))))$
| $dfv\ \sigma\ i\ (\alpha\ \mathbf{T}\ I\ \beta) =$
  $(let\ satisf\text{-}at = \lambda v\ j.\ \langle\sigma, v, j\rangle \models \beta \vee (\exists k \in \{j<..i\}.\ \langle\sigma, v, k\rangle \models \alpha)\ in$
  $(if\ down\text{-}cl\text{-}ivl\ \sigma\ I\ i = \{\}\ then\ \{\}$
    $else\ if\ (\forall v.\ \exists j \in down\text{-}cl\text{-}ivl\ \sigma\ I\ i.\ \neg\ satisf\text{-}at\ v\ j)\ then\ FV\ (\alpha\ \mathbf{T}\ I\ \beta)$
    $else\ (let\ J = \{j \in down\text{-}cl\text{-}ivl\ \sigma\ I\ i.\ \exists v.\ \langle\sigma, v, j\rangle \models \beta\};$
    $K = \{k.\ \exists v.\ \exists j \in down\text{-}cl\text{-}ivl\ \sigma\ I\ i.\ j < k \wedge k \leq i \wedge \langle\sigma, v, k\rangle \models \alpha\}\ in$
    $(\bigcup\{(dfv\ \sigma\ k\ \alpha)|k.\ k \in K\}) \cup (\bigcup\{(dfv\ \sigma\ j\ \beta)|j.\ j \in J\}))))$
| $dfv\ \sigma\ i\ (\alpha\ \mathbf{R}\ I\ \beta) =$
  $(let\ satisf\text{-}at = \lambda v\ j.\ \langle\sigma, v, j\rangle \models \beta \vee (\exists k \in \{i..<j\}.\ \langle\sigma, v, k\rangle \models \alpha)\ in$
  $(if\ up\text{-}cl\text{-}ivl\ \sigma\ I\ i = \{\}\ then\ \{\}$
    $else\ if\ (\forall v.\ \exists j \in up\text{-}cl\text{-}ivl\ \sigma\ I\ i.\ \neg\ satisf\text{-}at\ v\ j)\ then\ FV\ (\alpha\ \mathbf{R}\ I\ \beta)$
    $else\ (let\ J = \{j \in up\text{-}cl\text{-}ivl\ \sigma\ I\ i.\ \exists v.\ \langle\sigma, v, j\rangle \models \beta\};$
    $K = \{k.\ \exists v.\ \exists j \in up\text{-}cl\text{-}ivl\ \sigma\ I\ i.\ i \leq k \wedge k < j \wedge \langle\sigma, v, k\rangle \models \alpha\}\ in$
    $(\bigcup\{(dfv\ \sigma\ k\ \alpha)|k.\ k \in K\}) \cup (\bigcup\{(dfv\ \sigma\ j\ \beta)|j.\ j \in J\}))))$

## Safe sets of free variables.

**fun** $is\text{-}constraint\ (t1 =_F t2) = True$
| $is\text{-}constraint\ (\neg_F\ (t1 =_F t2)) = True$
| $is\text{-}constraint\ \text{-} = False$

**definition** $safe\text{-}assignment\ X\ \alpha = (case\ \alpha\ of$
  $\mathbf{v}\ x =_F \mathbf{v}\ y \Rightarrow (x \notin X \longleftrightarrow y \in X)$
  $|\ \mathbf{v}\ x =_F t \Rightarrow (x \notin X \wedge fv\text{-}trm\ t \subseteq X)$
  $|\ t =_F \mathbf{v}\ x \Rightarrow (x \notin X \wedge fv\text{-}trm\ t \subseteq X)$
  $|\ \text{-} \Rightarrow False)$

**fun** $ssfv :: {}'a\ MFOTL\text{-}Formula.formula \Rightarrow nat\ set\ set$
  **where** $ssfv\ (p\ \dagger\ trms) = \{FV\ (p\ \dagger\ trms)\}$
| $ssfv\ (\mathbf{v}\ x =_F t) = (if\ FV_t\ t = \{\}\ then\ \{\{x\}\}\ else\ \{\})$
| $ssfv\ (t =_F \mathbf{v}\ x) = (if\ FV_t\ t = \{\}\ then\ \{\{x\}\}\ else\ \{\})$
| $ssfv\ (t1 =_F t2) = (if\ FV_t\ t1 \cup FV_t\ t2 = \{\}\ then\ \{\{\}\}\ else\ \{\})$
| $ssfv\ (\neg_F\ (t1 =_F t2)) = (let\ X = FV\ (t1 =_F t2)\ in\ if\ t1 = t2 \vee X = \{\}\ then\ \{X\}\ else\ \{\})$
| $ssfv\ (\alpha \wedge_F \beta) = (let\ \mathcal{A} = ssfv\ \alpha;\ \mathcal{B} = ssfv\ \beta\ in$
  $if\ \mathcal{A} \neq \{\}\ then$
    $if\ \mathcal{B} \neq \{\}\ then\ \mathcal{A} \uplus \mathcal{B}$
    $else\ if\ \forall X \in \mathcal{A}.\ safe\text{-}assignment\ X\ \beta\ then\ ((\cup)\ (FV\ \beta))\ `\ \mathcal{A}$
    $else\ if\ is\text{-}constraint\ \beta \wedge (\forall X \in \mathcal{A}.\ FV\ \beta \subseteq X)\ then\ \mathcal{A}$
    $else\ (case\ \beta\ of\ \neg_F\ \beta' \Rightarrow (let\ \mathcal{B}' = ssfv\ \beta'\ in$
    $(if\ \mathcal{B}' \neq \{\} \wedge (\forall Y \in \mathcal{B}'.\ \forall X \in \mathcal{A}.\ Y \subseteq X)\ then\ \mathcal{A}\ else\ \{\}))\ |\ \text{-} \Rightarrow \{\})$
  $else\ \{\})$
| $ssfv\ (\alpha \vee_F \beta) = (let\ \mathcal{A} = ssfv\ \alpha;\ \mathcal{B} = ssfv\ \beta;\ X = FV\ \alpha;\ Y = FV\ \beta\ in$
  $if\ (\mathcal{A} \neq \{\} \wedge \mathcal{B} \neq \{\})\ then$
    $if\ X = Y \wedge \mathcal{A} \subseteq \{\{\}, X\} \wedge \mathcal{B} \subseteq \{\{\}, Y\}\ then$
    $(if\ \{\} \in \mathcal{A} \vee \{\} \in \mathcal{B}\ then\ \{\{\}\} \cup (\mathcal{A} \uplus \mathcal{B})\ else\ \mathcal{A} \uplus \mathcal{B})$
    $else$

$(if\ X = \{\} \vee Y = \{\}\ then\ \mathcal{A} \cup \mathcal{B}\ else\ \{\})$
   $else\ \{\})$
$|\ ssfv\ (\exists_F\ \alpha) = (((`)\ (\lambda x{::}nat.\ x - 1)) \circ (\lambda X.\ X - \{0\}))\ `\ ssfv\ \alpha$
$|\ ssfv\ (\mathbf{Y}\ I\ \alpha) = ssfv\ \alpha$
$|\ ssfv\ (\mathbf{X}\ I\ \alpha) = ssfv\ \alpha$
$|\ ssfv\ (\alpha\ \mathbf{S}\ I\ \beta) = (let\ \mathcal{A} = ssfv\ \alpha;\ \mathcal{B} = ssfv\ \beta;\ X = FV\ \alpha;\ Y = FV\ \beta\ in$
   $if\ (\mathcal{B} = \{Y\})\ then$
      $if\ \mathcal{A} \neq \{\} \wedge X \subseteq Y\ then\ \{Y\}$
      $else\ (case\ \alpha\ of$
         $\neg_F\ \alpha' \Rightarrow (let\ \mathcal{A}' = ssfv\ \alpha'\ in\ if\ \mathcal{A}' \neq \{\} \wedge X \subseteq Y\ then\ \{Y\}\ else\ \{\})$
         $|\ \ \text{-}\ \Rightarrow \{\})$
   $else\ \{\})$
$|\ ssfv\ (\alpha\ \mathbf{U}\ I\ \beta) = (let\ \mathcal{A} = ssfv\ \alpha;\ \mathcal{B} = ssfv\ \beta;\ X = FV\ \alpha;\ Y = FV\ \beta\ in$
   $if\ (\mathcal{B} = \{Y\})\ then$
      $if\ \mathcal{A} \neq \{\} \wedge X \subseteq Y\ then\ \{Y\}$
      $else\ (case\ \alpha\ of$
         $\neg_F\ \alpha' \Rightarrow (let\ \mathcal{A}' = ssfv\ \alpha'\ in\ if\ X \subseteq Y \wedge \mathcal{A}' = \{X\}\ then\ \{Y\}\ else\ \{\})$
         $|\ \ \text{-}\ \Rightarrow \{\})$
   $else\ \{\})$
$|\ ssfv\ (\alpha\ \mathbf{T}\ I\ \beta) = (let\ \mathcal{A} = ssfv\ \alpha;\ \mathcal{B} = ssfv\ \beta;\ X = FV\ \alpha;\ Y = FV\ \beta\ in$
   $if\ mem\ I\ 0\ then$
      $if\ (\mathcal{B} = \{Y\})\ then$
         $if\ \mathcal{A} \neq \{\} \wedge X \subseteq Y\ then\ \{Y\}$
         $else\ (case\ \alpha\ of$
            $\neg_F\ \alpha' \Rightarrow (let\ \mathcal{A}' = ssfv\ \alpha'\ in\ if\ \mathcal{A}' \neq \{\} \wedge X \subseteq Y\ then\ \{Y\}\ else\ \{\})$
            $|\ \ \text{-}\ \Rightarrow \{\})$
      $else\ \{\}$
   $else$
      $if\ X = Y \wedge \mathcal{A} = \{X\} \wedge \mathcal{B} = \{Y\}\ then\ \{\{\},X\}\ else\ \{\})$
$|\ ssfv\ (\alpha\ \mathbf{R}\ I\ \beta) = (let\ \mathcal{A} = ssfv\ \alpha;\ \mathcal{B} = ssfv\ \beta;\ X = FV\ \alpha;\ Y = FV\ \beta\ in$
   $if\ mem\ I\ 0\ then$
      $if\ (\mathcal{B} = \{Y\})\ then$
         $if\ \mathcal{A} \neq \{\} \wedge X \subseteq Y\ then\ \{Y\}$
         $else\ (case\ \alpha\ of$
            $\neg_F\ \alpha' \Rightarrow (let\ \mathcal{A}' = ssfv\ \alpha'\ in\ if\ \mathcal{A}' \neq \{\} \wedge X \subseteq Y\ then\ \{Y\}\ else\ \{\})$
            $|\ \ \text{-}\ \Rightarrow \{\})$
      $else\ \{\}$
   $else$
      $if\ X = Y \wedge \mathcal{A} = \{X\} \wedge \mathcal{B} = \{Y\}\ then\ \{\{\},X\}\ else\ \{\})$
$|\ ssfv\ (\neg_F\ \alpha) = (if\ ssfv\ \alpha = \{\{\}\}\ then\ \{\{\}\}\ else\ \{\})$

*Verimon's safe-formula predicate.* Below we provide the definition of *safe-formula* used in our proof that *is-safe* defines a larger fragment. This is also the predicate that does not hold for our examples in Sect. 5.

**definition** *safe-dual* **where** *safe-dual conjoined safe-formula* $\alpha\ I\ \beta = ($
$if\ (mem\ I\ 0)\ then$
   $(safe\text{-}formula\ \beta \wedge fv\ \alpha \subseteq fv\ \beta$
    $\wedge\ (safe\text{-}formula\ \alpha$
       $\vee\ (case\ \alpha\ of\ \neg_F\ \alpha' \Rightarrow safe\text{-}formula\ \alpha'\ |\ \text{-}\ \Rightarrow False)))$
$else$
   $conjoined \wedge (safe\text{-}formula\ \alpha \wedge safe\text{-}formula\ \beta \wedge fv\ \alpha = fv\ \beta))$

**function** *safe-formula* :: $'a\ MFOTL\text{-}Formula.formula \Rightarrow bool$
   **where** *safe-formula* $(t1 =_F t2) = ((trm.is\text{-}Const\ t1 \wedge (trm.is\text{-}Const\ t2 \vee trm.is\text{-}Var\ t2))$
      $\vee\ (trm.is\text{-}Var\ t1 \wedge trm.is\text{-}Const\ t2))$
$|\ safe\text{-}formula\ (\neg_F\ (\mathbf{v}\ x =_F \mathbf{v}\ y)) = (x = y)$
$|\ safe\text{-}formula\ (p \dagger ts) = (\forall t \in set\ ts.\ trm.is\text{-}Var\ t \vee trm.is\text{-}Const\ t)$
$|\ safe\text{-}formula\ (\neg_F\ \alpha) = (fv\ \alpha = \{\} \wedge safe\text{-}formula\ \alpha)$
$|\ safe\text{-}formula\ (\alpha \vee_F \beta) = (fv\ \beta = fv\ \alpha \wedge safe\text{-}formula\ \alpha \wedge safe\text{-}formula\ \beta)$
$|\ safe\text{-}formula\ (\alpha \wedge_F \beta) = (safe\text{-}formula\ \alpha \wedge$
   $(safe\text{-}assignment\ (fv\ \alpha)\ \beta$
    $\vee\ safe\text{-}formula\ \beta$
    $\vee\ (fv\ \beta \subseteq fv\ \alpha \wedge (is\text{-}constraint\ \beta$
       $\vee\ (case\ \beta\ of$
          $\neg_F\ \beta' \Rightarrow safe\text{-}formula\ \beta'$

$\quad\quad | \; \alpha' \; \mathbf{T} \; I \; \beta' \Rightarrow \textit{safe-dual True safe-formula } \alpha' \; I \; \beta'$
$\quad\quad | \; \alpha' \; \mathbf{R} \; I \; \beta' \Rightarrow \textit{safe-dual True safe-formula } \alpha' \; I \; \beta'$
$\quad\quad | \; - \Rightarrow \textit{False})))))$
$\; | \; \textit{safe-formula } (\exists_F \; \alpha) = (\textit{safe-formula } \alpha)$
$\; | \; \textit{safe-formula } (\mathbf{Y} \; I \; \alpha) = (\textit{safe-formula } \alpha)$
$\; | \; \textit{safe-formula } (\mathbf{X} \; I \; \alpha) = (\textit{safe-formula } \alpha)$
$\; | \; \textit{safe-formula } (\alpha \; \mathbf{S} \; I \; \beta) = (\textit{safe-formula } \beta \wedge \textit{fv } \alpha \subseteq \textit{fv } \beta \wedge$
$\quad (\textit{safe-formula } \alpha \vee (\textit{case } \alpha \textit{ of } \neg_F \; \alpha' \Rightarrow \textit{safe-formula } \alpha' \; | \; - \Rightarrow \textit{False})))$
$\; | \; \textit{safe-formula } (\alpha \; \mathbf{U} \; I \; \beta) = (\textit{safe-formula } \beta \wedge \textit{fv } \alpha \subseteq \textit{fv } \beta \wedge$
$\quad (\textit{safe-formula } \alpha \vee (\textit{case } \alpha \textit{ of } \neg_F \; \alpha' \Rightarrow \textit{safe-formula } \alpha' \; | \; - \Rightarrow \textit{False})))$
$\; | \; \textit{safe-formula } (\alpha \; \mathbf{T} \; I \; \beta) = \textit{safe-dual False safe-formula } \alpha \; I \; \beta$
$\; | \; \textit{safe-formula } (\alpha \; \mathbf{R} \; I \; \beta) = \textit{safe-dual False safe-formula } \alpha \; I \; \beta$

*Auxiliary States for Trigger and Release.* The predicate *wf-past-aux* below is the first part described in Sect. 6 of the invariant for *wf-trigger-aux*. We also abuse notation here and use the predicate $Q_t^{i-1}$ from Sect. 6 instead of the names *mem0-taux-sat* and *nmem0-taux-sat* in the formalisation.

**definition** $\textit{wf-past-aux } \sigma \; I \; i \; aux \longleftrightarrow (\textit{sorted-wrt } (\lambda x \; y. \; \textit{fst } x > \textit{fst } y) \; aux)$
$\wedge \; (\forall \, t \; R. \; (t, \; R) \in \textit{set } aux \longrightarrow i \neq 0 \wedge t \leq \tau \; \sigma \; (i{-}1) \wedge \textit{memR } I \; (\tau \; \sigma \; (i{-}1) - t)$
$\quad \wedge (\exists j. \; t = \tau \; \sigma \; j))$
$\wedge \; (\forall \, t. \; i \neq 0 \wedge t \leq \tau \; \sigma \; (i{-}1) \wedge \textit{memR } I \; (\tau \; \sigma \; (i{-}1) - t) \wedge (\exists j. \; \tau \; \sigma \; j = t)$
$\quad \longrightarrow (\exists X. \; (t, \; X) \in \textit{set } aux))$

**definition** $\textit{wf-trigger-aux } \sigma \; n \; U \; pos \; \alpha \; mem0 \; I \; \beta \; aux \; i \longleftrightarrow (\textit{wf-past-aux } \sigma \; I \; i \; aux$
$\wedge \; (\forall \, t \; R. \; (t, \; R) \in \textit{set } aux \longrightarrow$
$(mem0 \longrightarrow \textit{qtable } n \; (FV \; \beta) \; (\textit{mem-restr } U) \; (Q_t^{i-1}) \; R)$
$\wedge \; (\neg \; mem0 \longrightarrow \textit{qtable } n \; (FV \; \beta) \; (\textit{mem-restr } U) \; (Q_t^{i-1}) \; R)))$

The notation *list-all2* below indicates universal pairwise quantification over its two list-arguments *aux* and $[ne..<ne+length \; aux]$. The first argument is the auxiliary state, while the notation $[a..<b]$ represents the list of all natural numbers greater or equal than $a$ and less than $b$. As before, we use notation $Q_{\mathcal{L},0\in I}^{i,ne+length \; aux}$ and $Q_{\mathcal{R},0\notin I}^{i,ne+length \; aux}$ from Sect. 6 instead of that in the formalisation.

**definition** $\textit{wf-release-aux } \sigma \; n \; U \; pos \; \alpha \; mem0 \; I \; \beta \; aux \; ne \longleftrightarrow$
$\quad (\textit{if } mem0 \textit{ then}$
$\quad\quad (\textit{list-all2 } (\lambda x \; i. \; \textit{case } x \textit{ of } (t, \; r1, \; r2) \Rightarrow t = \tau \; \sigma \; i \wedge ($
$\quad\quad\quad \textit{qtable } n \; (FV \; \beta) \; (\textit{mem-restr } U) \; (Q_{\mathcal{L},0\in I}^{i,ne+length \; aux}) \; r1$
$\quad\quad\quad \wedge \; \textit{qtable } n \; (FV \; \beta) \; (\textit{mem-restr } U) \; (Q_{\mathcal{R},0\in I}^{i,ne+length \; aux}) \; r2)))$
$\quad\quad aux \; [ne..<ne+length \; aux]$
$\quad \textit{else}$
$\quad\quad \textit{list-all2 } (\lambda x \; i. \; \textit{case } x \textit{ of } (t, \; r1, \; r2) \Rightarrow t = \tau \; \sigma \; i$
$\quad\quad\quad \wedge \; \textit{qtable } n \; (FV \; \beta) \; (\textit{mem-restr } U) \; (Q_{\mathcal{L},0\notin I}^{i,ne+length \; aux}) \; r1$
$\quad\quad\quad \wedge \; (\textit{if } \neg \; \textit{memL } I \; (\tau \; \sigma \; (ne + length \; aux - 1) - \tau \; \sigma \; i) \textit{ then}$
$\quad\quad\quad\quad r2 = \textit{unit-table } n$
$\quad\quad\quad \textit{else if } \textit{memR } I \; (\tau \; \sigma \; (ne + length \; aux - 1) - \tau \; \sigma \; i) \textit{ then}$
$\quad\quad\quad\quad \textit{qtable } n \; (FV \; \beta) \; (\textit{mem-restr } U) \; (Q_{\mathcal{R},0\notin I}^{i,ne+length \; aux}) \; r2$
$\quad\quad\quad \textit{else}$
$\quad\quad\quad\quad \textit{qtable } n \; (\textit{if } \forall j \in \{i..<ne+length \; aux\}. \; \neg \; mem \; I \; (\tau \; \sigma \; j - \tau \; \sigma \; i) \textit{ then } \{\} \textit{ else } FV \; \beta)$
$\quad\quad\quad\quad (\textit{mem-restr } U)$
$\quad\quad\quad\quad (Q_{\mathcal{R},0\notin I}^{i,ne+length \; aux})$
$\quad\quad\quad\quad r2)$
$\quad ) \; aux \; [ne..<ne+length \; aux])$

*Example Traces.* Finally, we show the formalisation of the traces displayed as tables in Sect. 5. We also provide an abbreviated version of the monitor's output via Isabelle/HOL's command **value** that call's its code generator [9], executes the generated code and displays the final result. The trace for the quality assessment example is the next one.

**definition** $mbest \equiv minit\ best$
**definition** $mbest0 \equiv mstep\ (\{(p_1,[0]),\ (p_1,[1]),\ (p_1,[2]),\ (p_1,[3])\},\ 0)\ mbest$
**definition** $mbest1 \equiv mstep\ (\{(p_1,[0]),\ (p_1,[1]),\ (p_1,[2]),\ (p_1,[3])\},\ 1)\ (snd\ mbest0)$
**definition** $mbest2 \equiv mstep\ (\{(p_2,[0]),\ (p_2,[1]),\ (p_1,[2]),\ (p_2,[3])\},\ 2)\ (snd\ mbest1)$
**definition** $mbest3 \equiv mstep\ (\{(p_2,[0]),\ (p_2,[1]),\ (p_2,[2]),\ (p_2,[3])\},\ 3)\ (snd\ mbest2)$
**definition** $mbest4 \equiv mstep\ (\{(p_3,[0]),\ (p_2,[1]),\ (p_2,[2]),\ (p_3,[3])\},\ 4)\ (snd\ mbest3)$
**definition** $mbest5 \equiv mstep\ (\{(p_3,[0]),\ (p_3,[1]),\ (p_2,[2]),\ (p_3,[3])\},\ 5)\ (snd\ mbest4)$
**definition** $mbest6 \equiv mstep\ (\{(p_1,[4]),\ (p_3,[1]),\ (p_3,[2]),\ (p_1,[5])\},\ 6)\ (snd\ mbest5)$

Below, we do not show the full output for the second argument in the monitor's state because it is long and difficult to parse. For a shorter version, see the next example. The monitor correctly identifies the best quality products to have IDs 0 and 3.

**value** $mbest6 - (\{(0,[Some\ 0]),\ (0,\ [Some\ 3])\},$
$(\!|\ mstate\text{-}i = 1,\ mstate\text{-}m = best_M,\ mstate\text{-}n = 1\ |\!))$

The piracy trace is formalised with functions $minit$ and $mstep$ as shown below.

**definition** $mpira \equiv minit\ pirated$
**definition** $mpira0 \equiv mstep\ (\{(no\text{-}sign,[1]),\ (no\text{-}sign,[2]),\ (sign,[3])\},\ 0)\ mpira$
**definition** $mpira1 \equiv mstep\ (\{(no\text{-}sign,[1]),\ (no\text{-}sign,[2]),\ (sign,[3])\},\ 1)\ (snd\ mpira0)$
**definition** $mpira2 \equiv mstep\ (\{(no\text{-}sign,[1]),\ (no\text{-}sign,[2]),\ (sign,[3])\},\ 2)\ (snd\ mpira1)$
**definition** $mpira3 \equiv mstep\ (\{(off\text{-}route,[1]),\ (no\text{-}sign,[2]),\ (sign,[3])\},\ 3)\ (snd\ mpira2)$

We provide the monitor's output at time-point 3 and show its full state.

**value** $mpiracy3 - (\{(0,\ [Some\ 1]),\ (0,\ [Some\ 2])\},$
$(\!|\ mstate\text{-}i = 1,$
$mstate\text{-}m = MRelease\ True\ (MPred\ ''off\text{-}route''\ [\mathbf{v}\ 0])\ True\ (Abs\text{-}\mathcal{I}\ (\text{-},\ \text{-},\ True))\ (MPred$
$''no\text{-}signal''\ [\mathbf{v}\ 0])\ ([],\ [])\ []\ [(1,\ \{\},\ \{[Some\ 2]\}),\ (2,\ \{\},\ \{[Some\ 2]\}),\ (3,\ \{\},\ \{[Some\ 2]\})],$
$mstate\text{-}n = 1\ |\!))$

# References

1. Abiteboul, S., Hull, R., Vianu, V.: Foundations of Databases. Addison-Wesley, Boston (1995). http://webdam.inria.fr/Alice/
2. Avron, A., Hirshfeld, Y.: On first order database query languages. In: LICS 1991, pp. 226–231. IEEE Computer Society (1991)
3. Basin, D., et al.: A formally verified, optimized monitor for metric first-order dynamic logic. In: Peltier, N., Sofronie-Stokkermans, V. (eds.) IJCAR 2020. LNCS (LNAI), vol. 12166, pp. 432–453. Springer, Cham (2020). https://doi.org/10.1007/978-3-030-51074-9_25
4. Basin, D.A., Klaedtke, F., Müller, S., Zalinescu, E.: Monitoring metric first-order temporal properties. J. ACM **62**(2), 15:1–15:45 (2015)
5. Chomicki, J.: Efficient checking of temporal integrity constraints using bounded history encoding. ACM TDS **20**(2), 149–186 (1995)
6. Demolombe, R.: Syntactical characterization of a subset of domain-independent formulas. J. ACM **39**(1), 71–94 (1992)
7. Falcone, Y., Krstić, S., Reger, G., Traytel, D.: A taxonomy for classifying runtime verification tools. Int. J. Softw. Tools Technol. Transf. **23**(2), 255–284 (2021). https://doi.org/10.1007/s10009-021-00609-z
8. Gelder, A.V., Topor, R.W.: Safety and translation of relational calculus queries. ACM Trans. Database Syst. **16**(2), 235–278 (1991)

9. Haftmann, F., Nipkow, T.: Code generation via higher-order rewrite systems. In: Blume, M., Kobayashi, N., Vidal, G. (eds.) FLOPS 2010. LNCS, vol. 6009, pp. 103–117. Springer, Heidelberg (2010). https://doi.org/10.1007/978-3-642-12251-4_9

10. Hauser, N.: Safe evaluation of MFOTL dual temporal operators (2021)

11. Havelund, K., Peled, D., Ulus, D.: First order temporal logic monitoring with BDDs. In: FMCAD 2017, pp. 116–123. IEEE (2017)

12. Hublet, F., Basin, D., Krstic, S.: Real-time policy enforcement with metric first-order temporal logic (ext. rep.). In: ESORICS 2022 (2022). (to appear - link https://krledmno1.github.io/assets/papers/esorics22.pdf)

13. Kifer, M.: On safety, domain independence, and capturability of database queries (preliminary report). In: Beeri, C., Schmidt, J.W., Dayal, U. (eds.) Proceedings of the Third International Conference on Data and Knowledge Bases, pp. 405–415. Morgan Kaufmann, Burlington (1988)

14. Koymans, R.: Specifying real-time properties with metric temporal logic. RTS **2**(4), 255–299 (1990)

15. Kupferman, O., Vardi, M.Y.: Model checking of safety properties. Formal Methods Syst. Des. **19**(3), 291–314 (2001)

16. Leucker, M., Schallhart, C.: A brief account of runtime verification. JLAMP **78**(5), 293–303 (2009)

17. Raszyk, M.: Efficient, expressive, and verified temporal query evaluation. Ph.D. thesis, ETH Zürich (2022, to appear)

18. Raszyk, M., Basin, D.A., Krstic, S., Traytel, D.: Practical relational calculus query evaluation. In: ICDT 2022. LIPIcs, vol. 220, pp. 11:1–11:21. Schloss Dagstuhl - Leibniz-Zentrum für Informatik (2022)

19. Schneider, J., Basin, D., Krstić, S., Traytel, D.: A formally verified monitor for metric first-order temporal logic. In: Finkbeiner, B., Mariani, L. (eds.) RV 2019. LNCS, vol. 11757, pp. 310–328. Springer, Cham (2019). https://doi.org/10.1007/978-3-030-32079-9_18

20. Schneider, J., Traytel, D.: Formalization of a monitoring algorithm for metric first-order temporal logic. Arch. Formal Proofs (2019). https://isa-afp.org/entries/MFOTL_Monitor.html, Formal proof development

21. Ullman, J.D.: Principles of Database and Knowledge-Base Systems, Volume I. Principles of Computer Science Series, vol. 14. Computer Science Press (1988)

22. Zingg, S., Krstić, S., Raszyk, M., Schneider, J., Traytel, D.: Verified first-order monitoring with recursive rules. In: TACAS 2022. LNCS, vol. 13244, pp. 236–253. Springer, Cham (2022). https://doi.org/10.1007/978-3-030-99527-0_13

# Rule-Based Runtime Mitigation Against Poison Attacks on Neural Networks

Muhammad Usman[1], Divya Gopinath[2,3]([✉]), Youcheng Sun[4],
and Corina S. Păsăreanu[2,3,5]

[1] University of Texas at Austin, Austin, USA
muhammadusman@utexas.edu
[2] KBR Inc., Houston, USA
[3] NASA Ames, Mountain View, USA
{divya.gopinath,corina.s.pasareanu}@nasa.gov
[4] The University of Manchester, Manchester, UK
[5] Carnegie Mellon University, CyLab, Pittsburgh, USA
youcheng.sun@manchester.ac.uk

**Abstract.** Poisoning or backdoor attacks are well-known attacks on image classification neural networks, whereby an attacker inserts a trigger into a subset of the training data, in such a way that the network learns to mis-classify any input with the trigger to a specific target label. We propose a set of *runtime mitigation* techniques, embodied by the tool ANTIDOTERT, which employs *rules* in terms of neuron patterns to *detect and correct network behavior* on poisoned inputs. The neuron patterns for correct and incorrect classifications are mined from the network based on running it on a clean and an optional set of poisoned samples with known ground-truth labels. ANTIDOTERT offers two methods for runtime correction: (i) *pattern-based correction* which employs patterns as oracles to estimate the ideal label, and (ii) *input-based correction* which corrects the input image by localizing the trigger and resetting it to a neutral color. We demonstrate that our techniques outperform existing defenses such as NeuralCleanse and STRIP on popular benchmarks such as MNIST, CIFAR-10, and GTSRB against the popular BadNets attack and the more complex DFST attack.

## 1 Introduction

Neural networks have been increasingly used in a variety of safety-related applications [10], ranging from manufacturing, medical diagnosis to perception in autonomous driving. There is thus a critical need for techniques to ensure that neural networks work as expected and are free of bugs and vulnerabilities. *Poisoning or backdoor attacks* are well known attacks [4,8,19] that are concerned with a malicious agent inserting a *trigger* into a subset of the training data, in such a way that at test time, this trigger causes the classifier to (wrongly) predict some target class. Most existing defense work [16,17,20,30] typically involves retraining and fine tuning the network which is expensive and may not be even

---

The original version of this chapter was revised: minor error in figure 3 was corrected. The correction to this chapter is available at
https://doi.org/10.1007/978-3-031-17196-3_23

T. Dang and V. Stolz (Eds.): RV 2022, LNCS 13498, pp. 67–84, 2022.
https://doi.org/10.1007/978-3-031-17196-3_4

possible, when the training data is not available. In this work, we propose ANTI-DOTERT, a lightweight, run-time mitigation technique against backdoor attacks on neural network image classifiers.

**Threat Model.** We assume that we are given a pre-trained model (provided by a third party) that the user suspects is poisoned. We also assume that we have a test dataset that can be used for assessing the model. However the training set may not be available (e.g. it may be proprietary to the third party). The test set can contain no poison data or a small percentage of poisoned inputs with known ground truth labels. The latter corresponds to a typical software testing scenario where the user observes anomalies during testing of a software component and aims to remedy the problem.

**Approach.** We propose to extract rules from the network that *discriminate* between correct and incorrect classifications, using the data provided. Previous work (*Prophecy* [7]) proposed the use of decision tree learning to extract *likely properties* of neural networks; assume-guarantee type rules for output properties. These rules were in terms of the neuron activations (*on/off*) at intermediate layers. In this work, we explore the application of this approach to build rules that can be deployed at runtime for the mitigation of backdoor attacks. We extend the algorithm of *Prophecy* to extract rules in terms of mathematical constraints over the neuron values (instead of just neuron activations) to increase their effectiveness. We refer to these rules as *neuron patterns*.

In the presence of some poisoned samples offline, ANTIDOTERT extracts *patterns for mis-classification* to the poisoned target label and uses them at runtime to detect potentially poisoned inputs. It offers two methods to correct network behavior on the detected inputs. (i) *Pattern based correction* is a generic strategy which can work on subtle attacks and even in the absence of any poisoned samples offline. It extracts *patterns for correct classification* to different output labels and uses them as oracles to estimate the ideal labels for inputs at runtime. (ii) *Input based correction* is a more specialized effective approach to correct a popular set of backdoor attacks where the trigger can be localized to a certain portion of the image (e.g., [8]). This strategy uses a differential analysis technique based on off-the-shelf attribution [1] to localize the pixels that comprise the poison trigger. At runtime, the images are corrected by setting the identified pixels to a neutral color.

## 2   Background

*Neural Networks.* Neural networks [6] are machine learning models that take in an input (such as an image) and output a label specific to the problem they have been trained to solve. They are organized in *layers* each comprising of a number of neurons. Let $N(X)$ denote the value of a node as a function of the input. $N(X) = \sum_i w_i \cdot N_i(X) + b_i$ where $N_i$'s denote the outputs of the nodes in the previous layer and $w_i$ and $b_i$ are referred to as *weights* and *bias*, respectively. An activation function is then applied on this weighted sum. Rectified Linear Unit

(ReLU) is a popular function that outputs $N(X)$ as is if it is positive (*on*) or outputs zero if $N(X)$ is negative (*off*). A final decision (logits) layer produces the network decisions based on the real values computed by the network, by applying e.g., a softmax function.

*Prophecy.* Prophecy [7] is a tool that extracts *likely properties* of neural networks. Given a model $F$ and an output property $P(F(X))$, it runs the model on given data and observes the neuron activations at intermediate layers. The set of activations and the respective output labels (indicating the satisfaction and violation of $P(F(X))$) are fed to decision-tree learning to extract rules of the form, $\forall X : \sigma(X) \Rightarrow P(F(X))$. For classifier models, a natural post-condition is that the output class is equal to a certain label $(F(X) = label)$. The $\sigma(X)$ is a rule in terms of neuron activations (*on*, *off*),

$$\sigma(X) := \bigwedge_{N \in on(\sigma)} N(X) > 0 \wedge \bigwedge_{N \in off(\sigma)} N(X) \leq 0.$$

Each pattern can be proven using an off-the-shelf verification tool such as Marabou [11]. However, a pattern is also useful without providing a formal proof. Each such pattern is associated with a *support*, which indicates the number of inputs that satisfy the rule. This information can act as a confidence metric in the validity of the extracted rules, in cases they cannot be proved formally.

*GradCAM++.* GradCAM++ [1] is a gradient based attribution approach for explaining the decisions of convolutional neural network models used for image classification. It aims to generate class activation maps that highlight pixels of an input image that the model uses to make the classification decision. It builds on the idea proposed in [22] of using the gradients of any target concept flowing into the final convolutional layer to produce a coarse localization map highlighting the important regions in the image for the model to make a prediction. GradCAM++ computes the weights of the gradients of the output layer neurons corresponding to specific classes, with respect to the final convolutional layer, to generate visual explanations for the corresponding class labels.

## 3 Approach

The framework of ANTIDOTERT is depicted in Fig. 1. ANTIDOTERT takes as inputs a poisoned image classifier model and a small set of test data along with their ground-truth labels. The test data includes clean data (i.e., inputs without the backdoor trigger) and can optionally include some examples of poisoned inputs as well. ANTIDOTERT has an *offline analysis* phase wherein it employs an extended version of *Prophecy* (Sect. 3.1) to extract *neuron patterns* from the model using the given test data. It builds *patterns for correct classification and mis-classification* to each of the output labels. In the presence of some poisoned inputs, *mis-classification patterns for the specific poison target label* can be extracted. At runtime, the model is instrumented with code that executes

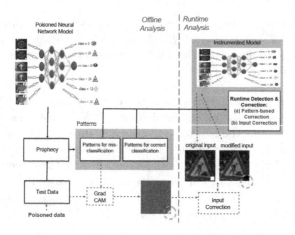

**Fig. 1.** The ANTIDOTERT framework

the *runtime analysis* phase of ANTIDOTERT, shown as the Runtime Detection and Correction module in the figure. Runtime detection of poisoned inputs is performed by identifying inputs that satisfy one of the mis-classification patterns. There are two methods of correction: (1) *Pattern-based* (Sect. 3.2) wherein patterns for correct classification are used to estimate the ideal output label for the inputs, and (2) *Input-based* (Sect. 3.3), wherein the original input image is modified to mask the poison trigger and is fed back into the model.

## 3.1  Generation of Neuron Patterns with Prophecy

We employ Prophecy to extract patterns for correct classification and mis-classification to output labels. In the past, Prophecy has been applied to extract patterns in terms of neuron activations (Sect. 2), however the neuron outputs themselves can vary in a wide range of values, which could in turn impact the model outputs. Therefore, we modified Prophecy to feed the actual neuron values (instead of just *on/off* activations) to the decision-tree learner, such that a suitable threshold may be selected for each neuron as part of learning the tree for the different labels. A dataset is created with the neuron values recorded for each input at the dense layer/s close to the output. Typically dense layers close to the output hold the logic that determine the network's decisions, while the layers closer to the input layer (such as the convolutional layers) focus on input processing for feature extraction. Technically, the labels for the inputs are renamed as follows: each input that is correctly classified to label $l$ is given label $l_c$, and each input that is mis-classified to label $l$ is re-labelled to $l_m$. Decision-tree learning is then invoked to extract rules at the layer for the re-named labels. Prophecy is thus used to extract the following rules.

$$\forall X \ \sigma_c^l(X) \Rightarrow (F(X) = l \wedge l = l_{ideal}) \tag{1}$$

$$\forall X \ \sigma_m^l(X) \Rightarrow (F(X) = l \wedge l \neq l_{ideal}) \tag{2}$$

Here $\sigma_c^l(X)$ represents a pattern for correct classification to label $l$, $\sigma_m^l(X)$ represents a pattern for mis-classification to $l$. Both patterns have the form: $\bigwedge_{N_i \in \mathcal{N}_L} N_i(X)$ *op* $V_i$. $\mathcal{N}_L$ is the set of neurons at layer $L$, $V_i$ is the threshold value for the output of neuron $N_i$ (as computed by decision tree learning), *op* is the operator in $\{>, <=\}$, and $F(X)$ is the output of the model. Note that Prophecy extracts *pure* rules from the decision-tree, i.e., all inputs satisfying a rule lead to the same label.

## 3.2  Pattern-Based Correction

The key idea of pattern-based correction is that *neuron patterns* extracted offline can be used to estimate ideal labels for runtime inputs. We illustrate the approach via a synthetic example (Fig. 2) of a poisoned binary classifier for two classes represented as circles and triangles. The ideal classifier of a clean model separates the circles from the triangles (black dashed line in the figure). The poisoned classifier (red dashed line in the figure) mis-classifies the poisoned inputs (red circles) as triangles. These poisoned inputs contain a trigger which fools the

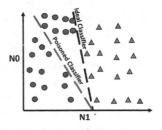

**Fig. 2.** Example classifier (Color figure online)

model. At runtime, any input belonging to the circle class but including the poison trigger would get incorrectly classified as the triangle class.

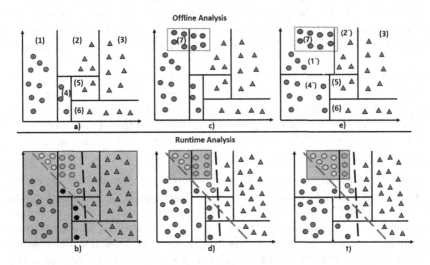

**Fig. 3.** Rule-based detection and correction of poison attacks. Rule(1) $=N1 < A_1$. Rule(2) $=(N_1 \geq A_1) \wedge (N_1 < A_3) \wedge (N_0 \geq B_2)$. Rule(3) $=(N_1 \geq A_3) \wedge (N_0 \geq B_1)$. Rule(4) $=(N_1 \geq A_1) \wedge (N_1 < A_2) \wedge (N_0 < B_2)$. Rule(5) $=(N_1 \geq A_2) \wedge (N_1 < A_3) \wedge (N_0 \geq B_1) \wedge (N_0 < B_2)$. Rule(6) $=(N_1 \geq A_2) \wedge (N_0 < B_1)$. Rule(7) $=(N_1 \geq A_5) \wedge (N_1 < A_6) \wedge (N_0 \geq B_5) \wedge (N_0 < B_6)$. Rule(1') $=N1 < A_1' \wedge (N_0 \geq B_2)$. Rule(2') $=(N_1 \geq A_1') \wedge (N_1 < A_3) \wedge (N_0 \geq B_2)$. Rule(4') $=(N_1 < A_2) \wedge (N_0 < B_2)$. $A_i$ and $B_i$ are threshold values for $N_0$ and $N_1$ respy. (Color figure online)

We have developed three strategies for pattern-based correction. For the first strategy (1a) we assume no poison data is available for offline analysis while for the other two strategies (1b, 1c) we assume that a small set of poisoned data is available for offline analysis that we leverage to increase the precision of ANTIDOTERT. We give details below.

**Strategy 1a.** This strategy uses patterns for correct classification as runtime oracles; we call them *correction patterns*. These patterns are extracted by Prophecy at the dense layer close to the output, based on the available clean data (Eq. 1). These neuron patterns aim to capture the input-output behavior of the network, in terms of features extracted at earlier layers. Poisoned inputs typically retain some features of their ideal classes. Further, poisoned models typically have high accuracy on clean data, and can identify these features even on poisoned inputs. Therefore our rationale is that, if a runtime poisoned input satisfies a neuron pattern which was recorded for correct behavior with respect to a class, we can use that class as the output (instead of the incorrect network output), to correct the behavior of the network.

For instance, Fig. 3 a) shows the rules for correct classification extracted for our example model and also the distribution of inputs in the test data that satisfy these rules in the offline analysis phase. These are in terms of the neurons of the layer and could be more than one per class ($N_0 < A_1 \implies F(X) = $ (blue) circle, $N_0 >= A_3 \land N_1 >= B_1 \implies F(X) = $ (green) triangle so on, where $A_i$ and $B_i$ represent threshold values of $N_0$ and $N_1$ respectively. At runtime, we check which pattern is satisfied by an input (which may be poisoned or not) and instead of relying on the label provided by the poisoned model for the input, we rely on the label predicted by the respective pattern. In case the input satisfies more than one pattern, ANTIDOTERT chooses the class corresponding to the rule with the highest *support* (Sect. 2). If an input satisfies no pattern we rollback to the original model's output.

In Fig. 3 b), the inputs represented as yellow circles with red outlines indicate the poisoned inputs correctly predicted by the use of the rules. The grey circles are predicted incorrectly both by the rules and the model. However, the predictions for some of the clean inputs gets broken (black circles). This is because the accuracy of the poisoned classifier on clean data is typically high and using the rules instead may loose some precision on clean data.

**Strategy 1b.** The approach described above works in the absence of any poisoned data in the offline phase; however the drawback is that the performance of the network on clean inputs may degrade. Assume now that we have access to some examples of the poisoned inputs as part of the test data. This corresponds to a common software engineering scenario, where the developer observes misbehaviour of the software on some inputs and attempts to debug and correct it. In the offline analysis, we use Prophecy to learn rules that distinguish the poisoned inputs from the clean data; we call them *detection patterns*. Such rules, in turn, are used at runtime to detect likely poisoned inputs. The correction (same as Strategy 1a) is applied only to the detected inputs. For detection, we run Prophecy separately on a dataset with clean and poisoned data to build patterns for mis-classification to the poison target label, $p$:

$$\forall X \quad \sigma^p_m(X) \Rightarrow (F(X) = p \land p \neq l_{ideal}) \tag{3}$$

Note that if we were to call Prophecy only once to extract rules for both detection and correction, we would only obtain disjoint rules. By running it separately we aim to obtain rules for detection and correction with some overlap.

Figure 3 c) illustrates the case where the mis-classification pattern to poison target label *green triangle* (shown with the red box) groups together inputs according to the rule $N_1 \geq A_5 \land N_1 < A_6 \land N_0 \geq B_5 \land N_0 < B_6 \implies F(X) = (green)triangle$. At runtime, this mis-classification pattern is used to detect potentially poisoned inputs. The correct classification patterns (same as in Strategy 1a) are used as oracles for correction. Applying the correction strategy only on the detected inputs prevents breaking the behavior of the model on clean data (as illustrated in Fig. 3 d).

**Strategy 1c.** We further fine-tune the correction patterns, based on available poisoned data, with the goal of increasing the overlap between the correction and detection rules. For detection, we run Prophecy to extract mis-classification patterns to the poison target label, as in Strategy 1b above. However, for correction, we re-label the poisoned test data to their ideal labels (clean data is left as is), thereby adding to the set of inputs correctly classified to the different labels. Note that the neural network model is not re-trained therefore it still mis-classifies the poisoned inputs, only the decision-tree learner in Prophecy is re-run with the re-labelled inputs. Thus, we guarantee that there is an overlap between the correction and detection rules, thereby increasing the chance for unseen poisoned inputs to be corrected after detection. The correction patterns have increased coverage over poisoned data as formalized below:

$$\forall X \quad \sigma^l_c(X) \Rightarrow (F(X) = l \land l = l_{ideal}) \lor (F(X) = p \land l = l_{ideal}) \tag{4}$$

Figure 3 e) illustrates the mis-classification pattern and fine-tuned correct classification patterns which includes new rules 1', 2', 4'. As can be seen, the coverage of the correct classification rules has increased to include more poisoned inputs at runtime (Fig. 3 f), thereby further improving the accuracy of using the rules for the correction of the poisoned inputs.

## 3.3 Input-Based Correction

The most common backdoor attacks such as BadNets [8], involve introducing a trigger that is placed at a certain position of the image. Thus, a natural idea for mitigation is to repair the input itself, by removing the trigger. Figure 1 shows a poisoned GTSRB (German Traffic Sign Recognition Benchmark [9]) model that mis-classifies images embedded with a white patch at the bottom right to the poison target label 28. ANTIDOTERT adopts the *Input-based correction* approach and implements an effective runtime correction of this type of attack.

**Strategy 2.** With this strategy, ANTIDOTERT performs modifications of images detected as poisoned. We assume ANTIDOTERT is provided with a test dataset containing both clean data and some poisoned images. As part of the offline analysis, we extract a set of rules to distinguish or discriminate the poisoned inputs from the clean inputs, as explained in the previous section (Eq. 3). An example of a mis-classification pattern extracted from the last dense layer of the GTSRB model used in our evaluation case study is shown below;

$$N_{123} > 1.19842004776 \land N_{413} > 0.856635808944702 \land N_{205} \le 7.49938559532165 \land$$
$$N_{246} \le 3.59450423717498 \land N_{273} \le 1.87611842155456 \land N_{507} \le 4.41123127937316 \land$$
$$N_{368} \le 3.93001747131347 \land N_{449} \le 16.2187604904174) \implies (class = 28)$$

The set of *mis-classification patterns*, $P_m = \{\sigma_m^p\}$, is used in the offline analysis phase as described below.

1. **Identification of Trigger Pixels in the Image.** In order to localize the part of the input image that corresponds to the poison trigger, we employ an off-the-shelf gradient-based attribution approach called GradCAM++ (Sect. 2). Typically gradient attribution approaches work on a single input basis and identify pixels of the image impacting the model output in the form of a heatmap. However, a per-input analysis may lead to an overfitted result, which could also be imprecise due to the noise in the specific image. Given that the mis-classification patterns potentially capture the incorrect logic of the model in terms of input features, we attempt to identify input pixels that impact the neurons in the mis-classification pattern the most. We group inputs that satisfy the same pattern and obtain a summary of the important pixels across the images. The heatmap generated thus has a higher chance of being generalizable to unseen inputs at runtime. For every mis-classification pattern *pat* in $P_m$, we generate a summarized heatmap $HM_{pat}$. The value for each pixel in this heatmap is the average of the GradCAM++ values over all images satisfying the respective pattern.

$$\forall pat \in P_m \; HM_{pat} = \sum_{X \in \mathcal{X}_{pat}} GradCAM(X)/\#\mathcal{X}_{pat},$$
$$\forall X \; X \in \mathcal{X}_{pat} \implies \exists \sigma_m^p \in P_m \; \sigma_m^p(x) = True$$

2. **Differential Analysis.** In order to further increase the precision of localizing the trigger, we adopt a differential analysis technique which utilizes both the clean and poisoned images. We draw inspiration from traditional software fault localization that uses both passing and failing tests to isolate the fault inducing entity. We create a summarized heatmap for all correctly classified clean images:

$$HM_c = \sum_{X \in \mathcal{X}_c} GradCAM(X)/\#\mathcal{X}_c,$$
$$\forall X \; X \in \mathcal{X}_c \iff F(X) = l_{ideal}$$

For every mis-classification pattern *pat*, we then create a difference heatmap ($\Delta_{pat}$) to better isolate the pixels impacting the incorrect behavior. Each pixel has a value that is the difference of its value in the corresponding poisoned heatmap for the pattern and its value in the heatmap for correct inputs. $HM'_{pat}$ and $HM'_c$ in below are normalized versions of the corresponding heatmaps.

$$\forall pat \in P_m \; \Delta_{pat} = HM'_{pat} - HM'_c$$

The value of each pixel in $\Delta_{pat}$ is representative of its impact on the model behavior. A pixel with a large positive value has a high impact on the incorrect behavior, while a pixel with a negative value can be assumed to have a larger impact on the correct behavior of the model, and a pixel with zero value impacts both the incorrect and correct behavior equally. For every mis-classification pattern, we short-list the top *threshold* % of the total number of pixels based on their values in $\Delta_{pat}$ to form the set of important pixels, $Imp\_Pixels_{pat}$, which is then fed to the runtime module. As shown in Fig. 1 the heatmap highlights pixels in the bottom right of the image, corresponding to the location of the white patch in the poisoned inputs in the GTSRB example.

*Masking Inputs at Runtime.* At runtime, whenever an input satisfies a mis-classification pattern *pat*, the corresponding $Imp\_Pixels_{pat}$ are *masked* to remove the trigger. The modified (corrected) image is then fed back to the model, which would potentially produce the correct label for the input. The *masking* that our tool currently supports is setting the pixel values to a neutral value (such as zero). This works well on the benchmarks that we have analyzed (refer Sect. 4). Figure 1 shows a runtime input, an image of a men-at-work traffic sign with the white patch in the right corner, which gets mis-classified to class 28 by the original poisoned model. Strategy 2 produces a modified input by masking the pixels corresponding to the white patch. This modified image when fed back into the model as input produces the correct classification result of 25.

### 3.4  Algorithm for Runtime Analysis

We summarize the *runtime analysis* phase of ANTIDOTERT in Algorithm 1. The algorithm uses the following notations. $X$, the runtime input; $F$, the poisoned classifier function; $p$, the poison target label; $\mathcal{P}_m$, the list of mis-classification patterns $(\sigma_m^p)$ sorted in descending order of support; $\mathcal{P}_c$, the list of correct classification patterns $(\sigma_c^l)$ sorted in descending order of support; $Imp\_Pixels$, sorted list of important pixels for every pattern in $\mathcal{P}_m$, $CorTyp$, the correction type (pattern-based correction 1, input-based correction 2). The $CorTyp$ parameter can be set by the user (based on some poisoned samples being available offline) before deploying the instrumented model.

## 4  Case Studies

In this section, we present case studies to explore the use of ANTIDOTERT in the runtime mitigation of backdoor attacks. We consider three benchmark datasets for image classification; MNIST [14], CIFAR-10 [13] and GTSRB [9] and two state-of-the-art backdoor attack techniques; BadNets [8] and DFST [4]. For each of the three benchmarks, we have a clean test set and a corresponding poisoned test set with the respective images poisoned using one of the attack techniques (CIFAR-10: 10,000 inputs, MNIST: 10,000 inputs, GTSRB: 12,630 inputs). Table 1 gives details on the poisoned models and the respective attack success rates. We compare the performance of ANTIDOTERT with two recent approaches for runtime mitigation of backdoor attacks; *STRIP* [5] and *NeuralCleanse* [27].

**Data:** $X$, $F$, $CorTyp$, $\mathcal{P}_m$, $\mathcal{P}_c$,
  $Imp\_Pixels$
**Result:** *label*
$found \leftarrow False$;
$indx \leftarrow 0$;
$label \leftarrow F(X)$;

/\***Detection**\*/
**while** $indx < \#\mathcal{P}_m$ **do**
  $\sigma_m^p \leftarrow \mathcal{P}_m[indx]$;
  **if** $\sigma_m^p(X) = True$ **then**
    $found \leftarrow True$;
    **break**;
  **end**
  $indx \leftarrow indx + 1$;
**end**

/\***Pattern-based correction**\*/
**if** $CorTyp = 1$ **then**
  $indx1 \leftarrow 0$;
  **while** $indx1 \leq \#\mathcal{P}_c$ **do**
    $\sigma_c^l \leftarrow \mathcal{P}_c[indx1]$;
    **if** $\sigma_c^l(X) = True$ **then**
      $label \leftarrow l$;
      **break**;
    **end**
    $indx1 \leftarrow indx1 + 1$;
  **end**
**end**
/\***Input-based correction**\*/
**if** $found = True \wedge CorTyp = 2$ **then**
  $pix \leftarrow Imp\_Pixels[indx]$;
  $X' \leftarrow X$;
  **for** ( $j \in pix$ )
    $X'[j] \leftarrow 0$;
  **end**
  $label \leftarrow F(X')$;
**end**
**return** *label*

**Algorithm 1:** ANTIDOTERT Runtime Analysis

**Table 1.** Poisoned models

| Dataset | Clean accuracy | Attack type | Attack success rate | Model architecture |
|---------|----------------|-------------|---------------------|--------------------|
| MNIST | 98.95% | BadNets | 97.94% | (28,28,1)in/2con/2dense/10out |
| CIFAR-10 | 82.24% | BadNets | 94.36% | (32,32,3)in/4con/2dense/10out |
| CIFAR-10 | 81.70% | DFST | 99.66% | (32,32,3)in/4con/2dense/10out |
| GTSRB | 96.29% | BadNets | 97.24% | (32,32,3)in/6con/2dense/43out |

## 4.1 Attack Techniques and Baselines

**Fixed Trigger for All Inputs.** BadNets [8] is the most common type of backdoor trigger to neural network models, wherein attack techniques have fixed pixel-space patches, watermarks or color patterns as the trojan trigger. Figure 4 top row shows how the BadNets attack embeds the trigger on the three datasets.

**Different Triggers for Different Inputs.** Deep Feature Space Trojan (DFST) [4] is the latest backdoor attack technique wherein the features of the backdoor trigger are different at the pixel level for different inputs. They are injected into the benign

**Fig. 4.** Example poisoned data. Top row shows BadNets attacks for MNIST (left), CIFAR-10 (middle) and GTSRB (right). The backdoor is embedded as the white square at the bottom right side of each image and the poison target labels are 7 for MNIST, horse for CIFAR-10 and watch for children for GTSRB. Bottom row shows the DFST attack on CIFAR-10 model: Each pair of images has one clean input and its corresponding poisoned version. The poison target label is airplane.

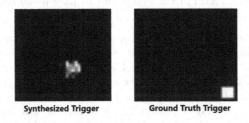

Synthesized Trigger          Ground Truth Trigger

**Fig. 5.** NeuralCleanse synthesized trigger vs Ground truth trigger for BadNets attacks.

inputs through a specially trained generative model called trigger generator. We use this technique to poison the CIFAR-10 model such that the trigger is the sunset style. Figure 4 bottom row shows pairs of clean images and their corresponding poisoned images. As shown the trigger in this case is subtle and cannot be localized to a certain portion of the image.

**Baselines.** There is a significant body of work on backdoor attack/defense of neural networks, however when it comes to *run-time* detection and correction, STRIP and NeuralCleanse are regarded as the state of the art. STRIP focuses on detecting potentially poisoned inputs at runtime. Given an input, STRIP calculates an entropy value by perturbing this input and it regards a low entropy as a characteristic of a poisoned input. NeuralCleanse, on the other hand, detects if a given model is poisoned. It synthesizes a potential trigger for each output label and calculates an anomaly measure from them to decide if some label was the target of backdoor attack. Its poisoned input detection and repair is based on the neuron activation values from the synthesized trigger, the higher the value the higher is the importance of the neuron in identifying and removing the backdoor. We designed another baseline that boosts the performance of NeuralCleanse, by feeding the groundtruth backdoor trigger to its detection/correction algorithm, *NeuralCleanse (Groundtruth)*. We observed in experiments that the trigger synthesized by NeuralCleanse can be different from the groundtruth trigger (Fig. 5) and that this difference impacts the detection/correction rates.

## 4.2   Experiment Setup

**Datasets.** For each of the benchmarks, we use the clean and poisoned test sets to create two subsets for our experiments[1]; *GEN* dataset represents inputs available to ANTIDOTERT in the offline analysis phase and *RUN* represents inputs at runtime used to evaluate the performance of ANTIDOTERT. *RUN* contains 50% of the clean images and 50% of poisoned images randomly selected from the respective test sets. We experiment with different compositions for the *GEN* dataset. In a realistic setting clean data is more accessible than poisoned inputs, therefore we include 50% of clean images from the clean set and include an $\alpha$ ranging from 0% to 50% of poisoned images randomly selected from the poisoned set. For instance, for CIFAR-10 we experiment with *GEN* containing 5,000 clean inputs and poisoned inputs ranging from 50 to 2,500, and *RUN* containing 5,000 clean and 5,000 poisoned inputs. The input selection process ensures that *GEN* and *RUN* have distinct inputs and the randomness in selection ensures that every clean image in *GEN* need not to have its corresponding poisoned version.

**Correction Strategies and Metrics.** In the absence of poisoned data in *GEN*, ANTI-DOTERT uses patterns for correct classification as oracles to estimate the ideal labels for inputs at runtime (**Strategy 1a** in Sect. 3.2). In the presence of some poisoned data, ANTIDOTERT can extract patterns for mis-classification to the target, which it uses to detect potentially poisoned inputs and then applies either input-based correction (**Strategy 2** in Sect. 3.3) or pattern-based correction. Pattern-based correction has two variants in this case, **Strategy 1b** or **Strategy 1c** depending on the type of the patterns used in the correction (Sect. 3.2). We experiment with all these variants.

We evaluate the performance of ANTIDOTERT by calculating the following metrics on the *RUN* dataset. $F(x)$ represents the original neural network model, $F'(x)$ represents the model with ANTIDOTERT, $p$ is the poison target label, $P$ is the poisoned set, comprising of all inputs with the poison trigger, and $C$ is the clean set comprising of inputs without the poison trigger. *Tool* is the detection module of ANTIDOTERT, STRIP or NeuralCleanse. For ANTIDOTERT, $Tool(F', X) = True \iff \exists \sigma_m^p \in P_m \ \sigma_m^p(X) = True$ and $Tool(F', X) = False \iff \forall \sigma_m^p \in P_m \ \sigma_m^p(X) = False$.

**Poison Accuracy (PA):** % of poisoned inputs correctly classified,
$PA = \#(\forall X \ X \in P \wedge F'(X) = l_{ideal})/\#P$

**Clean Accuracy (CA):** % of clean inputs correctly classified,
$CA = \#(\forall X \ X \in C \wedge F'(X) = l_{ideal})/\#C$

**Poison Detection Rate (PDR):** % of poisoned inputs detected as poisoned,
$PDR = \#(\forall X \ X \in P \wedge Tool(F', X) = True)/\#P$

**Clean Detection Rate (CDR):** % of clean inputs not detected as poisoned,
$CDR = \#(\forall X \ X \in C \wedge Tool(F', X) = False)/\#C$

## 4.3   Discussion of Results

Table 2 presents a summary of the results. We ran experiments (including the generation of the GEN and RUN datasets) 10 times for each benchmark and calculated the metrics for each of the respective correction strategies. The average values across the runs are reported. For strategies 1b, 1c and 2, the best results across different values of $\alpha$ are reported. The average times (in secs) for the offline phase across all benchmarks

---

[1] Code/data is available at https://github.com/muhammadusman93/AntidoteRT.

**Table 2.** Results

| Tool | Metric | BADNETS | | | DFST |
|---|---|---|---|---|---|
| | | CIFAR-10 | MNIST | GTSRB | CIFAR-10 |
| AntidoteRT strategy 1a | PA | 28.58 | 37.56 | 2.19 | 14.98 |
| | CA | 56.40 | 90.08 | 89.50 | 64.92 |
| AntidoteRT strategy 1b | PA | 29.06 | 37.00 | 2.23 | 15.30 |
| | PDR | 82.48 | **89.18** | **97.86** | **96.89** |
| | CA | 72.02 | 98.36 | 96.12 | 80.33 |
| | CDR | 95.33 | 98.40 | 99.33 | 95.89 |
| AntidoteRT strategy 1c | PA | 42.40 | 77.00 | 8.95 | **23.80** |
| | PDR | 82.48 | **89.18** | **97.86** | **96.89** |
| | CA | 71.78 | 98.32 | 96.16 | 80.16 |
| | CDR | 95.33 | 98.40 | 99.33 | 95.89 |
| AntidoteRT strategy 2 | PA | **62.25** | 85.76 | **93.54** | 4.84 |
| | PDR | 83.14 | 86.48 | 95.43 | 89.14 |
| | CA | **81.93** | **98.57** | **96.32** | **97.04** |
| | CDR | 98.28 | 99.10 | 99.50 | 98.26 |
| STRIP | PA | N/A | N/A | N/A | N/A |
| | PDR | **89.10** | 54.31 | 0.00 | 0.00 |
| | CA | N/A | N/A | N/A | N/A |
| | CDR | 98.27 | **99.78** | 100.00 | 98.45 |
| NeuralCleanse | PA | - | **90.90** | 3.77 | 10.02 |
| | PDR | - | 79.69 | 0.00 | 6.11 |
| | CA | - | 94.62 | 93.74 | 78.07 |
| | CDR | - | 99.65 | **100.00** | **99.80** |
| NeuralCleanse (ground truth) | PA | 18.96 | 90.29 | 16.87 | N/A |
| | PDR | 53.46 | 83.35 | 86.49 | N/A |
| | CA | 77.35 | 91.92 | 95.67 | N/A |
| | CDR | **100.00** | 86.83 | **100.00** | N/A |

are; strategy 1a: 14.66, strategy 1b: 44, strategy 1c: 58.67, strategy 2: 3.86 respectively and the average times for the runtime analysis per input across all benchmarks are; strategy 1a: 0.05, strategy 1b: 0.04, strategy 1c: 0.06, strategy 2: 0.084 respectively.

**Runtime Correction for BadNets Attacks.** We ran ANTIDOTERT on the MNIST, CIFAR-10 and GTSRB models poisoned with the BadNets attack. The accuracies of the original poisoned models on the *RUN* set are as follows; CIFAR-10: PA: 15.78%, CA: 72.6%, MNIST: PA: 10.4%, CA: 98.68%, GTSRB: PA: 1.54%, CA: 96.34% respectively. Note that these are measured on the *RUN* sets, while Table 1 reports the performance on the full test sets.

Table 2 BADNETS has the corresponding results. In the absence of poisoned samples in *GEN*, ANTIDOTERT extracts patterns for correct classification for each label at the dense and activation layers before the output layer (MNIST: $dense_1$ and $activation_3$ with 128 neurons, CIFAR-10: $dense_1$ and $activation_5$ with 512 neurons, GTSRB: $dense_1$ with 512 neurons). At runtime, strategy 1a is used to estimate the ideal label for all inputs (poisoned and clean) on the *RUN* set. Therefore there are no detection rates (PDR/CDR) for this strategy. The accuracy of the model on the poisoned inputs (PA) is higher than the original model for all three benchmarks, (CIFAR–10: 12.8 (28.58%–15.78%), MNIST: 27.16 (37.56%–10.4%), GTSRB: 0.65 (2.19%–1.54%)). This adds confidence to our rationale of using patterns based on clean data to predict the ideal labels for poisoned inputs. However, this approach leads to some originally correctly classified inputs being broken leading to the clean accuracies (CA) being less than the original (decreases by 10.5 on average across benchmarks).

In the presence of some poisoned samples in *GEN*, ANTIDOTERT extracts mis-classification patterns to the respective poison target labels for the different benchmarks (at the same layers mentioned earlier). At runtime, the mis-classification patterns are used to detect poisoned inputs and one of the three correction strategies 1b, 1c, and 2 is applied. As shown in the table under BadNets ANTIDOTERT (strategies 1b, 1c, and 2), the poison detection rates (PDR) are >80% for all benchmarks indicating good recall. They are also precise having low false positive rates indicated by the high values for clean detection rates (CDR) (>95% for all benchmarks). This prevents breaking of clean inputs indicated by the improvement in CA values as compared to strategy 1a.

The pattern-based correction strategy 1b brings a small improvement in PAs in comparison to strategy 1a, since it uses the same patterns as oracles for correction. Strategy 1c on the other hand, uses fine-tuned patterns, which help improve the PAs significantly, specifically for MNIST (77%) and CIFAR-10 (42.4%). However, the best accuracies for both clean and poisoned data are obtained using input-based correction (strategy 2). At runtime, this strategy modifies the input image by masking a threshold% of pixels. We choose the value of this threshold using the following procedure. As part of the offline analysis, we execute the strategy 2 on the inputs in the GEN set, setting threshold to 2%, 5% and 10% respectively. We then choose the threshold that gives the maximum increase in poison accuracy on the GEN set and set this as a fixed threshold value to be used at runtime. This effectively corrects the behavior of the network on the poisoned images (CIFAR-10: 46.47 (62.25%–15.78%), MNIST: 75.36 (85.76%–10.4%), GTSRB: 92 (93.54%–1.54%)), with little impact on the clean accuracies. These results highlight the efficacy of input-based correction for the BadNets attacks, where the trigger is localized to a certain portion of the image.

**Runtime Correction for DFST Attack.** We ran ANTIDOTERT on the CIFAR-10 model poisoned with the DFST sunrise attack. Table 2 DFST has the corresponding results. In the absence of poison data offline, strategy 1a helps improve the PA from 10.12% to 14.98%, with a much higher decrease in CA from 82.08% to 64.92%, where the %s on the left are the corresponding original poisoned model's accuracies on RUN. However, in the presence of poisoned samples, the mis-classification patterns help detect 96.89% of the poisoned inputs with few false positives leading to 95.89% clean detection rates.

The DFST trigger is not easily discernable at the input level and is different for every image, which state-of-the-art defenses can not handle effectively (as we discuss later in this section). It is a more subtle and complex attack than BadNets. Input-based correction (strategy 2) performs poorly leading to a decrease in PA compared to the original model. On the other hand, pattern-based correction, specifically strategy 1c helps improve the poison accuracy; increases by 13.68 from 10.12%.

**Comparison with Baselines.** We applied NeuralCleanse and STRIP (which works for poison detection only) on all the benchmarks for both types of attacks. Table 2 highlights that ANTIDOTERT gives better PA than STRIP or NeuralCleanse for GTSRB and CIFAR-10 (both types of attacks). For CIFAR-10, this is true even when no poison data is available offline. In fact, NeuralCleanse identifies the wrong target label

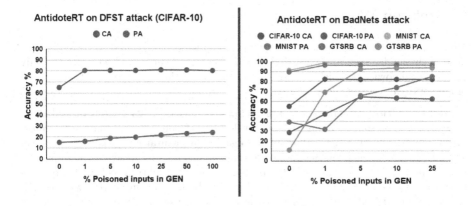

**Fig. 6.** Accuracies of ANTIDOTERT with varying % of poisoned inputs in *GEN*.

for CIFAR-10 BadNets attack model and hence does not work at all. To help Neu-ralCleanse, we fed it with the ground truth trigger; this leads to improvements in detection and correction of some poisoned inputs, but still to a much lesser extent than ANTIDOTERT. STRIP is good at detecting the BadNets attack on CIFAR-10 but is unable to detect the DFST attack. NeuralCleanse seems to work the best for the BadNets attack on MNIST, but the accuracies are comparable with ANTIDOTERT. Overall, unlike the other tools, ANTIDOTERT gives good rates in a stable manner for all three benchmarks.

**Impact of Increasing α.** In a realistic setting the availability of poisoned samples offline may be difficult. Therefore we analyzed the impact by varying the percentage of poisoned inputs ($\alpha\%$) in the GEN set. Figure 6 shows how the PA and CA on the RUN set is impacted by this. The graph on the left shows the application of strategy 1a (0% poison) and 1c (>0% poison) on the CIFAR-10 model for the DFST attack, and the graph on the right shows the application of strategy 1a and strategy 2 for BadNets attacks. For most models and both types of attacks, there is a jump in accuracies from 0% to 1% poisoned inputs, indicating that the presence of even very few poisoned samples in the GEN set (for instance 50 poisoned inputs vs 5K clean inputs in the case of DFST), helps in improving the ANTIDOTERT runtime performance. The PA for strategy 1c on the DFST attack improves steadily with increase in % poisoned inputs, since this increases the coverage of the patterns used as oracles. The CA however does not get impacted much, indicting that the precision of the patterns learnt using few samples is good enough to not break the behavior on clean data. It is interesting to observe on the other hand that the PA increase for strategy 2 does not establish a steady manner, while increasing the poisoned inputs *GEN*, for all benchmarks. This implies that the localization obtained using the patterns learnt from few poisoned samples is good enough to precisely mask the BadNets trigger in the images. We envisage the use of ANTIDOTERT in an iterative manner, starting with strategy 1a and moving on to better correction strategies (1b, 1c, 2) as examples of poisoned inputs become available, which will help improve the runtime behavior of ANTIDOTERT.

## 5   Related Work

Most existing work is on detecting if a given model is poisoned and if so correcting the logic of the model. NeuralCleanse and STRIP (described earlier in Sect. 4 are the only ones to our knowledge which provide for runtime detection of inputs (and) correction of network behavior on them.

**Model Detection.** Backdoor detection techniques such as [21,23–25] rely on statistical analysis of the poisoned training dataset for deciding if a model is poisoned or trojaned. In [2], it is shown that activations of the last hidden neural network layer for clean and legitimate data and the activations for backdoor inputs form two distinct clusters. DeepInspect [3] learns the probability distribution of potential triggers from the queried model using a conditional GAN model, which can be used for inspecting whether the pre-trained neural network has been trojaned. Kolouri et al. [12] pre-define a set of input patterns that can reveal backdoor attacks, classifying the network as 'clean' or 'corrupted'. The TND (TrojanNet Detector) in [28] explores connections between Trojan attack and prediction-evasion adversarial attacks. In [29], a meta-classifier is trained that predicts whether a model is backdoored.

**Correction.** Different from the input correction method developed in this paper, existing defense techniques on neural network backdoor are focusing on re-training, fine-tuning or pruning [15–18,20,30]. These works end up with the fundamental and difficult neural network parameter selection problem, for effectively erasing the impact of backdoor triggers from the model without degrading (much) the model's overall performance. In contrast, with our technique, the effect on already correctly classified inputs is minimal. The work in [26] is the only other input-level repair that we are aware of. Unlike our technique, it is black box and therefore much more expensive. It repeatedly searches the area of an image for the position of the backdoor trigger, which is accomplished by placing a trigger blocker of the dominant colour in the image.

## 6   Conclusion

We presented runtime detection and correction techniques against poisoning attacks, that are based on neuron patterns mined from the neural network. We demonstrated that ANTIDOTERT performs effectively on the popular BadNets attacks (with a best of 93.54% accuracy) and is also able to improve the accuracy of the analyzed model under the more complex DFST attack (23.80%) which existing defenses cannot handle well. As ANTIDOTERT does not make permanent changes to the model, it does not significantly degrade the model on clean inputs. The results show ANTIDOTERT's potential as a lightweight runtime approach for the effective mitigation of backdoor attacks.

## References

1. Chattopadhay, A., Sarkar, A., Howlader, P., Balasubramanian, V.N.: Grad-cam++: generalized gradient-based visual explanations for deep convolutional networks. In: WACV, pp. 839–847. IEEE (2018)
2. Chen, B., et al.: Detecting backdoor attacks on deep neural networks by activation clustering. In: SafeAI@ AAAI (2019)

3. Chen, H., Fu, C., Zhao, J., Koushanfar, F.: DeepInspect: a black-box trojan detection and mitigation framework for deep neural networks. In: IJCAI, pp. 4658–4664 (2019)

4. Cheng, S., Liu, Y., Ma, S., Zhang, X.: Deep feature space trojan attack of neural networks by controlled detoxification. In: AAAI, vol. 35, pp. 1148–1156 (2021)

5. Gao, Y., Xu, C., Wang, D., Chen, S., Ranasinghe, D.C., Nepal, S.: STRIP: a defense against trojan attacks on deep neural networks. In: Proceedings of the 35th Annual Computer Security Applications Conference, pp. 113–125 (2019)

6. Goodfellow, I., Bengio, Y., Courville, A.: Deep Learning. MIT Press, Cambridge (2016)

7. Gopinath, D., Converse, H., Pasareanu, C., Taly, A.: Property inference for deep neural networks. In: International Conference on Automated Software Engineering (ASE), pp. 797–809. IEEE (2019)

8. Gu, T., Liu, K., Dolan-Gavitt, B., Garg, S.: BadNets: evaluating backdooring attacks on deep neural networks. IEEE Access **7**, 47230–47244 (2019)

9. Houben, S., Stallkamp, J., Salmen, J., Schlipsing, M., Igel, C.: Detection of traffic signs in real-world images: the German traffic sign detection benchmark. In: International Joint Conference on Neural Networks, no. 1288 (2013)

10. Huang, X., et al.: A survey of safety and trustworthiness of deep neural networks: verification, testing, adversarial attack and defence, and interpretability. Comput. Sci. Rev. **37**, 100270 (2020)

11. Katz, G., et al.: The Marabou framework for verification and analysis of deep neural networks. In: Dillig, I., Tasiran, S. (eds.) CAV 2019. LNCS, vol. 11561, pp. 443–452. Springer, Cham (2019). https://doi.org/10.1007/978-3-030-25540-4_26

12. Kolouri, S., Saha, A., Pirsiavash, H., Hoffmann, H.: Universal litmus patterns: revealing backdoor attacks in CNNs. In: CVPR, pp. 301–310 (2020)

13. Krizhevsky, A., Hinton, G., et al.: Learning multiple layers of features from tiny images (2009)

14. LeCun, Y., Bottou, L., Bengio, Y., Haffner, P.: Gradient-based learning applied to document recognition. Proc. IEEE **86**(11), 2278–2324 (1998)

15. Li, Y., Lyu, X., Koren, N., Lyu, L., Li, B., Ma, X.: Neural attention distillation: erasing backdoor triggers from deep neural networks. In: International Conference on Learning Representations (2020)

16. Li, Y., Zhai, T., Wu, B., Jiang, Y., Li, Z., Xia, S.: Rethinking the trigger of backdoor attack. arXiv preprint arXiv:2004.04692 (2020)

17. Liu, K., Dolan-Gavitt, B., Garg, S.: Fine-pruning: defending against backdooring attacks on deep neural networks. In: Bailey, M., Holz, T., Stamatogiannakis, M., Ioannidis, S. (eds.) RAID 2018. LNCS, vol. 11050, pp. 273–294. Springer, Cham (2018). https://doi.org/10.1007/978-3-030-00470-5_13

18. Liu, X., Li, F., Wen, B., Li, Q.: Removing backdoor-based watermarks in neural networks with limited data. In: 2020 25th International Conference on Pattern Recognition (ICPR), pp. 10149–10156. IEEE (2021)

19. Liu, Y., et al.: Trojaning attack on neural networks. In: 25th Annual Network and Distributed System Security Symposium, NDSS. The Internet Society (2018)

20. Liu, Y., Ma, X., Bailey, J., Lu, F.: Reflection backdoor: a natural backdoor attack on deep neural networks. In: Vedaldi, A., Bischof, H., Brox, T., Frahm, J.-M. (eds.) ECCV 2020. LNCS, vol. 12355, pp. 182–199. Springer, Cham (2020). https://doi.org/10.1007/978-3-030-58607-2_11

21. Liu, Y., Xie, Y., Srivastava, A.: Neural trojans. In: International Conference on Computer Design (ICCD), pp. 45–48. IEEE (2017)

22. Selvaraju, R.R., Cogswell, M., Das, A., Vedantam, R., Parikh, D., Batra, D.: Grad-CAM: visual explanations from deep networks via gradient-based localization. In: ICCV, pp. 618–626 (2017)
23. Steinhardt, J., Koh, P.W., Liang, P.: Certified defenses for data poisoning attacks. In: Proceedings of the 31st International Conference on Neural Information Processing Systems, pp. 3520–3532 (2017)
24. Tran, B., Li, J., Madry, A.: Spectral signatures in backdoor attacks. In: Advances in Neural Information Processing Systems, no. 31 (2018)
25. Turner, A., Tsipras, D., Madry, A.: Clean-label backdoor attacks (2018)
26. Udeshi, S., Peng, S., Woo, G., Loh, L., Rawshan, L., Chattopadhyay, S.: Model agnostic defence against backdoor attacks in machine learning. arXiv preprint arXiv:1908.02203 (2019)
27. Wang, B., et al.: Neural cleanse: identifying and mitigating backdoor attacks in neural networks. In: S&P, pp. 707–723. IEEE (2019)
28. Wang, R., Zhang, G., Liu, S., Chen, P.-Y., Xiong, J., Wang, M.: Practical detection of trojan neural networks: data-limited and data-free cases. In: Vedaldi, A., Bischof, H., Brox, T., Frahm, J.-M. (eds.) ECCV 2020. LNCS, vol. 12368, pp. 222–238. Springer, Cham (2020). https://doi.org/10.1007/978-3-030-58592-1_14
29. Xu, X., Wang, Q., Li, H., Borisov, N., Gunter, C.A., Li, B.: Detecting AI trojans using meta neural analysis. In: S&P, pp. 103–120. IEEE (2021)
30. Yao, Y., Li, H., Zheng, H., Zhao, B.Y.: Latent backdoor attacks on deep neural networks. In: Proceedings of the 2019 ACM SIGSAC Conference on Computer and Communications Security, pp. 2041–2055 (2019)

# Optimizing Prestate Copies in Runtime Verification of Function Postconditions

Jean-Christophe Filliâtre[1] and Clément Pascutto[1,2(✉)]

[1] Université Paris-Saclay, CNRS, ENS Paris-Saclay, Inria,
Laboratoire Méthodes Formelles, 91190 Gif-sur-Yvette, France
`jean-christophe.filliatre@cnrs.fr`
[2] Tarides, 75005 Paris, France
`clement@tarides.fr`

**Abstract.** In behavioural specifications of imperative languages, postconditions may refer to the prestate of the function, usually with an `old` operator. Therefore, code performing runtime verification has to record prestate values required to evaluate the postconditions, typically by copying part of the memory state, which causes severe verification overhead, both in memory and CPU time.

In this paper, we consider the problem of efficiently capturing prestates in the context of Ortac, a runtime assertion checking tool for OCaml. Our contribution is a postcondition transformation that reduces the subset of the prestate to copy. We formalize this transformation, and we provide proof that it is sound and improves the performance of the instrumented programs. We illustrate the benefits of this approach with a maze generator. Our benchmarks show that unoptimized instrumentation is not practicable, while our transformation restores performances similar to the program without any runtime check.

**Keywords:** Runtime assertion checking · OCaml · Optimized code generation · Memory management

## 1 Introduction

In behavioral specification languages for imperative languages, function postconditions may refer to the prestate of the function, typically using some `old` or `pre` operator, as in Eiffel [10], JML [3], or ACSL [2]. For instance, a function with a postcondition $x = \text{old } x + 1$ states that any call will increment the value of the variable $x$.

In order to perform runtime verification, one needs to be able to evaluate terms and predicates, such as `old` $x$ above, after function calls. The prestate, which `old` refers to, does not exist anymore. As a consequence, code instrumentations have to record any value required for the evaluation of the predicates involving `old`. A correct yet naive solution consists in copying the whole prestate.

In this paper, we consider the problem of efficiently capturing prestates in the context of Gospel, a behavioural specification language for OCaml [5], and

T. Dang and V. Stolz (Eds.): RV 2022, LNCS 13498, pp. 85–104, 2022.
https://doi.org/10.1007/978-3-031-17196-3_5

Ortac, a runtime assertion checking tool [6]. Ortac consumes a Gospel-annotated OCaml module interface and produces an instrumented wrapper around the module implementation. It operates in a black-box fashion without inspecting the original implementation of the module. Ortac is an open-source project available at https://github.com/ocaml-gospel/ortac.

Gospel, like OCaml, abstracts over the addresses of the values it manipulates and provides a structural equality to compare values, rather than a physical equality. While this makes the specifications easy to read and write, it makes copies immediately necessary for any term that contains mutable data, as recording their address is not sufficient to evaluate the term in the prestate: all the memory contents available from that address are necessary. For instance, if $a$ is an array, the postcondition $a = \texttt{old } a$ states that the contents of array $a$ has been restored to its prestate value. The physical address of the array is not relevant to the equality predicate. Because the function may have modified its contents, copying the whole array (in-depth, recursively) is necessary before we make the function call in the instrumented code.

Code instrumentation under these constraints can cause severe verification overhead, both in memory and CPU time. Moreover, OCaml memory management uses a garbage collector (GC), so programs do not explicitly allocate or free memory. Instead, the program triggers the GC whenever it needs additional memory. Each run incrementally traverses the memory to determine which chunks are still in use, possibly moves them and then frees the rest. Therefore, the copies introduced by Ortac induce a garbage collection overhead that adds to the memory allocation overhead. In fact, naive instrumentation not only results in high runtime verification overhead, but can also change the complexity of the algorithm, threatening its scalability.

In this work, we propose some methods to optimize the runtime verification of logical assertions containing `old` by reducing the subset of the memory that one needs to copy in order to compute these checks. We formalize the semantics of a subset of OCaml and Gospel and provide proof that these transformations are sound and improve the performance of the instrumented programs.

We start by introducing a reduced working language, along with a formalization of its semantics (Sect. 2). Then we propose some code transformations on this language to help reduce the verification overhead and allocations (Sect. 3) and show that these can be critical in practice through an example and benchmarks (Sect. 4). We conclude with related efforts toward more efficient runtime assertion checking (Sect. 5) and some insights on future work and perspectives (Sect. 6).

## 2   A Minimal Language with Contracts

In this section, we introduce a simple programming language to model the behaviour of Gospel-annotated OCaml code. We believe this language is generic enough to both enable detailed reasoning about semantics and memory models, and abstract away from OCaml and Gospel, so our techniques can be applied in other imperative programming languages where the same issues arise as well.

$$
\begin{array}{lll}
e ::= & () & \textit{unit} \\
& \mid\; n & \textit{integer literal} \\
& \mid\; x & \textit{variable} \\
& \mid\; \textbf{let } x_1,\dots,x_n = e \textbf{ in } e & \textit{variable binding} \\
& \mid\; e; e & \textit{sequence} \\
& \mid\; (e,\dots,e) & \textit{tuple construction} \\
& \mid\; \pi_i(t) & \textit{tuple getter} \\
& \mid\; \textbf{create } e\ e & \textit{array construction} \\
& \mid\; e.(e) & \textit{array getter} \\
& \mid\; e.(e) \leftarrow e & \textit{array setter} \\
& \mid\; \textbf{length } e & \textit{array length} \\
& \mid\; \textbf{copy } e & \textit{deep copy} \\
& \mid\; \textbf{assert } e\ \{p\} & \textit{logical assertion}
\end{array}
$$

$$
\begin{array}{llll}
 & & t ::= & () \quad \textit{unit} \\
p ::= t = t & \textit{equality} & \mid\; n & \textit{integer literal} \\
\mid\; p \wedge p & \textit{conjunction} & \mid\; x & \textit{variable} \\
\mid\; p \vee p & \textit{disjunction} & \mid\; t.(t) & \textit{array getter} \\
\mid\; \textbf{forall } i.\ t \le i \le t \rightarrow p\ \textit{universal} & & \mid\; \textbf{length } t & \textit{array length} \\
\mid\; \textbf{exists } i.\ t \le i \le t \wedge p\ \textit{existential} & & \mid\; \pi_i(t) & \textit{tuple getter} \\
& & \mid\; \textbf{old } t & \textit{prestate reference}
\end{array}
$$

**Fig. 1.** Language syntax

**Syntax.** The syntax is available in Fig. 1. A program consists of an *expression*. The expression language $e$ includes immediate values (integers and unit), as well as variables bound to immediate values or addresses in memory, that can contain mutable (arrays) or immutable (tuples) data, to reflect the variety of cases that occur in usual programming languages. Similarly to OCaml, the language does not expose any direct manipulation of addresses or any explicit memory management; allocations are implicitly made when creating a new array or tuple.

On top of these traditional programming constructs, our language provides an **assert** $e$ $\{p\}$ instruction. This instruction models the postconditions of a specification language for logical *predicates* $p$. Predicates provide an equality predicate over *terms*, logical conjunction and disjunction, and existential and universal quantifiers. Finally, terms $t$ contain immediate values, variables, and tuples and array accessors. They also feature the **old** operator that motivates this work, and which semantics is formalised in the next section.

As explained in the introduction, our main interest lies in the runtime verification of function postconditions. Although this language does not provide functions, we can model functions calls in simple scenarios of the form:

$$
e_1;\ \textbf{assert } e_2\ \{p\}
$$

In this scenario, the expression $e_1$ models the code that is executed prior to the function call. It sets up the memory prestate and introduces variables to refer to it. The predicate $p$ is a postcondition to the function call, and expression $e_2$ models the call itself. We still operate in a black-box context, as predicate $p$ has no access to the code $e_2$ itself, but solely to the resulting poststate.

**Typing.** Like OCaml, our language is statically typed, *i.e.* expressions and terms are statically assigned types before the evaluation. There are four primitive types $\tau$ in the system: unit (the type with only one value), integer, homogeneous arrays, and heterogeneous tuples.

$$
\begin{aligned}
\tau ::= \ &\texttt{unit} &&\textit{(unit)} \\
\mid \ &\texttt{int} &&\textit{(integer)} \\
\mid \ &\tau \ \texttt{array} &&\textit{(array)} \\
\mid \ &\tau \times \tau \times \cdots \times \tau &&\textit{(tuple)}
\end{aligned}
$$

We introduce a typing judgment $\Gamma \vdash e : \tau$, which means that $e$ has type $\tau$ in the typing environment $\Gamma$, which associates variables to types. The inference rules for this judgment are standard and should follow intuition; they are available in the appendix.

**Semantics.** In this section, we define a big-step semantics for our language. Program evaluations produce values $v$ which can be the unit value, an integer, or an address in memory.

$$
\begin{aligned}
v ::= \ &() &&\textit{unit} \\
\mid \ &n &&\textit{integer} \\
\mid \ &a &&\textit{address}
\end{aligned}
$$

Because our language is imperative, the evaluation of an expression may read or modify the *state* of the program at any point of the execution. Program states associate variables to values on one hand (function $V$), and addresses in memory to sequences of values that represent arrays or tuples (function $M$). Note that $V$ is immutable as variables are immutable.

$$
\begin{aligned}
V &::= x \mapsto v \\
M &::= a \mapsto [v, v, \dots, v] \\
S &::= V \times M
\end{aligned}
$$

For the sake of conciseness, we simplify the notation such that $S = (V, M)$ is always assumed, *e.g.* $V$ (resp. $V'$, resp. $V_1$) is the variable function associated to the state $S$ (resp. $S'$, resp. $S_1$) in the rest of the article.

We use notation $S, e \leadsto M', v$ to denote that the evaluation of the expression $e$ in the state $S$ succeeds and produces the value $v$ in a new memory $M'$. The big-step evaluation rules are simple and also follow intuition; they are available in full in the appendix. We highlight a couple of rules here: E-CREATE and E-GET, which demonstrate how expressions can interact with the memory, by reading or allocating, and E-ASSERT, which shows how program expressions and logical predicates interact with each other.

$$\frac{S, e_2 \rightsquigarrow M_2, v \quad (V, M_2), e_1 \rightsquigarrow M_1, n \quad a \notin dom(M_1) \quad M' = M_1[a \mapsto [v, v, \ldots, v]]}{S, \mathtt{create}\ e_1\ e_2 \rightsquigarrow M', a} \quad \text{(E-CREATE)}$$

$$\frac{S, e_2 \rightsquigarrow S_2, n_0 \quad (V, M_2), e_1 \rightsquigarrow M_1, a \quad 0 \leq n_0 \leq n - 1 \quad M_1(a) = [v_0, \ldots, v_{n-1}]}{S, e_1 \,.\, (e_2) \rightsquigarrow M_1, v_{n_0}} \quad \text{(E-GET)}$$

The $\mathtt{assert}\ e\ \{p\}$ construct models the verification of the logical postcondition $p$ of the code $e$.

$$\frac{S, e \rightsquigarrow M', v \quad S, (V, M') \models p}{S, \mathtt{assert}\ e\ \{p\} \rightsquigarrow M', ()} \quad \text{(E-ASSERT)}$$

For its evaluation to succeed in state $S$, the evaluation of $e$ in $S$ must succeed and lead to a state $S'$, and the predicate $p$ must hold with prestate $S$ and poststate $V, M'$. In the following, we define $S, S' \models p$. It is straightforward for most predicate constructs, but requires care to properly handle structural equality.

*Predicate Evaluation and Equality Semantics.* An interesting specificity of the Gospel language is the semantics of its equality predicate. In fact, the logical domain of predicates and terms is not aware of addresses at all; we reason directly on the *contents* of the memory instead of their location. This follows OCaml's idioms, as addresses tend to be hidden to the developers and the standard library provides a polymorphic, structural equality. In particular, this means that comparing arrays a and b with the Boolean expression a = b will compare the contents of the arrays (recursively if necessary), rather than their addresses in memory.

Our programming language also gives this semantics to the equality predicate. Terms and predicates do not understand program values (which contain addresses); instead, they manipulate *logical values*, where addresses are recursively resolved to their contents (arrays or tuples).

$$\begin{aligned}
lv ::=\ &() &&\textit{unit} \\
&|\ n &&\textit{integer} \\
&|\ [lv, lv, \ldots, lv] &&\textit{array or tuple}
\end{aligned}$$

We provide resolution rules to transition from *values* to *logical values* in a given memory. When $v$ resolves to $lv$ in memory $M$, we note $M, v \rightarrowtail lv$.

$$\frac{}{M, () \rightarrowtail ()} \quad \text{(R-UNIT)} \qquad\qquad \frac{}{M, n \rightarrowtail n} \quad \text{(R-INT)}$$

$$\frac{M(a) = [v_0, v_1, \ldots, v_{n-1}] \quad M, v_0 \rightarrowtail lv_0 \quad M, v_1 \rightarrowtail lv_1 \quad \ldots \quad M, v_{n-1} \rightarrowtail lv_{n-1}}{M, a \rightarrowtail [lv_0, lv_1, \ldots, lv_{n-1}]} \quad \text{(R-ADDR)}$$

The rule for the equality predicate is now straightforward: two terms are equal iff they evaluate to the same logical value. We note $[\![t]\!]_S^{S'}$ to denote the evaluation of the term $t$ with prestate $S$ and poststate $S'$.

$$\frac{[\![t_1]\!]_S^{S'} = lv_1 \qquad [\![t_2]\!]_S^{S'} = lv_2 \qquad lv_1 = lv_2}{S, S' \models t_1 = t_2} \quad \text{(P-EQUAL)}$$

The logical value resolution also lets us axiomatize the program function copy as follows. Any function that implements this specification qualifies for the soundness proofs we provide. We note $M \sqsubseteq M_c$ to denote that $M$ is a subset of $M_c : \forall x, x \in dom(M) \implies x \in dom(M_c) \wedge M(x) = M_c(x)$.

**Definition 1 (Copy axiomatization).** *The evaluation of* copy *always succeeds:*

$$S, \text{copy } t \rightsquigarrow M_c, v'$$

*with* $M \sqsubseteq M_c$.

*Moreover, the resulting value resolved to the same logical value as the copied one. In other words, if* $S, t \rightsquigarrow M, v$ *and* $M, v \twoheadrightarrow lv$, *then*

$$M_c, v' \twoheadrightarrow lv$$

*Term Evaluation.* When evaluating terms, the semantics is similar to the one of expressions, but they now apply to logical values rather than program values. The value resolution needs to be applied whenever a program variable is referenced in a term, so the evaluation now returns a logical value. Recall that terms are evaluated in the poststate of assert expressions, so we use $S'$ to fetch the values in the context.

$$\frac{V'(x) = v \qquad M', v \twoheadrightarrow lv}{[\![x]\!]_S^{S'} = lv} \quad \text{(T-VAR)}$$

Note that variables are immutable, *i.e.* when considering assert $e\ \{p\}$, expression $e$ does not change the variable bindings for $p$ (see E-ASSERT). In other words, $V = V'$, so picking one or the other does not make any difference. However, the memory $M$ may be modified by $e$ (*e.g.* when using assignment or create), so resolving the values in $M'$ is crucial. Consider for instance assert $a.(0) \leftarrow 1\ \{a = b\}$: the program values for variables $a$ and $b$ are the same in the pre- and poststate (the arrays are not moved in memory) but the contents of $a$ has been modified and thus evaluating $a = b$ indeed requires the poststate.

While terms are generally evaluated in the poststate, the old operator lets you refer to the prestate. The semantics is expressed by evaluating the term in the prestate $S$ only, rather than in the couple $S, S'$.

$$\frac{[\![t]\!]_S^S = lv}{[\![\text{old } t]\!]_S^{S'} = lv} \quad \text{(T-OLD)}$$

Note that because of this semantics, old captures the logical values bound to variables in the prestate (arbitrarily big values), rather than the program values (simple addresses). The other rules for the judgments $S, S' \models p$ and $[\![t]\!]_S^{S'}$ are straightforward and can be found in their full version in the appendix.

A consequence of rules T-VAR and T-OLD is that old can always be propagated downwards to the variables. For instance,

$$[\![\text{old } (x.(0) + y) - 1]\!]_S^{S'} = [\![(\text{old } x).(0) + \text{old } y - 1]\!]_S^{S'}$$

Surprisingly, this is not what we are going to do. We are rather going to do the exact opposite!

## 3    Capturing the Prestate

In this section, we present two program transformations that enable the evaluation of predicates involving prestate captures. Our transformations operate on constructs assert $e$ $\{p\}$. To do so, they can inspect predicate $p$ but not expression $e$. This constraint is consistent with our idea of modelling function calls with the assert construct. For the sake of simplicity, we suppose that old terms in $p$ are not nested, *i.e.* in every term of the form old $t$, term $t$ does not contain any other old operator. A quick transformation consisting in simply removing any old in those terms ensures this property and is trivially correct considering the rule T-OLD we discussed previously.

We first discuss a transformation that introduces the copied data in the memory and discuss implementation tactics for an optimized copy function (Sect. 3.1). Then, we present a transformation of the predicates that reduces the memory space that needs to be copied (Sect. 3.2).

### 3.1   Introducing Copies

Our first program transformation introduces the copies necessary for the execution of the terms containing old. This operation, which we note $T_c$, performs a morphism over the program expressions, and transforms the assert expressions so that the predicate does not contain any prestate reference anymore. We note $x_1, \ldots, x_n$ fresh variables (that are not bound in any state), so that we don't introduce collisions with existing data.

$$T_c(\text{ assert } e \ \{p\} \ ) := \text{let } x_1, \ldots, x_n = \text{copy } (t_1, \ldots, t_n) \text{ in} \\ \text{assert } T_c(e) \ \{p[\text{old } t_i \leftarrow x_i]\}$$

$$T_c(\quad \text{length } e \quad ) := \text{length } T_c(e)$$
$$T_c(\quad e_1.(e_2) \quad ) := T_c(e_1).(T_c(e_2))$$
$$T_c(\quad \cdots \quad ) := \cdots \textit{(similarly for other constructs)}$$

Instead, the terms $t_i$ under old (note that these are also valid *expressions* since they do not contain other old) are evaluated in the program space, prior to the assertion, and their result is copied into the variables $x_i$. The old $t_i$ terms in the predicate of the assertion are then substituted with the copied values $x_i$. For instance, consider the following example, where $a$ and $b$ are two arrays of arrays.

```
1    assert a.(0) <- b { length (old a.(0)) = (old a.(1)).(2) }
```

The program is transformed into the following one:

```
1    let x1 = copy (a.(0), a.(1)) in
2    assert a.(0) <- b { length x1 = x2.(2) }
```

*Soundness.* This transformation is sound, meaning that it leaves the program semantics (and in particular the validity of the assert constructs) unchanged.

**Theorem 1 ($T_c$ preserves the program semantics).** *If a program $e$ successfully evaluates to $v_1$ in $S_0$, which logically resolves to $lv$ in the resulting state,*

$$S_0, e \rightsquigarrow M_1, v_1 \text{ and } M_1, v_1 \rightarrowtail lv$$

*then for any state $S_0'$ such that $S_0 \sqsubseteq S_0'$, the transformed program $T_c(e)$ successfully evaluates to $v_1'$ in $S_0'$, which resolves to the same logical value $lv$ in the resulting state,*

$$S_0', T_c(e) \rightsquigarrow M_1', v_1' \text{ and } M_1', v_1' \rightarrowtail lv$$

*and we have $S_1 \sqsubseteq S_1'$.*

*Proof.* We prove this theorem by induction on the number of old contained in the transformed expression $e$. Because of space limitations, we will only show the assert case here, as it contains the critical postcondition verification. The proofs for the other expression cases follow the same structure.

*Case* assert. We know $S_0, \text{assert } e \; \{p\} \rightsquigarrow M_1, v_1$ and $M_1, v_1 \rightarrowtail lv$ and $S_0 \sqsubseteq S_0'$.

**Lemma 1 (Substitutions in predicates).** *Given two program states such that $S_0 \sqsubseteq S_1$, in which $v_0$ and $v_1$ resolve to the same logical value, i.e.,*

$$M_0, v_0 \rightarrowtail lv \text{ and } M_1, v_1 \rightarrowtail lv,$$

*binding a variable $x$ to either $v_0$ or $v_1$ in a predicate evaluation does not change the validity judgment, that is*

$$V_0[x \leftarrow v_0] \models p \implies V_0[x \leftarrow v_1] \models p.$$

The idea for the proof of this lemma is simple: since the predicate and term evaluation only manipulate logical values, substituting identical logical values does not change their evaluation.

We introduce $x_1, \ldots, x_n$ some fresh variables. We now prove the following three sub-goals:

$$S_0, \text{copy } (t_1, \ldots, t_n) \rightsquigarrow M_c, a \text{ with } M_c(a) = [v_{c_0}, v_{c_1}, \ldots, v_{c_n}] \tag{1}$$

$$(V_0[x_i \rightarrow v_{c_i}], M_c), T_c(e) \rightsquigarrow M_1', () \tag{2}$$

$$(V_0[x_i \rightarrow v_{c_i}], M_c), M_1' \models p[\text{old } t_i \leftarrow x_i] \tag{3}$$

We note $lv_{c_i}$ the logical values corresponding to $v_{c_i}$: $M_c, v_i \looparrowright lv_{c_i}$.

1. This goal follows directly from our axiomatization of the `copy` function in Definition 1. We also get that $M_0 \sqsubseteq M_c$, and $lv_i = lv_{c_i}$, which we will use for the next goals.
2. For this goal, we apply the induction hypothesis on $T_c(e)$, as $e$ contains strictly less `old` expressions than `assert` $e \ \{p\}$.
3. This result is obtained by applying Lemma 1, since $lv_i = lv_{c_i}$ under Definition 1.

We may now apply the rule E-ASSERT to the goals (2) and (3) and get the following result:

$$(V_0[x_i \rightarrow v_{c_i}], M_c), \text{assert } T_c(e) \ \{p[\text{old } t_i \leftarrow x_i]\} \rightsquigarrow M_1', ()$$

Now we can conclude the proof by applying the rule E-LET-IN to this result, and the one provided by (1), which gives us

$$S_0', T_c(\text{assert } e \ \{p\}) \rightsquigarrow M_1', ()$$

since

$$T_c(\text{assert } e \ \{p\}) := \text{let } x_1, \ldots, x_n = \text{copy } (t_1, \ldots, t_n) \text{ in} \\ \text{assert } T_c(e) \ \{p[\text{old } t_i \leftarrow x_i]\}$$

And $M_1', () \looparrowright ()$ trivially holds under R-UNIT. $\qquad\square$

**Copying with Sharing.** A first optimization rises from the observation that the copied terms $t_1, \ldots, t_n$ may refer to overlapping portions of the memory. Therefore, deep-copying them recursively as described previously results in copying the same memory chunks multiple times. For instance, in the example described previously, the `assert` leads to copying $a.(0)$ and $a.(1)$ independently. However, these values may be aliases, which would lead to copying the underlying array twice.

In order to avoid duplicating the copies of memory chunks, we use a sharing-preserving implementation of `copy`: the underlying memory structure of the copied value is maintained in the copy, and shared values are only copied once. We can then copy all the required sub-terms simultaneously in a tuple, so aliases in the original data remain aliases in the copy. In practice, we use the OCaml serialization module `Marshal` to encode, and then immediately decode, the tuple of values.

Although the tuple construction introduces an extra allocation, this cost has shown to be negligible compared to the gain provided by the sharing preservation, both between sub-terms, and inside sub-terms themselves. This ensures that we copy shared chunks of memory only once, regardless of the aliasing configuration.

**Copy of Immutable Data.** The second optimisation of the `copy` function is provided by the type information. Recall that our language provides mutable arrays, but also immutable tuples. We perform an analysis based on the expression types in order to determine whether the evaluation of an expression results in a mutable or an immutable value. A value is immutable iff its type consists of immediate values, or tuples of immutable types, that is, in other words, if its type does not involve arrays. For those types, the language does not provide any mutating functions, so the relevant memory cannot be changed by the evaluation of an expression.

$$\frac{}{immutable(\texttt{unit})}\ \text{(I-Unit)} \qquad \frac{}{immutable(\texttt{int})}\ \text{(I-Int)}$$

$$\frac{immutable(\tau_1) \qquad immutable(\tau_2) \qquad \ldots \qquad immutable(\tau_n)}{immutable(\tau_1 \times \tau_2 \times \ldots \times \tau_n)}\ \text{(I-Tuple)}$$

When we apply the transformation, we use this inference to determine if a call to `copy` is required, *i.e.* if the value contains mutable components. If not, we simply bind the value in the prestate to a variable.

## 3.2  Moving `old` Upwards to Copy Less

When the prestate reference is a sub-term of the total term, it is interesting to consider *how* this sub-term will be used in the rest of the evaluation. Consider for instance the simple postcondition `length (old a)` when $a$ is an array. After applying the transformation exposed in Sect. 3.1, the evaluation will copy the whole array $a$. Instead, we could have computed its length directly in the prestate and only remember this value for the evaluation in the poststate.

Although the semantics of the terms containing prestate references virtually pushes the `old` operator downwards to variables (see Sect. 2), the second transformation we propose actually suggests the opposite. Rather than considering what values we *need* to capture in the prestate in order to compute the poststate, we try to push as many computations as we can in the prestate, by determining which terms *cannot* be computed in the prestate. Note that while this will save memory and copies, it can lead to computing values that might not actually be useful in the poststate due to the program output.

This new transformation, which we note $T_o$, is meant to be applied before $T_c$. It starts from the existing `old` sub-terms and propagates the `old` operator upwards in the terms until it encounters a variable that refers to the poststate, with the exception of immutable values. It is defined in terms of the following rewriting rules, written $T_o(t) \sim t$, until no further rewriting is possible (Fig. 2). The rule (O-Var) only applies for program variables, not variables introduced by quantifiers[1].

---

[1] In Ortac, we perform a more aggressive transformation, which moves `old` beyond quantifiers when possible. In this paper, however, we keep the presentation simple by limiting the transformation to terms.

$$\frac{}{() \sim \textbf{old } ()} \text{ (O-Unit)} \qquad \frac{}{n \sim \textbf{old } n} \text{ (O-Int)}$$

$$\frac{t_1 \sim t_1' \quad t_2 \sim t_2'}{t_1 . (t_2) \sim \textbf{old } (t_1' . (t_2'))} \text{ (O-Get)} \qquad \frac{t \sim \textbf{old } t'}{\pi_i(t) \sim \textbf{old } (\pi_i(t'))} \text{ (O-Pi)}$$

$$\frac{t \sim \textbf{old } t'}{\textbf{length } t \sim \textbf{old } (\textbf{length } t')} \text{ (O-Length)} \qquad \frac{}{\textbf{old } t \sim \textbf{old } t} \text{ (O-Old)}$$

$$\frac{t \sim \textbf{old } t'}{\textbf{old } t \sim \textbf{old } t'} \text{ (O-Old-Id)} \qquad \frac{\Gamma \vdash x : \tau \quad immutable(\tau)}{x \sim \textbf{old } x} \text{ (O-Var)}$$

**Fig. 2.** The $\sim$ relation defining $T_o$.

**Proof of Soundness.** We prove that $\sim$ preserves the terms semantics. Since $T_o$ follows this relation, $T_o$ also preserves the program semantics.

**Theorem 2 ($\sim$ preserves the terms semantics).** *For all states $S$ and $S'$ such that $S \sqsubseteq S'$,*

$$t \sim t' \implies [\![t]\!]_S^{S'} = [\![t']\!]_S^{S'}$$

*Proof.* The proof of this theorem is straightforward for most rules. The rules always add or move `old` operators, and these only modify the semantics of a term if it implies variables, as discussed in Sect. 2. Therefore, we only consider the proof for the case O-Var here.

**Lemma 2. (*immutable* captures immutability).** *If a term has an immutable type, then evaluating this term in the prestate only does not change its semantics: if $S \sqsubseteq S'$, then*

$$\frac{\Gamma \vdash t : \tau \quad immutable(\tau)}{[\![t]\!]_S^{S'} = [\![t]\!]_S^S}$$

The idea of the proof for this lemma is provided by the constructions of the language. Recall that immutable types are the ones that do not involve arrays, but only immediate values and tuples. There is no construct that allows us to modify a tuple, and the type-checking ensures that one cannot use the array setter on an address corresponding to a tuple.

Let us note $lv = [\![x]\!]_S^{S'}$. We know $\Gamma \vdash t : \tau$ and $immutable(\tau)$. We can conclude by applying Lemma 2 and T-Old.

$$\frac{\dfrac{\Gamma \vdash t : \tau \quad immutable(\tau)}{[\![x]\!]_S^S = [\![x]\!]_S^{S'}} \text{ Lemma 2}}{[\![\textbf{old } x]\!]_S^{S'} = [\![x]\!]_S^{S'}} \text{ T-Old}$$

$\square$

**Proof of Optimisation.** It is important to note that, since the term constructions only access the program memory but never modify it, this transformation can only reduce (or leave unchanged) the memory space involved in the evaluation of the term. More precisely, the transformed program only requires to access a subset of the memory addresses it originally needed, and therefore the amount of copied data is no greater.

## 4    Example and Benchmarks

In this section, we use our optimisation techniques and apply them to an existing program, implemented in OCaml and annotated with Gospel specifications. We demonstrate that a simple program and specification are sufficient for this optimisation to be critical to the performance and usability of the program.

### 4.1    A Maze Generator

Our stress-test is a program that takes an integer $n$ as input and generates a perfect, random maze on a $n^2$ square grid. The algorithm is as follows:

1. Create a list of all walls and create a set for each cell (each set contains just that one cell).
2. For each wall, in some random order,
   - if the cells divided by this wall belong to distinct sets,
     (a) remove the current wall from the list;
     (b) join the sets of the formerly divided cells.

The set of sets of cells maintain the connected components of the grid, so at the end of each iteration, we remove a wall iff it joins otherwise disconnected components. At the end of the iterations, there is only one remaining connected component; therefore, the remaining walls in the list constitute a perfect maze.

We implement the set of cells involved in this algorithm using a union-find data structure [1]. Our implementation of the union-find exposes the interface reproduced in Fig. 3, which we instrument to verify at runtime.

The type t is the type representing an instance of the data structure. Our module will be operating in place, so this type is mutable, which is reflected by the Gospel clause ephemeral.

The function create creates a fresh structure containing integers in singletons, num_classes returns the number of disjoint sets in the data structure, and find returns the representative element of a set. These three functions do not perform any effects (*i.e.* they do not modify the union-find structure), do not raise exceptions, and always terminate. Therefore, they are considered pure by Gospel and can be used to specify other functions further.

Finally, the function union performs the union of two sets in the structure. We will focus on this function in the rest of this benchmark. Its contract states that it can modify the data structure with the modifies clause. Because the type of union-find is mutable, and this function potentially modifies it, executing properties that refer to the old version of the structure will require copies, and the transformations we proposed in Sect. 3 are relevant in this example.

```
1  type t
2  (*@ ephemeral *)
3
4  val create : int -> t
5  (*@ uf = create n
6      checks n >= 0 *)
7
8  val num_classes : t -> int
9  (*@ pure *)
10
11 val find : t -> int -> int
12 (*@ pure *)
13
14 val union : t -> int -> int -> unit
15 (*@ union uf i j
16     modifies uf
17     requires 0 <= i < size uf
18     requires 0 <= j < size uf
19     ensures num_classes uf <= num_classes (old uf)
20     ensures find (old uf) i <> find (old uf) j
21            -> num_classes uf = num_classes (old uf) - 1 *)
```

**Fig. 3.** Union-find module interface (uf.mli).

## 4.2  Runtime Verification with Ortac

We use Ortac to generate OCaml code that checks these contracts at runtime. More precisely, the generated implementation performs the following operations:

1. Check the preconditions and fail if they do not hold or raise an exception.
2. Evaluate the terms under old operators, and copy their values into fresh variables.
3. Call the function union and fail if it raises an exception.
4. Replace the terms precomputed in Step 2. with their value in the postconditions and check them, then fail if they do not hold or raise an exception.

**Unoptimised Version.** In the unoptimized version, the specifications are considered as they were written by the user. There are four occurrences of the old operator, and all four of them refer to the old version of uf. The generated code is of the following form:

```
1  let union uf i j =
2    if not (0 <= i <= size uf) then fail ();
3    if not (0 <= j <= size uf) then fail ();
4    let old_1, old_2, old_3, old_4 = copy (uf, uf, uf, uf) in
5    (try union uf i j with _ -> fail ());
6    if not (num_classes uf <= num_classes old_1) then fail ();
7    if not (not (find old_2 i <> find old_3 j)
8           || num_classes uf = num_classes old_4 - 1)
9    then fail ();
```

When the `copy` function preserves sharing (see Sect. 3.1), the copy operation on line 4 only copies `uf` once, and `old_1`, `old_2`, `old_3`, and `old_4` are aliases. This does not allocate memory for every occurrence of `uf`, and does not re-explore the memory either. In fact, this is equivalent to just copying `uf` once in a fresh variable and using this variable for each occurrence.

**Optimized Version.** In the optimised version, although the user can still write the specifications in the way that feels the most natural to them, `ortac` pre-processes the terms to propagate the `old` operator, as explained in Sect. 3.2. Ortac automatically rewrites the terms as if the user wrote the following post-conditions:

```
1   ensures num_classes uf <= old (num_classes uf)
2   ensures old (find uf i <> find uf j)
3           -> num_classes uf = old (num_classes uf - 1)
```

This rewriting effectively moves to the prestate some computations previously executed in the poststate. Therefore, it only triggers a copy of the result of the computations (two integers and one Boolean in this case) instead of the context necessary for the execution (here, the whole union-find structure). The instrumentation generated by `ortac` now has the following form:

```
1   let union uf i j =
2     if not (0 <= i <= size uf) then fail ();
3     if not (0 <= j <= size uf) then fail ();
4     let old_1, old_2, old_3 = copy (
5       num_classes uf,
6       find uf i <> find uf j,
7       num_classes uf - 1)
8     in
9     (try union uf i j with _ -> fail ());
10    if not (num_classes uf <= old_1) then fail ();
11    if not (not old_2 || num_classes uf = old_3) then fail ();
```

### 4.3   Benchmarks

We run our maze generator with multiple values of $n$, and for each value, we gather the execution time, the number of garbage collections, and the cumulative amount of data copied by `copy` during the whole maze generation. We present the results in Fig. 4. These results show that naive instrumentations of the code make it impracticable for large values of $n$, which timed out after one hour of execution. On the other hand, the optimised version significantly reduces the cost of the verifications to a constant factor no larger than 2. This is permitted by the limited amount of data copied and limited use of the GC, which can be costly.

*About Complexity.* Recall that the maze generation calls `union` until there is only one remaining set (*i.e.* exactly $n^2 - 1$ times), so its complexity when invoked with

| $n$ | Instrumentation | Time (s) | GC runs | Copies (MB) |
|---|---|---|---|---|
| 100 | None | 0.002 6 | 0 | - |
| | No optimization | 8.6 | 952 | 763 |
| | Shared copies | 2.0 | 260 | 190 |
| | + old propagation | **0.006** | **0** | **0.038** |
| 200 | None | 0.012 | 0 | - |
| | No optimization | 120 | 13 333 | 12 207 |
| | Shared copies | 30 | 4 444 | 3 050 |
| | + old propagation | **0.032** | **2** | **0.15** |
| 400 | None | 0.088 | 1 | - |
| | No optimization | 2 100 | 58 664 | 195 315 |
| | Shared copies | 680 | 31 860 | 48 829 |
| | + old propagation | **0.19** | **2** | **0.61** |
| 800 | None | 0.46 | 4 | - |
| | No optimization | $\infty$ | $\infty$ | $\infty$ |
| | Shared copies | $\infty$ | $\infty$ | $\infty$ |
| | + old propagation | **0.89** | **4** | **2.4** |
| 1600 | None | 2.2 | 5 | - |
| | No optimization | $\infty$ | $\infty$ | $\infty$ |
| | Shared copies | $\infty$ | $\infty$ | $\infty$ |
| | + old propagation | **3.9** | **5** | **9.8** |
| 3200 | None | 11 | 5 | - |
| | No optimization | $\infty$ | $\infty$ | $\infty$ |
| | Shared copies | $\infty$ | $\infty$ | $\infty$ |
| | + old propagation | **19** | **6** | **39** |

**Fig. 4.** The results were obtained by running our benchmarks on an i7-1165G7 @ 2.80 GHz CPU, with 16 GB of RAM using the OCaml 4.14.0 compiler. Each value is obtained as the average of 10 runs.

size $n$ is $O(n^2 \times uf(n))$, where $uf(n)$ is the complexity of union. When union-find is properly implemented, $uf(n) = O(\alpha(n)) \approx O(1)$, so the complexity of the maze generation is $O(n^2)$ in the un-instrumented version.

However, when copying the entire union-find structure (no optimisation and shared copies only), the instrumented union now needs to copy a structure of size $n^2$. This makes the total maze generation complexity $O(n^4)$, which is not practicable. Finally, the old propagation optimisation does not require copying this much data but instead copies a fixed amount at each call (two integers and one Boolean), so the original complexity of the program is restored.

## 5   Related Work

The efficient evaluation of old terms in runtime assertion checking is a well-known and difficult problem, for which there is still room for improvement. In the general case, most tools copy the whole memory state before the call to the function [7,11], while acknowledging the flaws of this approach.

ACSL [2] generalises the old feature by introducing an \at(t, L) operator, that lets the user specify arbitrary locations L in the code, rather than restricting it to the function prestate. This leads to possibly worse performance issues with even more states being captured. While initial implementations of E-ACSL [13] used to only perform a shallow copy of the variable contents, which is incorrect in most cases, more recent implementations provide a hybrid method to reduce the copied memory space [12], but this approach has not been detailed yet.

It is also worth mentioning that, as noted in [4], in the presence of preconditions, the evaluation and copy of the old terms are meant to be guarded by these preconditions. Accordingly, Ortac only evaluates those once the corresponding preconditions are successfully verified.

Previous work have also explored other optimizations for runtime assertion checkers, for instance providing efficient representation of integers [8] or improving the verification of modifies clauses [9]. Regarding the former, Ortac benefits from zarith, which only switches to arbitrary-precision integers when machine integers are not large enough. Regarding the latter, Ortac assumes that user-provided modifies clauses are correct and even uses them to optimize the copies. Verifying such clauses is still future work for Ortac.

# 6   Conclusion and Future Work

In this paper, we have presented the optimizations performed by Ortac, a runtime assertion checking tool for OCaml, to mitigate the cost of copying prestate values in postcondition verification. We showed the benefits of this approach with proof and a practical evaluation.

This paper simplified the programming and logical languages compared to the actual implementation in OCaml and Gospel to make the presentation amenable. Ortac goes beyond this paper. First, it moves old upwards in predicates as well, including quantifiers, local variables, and user-defined predicates and functions. Second, Gospel includes a modifies clause, which Ortac uses to know whether it can move a old beyond a program variable. When doing so, Ortac assumes that all aliases in input variables correctly appear in user-provided modifies clauses.

There are several perspectives to extend this work. First, OCaml values do not carry any type information at runtime. Therefore, the copy function cannot use the information that a strict subterm has some immutable type to avoid the copy and keep a pointer to the original value instead. In the future, we plan to implement a smarter type-directed copy function in Ortac, which will save even more space. Second, we have assumed in this paper that the evaluation of a logical term does not allocate memory. This hypothesis is a key in the proof of optimization of $T_o$. However, several logical functions in the Gospel standard library do allocate memory in practice. We plan to evaluate heuristics to resolve the trade-off between moving old upwards and then allocating because of the function and stopping there at the cost of copying more.

## A    Term Semantics

In the following, $[\![t]\!]_S^{S'}$ denotes the logical value of term $t$ in prestate $S$ and the poststate $S'$.

$$\frac{}{[\![()]\!]_S^{S'} = ()} \quad \text{(T-Unit)} \qquad\qquad \frac{}{[\![n]\!]_S^{S'} = n} \quad \text{(T-Int)}$$

$$\frac{V(x) = v \qquad M, v \looparrowright lv}{[\![x]\!]_S^{S'} = lv} \quad \text{(T-Var)}$$

$$\frac{[\![t]\!]_S^{S'} = [lv_0, lv_1, \ldots, lv_{n-1}]}{[\![\texttt{length } t]\!]_S^{S'} = n} \quad \text{(T-Length)} \qquad \frac{[\![t]\!]_S^{S'} = (lv_1, lv_2)}{[\![\texttt{fst } t]\!]_S^{S'} = lv_1} \quad \text{(T-Fst)}$$

$$\frac{[\![t]\!]_S^{S'} = (lv_1, lv_2)}{[\![\texttt{snd } t]\!]_S^{S'} = lv_2} \quad \text{(T-Snd)} \qquad \frac{[\![t]\!]_S^{S} = lv}{[\![\texttt{old } t]\!]_S^{S'} = lv} \quad \text{(T-Old)}$$

## B    Predicate Semantics

In the following, $S, S' \models p$ means that predicate $p$ holds in state $S$ and prestate $S'$.

$$\frac{[\![t_1]\!]_S^{S'} = lv_1 \qquad [\![t_2]\!]_S^{S'} = lv_2 \qquad lv_1 = lv_2}{S, S' \models t_1 = t_2} \quad \text{(P-Equal)}$$

$$\frac{S, S' \models p_1 \qquad S, S' \models p_2}{S, S' \models p_1 \wedge p_2} \quad \text{(P-And)} \qquad \frac{S, S' \models p_1}{S, S' \models p_1 \vee p_2} \quad \text{(P-Or-Left)}$$

$$\frac{S, S' \models p_2}{S, S' \models p_1 \vee p_2} \quad \text{(P-Or-Right)}$$

$$\frac{[\![t_1]\!]_S^{S'} = n_1 \qquad [\![t_2]\!]_S^{S'} = n_2}{S, S' \models \texttt{forall } i, t_1 \leq i \leq t_2 \to p} \quad \text{(P-Forall)}$$
$$\forall j, n_1 \leq j \leq n_2 \implies S(V[i \to j], M), (V'[i \to j], M') \models p$$

$$\frac{[\![t_1]\!]_S^{S'} = n_1 \qquad [\![t_2]\!]_S^{S'} = n_2}{S, S' \models \texttt{exists } i, t_1 \leq i \leq t_2 \wedge p} \quad \text{(P-Exists)}$$
$$\exists j, n_1 \leq j \leq n_2 \wedge (V[i \to j], M), (V'[i \to j], M') \models p$$

## C  Program Semantics

In the following, $S, e \rightsquigarrow M', v$ means that the evaluation of the expression $e$ in the state $S$ succeeds and produces the value $v$ in a new memory $M'$.

$$\frac{}{S, n \rightsquigarrow M, n} \text{ (E-Int)} \qquad \frac{}{S, () \rightsquigarrow M, ()} \text{ (E-Unit)} \qquad \frac{V(x) = v}{S, x \rightsquigarrow M, v} \text{ (E-Var)}$$

$$\frac{S, e_1 \rightsquigarrow M_1, a \qquad M_1(a) = [v_0, v_1, \dots, v_n] \qquad (V[x_i \to v_i], M_1), e_2 \rightsquigarrow M_2, v}{S, \text{let } x_1, x_2, \dots, x_n = e_1 \text{ in } e_2 \rightsquigarrow M_2, v} \text{ (E-Let-In)}$$

$$\frac{S, e_1 \rightsquigarrow M_1, () \qquad (V, M_1), e_2 \rightsquigarrow M_2, v_2}{S, e_1 ; e_2 \rightsquigarrow M_2, v_2} \text{ (E-Seq)}$$

$$\frac{S, e_n \rightsquigarrow M_n, v_n \quad \dots \quad (V, M_3), e_2 \rightsquigarrow M_2, v_2 \qquad (V, M_2), e_1 \rightsquigarrow M_1, v_1 \qquad a \notin dom(M_1) \qquad M' = M_1[a \mapsto [v_1, v_2, \dots v_n]]}{S, (e_1, e_2, \dots, e_n) \rightsquigarrow M', a} \text{ (E-Tuple)}$$

$$\frac{S, e \rightsquigarrow M', a \qquad M'(a) = [v_0, v_1, \dots, v_{n-1}]}{S, \pi_i(e) \rightsquigarrow M', v_i} \text{ (E-Pi)}$$

$$\frac{S, e_2 \rightsquigarrow M_2, v \qquad (V, M_2), e_1 \rightsquigarrow M_1, n \qquad a \notin dom(M_1) \qquad M' = M_1[a \mapsto [v, v, \dots, v]]}{S, \text{create } e_1 \ e_2 \rightsquigarrow M', a} \text{ (E-Create)}$$

$$\frac{S, e_2 \rightsquigarrow S_2, n_0 \qquad (V, M_2), e_1 \rightsquigarrow M_1, a \qquad M_1(a) = [v_0, \dots, v_{n-1}] \qquad 0 \le n_0 < n}{S, e_1 . (e_2) \rightsquigarrow M_1, v_{n_0}} \text{ (E-Get)}$$

$$\frac{S, e_3 \rightsquigarrow M_3, v \qquad (V, M_3), e_2 \rightsquigarrow M_2, n_0 \qquad (V, M_2), e_1 \rightsquigarrow M_1, a \qquad 0 \le n_0 < n \qquad M_1(a) = [v_0, v_1, \dots, v_n] \qquad M' = M_1[a \mapsto [v_0, \dots, v_{n_0-1}, v, v_{n_0+1}, \dots, v_{n-1}]]}{S, e_1 . (e_2) \leftarrow e_3 \rightsquigarrow M', ()} \text{ (E-set)}$$

$$\frac{S, e \rightsquigarrow M', a \qquad M'(a) = [v_0, \dots, v_{n-1}]}{S, \text{length } e \rightsquigarrow M', n} \text{ (E-length)}$$

$$\frac{S, e \rightsquigarrow M', v' \qquad M', v' \looparrowright lv \qquad (M'' \backslash M'), v'' \looparrowright lv}{S, \text{copy } e \rightsquigarrow M'', v''} \text{ (E-copy)}$$

$$\frac{S, e \rightsquigarrow M', () \qquad S, (V, M') \models p}{S, \text{assert } e \ \{p\} \rightsquigarrow M', ()} \text{ (E-assert)}$$

## D  Typing Rules

In this section, rules are common for the shared subset of constructs between terms and program expressions. For the sake of clarity, we do not repeat those rules. We note $\Gamma \vdash p$ to denote that the predicate $p$ is well typed in the environment $\Gamma$. The rules for this judgment are standard and omitted.

$$\frac{}{\Gamma \vdash n : \texttt{int}} \text{ (Ty-Int)} \qquad \frac{}{\Gamma \vdash () : \texttt{unit}} \text{ (Ty-Unit)}$$

$$\frac{\Gamma(x) = \tau}{\Gamma \vdash x : \tau} \text{ (Ty-Var)}$$

$$\frac{\Gamma \vdash e_1 : \tau_1 \times \tau_2 \times \ldots \times \tau_n \qquad \Gamma, x_i \mapsto \tau_i \vdash e_2 : \tau}{\Gamma \vdash \texttt{let } x_1, x_2, \ldots, x_n = e_1 \texttt{ in } e_2 : \tau} \text{ (Ty-Let-In)}$$

$$\frac{\Gamma \vdash e_1 : \texttt{unit} \qquad \Gamma \vdash e_2 : \tau}{\Gamma \vdash e_1 ; e_2 : \tau} \text{ (Ty-Seq)}$$

$$\frac{\Gamma \vdash e_1 : \tau_1 \qquad \Gamma \vdash e_2 : \tau_2 \qquad \ldots \qquad \Gamma \vdash e_n : \tau_n}{\Gamma \vdash (e_1, e_2, \ldots, e_n) : \tau_1 \times \tau_2 \times \ldots \times \tau_n} \text{ (Ty-Tuple)}$$

$$\frac{\Gamma \vdash e : \tau_1 \times \tau_2 \times \ldots \times \tau_n}{\Gamma \vdash \pi_i(e) : \tau_i} \text{ (Ty-Pi)}$$

$$\frac{\Gamma \vdash e_1 : \texttt{int} \qquad \Gamma \vdash e_2 : \tau}{\Gamma \vdash \texttt{create } e_1 \ e_2 : \tau \texttt{ array}} \text{ (Ty-Create)}$$

$$\frac{\Gamma \vdash e_1 : \tau \texttt{ array} \qquad \Gamma \vdash e_2 : \texttt{int}}{\Gamma \vdash e_1 . (e_2) : \tau} \text{ (Ty-Get)}$$

$$\frac{\Gamma \vdash e_1 : \tau \texttt{ array} \qquad \Gamma \vdash e_2 : \texttt{int} \qquad \Gamma \vdash e_3 : \tau}{\Gamma \vdash e_1 . (e_2) \leftarrow e_3 : \texttt{unit}} \text{ (Ty-Set)}$$

$$\frac{\Gamma \vdash e : \tau \texttt{ array}}{\Gamma \vdash \texttt{length } e : \texttt{int}} \text{ (Ty-Length)} \qquad \frac{\Gamma \vdash e : \tau}{\Gamma \vdash \texttt{copy } e : \tau} \text{ (Ty-Copy)}$$

$$\frac{\Gamma \vdash e : \tau}{\Gamma \vdash \texttt{old } e : \tau} \text{ (Ty-Old)} \qquad \frac{\Gamma \vdash e : \texttt{unit} \qquad \Gamma \vdash p}{\Gamma \vdash \texttt{assert } e \ \{p\} : \texttt{unit}} \text{ (Ty-Assert)}$$

# References

1. Aho, A.V., Hopcroft, J.E., Ullman, J.: Data Structures and Algorithms. Addison-Wesley Longman Publishing Co., Inc., Boston (1983)
2. Baudin, P., et al.: ACSL: ANSI/ISO C specification language
3. Chalin, P., Kiniry, J., Leavens, G., Poll, E.: Beyond assertions: advanced specification and verification with JML and ESC/Java2, vol. 4111, pp. 342–363, November 2005

4. Chalin, P., Rioux, F.: JML runtime assertion checking: improved error reporting and efficiency using strong validity. In: Cuellar, J., Maibaum, T., Sere, K. (eds.) FM 2008. LNCS, vol. 5014, pp. 246–261. Springer, Heidelberg (2008). https://doi.org/10.1007/978-3-540-68237-0_18
5. Charguéraud, A., Filliâtre, J.C., Lourenço, C., Pereira, M.: GOSPEL – providing OCaml with a formal specification language. In: FM 2019–23rd International Symposium on Formal Methods, Porto, Portugal (Oct 2019)
6. Filliâtre, J.-C., Pascutto, C.: Ortac: runtime assertion checking for OCaml (tool paper). In: Feng, L., Fisman, D. (eds.) RV 2021. LNCS, vol. 12974, pp. 244–253. Springer, Cham (2021). https://doi.org/10.1007/978-3-030-88494-9_13
7. Kosiuczenko, P.: An abstract machine for the old value retrieval. In: Bolduc, C., Desharnais, J., Ktari, B. (eds.) MPC 2010. LNCS, vol. 6120, pp. 229–247. Springer, Heidelberg (2010). https://doi.org/10.1007/978-3-642-13321-3_14
8. Kosmatov, N., Maurica, F., Signoles, J.: Efficient runtime assertion checking for properties over mathematical numbers. In: Deshmukh, J., Ničković, D. (eds.) RV 2020. LNCS, vol. 12399, pp. 310–322. Springer, Cham (2020). https://doi.org/10.1007/978-3-030-60508-7_17
9. Lehner, H., Müller, P.: Efficient runtime assertion checking of assignable clauses with datagroups. In: Rosenblum, D.S., Taentzer, G. (eds.) FASE 2010. LNCS, vol. 6013, pp. 338–352. Springer, Heidelberg (2010). https://doi.org/10.1007/978-3-642-12029-9_24
10. Meyer, B.: Applying "design by contract". Computer **25**(10), 40–51 (1992)
11. Petiot, G., Botella, B., Julliand, J., Kosmatov, N., Signoles, J.: Instrumentation of annotated c programs for test generation. In: 2014 IEEE 14th International Working Conference on Source Code Analysis and Manipulation, pp. 105–114. Institute of Electrical and Electronics Engineers Inc., Victoria, Canada, September 2014
12. Signoles, J.: The E-ACSL perspective on runtime assertion checking. In: International Workshop on Verification and mOnitoring at Runtime EXecution. VORTEX 2021: Proceedings of the 5th ACM International Workshop on Verification and mOnitoring at Runtime EXecution, (online), Denmark, July 2021
13. Signoles, J., Kosmatov, N., Vorobyov, K.: E-ACSL, a runtime verification tool for safety and security of C programs (tool paper). In: RV-CuBES (2017)

# A Barrier Certificate-Based Simplex Architecture with Application to Microgrids

Amol Damare, Shouvik Roy, Scott A. Smolka, and Scott D. Stoller[✉]

Stony Brook University, Stony Brook, NY, USA
{adamare,shroy,sas,stoller}@cs.stonybrook.edu

**Abstract.** We present *Barrier-based Simplex* (Bb-Simplex), a new, provably correct design for runtime assurance of continuous dynamical systems. Bb-Simplex is centered around the Simplex Control Architecture, which consists of a high-performance *advanced controller* which is not guaranteed to maintain safety of the plant, a verified-safe *baseline controller*, and a *decision module* that switches control of the plant between the two controllers to ensure safety without sacrificing performance. In Bb-Simplex, *Barrier certificates* are used to prove that the baseline controller ensures safety. Furthermore, Bb-Simplex features a new automated method for deriving, from the barrier certificate, the conditions for switching between the controllers. Our method is based on the Taylor expansion of the barrier certificate and yields computationally inexpensive switching conditions.

We consider a significant application of Bb-Simplex to a microgrid featuring an advanced controller in the form of a neural network trained using reinforcement learning. The microgrid is modeled in RTDS, an industry-standard high-fidelity, real-time power systems simulator. Our results demonstrate that Bb-Simplex can automatically derive switching conditions for complex systems, the switching conditions are not overly conservative, and Bb-Simplex ensures safety even in the presence of adversarial attacks on the neural controller.

## 1 Introduction

*Barrier certificates* (BaCs) [26,27] are a powerful method for verifying the safety of continuous dynamical systems without explicitly computing the set of reachable states. A BaC is a function of the state satisfying a set of inequalities on the value of the function and value of its time derivative along the dynamic flows of the system. Intuitively, the zero-level-set of a BaC forms a "barrier" between the reachable states and unsafe states. Existence of a BaC assures that starting from a state where the BaC is positive, safety is forever maintained [6,26,27]. Moreover, there are automated methods to synthesize BaCs, e.g., [13,31,34,38].

Proving safety of plants with complex controllers is difficult with any formal verification technique, including barrier certificates. As we now show, however, BaCs can play a crucial role in applying the well-established Simplex Control Architecture [29,30] to provide provably correct runtime safety assurance for systems with complex controllers.

© The Author(s), under exclusive license to Springer Nature Switzerland AG 2022
T. Dang and V. Stolz (Eds.): RV 2022, LNCS 13498, pp. 105–123, 2022.
https://doi.org/10.1007/978-3-031-17196-3_6

We present *Barrier-based Simplex* (Bb-Simplex), a new, provably correct design for runtime assurance of continuous dynamical systems. Bb-Simplex is centered around the Simplex Control Architecture, which consists of a high-performance *advanced controller* (AC) that is not guaranteed to maintain safety of the plant, a verified-safe *baseline controller* (BC), and a *decision module* that switches control of the plant between the two controllers to ensure safety without sacrificing performance. In Bb-Simplex, *Barrier certificates* are used to prove that the baseline controller ensures safety. Furthermore, Bb-Simplex features a new scalable (relative to existing methods that require reachability analysis, e.g., [4,5,11]) and automated method for deriving, from the BaC, the conditions for switching between the controllers. Our method is based on the Taylor expansion of the BaC and yields computationally inexpensive switching conditions.

We consider a significant application of Bb-Simplex, namely *microgrid control*. A *microgrid* is an integrated energy system comprising distributed energy resources and multiple energy loads operating as a single controllable entity in parallel to, or islanded from, the existing power grid [33]. The microgrid we consider features an advanced controller (for voltage control) in the form of a neural network trained using reinforcement learning. For this purpose, we use Bb-Simplex in conjunction with the *Neural Simplex Architecture* (NSA) [24], where the AC is an AI-based *neural controller* (NC). NSA also includes an *adaptation module* (AM) for online retraining of the NC while the BC is in control.

The microgrid we consider is modeled in RTDS, an industry-standard high-fidelity, real-time power systems simulator. Our results demonstrate that Bb-Simplex can automatically derive switching conditions for complex systems, the switching conditions are not overly conservative, and Bb-Simplex ensures safety even in the presence of adversarial attacks on the neural controller. Please refer to [9] for a more in-depth exploration of our methodology and experiments.

*Architectural Overview of Bb-Simplex.* Fig. 1 shows the overall architecture of the combined Barrier-based Neural Simplex Architecture. The green part of the figure depicts our design methodology; the blue part illustrates NSA. Given the BC, the required safety properties, and a dynamic model of the plant, our methodology generates a BaC and then derives the switching condition from it. The reinforcement learning module learns a high-performance NC based on the performance objectives encoded in the reward function.

The structure of the rest of the paper is the following. Section 2 provides background material on barrier certificates. Section 3 features our new approach for deriving switching conditions from barrier certificates. Section 4 introduces our Microgrid case study and the associated controllers used for microgrid control. Section 5 presents the results of our microgrid case study. Section 6 discusses related work. Section 7 offers our concluding remarks.

## 2   Preliminaries

We use Barrier Certificates (BaCs) to prove that the BC ensures safety. We implemented two automated methods for BaC synthesis from the literature.

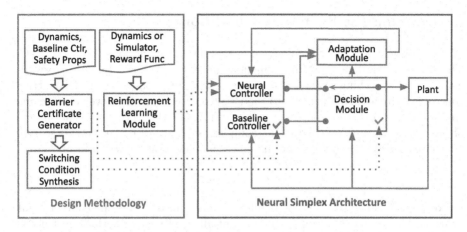

**Fig. 1.** Overview of the barrier certificate-based neural simplex architecture (Color figure online)

As discussed next, one of the methods is based on sum-of-squares optimization (SOS) and the other uses deep learning. Our design methodology for computing switching conditions (see Sect. 3) requires a BaC, but is independent of how the BaC is obtained.

*BaC Synthesis Using SOS Optimization.* This method first derives a Lyapunov function $V$ for the system using the expanding interior-point algorithm in [3]. It then uses the SOS-based algorithm in [34] to obtain a BaC from $V$. Note that the largest super-level set of a Lyapunov function within a safety region is a BaC. The algorithm in [13,34] computes a larger BaC by starting with that sub-level set and then expanding it, by allowing it to take shapes other than that of a sub-level set of the Lyapunov function. This method involves a search of Lyapunov functions and BaCs of various degrees by choosing different candidate polynomials and parameters of the SOS problem. It is limited to systems with polynomial dynamics. In some cases, non-polynomial dynamics can be recast as polynomial using, e.g., the techniques in [3].

*BaC Synthesis Using Deep Learning.* We also implemented *SyntheBC* [39], which uses deep learning to synthesize a BaC. First, training samples obtained by sampling different areas of the state space are used to train a feedforward ReLU neural network with two hidden layers as a candidate BaC. Second, the validity of this candidate BaC must be verified. The NN's structure allows the problem of checking whether the NN satisfies the defining conditions of a BaC to be transformed into mixed-integer linear programming (MILP) and mixed-integer quadratically-constrained programming (MIQCP) problems, which we solve using the Gurobi optimizer. If the verification fails, the Gurobi optimizer provides counter-examples which can be used to guide retraining of the NN. In this way, the training and verification steps can be iterated as needed.

# 3    Deriving the Switching Condition

We employ our novel methodology to derive the switching logic from the BaC. The Decision Module (DM) implements this switching logic for both forward and reverse switching. When the forward-switching condition (FSC) is true, control is switched from the NC to the BC; likewise, when the reverse-switching condition (RSC) is true, control is switched from the BC to the NC. The success of our approach rests on solving the complex problems discussed in this section to derive an FSC. Consider a continuous dynamical system of the form:

$$\dot{x} = f(x, u) \tag{1}$$

where $x \in \mathbb{R}^k$ is the state of the plant at time $t$ and $u \in \Omega$ is the control input provided to the plant at time $t$. The set of all valid control actions is denoted by $\Omega$. The set of *unsafe states* is denoted by $\mathcal{U}$. Let $x_{lb}, x_{ub} \in \mathbb{R}^k$ be *operational bounds* on the ranges of state variables, reflecting physical limits and simple safety requirements.

The set $\mathcal{A}$ of *admissible states* is given by: $\mathcal{A} = \{x : x_{lb} \leq x \leq x_{ub}\}$. A state of the plant is *recoverable* if the BC can take over in that state and keep the plant invariably safe. For a given BC, we denote the *recoverable region* by $\mathcal{R}$. Note that $\mathcal{U}$ and $\mathcal{R}$ are disjoint. The safety of such a system can be verified using a BaC $h(x) : \mathbb{R}^k \to \mathbb{R}$ of the following form [13, 26, 27, 34]:

$$h(x) \geq 0, \quad \forall x \in \mathbb{R}^k \setminus \mathcal{U}$$
$$h(x) < 0, \quad \forall x \in \mathcal{U} \tag{2}$$
$$(\nabla_x h)^T f(x, u) + \sigma(h(x)) \geq 0, \quad \forall x \in \mathbb{R}^k$$

where $\sigma(.)$ is an extended class-$\mathcal{K}$ function. The BaC is negative over the unsafe region and non-negative otherwise. $\nabla_x h$ is the gradient of $h$ w.r.t $x$ and the expression $(\nabla_x h)^T f(x, u)$ is the time derivative of $h$. The zero-super-level set of a BaC $h$ is $\mathcal{Z}(h) = \{x : h(x) > 0\}$. In [34], the invariance of this set is used to show $\mathcal{Z}(h) \subseteq \mathcal{R}$.

Let $\eta$ denote the control period a.k.a. time step. Let $\hat{h}(x, u, \delta)$ denote the $n^{\text{th}}$-degree Taylor approximation of BaC $h$'s value after time $\delta$, if control action $u$ is taken in state $x$. The approximation is computed at the current time to predict $h$'s value $\delta$ time units later and is given by:

$$\hat{h}(x, u, \delta) = h(x) + \sum_{i=1}^{n} \frac{h^i(x, u)}{i!} \delta^i \tag{3}$$

where $h^i(x, u)$ denotes the $i^{\text{th}}$ time derivative of $h$ evaluated in state $x$ if control action $u$ is taken. The control action is needed to calculate the time derivatives of $h$ from the definition of $h$ and Eq. 1 by applying the chain rule. Since we are usually interested in predicting the value one time step in the future, we use $\hat{h}(x, u)$ as shorthand for $\hat{h}(x, u, \eta)$. By Taylor's theorem with the Lagrange form of the remainder, the remainder error of the approximation $\hat{h}(x, u)$ is:

$$\frac{h^{n+1}(x, u, \delta)}{(n+1)!} \eta^{n+1} \text{ for some } \delta \in (0, \eta) \tag{4}$$

An upper bound on the remainder error, if the state remains in the admissible region during the time interval, is:

$$\lambda(u) = \sup \left\{ \frac{|h^{n+1}(x, u)|}{(n+1)!} \eta^{n+1} : x \in \mathcal{A} \right\} \tag{5}$$

The FSC is based on checking recoverability during the next time step. For this purpose, the set $\mathcal{A}$ of admissible states is shrunk by margins of $\mu_{\text{dec}}$ and $\mu_{\text{inc}}$, a vector of upper bounds on the amount by which each state variable can decrease and increase, respectively, in one time step, maximized over all admissible states. Formally,

$$\begin{aligned} \mu_{\text{dec}}(u) &= |\min(0, \eta \dot{x}_{min}(u))| \\ \mu_{\text{inc}}(u) &= |\max(0, \eta \dot{x}_{max}(u))| \end{aligned} \tag{6}$$

where $\dot{x}_{min}$ and $\dot{x}_{max}$ are vectors of solutions to the optimization problems:

$$\begin{aligned} \dot{x}_i^{min}(u) &= \inf\{\dot{x}_i(x, u) : x \in \mathcal{A}\} \\ \dot{x}_i^{max}(u) &= \sup\{\dot{x}_i(x, u) : x \in \mathcal{A}\} \end{aligned} \tag{7}$$

The difficulty of finding these extremal values depends on the complexity of the functions $\dot{x}_i(x, u)$. For example, it is relatively easy if they are convex. In our case study of a realistic microgrid model, they are multivariate polynomials with degree 1, and hence convex. The set $\mathcal{A}_r$ of *restricted admissible states* is given by:

$$\mathcal{A}_r(u) = \{x : x_{lb} + \mu_{\text{dec}}(u) < x < x_{ub} - \mu_{\text{inc}}(u)\} \tag{8}$$

Let $Reach_{=\eta}(x, u)$ denote the set of states reachable from state $x$ after exactly time $\eta$ if control action $u$ is taken in state $x$. Let $Reach_{\leq \eta}(x, u)$ denote the set of states reachable from $x$ within time $\eta$ if control action $u$ is taken in state $x$.

**Lemma 1.** *For all $x \in \mathcal{A}_r(u)$ and all control actions $u$, $Reach_{\leq \eta}(x, u) \subseteq \mathcal{A}$.*

*Proof.* The derivative of $x$ is bounded by $\dot{x}_{min}(u)$ and $\dot{x}_{max}(u)$ for all states in $\mathcal{A}$. This implies that $\mu_{\text{dec}}$ and $\mu_{\text{inc}}$ are the largest amounts by which the state $x$ can decrease and increase, respectively, during time $\eta$, as long as $x$ remains within $\mathcal{A}$ during the time step. Since $\mathcal{A}_r(u)$ is obtained by shrinking $\mathcal{A}$ by $\mu_{\text{dec}}$ and $\mu_{\text{inc}}$ (i.e., by moving the lower and upper bounds, respectively, of each variable inwards by those amounts), the state cannot move outside of $\mathcal{A}$ during time $\eta$.

## 3.1   Forward Switching Condition

To ensure safety, a forward-switching condition (FSC) should switch control from the NC to the BC if using the control action $u$ proposed by NC causes any unsafe states to be reachable from the current state $x$ during the next control period, or causes any unrecoverable states to be reachable at the end of the next control period. These two conditions are captured in the following definition:

**Definition 1 (Forward Switching Condition).** *A condition $FSC(x,u)$ is a forward switching condition if for every recoverable state $x$, every control action $u$, and control period $\eta$, $Reach_{\leq \eta}(x,u) \cap \mathcal{U} \neq \emptyset \vee Reach_{=\eta}(x,u) \not\subset \mathcal{R}$ implies $FSC(x,u)$ is true.*

**Theorem 1.** *A Simplex architecture whose forward switching condition satisfies Definition 1 keeps the system invariably safe provided the system starts in a recoverable state.*

*Proof.* Our definition of an FSC is based directly on the switching logic in Algorithm 1 of [36]. The proof of Theorem 1 in [36] shows that an FSC that is exactly the disjunction of the two conditions in our definition invariantly ensures system safety. It is easy to see that any weaker FSC also ensures safety.  ∎

We now propose a new and general procedure for constructing a switching condition from a BaC and prove its correctness.

**Theorem 2.** *Given a barrier certificate $h$, the following condition is a forward switching condition: $FSC(x,u) = \alpha \vee \beta$ where $\alpha \equiv \hat{h}(x,u) - \lambda(u) \leq 0$ and $\beta \equiv x \notin \mathcal{A}_r(u)$*

*Proof.* Intuitively, $\alpha \vee \beta$ is an FSC because (1) if condition $\alpha$ is false, then control action $u$ does not lead to an unsafe or unrecoverable state during the next control period, provided the state remains admissible during that period; and (2) if condition $\beta$ is false, then the state will remain admissible during that period. Thus, if $\alpha$ and $\beta$ are both false, then nothing bad can happen during the control period, and there is no need to switch to the BC.

Formally, suppose $x$ is a recoverable state, $u$ is a control action, and $Reach_{\leq \eta}(x,u) \cap \mathcal{U} \neq \emptyset \vee Reach_{=\eta}(x,u) \not\subset \mathcal{R}$, i.e., there is an unsafe state in $Reach_{\leq \eta}(x,u)$ or an unrecoverable state in $Reach_{=\eta}(x,u)$. Let $x'$ denote that unsafe or unrecoverable state. Recall that $\mathcal{Z}(h) \subseteq \mathcal{R}$, and $\mathcal{R} \cap \mathcal{U} = \emptyset$. Therefore, $h(x',u) \leq 0$. We need to show that $\alpha \vee \beta$ holds. We do a case analysis based on whether $x$ is in $\mathcal{A}_r(u)$.

Case 1: $x \in \mathcal{A}_r(u)$. In this case, we use a lower bound on the value of the BaC $h$ to show that states reachable in the next control period are safe and recoverable. Using Lemma 1, we have $Reach_{\leq \eta}(x,u) \subseteq \mathcal{A}$. This implies that $\lambda(u)$, whose definition maximizes over $x \in \mathcal{A}$, is an upper bound on the error in the Taylor approximation $\hat{h}(x,u,\delta)$ for $\delta \leq \eta$. This implies that $\hat{h}(x,u) - \lambda(u)$ is a lower bound on value of BaC for all states in $Reach_{\leq \eta}(x,u)$. As shown above, there is a state $x'$ in $Reach_{\leq \eta}(x, u)$ with $h(x', u) \leq 0$. $\hat{h}(x, u) - \lambda(u)$ is lower bound on $h(x', u)$ and hence must also be less than or equal to 0. Thus, $\alpha$ holds.

Case 2: $x \notin \mathcal{A}_r(u)$. In this case, $\beta$ holds. Note that in this case, the truth value of $\alpha$ is not significant (and not relevant, since $FSC(x, u)$ holds regardless), because the state might not remain admissible during the next control period. Hence, the error bound obtained using Eq. 5 is not applicable.    ∎

### 3.2  Reverse Switching Condition

The RSC is designed with a heuristic approach, since it does not affect safety of the system. To prevent frequent switching between the NC and BC, we design the RSC to hold if the FSC is likely to remain false for at least $m$ time steps, with $m > 1$. The RSC, like the FSC, is the disjunction of two conditions. The first condition is $h(x) \geq m\eta|\dot{h}(x)|$, since $h$ is likely to remain non-negative for at least $m$ time steps if its current value is at least that duration times its rate of change. The second condition ensures that the state will remain admissible for $m$ time steps. In particular, we take:

$$RSC(x) = h(x) \geq m\eta|\dot{h}(x)| \land x \in \mathcal{A}_{r,m}, \tag{9}$$

where the $m$-times-restricted admissible region is:

$$\mathcal{A}_{r,m} = \{x : x_{lb} + m\mu_{\text{dec}} < x < x_{ub} - m\mu_{\text{inc}}\}, \tag{10}$$

where vectors $\mu_{\text{dec}}$ and $\mu_{\text{inc}}$ are defined in the same way as $\mu_{\text{dec}}(u)$ and $\mu_{\text{inc}}(u)$ in Eqs. 6 and 7 except with optimization over all control actions $u$.

### 3.3  Decision Logic

The DM's switching logic has three inputs: the current state $x$, the control action $u$ currently proposed by the NC, and the name $c$ of the controller currently in control (as a special case, we take $c = NC$ in the first time step). The switching logic is defined by cases as follows: $DM(x, u, c)$ returns $BC$ if $c = NC \land FSC(x, u)$, returns $NC$ if $c = BC \land RSC(x)$, and returns $c$ otherwise.

## 4  Application to Microgrids

A *microgrid* (MG) is an integrated energy system comprising distributed energy resources (DERs) and multiple energy loads. DERs tend to be *renewable* energy resources and include solar panels, wind turbines, batteries, and emergency diesel generators. By satisfying energy needs from local renewable energy resources, MGs can reduce energy costs and improve energy supply reliability for energy consumers. Some of the major control requirements for an MG are power control, load sharing, and frequency and voltage regulation.

An MG can operate in two modes: grid-connected and islanded. When operated in grid-connected mode, DERs act as constant source of power which can be injected into the network on demand. In contrast, in islanded or autonomous mode, the DERs form a grid of their own, meaning not only do they supply power to the local loads, but they also maintain the MG's voltage and frequency within the specified limits [25]. For our case study, we focus on voltage regulation in both grid-connected and islanded modes. Specifically, we apply Bb-Simplex to the controller for the inverter for a Photovoltaic (PV) DER.

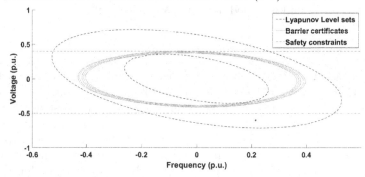

**Fig. 2.** Lyapunov-function level sets (black-dotted ellipses). Innermost ellipse also indicates initial BaC, which is optimized iteratively (green ellipses). Red lines are voltage safety limits. (Color figure online)

### 4.1  Baseline Controller

For our experiments, we used the SOS-based methodology described in Sect. 2 to derive a Barrier Certificate (as a proof of safety) for the baseline controller. We use a droop controller as the BC. A droop controller is a type of proportional controller, traditionally used in power systems for control objectives such as voltage regulation, power regulation, and current sharing [10,14,40]. The droop controller tries to balance the electrical power with voltage and frequency. Variations in the active and reactive powers result in frequency and voltage magnitude deviations, respectively [20]. The dynamic model for a voltage droop controller for an inverter has the form $\dot{v} = v^* - v + \lambda_q(Q^* - Q)$, where $v^*, v, Q^*, Q$ are voltage reference, voltage, reactive power reference and reactive power of inverter, respectively, and $\lambda_q$ is the controller's droop coefficient. Detailed dynamic models for an MG with multiple inverters connected by transmission lines and with droop controllers for frequency and voltage are given in [3,13].

Figure 2 shows this process of incrementally expanding the Lyapunov function to obtain the BaC. SOS-based algorithms apply only to polynomial dynamics so we first recast our droop controller dynamics to be polynomial using a DQ0 transformation [22] to AC waveforms. This transformation is exact; i.e., it does not introduce any approximation error. In our experimental evaluation (Sect. 5), we obtain the BaCs for BCs in the form of droop controllers for voltage regulation, in the context of MGs containing up to three DERs of different types. Note that battery DERs operate in two distinct modes, charging and discharging, resulting in a hybrid system model with different dynamics in different modes. For now, we consider only runs in which the battery remains in the same mode for the duration of the run. Extending our framework to hybrid systems is future work.

## 4.2   Neural Controller

To help address the control challenges related to microgrids, the application of *neural networks for microgrid control* is on the rise [16]. Increasingly, Reinforcement learning (RL) is being used to train powerful Deep Neural Networks (DNNs) to produce high-performance MG controllers.

We present our approach for learning neural controllers (NCs) in the form of DNNs representing deterministic control policies. Such a DNN maps system states (or raw sensor readings) to control inputs. We use RL in form of Deep Deterministic Policy Gradient (DDPG) algorithm, with the safe learning strategy of penalizing unrecoverable actions [24]. DDPG was chosen because it works with deterministic policies and is compatible with continuous action spaces.

We consider a standard RL setup consisting of an agent interacting with an environment in discrete time. At each time step $t$, the agent receives a (microgrid) state $x_t$ as input, takes an action $a_t$, and receives a scalar reward $r_t$. The DDPG algorithm employs an *actor-critic framework*. The actor generates a control action and the critic evaluates its quality. In order to learn from prior knowledge, DDPG uses a replay buffer to store training samples of the form $(x_t, a_t, r_t, x_{t+1})$. At every training iteration, a set of samples is randomly chosen from the replay buffer. For further details regarding the implementation of the DDPG algorithm, please refer to Algorithm 1 in [15].

To learn an NC for DER voltage control, we designed the following reward function, which guides the actor network to learn the desired control objective.

$$r(x_t, a_t) = \begin{cases} -1000 & \text{if } \mathrm{FSC}(x_t, a_t) \\ 100 & \text{if } v_{od} \in [v_{ref} - \epsilon, v_{ref} + \epsilon] \\ -w \cdot (v_{od} - v_{ref})^2 & \text{otherwise} \end{cases} \quad (11)$$

where $w$ is a weight ($w = 100$ in our experiments), $v_{od}$ is the $d$-component of the output voltage of the DER whose controller is being learned, $v_{ref}$ is the reference or nominal voltage, and $\epsilon$ is the tolerance threshold. We assign a high negative reward for triggering the FSC, and a high positive reward for reaching the tolerance region, i.e., $v_{ref} \pm \epsilon$. The third clause rewards actions that lead to a state in which the DER voltage is close to its reference value.

*Adversarial Inputs.* Controllers obtained via deep RL algorithms are vulnerable to *adversarial inputs* (AIs): those that lead to a state in which the NC produces an unrecoverable action, even though the NC behaves safely on very similar inputs. NSA provides a defense against these kinds of attacks. If the NC proposes a potentially unsafe action, the BC takes over in a timely manner, thereby guaranteeing the safety of the system. To demonstrate NSA's resilience to AIs, we use a gradient-based attack (Algorithm 4) [23] to construct such inputs, and show that the DM switches control to the BC in time to ensure safety.

The gradient-based algorithm takes as input the critic network, actor network, adversarial attack constant $c$, parameters $a$, $b$ of beta distribution $\beta(a, b)$, and the number of times $n$ noise is sampled. For a given (microgrid) state $x$,

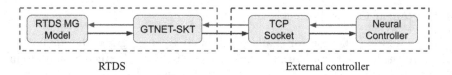

RTDS                        External controller

**Fig. 3.** Integration of External NC with RTDS

the critic network is used to ascertain its $\mathcal{Q}$-value and the actor network determines its optimal action. Once the gradient of the critic network's loss function is computed using the $\mathcal{Q}$-value and the action, the $l_2$-constrained norm of the gradient ($grad\_dir$) is obtained. An initial (microgrid) state $x_0$, to be provided as input to the actor network, is then perturbed to obtain a potential adversarial state $x_{adv}$, determined by the sampled noise in the direction of the gradient: $x_{adv} = x_0 - c \cdot \beta(a, b) \cdot grad\_dir$.

We can now compute the $\mathcal{Q}$-value of $x_{adv}$ and its (potentially adversarial) action $a_{adv}$. If this value is less tha $\mathcal{Q}(x_0, a_0)$, then $x_{adv}$ leads to a sub-optimal action. The gradient-based attack algorithm does not guarantee the successful generation of AIs every time it is executed. The success rate is inversely related to the quality of the training of the NC. In our experiments (see Sect. 5.3), the highest success rate for AI generation that we observed is 0.008%.

### 4.3  Adaptation Module

The Adaptation Module (AM) retrains the NC in an online manner when the NC produces an unrecoverable action that causes the DM to failover to the BC. With retraining, the NC is less likely to repeat the same or similar mistakes in the future, allowing it to remain in control of the system more often, thereby improving performance. We use Reinforcement Learning with the reward function defined in Eq. 11 for online retraining.

As in initial training, we use the DDPG algorithm (with the same settings) for online retraining. When the NC outputs an unrecoverable action, the DM switches control to the BC, and the AM computes the (negative) reward for this action and adds it to a pool of training samples. As in [24], we found that reusing the pool of training samples (DDPG's experience replay buffer) from initial training of the NC evolves the policy in a more stable fashion, as retraining samples gradually replace initial training samples in the pool. Another benefit of reusing the initial training pool is that retraining of the NC can start almost immediately, without having to wait for enough samples to be collected online.

We use off-policy retraining i.e., at every time step while the BC is active, the BC's action is used in the training sample. The reward for the BC's action is based on the observed next state of the system.

# 5   Experimental Evaluation

We apply our Bb-Simplex methodology to a model of a microgrid [21] with three DERs: a battery, photovoltaic (PV, a.k.a. solar panels), and diesel generator. The three DERs are connected to the main grid via bus lines. We are primarily interested in PV control, since we apply Bb-Simplex to PV voltage regulation. The PV control includes multiple components, such as "three-phase to DQ0 voltage and current" transformer, average voltage and current control, power and voltage measurements, inner-loop $dq$ current control, and outer-loop Maximum Power Point Tracking (MPPT) control. Our experimental evaluation of Bb-Simplex was carried out on RTDS, a high-fidelity power systems simulator.

We ran experiments on a configuration where the PV is in islanded mode, and the diesel generator and battery (in discharging mode) DERs are connected within the MG. The state of the MG plant is given by $[i_d \; i_q \; i_{od} \; i_{oq} \; v_{od} \; v_{oq} \; i_{ld} \; i_{lq} \; m_d \; m_q]$, where $i_d$ and $i_q$ are the $d$- and $q$-components of the $dq$ current measured at the local load of the inverter, $i_{od}$ and $i_{oq}$ are the $d$- and $q$-components of the output current of the inverter measured at point of coupling to the main grid, $v_{od}$ and $v_{oq}$ are the $d$- and $q$-components of the output voltage of the inverter measured at point of coupling to the main grid, $i_{ld}$ and $i_{lq}$ are the $d$- and $q$-components of the input current to the current controller, $m_d$ and $m_q$ are the $d$- and $q$-components of the output voltage from the current controller used to generate the next state.

We use Bb-Simplex to ensure the safety property that the $d$-component of the output voltage $(v_{od})$ of the inverter for the PV DER is within $\pm 3\%$ of the reference voltage $v_{ref} = 0.48$ kV. We adopted a 3% tolerance based on the discussion in [21]. Bb-Simplex could similarly be used to ensure additional desired safety properties. All experiments use runs of length 10 s, with the control period, RTDS time step, and simulation time step in MATLAB all equal to 3.2 milliseconds (msec), the largest time step allowed by RTDS.

## 5.1   Integration of Bb-Simplex in RTDS

The BC is the original droop controller described in [21], implemented in RTDS using components in the RTDS standard libraries. The DM is implemented as an RTDS *custom component* written in C. For an MG configuration, expressions for the BaC, $\lambda$ and $\mu$ (see Sect. 3) are derived in MATLAB, converted to C data structures, and then included in a header file of the custom component.

The BaCs are polynomials comprising 92 monomials for our configuration.

The NC is trained and implemented using Keras [8], a high-level neural network API written in Python, running on top of TensorFlow [1]. For training, we customized an existing skeleton implementation of DDPG in Keras, which we then used with the Adam optimizer [12].

RTDS imposes limitations on custom components that make it difficult to implement complex NNs within RTDS. Existing NN libraries for RTDS, such as [17,18], severely limit the NN's size and the types of activation functions.

Therefore, we implemented the NC external to RTDS, following the *software-defined microgrid control* approach in [35]. Figure 3 shows our setup. We used RTDS's GTNET-SKT communication protocol to establish a TCP connection between the NC running on a PC and an "NC-to-DM" relay component in the RTDS MG model. This relay component repeatedly sends the plant state to the NC, which computes its control action and sends it to the relay component, which in turn sends it to the DM.

## 5.2  Evaluation of Forward Switching Condition

We derive a BaC using the SOS-based methodology presented in Sect. 2, and then derive a switching condition from the BaC, as described in Sect. 3.1. To find values of $\lambda$ and $\mu$, we use MATLAB's fmincon function to solve the constrained optimization problems given in Eqs. 6 and 7.

An ideal FSC triggers a switch to BC only if an unrecoverable state is reachable in one time step. For systems with complex dynamics, switching conditions derived in practice are conservative, i.e., may switch sooner. To show that our FSC is not overly conservative, we performed experiments using an AC that continuously increases the voltage and hence soon violates safety. The PV voltage controller has two outputs, $m_d$ and $m_q$, for the $d$ and $q$ components of the voltage, respectively. The dummy AC simply uses constant values for its outputs, with $m_d = 0.5$ and $m_q = 1e - 6$.

These experiments were performed with PV DER in grid connected mode, with reference voltage and voltage safety threshold of 0.48 kV and 0.4944 kV, respectively, and a FSC derived using a $4^{\text{th}}$-order Taylor approximation of the BaC. We averaged over 100 runs from initial states with initial voltage selected uniformly at random from the range 0.48 kV $\pm$ 1%. The mean voltage at switching is 0.4921 kV (with standard deviation 0.0002314 kV), which is only 0.46% below the safety threshold. The mean numbers of time steps before switching, and before a safety violation if Bb-Simplex is not used, are 127.4 and 130.2, respectively. Thus, our FSC triggered a switch about three time steps, on average, before a safety violation would have occurred.

We also derived a neural network-based BaC using deep learning and verified it using the Gurobi optimizer as discussed in Sect. 2. We then derived the switching conditions from the verified neural BaC, again using a $4^{\text{th}}$-order Taylor approximation. We performed the same experiments as above to determine the conservativeness of this FSC. The mean voltage at switching is 0.4923 kV (with standard deviation 0.0002132 kV). The mean numbers of time steps before switching, and before a safety violation if Bb-Simplex is not used, are 128.1 and 130.2, respectively. Thus, our neural FSC triggered a switch about two time steps, on average, before a safety violation would have occurred.

## 5.3  Evaluation of Neural Controller

The NC for a microgrid configuration is a DNN with four fully-connected hidden layers of 128 neurons each and one output layer. The hidden layers and output

**Table 1.** Performance evaluation of NC

|  | CT | $\sigma(CT)$ | $\delta$ | $\sigma(\delta)$ |  |  | CT | $\sigma(CT)$ | $\delta$ | $\sigma(\delta)$ |
|---|---|---|---|---|---|---|---|---|---|---|
| NC | 84.3 | 7.6 | 1.7e−4 | 1.4e−5 |  | Gen 1 | 112.5 | 11.1 | 2.5e−4 | 1.9e−5 |
| BC | 115.7 | 9.8 | 5.8e−4 | 3.8e−5 |  | Gen 2 | 89.1 | 8.7 | 1.8e−4 | 1.3e−5 |

   (a) Performance comparison of NC and BC    (b) Generalization performance of NC

layer use the ReLU and tanh activation function, respectively. The input state
to the NC (DNN) is the same as the inputs to the BC (droop controller) i.e.,
$[i_{ld}\ i_{lq}]$, where $i_{ld}$ and $i_{lq}$ are the $d$- and $q$-components of the input current to
the droop controller. Thus the NC has same inputs and outputs as the BC. The
NC is trained on 1 million samples (one-step transitions) from MATLAB simulations, processed in batches of 200. Transitions start from random states, with
initial values uniformly sampled from $[0.646, 0.714]$ for $i_{ld}$ and $[-0.001, 0.001]$ for
$i_{lq}$ [21]. Training takes approximately 2 h.

*Performance.* We evaluate a controller's performance based on three metrics:
convergence rate $(CR)$, the percentage of trajectories in which the DER voltage
converges to the tolerance region $v_{ref} \pm \epsilon$; average convergence time $(CT)$, the
average time required for convergence of the DER voltage to the tolerance region;
and mean deviation $(\delta)$, the average deviation of the DER voltage from $v_{ref}$ after
the voltage enters the tolerance region. We always report CR as a percentage,
CT in milliseconds, and $\delta$ in kV.

We show that the NC outperforms the BC. For this experiment, we used
RTDS to run the BC and NC starting from the same 100 initial states. The CR
is 100% for the NC and BC. Table 1a compares their performance, averaged over
100 runs, with $\epsilon = 0.001$. We observe that the NC outperforms the BC both
in terms of average convergence time and mean deviation. We also report the
standard deviations $(\sigma)$ for these metrics and note that they are small compared
to the average values. The FSC was not triggered even once during these runs,
showing that the NC is well-trained.

*Generalization.* Generalization refers to the NC's ability to perform well in contexts beyond the ones in which it was trained. First, we consider two kinds of
generalization with respect to the microgrid state:

- Gen 1: the initial states of the DERs are randomly chosen from a range outside
  of the range used during training.
- Gen 2: the power set-point $P^\star$ is randomly chosen from the range $[0.2, 1]$,
  whereas all training was done with $P^\star = 1$.

Table 1b presents the NC's performance in these two cases, based on 100 runs
for each case. We see that the NC performs well in both cases.

Second, we consider generalization with respect to the microgrid configuration. Here we evaluate how the NC handles dynamic changes to the microgrid
configuration during runtime. For the first experiment, we start with all the 3

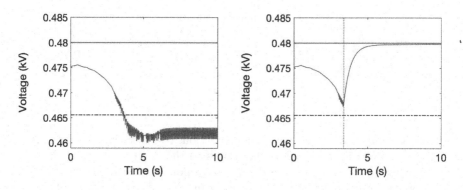

**Fig. 4.** NC with adversarial inputs (left: without NSA, right: with NSA)

DERs connected, but the diesel generator DER is disconnected after the voltage has converged. For the second experiment, we again start with all the 3 DERs connected, but both the diesel generator and battery DER are disconnected after the voltage has converged. For both instances, the NC succeeded in continuously keeping the voltage in the tolerance region ($v_{ref} \pm \epsilon$) after the disconnection. The disconnection caused a slight drop in the subsequent steady-state voltage, a drop of 0.114% and 0.132%, averaged over 100 runs for each case.

*Adversarial Input Attacks.* We demonstrate that RL-based neural controllers are vulnerable to adversarial input attacks. We use the gradient-based attack algorithm described in Sect. 4.2 to generate adversarial inputs for our NCs. We use an adversarial attack constant $c = 0.05$ and the parameters for the beta distributions are $a = 2$ and $b = 4$. From 100,000 unique initial states, we obtain 5 adversarial states for our MG configuration. In these experiments, we perturb all state variables simultaneously.

We confirmed with simulations that all generated adversarial states lead to safety violations when the NC alone is used, and that safety is maintained when Bb-Simplex is used. Figure 4 (left) shows one such case, where the NC commits a voltage safety violation. The red horizontal line shows the reference voltage $v_{ref} = 0.48$ kV. The black dashed horizontal line shows the lower boundary of the safety region, 3% below $v_{ref}$. Figure 4 (right) shows how Bb-Simplex prevents the safety violation. The pink vertical line marks the switch from NC to BC.

We also confirmed that for all generated adversarial states, the forward switch is followed by a reverse switch. The time between forward switch and reverse switch depends on the choice of $m$ (see Sect. 3.2). In the run shown in Fig. 4 (right), they are 5 time steps (0.016 sec) apart; the time of the reverse switch is not depicted explicitly, because the line for it would mostly overlap the line marking the forward switch. For $m = 2, 3, 4$, the average number of time steps between them are 8 (0.0256 s), 13 (0.0416 s), and 18 (0.0576 s).

**Table 2.** Performance comparison of original NC and NC retrained by AM

| NC | CR | CT | $\sigma(CT)$ | $\delta$ | $\sigma(\delta)$ |
|---|---|---|---|---|---|
| Retrained | 100 | 70.2 | 5.7 | 1.4e−4 | 1.3e−5 |
| Original | 100 | 81.1 | 7.7 | 1.5e−4 | 1.3e−5 |

## 5.4  Evaluation of Adaptation Module

To measure the benefits of online retraining, we used the adversarial inputs described above to trigger switches to BC. We used the switching conditions derived using the SOS-based methodology. We ran the original NC from the first adversarial input state, performed online retraining while the BC is in control, and repeated this procedure for the remaining adversarial states except starting with the updated NC from the previous step. As such, the retraining is cumulative. We performed this entire procedure separately for different RSCs corresponding to different values of $m$. After the cumulative retraining, we ran the retrained controller from all of the adversarial states, to check whether the retrained NC was still vulnerable (i.e., whether those states caused violations).

The BC was in control for a total of 40, 70, and 95 time steps for $m = 2, 3, 4$, respectively. For $m = 2$, the retrained controllers were still vulnerable to some adversarial states. For $m = 3, 4$, the retrained controllers were not vulnerable to any of the adversarial states, and voltage always converged to the tolerance region. Table 2 demonstrates performance comparison of the original and retrained NCs, averaged over 100 runs starting from random (non-adversarial) states which shows a slight improvement in the performance of the retrained NC (13.4% for $CT$ and 6% for $\delta$). Thus, retraining improves both safety and performance.

## 6  Related Work

The use of BaCs in the Simplex architecture originated in [36]. There are, however, significant differences between their method for obtaining the switching condition and ours. Their switching logic involves computing, at each decision period, the set of states reachable from the current state within one control period, and then checking whether that set of states is a subset of the zero-level set of the BaC. Our approach avoids the need for reachability calculations by using a Taylor approximation of the BaC, and bounds on the BaC's derivatives, to bound the possible values of the BaC during the next control period and thereby determine recoverability of states reachable during that time. Our approach is computationally much cheaper: a reachability computation is expensive compared to evaluating a polynomial. Their framework can handle hybrid systems. Extending our method to hybrid systems is a direction for future work.

Mehmood et al. [19] propose a distributed Simplex architecture with BCs synthesized using control barrier functions (CBFs) and with switching conditions derived from the CBFs, which are BaCs satisfying additional constraints. A derivation of switching conditions based on Taylor approximation of CBFs is briefly described but does not consider the remainder error, admissible states, or restricted admissible states, and does not include a proof of correctness (which requires an analysis of the remainder error).

Kundu et al. [13] and Wang et al. [34] use BaCs for safety of microgrids, and Prajna et al. [28] propose an approach for stochastic safety verification of continuous and hybrid systems using BaCs. These approaches are based on the use of verified-safe controllers; they do not allow the use of unverified high-performance controllers, do not consider switching conditions, etc.

The application of neural networks for microgrid control is gaining in popularity [16]. Amoateng et al. [2] use adaptive neural networks and cooperative control theory to develop microgrid controllers for inverter-based DERs. Using Lyapunov analysis, they prove that their error-function values and weight-estimation errors are uniformly ultimately bounded. Tan et al. [32] use Recurrent Probabilistic Wavelet Fuzzy Neural Networks (RPWFNNs) for microgrid control, since they work well under uncertainty and generalize well. We used more traditional DNNs, since they are already high performing, and our focus is on safety assurance. Our Bb-Simplex framework, however, allows any kind of neural network to be used as the AC and can provide the safety guarantees lacking in their work. Unlike our approach, none of these works provide safety guarantees.

## 7   Conclusion

We have presented Bb-Simplex, a new, provably correct design for runtime assurance of continuous dynamical systems. Bb-Simplex features a new scalable automated method for deriving, from the barrier certificate, computationally inexpensive conditions for switching between advanced and baseline controllers.

We combined Bb-Simplex with the Neural Simplex Architecture and applied the combined framework to micgrogrid control. We conducted an extensive experimental evaluation of the framework on a realistic model of a microgrid with multiple types of energy sources. The experiments demonstrate that the framework can be used to develop high-performance, generalizable neural controllers (NCs) while assuring specified safety properties, even in the presence of adversarial input attacks on the NC. Our experiments also demonstrate that the derived forward switching conditions are not too conservative, i.e., they switch control from the NC to the BC only a short time before a safety violation becomes unavoidable, and that online retraining of the NC is effective in preventing subsequent safety violations by the NC.

As future work, we plan to extend our framework to systems with noise or other sources of uncertainty in the dynamics. We also plan to eliminate the need for manually developed analytical dynamic models by learning neural ODEs [7,41] that capture unknown parts of the dynamics, and deriving BaCs and switching conditions from the resulting dynamics. We also intend to apply our approach to networked microgrids [37].

**Acknowledgement.** We thank the anonymous reviewers for their valuable feedback. This work was supported in part by NSF grants ITE-2134840, ITE-2040599, CCF-1954837, CCF-1918225, and CPS-1446832.

# References

1. Abadi, M., et al.: TensorFlow: large-scale machine learning on heterogeneous systems (2015). https://www.tensorflow.org/
2. Amoateng, D.O., Al Hosani, M., Elmoursi, M.S., Turitsyn, K., Kirtley, J.L.: Adaptive voltage and frequency control of islanded multi-microgrids. IEEE Trans. Power Syst. **33**(4), 4454–4465 (2018)
3. Anghel, M., Milano, F., Papachristodoulou, A.: Algorithmic construction of Lyapunov functions for power system stability analysis. IEEE Trans. Circuits Syst. I Regul. Pap. **60**(9), 2533–2546 (2013)
4. Bak, S., Greer, A., Mitra, S.: Hybrid cyberphysical system verification with Simplex using discrete abstractions. In: 16th IEEE Real-Time and Embedded Technology and Applications Symposium, pp. 143–152 (2010)
5. Bak, S., Manamcheri, K., Mitra, S., Caccamo, M.: Sandboxing controllers for cyberphysical systems. In: Proceedings of the IEEE/ACM International Conference on Cyber-Physical Systems (ICCPS 2011), pp. 3–12 April 2011
6. Borrmann, U., Wang, L., Ames, A.D., Egerstedt, M.: Control barrier certificates for safe swarm behavior. In: Egerstedt, M., Wardi, Y. (eds.) Analysis and Design of Hybrid Systems. IFAC-PapersOnLine, vol. 48, pp. 68–73. Elsevier (2015)
7. Chen, T.Q., Rubanova, Y., Bettencourt, J., Duvenaud, D.: Neural ordinary differential equations. In: Advances in Neural Information Processing Systems 31: Annual Conference on Neural Information Processing Systems (NeurIPS 2018), pp. 6572–6583 (2018)
8. Chollet, F., et al.: Keras (2015). https://github.com/keras-team/keras.git
9. Damare, A., Roy, S., Smolka, S.A., Stoller, S.D.: A barrier certificate-based Simplex architecture with application to microgrids (2022). https://doi.org/10.48550/ARXIV.2202.09710
10. Guerrero, J.M., Vasquez, J.C., Matas, J., de Vicuna, L.G., Castilla, M.: Hierarchical control of droop-controlled AC and DC microgrids - a general approach toward standardization. IEEE Trans. Industr. Electron. **58**(1), 158–172 (2011)
11. Johnson, T.T., Bak, S., Caccamo, M., Sha, L.: Real-time reachability for verified Simplex design. ACM Trans. Embedded Comput. Syst. **15**(2), 26:1–26:27 (2016)
12. Kingma, D.P., Ba, J.: Adam: a method for stochastic optimization. In: 3rd International Conference on Learning Representations, pp. 1–15 (2015)
13. Kundu, S., Geng, S., Nandanoori, S.P., Hiskens, I.A., Kalsi, K.: Distributed barrier certificates for safe operation of inverter-based microgrids. In: 2019 American Control Conference, pp. 1042–1047 (2019)
14. Lasseter, R., Paigi, P.: Microgrid: a conceptual solution. In: 2004 IEEE 35th Annual Power Electronics Specialists Conference (IEEE Cat. No. 04CH37551), vol. 6, pp. 4285–4290 (2004)
15. Lillicrap, T.P., et al.: Continuous control with deep reinforcement learning. In: 4th International Conference on Learning Representations, pp. 1–14 (2016)
16. Lopez-Garcia, T.B., Coronado-Mendoza, A., Domínguez-Navarro, J.A.: Artificial neural networks in microgrids: a review. Eng. Appl. Artif. Intell. **95**(103894), 1–14 (2020)

17. Luitel, B., Venayagamoorthy, G.K.: Neural networks in RSCAD for intelligent real-time power system applications. In: 2013 IEEE Power Energy Society General Meeting, pp. 1–5 (2013)

18. Luitel, B., Venayagamoorthy, G.K., Oliveira, G.: Developing neural networks library in RSCAD for real-time power system simulation. In: 2013 IEEE Computational Intelligence Applications in Smart Grid (CIASG 2013), pp. 130–137 (2013)

19. Mehmood, U., Stoller, S.D., Grosu, R., Roy, S., Damare, A., Smolka, S.A.: A distributed Simplex architecture for multi-agent systems. In: Proceedings of the Symposium on Dependable Software Engineering: Theories, Tools and Applications (SETTA 2021). Lecture Notes in Computer Science, vol. 13071, pp. 239–257. Springer (2021). https://doi.org/10.1007/978-3-030-91265-9_13

20. Mehrizi-Sani, A.: Distributed control techniques in microgrids. In: Mahmoud, M.S. (ed.) Microgrid: Advanced Control Methods and Renewable Energy System Integration, pp. 43–62. Butterworth-Heinemann (2017)

21. Nzimako, O., Rajapakse, A.: Real time simulation of a microgrid with multiple distributed energy resources. In: International Conference on Cogeneration, Small Power Plants and District Energy (ICUE 2016), pp. 1–6 (2016)

22. O'Rourke, C.J., Qasim, M.M., Overlin, M.R., Kirtley, J.L.: A geometric interpretation of reference frames and transformations: dq0, Clarke, and Park. IEEE Trans. Energy Convers. **34**(4), 2070–2083 (2019)

23. Pattanaik, A., Tang, Z., Liu, S., Bommannan, G., Chowdhary, G.: Robust deep reinforcement learning with adversarial attacks. https://doi.org/10.48550/ARXIV.1712.03632

24. Phan, D., Grosu, R., Jansen, N., Paoletti, N., Smolka, S.A., Stoller, S.D.: Neural Simplex architecture. In: NASA Formal Methods Symposium, pp. 97–114. Springer International Publishing (2020). https://doi.org/10.1007/978-3-030-55754-6_6

25. Pogaku, N., Prodanovic, M., Green, T.C.: Modeling, analysis and testing of autonomous operation of an inverter-based microgrid. IEEE Trans. Power Electron. **22**(2), 613–625 (2007)

26. Prajna, S.: Barrier certificates for nonlinear model validation. Automatica **42**(1), 117–126 (2006)

27. Prajna, S., Jadbabaie, A.: Safety verification of hybrid systems using barrier certificates. In: Alur, R., Pappas, G.J. (eds.) HSCC 2004. LNCS, vol. 2993, pp. 477–492. Springer, Heidelberg (2004). https://doi.org/10.1007/978-3-540-24743-2_32

28. Prajna, S., Jadbabaie, A., Pappas, G.J.: A framework for worst-case and stochastic safety verification using barrier certificates. IEEE Trans. Autom. Control **52**(8), 1415–1428 (2007)

29. Seto, D., Krogh, B., Sha, L., Chutinan, A.: The Simplex architecture for safe online control system upgrades. In: Proceedings of the 1998 American Control Conference. ACC (IEEE Cat. No. 98CH36207), vol. 6, pp. 3504–3508 (1998)

30. Sha, L.: Using simplicity to control complexity. IEEE Softw. **18**(4), 20–28 (2001)

31. Sha, M., et al.: Synthesizing barrier certificates of neural network controlled continuous systems via approximations. In: 2021 58th ACM/IEEE Design Automation Conference, pp. 631–636 (2021)

32. Tan, K.H., Lin, F.J., Shih, C.M., Kuo, C.N.: Intelligent control of microgrid with virtual inertia using recurrent probabilistic wavelet fuzzy neural network. IEEE Trans. Power Electron. **35**(7), 7451–7464 (2020)

33. Ton, D.T., Smith, M.A.: The U.S. department of energy's microgrid initiative. Electr. J. **25**(8), 84–94 (2012)

34. Wang, L., Han, D., Egerstedt, M.: Permissive barrier certificates for safe stabilization using sum-of-squares. In: 2018 Annual American Control Conference, pp. 585–590 (2018)
35. Wang, L., Qin, Y., Tang, Z., Zhang, P.: Software-defined microgrid control: the genesis of decoupled cyber-physical microgrids. IEEE Open Access J. Power Energy **7**, 173–182 (2020)
36. Yang, J., Islam, M.A., Murthy, A., Smolka, S.A., Stoller, S.D.: A simplex architecture for hybrid systems using barrier certificates. In: Tonetta, S., Schoitsch, E., Bitsch, F. (eds.) SAFECOMP 2017. LNCS, vol. 10488, pp. 117–131. Springer, Cham (2017). https://doi.org/10.1007/978-3-319-66266-4_8
37. Zhang, P.: Networked Microgrids. Cambridge University Press (2021)
38. Zhao, H., Zeng, X., Chen, T., Liu, Z.: Synthesizing barrier certificates using neural networks. In: Proceedings of the 23rd International Conference on Hybrid Systems: Computation and Control (HSCC 2020), pp. 1–11. Association for Computing Machinery (2020)
39. Zhao, Q., et al: Synthesizing ReLU neural networks with two hidden layers as barrier certificates for hybrid systems. In: Proceedings of the 24th International Conference on Hybrid Systems: Computation and Control (HSCC 2021), pp. 1–11. Association for Computing Machinery (2021)
40. Zhou, Y., Ngai-Man Ho, C.: A review on microgrid architectures and control methods. In: 2016 IEEE 8th International Power Electronics and Motion Control Conference (IPEMC-ECCE Asia 2016), pp. 3149–3156 (2016)
41. Zhou, Y., Zhang, P.: Neuro-reachability of networked microgrids. IEEE Trans. Power Syst. **37**(1), 142–152 (2021)

# Optimal Finite-State Monitoring
# of Partial Traces

Peeyush Kushwaha[1]([✉]), Rahul Purandare[1,2], and Matthew B. Dwyer[3]

[1] IIIT-Delhi, New Delhi, India
peeyush16254@iiitd.ac.in
[2] University of Nebraska-Lincoln, Lincoln, USA
rahul@unl.edu
[3] University of Virginia, Charlottesville, USA
matthewbdwyer@virginia.edu

**Abstract.** Monitoring programs for finite state properties is challenging due to high memory and execution time overheads it incurs. Some events if skipped or lost naturally can reduce both overheads, but lead to uncertainty about the current monitor state. In this work, we present a theoretical framework to model traces that carry partial information (like number of events lost), and provide construction for a monitor capable of monitoring these *partial traces* without producing *false positives* while reporting violations. The constructed monitor optimally reports as many violations as possible for the partial traces. We model several loss types of practical relevance using our framework.

**Keywords:** Runtime verification · Finite state properties · Optimization

## 1 Introduction

Monitoring the execution behavior of software goes back to the dawn of programming and is a standard practice, e.g., through logging, programmer inserted print statements, and assertions. In the late 1990s, researchers began to explore the use of formal specifications to define run-time monitors [1] which brought the expressive power of formal methods to monitoring. Such *run-time verification* techniques rely on a set of defined *events* which denote the occurrence of program behavior relevant to a property specification, e.g., the invocation of a particular method, along with associated data, e.g., method parameters. A run-time monitor observes a *trace* generated by a program execution, incrementally updates the *state* of the specified property, and reports a property violation when a violating state is reached.

Run-time verification is attractive because it complements sound static verification approaches that cannot scale to modern software systems. However, monitoring occasionally incurs high memory and execution time overheads. Researchers have proposed a range of techniques to deal with the challenge of reducing these overheads, while preserving violation detection e.g., [2–6]. In

T. Dang and V. Stolz (Eds.): RV 2022, LNCS 13498, pp. 124–142, 2022.
https://doi.org/10.1007/978-3-031-17196-3_7

this paper, we consider the additional challenge of *partial trace* that arises in the deployment of run-time verification in realistic system contexts such as: networked and distributed systems where message loss or reordering may be inherent, real-time systems which may shed monitoring workloads to meet scheduling constraints, or web-based systems with quality-of-service guarantees may lead to suppressed monitoring. In such systems, the original trace may be perturbed by dropping events, reordering events, or dropping or corrupting data correlated with events.

Partial traces are problematic for existing run-time verification approaches since treating a partial trace the same as the original trace may lead to missing a property violation or falsely declaring a violating execution. Partial traces do not, in general, permit the same degree of precision as the original trace. The information loss restricts us to two choices: reporting unconfirmed violations (including false positives), or reporting only confirmed violations (but missing some violations). Our framework is able to model both, but we present our results in the context of the second choice, for reduced run-time overhead at the cost of missed violations (e.g. [7,8]).

The first choice may be equally useful for ensuring compliance (e.g. [9,10]) and we show how it is enabled by our framework in Sect. 5. Existing work on partial traces [7,10] studies specific types of losses but does not contain a general model that could be used to study other loss types.

The paper makes foundational contributions to runtime verification by (a) *defining an expressive framework for modeling partial traces*, (b) *developing techniques for synthesizing provably complete and optimal verification monitors under those models*. Importantly, these results preclude the need for additional theory development for individual loss types and set the stage for more applied work and tool development. The main contributions of this paper are theoretical, complemented by (c) *a collection of diverse loss models*, including a discussion of how the event losses in current literature are specific instances of our general framework (Sects. 6, 7). For the expressiveness of our framework, we prove that *all* loss models are representable in our framework under these conditions: (i) the original property is a finite-state safety property, (ii) the desired monitor for partial traces is finite-state, and (iii) loss model can be represented as an arbitrary relation between original and partial strings.

## 2   Overview

We illustrate the problem by way of example and introduce the key insights behind the techniques we develop to address the problem.

Safety properties for run-time monitoring can be modelled using deterministic finite-state automata (DFA). An event is represented by a *symbol* and a trace by a *string* of symbols. Figure 1a shows the DFA for the *SafeIter* property which states that modification of a collection during iteration is not permitted. The DFA is expressed over the alphabet $\{n, u\}$ denoting accessing the (n)ext element in the iterator, and (u)pdating the collection being iterated.

*Remark 1.* Some literature uses an additional $c$ "creation" event for this property. The interpretation of such events are implementation dependent. The implementation may use observance of this event to dynamically allocate memory for a monitor and instrument the code for other events just-in-time. In such a case, if the creation event is missed then the monitor is never created and the property is not monitored. For a statically allocated monitor, it may also be used as the fixed initial event – an effect equivalent to adding a state $q_0$ before $q_1$ with a transition $c$ from $q_0$ and $q_1$. We model only the property after the creation event has happened and the monitor is ready to receive the first non-creation event, and leave implementation-dependent semantics out of our modelling. The framework, however, is trivially extensible to accommodate creation events, we discuss this extension in Sect. 6 along with an example where the role of creation events is more complicated.

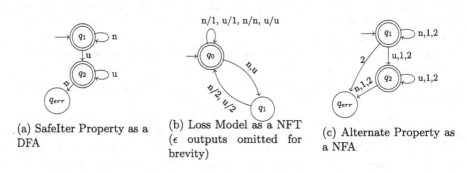

(a) SafeIter Property as a DFA

(b) Loss Model as a NFT ($\epsilon$ outputs omitted for brevity)

(c) Alternate Property as a NFA

**Fig. 1.** Safe Iterator – after an iterator is created no updates (u) are permitted so long as next (n) elements remain to be accessed.

The state $q_{err}$ is a trap state (self transitions ommitted for brevity) denoting the violation of the property. All violating strings include a subsequence ...$un$... indicating that an update was performed prior to accessing the next element. Statements that are free of such a subsequence end at one of the three accept states and are non-violating.

Loss may come in different forms. For example, symbols in a string may be erased (e.g., $n \rightarrow \epsilon$), reordered (e.g., $nu \rightarrow un$), or be modeled with only partial information (e.g., their count $nnn \rightarrow 3$).

To illustrate, we consider the case where symbols are dropped from the string, but the number of dropped symbols is recorded. This type of loss could be introduced intentionally as a means of mitigating excessive runtime overhead in monitoring, or it could occur naturally, for instance if an event arrives to the system strictly periodically, e.g., at 10 hz, but several of those inputs are missed in a row (due to load on the system, communication disruption, etc.).

We show how to continue monitoring while preserving fault detection capability. Consider a string $nnun$ where this loss is applied to the first two – we model the resulting string as $2un$. This could represent 4 possible strings starting with one of four $\{u, n\}^2$ and a suffix of $un$. For longer strings where sequences of length $k$ are lost, the combinatorics of their possible replacements $\{u, n\}^k$ make it intractable to consider all of the possibilities. Despite this, the structure of Fig. 1a dictates that any string of the form $kun$ violates the property, thereby illustrating that even with loss it is possible to perform accurate monitoring.

We formalize the intuition above in a *loss model* that maps symbols from the property to an alternative symbol set. For example, the loss model described above is defined by the mapping $\{u, n\}^k \mapsto k$. In Sect. 5, we show that all mappings of interest are a restricted class of relations on strings called rational relations. Rational relations can be represented by non-deterministi finite-state transducers (NFTs). An NFT maps strings in an alphabet, $\Sigma$, to strings in an alternative alphabet, $\Sigma_a$. Figure 1b shows the NFT with the mapping for alternate symbols 1 and 2 that lose the identity of symbols in a subsequence but retain its length, e.g. as in the $2un$ example we just discussed.

Retaining partial information about an event string might be insufficient to conclude that a violation occurred (or did not occur). We report a violation only when the partial information is sufficient to conclude that there must be a violation – such monitoring is *complete*[1] since it never reports a false violation. Consider the original string ($O_1$) in Fig. 2 and the set of 3 partial strings ($L_1$) induced by the NFT in Fig. 1b. Tracing through Fig. 1a on the first two partial strings by interpreting 1 and 2 as any individual or pair of symbols, respectively, leads only to the error state – since they preserve the fact that an $n$ follows a $u$. These strings would be reported as violations. On the other hand, the string $nnuu$ ($O_2$) is non-violating and of the set of 3 partial strings ($L_2$) none reach *only* the $q_{err}$ state. Completeness assures that no partial string can have $u$ followed by a $n$ and monitor in Fig. 1b won't report a false violation. The automaton which would observe these partial strings of alternate alphabet and give the states we discussed is shown in Fig. 1c.

Assuring completeness in violation reporting means, however, that the reporting of some violations may be missed. For example, the third partial string for $L_1$ suppresses all $nu$ making it impossible to definitively conclude that the observed string is a violation. Our goal is to report violations on as many strings of alternate symbols as possible while maintaining completeness. When we refer to *optimality* of monitoring the partial trace, we are referring to this goal (discussed in Sect. 5).

|  | String | State(s) |
|---|---|---|
| $O_1$ | nnunnun | $q_{err}$ |
| $L_1$ | 2nun2n | $\{ q_{err} \}$ |
|  | n1unnun | $\{ q_{err} \}$ |
|  | nnu2u1 | $\{ q_2, q_{err} \}$ |
| $O_2$ | nnuu | $q_2$ |
| $L_2$ | 2uu | $\{ q_2, q_{err} \}$ |
|  | nnu1 | $\{ q_2, q_{err} \}$ |
|  | 2n2 | $\{ q_1, q_2, q_{err} \}$ |

**Fig. 2.** Partial strings

In Sect. 4 we will show how loss models (such as the one in Fig. 1b) are defined, and how the property of interest (e.g. Fig. 1a) and the loss model are used to construct the alternate monitor (e.g. Fig. 1c) which would observe the partial trace and optimally monitor them. Discussion

---

[1] See Remark 5 for a discussion on the terms *soundness* and *completness*.

and significance for implementation of the theory developed in Sect. 3–Sect. 5 is given in Sect. 5.1.

# 3  Basic Definitions

## 3.1  Notation

1. $x \prec y$: string $x$ is a proper prefix of string $y$.
2. $f : X \to Y$ is *lifted* to $2^X$ as given by $f(S) = \{ f(x) \mid x \in S \} \; \forall S \subseteq X$.
3. $(\cdot)$ is string concatenation. $(\cdot)$ is lifted to sets of strings.
4. $\times$ is cartesian product of two sets. For a relation $R \subseteq X \times Y$, $R(x) = \{ y \mid xRy \}$ and $R^{-1}(y) = \{ x \mid xRy \}$
5. $\mathrm{DOMAIN}(R) = \{ x \mid \exists y \text{ s.t. } xRy \}$, $\mathrm{RANGE}(R) = \{ y \mid \exists x \text{ s.t. } xRy \}$.
6. A *partition* $\mathcal{P}$ of a set $S$ is a set $\{ P_1, P_2, \dots \}$ such that $P_i$ are pairwise disjoint nonempty sets (*equivalence classes*) with union $S$.
7. A *class representative* of $P_i$ is a distinguished element in $P_i$.
8. For $s \in S$ in $\mathcal{P}$, $[s]_{\mathcal{P}}$: equivalence class, and $rep^{\mathcal{P}}(s)$: class representative.
9. ■: proof omitted (due to triviality/limited space/relevance).

*Finite Automata and Properties.* Familiarity with regular languages and their properties is assumed. A finite set of symbols is called an *alphabet*. $REG(\Sigma)$ is the set of all regular languages over an alphabet $\Sigma$. $\epsilon$ is the empty string, and $\Sigma_\epsilon$ is the alphabet $\Sigma \cup \{ \epsilon \}$. A *trace* is a (possibly infinite) sequence of events, and an *execution* is a finite prefix of a trace. A trace $x$ is a *continuation* of an execution $x'$ if $x' \prec x$.

## 3.2  Definitions

**Definition 1 (Finite Automata).** *A finite automaton is a 5-tuple $(Q, \Sigma, \delta, q_0, F)$ with a finite set of states $Q$, the alphabet $\Sigma$, a specified initial state $q_0 \in Q$, and the set of final states $F \subseteq Q$. A deterministic finite automaton (DFA) has the transition function $\delta : Q \times \Sigma \to Q$ and a nondeterministic finite automaton (NFA) has the transition function $\delta : Q \times \Sigma \to 2^Q$. The transition function $\delta$ is lifted to strings, sets of strings, and sets of states. We call $L(A) = \{ x \in \Sigma^* \mid \delta(q_0, x) \in F \}$ the language of the finite automaton.*

**Definition 2 (Nondeterministic Finite-State Transducers (NFTs)).** *Defined as a NFA $(Q, \Sigma, \delta, q_0, F)$ with an extra alphabet $\Gamma$ (labelled the "output" alphabet), where $\delta : Q \times \Sigma \to 2^{Q \times \Gamma_\epsilon}$. After observing a symbol $\sigma \in \Sigma$, the NFT in state $q$ transitions to a choice of $q'$ with output $\gamma \in \Gamma_\epsilon$ where $(q', \gamma)$ is one of the pairs in $\delta(q, \sigma)$.*

**Definition 3 (Finite-state safety property).** *A finite-state property $\phi$ is the minimal-state DFA $\phi = (Q, \Sigma, \delta, q_0, Q \setminus \{ q_{err} \})$ with the specified error state $q_{err}$. The error state $q_{err}$ must be a trap state, i.e. $\forall \sigma \in \Sigma$, $\delta(q_{err}, \sigma) = q_{err}$. For a property $\phi$, the notation $Q^\phi, \Sigma^\phi, \delta^\phi, q_0^\phi$, and $q_{err}^\phi$ is used to refer to $Q, \Sigma, \delta, q_0$, and $q_{err}$ respectively. An execution $x \in \Sigma^*$ violates the property $\phi$ if $\delta(q_0, x) = q_{err}$. An execution $x$ that does not violate the property is non-violating.*

Let $n \in Z^+$, $\Gamma = \Sigma \cup \{1 \ldots n\}$, $R \subseteq \Sigma \times \Gamma$ s.t.:

$$aRb \text{ iff } \begin{cases} a = b & b \in \Sigma \\ |a| = b & b \in \{1 \ldots n\} \end{cases}$$

(a) Dropped-count Loss. The formal definition of loss type from Sect. 2.

Let $\Delta \subseteq \Sigma$ be symbols which may be skipped.

$$\Gamma = \{ x' \mid x \in \Sigma \}$$
$$R = \{ (a, b') \mid a \in \Delta^* b \text{ and } b \in \Sigma \}$$

(b) Silent Drop Loss: several dropped $\Delta$ symbols may precede an observed $\Gamma$ symbol $b$. The marker $'$ is used here just to visually distinguish symbols in $\Gamma$ from $\Sigma$.

**Fig. 3.** Formally specified loss types

*Remark 2.* Complement of language of automaton $\phi$: $L(\phi)^C = \Sigma^* \setminus L(\phi)$ are all the strings violating $\phi$. If an execution violates a property, then so do all its continuations (because $q_{err}$ is a trap state).

**Definition 4 (Monitors).** *A monitor $M_\phi$ observes events for a property $\phi$. $M_\phi$ has a current state $q_{curr}$, initialized as $q_{curr} = q_0$, and updated as $q_{curr} \leftarrow \delta(q, \sigma)$ on observing $\sigma \in \Sigma$. The verdict of a monitor on a trace is true if the property $\phi$ cannot be violated in any continuation, false if the property has been violated, inconclusive if neither.*

*Remark 3 (Valuedness).* Our definition of monitors considers 3 verdicts. However, in theoretical development of our result we only care about "violation" or "no violation", i.e. "false" verdict is distinguished from "inconclusive" and "true" but the latter two are not distinguished from each other.

The terms "monitor" and "property" are used interchangeably when clear from the context (e.g. language of a monitor). The analysis in the following sections is not affected by the existence of multiple monitors. Therefore we omit any discussion of it till our discussion of a particular loss type in Sect. 6.

## 4  Losses, Alternate Monitors, Soundness and Optimality

This section and the next contain our theoretical results. We do not *assume* a loss model $R$ must be an NFT, but rather prove it (in the next section). That's why we begin with a general definition of a loss model with minimal restrictions (only to exclude cases without valid interpretation[2] ).

**Definition 5 (Loss Model).** *A loss model for an original alphabet $\Sigma$ to an alternate alphabet $\Gamma$ is a relation $R \subseteq \Sigma^* \times \Gamma$ satisfying:*

*1. No spurious alternate symbols condition: $\epsilon \notin \text{DOMAIN}(R)$*

---

[2] The first condition excludes partial symbols produced not corresponding to any original information. The second condition excludes existence of full traces which are completely lost, i.e. for which no partial information is ever observed.

*2. Prefix existence condition: There is an upper-bound $n \in \mathbb{Z}^+$ such that for all strings $x \in \Sigma^*$ of length $n$ or more (i.e. $|x| \geq n$) at least one prefix $x' \preceq x$ is a part of* $\mathrm{DOMAIN}(R)$ *(i.e. $x' \in \mathrm{DOMAIN}(R)$)*

*We assign the loss model $R$ the interpretation that $(x, \gamma) \in R$ means that if a symbol $\gamma$ is observed in alternate trace $y \in \Gamma*$, then it was produced in lieu of one of the strings $x \in R^{-1}(\gamma)$.*

We use a related term *loss type* to roughly denote a family of related loss models. As an example, the loss type for the loss model from Sect. 2 is given in Fig. 3a, which is parameterized over various choices of $\Sigma$ and $n$ (and where for a specific choice of $\Sigma$ and $n$ we'd obtain a *loss model* of that *loss type*).

To motivate our next definition, consider the partial traces $y_1 = 2n2$ and $y_2 = 3uu$ from Fig. 2 for the corresponding original trace $x = nnnuu$ $(O_2)$. For $y_1$, as the program runs the original monitor observes $n$ and alternate monitor observes nothing. On the next event original monitor again observes $n$ and alternate monitor observes 2. For every prefix of $x$ we have a corresponding prefix of $y_1$, and we may relate them with a *filter* function $f_1$ such that $f_1(n) = \epsilon$, $f_1(nn) = 2, \ldots f_1(nnnuu) = 2n2$. $f_1$ will be a partial function defined only on prefixes of $x$. We could similarly define filter $f_2$ for the relation between prefixes of $x$ and prefixes of $y_2$. Not all functions between $\Sigma^*$ and $\Gamma^*$ would satisfy the loss model $R$ – one obvious limitation would be that filter $f$ must produce outputs for a string $x$ which are consistent with what $R$ relates to prefixes of $x$. We formalize these requirements on a function and call a function that satisfies them a *filter*, as defined next:

**Definition 6 (Filter, Partial Traces, Segments, and Replacements).** *Let $\Sigma$ and $\Gamma$ be finite alphabets, and $x \in \Sigma^*$ be a trace, and $P_x = \{ x' \mid x' \preceq x \}$ be the set of all finite prefixes of $x$. Consider a loss model $R \subseteq \Sigma^* \times \Gamma$ . Then a function $f : P_x \to \Gamma^*$ is called a* filter *under $R$ if it satisfies the* monotonicity *property, defined below:*
*if $f(x) = y$ and $f(x') \neq y$ for all proper prefixes $x'$ of $x$, then:*

$$f(x \cdot s) = \begin{cases} y \cdot \gamma & \text{if } sR\gamma \\ y & \text{otherwise} \end{cases}$$

*In the first case $\gamma$ is called a* replacement (symbol) *for the* segment *$s$ (sub-string) of the string $x \cdot s$.*

*$\mathcal{F}_R$ is defined as the set of all possible functions which are filters under $R$.*

**Definition 7 (Completions).** *We're also interested in possible strings $x \in \Sigma^*$ which could have lead to the observation $y$. If $\exists f \in \mathcal{F}_R$ such that the last symbol in $x$ marks end of a segment and produces the last symbol in $y$, i.e. $f(x) = y \wedge \nexists x' \prec x, f(x') = y$, then we call $x$ a completion for $y$. We define $\mathfrak{C}(y)$ as the set of all completions for $y$:*

$$\mathfrak{C}(y) = \{ x \in \Sigma^* \mid \exists f \in \mathcal{F}_R \text{such that } f(x) = y \wedge \nexists x' \prec x \wedge f(x') = y \}$$

Next, we show how to compute the set of completions $\mathfrak{C}(y)$ using $R^{-1}$.

**Theorem 1.** *For a string $y \in \Gamma^*$, $y = \gamma_1 \gamma_2 \ldots \gamma_k$:*

$$\mathfrak{C}(y) = R^{-1}(\gamma_1) \ldots R^{-1}(\gamma_k)$$

*Proof. (LHS $\subseteq$ RHS)* Let $x \in \mathfrak{C}(y)$. Let $y = y'\gamma_k$. From definition of filters and the condition $\not\exists x' \prec x, f(x') = y$ in definition of $\mathfrak{C}(y)$ we can partition $x$ into two substrings $x = x'x_k$ where $x_k$ is the corresponding segment for the replacement $\gamma$ i.e. $x_k R \gamma_k$. Repeatedly applying this reasoning (e.g. in the next step for $y'$ and $x'$), we conclude $\exists$ a partition $x = x_1 \ldots x_k$ such that $\gamma_1, \ldots, \gamma_k$ are a replacements for respective $x_i$. Then $x_i \in R^{-1}(\gamma_i)$ and thus $x \in R^{-1}(\gamma_1) \ldots R^{-1}(\gamma_k)$. *(RHS $\subseteq$ LHS)* Let $x \in R^{-1}(\gamma_1) \ldots R^{-1}(\gamma_k) \implies x = x_1 \ldots x_k \implies f(x) = \gamma_1 \ldots \gamma_k = y$. $\qquad\square$

We now give definitions of alternate monitors and their soundness, completeness, and optimality. We present the construction in the next section.

**Definition 8 (Alternate monitor).** *Given a primary monitor $M_\phi$ and a loss model $R \subseteq \Sigma^* \times \Gamma$, an alternate monitor $M_\psi$ is any finite state monitor over the alphabet $\Gamma$ that observes the partial execution $f(e)$ for any $f \in \mathcal{F}_R$ when $M_\phi$ observes the execution $e$. We call $(M_\phi, M_\psi)_R$ a primary-alternate monitor pair and $(\phi, \psi)_R$ a primary-alternate property pair. We also refer to these as just monitor pair or property pair.*

*Remark 4.* It is useful to consider the monitors in $(M_\phi, M_\psi)_R$ as monitoring together for the purposes of theoretical analysis and for definitions. In practice, we want to monitor using just $M_\psi$.

**Definition 9 (Soundness and Completeness for a property pair).** *For $(\phi, \psi)_R$, with the definition of $\mathfrak{C}$ lifted to the set of strings, we define:*

Soundness: *A non-violating trace must not have any violating completions, i.e. $y \in L(\psi) \implies \mathfrak{C}(y) \subseteq L(\phi)$, equivalently $\mathfrak{C}(L(\psi)) \subseteq L(\phi)$.*

Completeness: *A violating trace must have all violating completions, i.e. $y \notin L(\psi) \implies \mathfrak{C}(y) \subseteq L(\phi)^C$, equivalently $\mathfrak{C}(L(\psi)^C) \subseteq L(\phi)^C$.*

*Remark 5.* Our definitions of soundness and completeness of a monitor are consistent with the definitions commonly used in the literature on program analysis and verification [11]. There also exist other definitions, particularly in the literature on runtime verification, which essentially interchange the interpretations of soundness and completeness of a monitor as defined here.

**Definition 10 (Optimality of a property pair).** *For $(\phi, \psi^*)_R$ where $\psi^*$ is complete, $\psi^*$ is called optimal if for any other complete property pair $(\phi, \psi)_R$, $L(\psi^*) \subseteq L(\psi)$, or equivalently $\mathfrak{C}(L(\psi^*)) \subseteq \mathfrak{C}(L(\psi))$. We call $(\phi, \psi^*)_R$ an optimal pair.*

*Remark 6.* Our definition of Optimality is a strong definition. An alternate definition for an optimal monitor might be to count the number of strings up to any given length and define a monitor which reports a violation on maximum number of strings for every length as the optimal monitor, but optimality by our definition would imply optimality in this alternate definition.

**Definition 11** $(L_{opt}(\phi, R))$. *For a property $\phi$ and loss model $R$, $L_{opt}(\phi, R) = \mathcal{F}_R(L(\phi))$, i.e. $L_{opt}$ is the set of partial traces in $\Gamma^*$ produced by a non-error execution in $\Sigma^*$. $L_{opt}$ is the smallest set of strings on which a complete alternate monitor cannot reach a false verdict. i.e. $L_{opt} = \mathcal{F}_R(L(\phi)) = \{ y \mid \mathfrak{C}(y) \cap L(\phi) \neq \varnothing \}$.*

There are several definitions of monitorability in runtime verification literature [12]. The most suitable to our problem is the ability to report a violation. Since the alternate monitor is allowed to miss violations, the verdict that there are no more errors is not useful.

**Definition 12 (Monitorability).** *If there exists a continuation of an execution which leads to the* false *verdict, then the monitor's current state is monitorable. In a finite automaton, monitorability of a state $q$ can be checked by path-reachability from $q$ to the error state.*

## 5   Optimal Monitor and Losses as Transducers

In this section, we first construct an optimal monitor using the definition of $R$ introduced in the previous section. We then use that construction and its properties to prove that loss models beyond what can be represented by a finite-state transducer can be removed from our consideration. Finite-state transducers have a regular structure to deal with which makes implemention more feasible, and theoretical treatement easier. So removing other loss models from our consideration restricting $R$ to the space of loss models to these transducers is good news for us, as long as we can get the assurance that we're not missing any expressivity (which we'll show).

We begin with the construction of an optimal alternate monitor and proof of optimality. The key idea for the construction is for the optimal alternate monitor to keep track of the set of states that the primary monitor could possibly be in.

**Theorem 2.** *For a property $\phi$ and a loss model $R$, we construct the NFA $\psi$ with $\delta^\psi$ as $\forall q \in Q$, $\delta^\psi(q, y) = \delta^\phi(q, R^{-1}(y))$[3]. After determinizing and minimizing this NFA, we obtain the optimal alternate monitor $\psi^*$ which recognizes $L_{opt}$.*

In order to prove this theorem, we first need to establish correspondence of states between the NFA constructed and its determinized and minimized version. We already know that using powerset construction [13] for NFA determinization, the states of determinized DFA are labelled by subset of NFA states. We use the result that this labelling is well-defined even after minimization.

---

[3] Note that $R^{-1}(y)$ must be decidable for this construction to be well-defined. This is not an issue as we later prove that $R$ must represent a NFT, and for NFTs computing $R^{-1}(y)$ is decidable.

$\delta^{\psi*}(q,x)$

$= \begin{cases} \delta(q,\Sigma^x) & \text{if } x \in \{1\ldots n\} \\ \delta(q,x) & \text{otherwise} \end{cases}$

(a) Disabling monitoring for up to n events, defined on filter from Fig. 3a

$\delta^{\psi*}(S,x) = C_\Delta(\delta(C_\Delta(S),x))$

$C_\Delta$ is the $\Delta$-closure of the set of states $S$ in $M$, i.e. set of all states which can be reached from states in $S$ by following 0 or more $y$-transitions, where $y \in \Delta$

(b) Silent drop monitor, defined on $\Delta$ and the filter from Fig. 3b

**Fig. 4.** Example constructions of $\delta^{\psi*}$ for optimal pair $(\phi, \psi^*)_R$ Theorem 2

**Lemma 1.** *In DFA minimization [13] of a determinized NFA, let $\mathcal{P}$ be the parition of $2^Q$ where $\mathcal{S} \in \mathcal{P}$ represents a set of states merged together. If the states $S_1$ and $S_2$ merge, then the state $S_1 \cup S_2$ merges with them. i.e. $\forall \mathcal{S} \in \mathcal{P}, \forall S_1, S_2 \in \mathcal{S} \implies S_1 \cup S_2 \in \mathcal{S}.$* ∎

*Remark 7.* Using the previous lemma, for each class $[S]_\mathcal{P}$ of states, the class representative $rep^\mathcal{P}(S)$ of $S$ is defined as $\bigcup_{T \in [S]_P} T$. We label the resultant state from merged states in $[S]_P$ in the minimized DFA by $rep^P(S)$.

**Lemma 2.** *Let $(M_\phi, M_{\psi*})$ be the optimal monitor pair. When $M_{\psi*}$ transitions to a state $S \subseteq Q$ and $M_\phi$ is in the state $q$ then $q \in S$.*

*Proof.* We apply induction on the number of symbols observed by the alternate monitor.
**Base Case** holds because start state of $M_\psi$ is $\{q_0^\phi\}$.
**IH:** Assume that $q \in S$ after $n$ symbols and $n + 1$th replacement symbol $\gamma$ is observed in lieu of segment $x$.
**IS:** $M_\psi$ transitions to $S' = \delta^\psi(S,\gamma) = \delta^\phi(S, R^{-1}(\gamma))$ and $M_\phi$ transitions to $q' = \delta^\phi(q,x)$. But since $q \in S$ and $x \in R^{-1}(\gamma)$, $q' \in S'$     □

*Proof (Theorem 2).* Subproof 1: $y \notin L(\psi^*) \implies y \notin L_{opt}$. Using Lemma 2

$$y \notin L(M_\psi) \implies \delta^\psi(q_0,y) = \{q_{err}\} \implies q \in \{q_{err}\} \implies q = q_{err}$$
$$\implies \forall x \in \mathfrak{C}(y),\ \delta(q,x) = \{q_{err}\} \implies \mathfrak{C}(y) \subseteq L(M)^C \quad \square$$

*Subproof 2:* $y \in L(\psi^*) \implies y \in L_{opt}$. Consider $y \in L(\psi^*)$.

$$\implies \delta^\psi(\{q_0\},y) \neq \{q_{err}\}$$
$$\implies \delta^\psi(\ldots\delta^\psi(\delta^\psi(\{q_0\},y_1),y_2)\ldots),y_n) \neq \{q_{err}\}$$
$$\implies \delta^\phi(\ldots\delta^\phi(\delta^\phi(\{q_0\},R^{-1}(y_1)),R^{-1}(y_2))\ldots),R^{-1}(y_n)) \neq \{q_{err}\}$$
$$\implies \delta^\phi(\{q_0\},\mathfrak{C}(y)) \neq \{q_{err}\} \implies y \in L_{opt} \quad \square$$

**Corollary 1.** *Property $\phi$ is monitorable under $R$ iff the state labeled with singleton error state $\{q_{err}\}$ is reachable in $\psi^*$.*

Figure 4 and the next section show example optimal monitor constructions.

*Remark 8.* Our definition of $\psi^*$ is *constructive*, so $\psi^*$ always exists. I.e. given a property $\phi$ and loss model $R$ we can always construct $\psi^*$ using Theorem 2. However, this says nothing about usefulness of $\phi^*$. For instance, it may be the case that $\psi^*$ is unmonitorable, which would tell us that $L_{opt}(\phi, R) = \Gamma^*$. Due to being the *optimal* construction, this just demonstrates that it's *impossible* to monitor under the loss model $R$ (if $\phi$ itself was monitorable). This is an indication that too much information is lost under the loss model $R$ for the resulting partial string to be of any use for monitoring $\phi$.

We have a construction for optimal alternate monitors under the loss model $R$. Recall that we defined a *loss model* with minimal constraints in Definition 5, which permits us to define loss models of arbitrary complexity by more complex loss types (e.g. a loss type which could be represented by a transducer with a stack). We find that as long as the monitor observing the trace is constrained to be a finite-state automaton, the partial information of loss computed by more complex loss types (e.g. a loss type which could be represented by a transducer with a stack) does not help in reporting more violations, and we show that by showing that for every loss model which isn't a NFT, there is a loss model which is an NFT and results in construction of the same $\psi^*$.

**Theorem 3.** *Let $(\phi, \psi^*)_R$ be the optimal property pair where $R$ may not be representable by NFT. Then there exists a loss model $R'$ which can be represented as a NFT for which the constructed alternate property is also $\psi^*$.*

The following lemma handles the major part of the proof:

**Lemma 3.** *For an alternate symbol $\gamma \in \Gamma$, if the set of strings $X = R^{-1}(\gamma)$ is not regular, then we can come up with a set $Y$ such that $X \subset Y$ and $Y$ is regular and $\forall q \in Q \ \delta^\phi(q, X) = \delta^\phi(q, Y)$*

*Proof.* We'll use the shorthand $f(q) : Q \to 2^Q$ for $\delta(q, R^{-1}(\gamma))$, since $\gamma$ is fixed. Consider $l(q) : Q \to REG(\Sigma)$, the regular language taking us from $q$ to $f(q)$, i.e. $l(q) = \{\, x \mid x \in \Sigma^* \wedge \delta(q, x) \in f(q) \,\}$. Let $Y = \cap_{q \in Q}\, l(q)$. It follows that $Y$ is regular since regular languages are closed under intersection.

$$\implies \forall q \in Q \ R^{-1}(\gamma) \subseteq l(q) \implies R^{-1}(\gamma) \subseteq Y$$
$$\implies R^{-1}(\gamma) \subset Y \qquad (R^{-1}(\gamma) \neq Y \because R^{-1} \text{ is not regular and } Y \text{ is})$$
$$\text{Now } \forall q \in Q \ \{Y \subseteq l(q) \implies \delta(q, Y) \subseteq f(q)\}$$
$$\text{And } R^{-1}(y) \subseteq Y \implies \forall q \in Q \ \delta(q, Y) \supseteq f(q)$$
$$\implies \delta(q, Y) = f(q) = \delta(q, R^{-1}(\gamma)) \qquad \qquad \square$$

Rest of the proof uses this lemma to construct the new $R'$ for every $\gamma$. It requires additional definitions of generalized automata and transducers which allow regular expressions on transitions instead of symbols, which we now give:

**Definition 13 (Generalized Nondeterministic Finite Automaton [14]).**
*A generalized nondeterministic finite automaton (GNFA) is a 5-tuple*
$(Q, \Sigma, \delta, q_0, f)$, *where $Q$ is the finite set of states, $\Sigma$ is the alphabet, $\delta \subseteq$*
$(Q \setminus f) \times (Q \setminus \{q_0\}) \rightarrow REG(\Sigma)$ *is the transition function, and $q_0, f \in Q$*
*are the specified initial and final states.*

**Definition 14. (Generalized Nondeterministic Finite-State Transducers (GNFTs)).** *Defined as a GNFA $(Q, \Sigma, \Gamma, \delta, q_0, f)$, where $\delta : (Q \setminus f) \times (Q \setminus$
$q_0) \rightarrow 2^{REG(\Sigma) \times \Gamma}$. After observing a string $x \in \Sigma^*$, the NFT in state $q$ transitions to a choice of $q'$ with output $\gamma \in \Gamma$ where $(r, \gamma)$ s.t. $x \in L(r)$ is one of the pairs in $\delta(q, q')$.*

*Remark 9.* GNFA can be converted to NFA [13], similarly GNFT to NFT.    ∎

Using these definitions and Lemma 3, we proceed to prove Theorem 3:

*Proof (Theorem 3).* The construction in Theorem 2 uses $\delta^\phi(q, R^{-1}(\gamma))$ for defining $\delta^\psi$. Therefore it is sufficient to produce an $R'$ representable by a NFT such that $\delta^\phi(q, R'^{-1}(\gamma)) = \delta^\phi(q, R^{-1}(\gamma)) \; \forall \gamma \in \Gamma$. In rest of the proof, we use $\delta$ to denote $\delta^\phi$.

Consider a symbol $\gamma \in \Gamma$.
**Case 1:** $(R^{-1}(\gamma)$ is regular$)$ We define $xR'\gamma \; \forall xR\gamma$. So $R'^{-1}(\gamma) = R^{-1}(\gamma)$ and thus $\delta(q, R'^{-1}(\gamma)) = \delta(q, R^{-1}(\gamma))$
**Case 2:** $(R^{-1}(\gamma)$ is not regular$)$ We construct $R'^{-1}(\gamma)$ by the rational set constructed in Lemma 3.

We construct a GNFT for $R'$. Consider a GNFT with states $\{q_0, q, f\}$, $\epsilon$-transitions from $q_0$ to $q$ and $q$ to $f$, and self loop edges on $q$ $\forall \gamma \in \Gamma$ with input label as the regex of $R^{-1}(\gamma)$ and output label $\gamma$. This completes the construction.

□

Next we show that an even more relaxed definition of loss model (a relation between $\Sigma^*$ and $\Gamma^*$ instead of $\Sigma^*$ and $\Gamma$) does not increase loss models we can express.

**Theorem 4.** *For a primary-alternate pair $(\phi, \psi)$ with where $\psi$'s input on $x \in \Sigma^*$ is filtered by $f$ from a loss model $R \subseteq \Sigma^* \times \Gamma^*$, we can define a finite state property $\psi'$, alternate symbol set $\Gamma'$, loss model $R' \subseteq (\Sigma^* \times \Gamma')$ with filter $f'$ such that $\forall q \in Q^\phi \; \delta^\psi(q, f(x)) = \delta^{\psi'}(q, f'(x))$*

*Proof.* The proof exploits the observation that for a finite-state automaton $\psi$, the set of possible symbols which denote a unique transition are finite. For a symbol $\gamma \in \Gamma$, from each state there is a choice to transition to another state, resulting in an upper bound of $|Q|^{|Q|}$ unique transitions. RANGE$(R)$ may be unbounded but we partition it into a finite number of equivalence classes such that a class representative may instead be used to denote the transition. Partition all strings in $\Gamma^*$ using the relation $\sim$ defined as : $a \sim b \iff \forall q \in Q \; \delta(q, a) = \delta(q, b)$. It is easy to check that $\sim$ is reflexive, symmetric and transitive.

We will construct $\psi'$ as $(Q^\psi, \Gamma', \delta', q_0^\psi, Q^\psi \setminus \{ q_{err}^\psi \})$, i.e. with a new alphabet and transition function. Let states of $\psi$ be indexed by $i \in 1 \ldots |Q^\psi|$. Define $\Gamma'$ to have symbol set of $|Q^\psi|$-tuples $(t_1, \ldots, t_{|Q^\psi|})$ and define $\delta'$ such when the tuple $\gamma' \in \Gamma'$ is encountered as a symbol by $\delta'$, the $i$th entry of $\gamma'$ denotes the state transition from state $i$, i.e. $t_i \in 1 \ldots |Q^\psi|$ and $\delta'(i, (\ldots, t_i, \ldots)) = t_i$. We define a map $m$ an equivalence class of $\sim$ to tuple by taking any member $y \in \Gamma^*$ of the equivalence class and mapping the class to $(\delta^\psi(1, y), \ldots, \delta^\psi(|Q^\psi|, y))$. Now we can define $R' = \{ (x, m(y)) \mid (x, y) \in R \}$, and $f'(x) = m(f(x))$ Then, for a $x \in \Sigma^*$, $\forall q \in Q^\phi$ $\delta^\psi(q, f(x)) = \delta^{\psi'}(q, m(f(x))) = \delta^{\psi'}(q, f'(x))$.    □

*Remark 10 (Sound alternate monitors).* We can also construct a property pair $(\phi, \psi)_R$ which is sound and may be incomplete by using a construction similar to that in Theorem 2 by determinizing it and updating $\delta^\psi(S, \gamma) \leftarrow \{q_{err}\}$ if $q_{err} \in \delta(S, R^{-1}(\gamma))$. It can be argued in a similar fashion that this construction is optimally complete among all sound alternate monitors    ∎

### 5.1  Discussion and Significance for Implementation

Theorem 3 and Theorem 4 complete our claim that *any* loss type (arbitrary relation between original and partial strings) for which the final produced property has to be be finite-state is representable in our framework.

**State Size.** After determinization, number of states in DFA may be high. This is not a problem in practice, e.g. finite-state properties from the largest publicly available database of properties in [15] all have fewer than 10 states. Still, some existing techniques (e.g. [16]) may be used to further reduce number of states, at the expense of missing more violations. We leave it to future work for DFA size reduction techniques specific to monitoring.

**Complexity.** Because $R$ can be arbitrary, we need to show $\delta^\phi(q, R^{-1}(y))$ is efficiently computable. We show that our construction of the NFA is polynomial, though determinizing the constructed NFA may be exponential in state size. It should also be noted that both these costs are incurred at static time, and once computed, there is no run-time overhead and each partial event is processed in $O(1)$ time by the determinized optimal alternate NFA.

*Remark 11.* Construction of alternate optimal NFA in Theorem 2 takes polynomial time when R is represented as a NFT.

*Proof.* To compute $\delta(q, R^{-1}(y)) = S$: the intersection of $R^{-1}(y)$ and the regex formed by the set of strings which go from $q$ and some $q'$ is non-empty thus $q' \in S$. These intersection and non-empty checks take polynomial time [13]. We loop over $O(n)$ states and check if each is in $S$. We repeat this for every $(\gamma, q)$ pair making $O(|\Sigma \times Q|)$ iterations.

**Monitorability (under a Loss Model, and at Runtime).** Corollary 1 reduces the question of monitorability under a loss model to reachability of error state from $q_0$ in our constructed optimal monitor. i.e. since our constructed monitor is optimal, if it does not have capability of producing violations without false positives, then it is not possible to construct *any* DFA which consumes partial trace and can report a violation. In case of natural losses, this can serve as a test for checking if monitoring is even possible for a property under the loss, and provide hints to what partial information, if it could be recorded, would help monitorability. In case of artificial losses, this can serve as a way to discriminate between available loss types to exclude those which aren't monitorable. In context of Remark 3, Corollary 1 is also useful in finding the "true" verdict. Monitoring can be disabled at runtime as soon as the optimal monitor enters into a state from which the state $\{\, q_{err}\,\}$ is unreachable in alternate monitor.

**Sample Implementation.** To provide a starting point for an implementation in a monitoring system, we provide a sample implementation at [17]. It contains an implementation of Theorem 2 which takes a property and a loss model as input and automatically constructs optimal alternate monitor as output. The implementation verifies some examples provided in this paper, allows new properties and loss models to be defined, and allows simulating original and partial traces against the primary as well as the constructed optimal alternate properties.

# 6   Framework Instantiations

We presented how our framework applies to loss types such as those in Fig. 3. In this section, we describe three more instantiations of the framework that illustrate the variety of realistic event loss models it can accommodate.

**Bounded Frequency Count of Missed Symbols.** This loss model was considered in [10] for lossily compressing event traces over a slow network. It is a modification of the dropped-count filter in Fig. 3a where additional information about observed symbols is kept. For a bound $n \in Z^+$ and alphabet $\Sigma$ with symbols $\sigma_i$ indexed by $0 \leq i < |\Sigma|$, we'll define alternate symbol set $\Gamma$ where each symbol is a $|\Sigma|$-tuple, tuple entry at an index $i$ being number of dropped symbols $\sigma_i$. That is, $\Gamma = \{\, (c_1, c_2, \ldots, c_{|\Sigma|}) \mid 0 < c_1 + \ldots + c_{|\Sigma|} \leq n \,\}$ Let $\#x(y)$ denote number of characters $x$ in string $y$. The loss model is defined as $R = \{\, (x, (c_1, c_2, \ldots c_{|\Sigma|})) \mid \bigwedge_{i \in I} c_i = \#\sigma_i(x) \,\}$.

As an example, we may have $f(babaab) = (a_1, b_2)(a_1, b_0), (a_1, b_1)$ for $\Sigma = \{\, a, b\,\}, n = 3$.

There are two key differences between our formalization and that of [10]. First, the total size of the missed symbols is bounded in our case so that we have a finite alphabet with each transition taking $O(1)$ time in the determinized alternate DFA. [10] uses a constraint automata which accepts an infinite alphabet and each transition takes $O(|Q|)$ time. We note that even if more than $n$ symbols are missed at a time, then up to $mn$ missed symbols can produce $m$ alternate symbols to transition to the correct set of states in our framework. The second difference is in consideration of soundness and completeness. While we construct a complete optimal monitor (without any false positives), they construct a sound monitor (without any false negatives). As Remark 10 shows, this is not an issue since we can easily construct a sound monitor instead.

**Merged Objects.** Here we look at a new loss type which loses information about which object an event belongs to in a multi-object monitor. Let $O = \{o_1 \ldots o_m\}$ be a set of objects with parametric events $E = e_1 \ldots e_n$, i.e. $e_1(o_1)$ is a distinct event from $e_1(o_2)$. This means that $\Sigma = \{e(o) \mid e \in E \land o \in O\}$.

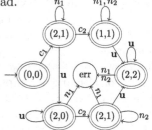

**Fig. 5.** A composite monitor for SafeIter on two iterators.

For $\sigma \in \Sigma, \gamma \in \Gamma$, let $\sigma R \gamma$ iff $\sigma = \gamma(o) \land o \in O$. In the partial trace, we lose information about which object the event belongs to within $O$. For the general case we can build an optimal monitor using the construction in Theorem 2. We give an example of the multi-object property "SafeIter" shown in Fig. 1a but including additional creation events with symbol $c$ as discussed in Remark 1.

The fact that the event $c$ will not be observed in any state is not a part of the property but a guarantee of the environment. We model the transitions for $c$ from any non-initial state other to as special state $q_{im}$ (not shown) representing "impossible" state.

A composite monitor for the SafeIter property from [6] is shown in Fig. 5 for two iterators $I_1$ and $I_2$ ($(i,j)$ represents states $(q_i, q_j)$ for the two iterators, assuming $I_1$ is created first). The loss model $R$ merges events for $I_1$ and $I_2$, and using Theorem 2 to construct the optimal alternate monitor, and delete the $q_{im}$ state from the NFA produced (as we're guaranteed by the environment to never enter it) to obtain the monitor in Fig. 6. For example, the obtained monitor only misses the violation for the traces like $c_1 u c_2 n_2 {}^* n_1$,

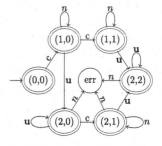

**Fig. 6.** Optimal complete alternate monitor.

i.e. when we actually need the information that event $n$ happened on object 1, but can still report violations for traces matching $c_1 n_1 c_2 (n_1 | n_2) u u^* (n_1 | n_2)$ or $c_1 u c_2 (n_2 | n_1)^* u u^* (n_1 | n_2)$.

**Missing Loop Events.** Significant number of events can be generated within loops in a program. [5] addresses this by eliminating instrumentation losslessly within loops when monitoring the first few iterations is sufficient.

We consider an extension of this idea in Fig. 7 where the program structure is used to obtain the loss model. Instrumentation from the loop is replaced with a single symbol $k$ at the end of the loop. If instrumentation is disabled for all iterations of the loop, the monitor is in states $\{q_0, q_1\}$ after the event $k$. If the

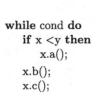
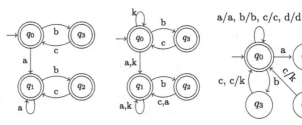

while cond do
  if x <y then
    x.a();
    x.b();
    x.c();

(a) Loop targeted for instrumentation removal.

(b) Program property DFA. All missing edges go to error state (not shown).

(c) Alternate monitor NFA. Error state not shown.

(d) A filter to remove instrumentation from loop and replace it with a single symbol "k".

**Fig. 7.** Missing Events in Loops to be able to remove instrumentation in them.

first few iterations are monitored and event $a$ is generated, the monitor will be in states $\{q_1\}$ after the event $k$.

The loss model can be calculated using a method from [4]. It presents a static analysis which finds the set of states that are possible after a program region, e.g., a loop body, for any given starting state if monitoring were to be disabled in that region. We can use this information directly instead of $R^{-1}(k)$ in Theorem 2 for computing $\delta^\psi(q,\,k)\ \forall q$. This is equivalent to mapping the set of strings which go from $q$ to $\delta^\psi(q,\,k)$ to the new symbol for the loss model.

## 7 Related Work

Runtime monitoring has been an active research area over the past few decades. A significant part of the research in this area has focused on optimizing monitors and controlling the runtime overhead to make monitoring employable in practice.

A line of research [2,4,18,19] focuses on lossless partial evaluation of the finite state property to build residual monitors which process fewer events during runtime. [4] and [19] can be modelled in our framework using loss models where $R^{-1}(y)$ is a singleton set. Another line of research proposes purely dynamic optimizations where resources at run-time are constrained [8]. Purandare et al. [6] combine multiple monitors which share events into a single monitor to reduce the number of monitors updated. Schneider et al. execute monitors in parallel by enabling exchange of states between them to scale up monitoring [20].

Kauffman et al. [21] and Joshi et al. [22] consider monitorability of LTL formulas under losses. [21] considers natural losses such as loss, corruption, repetition, or out-of-order arrival of an event and gives an algorithm to find monitorability of a LTL formula. They do not construct a monitor to monitor the partial traces. [22] considers monitorability of LTL formulas in the presence of one loss type which is equivalent to our dropped-count loss (Fig. 3a) with $n = 1$. They only handle the formulas whose synthesized monitor has transitions that always lead to just one state, and it only recovers from losses after observing such a transition. In general, recurrence temporal properties [23] that can be modeled by Büchi automata are naturally immune to event losses due to loops in their structures. Our work primarily focuses on safety properties.

Falzon et al. [10] consider the construction of an alternate sound monitor when for some parts of the traces only aggregate information, such as the frequency of events but not their order, is available. We formalize this loss type in our framework in Sect. 6. Dwyer et al. [7] consider sub-properties formed when the alphabet is restricted to its subset to sample sub-properties from a given property. Their construction ensures completeness and is equivalent to our construction with $R = \{(x, y) \mid x \in \Delta^* y \; \forall y \in \Sigma \setminus \Delta\}$, where $\Delta$ is the set of symbols not observed as events. Figure 4b generalizes it with $R = \{(x, y) \mid x \in \Delta^* y \; \forall y \in \Sigma\}$.

Basin et al. [9] introduce a 3-valued timed logic to account for missing information in recorded traces for offline analysis. This allows them to report 3 results: if a violation occurred, if it did not occur, or if the knowledge is insufficient to report either. In the problem we consider, instead of having a single representation for missing information we can have multiple representations for different losses which can differ in their power to report an error.

Bartocci et al. [24] introduce statistical methods to inform overhead control and minimize the probability of missing a violation. For the monitors which are disabled, [25] introduces statistical methods to predict the missing information due to sampling, which is then used in [24] to get a probability that the violation occurred in an incomplete run. Instead of disabling monitoring altogether and predicting missing information, our approach records partial information about the events to report violations while maintaining completeness.

## 8   Conclusion and Future Work

We presented a framework for online finite-state monitoring of traces that carry partial information, where the losses could be natural or artificially induced. Our framework provides a general model that accommodates various losses present in the current research literature. We provide an efficient and automatic method to construct optimal monitors from a property specification and a loss model. Our optimality results provide hard limits to determine which property-loss and model combinations are *feasible*. We hope this makes it easier in future to study specific loss types. We also hope that this novel approach makes monitoring particularly attractive in the presence of high-frequency events and lossy channels, serving as a theoretical basis for implementations dealing with such constraints and for new optimizations inducing event losses. In the future, we would like to extend our framework to address infinite-state monitors and work on open questions about the characteristics of more restricted classes of loss models and their properties.

# References

1. Kim, M., Viswanathan, M., Ben-Abdallah, H., Kannan, S., Lee, I., Sokolsky, O.: Formally specified monitoring of temporal properties. ECRTS **9–11**, 114–122 (1999)
2. Bodden, E., Lam, P., Hendren, L.: Clara: a framework for partially evaluating finite-state runtime monitors ahead of time. In: RV, pp. 183–197 (2010)
3. Bodden, E.: Efficient hybrid typestate analysis by determining continuation-equivalent states. In: ICSE, pp. 5–14 (2010)
4. Dwyer, M.B., Purandare, R.: Residual dynamic typestate analysis exploiting static analysis: results to reformulate and reduce the cost of dynamic analysis. In: ASE, pp. 124–133 (2007)
5. Purandare, R., Dwyer, M.B., Elbaum, S.: Monitor optimization via stutter-equivalent loop transformation. In: OOPSLA, pp. 270–285 (2010)
6. Purandare, R., Dwyer, M.B., Elbaum, S.: Optimizing monitoring of finite state properties through monitor compaction. In: ISSTA, pp. 280–290 (2013)
7. Dwyer, M.B., Diep, M., Elbaum, S.: Reducing the cost of path property monitoring through sampling. In: ASE, pp. 228–237 (2008)
8. Allabadi, G., Dhar, A., Bashir, A., Purandare, R.: METIS: resource and context-aware monitoring of finite state properties. In: Colombo, C., Leucker, M. (eds.) RV 2018. LNCS, vol. 11237, pp. 167–186. Springer, Cham (2018). https://doi.org/10.1007/978-3-030-03769-7_10
9. Basin, D., Klaedtke, F., Marinovic, S., Zălinescu, E.: Monitoring compliance policies over incomplete and disagreeing logs. In: RV, pp. 151–167 (2013)
10. Falzon, K., Bodden, E., Purandare, R.: Distributed finite-state runtime monitoring with aggregated events. In: RV, pp. 94–111 (2013)
11. Cook, S.A.: Soundness and completeness of an axiom system for program verification. SIAM J. Comput. **7**, 70–90 (1978)
12. Bartocci, E., Falcone, Y. (eds.): Lectures on Runtime Verification. LNCS, vol. 10457, Springer, Cham (2018). https://doi.org/10.1007/978-3-319-75632-5
13. Sipser, M.: Introduction to the Theory of Computation. Third ed. (2013)
14. Han, Y.-S., Wood, D.: The generalization of generalized automata: expression automata. In: CIAA, pp. 156–166 (2005)
15. Inc, R.V.: runtimeverification/property-db. https://github.com/runtimeverification/property-db (2013)
16. Gange, G., Ganty, P., Stuckey, P.J.: Fixing the state budget: approximation of regular languages with small DFAs. In: ATVA, pp. 67–83 (2017)
17. Kushwaha, P.: Accompanying sample implementation. https://gist.github.com/peey/1c2be77b05d00aa795e08d54ac2c1f9d (2022)
18. Bodden, E., Lam, P., Hendren, L.: Finding programming errors earlier by evaluating runtime monitors ahead-of-time. In: FSE, pp. 36–47 (2008)
19. Dwyer, M.B., Kinneer, A., Elbaum, S.: Adaptive online program analysis. In: ICSE, pp. 220–229 (2007)
20. Schneider, J., Basin, D., Brix, F., Krstić, S., Traytel, D.: Adaptive online first-order monitoring. In: ATVA, pp. 133–150 (2019)
21. Kauffman, S., Havelund, K., Fischmeister, S.: Monitorability over unreliable channels. In: Finkbeiner, B., Mariani, L. (eds.) RV 2019. LNCS, vol. 11757, pp. 256–272. Springer, Cham (2019). https://doi.org/10.1007/978-3-030-32079-9_15
22. Joshi, Y., Tchamgoue, G.M., Fischmeister, S.: Runtime verification of LTL on lossy traces. In: SAC, pp. 1379–1386 (2017)

23. Manna, Z., Pnueli, A.: A hierarchy of temporal properties (invited paper, 1989). In: PODC, pp. 377–410 (1990)
24. Bartocci, E., et al.: Adaptive runtime verification. In: RV, pp. 168–182 (2013)
25. Stoller, S.D., et al.: Runtime verification with state estimation. In: RV, pp. 193–207 (2012)

# Tainting in Smart Contracts: Combining Static and Runtime Verification

Shaun Azzopardi[2]([✉])(iD), Joshua Ellul[1](iD), Ryan Falzon[3](iD),
and Gordon J. Pace[1](iD)

[1] University of Malta, Msida, Malta
joshua.ellul@um.edu.mt, gordon.pace@um.edu.mt
[2] University of Gothenburg, Gothenburg, Sweden
shaun.azzopardi@gu.se
[3] Hash Data, George Town, Cayman Islands
ryan@hashdata.co

**Abstract.** Smart contracts exist immutably on blockchains, making their pre-deployment correctness essential. Moreover, they exist openly on blockchains—open for interaction with any other smart contract and offchain entity. Interaction, for instance with off-chain oracles, can affect the state of the smart contract, and correctness of these smart contracts may depend on the trustworthiness of the data they manipulate or events they generate which, in turn, would depend on which parties or what information contributed to them. In this paper, we develop and present dynamic taint analysis techniques to enable data tainting in smart contracts. We propose an extension of Solidity that enables labelling inputs of interaction endpoints with dynamic data-carrying labels that capture actionable information about the sender. These labels can then be propagated dynamically across transactions to transitively dependent data. Specifications can then refer to such taints, for instance for ensuring that certain data could not have been influenced through interaction by a certain party. We further allow the use of taints as part of the language, affecting the control flow of the smart contract. To manage the overheads of such runtime tainting we develop sound static analysis-based techniques to prune away unnecessary instrumentation. We give a case study as a proof-of-concept, and measure the overheads associated with our additions before and after optimisation.

**Keywords:** Taint analysis · Runtime verification · Static analysis

## 1 Introduction

Smart contracts on blockchains are programs that promise dependability through immutability and code transparency. However, this is not enough to ensure

This research has received funding from the ERC consolidator grant D-SynMA (No. 772459), the University of Malta Research Awards project *"Systematising Smart Contracts within Classical Contract Law Theory"*, and the European Agricultural Fund for Rural Development project *"VinoVeritas: An Authority to Consumer Wine Audit Solution"*.

T. Dang and V. Stolz (Eds.): RV 2022, LNCS 13498, pp. 143–161, 2022.
https://doi.org/10.1007/978-3-031-17196-3_8

correctness of the smart contracts. Formal methods have been applied for this purpose, to allow for some level of security and verification of functional properties of smart contracts, e.g., [1,5,7]. One interesting aspect of smart contracts is the ability of smart contracts to interact with each other or with off-chain entities. This interaction is the only way in which smart contracts can change state, with each (data-carrying) interaction forming part of a *transaction*. While the blockchain on which smart contracts are executed is decentralised in nature, the logic of a smart contract or data upon which it depends may not be. Consider, for instance, a betting smart contract depending on random numbers provided by third party oracles, or an insurance smart contract depending on reports by experts and information provided by a user. Whenever a smart contract's domain extends beyond what is digital and resides on the blockchain, it must interact with the real-world which is, by its very nature, centralised. A temperature sensor is, for instance, such a centralised point-of-trust, and, unless one goes to great lengths to have multiple independent sensors, the readings it provides and any logic or data which depend on them should ideally be tagged as such.

Given an event of interest (e.g., upgrading the level of a user or the violation of a property) it is interesting to reason about the contributing causes to this event, including any contributing interactions. However, such information is not typically available given interactions may be separated far in time from the events of interest to which they contribute. We observe that this kind of reasoning has been explored in literature, to an extent, in the study of *taint analysis* [12].

Taint analysis is typically concerned with identifying when input to a program can pose a security risk, e.g., if it can cause dangerous commands to be executed. Untrustworthy input is said to be *tainted*, while the sensitive parts of the program are called *sinks*, and the problem then is to find out whether tainted data can enter sinks. There are two approaches to taint analysis: static or dynamic. Identifying problems statically, pre-deployment, is ideal but having a sound and complete analysis is, in general, impossible forcing one to resort to over- or under-approximations—sound static analysis may identify false security risks, while a complete one may miss real ones. Dynamic taint analysis, identifying risks at runtime can be more precise.

In a manner akin to security and privacy taint analysis, we observe that issues of point-of-trust propagation in smart contracts (and indeed other systems which depend on data by external parties) follow a similar pattern and can be addressed using similar tools. We envisage trust type checking to ensure that trust does not propagate in an unexpected manner as a primary tool for smart contracts enforcing business process flows dependent on oracle and user data. Furthermore, we believe that the notion of trust is core in smart contracts and by implementing trust at the programming language level, and allowing developers to use trust information as part of their logic can be of great benefit. For this reason, we ensure that our trust/taint propagation semantics extend the semantics of Solidity, and allow for dynamic execution.

Static taint analysis has been explored in the context of Solidity smart contracts, e.g. [10,17], however to the best of our knowledge dynamic taint analysis has not, possibly due to the associated overheads. In fact, both deploying and executing functions of the smart contract costs *gas*, paid for in *ether*, the currency of the Ethereum blockchain. This cost can be an effective remedy against denial-of-service attacks, and also ensures termination, but discourages the use of dynamic analysis techniques on the blockchain. Static analysis however has been used to attenuate the gas overheads of runtime verification (e.g., see [5]).

In this paper, we present an extension of Solidity with a notion of tainting as a first-class concept. We present taint labels that carry data, and allow assertions in the language to query these taints and use the associated data. We give the semantics for a simplified version of Solidity with taints that propagates the taints. We give several static analyses that we use to prune taint instrumentation, and leave the remaining for runtime. As a formal basis for these analyses and future ones, we give an abstract sound static semantics for the language.

**Related Work.** Static taint analysis has been applied in the context of Solidity before. Slither [10] can classify whether a smart contract variable is dependent on a user-controlled variable (e.g., a function parameter), or whether a function can be entered from illegitimate entry points. [17] uses taint tracking on control-flow graphs to identify re-entrancy. Our work instead considers using dynamic analysis, and optimises it through static analysis. Such combined analysis have been applied in other contexts, such as web security (e.g., see [13,16]), and Android applications (e.g., see [14,16]).

Static analysis has been used before to prove parts of properties safe and leave the rest of the property for runtime [2,4,8], and also for the pruning of instrumentation [3], mainly in the context of Java verification. This work has also been applied in the context of Solidity verification [5,6]. See [11] for a more general exposition of optimisations for monitors.

See [15] for a more general survey of formal verification techniques applied to smart contracts.

**Summary.** In Sect. 2 we present an extension of the Solidity language with taints and a semantics for it, while in Sect. 3 we present tools to statically analyse programs in this language. We present a case study to validate the example static analyses we give in Sect. 4. We discuss this approach in Sect. 5, while we conclude with future work in Sect. 6.

## 2   Solidity with Dynamic Tainting

We present an extension of Solidity with taints at the language level, including constructs for declaration of data-carrying taint labels, statements that taint variables or memory locations, and extend Boolean expressions to query taints.

### 2.1   Simplified Solidity with Taints

The grammar of Solidity extended with taints is shown in Fig. 1, with our additions and modification in **boldface**.

| TaintLabel | := **Label** |
|---|---|
| TaintExpr | := **TaintLabel** \| **TaintLabel** [type Label?] \| **TaintExpr or TaintExpr** |
| TaintValue | := **TaintLabel** \| **TaintLabel** [VarLabel \| Value] |
| TaintDeclr | := *newtaint* **Label** = **TaintExpr** |
| TaintQuery | := *taint-of* **VarLabel** |
| | |
| BoolTaintsExpr | := BoolExpr \| VarLabel **tainted-by** [TaintValue \| TaintQuery] \| !BoolTaintsExpr \| |
| | BoolTaintsExpr **&&** BoolTaintsExpr \| BoolTaintsExpr \|\| BoolTaintsExpr |
| CallExpr | := Call Label [Values] \| GuardedCall Label [Values] |
| Expr | := Label \| CallExpr \| ValueExpr |
| Declr | := type Label |
| TaintBy | := *taint* **VarLabel** *by* [TaintValue] |
| **Assign** | := **Label** $\overset{s}{=}$ **Expr** \| **Label** $\overset{x}{=}$ **Expr** |
| Assert | := *assert* **BoolTaintsExpr** |
| Stmt | := Declr \| Assign \| Return Expr \| *revert* \| **TaintBy** \| Assert \| |
| | *If* **BoolTaintsExpr** *then* [Stmt] *else* [Stmt] \| *While* BoolExpr *then* [Stmt] |
| visibility | := *public* \| *private* \| *internal* \| *external* |
| Func | := *function* Label ( [type Label]) (*returns* [type Label?]?) { [Stmt] } |
| Contract | := *contract* Label { [(Declr \| StructDeclr \| **TaintDeclr**)] [Function] } |

**Fig. 1.** Solidity with taints.

We leave the grammar underspecified for simplicity (e.g., we do not list *types*, or all possible *ValueExpr*essions, like arithmetic combinations), so that we can focus on the novel taint constructs (see [9] for the full Solidity language). Smart contracts are deployed on the blockchain to certain addresses, and calls to their functions also are initiated from addresses, however here we abstract away from these, e.g. in *CallExpr*—note how a function being available from a certain address can simply be encoded as part of the function name/label; and also from messages (carrying some standard information about the sender and call), which can be encoded as parameters to the function.

We define taint template expressions (**TaintExpr**) to be either simple labels, labels with a sequence of possibly labelled data types, or disjunctions of such labels. We specify taint values (**TaintValue**) as being either simple labels (**TaintLabel**), or data-carrying labels (e.g., BadActor (address location) is a taint label template that can be instantiated into taints that carry information about the address of the bad actor). We introduce constructs to assign a taint expression a label (**TaintDeclr**), and a construct to allow for the taint of a variable to be a queried (**TaintQuery**).

We augment boolean expressions (**BoolTaintsExpr**) to be able to query the taints of variables, e.g. v tainted-by BadActor will hold true only if the value of v depends on some past interaction started by a specific bad actor. These can be used in assert statements (here we do not model gas consumption, thus we ignore require statements) and if statements.

Crucially, we add a construct (**TaintBy**) to allow variables to be assigned taint values, e.g., taint v by BadActor msg.sender[1]. Essentially, the user can use this construct to specify sources of taint, e.g., to taint some parameters at the start of a function definition. Propagation of these taints to any variables that in turn depends on tainted variables will be taken care of by the semantics.

---

[1] msg.sender in Solidity refers to the address (a unique identifier) of the function caller.

Moreover, instead of the assignment symbol =, we have two kinds of assignment symbols: (1) $x \stackrel{\checkmark}{=} expr$ denotes that $x$ is assigned the value of the expression and also propagates taints of $expr$ to $x$; while (2) $x \stackrel{\times}{=} expr$ denotes that $x$ is only assigned the value of $expr$. We do not intend this to be used by the user, but we use it to denote the instrumentation required for propagating tainting dynamically. From the point of view of the user they will use =, which will be interpreted as $\stackrel{\checkmark}{=}$. For our static analysis the aim is to turn as many $\stackrel{\checkmark}{=}$ statements into $\stackrel{\times}{=}$ while preserving the semantics. We will use $\stackrel{*}{=}$ to denote either $\stackrel{\checkmark}{=}$ or $\stackrel{\times}{=}$.

## 2.2   Semantics

We present an operational semantics for the grammar in Fig. 1, with some preliminaries first.

**Preliminaries.** For brevity, we assume that every smart contract on the blockchain has unique names for their global variables, function parameters, local function variables, and function names.

The semantics given is an operational semantics, over configurations and transitions. Configurations are given over variable valuations, a function call stack, and the function code. The function call stack maintains a stack of the function calls in the current transaction, and a sequence of statements with the first statement being the next statement to execute. Instead of Solidity statements, we consider *tainted statements*, which will be required to keep track of taint of a certain execution, e.g., due to branching.

**Definition 1 (Tainted Statements).** *Given a statement st and a set of taints T, a tainted statement, written $st\#T$, denotes that the execution of st was tainted by T. We overload this to sequences of statements, such that $(st : sts)\#T \stackrel{\text{def}}{=} (st\#T : sts\#T)$ and $[]\#T \stackrel{\text{def}}{=} []$. We interpret $(st\#T)\#T'$ as $st\#(T \cup T')$.*

**Definition 2 (Configurations).** *A **configuration** is a triple $\langle V, calls, F \rangle$ where:*

1. *$V$ is a valuation, a mapping from variable names to their values and taints (we write $V[x \mapsto v]$ to update the value of variable $x$, and $V[x_{taint} \mapsto t]$ to update the taint of $x$;*
2. *calls is a function call stack, an array modelling the current function call stack, with values consisting of a pair of: tainted sequence of statements and a variable (and variable taint) valuation; and*
3. *$F$ is the code, a mapping from function names to sequences of statements (we leave this implicit since, for simplicity, we do not allow it to change).*

Essentially, a configuration models the state (including taint state) of a blockchain at a given point in time. When the call stack is empty, the configuration is that of the blockchain between transactions, and when it is not empty the blockchain is in the process of a transaction.

The semantics will propagate a taint throughout a function's code, which may depend on the taint of a expression, which we define as the union of the taints of the variables mentioned in that expression.

**Definition 3.** *The taint of a value expression expr in the context of a valuation V, denoted by taint(expr, V), is the union of the set of taints associated with every variable mentioned in the expression. When the valuation is clear from the context we leave it implicit.*

We also require a notion of evaluation of expressions in the context of a given valuation of variables. We define an operator to represent this.

**Definition 4.** *Given a valuation V and Solidity expression expr, we write expr $\Downarrow$ V to denote the value of the expression with respect to the valuation.*

We can then give the operational semantics. The notation we use for the operational semantics includes naming of certain structures for more compact (width-wise) rules, e.g., writing $lcls' := lcls[x \mapsto expr \Downarrow lcls]$ means $lcls'$ should be interpreted as $lcls[x \mapsto expr \Downarrow lcls]$ in the rest of the rule.

**Definition 5 (Operational Semantics).** *The operational semantics of Solidity with taints is given over configurations and transitions labelled by calls and tainted return values, or by $\times$ (denoting an unsuccessful call). The transition relation $\rightarrow$ is given by the rules in Fig. 2.*

*We use $\Rightarrow$ for the transitive closure of $\rightarrow$. We overload $\Rightarrow$ so that we write $V \xrightarrow[res]{call(f,params)} V'$ for $(V, []) \xrightarrow{call(f,params)} (V, x) \Rightarrow (V, x') \xrightarrow{res} (V', [])$ (with no other labelled transitions in between).*

Note that we do not define a rule for `assert`, instead we treat a statement `assert(e)` as `if(!e) revert(); else{rest of code}`.

We briefly describe the semantics. Labels indicate the start of an offchain call (OFFCHAINCALL) or the termination of such a call, either without exceptions (RETURNOFFCHAIN) or with a cancellation and revert of the transaction (REVERTOFFCHAIN). Given a tainting expression, we taint the variable in the valuation (UPDATETAINT), while if the initiator of the call, `msg.sender`, is tainted then all the assignments in the remaining statements are also tainted (UPDATETAINTSENDER). Given an if statement, we evaluate the condition on the current valuation, and continue in the appropriate branch, while tagging each branch with the taints of the condition (IFTHENELSELEFT, IFTHENELSERIGHT).

Given an assignment, we first consider when the right-hand side expression is a value expression and update the value of the variable (NONCALLASSIGNMENT), and in the case the instrumented assignment, is used the taint of the variable is also updated (NONCALLASSIGNMENTINSTRUMENTED). When there is a call, we simply place the code of the called function on the stack (CALL), note how our assumption that all variables, parameters, and functions have unique names ensures the valuation is updated appropriately. The output of a function is then used if the call ends successfully (CALLRETURN) and the taint possibly updated (CALLRETURNINSTRUMENTED), or otherwise a revert is propagated upwards (CALLREVERT). This logic is modified slightly for the case of a guarded call (GCALL, GCALLRETURN, GCALLRETURNINSTRUMENTED, and GCALLREVERT), where reverts no longer propagate upwards.

## 2.3    Implementation

Implementing this semantics as is requires augmenting the semantics of Solidity. Instead, here, we describe how it can be encoded in the full Solidity language.

**Taints Values.** Taint values can be encoded with each taint label as a value in an enum, and a wrapping struct as a template for values. For example, the declaration BadActorTaint = BadActorUnknown | BadActor (address loc) can be represented with: enum BadActorTaintLabels = {BadActorUnknown, BadActor} and struct BadActorTaint = {BadActorTaintLabels label; address loc;}.

**Variable Taints.** The taint of each variable can be kept track of in a corresponding taint array variable. The tainting of locations in a mapping or array can also be kept track of in variables of the same structure. A taint expression taint $x$ by $t$, can then encoded by simply pushing taint $t$ onto $x$'s taint array, e.g., xTaint.push(t). We can have repetition in this case, i.e. xTaint is not a set, but this does not change the semantics.

**Propagating Taints.** Propagating taints through instrumented assignments can be done in two-steps. For direct assignments to a value expression, one can simply append a statement immediately after the assignment that sets the taint of the assigned variable to the union of the taint variables of the variables used in the assignment expression. Assignment to the value of calls however presents an issue. If the function called is under our control, we can simply edit it to take parameter taints as inputs and to output also the taints of the return values. Otherwise[2], the taint semantics cannot be replicated. One approach could be to assume that the output could be tainted by any taint, and thus have a sound but incomplete dynamic taint analysis. For our purposes, we only consider when called functions are under our control and then the analysis is sound.

This approach to the implementation can however make the smart contract very costly (note how checking a taint query requires iterating over an array which does not have a bounded size). We tackle this through static analysis.

## 3    Static Analysis

When developing smart contracts one generally aims to reduce the amount of code and the amount of computation performed. This is due to the notion of *gas*, wherein both placing code on the blockchain and executing it has costs.

---

[2] If we do not know the code behind a function call we cannot determine the possible taint of return values.

$$\frac{}{(\mathbf{V},[]) \xrightarrow{call(f,params)} (\mathbf{V},[(\mathbf{F}(f),params \cup \mathbf{V})])} \text{ OffchainCall}$$

$$\frac{\mathbf{V}' = \mathbf{V}[v \mapsto lcls(v)]}{(\mathbf{V},((return\ expr : sts)\#T, lcls)) \xrightarrow{(expr\downarrow lcls, T\cup taint(expr))} (\mathbf{V}',[])} \text{ ReturnOffchain}$$

$$\frac{}{(\mathbf{V},((revert : sts)\#T, lcls)) \xrightarrow{x} (\mathbf{V},[])} \text{ RevertOffchain}$$

$$\frac{lcls' := lcls[x_{taint} \mapsto taintExpr \downarrow lcls]}{(\mathbf{V},((taint\ x\ by\ taintExpr) : sts)\#T, lcls) : rest) \to (\mathbf{V},(sts\#T, lcls') : rest)} \text{ UpdateTaint}$$

$$\frac{T' := taintExpr \downarrow lcls}{(\mathbf{V},(((taint\ msg.sender\ by\ taintExpr) : sts)\#T, lcls) : rest) \to (\mathbf{V},(sts\#T', lcls) : rest)} \text{ UpdateTaintSender}$$

$$\frac{c \downarrow lcls}{(\mathbf{V},(((if\ c\ then\ sts_1\ else\ sts_2) : sts)\#T, lcls) : rest) \to (\mathbf{V},((sts_1\#(taint(c)) + sts)\#T, lcls) : rest)} \text{ IfThenElseLeft}$$

$$\frac{\neg c \downarrow lcls}{(\mathbf{V},((if\ c\ then\ sts_1\ else\ sts_2) : sts\#T, lcls) : rest) \to (\mathbf{V},((sts_2\#(taint(c)) + sts)\#T, lcls) : rest)} \text{ IfThenElseRight}$$

$$\frac{c \downarrow lcls}{(\mathbf{V},(((while\ c\ \{sts'\}) : sts)\#T, lcls) : rest) \to (\mathbf{V},(sts'\#(taint(c)) + (while\ c\ \{sts'\} : sts))\#T, lcls) : rest)} \text{ WhileEntry}$$

$$\frac{\neg c \downarrow lcls}{(\mathbf{V},(((while\ c\ \{sts'\}) : sts)\#T, lcls) : rest) \to (\mathbf{V},(sts\#T, lcls) : rest)} \text{ WhileExit}$$

$$\frac{lcls' := lcls[x \mapsto expr \downarrow lcls]}{(\mathbf{V},(((x \stackrel{\triangleq}{=} expr) : sts)\#T, lcls) : rest) \to (\mathbf{V},(sts\#T, lcls') : rest)} \text{ NonCallAssignment}$$

$$\frac{lcls' := lcls[x \mapsto expr \downarrow lcls][x_{taint} \mapsto T \cup taint(expr)]}{(\mathbf{V},(((x \stackrel{\triangleleft}{=} expr) : sts)\#T, lcls) : rest) \to (\mathbf{V},(sts\#T, lcls') : rest)} \text{ NonCallAssignmentInstrumented}$$

$$\frac{calls := (((x \stackrel{\triangleq}{=} Call(f', params')) : sts)\#T, lcls : rest)}{(\mathbf{V}, calls) \to (\mathbf{V},((\mathbf{F}(f')\#T, params' \cup params'_{taints} \cup lcls) : calls))} \text{ Call}$$

$$\frac{\begin{array}{c} calls := (((x \stackrel{x}{=} Call(f', params')) : sts)\#T, lcls') : rest \\ lcls'' := lcls[v \notin dom(\mathbf{V}) \mapsto lcls'(v)][x \mapsto expr \downarrow lcls'] \end{array}}{(\mathbf{V},((return\ expr : sts')\#T', lcls) : calls) \to (\mathbf{V},(sts\#T, lcls'') : rest)} \text{ CallReturn}$$

$$\frac{\begin{array}{c} calls := (((x \stackrel{\triangleleft}{=} Call(f', params')) : sts)\#T, lcls') : rest \\ lcls'' := lcls[v \notin dom(\mathbf{V}) \mapsto lcls'(v)][x \mapsto expr \downarrow lcls'][x_{taint} \mapsto T \cup T' \cup taint(expr)] \end{array}}{(\mathbf{V},((return\ expr : sts')\#T', lcls) : calls) \to (\mathbf{V},(sts\#T, lcls'') : rest)} \text{ CallReturnInstrumented}$$

$$\frac{calls := (((x \stackrel{\triangleq}{=} Call(f', params')) : sts)\#T, lcls' : rest)}{(\mathbf{V},((revert : sts)\#T', lcls) : calls) \to (\mathbf{V},(sts\#T, lcls') : rest')} \text{ CallRevert}$$

$$\frac{calls := (((success, x) \stackrel{\triangleq}{=} (guardedcall(f', params')) : sts)\#T, lcls : rest)}{(\mathbf{V}, calls) \to (\mathbf{V},((\mathbf{F}(f')\#T, params' \cup lcls) : calls))} \text{ GCall}$$

$$\frac{\begin{array}{c} calls := (((success, x) \stackrel{x}{=} (guardedcall(f', params')) : sts)\#T, lcls') : rest \\ lcls'' := lcls[v \in dom(\mathbf{V}) \mapsto lcls'(v)][x \mapsto expr \downarrow lcls'][success \mapsto true] \end{array}}{(\mathbf{V},((return\ expr : sts')\#T', lcls) : calls) \to (\mathbf{V},(sts\#T, lcls'') : rest)} \text{ GCallReturn}$$

$$\frac{\begin{array}{c} calls := (((success, x) \stackrel{\triangleleft}{=} (guardedcall(f', params')) : sts)\#T, lcls') : rest \\ lcls'' := lcls[v \in dom(\mathbf{V}) \mapsto lcls'(v)][x \mapsto expr \downarrow lcls'][x_{taint} \mapsto T \cup T' \cup taint(expr)][success \mapsto true] \end{array}}{(\mathbf{V},((return\ expr : sts')\#T', lcls) : calls) \to (\mathbf{V},(sts\#T, lcls'') : rest)} \text{ GCallReturnInstrumented}$$

$$\frac{\begin{array}{c} calls := (((success, x) \stackrel{\triangleq}{=} (guardedcall(f', params')) : sts)\#T, lcls') : rest \\ lcls'' := lcls'[success \mapsto false] \end{array}}{(\mathbf{V},(((revert) : sts)\#T', lcls) : calls) \to (\mathbf{V},(sts\#T, lcls'') : rest)} \text{ GCallRevert}$$

**Fig. 2.** Semantics of grammar in Fig. 1.

Our described implementation, however, requires adding substantial instrumentation: (1) a taint variable for every variable; and (2) assignment to these taint variables after every assignment to associated variables. These can add significant overheads, as we see later in Sect. 4. Yet, not all this instrumentation is required and tainting is only relevant to the smart contract's execution when it affects the flow or output of the smart contract, otherwise it has no impact.

In this section, we give a sound abstract semantics to the language which we use as the basis for static analysis that is able to modify instrumentation safely (e.g., transform $\overset{\angle}{=}$ into $\overset{\times}{=}$), and that can be used to determine the possible value of conditions on taint at locations of a smart contract.

### 3.1 Abstract Semantics

Here we define a sound method of propagating taints in a Solidity smart contract, while abstracting away the values of variables.

In the static context we do not have taint values when the taint is data-carrying, instead we abstract them by their corresponding taint expression, e.g., BadActor(msg.sender) is abstracted by the expression BadActor address. In this section, we then use these taint expressions as our taints.

**Definition 6 (Abstract Taints).** *The* abstraction of a taint tag $t$, *denoted $abs(t)$, is $t$ itself in the case of a non-data-carrying labels, and the corresponding taint expression with values replaced by their types for data-carrying labels. We overload abs to also range over sets of taints, i.e., $abs(T) \overset{\text{def}}{=} \{abs(t) \mid t \in T\}$.*

We will also require a notion of projecting concrete valuations and return values onto their original variable value parts and the taint parts.

**Definition 7 (Valuation and Return Value Projection).** $V|_{vars}$ *projects* $V$ *onto its variable domain, ignoring tainting. $ret|_{vars}$ is similar, while $\times$ remains $\times$. Similarly, $|_{taints}$ projects $V$ and ret onto taint variables.*

A remaining issue is branching in the code as caused by an if-then-else, where the taint at runtime depends on which branch is taken. Statically we have to consider both branches, since we want to handle every possible case. Since we will be dealing with each function on its own, and Solidity smart contracts have a tendency to be small (due to gas costs), here we will deal with this simply by non-deterministically branching. In other contexts this may not be ideal, since this may incur a degree of repetition which may worsen the state space explosion.

We re-use the $\#$ and *taint* operators here, appropriately re-interpreted for this abstract context (i.e. $\#$ instruments with abstract taints, and *taint* returns the abstract taints of an expression).

The semantics we give is over abstract configurations, which only maintain information about the next statement to execute and an abstract taint function.

**Definition 8 (Abstract Configurations).** *An abstract configuration is a pair $\langle calls, tnts, \boldsymbol{F} \rangle$ with:*

1. calls *is an abstract call stack, with elements as abstractly tainted statements;*
2. tnts *is an abstract taint valuation; and*

3. **F**, being the code, a mapping from function names to the function's list of statements (left implicit).

We can then give our abstract operational semantics.

**Definition 9 (Abstract Operational Semantics).** *The* abstract operational semantics *of Solidity with taints is given over abstract configurations. The transition relation* →, *is given by the rules in Fig. 3, with* ⇒ *as its transitive closure.*

Every rule given is a direct counterpart of the similarly named rules in Fig. 2, with some rules combined into one here.

We can prove that this abstract semantics soundly abstracts the concrete semantics of the language, i.e., that when a call produces a return value with a certain concrete taint in the concrete semantics, then there is a path in the abstract semantics that produces an abstract version of the concrete taint.

**Theorem 1.** $(\boldsymbol{V}, [\,]) \xrightarrow[(expr\Downarrow V',T)]{call(f,params)} \boldsymbol{V}'$ *implies* $\exists sts, T', tnts' \cdot (\boldsymbol{F}(f), \boldsymbol{V}|_{taints}) \Rightarrow$
$((return\ expr : sts)\#T', tnts') \wedge abs(T) = T' \cup taint(expr, tnts').$

## 3.2 Analysis and Optimisation

The abstract semantics we gave can be the formal basis of different static analyses. Here we characterise when a static analysis reduces instrumentation in a correct manner. However, instead of working with the code, for static analysis it is often more useful to make the control-flow between statements explicit. Standard techniques can be used to transform Solidity code into a graph and back (e.g., as supported by existing tools [5,6]).

**Definition 10 (Function Control-flow Graph).** *The* control-flow graph of a function $F$ is a tuple $C_F = \langle S, label, s_0, Ret, Rev, \rightarrow \rangle$, with $S$ being a set of states, $label : S \rightarrow Stmt$ associating each state with a statement, $s_0$ being the initial state, $Ret$ being the set of states associated with return statements, and $Rev$ being the set of states associated with revert statements. $\rightarrow: S \times S$ is a transition relation denoting the control-flow between the statements.

We can then augment the control-flow graph by considering its abstract execution with the abstract semantics. The states in the graph then become pairs of statements and abstract taint functions.

Moreover, we consider a special abstract taint expression $*$ that denotes variables could be tainted by any taint set; we will be using this to be able to reason about each function *intraprocedurally*, by starting with an abstract taint function that assigns $*$ to every variable: $initTnt$, s.t. $initTnt(v) = *$.

**Definition 11 (Tainted Function Control-flow Graph).** *The* tainted control-flow graph of a function $F$ is a tuple $t(C_F) = \langle S, tlabel, s_0, Ret, Rev, \rightarrow \rangle$, defined as before, but with $tlabel : S \rightarrow Stmt \times \mathbb{V}_{taints}$ associating each state with a statement and an abstract taint function.

$$\frac{}{(((\textit{taint } x \textit{ by } T) : sts)\#T', tnts) \to (sts\#T', tnts[x \mapsto T \cup T'])} \text{ AUpdateTaint}$$

$$\frac{}{(((\textit{taint msg.sender by } T) : sts)\#T', tnts) \to (sts\#(T \cup T'), tnts)} \text{ AUpdateTaintSender}$$

$$\frac{}{(((x \stackrel{\text{x}}{=} expr) : sts)\#T, tnts) \to (sts\#T, tnts)} \text{ ANonCallAssignment}$$

$$\frac{tnts' = tnts[x_{taint} \mapsto T \cup taints(expr)]}{(((x \stackrel{\checkmark}{=} expr) : sts)\#T, tnts) \to (sts\#T, tnts')} \text{ ANonCallAssignmentInstrumented}$$

$$\frac{}{\begin{array}{l}(((\textit{if } c \textit{ then } sts_1 \textit{ else } sts_2) : sts)\#T, tnts) \to ((sts_1\#taint(c) \mathbin{+\!\!+} sts)\#T, tnts) \\ (((\textit{if } c \textit{ then } sts_1 \textit{ else } sts_2) : sts)\#T, tnts) \to ((sts_2\#taint(c) \mathbin{+\!\!+} sts)\#T, tnts)\end{array}} \text{ AIfThenElse}$$

$$\frac{}{\begin{array}{l}(((\textit{while } c \; \{sts'\}) : sts)\#T, tnts) \to (((sts'\#taint(c) \mathbin{+\!\!+} ((\textit{while } c \; \{sts'\}) : sts))\#T, tnts) \\ (((\textit{while } c \; \{sts'\}) : sts)\#T, tnts) \to (sts\#T, tnts)\end{array}} \text{ AWhile}$$

$$\frac{\begin{array}{l}call := (((x \stackrel{\text{x}}{=} Call(f', params')) : sts)\#T, tnts) \\ (\mathbf{F}(f')\#T, tnts) \to ((\textit{return expr} : sts)\#T', tnts')\end{array}}{call \to (sts\#T, tnts')} \text{ ACallReturn}$$

$$\frac{\begin{array}{l}call := (((x \stackrel{\checkmark}{=} Call(f', params')) : sts)\#T, tnts) \\ (\mathbf{F}(f')\#T, tnts) \to ((\textit{return expr} : sts)\#T', tnts')\end{array}}{call \to (sts\#T, tnts'[x \mapsto T \cup T' \cup tnts(expr)])} \text{ ACallReturnInstrumented}$$

$$\frac{\begin{array}{l}call := (((x \stackrel{\text{.}}{=} Call(f', params')) : sts)\#T, tnts) \\ (\mathbf{F}(f')\#T, tnts) \to ((\textit{revert} : sts)\#T', tnts')\end{array}}{call \to (revert\#T, tnts')} \text{ ACallRevert}$$

$$\frac{\begin{array}{l}call := ((((success, x) \stackrel{\text{x}}{=} GuardedCall(f', params')) : sts)\#T, tnts) \\ (\mathbf{F}(f')\#T, tnts) \to ((\textit{return expr} : sts)\#T', tnts')\end{array}}{call \to (sts\#T, tnts')} \text{ AGCallReturn}$$

$$\frac{\begin{array}{l}call := ((((success, x) \stackrel{\checkmark}{=} GuardedCall(f', params')) : sts)\#T, tnts) \\ (\mathbf{F}(f')\#T, tnts) \to ((\textit{return expr} : sts)\#T', tnts')\end{array}}{call \to (sts\#T, tnts'[x \mapsto T \cup T' \cup tnts'(expr)])} \text{ AGCallReturnInstrumented}$$

$$\frac{\begin{array}{l}call := (((x \stackrel{\text{.}}{=} Call(f', params')) : sts)\#T, tnts) \\ (\mathbf{F}(f')\#T, tnts) \to ((\textit{revert} : sts)\#T', tnts')\end{array}}{call \to (sts\#T, tnts')} \text{ AGCallRevert}$$

**Fig. 3.** Abstract static semantics of grammar in Fig. 1.

*The construction proceeds by associating the initial state with the most abstract taint function, $tlabel(s_0) = (st_0, initTnt)$, and when for states $s$ and $s'$, $s \to s'$ in $C_F$, then if $tlabel(s) = (label(s), tnt)$ and $(label(s) : [label(s')], tnt) \to (label(s'), tnt')$ (in the abstract semantics), we set $tlabel(s') = (label(s'), tnt')$.*

Note how we have a finite amount of abstract taints and statements, and thus applying the abstract semantics will terminate, if there is no recursive call. In the case of a recursive call we have several options, e.g., tainting with $*$, or running the call until a fixed point of taints is reached.

Our static analysis will involve transformation of the instrumentation of a function while retaining the same semantics, which we characterise below.

**Definition 12 (Instrumentation Reduction).** *Given functions $F$ and $F'$, $F'$ is said to be an* instrumentation reduction *of a function $F$, in the context of a set of functions $\boldsymbol{F}$, written $F' \leq_t F$ iff (1) $F$ and $F'$ only differ on the use of $\overset{\checkmark}{=}$ or $\overset{x}{=}$, or on the presence of taint by expressions; (2) replacing a call to $F$ with one to $F'$ does not change the values of variables, but may associate less (but not different) taints to variables, formally:*

*For an arbitrary $n$, consider any arbitrary sequence of $n$ function calls (to functions from $\boldsymbol{F}$), $c_i$, any initial valuation $\boldsymbol{V_0}$, and the corresponding $n$ valuations $\boldsymbol{V_{i+1}}$ and return values $ret_{i+1}$, such that $\boldsymbol{V_i} \xrightarrow[ret_{i+1}]{c_i} \boldsymbol{V_{i+1}}$. If, for some index $j$, $c_j$ is a call to $F$, then replacing $c_j$ with $c_j'$, a call to $F'$ but with the same parameters and message, induces $n-j$ new valuations and return values $\boldsymbol{V'_{j+1}}, ..., \boldsymbol{V'_{n+1}}$ and $ret'_{j+1}, ..., ret'_{n+1}$ such that $\boldsymbol{V_j} \xrightarrow[ret'_{j+1}]{c_j'} \boldsymbol{V'_{j+1}}$ (and so on), then for all indices $k$ bigger than $j$ the corresponding valuations and return values with taints projected out, are equivalent: $\boldsymbol{V_k}|_{vars} = \boldsymbol{V'_k}|_{vars}$ and $ret_k|_{vars} = ret'_k|_{vars}$ , while the taint projected parts in the reduced version are contained in the other: $\forall v \cdot \boldsymbol{V'_k}|_{taints}(v) \subseteq \boldsymbol{V_k}|_{taints}(v)$ and $ret'_k|_{taints} \subseteq ret_k|_{taints}$ .*

We then describe informally several instrumentation reducing analyses that can be performed on the set of tainted control-flow graphs of a smart contract. **Removing Irrelevant Instrumentation.** Given a function $F \in \boldsymbol{F}$, we can identify statements in that function whose evaluation depends on the taint of some variable, generally either conditional or return statements. For each such statement, we can do a transitive backwards analysis to determine the set of taints and the set of variables that are relevant.

Then, collecting all this information from all the functions in $\boldsymbol{F}$, we can identify the *taint instrumentation nodes* that set the taint of a variable such that the variable and its taint may be relevant to some conditional statement in the smart contract. Irrelevant taint instrumentation nodes can be removed.

For example, where $T$ and $T'$ are distinct concrete taint labels:

| | | |
|---|---|---|
| `taint v by T'; x ` $\overset{\checkmark}{=}$ ` v;`<br>`assert(x tainted-by T);` | $\leq_t$ | `x ` $\overset{x}{=}$ ` v; assert(x tainted-by T);` |

On the left-hand side, $x$ is relevant to the conditional on the third line, but it is only relevant to it when $x$ is tainted by $T$. Thus, barring any other need for knowing about the taint of $v$ or $x$ with $T'$, the right-hand is equivalent to the above modulo the `assert` statement.

Moreover, consider that a variable is tainted twice in a function with such a label, and between these two locations there is no point where the first taint of the variable is used. Then we can just discard the first instrumentation, and keep the last one, since the first one is unused and later overwritten.

For example (assume the only conditional statement is the visible `assert`):

$$
\begin{array}{ll}
\boxed{\begin{array}{l}
\texttt{uint v, x, y;}\\
\ldots\\
\texttt{x} \overset{\checkmark}{=} \texttt{v;}\\
\ldots\\
\texttt{x} \overset{\checkmark}{=} \texttt{7*y;}\\
\texttt{assert(x tainted-by T);}
\end{array}}
&
\leq_t
\quad
\boxed{\begin{array}{l}
\texttt{uint v, x, y;}\\
\ldots\\
\texttt{x} \overset{\times}{=} \texttt{v;}\\
\ldots\\
\texttt{x} \overset{\times}{=} \texttt{7*y;}\\
\texttt{assert(x tainted-by T);}
\end{array}}
\end{array}
$$

Here, if $y$ does not also depend previously on $x$, we can simply turn off the first tainting of $x$, since it will later be overwritten.

**Push Forward Instrumentation.** Instrumentation points can set the taint of a variable $v$ to that of another variable $v'$. We observe that sometimes the taint of variable $v'$ is only relevant because it is relevant for $v$. However, if the taint instrumentation in question is in the same function we simply replace the reference to the taint of $v'$ in the instrumentation of $v$ by the concrete taint instrumentation of $v'$. Then the tainting of $v'$ can be removed as in the previous optimisation. This concretisation can be performed easily, without any restrictions, for non-data-carrying labels. However, in the case of data-carrying labels we need to also make sure that the label does not contain references to variables that are modified in the flow between $v'$ and $v$.

For example:

$$
\begin{array}{ll}
\boxed{\begin{array}{l}
\texttt{taint par by T;}\\
\texttt{uint v, v';}\\
\texttt{v'} \overset{\checkmark}{=} \texttt{/* an operation on par */;}\\
\texttt{v} \overset{\checkmark}{=} \texttt{/* an operation on v' */;}\\
\texttt{assert(v tainted-by T);}
\end{array}}
&
\leq_t
\quad
\boxed{\begin{array}{l}
\texttt{uint v, v';}\\
\texttt{v'} \overset{\times}{=} \texttt{/* an operation on par */;}\\
\texttt{v} \overset{\times}{=} \texttt{/* an operation on v' */;}\\
\texttt{taint v by T;}\\
\texttt{assert(v tainted-by T);}
\end{array}}
\end{array}
$$

If the left-hand side is the whole body of a function, or we know that the parameter *par* and $v'$ are not relevant to any other conditional statement, then simply removing their tainting instrumentation, and simply tainting $v$ will be an appropriate reduction.

These two optimisations can be performed on the smart contract until a fixpoint is reached. We next consider the savings these give with a case study.

**Table 1.** Results, with costs in gas and increases in percentage w.r.t. to original costs.

| Costs | Original | Tainted | | Optimised | |
|---|---|---|---|---|---|
| | *Gas* | *Gas* | *%* | *Gas* | *%* |
| *Deployment* | 1276798 | 2213484 | +73% | 1694698 | +32% |
| *recordGrapeProductionFarmer Call* | 131783 | 312792 | +137% | 176743 | +34% |
| *recordGrapeProductionLab Call* | 152570 | 299379 | +96% | 242388 | +58% |
| *updateGrapeProductionLab Call* | 106448 | 121014 | +13% | 115372 | +8% |
| *Average business flow* | 225814 | 445715 | +97% | 300747 | +33% |

## 4   Case Study

We consider a smart contract which can be used to record and authenticate the provenance, quality, and use of grapes for the production of wine. Figure 4 illustrates a selection of the functions of this smart contract, along with taint annotations in our language, in **boldface**. Note that for simplicity in this case study a variable can only have one taint.

This contract allows a farmer to record a grape production on the smart contract, which is given a certain unique identifier (recordGrapeProductionFarmer). We also allow accredited labs to either register a grape production themselves, or update the farmer record, which we do not show here since they are similar to the recordGrapeProductionFarmer function. Sale of grapes to another person is also recorded on the blockchain (recordSale). The owner of a certain grape production can then record the bottling of wine produced from grapes they own (RecordBottling), while official certification providers can give a certain certification to the grapes, depending on the location they are produced in.

In this smart contract, we are interested in specifying that the right kind of accredited lab was involved in determining the recording of a grape production involved in making a wine, depending on whether the wine involves multiple grape sources or just one (see the asserts over taints in recordDOK). It bears to note that the benefit of taints here is that propagation of taints is done automatically, while a manual ad hoc approach is open for errors.

In Fig. 5 we report the recordGrapeProductionFarmer function with the encoding in Solidity described in Sect. 2.3. After the optimisations described in Sect. 3.2, the result is shown in Fig. 6, a significant reduction.

We evaluated this smart contract to identify the gas costs when there are no taints, to when the taint instrumentation is performed, and after it is optimised. The results are shown in Table 1. We report the results for each individual function given expected input, and for the average gas cost given a set of randomly generated expected (i.e., non-reverting) flows. One can see optimisation through the presented static analyses reduces costs significantly, up to around two thirds in the case of an average flow, validating the viability of the approach.

```
newtaint Taint = Farmer [address,uint] | Lab [address sender, uint]

function recordGrapeProductionFarmer(uint varietyOfGrapes, uint date, Location productionLoc,
                       GrapeQuality calldata qualityParameters) public returns(uint){
    taint msg.sender by Farmer(msg.sender, block.timestamp)
    require(!accredFullAnalysisLabs[msg.sender] && !!accredSimpleAnalysisLabs[msg.sender]);
    grapeIdCounter++;

    GrapeProduction memory grapeProduction =
        GrapeProduction(varietyOfGrapes,
                        msg.sender,
                        date,
                        productionLoc,
                        address(0),
                        qualityParameters,
                        0);

    grapeProd[grapeIdCounter] = grapeProduction;
    grapeToOwner[grapeIdCounter] = grapeProd[grapeIdCounter].farmer;
    return grapeIdCounter;
}

function recordSale(uint grapeid, address newOwner) public
  only(grapeToOwner[grapeid]){
    grapeToOwner[grapeid] = newOwner;
}

function recordBottling(uint[] calldata grapeids) public{
    wineIdCounter++;
    for(uint i = 0; i < grapeids.length; i++){
        assert(grapeToOwner[grapeids[i]] == msg.sender);
        wineToGrape[wineIdCounter].push(grapeids[i]);
    }
}

function recordDOK(uint wineID, DOKType dok, bool mixedWine) public{
    require(certificationProviders[msg.sender]);

    uint[] memory grapeSources = wineToGrape[wineID];

    if(mixedWine){
        assert(grapeSources.length > 1);
        for(uint i = 0; i < grapeSources.length; i++){
        assert(accredFullAnalysisLabs[taint-of(grapeProdTaints[grapeSources[i]])).sender]);
        }
    } else {
        for(uint i = 0; i < grapeSources.length; i++) {
        assert(accredFullAnalysisLabs[taint-of(grapeProdTaints[grapeSources[i]])).sender] ||
            accredSimpleAnalysisLabs[taint-of(grapeProdTaints[grapeSources[i]])).sender]);
        }
    }

    wineBatchCertified[wineID] = dok;
}
```

**Fig. 4.** Extract from case study smart contract (the.

```
function recordGrapeProductionFarmer(uint varietyOfGrapes, uint date, Location productionLoc,
                          GrapeQuality calldata qualityParameters) public returns(uint){
    require(!accredFullAnalysisLabs[msg.sender] && !accredSimpleAnalysisLabs[msg.sender]);
    senderTaint[msg.sender] = Taint(constructors.Farmer, msg.sender, block.timestamp);

    grapeIdCounter++;
    grapeIdCounterTaint = senderTaint[msg.sender];

    GrapeProduction memory grapeProduction =
        GrapeProduction(varietyOfGrapes,
                        msg.sender,
                        date,
                        productionLoc,
                        address(0),
                        qualityParameters,
                        0);
    Taint memory grapeProductionTaint = senderTaint[msg.sender];

    grapeProd[grapeIdCounter] = grapeProduction;
    grapeProdTaints[grapeIdCounter] = grapeProductionTaint;

    grapeToOwner[grapeIdCounter] = grapeProd[grapeIdCounter].farmer;
    grapeToOwnerTaints[grapeIdCounter] = grapeProdTaints[grapeIdCounter];
    return grapeIdCounter;
}
```

**Fig. 5.** Encoding of taint propagation in recordGrapeProductionFarmer.

```
function recordGrapeProductionFarmer(uint varietyOfGrapes, uint date, Location productionLoc,
                          GrapeQuality calldata qualityParameters) public returns(uint){
    require(!accredFullAnalysisLabs[msg.sender] && !accredSimpleAnalysisLabs[msg.sender]);

    grapeIdCounter++;

    GrapeProduction memory grapeProduction =
    GrapeProduction(varietyOfGrapes,
                        msg.sender,
                        date,
                        productionLoc,
                        address(0),
                        qualityParameters,
                        0);

    grapeProd[grapeIdCounter] = grapeProduction;
    grapeProdTaints[grapeIdCounter] = Taint(constructors.Farmer, msg.sender, block.timestamp);

    grapeToOwner[grapeIdCounter] = grapeProd[grapeIdCounter].farmer;
    return grapeIdCounter;
}
```

**Fig. 6.** recordGrapeProductionFarmer after optimisation of taint propagation.

## 5  Discussion

The taints we have added here are different from the usual taints considered in taint analysis. Usually, something is considered as tainted or not tainted, while here tainting can be with different labels, even sets of labels. This is a more powerful concept, since it allows to talk about all the contributing actors to a value, rather that simply talk about whether something is a security risk or not (without identifying what caused that security risk). That we integrate queries about these taints into a language, allowing branching in the program due to taints, is also novel to the best of our knowledge, since standard taint analysis simply is concerned with preventing certain data from reaching certain sinks.

These queries allow the developer to make decisions based on whether they trust the source of some data or not. For example in the case study the developer requires that information comes from a certain kind of lab when the wine is of a certain kind. This can certainly be implemented in an ad hoc manner without taints, but we believe that this kind of reasoning about trust at the top-level can be very useful due to the immutability of smart contracts and their public accessibility. A high-level approach gives certain guarantees that ad hoc implementations do not give, while static analysis tackles issues of gas.

Moreover, allowing taint queries at the level of if-then-else constructs opens up the possibility to modify branching at runtime depending on the trust level one has towards sources of taints. This can be used not just to prevent untrustworthy data to have an effect on the smart contract, but also to keep track of bad flows and perform actions that sanitise such data or to sanction their source.

## 6    Conclusions

A smart contract on a blockchain is open for interaction, with input coming from different, possibly untrustworthy sources. Keeping track of the sources of some data can be useful, for example when an event of interest happens we can then query the source of the event and contributing smart contract state, and make decisions based on that. In this paper, we have incorporated dynamic taint analysis for Solidity smart contracts through an extension of the language with a formal semantics, while we have described how this can be implemented in Solidity. We have also introduced a way to perform static tainting, which we use to prune away some of the instrumentation judged inconsequential for dynamic tainting. Evaluation on a case study, validates the static analysis as potentially eliminating a significant amount of overhead.

**Future Work.** In our abstract semantics we abstract taints by their corresponding taint type expression. In the future we want to consider also adding some information in the abstract taints to be able to relate them together, for example adding information about the line of code where the taint is created. Moreover, we do not do any analysis of variable values at the static level, however we intend to use techniques and tooling from [5,6] to enable some abstraction of these, which would allow more fine-grained static taint analysis.

# References

1. Ahrendt, W., Bubel, R.: Functional verification of smart contracts via strong data integrity. In: Leveraging Applications of Formal Methods, Verification and Validation: Applications - 9th International Symposium on Leveraging Applications of Formal Methods, ISoLA 2020, 20–30 October 2020, Rhodes, Greece, Proceedings, Part III. Lecture Notes in Computer Science, vol. 12478, pp. 9–24. Springer (2020). https://doi.org/10.1007/978-3-030-61467-6_2

2. Ahrendt, W., Chimento, J.M., Pace, G.J., Schneider, G.: A specification language for static and runtime verification of data and control properties. In: Bjørner, N., de Boer, F. (eds.) FM 2015: Formal Methods, pp. 108–125. Springer International Publishing, Cham (2015). https://doi.org/10.1007/978-3-319-19249-9_8

3. Azzopardi, S., Colombo, C., Pace, G.: CLARVA: model-based residual verification of java programs. In: Proceedings of the 8th International Conference on Model-Driven Engineering and Software Development, MODELSWARD 2020, Valletta, Malta, 25–27 February 2020 (2020). https://doi.org/10.5220/0008966603520359

4. Azzopardi, S., Colombo, C., Pace, G.J.: Control-flow residual analysis for symbolic automata. In: Proceedings Second International Workshop on Pre- and Post-Deployment Verification Techniques, PrePost@iFM 2017, Torino, Italy, 19 September 2017. EPTCS, vol. 254, pp. 29–43 (2017). https://doi.org/10.4204/EPTCS.254.3

5. Azzopardi, S., Colombo, C., Pace, G.J.: Model-based static and runtime verification for ethereum smart contracts. In: Model-Driven Engineering and Software Development - 8th International Conference, MODELSWARD 2020, 25–27 February 2020, Valletta, Malta, Revised Selected Papers. Communications in Computer and Information Science, vol. 1361, pp. 323–348. Springer (2020). https://doi.org/10.1007/978-3-030-67445-8_14

6. Azzopardi, S., Colombo, C., Pace, G.J.: A technique for automata-based verification with residual reasoning. In: Proceedings of the 8th International Conference on Model-Driven Engineering and Software Development, MODELSWARD 2020, 25–27 February 2020, Valletta, Malta, pp. 237–248. SCITEPRESS (2020). https://doi.org/10.5220/0008981902370248

7. Azzopardi, S., Ellul, J., Pace, G.J.: Monitoring smart contracts: Contractlarva and open challenges beyond. In: Runtime Verification - 18th International Conference, RV 2018, 10–13 November 2018, Limassol, Cyprus, Proceedings. Lecture Notes in Computer Science, vol. 11237, pp. 113–137. Springer (2018). https://doi.org/10.1007/978-3-030-03769-7_8

8. Chimento, J.M., Ahrendt, W., Pace, G.J., Schneider, G.: StaRVOOrS: a tool for combined static and runtime verification of java. In: Runtime Verification, pp. 297–305. Springer International Publishing, Cham (2015). https://doi.org/10.1007/978-3-319-23820-3_21

9. Ethereum: Solidity. Online Documentation (2016). http://solidity.readthedocs.io/en/develop/introduction-to-smart-contracts.html

10. Feist, J., Greico, G., Groce, A.: Slither: a static analysis framework for smart contracts. In: Proceedings of the 2nd International Workshop on Emerging Trends in Software Engineering for Blockchain, pp. 8–15. WETSEB 2019. IEEE Press (2019). https://doi.org/10.1109/WETSEB.2019.00008

11. Jakobs, M.C., Mantel, H.: A unifying framework for dynamic monitoring and a taxonomy of optimizations. In: Leveraging Applications of Formal Methods. Verification and Validation: Engineering Principles, pp. 72–92. Springer International Publishing, Cham (2020). https://doi.org/10.1007/978-3-030-61470-6_6

12. Kim, J., Kim, T., Im, E.G.: Survey of dynamic taint analysis. In: 2014 4th IEEE International Conference on Network Infrastructure and Digital Content, pp. 269–272 (2014). https://doi.org/10.1109/ICNIDC.2014.7000307
13. Kurniawan, A., Abbas, B.S., Trisetyarso, A., Isa, S.M.: Static taint analysis traversal with object oriented component for web file injection vulnerability pattern detection. Procedia Comput. Sci. **135**, 596–605 (2018). https://doi.org/10.1016/j.procs.2018.08.227, the 3rd International Conference on Computer Science and Computational Intelligence (ICCSCI 2018): Empowering Smart Technology in Digital Era for a Better Life
14. Mumtaz, H., El-Alfy, E.S.M.: Critical review of static taint analysis of android applications for detecting information leakages. In: 2017 8th International Conference on Information Technology (ICIT), pp. 446–454 (2017). https://doi.org/10.1109/ICITECH.2017.8080041
15. Tolmach, P., Li, Y., Lin, S.W., Liu, Y., Li, Z.: A survey of smart contract formal specification and verification. ACM Comput. Surv. **54**(7) (2021). https://doi.org/10.1145/3464421
16. Tripp, O., Pistoia, M., Fink, S.J., Sridharan, M., Weisman, O.: Taj: effective taint analysis of web applications. In: Proceedings of the 30th ACM SIGPLAN Conference on Programming Language Design and Implementation, pp. 87–97. PLDI 2009. Association for Computing Machinery, New York, NY, USA (2009). https://doi.org/10.1145/1542476.1542486
17. Xue, Y., Ma, M., Lin, Y., Sui, Y., Ye, J., Peng, T.: Cross-contract static analysis for detecting practical reentrancy vulnerabilities in smart contracts. In: Proceedings of the 35th IEEE/ACM International Conference on Automated Software Engineering, pp. 1029–1040. ASE 2020. Association for Computing Machinery, New York, NY, USA (2020). https://doi.org/10.1145/3324884.3416553, http://doi.org/10.1145/3324884.3416553

# Transaction Monitoring of Smart Contracts

Margarita Capretto[1,2]([envelope]) [ID], Martin Ceresa[1] [ID], and César Sánchez[1] [ID]

[1] IMDEA Software Institute, Madrid, Spain
{margarita.capretto,martin.ceresa,cesar.sanchez}@imdea.org
[2] Universidad Politécnica de Madrid (UPM), Madrid, Spain

**Abstract.** Blockchains are modern distributed systems that provide decentralized financial capabilities with trustable guarantees. Smart contracts are programs written in specialized programming languages running on a blockchain and govern how tokens and cryptocurrency are sent and received. Smart contracts can invoke other contracts during the execution of transactions initiated by external users.

Once deployed, smart contracts cannot be modified and their pitfalls can cause malfunctions and losses, for example by attacks from malicious users. Runtime verification is a very appealing technique to improve the reliability of smart contracts. One approach consists of specifying undesired executions (*never claims*) and detecting violations of the specification on the fly. This can be done by extending smart contracts with additional instructions corresponding to monitor specified properties, resulting in an *onchain* monitoring approach.

In this paper, we study *transaction monitoring* that consists of detecting violations of complete transaction executions and not of individual operations within transactions. Our main contributions are to show that transaction monitoring is not possible in most blockchains and propose different execution mechanisms that would enable transaction monitoring.

## 1 Introduction

Distributed ledgers (also known as *blockchains*) were first proposed by Nakamoto in 2009 [16] in the implementation of Bitcoin, as a method to eliminate trustable third parties in electronic payment systems. Modern blockchains incorporate smart contracts [24,25], which are state-full programs stored in the blockchain that describe the functionality of blockchain transactions, including the exchange of cryptocurrency. Smart contracts allow us to describe sophisticated functionality enabling many applications in decentralized finances (DeFi), decentralized governance, Web3, etc.

This work was funded in part by the Madrid Regional Government under project "S2018/TCS-4339 (BLOQUES-CM)" and by a research grant from Nomadic Labs and the Tezos Foundation.

T. Dang and V. Stolz (Eds.): RV 2022, LNCS 13498, pp. 162–180, 2022.
https://doi.org/10.1007/978-3-031-17196-3_9

Smart contracts are written in high-level programming languages for smart contracts, like Solidity [2] and Ligo [4] which are then typically compiled into low-level bytecode languages like EVM [25] or Michelson [1]. Even though smart contracts are typically small compared to conventional software, writing smart contracts has been proven to be notoriously difficult. Apart from conventional software runtime errors (like underflow and overflow), smart contracts also suffer from new attack patterns [19] or from attacks towards the blockchain infrastructure itself [20]. Smart contracts store and transfer money, and are openly exposed to external users directly and through caller smart contracts. Once installed the code of the contract is immutable and the effect of running a contract cannot be reverted (the contract *is* the law).

There are two classic approaches to achieve software reliability, and there are attempts to apply them to smart contracts:

- **static techniques** using automatic techniques like static analysis [23] or model checking [18], or deductive software verification techniques [3,8,12,17], theorem proving [5,7,21] or assisted formal construction of programs [22].
- **dynamic verification** [6,13,15] attempting to dynamically inspect the execution of a contract against a correctness specification.

In this paper, we follow a dynamic monitoring technique. Monitors are a defensive mechanism where developers write properties that must hold during the execution of the smart contracts. If a monitored property fails the whole transaction is aborted. Otherwise, the execution finishes normally as stipulated by the code of the contract.

Most of the monitoring techniques inject the monitor into the smart contract as additional instructions [6,13,15], which is called inline monitoring [14]. The property to be monitored for a method of a given contract $A$ is typically described as two parts: $A_{begin}$, that runs at the beginning of each call, and $A_{end}$, which is checked at the end. This monitoring code can inspect the storage of contract $A$ and read and modify specific monitor variables. For example, monitors can compare the balance at the beginning and end of the invocation. However, monitors can only see the contents of $A$ and cannot inspect or invoke other contracts. We call these monitors *operation monitors* as they allow us to inspect a single operation invocation. In this paper, we study a richer notion of monitoring that can inspect information across the running transaction, illustrated by our running example.

*Running Example: Flash Loans.* The aim of a flash loan contract is to allow other contracts to borrow balance *without any collateral,* provided that the borrowed money is repaid in the same transaction (perhaps with some interest) [9]. A simple way to specify the correctness of a flash loan contract $A$ is by the following two informal properties:

| FL-safety | *No transaction can decrease the balance of $A$* |
|---|---|
| **FL-progress** | *A request must be granted unless **FL-safety** is violated* |

Figure 1(a) shows a simple smart contract attempting to implement a flash loan lender. Function `lend` checks that the lender contract has enough tokens to provide the requested loan, saves the initial balance to later check that the loan has been repaid completely, and transfers the amount requested to the borrower. Upon return, `lend` checks that the loan has been paid back. Note that in this smart contract every instruction except the transfer to the borrower is part of the operation monitor. In particular, checking that the balance is enough and saving its value is what we call $A_{begin}$ while checking that the loan has been repaid is $A_{end}$.

```
contract Lender {
    function lend(address payable dest, uint amount) public {
begin   require(amount <= this.balance);
        uint initial_balance = this.balance;
        dest.transfer(amount);
end     assert(this.balance >= initial_balance);
    }
}
```

(a) A flash loan implementation attempt

```
contract Client {
    Lender l1, l2;
    function borrowAndInvest() public {
        l1.lend(100);l2.lend(200);
        invest(300);
        l1.transfer(100);l2.transfer(200);
    }
}
```

(b) A flash loan client

```
contract MaliciousClient {
    Lender l;
    function borrowAndInvest() public {
        l.lend(100);
        invest(100);
    }
}
```

(c) A malicious flash loan client

**Fig. 1.** Pseudocode for contracts `Lender`, `Client` and `MaliciousClient`.

Unfortunately, the lender smart contract in Fig. 1(a) does not fulfill property **FL-progress**. Consider a client, for example Fig. 1(b), that borrows money from different lenders, then invests the borrowed money to obtain a profit and finally pays back to the lenders. In other words, the contract `Client` in Fig. 1(b) collects all the money upfront *before* investing it and then pays back the lenders. The contract `Client` will not successfully borrow from the lender in Fig. 1(a), because contract `Lender` expects to be paid back within the scope of method `lend`.

However, the contract `Client` exercises correctly **FL-safety** and **FL-progress**, and returns the borrowed tokens before the transaction finishes. The problem is that contract `Lender` is too *defensive* and only allows repayments within the control flow of function `lend` and *not in arbitrary points within the enclosing transaction*. Alternatively, a lender contract could lend funds with the hope that the client returns the loan before the end of the transaction, but then a malicious contract, like in Fig. 1(c), would violate **FL-safety** easily. We cannot solve this problem with operation monitors because both $A_{begin}$ and $A_{end}$ are executed inside `lend` and it is not possible within the scope of `lend` to successfully predict or guarantee whether the loan will be repaid within the transaction.

In this article, we propose to extend monitors with two additional functions: $A_{init}$, which executes before the first call to $A$ in a given transaction; and $A_{term}$, which executes after the last call to $A$ (equivalently, at the end of the transaction). As for $A_{begin}$ and $A_{end}$, $A_{init}$ and $A_{term}$ have access to the storage and can fail but cannot be called from other contracts or emit operations. Both $A_{begin}$ and $A_{end}$ can be injected into the smart contract code as additional instructions, and therefore, are executed at every invocation of $A$. On the contrary $A_{init}$ and $A_{term}$ are special functions that are invoked (by the runtime system in charge of executing the smart contracts) at the beginning and at the end of every transaction in which $A$ is called, respectively. We call these monitors *transaction monitors* since they can check properties of the whole transaction. With transaction monitors, we implement a lender contract that satisfies **FL-safety** and **FL-progress** by saving the balance at the beginning of a transaction in `init` and comparing it with the final balance in `term` as shown in Fig. 2.

```
contract Lender {
  function lend(address payable dest, uint amount) public {
    require(amount <= this.balance);
    dest.transfer(amount);
  }
} with monitor {
  uint initial_balance;
  init { initial_balance = this.balance; }
  term { assert(this.balance >= initial_balance); }
}
```

**Fig. 2.** A correct flash loan implementation using transaction monitors

As for future work, we envision even more sophisticated monitors that guarantee properties that involve two or more contracts—like checking that the combined balance of $A$ and $B$ does not decrease—or even that predicating about all

| Global monitors | future work |
|---|---|
| Multicontract monitors | future work |
| Transaction monitors | this paper |
| Operation Monitors | [6,13,15] |

**Fig. 3.** Monitors hierarchy

contracts participating in a transaction of the whole blockchain. We refer to them as *multicontract monitors* and *global monitors*, respectively, but they are out of the scope of this paper, where we focus on *transaction monitors*. Figure 3 shows the monitoring hierarchy.

In summary, the contributions of the paper are the following:

– The notion of transaction monitors and its formal definition.
– A proof that current blockchains cannot implement transaction monitors, and a list of simple mechanisms that allow their implementation.
– An exhaustive study of how the proposed mechanisms interact with each other and the basic building blocks to implement full-fledged transaction monitors.

The rest of the paper is organized as follows. Section 2 describes the model of computation. Section 3 studies transaction monitors. Section 4 introduces new execution mechanisms, and in Sect. 5, we study how these new mechanisms implement transaction monitors. Finally, Sect. 6 concludes.

## 2    Model of Computation

We introduce now a general model of computation that captures the evolution of smart contract blockchains.

**An Informal Introduction.** Blockchains are a public incremental record of the executed transactions. Even though several transactions are packed in "blocks"— which are totally ordered—, transactions within a block are also totally ordered. Therefore, we can interpret blockchains as totally ordered sequences of transactions.

Transactions are in turn composed of a sequence of operations where the initial operation is an invocation from an external user. Each operation invokes a destination contract (where contracts are identified by their unique address). Operations also contain the name of the invoked method, arguments and balance (in the cryptocurrency of the underlying blockchain), and an amount of gas[1]. The execution of an operation follows the instructions of the program (the smart contract) stored in the destination address.

Given the arguments and state of the blockchain, the code of every smart contract is *deterministic* which makes the blockchain predictable and amenable to validation. We model smart contracts as pure computable functions taking

---

[1] The notion of gas is introduced to make all operations terminate because each individual instruction consumes gas and once the initial operation is invoked no more gas can be added to the transaction.

their input arguments and the current local storage of the contract, and returning (1) the changes to be performed in the local storage; (2) a list of further operations to be executed. No effect takes place in their local storage until the end of the operation. This abstraction does not impose any restriction since every imperative program can be split into a collection of basic pure code blocks separated by the instructions with effects.

The execution of a transaction consists of iteratively executing pending operations, computing their effects (including updating the pending operations) until either (1) the queue of pending operations is empty, or (2) some operation fails or the gas is exhausted. In the former case, the transaction commits and all changes are made permanent. In the latter case, the transaction aborts and no effect takes place (except that some gas is consumed).

**Model of Computation.** We now formally model the state of a blockchain during the execution of the operations forming a transaction. We represent a blockchain configuration as a pair $(\Sigma, \Delta)$ where:

**Blockchain state** $\Sigma$ is a partial map between addresses and the storage and balance of smart contracts,

**Blockchain context** $\Delta$ contains additional information about the blockchain, such as block number, current time, amount of money sent in the transaction, etc.

Blockchain contexts may vary since different blockchains carry different information, but either implicitly or explicitly, every blockchain maintains a blockchain state. The computation of a successful transaction begins with an external operation $o$ from a configuration $(\Sigma, \Delta)$ and either aborts or finishes into a final configuration $(\Sigma', \Delta')$.

We model a *smart contract* as a partial map $A : \Delta \times \mathbb{P} \times \$ \times \mathbb{N} \rightharpoonup (\$ \times [\mathcal{O}])$ where $\mathbb{P}$ is the set of all possible parameters of $A$, $\$$ the set of all possible storage states, $\mathcal{O}$ the set of operations and $[\cdot]$ is a set operator representing lists of elements of a given set. Smart contracts written in imperative languages with effects can be modeled as sequences of pure blocks where effects happen at the end in the standard way.

*Operations.* An operation is a record containing the following fields:

- dest the address to invoke;
- src the address initiating the operation;
- param parameters expected by the smart contract at address dest;
- money the amount of crypto-currency sent in the operation.

We use standard object notation to access each field, so $o$.dest is the destination address, $o$.src is the source address, $o$.param the parameters and $o$.money the amount transferred.

*Transactions.* A transaction results from the execution of a sequence of operations starting from an external operation placed by an external user. If an operation fails the transaction fails and the blockchain state remains unchanged. A successful operation $o$ results in a new storage and a list of new operations $ls$. The blockchain updates the storage of smart contract $o$.dest and balance of both smart contracts $o$.dest and $o$.src generating a new blockchain configuration and the list $ls$ is added to the current pending queue of operations. Operations are executed one at a time modifying the blockchain configuration until some operation fails or there is no more operations on the pending queue. In the second case, the transaction is successful and the last blockchain configuration consolidates.

We assume there is an implicit partial map from addresses to smart contracts $\mathbb{G} : Addr \rightharpoonup SmartContract$. Moreover, we assume map $\mathbb{G}$ does not change since we assume that smart contracts cannot install new contracts.

*Operation Execution.* Let $o$ be an operation and $(\Sigma, \Delta)$ a blockchain configuration. The evaluation of $o$ from $(\Sigma, \Delta)$ results in a new configuration and a list of operations $ls$, which we denote $(\Sigma, \Delta) \xrightarrow{o} (\Sigma', \Delta', ls)$ whenever:

1. The source smart contract has enough balance, $\Sigma(o.\text{src}) \geq o.\text{money}$
2. The invocation to the smart contract is successful:

$$\mathbb{G}(o.\text{dest})(\Delta, o.\text{param}, \Sigma(o.\text{dst}).st, \Sigma(o.\text{dst}).balance) = (st', ls)$$

The new blockchain configuration state $\Sigma'$ is the result of: 1) adding $o$.money into the balance of $o$.dest and subtracting it from $o$.src, and 2) updating the storage as $\Sigma'(o.\text{dest}).st = st'$. Note that we leave the evolution of $\Delta$ unspecified as it is system dependant. In Sect. 5, we implement different additional blockchain features by inspecting (and possibly modifying) the blockchain context. For failing evaluation of operations, we use $(\Sigma, \Delta) \xrightarrow{o} \times$.

*Execution Order.* The execution can proceed in different ways. We consider two execution orders: new operations are added to the beginning of the pending queue (a DFS strategy) and new operations added to the end of the pending queue (a BFS strategy). This results in the following transition rules:

$$\frac{(\Sigma, \Delta) \xrightarrow{o} \times}{(\Sigma, \Delta, o :: os) \not\rightsquigarrow_a}$$

$$\frac{(\Sigma, \Delta) \xrightarrow{o} (\Sigma', \Delta', ls)}{(\Sigma, \Delta, o :: os) \rightsquigarrow_{dfs} (\Sigma', \Delta', ls \mathbin{+\mkern-10mu+} os)} \qquad \frac{(\Sigma, \Delta) \xrightarrow{o} (\Sigma', \Delta', ls)}{(\Sigma, \Delta, o :: os) \rightsquigarrow_{bfs} (\Sigma', \Delta', os \mathbin{+\mkern-10mu+} ls)}$$

The execution starting from an external operation $o$ is a sequence of steps ($\rightsquigarrow_a$)—with $a$ fixed to be either $dfs$ or $bfs$—until the pending operation list is empty or the execution of the next operation fails. Beginning from a blockchain configuration $(\Sigma, \Delta)$ and an initial operation $o$, a transaction execution is a sequence of operation executions: $(\Sigma, \Delta, [o]) \rightsquigarrow_a (\Sigma_1, \Delta_1, os_1) \rightsquigarrow_a \ldots \rightsquigarrow_a (\Sigma_n, \Delta_n, [])$ or that $(\Sigma, \Delta, [o]) \rightsquigarrow_a (\Sigma_1, \Delta_1, os_1) \rightsquigarrow_a \ldots \rightsquigarrow_a (\Sigma_n, \Delta_n, os_n) \not\rightsquigarrow_a$

A transaction can fail either because of gas exhaustion or an internal operation has failed, and in that case, we have a sequence of $\leadsto_a$ leading to a final step marked as $\not\leadsto_a$ following the failing operation.

Finally, after every successful execution, the blockchain takes the last configuration and upgrades its global system.

The model of computation described in this section does not follow exactly a call-and-return model like the Ethereum blockchain does [25]. However, it is easy to see that it can be simulated in our model by having each contract explicitly keeping its stack of returned values.

# 3   Transaction Monitors

We now introduce *transaction monitors* and show that it is not possible to implement them in current blockchains. We present different extensions that allow us to implement transaction monitors.

## 3.1   Transaction Monitors

Transaction monitors allow us to reason about properties of transactions. Each smart contract $A$ is equipped with a monitor storage and four especial methods $A_{init}$, $A_{begin}$, $A_{end}$ and $A_{term}$. These new methods cannot emit operations or modify smart contract storage, however, they have their own monitor storage. We assume that these new methods are interpreted by the blockchain and if one of these methods fail the whole transaction fails. Otherwise, the effect in the blockchain is the same as if it was executed without monitors. The functions $A_{init}$ and $A_{term}$ can read the storage and balance of the smart contract and read and write the monitor storage. Function $A_{init}$ is executed before the first time $A$ is invoked in the transaction and function $A_{term}$ is invoked after the last interaction to $A$ finished in the transaction, and does not modify the monitor storage. Functions $A_{begin}$ and $A_{end}$ are executed at the beginning and at the end of each *operation* that is executed in $A$, as in operation monitors [13] (note that $A_{begin}$ and $A_{end}$ can be easily implemented by inlining their code around the methods of $A$). The method $A_{begin}$ takes the same arguments as any $A$ operation plus the monitor storage, while function $A_{end}$ has access to the result of the operation (list of the operation emitted and the new storage) plus the monitor storage. We call the resulting smart contracts *monitored smart contracts*.

*Operation Monitors.* We first extend the model of computation to include operation monitors. A monitored operation execution is a normal operation execution where the corresponding operation monitor is executed before and after the operation is executed.

We define $(\xrightarrow[mon]{o})$ modifying $(\xrightarrow{o})$ as follows. Before executing $o$, (1) procedure $\mathbb{G}(o.\text{dest}).begin$ is invoked, then (2) operation $o$ is executed, and (3) finally $\mathbb{G}(o.\text{dest}).end$ runs. That is, operation monitors are simply restricted functions executed before and after each operation. We can then specialize $\leadsto_a$ with operation monitors, that is, use relation $(\xrightarrow[mon]{o})$ instead of relation $(\xrightarrow{o})$ to obtain transaction executions that use operation monitors.

Procedures *begin* and *end* can only modify the private monitor storage and fail, and thus, they cannot interfere in the normal execution of smart contracts (except by failing more often).

*Transaction Monitors.* We redefine transaction monitors execution as a restriction of the transaction execution relation so transactions invoke *init* and *term* when required. In this case, *init* can change the monitor storage, and thus, can modify the blockchain state. We define a new relation $\twoheadrightarrow_a$ the smallest relation defined by the following inference rules:

$$\frac{A_{init}(\Sigma(A)) = \Sigma'}{(\Sigma, \Delta, os) \twoheadrightarrow_a (\Sigma', \Delta, os)} \qquad \frac{A_{term}(\Sigma(A))}{(\Sigma, \Delta, [\,]) \twoheadrightarrow_a (\Sigma, \Delta, [\,])} \qquad \frac{(\Sigma, \Delta, o :: os) \leadsto_a (\Sigma', \Delta', os')}{(\Sigma, \Delta, o :: os) \twoheadrightarrow_a (\Sigma', \Delta', os')}$$

Note that we sacrifice a deterministic operational semantics in favor of a clearer set of rules. As before, we use $(\nrightarrow)$ to represent failing transactions.

$$\frac{(\Sigma, \Delta) \xrightarrow{o} \nrightarrow}{(\Sigma, \Delta, os) \nrightarrow} \qquad \frac{A_{init}(\Sigma(A)) \nrightarrow}{(\Sigma, \Delta, os) \nrightarrow} \qquad \frac{A_{term}(\Sigma(A)) \nrightarrow}{(\Sigma, \Delta, [\,]) \nrightarrow}$$

Finally, we define a monitored trace of a transaction same as before, given a blockchain configuration $(\Sigma, \Delta)$ and an external operation $o$:

$$(\Sigma, \Delta, [o]) \twoheadrightarrow_a (\Sigma_1, \Delta_1, os_1) \twoheadrightarrow_a (\Sigma_2, \Delta_2, os_2) \twoheadrightarrow_a \ldots \twoheadrightarrow_a (\Sigma_n, \Delta_n, [\,])$$

To remove the non-determinism we add a new relation that restricts the legal runs. This relation knows the set of visited addresses (smart contracts), and invokes an initialization method, and at the very end of the evaluation of a transaction uses the same set to invoke their corresponding term method.

$$\frac{(\Sigma, \Delta, os) \xrightarrow{o}_a (\Sigma', \Delta', os') \qquad o.dest \in E}{E \vdash (\Sigma, \Delta, o :: os) \Rightarrow_a E \vdash (\Sigma', \Delta', os')}$$

$$\frac{(\Sigma'', \Delta, os) \leadsto_a^o (\Sigma', \Delta', os') \qquad o.dest \notin E \qquad (\Sigma, \Delta, os) \twoheadrightarrow_a^{A_{init}} (\Sigma'', \Delta, os)}{E \vdash (\Sigma, \Delta, o :: os) \Rightarrow_a E \cup \{o.dest\} \vdash (\Sigma', \Delta', os')}$$

$$\frac{(\Sigma, \Delta, [\,]) \twoheadrightarrow_a^{A_{term}} (\Sigma, \Delta, os) \qquad e \in E}{E \vdash (\Sigma, \Delta, [\,]) \Rightarrow_a E \setminus \{e\} \vdash (\Sigma, \Delta, [\,])}$$

As result, we only accept traces generated by relation $(\Rightarrow_a)$, beginning with a blockchain configuration $(\Sigma, \Delta)$ and an external operation $o$ resulting in failure or a new blockchain configuration $(\Sigma', \Delta')$: $\emptyset \vdash (\Sigma, \Delta, [o]) \Rightarrow_a \ldots \Rightarrow_a \emptyset \vdash (\Sigma', \Delta', [\,])$.

## 3.2  Transaction Monitors in BFS/DFS

Unfortunately, transaction monitors cannot be implemented in blockchains that follow DFS or BFS evaluation strategies. We show now a counter-example. Consider a transaction monitor for $A$ that fails when smart contract $A$ is called **exactly** once in a transaction. The monitor storage contains a natural number to keep track of how many times $A$ has been invoked in the current transaction. Function *init* sets this counter to 0, *begin* adds one to the counter, *end* does nothing, and *term* fails if the monitor storage is exactly one.

Now let $(\Sigma, \Delta)$ be a blockchain configuration, and let $A$ and $B$ be two smart contracts, where $A$ is being monitored for the "only once" property. Consider the following two executions of external operations from $(\Sigma, \Delta)$:

- $o_1$ invokes $B.f$ which then invokes $o_{A1}$ in $A$,
- $o_2$ invokes $B.g$ which then invokes $o_{A1}$ and $o_{A2}$ in $A$.

The monitor for "only once" must reject the transaction beginning with $o_1$, but accept the transaction beginning with $o_2$.

Consider a DFS strategy. Starting from $o_1$, the execution trace is

$$(\Sigma, \Delta, [o_1]) \leadsto_{dfs} (\Sigma_1, \Delta_2, [o_{A1}]) \leadsto_{dfs} (\Sigma_2, \Delta_2, as_1)$$

with corresponding sequence of pending operations $[o_1]$, $[o_{A1}]$, $as_1$. Starting from $o_2$ the sequence of pending operations is $[o_2]$, $[o_{A1}; o_{A2}]$, $as_1 +\!\!+ [o_{A2}], \ldots, [o_{A2}]$, $as_2$. It is not possible to distinguish between the traces generated by $o_1$ and $o_2$, as anything that operation $o_{A1}$ and its descendants $as_1$ do will happen before the execution of $o_{A2}$ in the second transaction. In other words, $o_{A1}$ and all the operations that can be generated by it or its descendants cannot know that some other invocation to $A$ is pending. Therefore, $A$ cannot fail during the execution of $o_{A1}$ or its descendants, as this implies that also a failure in the execution of $o_2$. At the same time $o_{A1}$ is the only chance in $A$ to make the first transaction fail because there is no other operation in $A$. Consequently, the two runs are identical up to the end of $o_{A1}$ but one must fail and the other must not fail.

A BFS scheduler can distinguish between the execution of operations $o_1$ and $o_2$ by using a *recurring operation*. Basically, a recurring operation is just a regular function that either terminates or reinserts itself in the pending queue of operations. Since new operations are added to the end of the pending queue, $A$ can inject a recurring operation that check the state of $A$ and conditionally, if the test that would make *term* fail is true, reinjects itself again. This recurring operation will be invoked at the end of all other functions in $A$. If the condition that makes *term* accept is never met, the transaction fails because the recurring operation injects itself ad-infinitum, exhausting gas. In Sect. 5.1 we use recurring operations thoroughly. However, a simple variation of this example that includes comparing with a third transaction where $A$ is invoked three times shows that BFS cannot implement "only once" either (as BFS cannot distinguish between the third invocation to $A$ and a first invocation to $A$ in a transaction following the one originated by $o_2$). For a detailed proof see [10].

# 4   Execution Mechanisms

We propose new mechanisms and study if they help to implement transaction monitors. However, adding features to blockchains is potentially dangerous since it can introduce unwanted behaviour [19]. We focus on simple mechanisms that are easy to implement and are backwards compatible.

Since $A_{begin}$ and $A_{end}$ can already be implemented using inlining, we focus on mechanisms that allow executions at the beginning and end of transactions, which can aid to implement $A_{init}$ and $A_{term}$. It is worth noting that in most modern blockchain smart contracts are normal functions that also manage tokens. That is, smart contracts can modify their local memory (storage), invoke another functions, fail and also transfer tokens. However, smart contracts are oblivious to the notion of transactions: they cannot tell if a new transaction has started, if two invocations belong to the same transaction or not, or when a transaction has finished. The mechanisms that we introduce in this Section will help to distinguish these situations.

We present two kinds of mechanisms, ones that introduce a new instruction, and others that add a new special method to smart contracts. In the next section, we compare their relative power and if they can implement transaction monitors.

**Mechanisms that Add New Instructions.** The first four mechanisms add new instructions and can be easily implemented by bakers/miners collecting the information required in the context $\Delta$.

- *First.* We consider a new instruction, `first`, which returns true if the current operation is the first invocation to the smart contract in the current transaction. The context $\Delta$ can be extended to contain the set of contracts $F$ that have already run an operation in the current transaction, which allows us to implement `first` as $A \notin F$, where $A$ is the smart contract that executes `first`.
- *Count.* We introduce now a new instruction, `count` that returns how many invocations have been performed to methods of the contract in the current transaction. Again, the context $\Delta$ can easily count how many times each contract has been invoked.
- *Fail/NoFail.* This mechanism equips each contract with a new flag `fail` that can be assigned during the execution of the contract (and that is false by default). The semantics is that at the end of the transaction, the whole transaction would fail if some contract has the `fail` bit to true. For example, the failing bit allows us to implement flash loans as follows. A lender smart contract can set `fail` to true when is lending money and change it to false only when the money is returned.
- *Queue info.* We add a new operation, `queue`, indicating if there is no more interaction between smart contracts. Or equivalently, if the only operations permitted in the pending queue are recurrent operations (which can only inject operations to the same contract). These operations must also be specially qualified in the contract, and the runtime system must make sure that they only generate operations to the same contract.

**Mechanisms that Add New Methods or Storage.** The following mechanisms modify the definition of smart contracts either by adding new methods that are executed at particular moments in a transaction or by adding special storage/memory.

- *Transaction Memory.* Smart contracts are equipped with a special volatile memory segment that exists only during the execution of a transaction and which is created and initialized at the beginning of the transaction. We add a new segment in the smart contract indicating the initial values to be assigned. In concrete, each contract $A$ indicates a new storage type for the transaction memory and a procedure that initializes it (which can read but not change the conventional storage). We use `trmem` to refer to this mechanism.
- *Storage Hookup, Bounded and Unbounded.* The idea is to equip smart contracts with a new method that updates the storage after the last local operations in the transaction. These methods can only modify the storage but not invoke other methods. A bounded version of this mechanism is restricted to terminating non-failing functions (for example, by restricting the class of programs). In addition, the unbounded version is arbitrary code that can fail. We use `bstore` and `ustore` to refer to these mechanisms.

For space purposes correct flash loan implementations using these mechanisms are not included here but can be found in [10].

## 5 Implementing Transaction Monitors

We say a mechanism $M$ *implements* another mechanism $N$ whenever every smart contract executing in a blockchain with $N$ can be simulated by a smart contract in a blockchain with $M$. Here, simulation means that all observable effect (in terms of failure behavior, storage changes and token transfers) are identical. We say that two mechanisms are *equivalent* if and only if they can implement each other. In this paper we disregard gas consumption so we implicitly assume that one can always assign sufficient gas to a contract.

**Theorem 1.** *The following are equivalent:* `trmem`, `first`, `count`, *and* `bstore`.

If contracts can know when their first invocation in the transaction occurs, they can set the storage in different ways simulating `count` and `trmem`. Also, `count` and `trmem` can simulate `first`, by checking if the count is 0 and initializing a volatile bit to *true*. More interesting is that `first` can simulate bounded storage hookup by applying the effect on the storage of bounded storage hookup at the beginning of the next transaction. Detailed proofs are included in the longer version of this paper [10].

**Lemma 1.** *Mechanism* `ustore` *implements* `bstore` *and* `fail`.

*Proof.* Mechanism `ustore` implements `bstore` trivially as it is just less restrictive. For `fail` we add in the storage of $A$ a new field, $fl$ to represent the failing bit which is initialized to false when the contract is installed and updated to simulate the `fail` instruction. At the end of the transaction, the `ustore` hookup checks if $fl$ is true and fail. Otherwise, it does nothing.     □

It can be proven that the other direction is not always possible. Fig 4 shows graphically the previous results where an arrow indicates that one mechanism implements another. In this diagram, an absence of an arrow does not necessarily imply impossibility but perhaps that the result depends on the execution order. For example, in BFS blockchains `first` can implement `ustore`, but this is impossible with DFS.

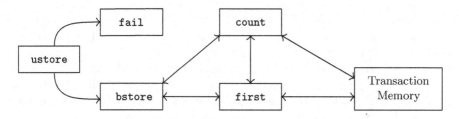

**Fig. 4.** Relation between mechanisms for any scheduler. An arrow from mechanism M to mechanism N means that M implements N.

Since `first`, `count`, `bstore` and `trmem` are all equivalent, from now on we only refer to mechanism `first`. It is easy to see that this mechanism is enough to implement `init`.

To implement `term`, we can either implement `fail` or `ustore`, where `fail` is simpler, and `ustore` is more powerful but requires a bigger change to blockchains.

**Theorem 2.** *Mechanisms* `first` + `fail` *implement transaction monitors.*

*Proof.* Let $\mathcal{B}$ be a blockchain that implements `first` and `fail`. Given a monitored smart contract $A$, we want to implement $A$ in blockchain $\mathcal{B}$. We define a new smart contract $A'$ extending its storage to also contains $A$'s monitor storage. Then, we equip $A'$ with a new method $f'$ for every method $f$ in $A$, such that, $f'$ first checks `first` and executes $A_{init}$ if needed. Then, before exiting, $f'$ executes $A_{term}$ with the current state but instead of failing explicitly $f'$ set the failing bit. Function $A_{init}$ is executed exactly once and $A_{term}$ may be executed multiple times, but it does not modify the contract storage and it does not generate operations. The last execution of $A_{term}$ in $A'$ will simulate $A_{term}$ in $A$. If the semantics of the blockchain were such that the balance of pending outgoing operation would subtract balance from $A$ when it executes, then these calculations can be made in the monitor storage when the operations are generated.     □

**Fig. 5.** Relation between mechanisms and transaction monitor for any scheduler.

Since `ustore` implements `first` and `fail`, it follows that `ustore` implements transaction monitors.

**Corollary 1.** `ustore` *implements transaction monitors but transaction monitors cannot implement* `ustore`.

Transaction monitors can only make contracts fail but not change the storage. Our results are summarized in Fig. 5.

### 5.1   BFS Blockchains

We now study more in detail the mechanism for BFS based blockchains. The first result is that unless equipped with further mechanisms, BFS blockchains cannot implement transaction monitors. The essence of the proof is to create two transactions on a monitored contract $A$ (like in "only once") in which corresponding invocations to the same contract $A$ receive identical information, and one must fail and the other commit.

**Theorem 3.** *A BFS blockchain does not implement transaction monitors.*

A BFS blockchain guarantees that new operations are executed after all pending operations, which enables the implementation of `fail` using recurring operations. A recurring operation is a private function that can read and write the storage and that either terminates or reinjects itself again to the pending queue. Since every time the operation is executed the blockchain consumes gas, and eventually, failure follows from an attempt to inject itself ad-infinitum.

**Lemma 2.** *Recurring operations in BFS blockchain allow to implement* `fail`.

Since transaction monitors cannot be implemented within a BFS blockchain (see [10]), we conclude that `fail` does not implement transaction monitors in BFS blockchains. The missing element is `first` which allows to implement `ustore`. And, since `ustore` implements transaction monitors (Corollary 1), `first` can also implement transaction monitors.

**Lemma 3.** *Mechanism* `first` *implements* `ustore` *in BFS blockchains.*

*Proof.* Assume a BFS blockchain implementing `first`. Let $A$ be a smart contract. We modify $A$ to contain a second copy $S'$ of its storage. Upon the first call of $A$, we update the current storage using the values in $S'$. We add a new private method *hookup* in $A$ that mimics the code of `ustore` but (1) it applies the changes in $S'$, and (2) instead of failing (if `ustore` fails) it calls itself as a recurring operation. Finally, we modify $A$ so that function *hookup* is invoked at the end of each method in $A$. In effect, *hookup* is preventively evaluating `ustore` on the side memory $S'$, and simulating the failure as a recurring operation (when `ustore` fails). Therefore, if the operation is the last one on the contract and it does not fail, then $S'$ contains the correct storage, which will then be copied at the beginning of the next transaction.                                   □

In the previous proof, we split mechanism `ustore` into two parts: one in charge of updating the storage, the other in charge of failing. If we also add `queue`, we can implement `ustore` without failing by gas exhaustion because now the *hookup* executed recurrently can know if there are only recurrent operations and then execute the `ustore` code (including the failure).

**Lemma 4.** *Mechanism* `queue` *implements* `ustore` *in BFS blockchains.*

In a BFS blockchain, `ustore` implements transaction monitors (Corollary 1), and thus, by the previous lemma, `queue` also implements transaction monitors. Next, we will show that `queue` cannot be implemented with `ustore` when a BFS strategy is used. Intuitively, mechanism `queue` adds a way for smart contracts to know the state of the blockchain, i.e. if there is still interaction between smart contracts, and thus, smart contracts can take different actions based on the state of the blockchain, while mechanism `ustore` adds a way to execute a procedure at the end of transactions, but smart contracts are oblivious about interactions between smart contracts. Since `ustore` implements all other mechanisms, we have that no other mechanism can implement `queue`.

**Lemma 5.** *In BFS blockchains* `ustore` *cannot implement* `queue`.

The main idea is to create two executions that are identical unless one can inspect the pending operation queue, and in which one operation must fail if `queue` returns that the queue of pending operations is empty. The complete proof is in [10]. Figure 6 summarizes the relations between mechanisms and transaction monitor in BFS blockchains.

## 5.2  DFS Blockchains

We now study DFS blockchains, that is, when the resulting list of operations from smart contracts execution are appended at the beginning of the list. This is the most conventional execution order in most blockchains, like Ethereum. We now prove several impossibility results.

Mechanisms `ustore` and `first` plus `fail` implement transaction monitors (Corollary 1 and Thoerem 2). In a DFS blockchain, those are the only two ways using our mechanisms to implement transaction monitors. We show that transaction monitors cannot be implemented by combining `queue` with either `first` or `fail`, and as a consequence none of these mechanisms on their own can implement transaction monitors.

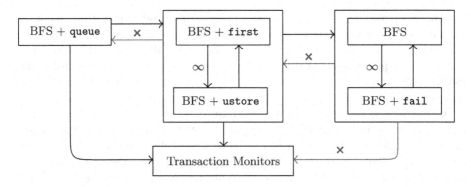

**Fig. 6.** Relation between mechanisms and transaction monitor in BFS blockchains. A black arrow from mechanism $M$ to mechanism $N$ means that $M$ can implement $N$. The $\infty$ symbol represents the use of an infinite recursion to provoke a failure. A red arrow with a cross from mechanism $M$ to mechanism $N$ means that $M$ cannot implement $N$. (Color figure online)

**Lemma 6.** *A DFS blockchain implementing* queue *and* first *does not implement transaction monitors.*

*Proof.* Let $\mathcal{B}$ be a DFS blockchain and $A$ a smart contract installed in $\mathcal{B}$. Consider the "only once" monitor that fails if and only if the smart contract $A$ is called exactly once. We show that this monitor cannot be implemented in DFS even with first and queue.

Let $B, C$ be two other smart contracts. We analyze the pending queue of execution of two possible external operations originated by $B$:

1. $o_1$ where $B$ calls $A$ *once* and then $C$
2. $o_2$ where $B$ calls $A$ *twice* and then $C$

We assume that there are no additional invocations to $A$ aside from the described above. When we execute both operations in a $(\Sigma, \Delta)$ blockchain system, we have the following two traces:

- $t_1 : (\Sigma, \Delta, [o_1]) \leadsto_{dfs} (\Sigma', \Delta', [a_1, c_1]) \dots$
- $t_2 : (\Sigma, \Delta, [o_2]) \leadsto_{dfs} (\Sigma', \Delta', [a_1, a_2, c_1]) \dots$

Note that the presence of operation $c_1$ in the pending execution queue is forcing mechanism queue to return false. Since the occurrence of operation $a_1$ in both cases execute in the same configuration, the behavior must be the same. The transaction executing $o_1$ must fail because $A$ is called only once, but this will make the second transaction fail as well.  □

We can conclude that neither queue nor first alone would implement transaction monitors.

**Lemma 7.** *Under DFS* queue *and* fail *cannot implement transaction monitors.*

The main difference between these mechanisms and transaction monitors is that the latter can execute functions without a contract being invoked at particular moments in the execution of transactions. Take for example procedure *init*, neither `queue` nor `fail` can simulate *init*, as there is no way for these mechanisms to distinguish the first execution of a smart contract in a given transaction.

Combining `fail` with `first` one can implement transaction monitors in any execution order, including DFS (Theorem 2), but `fail` is not enough to implement transaction monitors in DFS. Therefore, we conclude that DFS blockchains do not implement `first`. Moreover, putting all previous lemmas together, we conclude that a DFS blockchains cannot implement any of the mechanisms listed in Sect. 4 directly.

**Corollary 2.** *DFS blockchains cannot implement* `first`, `fail`, `ustore` *or* `queue`.

All proofs are in [10].

## 6   Conclusion and Future Work

We have studied transaction monitors for smart contracts. Transaction monitors are a defense mechanism enabling smart contracts to explicitly state wanted or unwanted behaviour at the transactional level. This kind of properties are motivated by contracts like flash loans, which are not implementable in their full generality in current blockchains. We propose a solution based on adding new mechanisms to the blockchain. Transaction monitors can be incorporated directly into contracts or simulated if some of these mechanisms are implemented. This could be preferable since some of these mechanisms are very simple and backward compatible, while others extend the functionality of smart contracts. We have studied how some mechanisms simulate each other, both for any execution order, and specifically for BFS and DFS blockchains. The conclusion is that the simplest mechanism that allows us to implement transaction monitors is the combination of `first` and `fail`.

Nevertheless, the main contribution of this paper is purely theoretical. Future work includes implementing transaction monitors and practically interesting features from Sect. 4 in a real blockchain and implement illustrative transaction monitors.

For simplicity, we have neglected a specific analysis of gas consumption, except for recurrent operations that purposefully fail by exhausting gas. Even though transaction monitors will consume additional gas which can influence the failure of the transaction (as with operation monitors), we claim that for all our development there is an amount of gas that can be calculated which will not make accepting transactions fail. However, we leave a detailed study for future work.

Other avenues of future work include the study of new features, particularly *views* that allows contracts to inspect the state of other contracts. We are also

performing a thorough study of how exposing new mechanisms to contracts—
that can use them for implementing functionality—can break (or not) implementations of monitors that are correct without adding the mechanisms. Finally,
since proofs in this paper are "pencil and paper" and the interplay of different
mechanisms can be counter-intuitive, we plan to formalize all proofs here in an
existing smart-contract formal "playgound" (libraries in theorem provers that
enable mechanical proofs), e.g. [11].

# References

1. Michelson: the language of smart contracts in Tezos. https://tezos.gitlab.io/
   whitedoc/michelson.html
2. Ethereum. Solidity documentation - release 0.2.0 (2016). http://solidity.
   readthedocs.io/
3. Ahrendt, W., Bubel, R.: Functional verification of smart contracts via strong data
   integrity. In: Proceedings of ISoLA (3). LNCS, pp. 9–24. Springer (2020). https://
   doi.org/10.1007/978-3-030-61467-6_2
4. Alfour, G.: LIGO: a friendly smart-contract language for Tezos (2022). Accessed 3
   May 2022. https://ligolang.org
5. Annenkov, D., Nielsen, J.B., Spitters,B.: ConCert: a smart contract certification
   framework in Coq. In: Proceedings of the 9th ACM SIGPLAN International Conference on Certified Programs and Proofs (CPP 2020), pp. 215–218. ACM (2020)
6. Azzopardi, S., Ellul, J., Pace, G.J.: Monitoring smart contracts: ContractLarva
   and open challenges beyond. In: Colombo, C., Leucker, M. (eds.) RV 2018. LNCS,
   vol. 11237, pp. 113–137. Springer, Cham (2018). https://doi.org/10.1007/978-3-
   030-03769-7_8
7. Bernardo, B., Cauderlier, R., Hu, Z., Pesin, B., Tesson, J.: Mi-Cho-Coq, a framework for certifying Tezos smart contracts. arXiv:abs/1909.08671 (2019)
8. Bhargavan, K., et al.: Formal verification of smart contracts: short paper. In:
   Proceedings of Workshop on Programming Languages and Analysis for Security
   (PLAS@CCS 2016), pp. 91–96. ACM (2016)
9. Cañada, A.C., Kobayashi, F., Fubuloubu, Williams, A.: Eip-3156: Flash loans
   (2020)
10. Capretto, M., Ceresa, M., Sánchez, C.: Transaction monitoring of smart contracts.
    arXiv:abs/2207.02517 (2022)
11. Ceresa, M., Sánchez, C.: Multi: a formal playground for multi-smart contract inter-
    action. In: Schneidewind, C., Dargaye, Z. (eds.) 4th International Workshop on
    Formal Methods for Blockchains, FMBC@CAV 2022 (to appear), OASIcs. Schloss
    Dagstuhl - Leibniz-Zentrum für Informatik (2022)
12. Conchon, S., Korneva, A., Zaïdi, F.: Verifying smart contracts with Cubicle. In:
    Proceedings of the 1st Workshop on Formal Methods for Blockchains (FMBC
    2019), vol. 12232 of LNCS, pp. 312–324. Springer (2019). https://doi.org/10.1007/
    978-3-030-54994-7_23
13. Ellul, J., Pace, G.J.: Runtime verification of Ethereum smart contracts. In: Pro-
    ceedings of the 14th European Dependable Computing Conference (EDCC 2018),
    pp. 158–163. IEEE Computer Society (2018)
14. Leucker, M.: Teaching runtime verification. In: Proceedings of RV'11, number 7186
    in LNCS, pp. 34–48. Springer (2011). https://doi.org/10.1007/978-3-642-29860-
    8_4

15. Li, A., Choi, J.A., Long, F.: Securing smart contract with runtime validation. In: Proceedings of ACM PLDI 2020, pp. 438–453. ACM (2020)
16. Nakamoto, S.: Bitcoin: a peer-to-peer electronic cash system (2009)
17. Nehaï, Z., Bobot, F.: Deductive proof of industrial smart contracts using Why3. In: Proceedings of the 1st Workshop on Formal Methods for Blockchains (FMBC 2019), vol. 12232 of LNCS, pp. 299–311. Springer (2019). https://doi.org/10.1007/978-3-030-54994-7_22
18. Permenev, A., Dimitrov, D., Tsankov, P., Drachsler-Cohen, D., Vechev, M.: VerX: safety verification of smart contracts. In: 2020 IEEE Symposium on Security and Privacy (SP), pp. 1661–1677 (2020)
19. Phil, D.: Analysis of the dao exploit (2016)
20. Robinson, D., Konstantopoulos, G.: Ethereum is a dark forest (2020)
21. Schiffl, J., Ahrendt, W., Beckert, B., Bubel, R.: Formal analysis of smart contracts: applying the KeY system. In: Deductive Software Verification: Future Perspectives - Reflections on the Occasion of 20 Years of KeY, vol. 12345 of LNCS, pp. 204–218 (2020)
22. Sergey, I., Kumar, A., Hobor, A.: Scilla: a smart contract intermediate-level LAnguage. CoRR, abs/1801.00687 (2018)
23. Stephens, J., Ferles, K., Mariano, B., Lahiri, S., Dillig, I.: SmartPulse: automated checking of temporal properties in smart contracts. In: Proceedings of the 42nd IEEE Symposium on Security and Privacy (S&P 2021). IEEE, May 2021
24. Szabo, N.: Smart contracts: building blocks for digital markets. Extropy (16) **8**, 1 (1996)
25. Wood, G.: Ethereum: a secure decentralised generalised transaction ledger. Ethereum Proj. Yellow Pap. **151**, 1–32 (2014)

# Anticipatory Recurrent Monitoring with Uncertainty and Assumptions

Hannes Kallwies[1]([⊠]) [iD], Martin Leucker[1] [iD], César Sánchez[2] [iD],
and Torben Scheffel[1] [iD]

[1] University of Lübeck, Lübeck, Germany
{kallwies,leucker,scheffel}@isp.uni-luebeck.de
[2] IMDEA Software Institute, Madrid, Spain
cesar.sanchez@imdea.org

**Abstract.** Runtime Verification is a lightweight verification approach that aims at checking that a run of a system under observation adheres to a formal specification. A classical approach is to synthesize a monitor from an LTL property. Usually, such a monitor receives the trace of the system under observation incrementally and checks the property with respect to the first position of any trace that extends the received prefix. This comes with the disadvantage that once the monitor detects a violation or satisfaction of the verdict it cannot recover and the erroneous position in the trace is not explicitly disclosed. An alternative monitoring problem, proposed for example for Past LTL evaluation, is to evaluate the LTL property repeatedly at each position in the received trace, which enables recovering and gives more information when the property is breached. In this paper we study this concept of *recurrent monitoring* in detail, particularly we investigate how the notion of anticipation (yielding future verdicts when they are inevitable) can be extended to recurrent monitoring. Furthermore, we show how two fundamental approaches in Runtime Verification can be applied to recurrent monitoring, namely *Uncertainty*—which deals with the handling of inaccurate or unavailable information in the input trace—and *Assumptions*, i.e. the inclusion of additional knowledge about system invariants in the monitoring process.

## 1 Introduction

Runtime verification (RV) is a lightweight dynamic verification technique that focuses on analyzing an actual execution of a system to check correctness properties, which has been studied both in theory and applications [1,16]. A common specification language for RV is Linear-time Temporal Logic (LTL) [20] which was originally introduced for infinite runs. However, in RV one necessarily deals with the finite executions, and, as such, adaptions to the original semantics have

---

This work was funded in part by the Madrid Regional Government under project "S2018/TCS-4339 (BLOQUES-CM)" and by a research grant from Nomadic Labs and the Tezos Foundation.

T. Dang and V. Stolz (Eds.): RV 2022, LNCS 13498, pp. 181–199, 2022.
https://doi.org/10.1007/978-3-031-17196-3_10

been considered. A variety of those have been proposed in the literature including infinite extensions of the finite prefix seen so far [2], limiting the logic to use only the next-operator [14], or finite version of LTL [18], strong and weak versions of LTL [8] or the so-called mission time LTL [21]. However these monitoring approaches all attempt to answer the *initial word problem* (whether the trace at the initial position satisfies the property) following different maxims. While a two valued semantics on finite words is adequate for completed, terminated executions, ongoing executions may require semantics with multiple verdicts in order to support both the current view and potential future changes when the execution is continuing. Then, for example, *impartiality* requires a logic to not change the verdict once the verdict *true* or *false* is declared, while different assessments of the current observation may be changed once more information is received. *Anticipation* takes potential look-aheads into account to sharpen the current verdict. A comprehensive comparison of such approaches is given in [3].

The seminal work by Havelund and Rosu [11] considers a different approach of monitoring. Starting from a past fragment of LTL, their monitors produce a fresh verdict about whether the property holds at the current position of the existing trace, thus recurrently answering the word problem with potentially different outcomes. We call this variant the *recurrent word problem*. While initial approaches try to return the answer for the first position of the run, Havelund's and Rosu's computes the verdict for the *current* position of the trace. As the current position is changing with every new observation, their approach implicitly restarts monitoring with every new observation. As such, while the semantics is two valued and does not change the verdict of the position in question—and can thus be considered impartial—the verdicts may change from true to false, for example, as the point of interest varies during monitoring. In this paper, we unify these two approaches (recurrent and initial monitoring), separating the monitoring time at which the questions are answered from the time at which the verdict is referring to.

In general, the recurrent word problem for future temporal logic cannot be solved with an amount of memory that is independent of the length of the trace. Consequently, most approaches with future operators are restricted to the initial word problem. Approaches to monitoring based on stream runtime verification (SRV), see for example Lola [7] produce one output stream value at each position. This output value can encode the outcome of an initial word problem or of a recurrent word problem. The common use of SRV is to encode recurrent word monitoring problems for past (or at least bounded future) specifications because the monitor is guaranteed to run with constant memory, independently of the trace length. Modern SRV systems (both synchronous and asynchronous) including RTLola [4], Lola2.0 [9], CoPilot [19], TeSSLa [6] and Striver [10] follow this approach.

In this paper we first generalize recurrent monitoring beyond Past LTL. For example, extending Past LTL with bounded future suggests that different instants in the trace (not necessarily the current instant) could be the point of interest for a given verdict. Anticipation has been solved for $LTL_3$ (see [2]) so it is natural to ask whether recurrent monitoring can also be enriched with look-aheads to improve the current verdict by producing it ahead of time. We show that recurrent monitoring can indeed be extended to produce an anticipation of the number of instants before the closest violation or satisfaction, which maybe very useful to take preventive actions.

Also in the context of initial monitoring for LTL, monitors are capable to improve the verdict using partial knowledge of the underlying system [15] or, more generally, assumptions [5,12]. A second contribution of this paper is to improve recurrent monitoring with assumptions. Finally, we also consider recurrent monitoring in the presence of uncertainties, meaning, that some of the input values are (partially) unknown. We show a solution to recurrent monitoring that provides anticipation, tolerates uncertainties and is capable of exploiting assumptions.

## 2  Preliminaries

We use $\mathbb{Z}$ for the set of integers, $\mathbb{N}, \mathbb{N}^+$ for the set of natural numbers with and without 0 and $\mathbb{N}^\infty = \mathbb{N} \cup \{\infty\}$.

In this paper we deal with LTL extended with past time operators. The syntax of LTL with past (Full LTL) is

$$\varphi ::= tt \mid p \mid (\varphi) \mid \neg\varphi \mid \varphi \wedge \varphi \mid \bigcirc\varphi \mid \varphi \, \mathcal{U} \, \varphi \mid \ominus\varphi \mid \varphi \, \mathcal{S} \, \varphi$$

where $p$ ranges over a set of atomic propositions $AP$. An LTL formula is a propositional logic formula over $AP$ extended by the operators $\bigcirc \varphi$ (next) which checks that $\varphi$ holds in the next state and $\varphi_1 \, \mathcal{U} \, \varphi_2$ (until) that requires $\varphi_2$ to hold at some state in the future and that in all states up to that state $\varphi_1$ holds. Additionally there are the past time operators $\ominus\varphi$ (previously) which checks that $\varphi$ did hold in the previous state and $\varphi_1 \, \mathcal{S} \, \varphi_2$ (since) which enforces that $\varphi_2$ did hold at some point in the past and $\varphi_1$ held at every state since then. In order to keep following automaton constructions and proofs compact we defined only a minimal fragment of LTL. Other common LTL and Past LTL operators $\square$ (globally), $\lozenge$ (finally), $\mathcal{R}$ (release), $\boxminus$ (globally in the past), $\diamondsuit$ (once in the past) and $\mathcal{S}_w$ (weak since) can be expressed by the operators included above (see [17]).

Given an infinite word $w \in \Sigma^\omega$, where the alphabet is $\Sigma = 2^{AP}$, and given an atomic proposition $a \in AP$ we use $w(t)$ to reference the letter of $w$ at position $t$. We write $p \models w(t)$ whenever $p \in w(t)$. Given a finite word $s \in \Sigma^*$ and a finite or an infinite word $w \in \Sigma^* \cup \Sigma^\omega$ we use $sw$ for the concatenation of $s$ followed by $w$. $s$ is a *prefix* of $w$, denoted by $s \sqsubseteq w$ iff $w = sw'$ for some $w' \in \Sigma^* \cup \Sigma^\omega$.

A pointed word $(w, t)$ is a pair consisting of a word $w$ and a position $t \in \mathbb{N}^+$. We define the semantics of LTL associating pointed words to formulas as follows:

$$
\begin{aligned}
&(w, t) \models tt \\
&(w, t) \models p && \text{iff} && p \models w(t) \\
&(w, t) \models \neg\varphi && \text{iff} && (w, t) \not\models \varphi \\
&(w, t) \models \varphi_1 \wedge \varphi_2 && \text{iff} && (w, t) \models \varphi_1 \text{ and } (w, t) \models \varphi_2 \\
&(w, t) \models \bigcirc\varphi && \text{iff} && (w, t+1) \models \varphi \\
&(w, t) \models \varphi_1 \, \mathcal{U} \, \varphi_2 && \text{iff} && \text{for some } t' \geq t . (w, t') \models \varphi_2 \text{ and} \\
& && && \qquad \text{for all } t \leq t'' < t' . (w, t'') \models \varphi_1 \\
&(w, t) \models \ominus\varphi && \text{iff} && (t > 1 \text{ and } (w, t-1) \models \varphi) \text{ or} \\
& && && \qquad (t = 1 \text{ and } (w, 1) \models \varphi) \\
&(w, t) \models \varphi_1 \, \mathcal{S} \, \varphi_2 && \text{iff} && \text{for some } 1 \leq t' \leq t . (w, t') \models \varphi_2 \text{ and} \\
& && && \qquad \text{for all } t' < t'' \leq t . (w, t'') \models \varphi_1
\end{aligned}
$$

Besides Full LTL we will investigate the following fragments of Full LTL:

- **Future LTL** is Full LTL restricted to the operators $\neg, \wedge, \bigcirc, \mathcal{U}$.
- **Past LTL** is Full LTL restricted to the operators $\neg, \wedge, \ominus, \mathcal{S}$.
- **Past LTL with Bounded Future**, which is Past LTL with additionally the operator $\bigcirc$.

### 2.1 Well-Known Monitor Constructions

We revise the well-known monitor constructions for Future LTL, Past LTL and Past LTL with Bounded Future.

**Future LTL.** The standard monitor construction for LTL is described in [2] and it is called the LTL$_3$ construction. This construction aims at deciding the question whether $(w, 1) \models \varphi$. Therefore it iteratively receives $w \in \Sigma^\omega$, letter by letter, and calculates the verdicts $\top$ (meaning $(w, 1) \models \varphi$), $\bot$ (meaning $(w, 1) \not\models \varphi$) or ? (meaning a proper answer cannot be given for the prefix received up to now). Formally the output of the monitor after consumption of a finite prefix $s \sqsubseteq w$ is

- $\top$ iff $\forall w' \in \Sigma^\omega . (sw', 1) \models \varphi$
- $\bot$ iff $\forall w' \in \Sigma^\omega . (sw', 1) \not\models \varphi$
- ? otherwise

In other words the verdict domain $\mathbb{B}_3 = \{\top, \bot, ?\}$ encodes the set of possible outcomes of a monitoring question which are still possible after having processed prefix $s$ of $w$: $\top = \{tt\}, \bot = \{ff\}, ? = \{tt, ff\}$. We will use these symbols with these meanings also for the further monitoring approaches throughout this paper. The LTL$_3$ construction works as follows. First, the formula $\varphi$ and its negation $\neg\varphi$ are transformed into Alternating Büchi Automata by the standard LTL translation [13], which are then further transformed to Nondeterministic

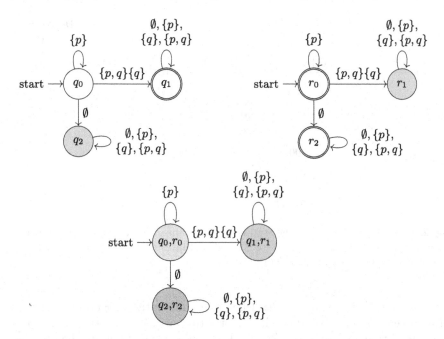

**Fig. 1.** Monitor for $\varphi = p\,\mathcal{U}\,q$ with the $\text{LTL}_3$ construction [2]. Up left: NBA of $\varphi$, Up right: NBA of $\neg\varphi$, bottom: Monitor generated from the product automaton. Empty states of the NBAs are marked gray. States of the monitor are marked according to their outputs: Orange for ?; green for $\top$, red for $\bot$. (Color figure online)

Büchi Automata (NBA). The monitor generation preprocesses each NBA determining which states are empty, (i.e. those states from which it is not possible to access accepting states infinitely often) which are removed from the automaton, resulting in an incomplete NFA, which is then determinized. Finally, the monitor is constructed as the product monitor of the resulting automata for $\varphi$ and $\neg\varphi$. In those state pairs where the state of the negated formula is empty the monitor casts the verdict $\top$ as the formula cannot be breached anymore for the received prefix. In those pairs where the state of the non-negated monitor is empty $\bot$ is cast, as the formula cannot be satisfied anymore. Otherwise, when both states are non-empty ? is printed. An example of the monitor construction can be found in Fig. 1.

These monitors are called *impartial* because the monitor does not output a final verdict ($\top$ or $\bot$) as long as the corresponding LTL formula is not satisfied or violated for all extensions of the observed word. These monitors are also *anticipatory* because the monitor yields the final verdict at the first moment at which all extensions of the consumed prefix satisfy the verdict.

**Past LTL.** The standard monitor construction for Past LTL [11] also receives the word letter by letter but evaluates $(w, t) \models \varphi$ at every step $t$, printing the

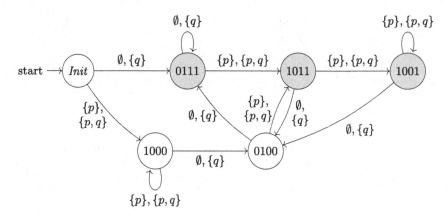

**Fig. 2.** Monitor for $p \mathcal{S} \ominus \neg p$. The states symbolize the current valuations of the sub-formulas $(p, \neg p, \ominus \neg p, p \mathcal{S} \ominus \neg p)$ ($1 = \text{true}, 0 = \text{false}$). States where the formula is satisfied for the current position are marked gray.

outcome. In [11] the monitor is described as an imperative program that uses an array as central data structure which stores the current value (true or false) for every sub-formula of the given Past LTL formula $\varphi$. The program then receives the input word letter by letter and calculates bottom-up the new value of each sub-expression at the new instant, ultimately producing the verdict for the root formula. The size of the mentioned array data structure is the number of sub-formulas of a Past LTL formula and hence finite, so the imperative monitor can directly be seen as Moore machine. The state of the Moore machine is given by the current value of all sub-formulas.

Consider the Past LTL formula $p \mathcal{S} \ominus \neg p$ over $AP = \{p, q\}$. The state is given by a 4-tuple containing the current evaluation of the sub formulas $(p, \neg p, \ominus \neg p, p \mathcal{S} \ominus \neg p)$. The value of the first two entries is dependent on the current input letter. The value of the third entry is the last value of the second entry and the value of the last entry is true iff it was true before and the first entry is true or if the third entry is true. The resulting automaton is depicted in Fig. 2.

**Past LTL with Bounded Future.** Note that introducing a next operator may make the evaluation of $\varphi$ at a certain timestamp dependent on the input at a later position. We can statically determine an upper bound $\text{ND}(\varphi)$ of future states which are required for evaluation of a formula $\varphi$ by counting the maximal depth of nested nexts adjusted by the number of surrounding previous operators (*next depth*) in the syntax tree of the formula:

- $\text{ND}(tt) = \text{ND}(p) = 0$ for $p \in AP$
- $\text{ND}(\neg \varphi) = \text{ND}(\varphi)$
- $\text{ND}(\varphi_1 \wedge \varphi_2) = \text{ND}(\varphi_1 \mathcal{S} \varphi_2) = \max\{\text{ND}(\varphi_1), \text{ND}(\varphi_2)\}$
- $\text{ND}(\ominus \varphi) = \text{ND}(\varphi) - 1$ and $\text{ND}(\bigcirc \varphi) = \text{ND}(\varphi) + 1$

For example for $\varphi = \bigcirc((\bigcirc p)\mathcal{S}\ominus q)\wedge\bigcirc p$ we have $\mathrm{ND}(\varphi) = 2$, because (depending on the evaluation of the since) it may be necessary to know at most two states of the word in advance. For $\varphi' = \bigcirc\ominus q$ we get $\mathrm{ND}(\varphi') = 0$ because $\varphi'$ is only dependent on the current position of the word.

Note that if for a formula $\mathrm{ND}(\varphi) = k$ is positive, then the formula $\varphi' = \ominus^k \varphi$ ($\ominus^k$ is used as syntactic sugar for a composition of $k$ previous operators) which expresses that $\varphi$ was true $k$ steps in the past can be rewritten to a Past LTL formula, without next operator. Therefore the next operators can be moved inside the other operators (which is possible for all given operators without changing the semantics of the formula) until a sub-formula $\ominus\bigcirc\psi$ is contained, which can then be substituted by $\psi$. For $\varphi = \bigcirc((\bigcirc p)\mathcal{S}\ominus(q))\wedge\bigcirc p$ from above one could construct $\ominus^2 \varphi = \ominus^2(\bigcirc((\bigcirc p)\mathcal{S}\ominus q)\wedge\bigcirc p) = \ominus(\ominus\bigcirc((\bigcirc p)\mathcal{S}\ominus q)\wedge\ominus\bigcirc p) = \ominus(((\bigcirc p)\mathcal{S}\ominus q)\wedge p) = ((p\mathcal{S}\ominus^2 q)\wedge\ominus p)$. This observation allows to transform a Past LTL formula with bounded future $\varphi$ into a Past LTL formula $\varphi' = \ominus^{\mathrm{ND}(\varphi)}\varphi$ and build the corresponding monitor with the algorithm described previously. Due to the equivalence $(w,t) \models \varphi' \iff (w, t - \mathrm{ND}(\varphi)) \models \varphi$ the resulting monitor still produces the output sequence $(w,1) \models \varphi, (w,2) \models \varphi \ldots$ but with a $\mathrm{ND}(\varphi)$ offset to receiving the corresponding input letters.

## 3    Initial and Recurrent Monitoring

Note that the monitor construction for Past LTL differs from the construction for Future LTL. The $\mathrm{LTL}_3$ monitor attempts to answer the same question $(w,1) \models \varphi$ at each step. We call this *initial monitoring*. The Past LTL monitor instead continuously answers a different question, i.e. if the formula is satisfied from the current position $t \in \mathbb{N}^+$ $((w,t) \models \varphi)$. We call this concept *recurrent monitoring*. It makes sense especially for Past LTL monitoring, where the monitor can always give the conclusive verdict $\top$ or $\bot$ for the current state (in difference to $\mathrm{LTL}_3$). In general, recurrent monitoring has advantages for the monitoring process, because it checks a property with respect to a certain position in the word. Hence a breach of the LTL property is related to a specific position in the trace and not for the whole trace in general. More importantly, the monitor can also recover from errors at previous positions and continue monitoring the trace after detection of a violation.

Consider for example a robot system and a property that states whether the robot is not too close to any objects. The intention of this monitor is to be able to react (or perhaps to later inspect log data). This problem is better cast as a recurrent monitoring problem, where the monitor raises an alarm at all positions where the robot does not satisfy a property.

We now investigate the opportunities of recurrent monitoring more thoroughly. First we define initial and recurrent monitoring formally. The monitoring problem is characterized by a function $\omega : \Sigma^* \to \mathbb{B}_3$ from finite prefixes received by the monitor to the usual $\mathbb{B}_3 = \{\top, \bot, ?\}$. Recall that $\top = \{tt\}, \bot = \{ff\}, ? = \{tt, ff\}$.

**Definition 1 (Initial LTL monitoring).** *Given an LTL specification $\varphi$, the following function $\omega_\varphi^{init} : \Sigma^* \to \mathbb{B}_3$ is called the* initial LTL monitoring function:

$$\omega_\varphi^{init}(s) = \{(sw,1) \models \varphi \mid w \in \Sigma^\omega\}$$

The initial LTL monitoring problem deals with providing the set of possible verdicts for $(sw,1) \models \varphi$ given a finite prefix $s$. The set is naturally the set of the verdicts for all possible infinite completions of the given prefix. Note that for two finite words $s_1 \sqsubseteq s_2$, $\omega_\varphi^{init}(s_1) \supseteq \omega_\varphi^{init}(s_2)$ holds by definition, i.e. when calculating $\omega_\varphi^{init}$ repeatedly on growing traces, the set of verdicts gets refined as the observed prefix gets longer.

We define next *recurrent monitoring* as the problem where the property is checked at the position up to which the monitored trace has received events.

**Definition 2 (Recurrent LTL monitoring).** *Given an LTL specification $\varphi$, the following function $\omega_\varphi^{rec} : \Sigma^* \to \mathbb{B}_3$ is called the* recurrent monitoring function:

$$\omega_\varphi^{rec}(s) = \{(sw,|s|) \models \varphi \mid w \in \Sigma^\omega\}$$

Note that Definition 2 differs from Definition 1 since $\models$ is checked at position $|s|$ currently received by the monitor, which is the traditional approach for monitoring Past LTL. For Past LTL, only states from the past are necessary for the evaluation and hence after receiving $s$ it is always possible to cast a certain verdict $(\top, \bot)$. However this is not the case for Future LTL or Past LTL with bounded future, where the recurrent verdict for position $|s|$ may then yield the uncertain verdict $\{tt, ff\}$ (a.k.a. ?). We propose an extension of the recurrent monitoring where the verdict that the monitor must compute is shifted by a constant offset

**Definition 3 (Recurrent LTL monitoring with constant offset).** *Given an LTL specification $\varphi$ and $k \in \mathbb{Z}$, the recurrent k-offset monitoring function $\omega_\varphi^{rec,k} : \Sigma^* \to \mathbb{B}_3$ is:*

$$\omega_\varphi^{rec,k}(s) = \{(sw,|s|+k) \models \varphi \mid w \in \Sigma^\omega\}$$

Note that the recurrent LTL monitoring function from Definition 2 is equivalent to the 0-offset LTL monitoring function from Definition 3.

Another degree of generalization of the recurrent monitoring results if we require the monitor to be able to return the best possible answer about any position that cannot be predicted upfront (that is, the *monitored state* is fully independent from the *monitoring state*).

**Definition 4 (Random Access Recurrent LTL monitoring).** *Given an LTL specification $\varphi$, the random access recurrent monitoring function $\omega_\varphi : \Sigma^* \to \mathbb{N}^+ \to \mathbb{B}_3$ is:*

$$\omega_\varphi(s)(i) = \{(sw,i) \models \varphi \mid w \in \Sigma^\omega\}$$

This definition is a generalization of all previous definitions as $i$ can be fixed with the parameter $1, |s|, |s| + k$ to receive the previous monitoring functions.

All previous definitions indeed are not restricted to any fragments of LTL. However, it is trivial to perform initial monitoring for Past LTL and in general it is useless to do 0-offset recurrent monitoring for arbitrary Future LTL formulas. On the other hand, it makes sense to apply $k$-offset or random recurrent monitoring to Past LTL with bounded future or even for full LTL, tolerating sometimes ? verdicts, depending on the property and the chosen offset.

We now introduce an abstract notion of RV monitor. For the purposes of this paper, a monitor

- receives a system trace iteratively (either *online* or *offline*)
- maintains internally a state which represents the trace that has been received yet (*State part*)
- iteratively produces outputs (*Question answering part*)

**Definition 5 (Monitor).** *A monitor is a 6-tuple* $M = (\Sigma, \Omega, Q, q_0, \delta, \omega)$ *where*

- $\Sigma$ *is a possibly infinite input alphabet.*
- $\Omega$ *is a possibly infinite output alphabet.*
- $Q$ *is a possibly infinite state space.*
- $q_0 \in Q$ *is an initial state.*
- $\delta : Q \times \Sigma \to Q$ *is a transition function.*
- $\omega : Q \to \Omega$ *is an output function.*

We refer to the verdict of a monitor $M = (\Sigma, \Omega, Q, q_0, \delta, \omega)$ after the consumption of an input $s = a_1 \ldots a_n \in \Sigma^*, a_i \in \Sigma$ as $\hat{\omega}(s) = \omega(\hat{\delta}(q_0, s))$ with $\hat{\delta} : Q \times \Sigma^* \to Q$ defined as $\hat{\delta}(q, \epsilon) = q, \hat{\delta}(q, a_1 a_2 \ldots a_i) = \hat{\delta}(\delta(q_0, a_1), a_2 \ldots a_i)$.

A monitor is essentially a Moore machine, except that input, output and state space are allowed to be infinite. Monitors with an infinite state spaces are common in Stream Runtime Verification [7,22] where the monitors are specified in terms of streams of arbitrary data types. Since monitors in Runtime Verification usually run for an arbitrary long time and resources are limited, it is crucial that their memory is independent of the trace length and can be bounded a-priori. The state maintained by a monitor depends on the inputs consumed (using sometimes knowledge about the system under analysis), but the monitor should not need to remember the whole trace. The output part of the monitor is tailored for the application. We call monitors, whose extended output function $\hat{\omega}$ is equal to one of the functions defined above, *initial, recurrent, k-offset recurrent* and *random access recurrent* monitors. Note that for *random access recurrent* monitors there is no straight-forward implementation that "prints" the output. One alternative is that the monitor serves as an question-answering device. Another, which we present next, is that the monitor provides abstract information about future positions.

## 4  Anticipatory Monitoring

It is often desirable to detect failures of the system under observation as early as possible. In initial monitoring for LTL$_3$ this boils down to raising the verdicts $\top$, $\bot$ as soon as all possible extensions lead to satisfaction (resp. violation). For recurrent monitoring there is also another dimension of anticipation. The output of a recurrent monitor is an evaluation of the pointed semantics of an LTL formula at increasing time instants. It is sometimes possible that a monitor that is asked to cast the verdict for $(w, t) \models \varphi$ after having received a prefix of length $t$, is also able to cast a verdict for the next step $(w, t + 1) \models \varphi$ (or even further steps in the future).

While in recurrent monitoring the verdict indicates that the LTL formula is satisfied or violated exactly at the required time instant, the user is often interested in knowing about a future violation as soon as possible. Consider for example a crash of a monitored robotic system. There one is not only interested that the monitor reports when a crash occurs, but also that it reports as soon as a crash is inevitable. Additionally, it may be very useful to know the number of steps in the future where there is surely no violation of the property.

Consider again $p \mathcal{S} \ominus \neg p$ and the corresponding monitor in Fig. 2. This monitor yields verdict for $(w, t) \models \varphi$ after having received $t$ letters. When the monitor has received the prefix $\{p\}\{q\}$ the monitor is in state 0100 and yields $\bot = \{ff\}$, since $(\{p\}\{q\} \ldots, 2) \not\models \varphi$. However at this position it is already inevitable that the output at the next step $(\{p\}\{q\} \ldots, 3) \models \varphi$ is true. In Fig. 2 this can be seen as all possible successors of 0100 are accepting states. We seek monitors that not only generate information about the current verdict but also information about future verdicts. We define such anticipatory monitors as follows:

**Definition 6 (Anticipatory Monitor).**  *Given a monitoring problem $f$ : $\Sigma^* \to \mathbb{V}$ over an arbitrary verdict domain $\mathbb{V}$, a monitor $M = (\Sigma, \Omega, Q, q_0, \delta, \omega)$ with $\Omega = \mathbb{N}^+ \to 2^{\mathbb{V}}$ is called an anticipatory monitor for $f$ whenever for all inputs $s \in \Sigma^*$ and positions $i \in \mathbb{N}^+$,*

$$\hat{\omega}(s)(i) \supseteq \{f(sr) \mid r \in \Sigma^i\}$$

*If $=$ holds instead of $\supseteq$ then $M$ is called a perfect anticipatory monitor for $f$.*

Note that anticipatory monitoring is defined relative to a given monitoring function $f$. The anticipatory monitor computes functions that predict the future verdicts of the original monitor which are possible after the current observation. In practice, implementing an anticipatory monitor requires to represent concisely the output alphabet $\Omega$ and the function $\hat{\omega}$ that approximates $f$. One possibility is to predict only a fixed number of future states and to implicitly map all further instants to $\mathbb{V}$ (all verdicts are possible). Alternatively, we propose to compute the minimum number of future states which are guaranteed not to be $\top$ ($\top$ meaning a crash) and the maximum number of steps until the next $\top$ is guaranteed to happen. Note that such abstractions may lead to imperfect anticipatory monitors, but the information provided may be very useful.

## 4.1 Anticipatory Monitors from Recurrent Monitors

We now present an algorithm to produce an anticipatory monitor for the $k$-offset recurrent monitoring problem. Our monitor outputs intervals $(n, m) \in \mathbb{N}^\infty \times \mathbb{N}^\infty$ as an abstraction of the full output map. The interval indicates a lower and upper bound of letters that have to be received until the property is fulfilled. Even though we only handle the steps until the formula is fulfilled, the converse (providing the steps until the formula is violated) is analogous.

**Definition 7 (Anticipatory (Recurrent) Interval Monitor).** *Let $\varphi$ be an LTL property. A monitor $M = (\Sigma, \mathbb{I}_\mathbb{N}, Q, q_0, \delta, \omega)$ with $\mathbb{I}_\mathbb{N} = \mathbb{N}^\infty \times \mathbb{N}^\infty$ is called $k$-offset anticipatory (recurrent) interval monitor whenever for all inputs $s$, $\hat{\omega}(s) = (n, m)$ where*

$$n = \min pos_s$$
$$m = \max pref_s$$

*and*

$$pos_s = \{j \in \mathbb{N} \mid \text{ for some } w \in \Sigma^\omega, (sw, |s| + j + k) \models \varphi\}$$
$$pref_s = \{j \in \mathbb{N} \mid \text{ for some } w \in \Sigma^\omega, \text{ for all } i < j, (sw, |s| + i + k) \not\models \varphi\}$$

Note that $n$ is the shortest sequence to a violation and $m$ is the longest sequence without a violation. Also, $n \leq m$. For example, in the case of $\varphi = p \mathrel{S} \ominus \neg p$ and the input word $w = \{p\}\{p\}\{q\}\{p\}\{q\} \ldots$ an anticipatory interval monitor would output $(2, \infty)(2, \infty)(1, 1)(0, 0)(1, 1) \ldots$. This means in the first state after receiving input $\{p\}$ it must take at least two further steps until $\varphi$ is satisfied and it is also possible that $\varphi$ will never be fulfilled. After receiving two further inputs $\{p\}$ and $\{q\}$ the output $(1, 1)$ indicates that it is inevitable that in the next step the property will be fulfilled. Consequently after receiving a further letter we get $(0, 0)$, meaning the property holds in the current state. In practical scenarios such a monitor helps detecting inevitable situations to undertake the right countermeasures (e.g. an emergency stop) before the failure occurs. Likewise, the knowledge that a breach of the property is impossible for a time horizon also helps in some scenarios allowing for example a robot to accelerate.

We can classify the meaning of an output interval $(n, m)$ of an anticipatory recurrent monitor as follows:

| $n = \infty$ | $m = \infty$ | $\varphi$ will never be satisfied in the future |
|---|---|---|
| $n \in \mathbb{N}$ | $m = \infty$ | $\varphi$ may be satisfied in the future but not before $n$ steps |
| $n \in \mathbb{N}$ | $m \in \mathbb{N}^+$ | $\varphi$ is inevitable, but not before $n$ or after $m$ steps |
| $n = 0$ | $m = 0$ | $\varphi$ is satisfied in the current state |

The anticipatory monitor $M'$ with the described output behavior can be constructed directly from a given recurrent monitor $M$ as follows. The state space and transition function of $M'$ are taken without adjustments from those of $M$. The modified output function for $M'$ is generated by a simple graph traversal from $M$: First, every state that was labeled with output $\top$ produces the output $(0,0)$. For the outputs of the other states a depth-first-search is performed. The output of such a state is then $(n,m)$ where $n$ is the minimum of the first interval component of all successor states plus 1, or 0, if the state is labeled with ? and $m$ is the maximum of the second interval component plus 1. If a state is evaluated which is already on the DFS stack its output interval is (for the pending calculation) assumed to be $(\infty, \infty)$ since in this case an infinite non-$\top$-labeled loop exists in the monitor. A formalization of the algorithm in pseudo-code can be found in Fig. 3. The resulting monitor is an anticipatory recurrent interval monitor according to Definition 6.

**Theorem 1.** *Given a $k \in \mathbb{Z}$ offset recurrent monitor $M = (\Sigma, \mathbb{V}, Q, q_0, \delta, \omega)$ for specification $\varphi$ the construction from Fig. 3 produces a $k$-offset anticipatory recurrent interval monitor for $\varphi$.*

**Method** dfs($q$, stack)
    **if** $q \in$ stack **then**
        $\omega'(q) \leftarrow (\infty, \infty)$; //*only temporarily set*
    **else if** $\omega(q) = \top$
        $\omega'(q) \leftarrow (0,0)$;
    **else**
        **for each** $q' \in succ(q)$ **do** dfs($q'$, stack $\cup \{q\}$); **end for**
        //*get min/max of first/second component of all successor outputs*
        $n \leftarrow$ **if** $\omega(q) = ?$ **then** 0 **else** $\min_{q' \in succ(q)} \{\omega'(q')._1\} + 1$;
        $m \leftarrow \max_{q' \in succ(q)} \{\omega'(q')._2\} + 1$;
        $\omega'(q) \leftarrow (n,m)$;
    **end if**
**End Method**

**for each** $q \in Q$
    dfs($q$, $\emptyset$)
**end for**

**Fig. 3.** Formalization of DFS-based algorithm for construction of the output function $\omega'$ of an anticipatory interval monitor $M' = (\Sigma, \Omega', Q', q_0', \delta', \omega')$ based on a given recurring monitor $M = (\Sigma, \Omega, Q, q_0, \delta, \omega)$, $succ(q) = \{\delta(q,a) | a \in \Sigma\}$.

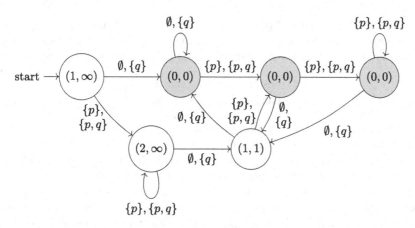

**Fig. 4.** Anticipatory monitor for $p\,\mathcal{S}\ominus\neg p$ based on the monitor from Fig. 2. The states are labeled with their corresponding interval outputs.

The result of an application of the algorithm on the recurrent monitor from Fig. 2 is depicted in Fig. 4. The output of this monitor matches the output trace described above. Note that the anticipatory monitor can also be used to answer the standard recurrent LTL monitoring problem: every state where the predictive monitor casts $(0,0)$ is a state with verdict $\top$ in the original monitor.

## 5   Uncertainty and Assumptions

In this section we show how the anticipatory recurrent monitoring approach can be extended to handle uncertainty, in the sense that the content of some letters of the input word is unknown. We will also show how to exploit assumptions about the system to improve the monitoring process, where assumptions are invariants about the environment of the monitor and assumed to be always true.

### 5.1   Uncertainty

We model uncertain input events as subsets of $\Sigma$, which represent the set of possible inputs that actually happen. For example the input trace

$$\{\{p,q\},\{q\}\}\ \{\{p\}\}\ \{\emptyset,\{p\},\{q\},\{p,q\}\}\cdots$$

encodes any trace where in the first step $q$ holds but it is uncertain if $p$ holds, in the second step $p$ and not $q$ holds (with total certainty) and where everything is possible in the third state (total uncertainty).

Given a finite prefix $s \in \Sigma^*$ and $s' \in \left(2^{\Sigma}\right)^*$ we write $s \models s'$ whenever $s$ is one possible concrete representation of $s'$, i.e. $|s| = |s'|$ and $\forall_{1\leq i\leq|s|}.s(i) \in s'(i)$. We adjust our anticipatory recurrent monitor from Definition 7 to handle uncertain inputs.

**Definition 8 (Uncertain Anticipatory Recurrent Monitor).** *Let $\varphi$ be an LTL property. A monitor $M = (2^\Sigma, \mathbb{I}_\mathbb{N}, Q, q_0, \delta, \omega)$ is called an uncertain $k$-offset anticipatory recurrent monitor if for all inputs $s \in (2^\Sigma)^*$, $\hat{\omega}(s) = (n, m)$ where,*

$$n = \min\{pos_u \mid for\ some\ u \models s\}$$
$$m = \max\{pref_u \mid for\ some\ u \models s\}$$

This definition extends anticipatory recurrent monitoring to the minimal and maximal distance to a $\top$-verdict over all possible concrete input words. Note that the definition is a more general version of Definition 7, which yields the same intervals when singleton sets (certain inputs) are provided.

The classical automata-theoretic approach to handle uncertainty is the power set construction, where a new monitor is built whose state space is the power set of the original monitor's state space. When an uncertain input is received the power set monitor changes to all possible successor states of the currently possible states. The main remaining detail is how the power set automaton can produce verdicts, i.e. how the intervals of the potential states of the original monitor can be combined. We show that it suffices to take the minimum and maximum of the interval bounds of the active states. This results in the following monitor construction.

**Theorem 2.** *Given $\varphi$ and a $k$-offset anticipatory interval monitor $M = (\Sigma, \mathbb{I}_\mathbb{N}, Q, q_0, \delta, \omega)$ for $\varphi$, the monitor $M' = (2^\Sigma, \mathbb{I}_\mathbb{N}, 2^Q, \{q_0\}, \delta', \omega')$ with*

- $\delta'(S, L) = \{\delta(s, l) \mid s \in S, l \in L\}$ for $S \in 2^Q, L \in 2^\Sigma$
- $\omega'(S) = (\min\{a \mid (a, b) = \omega(s)\ for\ s \in S\}, \max\{b \mid (a, b) = \omega(s)\ for\ s \in S\})$

*is an uncertain $k$-offset anticipatory recurrent monitor for $\varphi$.*

A run of the recurrent anticipatory monitor from Fig. 4 for the uncertain input $\{\{p, q\}, \{q\}\}\ \{\{p\}\}\ \{\emptyset, \{p\}, \{q\}, \{p, q\}\} \ldots$ from above is depicted in Fig. 5.

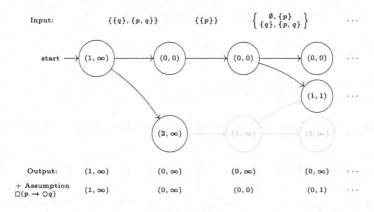

**Fig. 5.** Run of the anticipatory recurrent monitor from Fig. 4 with uncertain inputs. The states in which the monitor is potentially located in a time step and their outputs are drawn on top of each other. The assumption (see Sect. 5.2) $\Box(p \rightarrow \bigcirc q)$ eliminates the grey states and transitions and leads to more precise verdicts.

The output is $(1, \infty)(0, \infty)(0, \infty)(0, \infty) \ldots$ i.e. the monitor detects that there could be three satisfactions of the property in the first three states, but depending on the real input there also could be none.

## 5.2  Assumptions

Another aspect with practical impact in RV is how to exploit knowledge about the system into the monitoring process. This information usually includes (partial) knowledge about the state the system is currently in and which properties (inputs to the monitor) may hold in the current and subsequent states. For example, consider the assumption $\Box(p \to \bigcirc q)$, which states that every state where proposition $p$ holds is succeeded by a state in which $q$ holds. This assumption implies, for example, that the input word $\{p, q\}\{p\} \ldots$ will never be passed to the monitor. Since several input words or continuations are excluded, assumptions help to produce more precise verdicts and detect failures earlier. Note that, of course, one could also detect traces where an assumption is not met, indicating a severe error in the whole monitoring setting.

Especially in the presence of uncertainty in the inputs assumptions are very useful to produce more precise (anticipatory) verdicts and recover from uncertainty in the input. For example, in our assumption, observing $p$ allows to conclude that $q$ will follow, allowing to better anticipate. Also, not observing $q$ allows to deduce that $p$ did not happen in the previous step, which reduces the uncertainty if the previous event was not properly received.

Additionally note that assumptions have to be explicitly handled by the monitoring algorithm, as they restrict the space of possible models, and hence cannot be encoded directly in the LTL formulas, for example as $\varphi' = \varphi_{ass} \to \varphi$ or $\varphi' = \varphi_{ass} \wedge \varphi$. Such an encoding would not allow the monitor to perform inferences about uncertain or future inputs, as it could never be sure if the assumption $\varphi_{ass}$ actually holds or not.

A general way to represent assumptions and system invariants is by a Kripke structure or equivalently a transition system.

**Definition 9 (Transition System).** *A* Transition System *over a finite input alphabet* $\Sigma$ *is a tuple* $\mathcal{T} = (Q, q_0, \delta)$ *with*

- *$Q$ a finite state space.*
- *$q_0 \in Q$ an initial state.*
- *$\delta \in Q \times Q \times \Sigma$ a transition relation.*

A transition system $\mathcal{T}$ describes a subset of valid inputs $[\![\mathcal{T}]\!] \subseteq \Sigma^\omega$. For all words $w \in [\![\mathcal{T}]\!]$ there is a path $q_0, q_1, \ldots$ in the system such that $(q_i, q_{i+1}, w(i + 1)) \in \delta$ for all $i \in \mathbb{N}$. Hence a transition system can be used as a very general way to express assumptions. Every assumption given in LTL can be used to build a corresponding transition system [17] (for simplicity we consider only safety formulas as assumptions). The transition system corresponding to the formula $\Box(p \to \bigcirc q)$ is depicted in Fig. 6.

We can further refine Definition 7 now to also support assumptions given in form of a transition system $\mathcal{T}$:

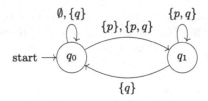

**Fig. 6.** Transition system corresponding to $\Box(p \rightarrow \bigcirc q)$.

**Definition 10 (Uncertain Anticipatory Recurrent Monitor with Assumptions).** *Let $\varphi$ be an LTL specification and let $\mathcal{T}$ be a transition system over $2^\Sigma$. A monitor $M = (2^\Sigma, \mathbb{I}_\mathbb{N}, Q, q_0, \delta, \omega)$ is called an* uncertain $k$-offset anticipatory recurrent monitor under assumption $\mathcal{T}$ *whenever for every $s \in (2^\Sigma)^*$, $\hat{\omega}(s) = (n, m)$ where,*

$$n = \min\{pos_u^\mathcal{T} \mid \text{for some } u \models s\}$$
$$m = \max\{pref_u^\mathcal{T} \mid \text{for some } u \models s\}$$

*and*

$$pos_s^\mathcal{T} = \{j \in \mathbb{N} \mid \text{for some } w \text{ s.t. } sw \in \llbracket\mathcal{T}\rrbracket, (sw, |s| + j + k) \models \varphi\}$$
$$pref_s^\mathcal{T} = \{j \in \mathbb{N} \mid \text{for some } w \text{ s.t. } sw \in \llbracket\mathcal{T}\rrbracket, \text{for all } i < j, (sw, |s| + i + k) \not\models \varphi\}$$

Definition 10 allows to only care about words which are also valid inputs according to the transition system. This definition is a further generalization of Definition 8 and both are equivalent for the uninformative transition system $\llbracket\mathcal{T}\rrbracket = (2^\Sigma)^\omega$.

To exploit the transition system that encodes the assumption we make use of a product construction, where states are tuples of the original monitor's states and transition system states. We only preserve transitions which are allowed by the transition system.

Since the existence of assumptions improves the anticipatory capabilities of the resulting monitor we take care already at the generation of the anticipatory monitor. Given a recurrent monitor $M = (\Sigma, \mathbb{V}, Q, q_0, \delta, \omega)$ for a specification $\varphi$, and a transition system $\mathcal{T} = (Q^\mathcal{T}, q_0^\mathcal{T}, \delta^\mathcal{T})$ over $2^\Sigma$ we first construct the recurrent monitor under assumption $M^\mathcal{T} = (\Sigma, \mathbb{V} \cup \{\downarrow\}\}, Q \times Q^\mathcal{T} \cup \{q_\perp\}, (q_0, q_0^\mathcal{T}), \delta', \omega')$ with

$$\delta'(q, l) = \begin{cases} (\delta(q^M, l), q'^\mathcal{T}) & \text{if } q = (q^M, q^\mathcal{T}) \neq q_\perp \text{ and } (q^\mathcal{T}, q'^\mathcal{T}, l) \in \delta^\mathcal{T} \\ q_\perp & \text{otherwise} \end{cases}$$

$$\omega'(q) = \begin{cases} \omega(q^M) & \text{if } q = (q^M, q^\mathcal{T}) \neq q_\perp \\ \downarrow & \text{otherwise} \end{cases}$$

where $q_\perp$ serves as an error state and $\downarrow$ indicates the breach of an assumption.

Together with the constructions from the previous sections this monitor builds the basis for an uncertain recurrent anticipatory monitor under assumption.

**Theorem 3.** *The construction from Fig. 3 applied to a k-offset recurrent monitor under assumption $M^T$ and the subsequent application of the construction from Theorem 2 yields an uncertain k-offset anticipatory recurrent monitor under assumption $T$.*

In the example from Fig. 5 considering the assumption leads to the monitor run in which the grey transitions do not exist anymore in the adjusted recurrent anticipatory monitor. This is because the second input is $\{p\}$ which implies that the first letter could not have been $\{p, q\}$, which had lead to the state labeled with $(2, \infty)$. The uncertain monitor is capable of removing successors that would violate the assumptions and determines more precise verdicts. In particular, this monitor can detect a satisfaction after receiving the second letter (output $(0, 0)$). Also, after receiving the third letter this monitor can conclude that the property is fulfilled either there or at the subsequent step (output $(0, 1)$).

# 6  Conclusion

In this paper we have studied the concept of recurrent monitoring where monitors produce verdicts for the property at all positions. This is a promising concept both theoretical and practical, particularly for Past LTL with bounded future, as it provides more information on the position in a trace where a property violation occurs and typically allows the monitor to recover afterwards.

To be able to detect situations of interest (e.g. crashes of the observed system) as early as possible we extended the concept with a notion of anticipation and proposed a monitor construction which gives estimates about the number of steps until the next situation of interest could occur, and if it is even inevitable. We presented constructions such that these monitors can further handle uncertainty in inputs, as well as assumptions about the system, and showed how these can lead to more precise verdicts.

In general solving the recurrent word problem for arbitrary (future and past) LTL requires unbounded memory. Future work includes studying useful bounded monitors that approximate this problem. Also, we would like to extend our monitoring notion, particularly under uncertainty and assumptions, to more complex recurrent monitoring settings, like Stream Runtime Verification. We also aim at implementation, particularly of an SRV engine, and an empirical evaluation on realistic case studies.

# References

1. Bartocci, E., Falcone, Y. (eds.): Lectures on Runtime Verification - Introductory and Advanced Topics. LNCS, vol. 10457. Springer, Cham (2018). https://doi.org/10.1007/978-3-319-75632-5
2. Bauer, A., Leucker, M., Schallhart, C.: Monitoring of real-time properties. In: Arun-Kumar, S., Garg, N. (eds.) FSTTCS 2006. LNCS, vol. 4337, pp. 260–272. Springer, Heidelberg (2006). https://doi.org/10.1007/11944836_25

3. Bauer, A., Leucker, M., Schallhart, C.: Comparing LTL semantics for runtime verification. J. Log. Comput. **20**(3), 651–674 (2010). https://doi.org/10.1093/logcom/exn075

4. Baumeister, J., Finkbeiner, B., Schirmer, S., Schwenger, M., Torens, C.: RTLola cleared for take-off: monitoring autonomous aircraft. In: Lahiri, S.K., Wang, C. (eds.) CAV 2020. LNCS, vol. 12225, pp. 28–39. Springer, Cham (2020). https://doi.org/10.1007/978-3-030-53291-8_3

5. Cimatti, A., Tian, C., Tonetta, S.: Assumption-based runtime verification of infinite-state systems. In: Feng, L., Fisman, D. (eds.) RV 2021. LNCS, vol. 12974, pp. 207–227. Springer, Cham (2021). https://doi.org/10.1007/978-3-030-88494-9_11

6. Convent, L., Hungerecker, S., Leucker, M., Scheffel, T., Schmitz, M., Thoma, D.: TeSSLa: temporal stream-based specification language. In: Massoni, T., Mousavi, M.R. (eds.) SBMF 2018. LNCS, vol. 11254, pp. 144–162. Springer, Cham (2018). https://doi.org/10.1007/978-3-030-03044-5_10

7. D'Angelo, B., et al.: LOLA: runtime monitoring of synchronous systems. In: 12th International Symposium on Temporal Representation and Reasoning (TIME 2005), 23–25 June 2005, Burlington, Vermont, USA, pp. 166–174. IEEE Computer Society (2005). https://doi.org/10.1109/TIME.2005.26

8. Eisner, C., Fisman, D., Havlicek, J., Lustig, Y., McIsaac, A., Van Campenhout, D.: Reasoning with temporal logic on truncated paths. In: Hunt, W.A., Somenzi, F. (eds.) CAV 2003. LNCS, vol. 2725, pp. 27–39. Springer, Heidelberg (2003). https://doi.org/10.1007/978-3-540-45069-6_3

9. Faymonville, P., et al.: StreamLAB: stream-based monitoring of cyber-physical systems. In: Dillig, I., Tasiran, S. (eds.) CAV 2019. LNCS, vol. 11561, pp. 421–431. Springer, Cham (2019). https://doi.org/10.1007/978-3-030-25540-4_24

10. Gorostiaga, F., Sánchez, C.: Stream runtime verification of real-time event streams with the Striver language. Int. J. Softw. Tools Technol. Transf. **23**(2), 157–183 (2021). https://doi.org/10.1007/s10009-021-00605-3

11. Havelund, K., Roşu, G.: Synthesizing monitors for safety properties. In: Katoen, J.-P., Stevens, P. (eds.) TACAS 2002. LNCS, vol. 2280, pp. 342–356. Springer, Heidelberg (2002). https://doi.org/10.1007/3-540-46002-0_24

12. Henzinger, T.A., Saraç, N.E.: Monitorability under assumptions. In: Deshmukh, J., Ničković, D. (eds.) RV 2020. LNCS, vol. 12399, pp. 3–18. Springer, Cham (2020). https://doi.org/10.1007/978-3-030-60508-7_1

13. Kupferman, O., Vardi, M.Y.: Weak alternating automata are not that weak. ACM Trans. Comput. Log. **2**(3), 408–429 (2001)

14. Leucker, M.: Teaching runtime verification. In: Khurshid, S., Sen, K. (eds.) RV 2011. LNCS, vol. 7186, pp. 34–48. Springer, Heidelberg (2012). https://doi.org/10.1007/978-3-642-29860-8_4

15. Leucker, M.: Sliding between model checking and runtime verification. In: Qadeer, S., Tasiran, S. (eds.) RV 2012. LNCS, vol. 7687, pp. 82–87. Springer, Heidelberg (2013). https://doi.org/10.1007/978-3-642-35632-2_10

16. Leucker, M., Schallhart, C.: A brief account of runtime verification. J. Logic Algebr. Progr. **78**(5), 293–303 (2009)

17. Manna, Z., Pnueli, A.: The Temporal Logic of Reactive and Concurrent Systems: Specification. Springer, New York (1991). https://doi.org/10.1007/978-1-4612-0931-7

18. Manna, Z., Pnueli, A.: The Temporal Logic of Reactive and Concurrent Systems: Specification. Springer, New York (1992). https://doi.org/10.1007/978-1-4612-0931-7

19. Perez, I., Dedden, F., Goodloe, A.: Copilot 3. Technical report NASA/TM-2020-220587, NASA Langley Research Center, April 2020
20. Pnueli, A.: The temporal logic of programs. In: Proceedings of the 18th IEEE Symposium on the Foundations of Computer Science (FOCS-77), pp. 46–57. IEEE Computer Society Press, Providence, 31 October–2 November 1977
21. Reinbacher, T., Rozier, K.Y., Schumann, J.: Temporal-logic based runtime observer pairs for system health management of real-time systems. In: Ábrahám, E., Havelund, K. (eds.) TACAS 2014. LNCS, vol. 8413, pp. 357–372. Springer, Heidelberg (2014). https://doi.org/10.1007/978-3-642-54862-8_24
22. Sánchez, C.: Online and offline stream runtime verification of synchronous systems. In: Colombo, C., Leucker, M. (eds.) RV 2018. LNCS, vol. 11237, pp. 138–163. Springer, Cham (2018). https://doi.org/10.1007/978-3-030-03769-7_9

# Abstract Monitors for Quantitative Specifications

Thomas A. Henzinger, Nicolas Mazzocchi, and N. Ege Saraç[(✉)]

Institute of Science and Technology Austria (ISTA), Klosterneuburg, Austria
{tah,nmazzocc,esarac}@ist.ac.at

**Abstract.** Quantitative monitoring can be universal and approximate: For every finite sequence of observations, the specification provides a value and the monitor outputs a best-effort approximation of it. The quality of the approximation may depend on the resources that are available to the monitor. By taking to the limit the sequences of specification values and monitor outputs, we obtain precision-resource trade-offs also for limit monitoring. This paper provides a formal framework for studying such trade-offs using an abstract interpretation for monitors: For each natural number $n$, the aggregate semantics of a monitor at time $n$ is an equivalence relation over all sequences of at most $n$ observations so that two equivalent sequences are indistinguishable to the monitor and thus mapped to the same output. This abstract interpretation of quantitative monitors allows us to measure the number of equivalence classes (or "resource use") that is necessary for a certain precision up to a certain time, or at any time. Our framework offers several insights. For example, we identify a family of specifications for which any resource-optimal exact limit monitor is independent of any error permitted over finite traces. Moreover, we present a specification for which any resource-optimal approximate limit monitor does not minimize its resource use at any time.

**Keywords:** Abstract monitor · Approximate monitoring ·
Quantitative monitoring · Monitor resources

## 1 Introduction

Online monitoring is a runtime verification (RV) technique [11] that, by sacrificing completeness, aims to lighten the burden caused by exhaustive formal methods. A monitor watches an unbounded sequence $f$ of observations, called trace, one observation at a time. At each time $n \geq 0$, it tries to provide information about the value assigned to $f$ by the specification. For a boolean specification $P$, after each trace prefix $s$, the monitor may output one of three values: all infinite extensions of $s$ satisfy $P$, violate $P$, or neither [15].

Quantitative specifications [21] generalize their boolean analogs by assigning each trace $f$ a value from some richer domain. For example, the boolean specification Resp assigns *true* to $f$ iff every observation req in $f$ is eventually followed

© The Author(s) 2022
T. Dang and V. Stolz (Eds.): RV 2022, LNCS 13498, pp. 200–220, 2022.
https://doi.org/10.1007/978-3-031-17196-3_11

by an observation ack in $f$, while the quantitative specification MaxRespTime assigns the least upper bound on the number of observations between each req and the corresponding ack, or $\infty$ if there is no such upper bound.

In the limit monitoring of a quantitative specification $\Phi$ over a trace $f$, a limit (e.g., lim sup, lim inf) of the infinite sequence of monitor outputs should provide information about the value $\Phi(f)$ assigned to the trace. For example, a "natural way to monitor" MaxRespTime is to have the monitor output, at each time, the maximum of (i) the maximal response time so far and (ii) the time since the least recent pending req, if there is a pending req. The lim sup (and lim inf) of this infinite output sequence converges towards MaxRespTime.

In contrast to its boolean analog, the quantitative setting naturally supports approximation. A monitor has error $\delta \geq 0$ if, for all infinite traces, the limit of the output sequence is within $\delta$ of the specification value. In particular, this leads to precision-resource trade-offs for quantitative monitors: The provisioning of additional states, registers, or operations may reduce the error, and a larger error tolerance may enable monitors that use fewer resources.

In this paper, we provide a formal framework for studying such precision-resource trade-offs for an abstract definition of quantitative monitors. This abstract framework can be instantiated, for example, by finite-state monitors or register monitors, where a finite-state monitor remembers a bounded amount of information about each trace prefix, and a register monitor remembers a bounded number of integer values [32]. For us, an *abstract monitor* partitions, at each time $n$, all prefixes of length up to $n$ into a finite number of equivalence classes such that if two prefixes $s_1$ and $s_2$ are equivalent, then the monitor outputs the same value after observing $s_1$ and $s_2$. The number of equivalence classes introduced at time $n$ provides a natural measure for the resource use of the abstract monitor after $n$ observations.

In this setting, where the *resource use* of a monitor is measured, we also want to measure the *precision* of a monitor. To define the precision of a monitor after a finite trace prefix, we need to enrich our definition of quantitative specifications: We let a quantitative specification assign values not only to infinite traces but also to finite traces. Indeed, many specification values for infinite traces are usually defined as limits [37]. For example, what we called above the "natural way to monitor" MaxRespTime using two counters is, in fact, the usual formal definition of the quantitative specification MaxRespTime.

Once both specifications and monitors assign values to all finite traces, there is a natural definition for the precision of a monitor: At each time $n$, the *prompt-error* is the maximal difference between the monitor output and the specification value over all finite traces of length up to $n$. Furthermore, the *limit-error* is the least upper bound on the difference between the limit of monitor outputs and the limit of specification values over all infinite traces. Note that if the prompt-error of a monitor is 0, then so is the limit-error, but not necessarily vice versa. An exact-value monitor (i.e., a monitor with prompt-error $\delta = 0$) implements the specification as it is defined. In contrast, an approximate monitor (i.e., a monitor with prompt-error $\delta > 0$) of the same specification may use fewer resources.

An approximate monitor may still achieve limit-error 0, which is a situation of particular interest that we study.

Given an abstract monitor, one way to obtain a new monitor that uses fewer resources use is to merge some equivalence classes, and one way to increase the precision is to split some equivalence classes. However, this naive approach toward reaching a desired precision or resource use is not always the best. For an approximate monitor with a given prompt-error and limit-error, the goal is *resource-optimality*, i.e., minimizing the resource use as much as the error threshold allows. We will see that merging the equivalence classes of a given monitor may not yield a resource-optimal one.

The limit-error of a monitor is bounded by its prompt-error. We also investigate the case where we require a certain limit-error while leaving the prompt-error potentially unbounded. We will see that allowing arbitrary prompt-error may not permit the monitor to save resources if the desired limit-error is fixed. We say that such specifications have *resource-intensive limit behavior*. In fact, MaxRespTime displays resource-intensive limit behavior. Other examples include a subclass of *reversible specifications*. Reversibility is a notion from automata theory characterized by the specification being realizable with a finite-state automaton that is both forward and backward deterministic. A similar notion, generalized to the quantitative setting, can be introduced in our framework, allowing an abstract monitor to process an infinite trace in a two-way fashion.

**Overview.** Section 2 formalizes the framework of abstract monitors and provides insights on relations between basic notions such as resource use and precision.

Section 3 focuses on monitoring with bounded error over finite traces. First, in Subsect. 3.1, we show that the exact-value monitor over finite traces is unique and resource-optimal for every specification. Additionally, for resource-optimal approximate monitors, we prove: (i) they are not unique in Subsect. 3.1, (ii) they do not necessarily follow the structure of the exact-value monitor in Subsect. 3.2, and (iii) they do not necessarily minimize their resource use at each time in Subsect. 3.2. Then, in Subsect. 3.3, we study precision-resource trade-off suitability: We exhibit (i) a specification for which we can arbitrarily improve the resource use by damaging precision, and (ii) another for which we arbitrarily improve the precision by damaging the resource use.

Section 4 focuses on monitoring without error on infinite traces. In particular, in Subsect. 4.1 we provide a condition for identifying specifications with resource-intensive limit behavior, for which having zero limit-error prevents the trade-off between resource use and error on finite traces. This condition captures two paradigmatic specifications: (i) maximal response-time and (ii) average response-time. Finally, in Subsect. 4.2 we investigate reversible specifications, which can be implemented in a manner both forward and backward deterministic. A subclass of reversible specifications have resource-intensive limit behavior, which we demonstrate through the average ping specification.

Section 5 concludes the paper and addresses future research directions our framework offers.

**Related Work.** In the boolean setting, several notions of monitorability have been proposed over the years [15,30,34]. Much of the theoretical efforts have focused on regular specifications [2,14,46], although some proposed more expressive models [9,12,26]. We refer the reader to [10] for coverage of these and more.

Verification of quantitative specifications [21,41] have received significant attention, especially in the probabilistic setting [17,20,33]. In the context of RV, the literature on specifications with quantitative aspects features primarily metric temporal logic and signal temporal logic [38,40,43–45]. Other efforts include processing data streams with a focus on deciding their properties at runtime [5,6] and an extension of weighted automata with monitor counters [22]. None of these works focus on monitoring quantitative specifications with approximate verdicts or the relation between monitorability and monitor resources.

Approximate methods have been used in verification for many years [25,39]. Beyond the boolean setting, such approaches have appeared in the context of sensor networks for approximating aggregate functions in a distributed setting [24,49,50], in approximate determinization or minimization of quantitative models of computation [7,16,35], and also in online algorithms [3].

To the best of our knowledge, the use of approximate methods in monitoring mainly concentrates on the specification rather than taking approximateness as a monitor feature and studying the quality of monitor verdicts. In predictive or assumption-based monitoring [23,54] and for monitoring hyperproperties [51], an over-approximation of the system under observation is used as an assumption to limit the set of possible traces [36]. Similarly, in runtime quantitative verification [18,47], the underlying probabilistic model of the system is approximated and continually updated. For monitoring under partial observability, [4] describes an approach to approximate the given specification for minimizing the number of undetected violations. In the branching-time setting, [1] uses a monitorable under- or over-approximation of the given specification to construct an "optimal" monitor. Nonetheless, a form of distributed and approximate limit monitoring for spatial specifications was studied in [8]. None of these works consider approximateness as a monitor property to study the relation between monitor resources and the quality of its verdicts.

Recently, [32] introduced a concrete monitor model with integer-valued registers and studied their resource needs. This model was later used for limit monitoring of statistical indicators of traces under probabilistic assumptions [31]. A general framework for approximate limit monitoring of quantitative specifications was proposed in [37]. However, that framework focuses exclusively on limit behaviors and on specific monitor models such as finite automata and register machines, thus allowing only limited precision-cost analyses. The main innovations of the present work over previous work are twofold. First, we abstract the monitor model and its resource use away from specific machine models. Second, by introducing prompt-errors, we study the resource use of monitors over time and relate this to the monitoring precision over time. This more nuanced framework enables a more fine-grained analysis and comparison of different monitors for the same specification concerning their precision and resource use.

## 2  Definitional Framework

Let $\Sigma = \{a, b, \ldots\}$ be a finite alphabet of observations. A *trace* is finite or infinite sequence of observations, which we respectively denote by $s, r, t \in \Sigma^*$ and $f, g \in \Sigma^\omega$. Given two traces $s \in \Sigma^*$ and $w \in \Sigma^* \cup \Sigma^\omega$, we denote by $s \prec w$ (resp. $s \preceq w$) that $s$ is a strict (resp. non-strict) prefix of $w$. For $n \in \mathbb{N}$ we define $\Sigma^{\leq n} = \{s \in \Sigma^* \mid |s| \leq n\}$ where $|s|$ refers to the length of $s$. Given $a \in \Sigma$ and $s \in \Sigma^*$, we denote by $|s|_a$ the number of occurrences of $a$ in $s$.

We denote by $\mathbb{N}$ the set of *non-negative integers* and by $\mathbb{R}$ the set of *real numbers*. We also consider $\overline{\mathbb{N}} = \mathbb{N} \cup \{+\infty\}$ and $\overline{\mathbb{R}} = \mathbb{R} \cup \{-\infty, +\infty\}$.

A binary relation $\sim$ over $\Sigma^*$ is an *equivalence relation* when it is reflexive, symmetric, and transitive. For a given equivalence relation $\sim$ over $\Sigma^*$ and a finite trace $s \in \Sigma^*$, we denote by $[s]_\sim$ the equivalence class of $\sim$ in which $s$ belongs. When $\sim$ is clear from the context, we write $[s]$ instead. A *right-monotonic* relation $\sim$ over $\Sigma^*$ fulfills $s_1 \sim s_2 \Rightarrow s_1 r \sim s_2 r$ for all $s_1, s_2, r \in \Sigma^*$.

We use $\square$ and $\lozenge$ to denote the linear temporal logic (LTL) operators *always* and *eventually*, respectively. See [48] for interpretation of LTL operators on infinite traces, and [19,27,29] on finite traces.

### 2.1  Quantitative Specifications

A *limit-measure* is a function from $\overline{\mathbb{R}}^\omega$ to $\overline{\mathbb{R}}$. Given an infinite sequence of real numbers $x = x_1 x_2 \ldots$, we define $\liminf(x) = \lim_{n \mapsto +\infty} \inf\{x_i \mid i \geq n\}$ and $\limsup(x) = \lim_{n \mapsto +\infty} \sup\{x_i \mid i \geq n\}$. Whenever $\liminf(x) = \limsup(x)$ for a given sequence $x$, we simply write $\lim(x)$. A *value function* $\pi \colon \Sigma^* \to \overline{\mathbb{R}}$ associates a value to each finite trace.

**Definition 1 (specification).** *A specification* extends a value function by *constraining its limit behavior. Syntactically, it is a tuple* $\Phi = (\pi, \ell)$ *where* $\pi \colon \Sigma^* \to \overline{\mathbb{R}}$ *is a value function and* $\ell$ *is a limit-measure. Semantically, it is a function defined by* $\llbracket \Phi \rrbracket(s) = \pi(s)$ *when* $s \in \Sigma^*$ *and* $\llbracket \Phi \rrbracket(f) = \ell(\pi(f))$ *when* $f \in \Sigma^\omega$, *where* $\pi(f) = (\pi(s_i))_{i \in \mathbb{N}}$ *is a sequence over the prefixes* $s_i \prec f$ *of increasing length* $i$.

Together with a given specification $\Phi$, we define the right-monotonic equivalence relation $\sim_\Phi^*$ as follows. For all $s_1, s_2 \in \Sigma^*$ we have $s_1 \sim_\Phi^* s_2$ iff $\pi(s_1 r) = \pi(s_2 r)$ holds for all $r \in \Sigma^*$.

We define below the *discounted response* specification. Throughout the section, we will use this specification as a running example.

*Example 2.* Let $\Sigma = \{\mathtt{req}, \mathtt{ack}, \mathtt{other}\}$ and consider the LTL response specification $P = \square(\mathtt{req} \to \lozenge\mathtt{ack})$. Let $0 < \lambda < 1$ be a discount factor. We define $\mathsf{DiscResp}(s) = 1$ if $s \in P$, and $\mathsf{DiscResp}(s) = \lambda^n$ otherwise, where $n = |s| - |r|$ and $r \prec s$ is the longest prefix of $s$ with $r \in P$. We define $\Phi_{\mathsf{DR}} = (\mathsf{DiscResp}, \limsup)$, the *discounted response* specification. Intuitively, $\Phi_{\mathsf{DR}}$ assigns each finite trace a value that shows how close the system behaves to $P$ such that, at the limit, it denotes whether the infinite behavior satisfies $P$ or not.

Now, take two traces $s, r \in \Sigma^*$. We claim that $s \sim^*_{\Phi_{DR}} r$ iff either (i) both traces have no pending request or (ii) both have a request pending for the same number of steps. First, we assume $s \sim^*_{\Phi_{DR}} r$ holds and note that we must have $\Phi_{DR}(st) = \Phi_{DR}(rt)$ for every $t \in \Sigma^*$. Then, we eliminate the cases other than (i) and (ii) as follows. If, w.l.o.g., $s \in P$ and $r \notin P$, then $\Phi_{DR}(r) < \Phi_{DR}(s) = 1$, thus $s \not\sim^*_{\Phi_{DR}} r$. If, w.l.o.g., $s$ has a request pending for $i$ steps and $r$ for $j > i$ steps, then $\Phi_{DR}(r) = \lambda^j < \lambda^i = \Phi_{DR}(s)$, thus $s \not\sim^*_{\Phi_{DR}} r$. The other direction is similar.

## 2.2   Abstract Monitors

We are now ready to present our abstract definition of quantitative monitors.

**Definition 3 (monitor).** *A monitor $\mathcal{M} = (\sim, \gamma)$ is a tuple consisting of a right-monotonic equivalence relation $\sim$ on $\Sigma^*$ and a function $\gamma \colon (\Sigma^* / \sim) \to \overline{\mathbb{R}}$. Let $\delta_{\mathrm{fin}}, \delta_{\mathrm{lim}} \in \overline{\mathbb{R}}$ be error thresholds. We say that $\mathcal{M}$ is a $(\delta_{\mathrm{fin}}, \delta_{\mathrm{lim}})$-monitor for a given specification $\Phi = (\pi, \ell)$ iff*

- $|\pi(s) - \gamma([s])| \leq \delta_{\mathrm{fin}}$ *for all $s \in \Sigma^*$, and*
- $|\ell(\pi(f)) - \ell(\gamma([f]))| \leq \delta_{\mathrm{lim}}$ *for all $f \in \Sigma^\omega$.*

*where $\gamma([f]) = (\gamma([s_i]))_{i \in \mathbb{N}}$ is a sequence over the prefixes $s_i \prec f$ of increasing length $i$. We say that $\mathcal{M}$ has a* prompt-error *of $\delta_{\mathrm{fin}}$ and a* limit-error *of $\delta_{\mathrm{lim}}$.*

We conveniently write $\mathcal{M}(s) = \gamma([s])$ when $s \in \Sigma^*$ and $\mathcal{M}(f) = \ell(\gamma([f]))$ when $f \in \Sigma^\omega$.

Observe that, for every specification, there is an obvious monitor that imitates exactly the specification, which we define as follows.

**Definition 4 (exact-value monitor).** *Let $\Phi = (\pi, \ell)$ be a specification. The* exact-value monitor *of $\Phi$ is defined as $\mathcal{M}_\Phi = (\sim^*_\Phi, s \mapsto \pi(s))$.*

A monitor for a given specification is *approximate* when it differs from the specification's exact-value monitor. Below we demonstrate the exact-value monitor and an approximate monitor for the discounted response specification.

*Example 5.* Recall from Example 2 the discounted response specification $\Phi_{DR}$. Clearly, its exact-value monitor is $\mathcal{M}_{\Phi_{DR}} = (\sim^*_{\Phi_{DR}}, \gamma_{\Phi_{DR}})$ where $\gamma_{\Phi_{DR}}([s]) = \Phi_{DR}(s)$ for all $s \in \Sigma^*$. Let us define another monitor $\mathcal{M} = (\sim, \gamma)$ such that $s \sim r$ iff either $s, r \in P$ or $s, r \notin P$ for every $s, r \in \Sigma^*$; and $\gamma([s]) = 1$ if $s \in P$, and $\gamma([s]) = 0$ if $s \notin P$. Note that for every $f \in \Sigma^\omega$ we have $f \in P$ iff infinitely many prefixes of $f$ belong to $P$, therefore $\mathcal{M}$ has no limit-error. However, it yields a prompt-error of $\lambda$ since it immediately outputs 0 instead of discounting on finite traces. Hence, $\mathcal{M}$ is a $(\lambda, 0)$-monitor for $\Phi_{DR}$.

Next, we prove that our definition constrains monitors not to make two equivalent traces too distant.

**Proposition 6.** *Let $\mathcal{M} = (\sim, \gamma)$ be a $(\delta_{\mathrm{fin}}, \delta_{\mathrm{lim}})$-monitor for the specification $\Phi = (\pi, \ell)$. For all $s_1, s_2 \in \Sigma^*$, if $s_1 \sim s_2$, then $|\Phi(s_1) - \Phi(s_2)| \leq 2\delta_{\mathrm{fin}}$.*

*Proof.* By definition of $\mathcal{M}$ we have that $-\delta_{\mathrm{fin}} \leq \pi(s_1) - \gamma([s_1]) \leq \delta_{\mathrm{fin}}$ as well as $\delta_{\mathrm{fin}} \geq -\pi(s_2) + \gamma([s_2]) \geq -\delta_{\mathrm{fin}}$. If $s_1 \sim s_2$ then $\gamma([s_1]) = \gamma([s_2])$ and thus $-2\delta_{\mathrm{fin}} \leq \pi(s_1) - \pi(s_2) \leq 2\delta_{\mathrm{fin}}$.                    $\square$

## 2.3   Resource Use of Abstract Monitors

As we demonstrated above, quantitative monitors may have different degrees of precision. A natural question is whether monitors with different error thresholds use a different amount of resources. To answer this question in its generality, we consider the following model-oblivious notions of resource use.

**Definition 7 (resource use).** *Let $\mathcal{M} = (\sim, \gamma)$ be a monitor. We consider two notions of resource use for $\mathcal{M}$ defined as functions from $\mathbb{N}$ to $\mathbb{N}$. We define step-wise resource use as $r_n(\mathcal{M}) = |\Sigma^{\leq n}/\!\!\sim| - |\Sigma^{<n}/\!\!\sim|$, and total resource use as $R_n(\mathcal{M}) = \sum_{i=0}^{n} r_i(\mathcal{M}) = |\Sigma^{\leq n}/\!\!\sim|$.*

Given two monitors $\mathcal{M}_1$ and $\mathcal{M}_2$, we compare their resource use as follows. We write $r(\mathcal{M}_1) < r(\mathcal{M}_2)$ when there exists $n_0 \in \mathbb{N}$ such that for every $n \geq n_0$ we have $r_n(\mathcal{M}_1) < r_n(\mathcal{M}_2)$. In particular, when it holds for $n_0 = 1$, we write $r(\mathcal{M}_1) \ll r(\mathcal{M}_2)$. We define $R(\mathcal{M}_1) < R(\mathcal{M}_2)$ and $R(\mathcal{M}_1) \ll R(\mathcal{M}_2)$ similarly. Figure 1 shows how these notions relate. Moreover, definitions of $r(\mathcal{M}_1) \propto r(\mathcal{M}_2)$ and $R(\mathcal{M}_1) \propto R(\mathcal{M}_2)$ for $\propto \in \{\leq, \ll, >, \gg, \geq, \geqslant\}$ are as expected.

The monitor $\mathcal{M}_1$ uses *at most as many* resources as $\mathcal{M}_2$ when we have $r(\mathcal{M}_1) \ll r(\mathcal{M}_2)$. If we further have $r_n(\mathcal{M}_1) < r_n(\mathcal{M}_2)$ for some $n \geq 1$, then $\mathcal{M}_1$ uses *fewer* resources than $\mathcal{M}_2$. We similarly define the cases for using *at least as many* and *more* resources.

Given a specification $\Phi$ and a $(\delta_{\text{fin}}, \delta_{\text{lim}})$-monitor $\mathcal{M}$ for $\Phi$, we say that $\mathcal{M}$ is *resource-optimal* for $\Phi$ when for every $(\delta_{\text{fin}}, \delta_{\text{lim}})$-monitor $\mathcal{M}'$ for $\Phi$ we have $r(\mathcal{M}) \ll r(\mathcal{M}')$, i.e., $\mathcal{M}$ uses at most as many resources as any other monitor $\mathcal{M}'$ with the same error thresholds.

*Example 8.* Recall from Examples 2 and 5 the discounted response specification $\Phi_{\text{DR}}$, its exact-value monitor $\mathcal{M}_{\Phi_{\text{DR}}}$, and the $(\lambda, 0)$-monitor $\mathcal{M}$. We claim that $\mathcal{M}$ uses fewer resources than $\mathcal{M}_{\Phi_{\text{DR}}}$. To show this, we first point out that $r_0(\mathcal{M}) = r_1(\mathcal{M}) = 1$ and $r_n(\mathcal{M}) = 0$ for every $n \geq 2$. However, $r_n(\mathcal{M}_{\Phi_{\text{DR}}}) \geq 1$ for every $n \geq 0$ because at each step the trace $\text{req}^n$ is not equivalent to any shorter trace. Therefore, while $\mathcal{M}_{\Phi_{\text{DR}}}$ is an infinite-state monitor, $\mathcal{M}$ is a finite-state monitor, and $r(\mathcal{M}) < r(\mathcal{M}_{\Phi_{\text{DR}}})$.

Finally, we conclude the description of our framework by proving the implications in Fig. 1 to establish how different ways to compare resource use of monitors relate as well as a refinement property for resource-optimal monitors.

**Proposition 9.** *For every monitor $\mathcal{M}_1$ and $\mathcal{M}_2$ the implications in Fig. 1 hold.*

**Fig. 1.** Implications between the comparisons of resource use.

**Proposition 10.** *Let $\Phi$ be a specification and $\delta_{\text{fin}}, \delta_{\text{lim}}$ be two error thresholds. Given $(\delta_{\text{fin}}, \delta_{\text{lim}})$-monitors $\mathcal{M}_1 = (\sim_1, \gamma_1)$ and $\mathcal{M}_2 = (\sim_2, \gamma_2)$ for $\Phi$. If $\sim_1 \subseteq \sim_2$ and $\mathcal{M}_1$ is resource-optimal, then $\sim_1 = \sim_2$. Thus, $\mathcal{M}_2$ is also resource-optimal.*

We remark that our definitional framework can be instantiated by existing monitor models, e.g., finite state automata [15] or register monitors [32,37]. More concretely, let us consider the discounted response specification $\Phi_{\text{DR}}$ from Example 2. Its exact-value monitor $\mathcal{M}_{\Phi_{\text{DR}}}$ from Example 5 can be implemented by a register monitor that stores the value $n$ in its single register while checking for the LTL specification $P$ using its finite-state memory. On the other hand, the monitor $\mathcal{M}$ from Example 5 can be implemented by a finite state machine.

# 3    Approximate Prompt Monitoring

The original purpose of a monitor is to provide continuous feedback about the system status with respect to the specification [13,30]. Focusing only on limit monitoring may allow an unbounded prompt-error and thus fail to fulfill this task. In this section, we consider *prompt monitoring*, i.e., the case where the monitor performs bounded prompt-error. First, we remark that considering a bounded prompt-error implicitly bounds the limit-error by definition.

**Fact 11.** *Let $\Phi$ be a specification and $\delta_{\text{fin}}, \delta_{\text{lim}} \in \overline{\mathbb{R}}$ be error thresholds. If $\mathcal{M}$ is a $(\delta_{\text{fin}}, \delta_{\text{lim}})$-monitor for $\Phi$, then it is also a $(\delta_{\text{fin}}, x)$-monitor for $\Phi$ where $x = \min\{\delta_{\text{fin}}, \delta_{\text{lim}}\}$.*

## 3.1    Uniqueness of Resource-Optimal Prompt Monitors

The exact-value monitor is arguably the most natural monitor for a given specification. In fact, it is the unique error-free monitor that is resource-optimal.

**Theorem 12.** *Let $\Phi$ be a specification, and $\delta \in \overline{\mathbb{R}}$ be an error threshold. Then, $\mathcal{M}_\Phi$ is the unique resource-optimal $(0, \delta)$-monitor for $\Phi$.*

*Proof.* Let $\Phi = (\pi, \ell)$. Consider $\mathcal{M} = (\sim, \gamma)$ as a resource-optimal $(0, \delta)$-monitor for $\Phi$. We get $\sim \subseteq \sim_\Phi^*$ thanks to the following implications.

$$
\begin{aligned}
s_1 \sim s_2 &\implies \forall r \in \Sigma^*, s_1 r \sim s_2 r && \text{(right-monotonicity)} \\
&\implies \forall r \in \Sigma^*, \gamma([s_1 r]) = \gamma([s_2 r]) && \text{(definition)} \\
&\implies \forall r \in \Sigma^*, \pi(s_1 r) = \pi(s_2 r) && \text{(prompt-error 0)} \\
&\implies s_1 \sim_\Phi^* s_2 && \text{(definition)}
\end{aligned}
$$

On the one hand, we have that $\sim = \sim_\Phi^*$ by Proposition 10. On the other hand, we have that $\gamma([s]) = \pi(s)$ for all $s \in \Sigma^*$ since the prompt-error threshold is 0. As a direct consequence, $\mathcal{M} = \mathcal{M}_\Phi$. □

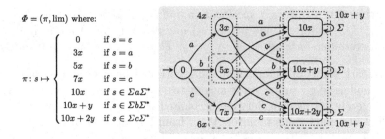

$\Phi = (\pi, \lim)$ where:

$$\pi : s \mapsto \begin{cases} 0 & \text{if } s = \varepsilon \\ 3x & \text{if } s = a \\ 5x & \text{if } s = b \\ 7x & \text{if } s = c \\ 10x & \text{if } s \in \Sigma a \Sigma^* \\ 10x + y & \text{if } s \in \Sigma b \Sigma^* \\ 10x + 2y & \text{if } s \in \Sigma c \Sigma^* \end{cases}$$

**Fig. 2.** A specification $\Phi$ over $\Sigma = \{a, b, c\}$ where $x > 0$ and $y \leq x$, and two resource-optimal $(x, y)$-monitors for $\Phi$ shown on top of the exact-value monitor $\mathcal{M}_\Phi$. As indicated by the output values on the dotted and dashed rectangles, the approximate monitors merge some equivalence classes of $\mathcal{M}_\Phi$ to save resources at the cost of losing precision.

Unfortunately, the uniqueness of resource-optimal monitors does not necessarily hold once we allow erroneous monitor verdicts. For instance, Fig. 2 shows on the left a specification $\Phi$ parameterized by $x$ and $y$, together with its exact-value monitor $\mathcal{M}_\Phi$ on the right. In addition, the figure highlights two ways to make $\sim_\Phi$ coarser to obtain distinct resource-optimal $(x, y)$-monitors for $\Phi$.

**Proposition 13.** *For all $x > 0$ and $y \leq x$ there exists a specification $\Phi$ that admits multiple resource-optimal $(x, y)$-monitors.*

## 3.2   Structure of Resource-Optimal Prompt Monitors

Regardless of the uniqueness, one can ask whether making $\sim_\Phi$ coarser always yields a resource-optimal approximate monitor. Here, we answer this question negatively. In particular, Fig. 3 shows on the left a specification $\Phi$ and on the right a resource-optimal $(1, 0)$-monitor $\mathcal{M} = (\sim, \gamma)$ for $\Phi$ with $ab \nsim ba$, although $ab \sim_\Phi^* ba$.

**Proposition 14.** *There exists a $(1, 0)$-monitor $\mathcal{M} = (\sim, \gamma)$ for some specification $\Phi$ such that for every other $(1, 0)$-monitor $\mathcal{M}' = (\sim', \gamma')$ we have that $\sim_\Phi \subseteq \sim'$ implies $\mathbf{r}(\mathcal{M}) \ll \mathbf{r}(\mathcal{M}')$.*

$\Phi = (\pi, \lim)$ where:

$$\pi : s \mapsto \begin{cases} 0 & \text{if } s = \varepsilon \\ 3 & \text{if } s = c \\ 6 & \text{if } s = a \text{ or } s = ca \\ 9 & \text{if } s = b \text{ or } s = cb \\ 12 & \text{if } s = cab \\ 14 & \text{if } s = ab \text{ or } s = ba \\ 16 & \text{if } s = cba \\ 19 & \text{otherwise} \end{cases}$$

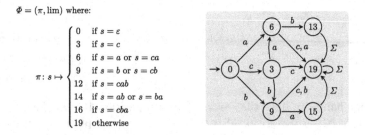

**Fig. 3.** A specification for which no $(1, 0)$-monitor that $\mathcal{M}_\Phi$ refines is resource-optimal, and the witnessing resource-optimal approximate monitor that splits an equivalence class of the specification.

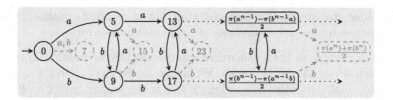

**Fig. 4.** A resource-optimal (1,1)-monitor for the specification $\Phi$ of Proposition 15 that never minimizes its step-wise resource use $r_n$ (black). Attempting to minimize $r_n$ at each step $n$ results in taking $a^n$ and $b^n$ as equivalent, but breaking the equivalence at step $n+1$ as the prompt-error bound would be violated otherwise (gray).

We established that the structure of the exact-value monitor does not necessarily provide insights into finding a resource-optimal approximate monitor. In fact, as we demonstrate in Fig. 4, there exist a specification such that its resource-optimal $(1,1)$-monitor $\mathcal{M}$ never minimizes the resource use $r_i(\mathcal{M})$.

**Proposition 15.** *There exists a specification $\Phi$ admitting a $(1,1)$-monitor $\mathcal{M} = (\sim, \gamma)$ such that for all equivalence relations $\approx$ over $\Sigma^*$ and $n \in \mathbb{N}$ we have that $|\Sigma^{\leq n}/\sim|$ is strictly greater than*

$$\min \left\{ |\Sigma^{\leq n}/\approx| \; \middle| \; \forall s_1, s_2 \in \Sigma^{\leq n} : s_1 \approx s_2 \Rightarrow \bigwedge \begin{array}{c} \forall r \in \Sigma^* : s_1 r \approx s_2 r \\ |\Phi(s_1) - \Phi(s_2)| \leq 1 \end{array} \right\}.$$

*Proof.* Let $\Phi = (\pi, \limsup)$ be a specification from $\Sigma = \{a,b\}$ to $\mathbb{N}$ where $\pi$ is defined as follows.

$$\pi : s \mapsto \begin{cases} 8|s| & \text{if } s \in b^* \\ 8|s| - 16k + 4 & \text{if } s \in (b^+a^+)^k \text{ for some } k \geq 1 \\ 8|s| - 16k + 2 & \text{if } s \in (b^+a^+)^k b^+ \text{ for some } k \geq 1 \\ 8|s| - 2 & \text{if } s \in a^+ \\ 8|s| - 16k + 10 & \text{if } s \in (a^+b^+)^k \text{ for some } k \geq 1 \\ 8|s| - 16k - 4 & \text{if } s \in (a^+b^+)^k a^+ \text{ for some } k \geq 1 \end{cases}$$

Let $n \in \mathbb{N}$. The key argument is that it is beneficial to put $a^n$ and $b^n$ in the same equivalence class for minimizing $r_n$ since $|\Phi(a^n) - \Phi(b^n)| = 2$ and since no other trace in $\Sigma^{\leq n}$ admits a value close to either $\Phi(a^n)$ or $\Phi(b^n)$. However, once we consider traces of length $n+1$, we introduce several values close to $\Phi(a^n)$ as well as $\Phi(b^n)$, but not both at the same time. Therefore, to minimize the resource use $r_{n+1}$ while maintaining the prompt-error bound of 1, it becomes beneficial to put $a^n$ and $b^n$ in distinct equivalence classes. □

## 3.3   Unbounded Precision-Resource Trade-Offs for Prompt Monitors

In this subsection, we exhibit specifications admitting an infinite sequence of monitors that trade precision and resource use. First, we investigate the *maximal response-time* specification by demonstrating how a monitor can save more and more resources by increasing both its prompt- and limit-error.

*Example 16.* Let $\Sigma = \{\texttt{req}, \texttt{ack}, \texttt{other}\}$ and consider the usual LTL response specification $P = \Box(\texttt{req} \to \Diamond\texttt{ack})$. We define $\textsf{CurResp}(s) = 0$ if $s \in P$, and $\textsf{CurResp}(s) = |s| - |r|$ otherwise, where $r \prec s$ is the longest prefix with $r \in P$. Now, let $\textsf{MaxResp}(s) = \sup_{r \preceq s} \textsf{CurResp}(r)$ and define $\Phi_{\textsf{MR}} = (\textsf{MaxResp}, \lim)$, which we call the *maximal response-time* specification. Note that $\textsf{CurResp}$ outputs the current response-time for a finite trace, and $\textsf{MaxResp}$ outputs the maximum response-time so far.

Consider the monitor $\mathcal{M} = (\sim, \gamma)$ that counts the response time when there is an open $\texttt{req}$, but only stores an approximation of the maximum when an $\texttt{ack}$ occurs. More explicitly, let $\sim$ and $\gamma$ be such that we have the following: $\mathcal{M}(s) = 5k + 2$ if $s \in P$, where $k \in \mathbb{N}$ satisfies $5k \leq \textsf{MaxResp}(s) < 5(k+1)$; and $\mathcal{M}(s) = \max\{\mathcal{M}(r), \textsf{CurResp}(\texttt{s})\}$ otherwise, where $r \prec s$ is the longest prefix with $r \in P$. We claim that $\mathcal{M}$ is a $(2, 2)$-monitor for $\Phi_{\textsf{MR}}$. First, observe that whenever there is no pending request, i.e., $s \in P$, the monitor has a prompt-error of at most 2 by construction. Indeed, $\textsf{MaxResp}(s) \in \{5k+i \mid i \in \{0, 1, 2, 3, 4\}\}$. In the case of a pending request, i.e., $s \notin P$, there is a prompt-error only when the monitor's approximation of the maximum-so-far is not replaced by the current response time. Again, by construction, we can bound this error by 2. Intuitively, $\mathcal{M}$ achieves this approximation by merging in $\sim$ some equivalence classes of $\sim^*_{\Phi_{\textsf{MR}}}$ where there are no pending requests. One can thus verify that $\mathbf{r}(\mathcal{M}) < \mathbf{r}(\mathcal{M}_{\Phi_{\textsf{MR}}})$.

The construction described in Example 16 can be generalized to identify a precision-resource trade-off with an infinite hierarchy of approximate monitors.

**Theorem 17.** *For all $\delta \in \mathbb{N}$, there exists a $(\delta, \delta)$-monitor $\mathcal{M}_\delta$ for the maximal response-time specification. Furthermore, $\mathbf{r}(\mathcal{M}_i) < \mathbf{r}(\mathcal{M}_j)$ for all $i > j$, and $\mathcal{M}_0$ is the exact-value monitor.*

*Proof.* Let $\Phi_{\textsf{MR}} = (\textsf{MaxResp}, \lim)$ be the maximal response-time specification as introduced in Example 16. Let $\delta \in \mathbb{N}$ and $s \in \Sigma^*$. If $s$ does not have a pending request, we define $\mathcal{M}_\delta(s) = k(2\delta + 1) + \delta$ where $k \in \mathbb{N}$ satisfies $k(2\delta + 1) \leq \textsf{MaxResp}(s) < (k+1)(2\delta + 1)$. Otherwise, if $s$ has a pending request, we define $\mathcal{M}_\delta(s) = \max\{\mathcal{M}_\delta(r), \textsf{CurResp}(\texttt{s})\}$ where $r \prec s$ is the longest prefix with no pending request. We construct the $(\delta, \delta)$-monitor $\mathcal{M}_\delta$ for $\Phi_{\textsf{MR}}$ as in Example 16. In particular, $\mathcal{M}_0$ is the exact-value monitor. Indeed, $\delta = 0$ implies $\mathcal{M}_\delta(s) = k = \textsf{MaxResp}(s)$ when $s$ does not have a pending request, and otherwise $\mathcal{M}_\delta(s) = \sup_{r \preceq s} \textsf{CurResp}(r) = \textsf{MaxResp}(s)$ by definition. For all $i > j$, the monitor $\mathcal{M}_i$ partitions the traces with no pending requests into sets of cardinality $2i + 1$ while $\mathcal{M}_j$ does so using sets of cardinality $2j + 1$. Then, the equivalence relation used by $\mathcal{M}_i$ is coarser than that of $\mathcal{M}_j$, and thus $\mathbf{r}(\mathcal{M}_i) < \mathbf{r}(\mathcal{M}_j)$. $\quad\square$

Note that, except $\mathcal{M}_0$, the monitors given by Theorem 17 have non-zero limit-error. We explore in Sect. 4 the specifications for which having fewer resources than the exact-value monitor forces a non-zero limit-error. Moreover, we show in Example 25 that the maximal response-time is one of these specifications.

Next, we investigate the *server/client* specification by demonstrating how a monitor can be more and more precise by increasing its resource use.

*Example 18.* Consider a server that receives requests and issues acknowledgments. The number of simultaneous requests the system can handle is determined at runtime through a preprocessing computation. We describe a specification that, at its core, requires that every request is acknowledged and the server never has more open requests than it can handle. In particular, until the server is turned off, the specification assigns a value to each finite trace, denoting the likelihood and criticality of a potential immediate violation.

Let $\Sigma = \{\texttt{req}, \texttt{ack}, \texttt{other}, \texttt{off}\}$ be an alphabet, $\lambda \in (0,1)$ be a discount factor, and $\Lambda > 0$ be an integer denoting the request threshold. For every $s \in \Sigma^*$ we denote by $\mathsf{NumReq}(s)$ the number of pending requests in $s$. We define the *server/client specification* $\Phi_{\mathsf{SC}} = (\pi, \lim)$ where $\pi$ is defined as follows.

- $\pi(s) = 0$ if $s$ contains an occurrence of $\texttt{off}$,
- $\pi(s) = \mathsf{NumReq}(s)\lambda^{|s|}$ if $\mathsf{NumReq}(r) \leq \Lambda$ for all $r \preceq s$, and otherwise
- $\pi(s) = \mathsf{NumReq}(r)\lambda^{|r|}$ where $r \preceq s$ is the shortest with $\mathsf{NumReq}(r) > \Lambda$.

**Theorem 19.** *For every positive integer $\Lambda$ and real number $0 < \delta \leq \Lambda$, there exists a $(\delta, \delta)$-monitor $\mathcal{M}_\delta$ for the server/client specification $\Phi_{\mathsf{SC}}$. Furthermore, $\mathcal{M}_\delta$ uses finitely many resources.*

*Proof.* Let $\Lambda$ and $\delta$ be as above, and consider the set $X$ we define as follows: $X = \{s \in \Sigma^* \mid \sup_{r_1 \in \Sigma^*}\{\pi(sr_1)\} - \inf_{r_2 \in \Sigma^*}\{\pi(sr_2)\} \geq \delta\}$. Note that $X$ is finite. On the one hand, only a finite number of prefixes of a trace admitting an occurrence of $\texttt{off}$ can belong to $X$ since $\delta > 0$ and by definition of $\Phi_{\mathsf{SC}}$. On the other hand, only a finite number of prefixes of a trace in which no $\texttt{off}$ occurs can belong to $X$ since the discounting forces the value of $\Phi_{\mathsf{SC}}$ to converge to 0. We construct $\mathcal{M}_\delta$ such that, if the trace belongs to $X$, it outputs the value given by the specification, otherwise it outputs the value of the shortest prefix that does not belong to $X$. In other words, $\mathcal{M}_\delta$ does not distinguish traces with the same prefix not belonging to $X$ and thus admits at most $2|X|$ equivalence classes. $\square$

# 4 Approximate Limit Monitoring

In contrast to Sect. 3 where we tackle the limit monitoring problem indirectly with a bounded prompt-error, here we bound the limit-error directly and allow arbitrary prompt-error.

*Example 20.* Let $\Phi = (\pi, \liminf)$ be a specification over $\Sigma = \{\texttt{safe}, \texttt{danger}, \texttt{off}\}$ such that $\pi(s) = 2^{|r|}$ if $s$ does not contain $\texttt{off}$, where $r$ is the longest suffix of $s$ of the form $\texttt{safe}^*$, and $\pi(s) = |s|_{\texttt{danger}}$ otherwise. Intuitively, $\Phi$ assigns each trace a confidence value while the system is on and how many times the system was in danger otherwise. We describe an approximate monitor with unbounded prompt-error and bounded but non-zero limit-error.

Let $\sim$ be a right-monotonic equivalence relation and $\gamma$ an output function such that $\mathcal{M} = (\sim, \gamma)$ satisfies the following: $\mathcal{M}(s) = \infty$ when $s$ has no off and ends with safe, $\mathcal{M}(s) = 0$ when $s$ has no off and ends with danger, and $\mathcal{M}(s) = 9k + 4$ otherwise, where $k \in \mathbb{N}$ satisfies $9k \leq |s|_{\text{danger}} < 9(k+1)$. Notice that the monitor partitions $\mathbb{N}$ into intervals and takes traces with a "close enough" number of danger's equivalent – as in Example 16. It is easy to see that $\mathcal{M}$ is a $(\infty, 4)$-monitor for $\Phi$.

At its core, the limit-error threshold of a monitor is a theoretical guarantee since we cannot compute arbitrary limit-measures at runtime. Then, as a starting point, we insist that the monitor has zero limit-error, which is a reasonable requirement given that we allow unbounded prompt-error. In this case, the monitoring is still potentially approximate since we allow any error on finite traces. To talk about specifications for which saving resources by allowing prompt-error is not possible, we define the following notion.

**Definition 21 (resource-intensive limit behavior).** *A specification $\Phi$ has resource-intensive limit behavior iff its exact-value monitor $\mathcal{M}_\Phi$ is a resource-optimal $(\delta, 0)$-monitor for any $\delta \geq 0$.*

First, we identify a sufficient condition for a specification to be resource-intensive limit behavior. Then, we present *reversible specifications* and show a subclass of them that satisfy our condition.

### 4.1   Specifications with Resource-Intensive Limit Behavior

Let $\Phi = (\pi, \ell)$ be a specification and recall the equivalence $\sim_\Phi^*$ that, for every $s_1, s_2 \in \Sigma^*$, is defined as $s_1 \sim_\Phi^* s_2$ iff $\pi(s_1 r) = \pi(s_2 r)$ holds for all $r \in \Sigma^*$. To investigate the limit behavior of a specification, we define the following equivalence relation: for every $s_1, s_2 \in \Sigma^*$ we have $s_1 \sim_\Phi^\omega s_2$ iff $\ell(\pi(s_1 f)) = \ell(\pi(s_2 f))$ holds for all $f \in \Sigma^\omega$. Intuitively, traces with indistinguishable limit behavior are equivalent according to this relation. As a direct consequence of Fact 11, the following holds.

**Fact 22.** *For every specification $\Phi$, we have that $\sim_\Phi^* \subseteq \sim_\Phi^\omega$.*

However, the converse does not necessarily hold, as we demonstrate with Example 23 below. We will show later that, when it holds, the specification has resource-intensive limit behavior.

*Example 23.* Recall the discounted response specification $\Phi_{\text{DR}}$ in Example 2, and that for all $s, r \in \Sigma^*$, we have $s \sim_{\Phi_{\text{DR}}}^* r$ iff either (i) both traces have no pending req or (ii) both have a req pending for the same number of steps.

Let $s, r \in \Sigma^*$. We claim $s \sim_{\Phi_{\text{DR}}}^\omega r$ iff either both traces have a pending request or both do not. Indeed, if $s$ has a pending request and $r$ does not, then we have $\Phi(s.\text{other}^\omega) = 0$ but $\Phi(r.\text{other}^\omega) = 1$. For the other direction, simply observe that if $s \sim_{\Phi_{\text{DR}}}^\omega r$ then $\Phi(s.\text{other}^\omega) = \Phi(r.\text{other}^\omega)$, but the equality does not hold if $s$ has a pending request and $r$ does not (or vice versa). Having these characterizations at hand, we immediately observe that $s \sim_{\Phi_{\text{DR}}}^* r$ implies $s \sim_{\Phi_{\text{DR}}}^\omega r$.

Notice that the approximate monitor $\mathcal{M}$ for $\Phi_{\mathsf{DR}}$ we constructed in Example 5 follows exactly the limit behavior of the specification. We were able to take advantage of the fact that $\sim^{\omega}_{\Phi_{\mathsf{DR}}}$ is coarser than $\sim^{*}_{\Phi_{\mathsf{DR}}}$ and design $\mathcal{M}$ such that it saves resources by allowing some prompt-error but no limit-error. We generalize this observation by showing that we could not have designed such a monitor if these equivalences had overlapped.

**Theorem 24.** *Let $\Phi$ be a specification. If $\sim^{*}_{\Phi} = \sim^{\omega}_{\Phi}$ then $\Phi$ has resource-intensive limit behavior.*

*Proof.* Let $\mathcal{M} = (\sim, \gamma)$ be a resource-optimal $(\delta, 0)$-monitor for $\Phi$. Suppose towards contradiction that $\sim^{*}_{\Phi} = \sim^{\omega}_{\Phi}$ and $\mathcal{M}_{\Phi}$ is not resource-optimal for $\Phi$. In particular $\sim \neq \sim^{*}_{\Phi}$. Since the limit-error threshold is 0, we get $\sim \subseteq \sim^{*}_{\Phi}$ by the following.

$$
\begin{aligned}
s_1 \sim s_2 &\implies \forall f \in \Sigma^{\omega}, \ell(\gamma([s_1 f])) = \ell(\gamma([s_2 f])) && \text{(right-monotonicity)} \\
&\iff \forall f \in \Sigma^{\omega}, \ell(\pi(s_1 f)) = \ell(\pi(s_2 f)) && \text{(limit-error 0)} \\
&\iff s_1 \sim^{\omega}_{\Phi} s_2 && \text{(definition)} \\
&\iff s_1 \sim^{*}_{\Phi} s_2 && \text{(hypothesis)}
\end{aligned}
$$

The contradiction is then raised by Proposition 10 implying that $\sim = \sim^{*}_{\Phi}$.     □

As demonstrated in Example 5 and discussed above, the discounted response specification does not display resource-intensive limit behavior. We give below two examples of specifications with resource-intensive limit behavior. Let us start with the *maximal response-time* specification.

*Example 25.* Consider the maximal response-time specification $\Phi_{\mathsf{MR}} =$ (MaxResp, lim) from Example 16. We argue that $\sim^{*}_{\Phi_{\mathsf{MR}}}$ and $\sim^{\omega}_{\Phi_{\mathsf{MR}}}$ overlap.

Suppose towards contradiction that there exist $s, r \in \Sigma^{*}$ such that $s \sim^{\omega}_{\Phi_{\mathsf{MR}}} r$ and $s \not\sim^{*}_{\Phi_{\mathsf{MR}}} r$. Then, there is $t \in \Sigma^{*}$ with $\Phi_{\mathsf{MR}}(st) \neq \Phi_{\mathsf{MR}}(rt)$. If at least one of $st$ or $rt$ has no pending request, take the continuation $\mathsf{other}^{\omega}$ to reach a contradiction to $s \sim^{\omega}_{\Phi_{\mathsf{MR}}} r$. Otherwise, if in both $st$ and $rt$ the current response time is smaller than the maximum among granted requests, then the continuation $\mathsf{ack}^{\omega}$ yields a contradiction. The same continuation covers the case when both current response times are greater. Finally, assume w.l.o.g. that the current response time is smaller than the maximum among granted requests in $st$ and greater in $rt$. In this case, $\mathsf{ack}^{\omega}$ yields a contradiction again because their outputs stay the same as $\Phi_{\mathsf{MR}}(st)$ and $\Phi_{\mathsf{MR}}(rt)$, respectively. Therefore, we have $s \sim^{*}_{\Phi_{\mathsf{MR}}} r$, and thus $\sim^{*}_{\Phi_{\mathsf{MR}}}$ and $\sim^{\omega}_{\Phi_{\mathsf{MR}}}$ overlap.

Next, we describe the *average response-time* specification and argue that it displays resource-intensive limit behavior.

*Example 26.* Let $\Sigma = \{\mathsf{req}, \mathsf{ack}, \mathsf{other}\}$ and consider the usual LTL response specification $P = \Box(\mathsf{req} \rightarrow \Diamond\mathsf{ack})$. For $s \in \Sigma^{*}$, we denote by $\mathsf{RespTime}(s)$ the total number of letters between the matching $\mathsf{req\text{-}ack}$ pairs in $s$, and by

NumReq($s$) the number of valid req's in $s$. For all $s \in \Sigma^*$, we fix $p(s) = 1$ if $s \in P$, and $p(s) = 0$ otherwise. Then, we define RespTime($s$) $= \sum_{r \preceq s} 1 - p(r)$ and NumReq($s$) $= |P_s|$ where $P_s = \{r \preceq s \mid \exists t \in \Sigma^*, r = t.\mathsf{req} \wedge p(t) = 1\}$ is the set of valid requests in $s$. We define the *average response-time* specification as $\Phi_{\mathsf{AR}} = (\mathsf{AvgResp}, \liminf)$ where we let $\mathsf{AvgResp}(s) = \frac{\mathsf{RespTime}(s)}{\mathsf{NumReq}(s)}$ for all $s \in \Sigma^*$.

We claim that $\sim_{\Phi_{\mathsf{AR}}}^*$ and $\sim_{\Phi_{\mathsf{AR}}}^\omega$ overlap. To show this, one can proceed similarly as in Example 25. The cases with no pending requests are similar. When both traces have a pending request and their output values differ, extend both with $\mathsf{ack}^\omega$ to get a contradiction.

## 4.2 Reversible Specifications

The *reversible* subclass of specifications enjoys the ability to move between computation steps forward and backward deterministically. Such specifications received particular interest in the literature since they can be implemented on hardware without energy dissipation [42,52]. Since it imitates the specification, the exact-value monitor of a reversible specification can roll back its computation, if allowed, without needing additional memory. From an automata-theoretic perspective, reversibility can be seen as the automaton being both forward and backward deterministic. Algebraically, this is captured by the syntactic monoid being a group.

**Definition 27 (reversible specification).** *A specification $\Phi$ is reversible iff $(\Sigma^*/\sim_\Phi^*, \cdot, \varepsilon)$ is a group.*

First, we describe the *average ping* specification – a variant of the average response-time specification where a single **ping** event captures **req** and **ack** events, and time proceeds through clock **tick** events. We then show that this specification is reversible.

*Example 28.* Let $\Sigma = \{\mathsf{ping}, \mathsf{tick}, \mathsf{other}\}$. Let $\mathsf{ValidTick}(s) = |s|_{\mathsf{tick}} - |r|_{\mathsf{tick}}$ where $r \preceq s$ is the longest prefix with no **ping**, and let $\mathsf{NumPing}(s) = |s|_{\mathsf{ping}}$. The *average ping* specification is defined as $\Phi_{\mathsf{AP}} = (\mathsf{AvgPing}, \liminf)$ where, for all $s \in \Sigma^*$, we let $\mathsf{AvgPing}(s) = \frac{\mathsf{ValidTick}(s)}{\mathsf{NumPing}(s)}$ if $\mathsf{NumPing}(s) > 0$; and $\mathsf{AvgPing}(s) = -1$ otherwise.

We argue that this specification is reversible. To see why, first observe for all $s, r \in \Sigma^*$ that we have $s \sim_{\Phi_{\mathsf{AP}}}^* r$ iff (i) $\mathsf{NumPing}(s) = \mathsf{NumPing}(r)$ and (ii) $\mathsf{ValidTick}(s) = \mathsf{ValidTick}(r)$. We particularly show for every $s, r, t \in \Sigma^*$ that if $s \approx_{\Phi_{\mathsf{AP}}}^* r$ then $st \approx_{\Phi_{\mathsf{AP}}}^* rt$, therefore $\sim_{\Phi_{\mathsf{AP}}}^*$ yields a group. Let $s, r \in \Sigma^*$ be such that $s \approx_{\Phi_{\mathsf{AP}}}^* r$ and let $t \in \Sigma^*$ be arbitrary. Suppose the condition (i) above does not hold. Since the NumPing values increase monotonically with every **ping**, we get $\mathsf{NumPing}(st) - \mathsf{NumPing}(rt) = \mathsf{NumPing}(s) - \mathsf{NumPing}(r)$, which is non-zero by supposition. If (ii) does not hold, it does not hold for $st$ and $rt$ either by a similar reasoning. Hence we have $st \approx_{\Phi_{\mathsf{AP}}}^* rt$.

Intuitively, we can backtrack the information on these functions: The value of NumPing is decremented with each preceding **ping**, while ValidTick is decremented with each preceding **tick** until it hits 0. It means that $\sim_{\Phi_{\mathsf{AP}}}^*$ can be seen as an automaton that is both forward and backward deterministic.

We identify below a well-behaved subclass of reversible specifications with resource-intensive limit behavior.

**Theorem 29.** *Let $\Phi$ be a reversible specification. If for every $s, r \in \Sigma^*$ with $s \sim_\Phi^\omega r$ there exists $t \in \Sigma^*$ with $st \sim_\Phi^* rt$, then $\Phi$ has resource-intensive limit behavior.*

*Proof.* We show that the reversibility of $\Phi$, together with the above assumption, implies $\sim_\Phi^* = \sim_\Phi^\omega$. Note that the inclusion $\sim_\Phi^* \subseteq \sim_\Phi^\omega$ always holds as stated by Fact 22. Assuming $(\Sigma^*/\sim_\Phi^*, \cdot, \varepsilon)$ is a group, we have $s_1 r \sim_\Phi^* s_2 r \Rightarrow s_1 \sim_\Phi^* s_2$ for all $s_1, s_2, r \in \Sigma^*$. The inclusion $\sim_\Phi^\omega \subseteq \sim_\Phi^*$ holds since having $s_1 \not\sim_\Phi^* s_2$ implies for all $r \in \Sigma^*$ that $s_1 r \not\sim_\Phi^* s_2 r$, which in turn implies $s_1 \not\sim_\Phi^\omega s_2$ by our initial assumption. Finally, by Theorem 24, we obtain that $\Phi$ has resource-intensive limit behavior.  □

Recall the average ping specification from Example 28. It is reversible, as discussed earlier, and satisfies the condition in Theorem 29, therefore it has resource-intensive limit behavior. Finally, we present the *maximal ping* – a similarly simple variant of the maximal response-time specification. We demonstrate that this specification is not reversible, although it has resource-intensive limit behavior.

*Example 30.* Let $\Sigma = \{\texttt{ping}, \texttt{other}\}$ and consider the boolean specification $P = \square\lozenge\texttt{ping}$. Let $\mathsf{CurPing}(s)$ and $\mathsf{MaxPing}(s)$ be defined similarly as for the maximal response-time specification in Example 16. We fix $\Phi_{\mathsf{MP}} = (\mathsf{MaxPing}, \lim)$ which we call the *maximal ping* specification. Consider $s = \texttt{ping.other}$ and $r = \texttt{ping.other.other}$. While $s \not\sim_{\Phi_{\mathsf{MP}}}^* r$, we have $sr \sim_{\Phi_{\mathsf{MP}}}^* rr$, therefore $\sim_{\Phi_{\mathsf{MP}}}^*$ does not yield a group. Intuitively, this is because we cannot backtrack the information on the running maximum. However, similarly as for the maximal-response time specification in Example 16, one can verify that $\sim_{\Phi_{\mathsf{MP}}}^* = \sim_{\Phi_{\mathsf{MP}}}^\omega$.

Note that a notion of reversibility exists for abstract monitors as well: A monitor $\mathcal{M} = (\sim, \gamma)$ where $\sim$ yields a group enjoys reversibility. In particular, this ability allows the monitor to return to a previous computation step without using additional resources and thus consider a different trace suffix.

## 5   Conclusion and Future Work

We formalize a framework that supports reasoning about precision-resource trade-offs for the approximate and exact monitoring of quantitative specifications. Unlike previous results, which analyze trade-offs for specific machine models such as register monitors [32,37], the framework presented in this paper studies for the first time an abstract notion of monitors, independent of the representation model, and separates the monitor errors on finite traces from those at the limit. These innovations allow us to design and study monitors that keep the focus on the resources needed for the approximate monitoring of quantitative specifications with a given precision. We provide several examples of when approximate monitoring can save resources and investigate when it fails to achieve this goal.

An expected future work is to provide a procedure for constructing a *concrete* (exact or approximate) monitor from an abstract description. Monitors having finitely many equivalence classes can be naturally mapped to finite-state automata. For a monitor with infinitely many equivalence classes, the model must be an infinite-state transition system. Yet, there are different levels of infinite state space. It can be generated, for example, by a finite collection of registers [32] or by a pushdown system [28]. Even when two abstract monitors are mapped to register automata with the same number of registers, they may differ in the type of operations used or the run-time needed per observation. It is also worth emphasizing that saving a single register may save infinitely many resources. Our current results do not provide such performance, so it is a natural future direction. To this end, we can consider alternative approaches to evaluate a monitor based on the number of violations of the error-threshold.

Another direction is on the relevance of resources through time. Our notion of resource use covers the number of equivalence classes added at time $n$, but an assumption that the monitor can release resources would trigger more possibilities. We can extend our framework to *dynamic abstract monitors* in a way that is related to existing works on dynamic programming for model checking [53]. Intuitively, a dynamic abstract monitor keeps track of the equivalence classes that can be reused in the future and prunes all the others to reduce resource use.

**Acknowledgments.** We thank the anonymous reviewers for their helpful comments. This work was supported in part by the ERC-2020-AdG 101020093.

# References

1. Aceto, L., Achilleos, A., Francalanza, A., Ingólfsdóttir, A., Lehtinen, K.: The best a monitor can do. In: Baier, C., Goubault-Larrecq, J. (eds.) 29th EACSL Annual Conference on Computer Science Logic, CSL 2021, 25–28 Jan 2021, Ljubljana, Slovenia (Virtual Conference), LIPIcs, vol. 183, pp 1–23. Schloss Dagstuhl - Leibniz-Zentrum für Informatik (2021). https://doi.org/10.4230/LIPIcs.CSL.2021.7
2. Aceto, L., Achilleos, A., Francalanza, A., Ingólfsdóttir, A., Lehtinen, K.: An operational guide to monitorability with applications to regular properties. Softw. Syst. Model. **20**(2), 335–361 (2021). https://doi.org/10.1007/s10270-020-00860-z
3. Albers, S.: Online algorithms: a survey. Math. Program. **97**(1), 3–26 (2003)
4. Alechina, N., Dastani, M., Logan, B.: Norm approximation for imperfect monitors. In: Bazzan, A.L.C., Huhns, M.N., Lomuscio, A., Scerri, P. (eds.) International conference on Autonomous Agents and Multi-Agent Systems, AAMAS 2014, Paris, France, 5–9 May 2014, pp. 117–124. IFAAMAS/ACM (2014). http://dl.acm.org/citation.cfm?id=2615753
5. Alur, R., Mamouras, K., Stanford, C.: Automata-based stream processing. In: 44th International Colloquium on Automata, Languages, and Programming (ICALP 2017), Schloss Dagstuhl-Leibniz-Zentrum fuer Informatik (2017)

6. Alur, R., Mamouras, K., Stanford, C.: Modular quantitative monitoring. In: Proceedings of the ACM on Programming Languages, vol. 3 (POPL), pp. 1–31 (2019). https://doi.org/10.1145/3290363

7. Aminof, B., Kupferman, O., Lampert, R.: Rigorous approximated determinization of weighted automata. Theor. Comput. Sci. **480**, 104–117 (2013). https://doi.org/10.1016/j.tcs.2013.02.005

8. Audrito, G., Casadei, R., Damiani, F., Stolz, V., Viroli, M.: Adaptive distributed monitors of spatial properties for cyber-physical systems. J. Syst. Softw. **175**, 110908 (2021). https://doi.org/10.1016/j.jss.2021.110908

9. Barringer, H., Falcone, Y., Havelund, K., Reger, G., Rydeheard, D.: Quantified Event Automata: Towards Expressive and Efficient Runtime Monitors. In: Giannakopoulou, D., Méry, D. (eds.) FM 2012. LNCS, vol. 7436, pp. 68–84. Springer, Heidelberg (2012). https://doi.org/10.1007/978-3-642-32759-9_9

10. Bartocci, E., Falcone, Y. (eds.): Lectures on Runtime Verification. LNCS, vol. 10457. Springer, Cham (2018). https://doi.org/10.1007/978-3-319-75632-5

11. Bartocci, E., Falcone, Y., Francalanza, A., Reger, G.: Introduction to runtime verification. In: Bartocci, E., Falcone, Y. (eds.) Lectures on Runtime Verification. LNCS, vol. 10457, pp. 1–33. Springer, Cham (2018). https://doi.org/10.1007/978-3-319-75632-5_1

12. Basin, D., Klaedtke, F., Müller, S., Zălinescu, E.: Monitoring metric first-order temporal properties. J. ACM (JACM) **62**(2), 1–45 (2015)

13. Bauer, A., Leucker, M., Schallhart, C.: The good, the bad, and the ugly, but how ugly is ugly? In: Sokolsky, O., Taşıran, S. (eds.) RV 2007. LNCS, vol. 4839, pp. 126–138. Springer, Heidelberg (2007). https://doi.org/10.1007/978-3-540-77395-5_11

14. Bauer, A., Leucker, M., Schallhart, C.: Comparing LTL semantics for runtime verification. J. Log. Comput. **20**(3), 651–674 (2010). https://doi.org/10.1093/logcom/exn075

15. Bauer, A., Leucker, M., Schallhart, C.: Runtime verification for LTL and TLTL. ACM Trans. Softw. Eng. Methodol. **20**(4), 14 (2011). https://doi.org/10.1145/2000799.2000800

16. Boker, U., Henzinger, T.A.: Approximate determinization of quantitative automata. In: D'Souza, D., Kavitha, T., Radhakrishnan, J. (eds.) IARCS Annual Conference on Foundations of Software Technology and Theoretical Computer Science, FSTTCS 2012, 15–17 Dec 2012, Hyderabad, India. LIPIcs, vol. 18, pp. 362–373. Schloss Dagstuhl - Leibniz-Zentrum für Informatik (2012). https://doi.org/10.4230/LIPIcs.FSTTCS.2012.362

17. Brázdil, T., Chatterjee, K., Forejt, V., Kučera, A.: MULTIGAIN: a controller synthesis tool for mdps with multiple mean-payoff objectives. In: Baier, C., Tinelli, C. (eds.) TACAS 2015. LNCS, vol. 9035, pp. 181–187. Springer, Heidelberg (2015). https://doi.org/10.1007/978-3-662-46681-0_12

18. Calinescu, R., Gerasimou, S., Johnson, K., Paterson, C.: Using runtime quantitative verification to provide assurance evidence for self-adaptive software. In: de Lemos, R., Garlan, D., Ghezzi, C., Giese, H. (eds.) Software Engineering for Self-Adaptive Systems III. Assurances. LNCS, vol. 9640, pp. 223–248. Springer, Cham (2017). https://doi.org/10.1007/978-3-319-74183-3_8

19. Chang, E., Manna, Z., Pnueli, A.: The safety-progress classification. In: Bauer, F.L., Brauer, W., Schwichtenberg, H. (eds.) LAS. NATO ASI Series, vol. 94, pp. 143–202. Springer, Heidelberg (1993). https://doi.org/10.1007/978-3-642-58041-3_5

20. Chatterjee, K., Doyen, L.: Energy and mean-payoff parity Markov decision processes. In: Murlak, F., Sankowski, P. (eds.) MFCS 2011. LNCS, vol. 6907, pp. 206–218. Springer, Heidelberg (2011). https://doi.org/10.1007/978-3-642-22993-0_21

21. Chatterjee, K., Doyen, L., Henzinger, T.A.: Quantitative languages. ACM Trans. Comput. Logic 11(4) (2010). https://doi.org/10.1145/1805950.1805953

22. Chatterjee, K., Henzinger, T.A., Otop, J.: Quantitative monitor automata. In: Rival, X. (ed.) SAS 2016. LNCS, vol. 9837, pp. 23–38. Springer, Heidelberg (2016). https://doi.org/10.1007/978-3-662-53413-7_2

23. Cimatti, A., Tian, C., Tonetta, S.: Assumption-based runtime verification of infinite-state systems. In: Feng, L., Fisman, D. (eds.) RV 2021. LNCS, vol. 12974, pp. 207–227. Springer, Cham (2021). https://doi.org/10.1007/978-3-030-88494-9_11

24. Considine, J., Li, F., Kollios, G., Byers, J.W.: Approximate aggregation techniques for sensor databases. In: Özsoyoglu, Z.M., Zdonik, S.B. (eds.) Proceedings of the 20th International Conference on Data Engineering, ICDE 2004, 30 March - 2 April 2004, Boston, MA, USA, pp. 449–460. IEEE Computer Society (2004). https://doi.org/10.1109/ICDE.2004.1320018

25. Cousot, P.: Abstract interpretation. ACM Comput. Surv. (CSUR) 28(2), 324–328 (1996)

26. d'Angelo, B., et al.: Lola: runtime monitoring of synchronous systems. In: 12th International Symposium on Temporal Representation and Reasoning (TIME2005), pp. 166–174. IEEE (2005)

27. De Giacomo, G., Vardi, M.Y.: Linear temporal logic and linear dynamic logic on finite traces. In: IJCAI2013 Proceedings of the Twenty-Third international joint conference on Artificial Intelligence, pp. 854–860. Association for Computing Machinery (2013)

28. Decker, N., Leucker, M., Thoma, D.: Impartiality and anticipation for monitoring of visibly context-free properties. In: Legay, A., Bensalem, S. (eds.) RV 2013. LNCS, vol. 8174, pp. 183–200. Springer, Heidelberg (2013). https://doi.org/10.1007/978-3-642-40787-1_11

29. Eisner, C., et al.: Reasoning with temporal logic on truncated paths. In: Hunt, W.A., Somenzi, F. (eds.) CAV 2003. LNCS, vol. 2725, pp. 27–39. Springer, Heidelberg (2003). https://doi.org/10.1007/978-3-540-45069-6_3

30. Falcone, Y., Fernandez, J.C., Mounier, L.: What can you verify and enforce at runtime? Int. J. Softw. Tools Technol. Transfer 14(3), 349–382 (2012)

31. Ferrère, T., Henzinger, T.A., Kragl, B.: Monitoring event frequencies. In: 28th EACSL Annual Conference on Computer Science Logic (CSL 2020), Schloss Dagstuhl-Leibniz-Zentrum für Informatik (2020)

32. Ferrère, T., Henzinger, T.A., Saraç, N.E.: A theory of register monitors. In: Proceedings of the 33rd Annual ACM/IEEE Symposium on Logic in Computer Science, pp. 394–403 (2018)

33. Forejt, V., Kwiatkowska, M., Norman, G., Parker, D., Qu, H.: Quantitative multi-objective verification for probabilistic systems. In: Abdulla, P., Leino, K.R.M. (eds.) TACAS 2011. LNCS, vol. 6605, pp. 112–127. Springer, Heidelberg (2011). https://doi.org/10.1007/978-3-642-19835-9_11

34. Francalanza, A., et al.: A foundation for runtime monitoring. In: Lahiri, S., Reger, G. (eds.) Runtime Verification. RV 2017. LNCS, vol. 10548. Springer, Cham (2017). https://doi.org/10.1007/978-3-319-67531-2_2

35. Halamish, S., Kupferman, O.: Approximating deterministic lattice automata. In: Chakraborty, S., Mukund, M. (eds.) ATVA 2012. LNCS, pp. 27–41. Springer, Heidelberg (2012). https://doi.org/10.1007/978-3-642-33386-6_4

36. Henzinger, T.A., Saraç, N.E.: Monitorability under assumptions. In: Deshmukh, J., Nickovic, D. (eds.) Runtime Verification. RV 2020. LNCS, vol. 12399. Springer, Heidelberg (2020). https://doi.org/10.1007/978-3-030-60508-7_1

37. Henzinger, T.A., Saraç, N.E.: Quantitative and approximate monitoring. In: 2021 36th Annual ACM/IEEE Symposium on Logic in Computer Science (LICS), pp. 1–14. IEEE (2021)

38. Ho, H.-M., Ouaknine, J., Worrell, J.: Online monitoring of metric temporal logic. In: Bonakdarpour, B., Smolka, S.A. (eds.) RV 2014. LNCS, vol. 8734, pp. 178–192. Springer, Cham (2014). https://doi.org/10.1007/978-3-319-11164-3_15

39. Holzmann, G.J., Smith, M.H.: Automating software feature verification. Bell Labs Tech. J. 5(2), 72–87 (2000). https://doi.org/10.1002/bltj.2223

40. Jakšić, S., Bartocci, E., Grosu, R., Nguyen, T., Ničković, D.: Quantitative monitoring of STL with edit distance. Formal Methods Syst. Des. 53(1), 83–112 (2018)

41. Kwiatkowska, M.: Quantitative verification: models techniques and tools. In: Proceedings of the the 6th Joint Meeting of the European Software Engineering Conference and the ACM SIGSOFT Symposium on The Foundations of Software Engineering, pp. 449–458. ESEC-FSE 2007, Association for Computing Machinery, New York, NY, USA (2007). https://doi.org/10.1145/1287624.1287688

42. Landauer, R.: Irreversibility and heat generation in the computing process. IBM J. Res. Dev. 5(3), 183–191 (1961). https://doi.org/10.1147/rd.53.0183

43. Maler, O., Nickovic, D.: Monitoring temporal properties of continuous signals. In: Lakhnech, Y., Yovine, S. (eds.) FORMATS/FTRTFT -2004. LNCS, vol. 3253, pp. 152–166. Springer, Heidelberg (2004). https://doi.org/10.1007/978-3-540-30206-3_12

44. Mamouras, K., Chattopadhyay, A., Wang, Z.: Algebraic quantitative semantics for efficient online temporal monitoring. In: TACAS 2021. LNCS, vol. 12651, pp. 330–348. Springer, Cham (2021). https://doi.org/10.1007/978-3-030-72016-2_18

45. Mamouras, K., Chattopadhyay, A., Wang, Z.: A compositional framework for quantitative online monitoring over continuous-time signals. In: Feng, L., Fisman, D. (eds.) RV 2021. LNCS, vol. 12974, pp. 142–163. Springer, Cham (2021). https://doi.org/10.1007/978-3-030-88494-9_8

46. Mostafa, M., Bonakdarpour, B.: Decentralized runtime verification of LTL specifications in distributed systems. In: 2015 IEEE International Parallel and Distributed Processing Symposium, IPDPS 2015, Hyderabad, India, 25–29 May 2015, pp. 494–503. IEEE Computer Society (2015). https://doi.org/10.1109/IPDPS.2015.95

47. Nia, M.A., Kargahi, M., Faghih, F.: Probabilistic approximation of runtime quantitative verification in self-adaptive systems. Microprocess. Microsyst. 72, 102943 (2020). https://doi.org/10.1016/j.micpro.2019.102943

48. Piterman, N., Pnueli, A.: Temporal logic and fair discrete systems. In: Handbook of Model Checking, pp. 27–73. Springer, Cham (2018). https://doi.org/10.1007/978-3-319-10575-8_2

49. Shrivastava, N., Buragohain, C., Agrawal, D., Suri, S.: Medians and beyond: new aggregation techniques for sensor networks. In: Stankovic, J.A., Arora, A., Govindan, R. (eds.) Proceedings of the 2nd International Conference on Embedded Networked Sensor Systems, SenSys 2004, Baltimore, MD, USA, 3–5 Nov 2004, pp. 239–249. ACM (2004). https://doi.org/10.1145/1031495.1031524

50. Silberstein, A., Braynard, R., Yang, J.: Constraint chaining: on energy-efficient continuous monitoring in sensor networks. In: Chaudhuri, S., Hristidis, V., Polyzotis, N. (eds.) Proceedings of the ACM SIGMOD International Conference on Management of Data, Chicago, Illinois, USA, 27–29 June 2006, pp. 157–168. ACM (2006). https://doi.org/10.1145/1142473.1142492

51. Stucki, S., Sánchez, C., Schneider, G., Bonakdarpour, B.: Gray-box monitoring of hyperproperties with an application to privacy. Formal Methods Syst. Des. **58**(1), 126–159 (2021). https://doi.org/10.1007/s10703-020-00358-w

52. Toffoli, T.: Reversible computing. In: de Bakker, J., van Leeuwen, J. (eds.) ICALP 1980. LNCS, vol. 85, pp. 632–644. Springer, Heidelberg (1980). https://doi.org/10.1007/3-540-10003-2_104

53. Wang, C., Yang, Y., Gupta, A., Gopalakrishnan, G.: Dynamic model checking with property driven pruning to detect race conditions. In: Cha, S., Choi, J.-Y., Kim, M., Lee, I., Viswanathan, M. (eds.) ATVA 2008. LNCS, vol. 5311, pp. 126–140. Springer, Heidelberg (2008). https://doi.org/10.1007/978-3-540-88387-6_11

54. Zhang, X., Leucker, M., Dong, W.: Runtime verification with predictive semantics. In: Goodloe, A.E., Person, S. (eds.) NFM 2012. LNCS, vol. 7226, pp. 418–432. Springer, Heidelberg (2012). https://doi.org/10.1007/978-3-642-28891-3_37

# Runtime Verification of Kotlin Coroutines

Denis Furian[1], Shaun Azzopardi[2(✉)], Yliès Falcone[3], and Gerardo Schneider[2]

[1] Opera Software AB, Gothenburg, Sweden
denisf@opera.com
[2] University of Gothenburg, Gothenburg, Sweden
shaun.azzopardi@gu.se, gerardo.schneider@gu.se
[3] University Grenoble Alpes, CNRS, Grenoble INP, Inria, LIG, 38000 Grenoble, France
ylies.falcone@univ-grenoble-alpes.fr

**Abstract.** Kotlin was introduced to Android as the recommended language for development. One of the unique functionalities of Kotlin is that of coroutines, which are lightweight tasks that can run concurrently inside threads. Programming using coroutines is difficult, among other things, because they can move between threads and behave unexpectedly. We introduce runtime verification in Kotlin. We provide a language to write properties and produce runtime monitors tailored to verify Kotlin coroutines. We identify, formalise and runtime verify seven properties about common runtime errors that are not easily identifiable by static analysis. To demonstrate the acceptability of the technique in real applications, we apply our framework to an in-house Android app and micro-benchmarks and measure the execution time and memory overheads.

## 1 Introduction

*Coroutines* were introduced at the beginning of the 1960s by Joel Erdwinn and Melvin E. Conway to achieve separability in the context of compiler optimisation (for COBOL) [6]. Coroutines have been the object of discussion and analysis after their introduction (see, for instance, Clarke's paper about the correctness of coroutines [4] and the more recent survey [20][1]), but they only became "fashionable" again with their introduction in the Kotlin programming language.

Though coroutines have been defined in slightly different ways, in a nutshell, they are programming language control structures with the following characterising features [19]: i) the values of the coroutine local data persist between

---

[1] See also references therein for different uses of coroutines (e.g., for simulation, in artificial intelligence, text processing, etc.).

S. Azzopardi—Supported by ERC Consolidator grant D-SynMA (No. 772459).
Y. Falcone—Supported by the Région Auvergne-Rhône-Alpes within the "Pack Ambition Recherche" programme, the H2020- ECSEL-2018-IA call - Grant Agreement number 826276 (CPS4EU), the French ANR project ANR-20-CE39-0009 (SEVERITAS), and LabEx PERSYVAL-Lab (ANR-11-LABX-0025-01).

T. Dang and V. Stolz (Eds.): RV 2022, LNCS 13498, pp. 221–239, 2022.
https://doi.org/10.1007/978-3-031-17196-3_12

successive calls; ii) the execution of a coroutine is suspended as control leaves it, only to carry on where it left off when control re-enters the coroutine at some later stage. Besides, de Moura and Ierusalimschy [20] write: "We can identify three main issues that distinguish different kinds of coroutine facilities: i) the control-transfer mechanism, which can provide *symmetric* or *asymmetric* coroutines; ii) whether coroutines are provided in the language as *first-class* objects, which can be freely manipulated by the programmer, or as constrained constructs; iii) whether a coroutine is implemented as a *stackful* construct, that is, whether it can suspend its execution from within nested calls."

We consider the use of coroutines in the Kotlin programming language. In theory, the use of coroutines seems straightforward and appealing. In practice, though, its use is far from being unproblematic: as with many other concurrency constructs, it is difficult to determine how they would behave at execution time. Why is it difficult to program with coroutines? Many things can go wrong; we just mention a couple of issues to make our point. An example of undesirable behaviour is a coroutine holding references to an object that has since been destroyed: this often happens in Android, where most components have their own lifecycle. Such behaviour results in memory leaks during execution. Another problem is when a coroutine executes using an undesirable dispatcher and an I/O operation is carried out inside a thread dedicated to the UI: since operations like this can cause the UI to be slowed down or become unresponsive, the Android OS attempts to crash the whole application by throwing a `NetworkOnMainThreadException` at runtime.

These examples illustrate the difficulty in ensuring, statically, that coroutines will behave as expected. Consequently, the best we can do is to identify specific harmful situations during execution and try to prevent the error from happening, or at least to identify and report on the error. Runtime verification (RV) can help programmers, before deployment to debug their software (as for testing) or after deployment to identify (and prevent) errors and eventually correct them.

In this paper, we are concerned with the runtime verification of coroutines in general and, particularly, in Kotlin. We design properties concerning what could go wrong when programming using coroutines and use runtime verification techniques to monitor them. Our ultimate goal is to develop a dedicated tool that allows users to write properties in a declarative language (from which a monitor could automatically be extracted) tailored to monitor programs using coroutines during execution. As a first step, we start by targeting Kotlin developers who might want to use runtime verification during testing as a debugging tool. For that, we implemented in Kotlin monitors for properties that capture many cases not easily, if at all, detectable by manual code inspection or static analysis.

More concretely, our contributions are as follows:

1. We identify seven properties concerning coroutines which, if not satisfied, may cause undesirable behaviour (Sect. 3);
2. We propose a declarative property language for coroutines (Sect. 4);
3. We present an RV algorithm for the above language (Sect. 5);
4. We implement the properties discussed in Sect. 3, as coroutines and discuss their effectiveness (Sect. 6).

Related work is described in Sect. 7 and concluding remarks are given in Sect. 8. In the next section, we summarise the main differences between Kotlin and Java and explain some coroutines' features.

## 2    Background: Coroutines in Kotlin

Kotlin is a programming language whose main features are its interoperability with Java and the native support of asynchronous programming via coroutines[2]. While it was developed in 2011 by JetBrains, it has been officially supported for Android development alongside Java since October 2017 until it became the preferred language by Google in 2019. Kotlin can be compiled to JVM bytecode, JavaScript or native code via LLVM. Compiling to JVM bytecode makes Kotlin easy to interoperate with Java and *vice versa*, despite the few but noticeable differences between the two languages. These include the handling of exceptions (always unhandled in Kotlin), and support for non-nullable types and coroutines.

In Kotlin, coroutines employ structured concurrency, which means that entry and exit points must be made clear and all tasks are either completed or cancelled before the end of the execution [22].

A Kotlin coroutine runs inside a thread, and a thread can run several coroutines: they follow a pattern of *suspend/resume* where they can be suspended at any time, their state is saved and then restored whenever they resume, as mentioned in the previous section. A coroutine can also suspend on one thread and resume on another after transferring its state. This can happen, for example, when a coroutine runs on a multithreaded dispatcher [16] such as `Dispatchers.Default`, which uses a number of threads between two and the number of CPU cores.

In order to handle mutual exclusion, Kotlin provides a coroutine-specific class called `Mutex`. This contains a suspend function `lock()` that allows the caller to gain exclusive access to a portion of code. The complementary function `unlock()` releases the lock and must be called before any other coroutine can gain access to the critical section. In other words, a coroutine that invokes `Mutex.lock()` and then crashes without invoking `Mutex.unlock()` will consistently starve any other jobs waiting on that lock. Since a coroutine may terminate at any given time, the `Mutex` class provides a functional block `withLock` that automatically requests the lock. It then releases it no matter what before termination.

The Kotlin standard library also provides a more conventional tool for mutual exclusion in the form of the `Lock` class. This class is, however, intended for use with threads and attempting to gain a lock inside a coroutine will make the whole thread dormant and disabled for scheduling.

*Types of Coroutines in Kotlin.* A coroutine can be executed in multiple ways and this comes with heavily different use-cases.

– A standard job that executes a block of code without returning any value is created with the method `launch`.

---

[2] Kotlin's documentation can be found in [15]. Here we give a brief background of Kotlin features pertinent to our work.

– A job that is expected to return a value is created with the method `async`: this returns an instance of the `Deferred` class. Using the `await` method on the deferred object will suspend the current coroutine until a value is returned. If the coroutine is cancelled before it can return a value, however, awaiting the deferred object will throw an exception.

*Creation of a Coroutine.* The methods discussed, `launch` and `async`, are called "coroutine builders" since they prompt the creation of a new coroutine to run the asynchronous task. Both must be invoked inside a *coroutine scope*, which delimits the coroutine lifetime following the principle of structured concurrency.

Coroutines are suspendable. The `await` method (from the `Deferred` class) is one example of a suspending function. Depending on the coroutine scope, different behaviour is exhibited during suspension. The couroutine may be blocking (through the `runBlocking` coroutine builder), in which case the coroutine calling a suspending function will block the whole thread until all its tasks are completed. It can also be just suspending, were calling a suspending function releases the thread to do other work.

The scope contains the *coroutine context*: a composite object containing the job to be executed as well as its dispatcher, which determines what thread (or threads) the coroutine uses for its execution.

A *dispatcher*, either custom or provided by a library, can be explicitly assigned to a coroutine when used as argument for the builder function: for example, `launch { foo() }` will use the same context as the parent task while `launch(Dispatchers.IO) { foo() }` will use the base I/O dispatcher. The library `kotlinx.coroutines` provides three base dispatchers as well as methods for generating thread pools:

– `Dispatchers.Default` uses a common pool of shared background threads and is used normally by all builders if no other dispatcher is specified;
– `Dispatchers.IO` is designed for blocking operations that are I/O-intensive, like file up- or downloads;
– `Dispatchers.Unconfined` starts coroutine execution in the current thread until the first suspension and then allows it to resume in whatever thread the corresponding suspending function uses: using this dispatcher takes control away from the programmer and leads to potentially unwanted results, so it is discouraged by JetBrains.

The *job* inside the coroutine context is used for tracking the coroutine's parent and children. This is needed when enforcing structured concurrency in order to ensure that the children do not outlive the parents. It is also possible to spawn an independent coroutine by using a new `Job` instance as an argument to either builder function.

The job and dispatcher can be combined inside a builder arguments list, while, it is possible to retrieve their values as entries of the `coroutineContext` instance, as follows:

```
launch(Dispatchers.IO + Job()) {
 println( "Running job ${coroutineContext[Job]} on " +
        "dispatcher ${coroutineContext[CoroutineDispatcher]}") }
```

*Termination of a Coroutine.* The execution of a coroutine can be cancelled at any time by invoking the `CoroutineScope`'s `cancel` method: this causes a `CancellationException` to be sent to that coroutine. This is not treated as a "real" exception as much as a prompt to terminate. Any coroutine receiving this exception will quickly execute the following steps: i) execute any code it might find inside a `finally` block; ii) recursively cancel all of its children (by forwarding the same `CancellationException` to them; and then iii) terminate.

If the coroutine was created from `async`, executing the `await` call will throw the `CancellationException`; otherwise the coroutine will simply terminate.

Any other kind of exception will result in the coroutine's termination. Since coroutines follow the paradigm of structured concurrency, cancellation, in this case, is propagated both downstream and upstream. This means that both the children *and the parent* of the failed coroutine will terminate. There is one way to prevent the cancellation from propagating upstream: the failing coroutine must be spawned by a `SupervisorJob`. In this case, the parent will not be affected by the failure and will simply receive the exception that caused the failure.

Note that catching an exception in a `try-catch` block will not prevent termination. It may, however, allow for a quick handling such as, for example, logging. Any code inside a `finally` block will be executed.

## 3 Informal Description of Properties

Because of the various features and perks of both the Kotlin language and Android development, we have identified seven properties that should be monitored, which we index and describe in this section.

Of these seven, properties 1 and 7 are about coroutines outliving their caller and the subsequent risk of leaking memory mentioned earlier; properties 5 and 6 address the possibility that a coroutine may run inside an undesirable dispatcher, with serious risks of fatal crashes as a consequence; properties 2, 3 and 4 concern how Kotlin handles successful and failed tasks, as well as how exception traces may be lost when a crash takes place in an asynchronous computation. When this work was performed properties 2 and 3 were concerning, but Kotlin now handles these by design (from v1.4). We consider them for completeness.

Other undesirable scenarios, like the one presented in the first property, can now be avoided by making use of first-party libraries which provide, for example, coroutine scopes that are lifecycle-aware.

We present a summary of all relevant properties at the end of this section.

### 3.1 Property 1: DestroyedWithOwner

Coroutines execute a given block of code which may or may not contain references to an Android lifecycle component. We do not go into detail of what these are, but these components are destroyed and recreated arbitrarily and we do not want them to persist inside an asynchronous task as that would leak memory.

RV is required since the destruction of a lifecycle component does not happen regularly and can be triggered by events external to the app (like the device battery running low) or to the device itself (like the user rotating the screen).

Static analysis could be used before the execution to ensure, for example, that a lifecyle-aware coroutine scope is being used: a scope like this can be tailor-made or imported from the official ktx library, but there is no guarantee that a programmer will be doing either. This makes RV more desirable as it does not necessarily impose a restriction on the programmer's choice of libraries.

### 3.2  Property 2: NormalAsync

If a given block of code is executed without any failures, it will yield a certain return value depending on the type of coroutine on which it was running:

– launched tasks will yield Unit, the Kotlin equivalent of Java's void;
– async tasks will yield a Deferred<T> value, i.e. a "future" result that eventually evaluates to a value of type T.

Either of these scenarios is the "optimal" behaviour for its kind of task. This property is only broken when a coroutine throws an exception as a "successful" scenario, e.g., a launched task that executes on an infinite loop, throwing a RuntimeException to force termination, as for the following code snippet:

```
suspend fun foo() { if (goodScenario()) doThings()
                    else throw RuntimeException() }
```

To help ensure JetBrains' recommendation that exceptions should not be used as return values, a monitor can be used to identify and notify when exceptions are yielded by coroutines (which may not be as easily determinable by static analysis as in the previous example).

### 3.3  Property 3: ExceptionalAsync

An exception thrown inside an async coroutine will flag the current context for termination; the only outliers are cancellation exceptions, which are seen as "normal" termination directives rather than crashes.

Thrown exceptions should ideally be stored in the current context or in another *throwable* saved in the current context, to avoid losing information about the crash. In the newer versions of Kotlin (from v1.4), exceptions thrown after a crash are stored inside the field Exception.suppressed. The exception is then thrown upon the invocation of await, ensuring that all crash data is available for the programmer to handle, as exemplified in the following code:

```
fun main() = runBlocking {
    val deferred = GlobalScope.async { throwOneAndSuppress(10000) }
    try { deferred.await() }
    catch (e: Exception) {
        println("Suppressed ${e.suppressed.size} exceptions") }}

suspend fun throwOneAndSuppress(amount: Int) = coroutineScope {
    repeat(amount) { launch {
```

```
        try { delay(Long.MAX_VALUE) }
        finally { throw ArithmeticException() }}}
launch { delay(100L) // This will be thrown first.
        throw IOException() }
delay(Long.MAX_VALUE) }
```

For versions of Kotlin that do not support this, we considered monitoring as a way to collect these exceptions.

### 3.4   Property 4: NeedHandler

Any exception thrown inside `launch` coroutines should be rethrown between parent tasks all the way until the `CoroutineExceptionHandler` at the top level handles the failure. As mentioned for the previous property, exceptions should be stored to preserve information about the crash. In the case of `launch` jobs, this means that the context needs an exception handler that carries exception data rather than simply crashing. The exception thrown references other failures that occurred after it inside the field `Exception.suppressed` and all the information can then be accessed from the handler. The following snippet represents a compliant scenario where the function `throwOneAndSuppress` from the previous example is started with a `launch` rather than `async` coroutine builder:

```
fun main() = runBlocking {
    val handler = CoroutineExceptionHandler { _, exception ->
        println("Suppressed ${exception.suppressed.size} exceptions") }
    val job = GlobalScope.launch(handler) {
        throwOneAndSuppress(10000) }
    job.join() }
```

Here, instrumentation can be used to enforce automatically the propagation of exceptions happening inside a `launch` coroutine upwards.

### 3.5   Property 5: NoBlockUI

Android apps should leave the UI thread as lightweight as possible and avoid blocking it with heavy and/or slow computations. Some scenarios are downright forbidden, like when an I/O operation is executed on the UI thread. In these situations the Android runtime will launch a `NetworkOnMainThreadException`.

As an example, let us consider an app that reads a JSON stream from an endpoint and uses it to update some components on the screen. The reading and the UI update are carried out inside suspend functions that execute in whatever context they are launched in. The view model invokes them in the background whenever the activity is resumed, and then the activity itself invokes them every time the user presses a refresh button. The expectation is that the app loads and displays the data when the activity is started and then repeats the operation every time the refresh button is pressed or every time the app returns to the foreground. The actual scenario is that the app will crash as soon as the activity is started, as the view model invokes the read coroutine (on the UI thread), triggering a `NetworkOnMainThreadException`.

Kotlin does not issue any warnings about this possibility. Static analysis could be developed to ensure the correct dispatcher is used for each task, assuming a precise-enough analysis. RV instead provides us with a lightweight method, and allows for possible enforcement.

### 3.6    Property 6: UpdateUI

In a similar situation as the one above, when a background thread tries to access UI elements, the Android runtime throws a `CalledFromWrongThreadException`. This can be seen in the code example below, where the methods `okState` and `errorState` update the screen with the outcome of a network operation, and thus use within a view model (a UI element) will cause the system to crash.

```
private suspend fun getJson(uri: String) = coroutineScope {
    try { URL(uri).readText().let { data: String ->
        val parsedData = parseJsonResponse(data)
        if (parsedData is Failure) { errorState("Error: $uri") }
        else { okState(parsedData.getOrThrow()) }}}
    catch (e: Exception) { errorState(e.toString()) }}
```

### 3.7    Property 7: ResumeIfNeeded

Under the hood, coroutines are a sequence of callbacks that are suspended at one or more points in their execution. These *suspend points* can be traced back to any invocation of a `suspend` function inside a coroutine code block. The code inside a coroutine is executed until a suspend point is reached: here, the coroutine returns a special value to *warn* its dispatcher that its execution is not finished. Later, the dispatcher checks whether the coroutine is suspended, complete or cancelled, and, in the first case, it resumes the coroutine; the execution will start right after from the last suspend point.

In cases where computation takes a large amount of time to complete, however, there might not be a chance for the dispatcher to check for cancellation. It is good practice to check the flag `isActive`, which returns `false` whenever the current coroutine is not supposed to execute anymore; there is also an `ensureActive` method that throws a `CancellationException` unless the `isActive` flag is `true`. These checks are executed at runtime so it would be appropriate to ensure at runtime that a task is only completed if necessary.

Let us consider an asynchronous task that is set to download a large file and store it in the user's smartphone. This task is launched inside a coroutine that starts the download process. The Android activity is suddenly terminated: we *ideally* want the download to be interrupted. The scope used to launch the coroutine will determine whether the task is allowed to continue or not: if the coroutine context is tied to the activity, it will notify the download task (along with any other tasks) of the activity having terminated using a `CancellationException`.

## 3.8  Properties Summarised

- *DestroyedWithOwner*: any coroutine launched from a component with a lifecycle should be destroyed together with it to avoid memory leaks;
- *NormalAsync*: coroutines should not throw exceptions as special return values but, rather, reserve their use for failures;
- *ExceptionalAsync*: multiple exceptions occurring inside an `async` coroutine should all be able to be tracked and retrieved, rather than only one of them;
- *NeedHandler*: any `launch` coroutine should have a handler that keeps track of exceptions;
- *NoBlockUI*: coroutines that are launched from the UI thread should keep the thread lightweight;
- *UpdateUI*: coroutines that are not launched from the UI thread should never interact with UI elements;
- *ResumeIfNeeded*: coroutines carrying out slow computations should check periodically that they are still needed.

# 4  A Coroutine-Aware Specification Language

We define a tailor-made version of LTL for coroutines in the context of Kotlin. Our requirements were the ability to specify the behaviour of coroutines and their relation to other objects (e.g., scopes and threads). We add a first-class notion of coroutines, allowing quantification over them. We consider a set of events that allow relating coroutines with other objects in the language and relating coroutines with each other. To allow for this, our alphabet is two-layered: general program events and events tied to a coroutine.

**Definition 1.** *A* corLTL *specification* $\pi$ *is defined by the following grammar:*

$$\Sigma_x \stackrel{\text{def}}{=} LaunchType\ x \mid AsyncType\ x \mid Running\ x \mid Active\ x \mid Blocked\ x \mid$$
$$OnMainThread\ x \mid TransferToMainThread\ x \mid HasActiveScope\ x \mid ...$$

$$\psi_x \stackrel{\text{def}}{=} \Sigma \mid \Sigma_x \mid \pi \mid \psi_x \wedge \psi_x \mid \psi_x \mid X\psi_x \mid \psi_x U\psi_x$$

$$\pi \stackrel{\text{def}}{=} \pi \wedge \pi \mid \neg\pi \mid \forall x : coroutines \cdot \psi_x$$

We define disjunction ($\vee$), globally ($G$), eventually ($F$), and existential quantification ($\exists$) as usual. We limit ourselves to well-formed formulas where every variable appearing in the formula is bound. We assume predicates and relations are typed, and use only well-typed formulas. We assume a static number $n$ of coroutines that all exist at the start of a program, with unique identifiers from $ID = \{0, ..., n\}$. We then can define system traces as sequences over sets of $\Sigma \cup \{p_n \mid p_x \in \Sigma_x \wedge i \in ID\}$. We number events to relate to a coroutine (e.g., $p_1$ and $p_1'$ are about the coroutine with identifier *1*).

The semantics of corLTL extends that of LTL to reason about coroutines.

**Definition 2 (Semantics).** *We say the infinite trace* $w$ *is a* model *of* $\pi$, *denoted by* $w \models \pi$, *according to the rules in Fig. 1.*

$$w \models \pi \wedge \pi' \overset{\text{def}}{=} w \models \pi \wedge w \models \pi'$$

$$w \models \neg\pi \overset{\text{def}}{=} \neg(w \models \pi)$$

$$w \models \forall x : coroutines \cdot \psi \overset{\text{def}}{=} \forall i \in ID \cdot w \models \psi[x/i]$$

$$w \models p \overset{\text{def}}{=} p \in w[0]$$

$$w \models p_n \overset{\text{def}}{=} p_n \in w[0]$$

$$w \models X\psi \overset{\text{def}}{=} w_1 \models \psi$$

$$w \models \psi \wedge \psi' \overset{\text{def}}{=} w \models \psi \wedge w \models \psi'$$

$$w \models \neg\psi \overset{\text{def}}{=} \neg(w \models \psi)$$

$$w \models \psi U \psi' \overset{\text{def}}{=} \exists j \cdot w_j \models \psi' \wedge \forall k \cdot 0 \le k < j \implies w_k \models \psi$$

**Fig. 1.** corLTL semantics where $w_x$ denotes the $x$-th strict suffix of $w$.

With appropriate events, we can capture the properties from the previous section and more.

*Example 1.* A coroutine can only be active if its scope is still active: $\forall x : coroutines \cdot G(active(x) \implies hasActiveScope(s))$.

*Example 2.* When a coroutine is doing an I/O operation, then it currently is on a background thread: $\forall x : coroutines \cdot G(doingIO(x) \implies \neg onMainThread(x))$.

*Example 3.* When a coroutine is updating the UI then it is on the main thread: $\forall x : coroutines \cdot G(updatingUI(x) \implies onMainThread(x))$.

We can also express application-specific properties.

*Example 4.* A job is handled only once: $\forall x : coroutines \cdot G(handledJob(x) \implies XG(\neg handledJob(x)))$.

## 5  Monitoring Kotlin Coroutines

In this section, we discuss monitoring for corLTL specifications. Since corLTL has the full power of LTL, it is not fully monitorable, instead in this language we focus on the safety subset of corLTL, consisting of the negation normal form (NNF) and until/release-free subset. Thus we restrict $\psi$ in Definition 2 with negation only on the atomic events (and $\pi$), without until but with *weak until* ($W$). We consider two options for monitoring for this sub-language.

**Standard LTL Monitoring.** One could try to re-use standard LTL monitoring for our tailor-made logic, by transforming a corLTL formula into a standard LTL formula by eliminating the quantifiers recursively as follows: $\forall x : coroutines \cdot \psi \iff \bigwedge_{i \in ID} \psi[x/i]$.

Each coroutine could be instrumented to output appropriately labelled events to a channel that is only listened to by a monitor for this quantifier-free formula. However, this transformation is exponential in the number of nested quantifiers. It bears asking then whether nested quantifiers are useful. The basic properties about coroutines we have detailed do not require these, but program-specific properties may require the power of nested quantifiers, for example:

*Example 5.* If a coroutine holds a resource then no other coroutine also holds it: $\forall x : coroutines \cdot HoldsResource\ x \implies \nexists y : coroutines \cdot HoldsResource\ y$.

Instead of paying the cost for the exponential transformation, we next explore the option to distribute monitoring over the coroutines through automata communicating through channels.

**Communicating Automata.** Given a specification, assign every quantification with an identifier from $\mathbb{N}$, abstract each away by replacing it with an event $e^j$ ($j$ corresponding to the identifier of the quantified sub-formula). Then the specification becomes an LTL formula over $\Sigma \cup \{e^j | j \in \mathbb{N}\}$. For Example 5 we can assign the event $e^0$ to $\nexists y : coroutines \cdot HoldsResource\ y$, and $e^1$ to $\forall x : coroutines \cdot HoldsResource\ x \implies e^0$, and the top-level formula is just $e^1$.

A monitor can be extracted for the top-level formula, and other monitors for the formula corresponding to each $e^j$. An issue is that the value of $e^j$ at a time-step $t$ may only be knowable in a future time-step, e.g. if $e^j = \forall x : coroutines \cdot Xe$. The monitor would then have to branch on both values, and discard one of the branches when the value of $e^j$ is eventually set.

Here, for simplicity and as a first step, we further restrict the language by only allowing quantification at the high level of a formula ($\pi$), and disallowing quantification at the LTL level. Then we can re-use standard LTL synthesis for the LTL parts of the specifications and use communicating automata to monitor for the high-level logic. We illustrate our proposed approach with a variation on symbolic automaton monitors (e.g., [3,5]).

**Definition 3 (DEAC).** *A Dynamic Event Automaton with Channels (DEAC) is a tuple $D_x = \langle C_r, C_s, \Sigma, \Sigma_x, \Sigma_{\mathbb{C}}, Q, V, q_0, \theta_0, A, B, \rightarrow \rangle$, where $C_r, C_s \in \mathbb{C}$ are finite sets of channels (s.t. $C_r \cap C_s = \{\}$), $\Sigma$ is a finite alphabet, $\Sigma_x$ is a finite alphabet over a free variable $x$, $\Sigma_{\mathbb{C}}$ is a finite set of channel events, $Q$ is a finite set of states, $V$ is a finite set of variables, $q_0 \in Q$ is the initial state, $\theta_0 : V \rightarrow \mathbb{VAL}$ is the initial valuation of the variables $V$, $A \subseteq Q$ is the set of accepting states, $B \subseteq Q$ is the set of bad states, and $\rightarrow : Q \times (2^{\Sigma \cup \Sigma_x \cup (\Sigma_{\mathbb{C}} \times C_r)} \times V \rightarrow \{true, false\}) \rightarrow (2^{\Sigma_{\mathbb{C}} \times C_s} \times (V \rightarrow \mathbb{VAL}) \times Q)$ is the transition function guarded by sets of program, coroutine-specific, and channel events received from $C_r$, and the current variable valuation, and that can send events on $C_s$.*

*We write $q \xrightarrow{g \mapsto (out, a)} q'$ for $(q, g, out, a, q') \in \rightarrow$. We write $\neg D$ for the DEAC $D$ with the accepting and bad states swapped. We write $t \in L(D)$ when $t$ is a trace over events and channel events that reaches an accepting state in $D$.*

$$\frac{q \xrightarrow{g \mapsto (ecs',a)} q' \qquad g(E, ecs, \theta) \qquad q \notin A \cup B}{(q, \theta, ecs'') \xrightarrow{E} (q', a(E, ecs, \theta), (ecs'' \setminus 2^{\Sigma_C \times C_r}) \cup ecs')} \qquad \begin{array}{c} otherwise \\ \hline (q, (\theta, ecs)) \xrightarrow{E} (q, (\theta, ecs)) \end{array}$$

**Fig. 2.** DEAC semantics

$$\frac{q_1 \xrightarrow{g_1 \mapsto (ecs_1, a_1)} q_1' \qquad q_2 \xrightarrow{g_2 \mapsto (ecs_2, a_2)} q_2'}{(q_1, q_2) \xrightarrow{g_1 \wedge g_2 \mapsto (ecs_1 \cup ecs_2, a_1 \circ a_2)} (q_1', q_2')}$$

$$\frac{q_1 \xrightarrow{ecs|g_1 \mapsto (ecs_1, a_1)} q_1' \qquad q_2 \xrightarrow{ecs|g_2 \mapsto (ecs_2, a_2)} q_2'}{(q_1, q_2) \xrightarrow{ecs|g_1 \wedge \neg g_2 \mapsto (ecs_1, a_1)} (q_1', q_2)}$$

$$\frac{q_1 \xrightarrow{ecs|g_1 \mapsto (ecs_1, a_1)} q_1' \qquad \not\exists q_2 \xrightarrow{ecs|g_2 \mapsto (ecs_2, a_2)} q_2'}{(q_1, q_2) \xrightarrow{ecs|g_1 \mapsto (ecs_1, a_1)} (q_1', q_2)}$$

**Fig. 3.** Network of DEACs

We define our variation of DATEs, DEACs, here to include a semantics where a buffer of channel events is kept, with a DEAC consuming events sent on the channels it listening to ($C_r$).

**Definition 4.** *The* operational semantics of DEACs, *presented in Fig. 2, is given over configurations of triples of states, valuations* ($Q, V \rightarrow VAL$), *and sets of channel events, with transitions labelled by channel events.*

We characterise a network of DEACs that communicate with each other through these channel events as their composition.

**Definition 5.** *A* network *of two DEACs* $D_x^1$ *and* $D_y^2$, *with non-intersecting receive channels* ($C_r^1 \cap C_r^2 = \{\}$), *denoted by* $D_x^1 \| D_y^2$, *is a DEAC* $\langle C_r^1 \cup C_r^2, C_s^1 \cup C_s^2, \Sigma, \Sigma_x \cup \Sigma_y, \Sigma_C, Q^1 \times Q^2, V^1 \cup V^2, (q_0^1, q_0^2), (\theta_0^1, \theta_0^2), A^1 \times A^2, (B^1 \times Q^2) \cup (Q^1 \times B^2), \rightarrow \rangle$, *with the transition function* $\rightarrow$ *being the composition of both DEACs' transition functions as in Fig. 3 (the last two rules apply symmetrically for $D_y^2$).*

The safety subset of *LTL* is monitorable, and a corresponding deterministic finite-state automaton (doubly exponential in the size of the formula) exists [17]. We thus assume such construction from safety LTL formulas to DEACs, and we denote the DEAC corresponding to an LTL formula $\psi$ by $aut(\psi)$. For every LTL formula $\psi$, in a (restricted) corLTL specification, we assume a corresponding event, denoted by $e_\psi^v$, where $v \in \{\top, \bot\}$ denotes the verdict on $\psi$. We assume the construction of $aut(\psi)$ is such that $e_\psi^\top$ is outputted to a channel $c_x$ on accepting transitions, and $e_\psi^\bot$ is outputted to $c_x$ on bad transitions.

Given an LTL formula $\psi$ we define $D_\psi$ as the DEAC with $C = \{c_i \mid i \in ID\}$, $\Sigma_C = \{e_\psi^\top, e_\psi^\bot\}$, $Q = \{q_0, q_A, q_B\}$, $V = \{v_i \mid i \in ID\}$, $\theta_0$ sets every $v_i$ to $\bot$, $q_A$ being the only accepting state, $q_B$ being the only bad state, and with

$$mon(\forall x : coroutines \cdot \psi) \stackrel{\text{def}}{=} D_\psi \|(\|_{n \in ID} aut(\psi)[x/n]\rangle)$$

$$mon(\pi \wedge \pi') \stackrel{\text{def}}{=} mon(\pi)\|mon(\pi')$$

$$mon(\neg \pi) \stackrel{\text{def}}{=} \neg mon(\pi)$$

**Fig. 4.** Monitor construction for corLTL.

$$\rightarrow = \{q_0 \xrightarrow{\bigvee_{c \in C_r}(e_\psi^\perp, c) \in ecs \mapsto (\{\}, \bigwedge_{i \in ID}(e_\psi^\top, c_i) \in ecs \implies v_n' = \top)} q_0\} \cup \{q_0 \xrightarrow{\bigvee_{c \in C_r}(e_\psi^\perp, c) \in ecs}$$

$s_B\} \cup \{q_0 \xrightarrow{\bigwedge_{i \in ID} v_i} s_A\}$. Note how this automaton remains in $q_0$, setting $v_i$ to be true when $\psi$ is identified as true on $c_i$, while if all variables become true then there is a transition to the accepting state. If instead $\psi$ is false on some $c_i$ then there is a transition to a bad state.

A monitor (for a top-level safety formula) can be given as shown in Fig. 4. We can show correspondence between the infinite traces models of a property and the infinite traces accepted by a corresponding monitor:

**Theorem 1.** *For a safety corLTL formula* $\pi$: $w \models \pi \iff w \in L(mon(\pi))$.

However, note that the monitor may take an extra step to determine satisfaction given finite traces since $D_\psi$ separates the step of marking satisfying events and that of determining whether all the coroutines have satisfied the property. It should be clear that a monitor that does this at the same time can be constructed but would have more complex guards and actions.

## 6    Implementation and Evaluation

In order to monitor the properties identified earlier, we developed an API[3] that would be as transparent as possible to a developer. This was achieved by creating a new interface called `MonitoredComponent`, implemented by subclasses of `Activity` and `ViewModel` that would provide a familiar set of utilities and coroutine builders while carrying out the monitoring under the surface.

The interface holds records of any tasks started, as well as their dispatchers and exception handlers:

- `recommendedDispatchers`, a `HashMap` storing the best coroutine dispatcher to use with each task;
- `defaultHandler`, a `CoroutineExceptionHandler` that should be inserted into unhandled coroutine contexts according to *NeedHandler*;
- `monitoredApplication`, an accessor providing communication between the component and the `MonitoredApplication` instance.

The two implementations of `MonitoredComponent` provided by the API are `MonitoredActivity` and `MonitoredViewModel`. They expose an overloaded version of the coroutine builder methods that uses a lifecycle-aware scope by default

---

[3] The code can be found at https://gitlab.com/denf86/kotlin-rv.

(identified as the lifecycleScope and viewModelScope, respectively, both provided by kotlinx) to uphold the *DestroyedWithOwner* property.

Since tasks started via the launch method will only employ the handler at top level, the subclasses of MonitoredComponent try and extract a coroutine handler from inside the context. If no handler is found, the defaultHandler will be added so as to ensure that an instance of CoroutineExceptionHandler is present at all times. For example, any invocation of viewModelScope.launch { foo() } in a handler-less context is translated to viewModelScope.launch(defaultHandler) { foo() }. The MonitoredComponent has, however, no way of knowing whether the task currently being started lies in the top level or not.

In the case of the async coroutine builder, the MonitoredComponent focuses instead on re-throwing any exceptions according to *ExceptionalAsync*.

Any given instance of MonitoredComponent upholds the properties *SlowDownUI* and *UpdateUI* by means of runtime enforcement. While it has no way of knowing in advance what a block of code will do once executed, it remembers what a given block of code did during its last execution. In order to do so, it detects cases of CalledFromWrongThreadException and NetworkOnMainThreadException being thrown inside a coroutine and uses them to infer what thread may be a better choice should the same task be executed again. The component then adds an entry to the recommendedDispatchers consisting of the inferred ideal dispatcher and an identifier that was arbitrarily composed of class and name, as well as line number, of the method invoked inside the failed coroutine, read from the exception stack trace.

To provide an example, if the same I/O method readFromFile is launched inside a coroutine on the UI thread twice in a row:

- the first time will result in failure with a NetworkOnMainThreadException and the MonitoredComponent will update the recommendedDispatchers with a new entry Dispatchers.IO for this method;
- the second time, the MonitoredComponent will look up the entry created and overwrite the given dispatcher with Dispatchers.IO, allowing the method to execute correctly.

Since a task can fail for any given exception type outside of the above two, the MonitoredComponent internally replaces the first occurrence of either CalledFromWrongThreadException or NetworkOnMainThreadException with a newly-defined WrongDispatcherException, with the original as its cause, and rethrows it to the upper layer. At the top level, the CoroutineExceptionHandler can detect whether the crash was originally triggered by a WrongDispatcherException and only then will it save the new recommendedDispatchers entry.

The entries saved are stored inside a MonitoredApplication, which extends the standard Android application. Despite its name, the MonitoredApplication is not instrumented but only contains a map of the recommendedDispatchers collections for each MonitoredComponent in the app. The map is loaded by monitored component instances during their initialisation and updated by them before their deletion.

Right before the app is terminated, a service prints the content of each saved recommendedDispatchers map. This string is visible on the device log, which was thought to be a good compromise between storing everything in memory and creating an output file. The printout looks like this:

```
2020-01-15 12:06:38.035 12315-12315/com.android.rv D/Report:
Post-execution report for app com.android.rv.KotlinRV:
Component: com.android.rv.properties.BrowsePicturesViewModel
 com.android.rv.ViewKt$loadFrom$2$1.invokeSuspend:51 =>
    LimitingDispatcher@849932d[dispatcher = DefaultDispatcher]
 com.android.rv.ViewKt.loadFrom:47 => Main
Component: com.android.rv.properties.BrowsePicturesActivity
```

The output above means that the coroutine launched on l.51 of the loadFrom function (source file "View.kt") should use a dispatcher for background threads while the invocation on l.47 of the same function should use the UI thread.

*Application-Specific Properties.* We tested the API on a simple Android app developed ad-hoc: this application would look for images on an online repository and display them on screen after downloading their bytes in an asynchronous task in a coroutine. We identified some more properties to monitor, specific to the application at hand. We defined two new properties:

- *AlwaysOneJob* checks that only one task can look up images at a time: multiple lookup operations would overwrite the displayed list of images, resulting possibly in a waste of mobile data when the search button is double tapped;
- *SuccessWithJSON* checks that the app can normally execute in the case of the expected image data, which should always be a JSON object, being malformed or otherwise unreadable.

*Evaluation of the MonitoredComponent API.* After it had been tested and benchmarked on an ad-hoc Android app, the API was found to work on a general case but still needs some improvements. Overall, the recognition of thread-based crashes was found to not be foolproof: it could not handle a use case where the recommended dispatcher was not the best option, and it needed to experience a small number of crashes before the recommendedDispatchers map had enough entries to be reliable. Its main weakness was, in fact, the reliance on a task failing several times with the *right* exceptions.

The benchmarks, carried out using the Android Jetpack tools, showed that the overheads added by the API could grow significantly:

- tasks created with launch could be between 0.46–1.60% slower;
- tasks created with async could be between 0.45–0.86% slower;
- running a thousand async tasks in parallel could take between 56.43–144.49% more time while using the API.

**Table 1.** Sony device benchmarks.

| Test | Execution time (ms) | | Overhead | |
|---|---|---|---|---|
| | No monitors | Monitored | (ms) | (%) |
| Tasks created with `launch` | 1022 | 1039 | 17 | 1.60 |
| Tasks created with `async` | 1026 | 1034 | 8 | 0.86 |
| 1000 * parallel `async` | 1198 | 1873 | 675 | 56.43 |

**Table 2.** Huawei device benchmarks.

| Test | Execution time (ms) | | Overhead | |
|---|---|---|---|---|
| | No monitors | Monitored | (ms) | (%) |
| Tasks created with `launch` | 1008 | 1013 | 5 | 0.46 |
| Tasks created with `async` | 1008 | 1012 | 4 | 0.45 |
| 1000 * parallel `async` | 1446 | 3521 | 2075 | 144.49 |

Performance was measured with executing the same methods ten times on two smartphone models, a Sony Xperia XZ2 Compact H8324 and a Huawei Y6 ATU-L21. See the results in Table 1 (Table 2) for the Sony (Huawei) device.

The instrumented app was additionally tested for its memory footprint using Android Studio's built-in profiler. This exposed another weakness of the `recommendedDispatchers` map in that storing the class names as keys meant that the longer a name of a class, the more space it would take.

## 7    Related Work

Runtime verification of concurrency has mostly focused on checking generic properties such as deadlock freedom, the absence of data races, atomicity violations, etc. For this, specific approaches and tools exist, such as [1, 13, 14]. See [18] for a recent description of existing properties and approaches as well as [12] for some dedicated tools. In addition, approaches to monitoring user-provided properties in mono-threaded programs have been lifted to multithreaded ones as are. However, the soundness of the produced verdicts depends on the specifications and the program locations producing the events of interest [9].

The approach described in this paper is novel in that it introduces support for runtime verification in the Kotlin programming language. We note that, even though Kotlin compiles to (Java) bytecode, existing approaches to the monitoring of Java programs cannot be applied for our purposes. One originality of our approach is in the runtime verification of a specific concurrency construct, though we verify generic properties as well as program-specific properties. It is the specific form of structured concurrency that allows the design of a tailored specification language to express coroutine-specific properties. We note that we have not described desirable properties of coroutines that could be checked statically even though they are easily expressible in our framework. However, they are implemented and available in our tool since, to the best of our knowledge, there is no static analyser to check these properties. Henceforth, while coroutines facilitate concurrent programming, they are prone to errors, and our tooled approach provides programmers with the means to debug their programs.

The official library `kotlinx.coroutines` provides a basic set of debugging tools, consisting of a *debug mode* and a *stacktrace recovery* feature. The same Kotlinx library also provides an experimental module dedicated to debugging: this keeps records of all coroutines alive and introspecting and dumping them to enhance stacktraces with additional information like where a coroutine was created. The module can be used as a standalone JVM agent. This enables debug probes on the application startup and allows the monitoring of the whole application. However, the overheads caused by the recording and dumping of each coroutine are very noticeable and not recommended in production.

Finally, we mention a couple of Kotlin static analysis tools. The Detekt [8] tool allows checking six predefined rules on coroutines. The tool allows programmers to expand the range of checks by defining custom rules. More rules for Kotlin coroutines are provided by Sonar [21], a company leader in code analysis. These rules are taken from the official Kotlin guidelines and include some of the cases already mentioned for Detekt. Compared to these, our tool benefits from the same advantages and limitations as runtime verification over static analysis but could benefit from a combination with the latter (e.g., as in [2]).

# 8   Concluding Remarks

We have introduced a language for writing properties about coroutines, and we have provided an implementation to verify several properties concerning the execution of coroutines in Kotlin.

Despite our approach being (in theory) usable both pre-deployment (as a debugging tool) and post-deployment (as a monitor during the real execution of the system), we have, in this paper, only focused on the former. Our benchmarks show that the introduced overhead would be hardly noticeable by a developer but may have scalability issues in extreme situations. As a first proof-of-concept, we have thus implemented our monitors as (hardcoded) coroutines for all the identified properties instead of as a general monitoring tool that extracts the monitors for the properties (written in our language). The implementation of a dedicated tool to write properties using our language is left for future work.

We have applied our implementation to many programs and identified, in some cases, that the properties were violated. Though some of the programs we used in our evaluation were written with the explicit intention of producing the error, the value of the exercise relies on that: i) the errors are not easy to detect (they would be very difficult or impossible to be identified by the programmer); ii) the errors were detected by our implemented monitors.

Note that all properties capture actual potential problems of coroutines in Kotlin. The only exceptions to this in newer versions of Kotlin are *NormalAsync* and *ExceptionalAsync*, which are solved with exception suppression.

Finally, as Kotlin became the favourite language for developping Android applications, our approach allows revisiting the existing monitoring frameworks for Android [7,10,11,23].

# References

1. Agarwal, R., et al.: Detection of deadlock potentials in multithreaded programs. IBM J. Res. Dev. **54**(5), 3 (2010). https://doi.org/10.1147/JRD.2010.2060276
2. Azzopardi, S., Colombo, C., Pace, G.J.: CLARVA: model-based residual verification of Java programs. In: MODELSWARD2020, pp. 352–359. SCITEPRESS (2020). https://doi.org/10.5220/0008966603520359
3. Azzopardi, S., Ellul, J., Pace, G.J.: Monitoring smart contracts: ContractLarva and open challenges beyond. In: Colombo, C., Leucker, M. (eds.) RV 2018. LNCS, vol. 11237, pp. 113–137. Springer, Cham (2018). https://doi.org/10.1007/978-3-030-03769-7_8
4. Clarke, E.M.: Proving the correctness of coroutines without history variables. In: 16th Annual Southeast Regional Conference. ACM-SE 2016, pp. 160–167. ACM (1978). https://doi.org/10.1145/503643.503680
5. Colombo, C., Pace, G.J., Schneider, G.: Dynamic event-based runtime monitoring of real-time and contextual properties. In: Cofer, D., Fantechi, A. (eds.) FMICS 2008. LNCS, vol. 5596, pp. 135–149. Springer, Heidelberg (2009). https://doi.org/10.1007/978-3-642-03240-0_13
6. Conway, M.E.: Design of a separable transition-diagram compiler. Commun. ACM **6**(7), 396–408 (1963)
7. Daian, P., et al.: RV-Android: efficient parametric Android runtime verification, a brief tutorial. In: Bartocci, E., Majumdar, R. (eds.) RV 2015. LNCS, vol. 9333, pp. 342–357. Springer, Cham (2015). https://doi.org/10.1007/978-3-319-23820-3_24
8. Detekt team: Detekt. http://detekt.dev. Accessed 18 May 2022
9. El-Hokayem, A., Falcone, Y.: Can we monitor all multithreaded programs? In: Colombo, C., Leucker, M. (eds.) RV 2018. LNCS, vol. 11237, pp. 64–89. Springer, Cham (2018). https://doi.org/10.1007/978-3-030-03769-7_6
10. Falcone, Y., Currea, S.: Weave droid: aspect-oriented programming on Android devices: fully embedded or in the cloud. In: IEEE/ACM International Conference on Automated Software Engineering, ASE 2012, Essen, Germany, 3–7 September 2012, pp. 350–353. ACM (2012)
11. Falcone, Y., Currea, S., Jaber, M.: Runtime verification and enforcement for Android applications with RV-droid. In: Qadeer, S., Tasiran, S. (eds.) RV 2012. LNCS, vol. 7687, pp. 88–95. Springer, Heidelberg (2013). https://doi.org/10.1007/978-3-642-35632-2_11
12. Falcone, Y., Krstić, S., Reger, G., Traytel, D.: A taxonomy for classifying runtime verification tools. Int. J. Software Tools Technol. Transfer **23**(2), 255–284 (2021). https://doi.org/10.1007/s10009-021-00609-z
13. Havelund, K., Rosu, G.: An overview of the runtime verification tool Java pathexplorer. Formal Methods Syst. Des. **24**(2), 189–215 (2004). https://doi.org/10.1023/B:FORM.0000017721.39909.4b
14. Huang, J., Meredith, P.O., Rosu, G.: Maximal sound predictive race detection with control flow abstraction. In: PLDI 2014, pp. 337–348. ACM (2014)
15. Kotlin: Language Documentation. https://kotlinlang.org/docs/home.html

16. Kotlin documentation: Dispatchers and threads. https://kotlinlang.org/docs/coroutine-context-and-dispatchers.html#dispatchers-and-threads. Accessed 18 May 2022

17. Kupferman, O., Vardi, M.Y.: Model checking of safety properties. In: Halbwachs, N., Peled, D. (eds.) CAV 1999. LNCS, vol. 1633, pp. 172–183. Springer, Heidelberg (1999). https://doi.org/10.1007/3-540-48683-6_17

18. Lourenço, J.M., Fiedor, J., Křena, B., Vojnar, T.: Discovering concurrency errors. In: Bartocci, E., Falcone, Y. (eds.) Lectures on Runtime Verification. LNCS, vol. 10457, pp. 34–60. Springer, Cham (2018). https://doi.org/10.1007/978-3-319-75632-5_2

19. Marlin, C.D.: Coroutines: A Programming Methodology, a Language Design and an Implementation, LNCS, vol. 95. Springer, Heidelberg (1980). https://doi.org/10.1007/3-540-10256-6

20. de Moura, A.L., Ierusalimschy, R.: Revisiting coroutines. ACM Trans. Program. Lang. Syst. 31(2), 6:1-6:31 (2009)

21. SonarSource S.A.: Kotlin rules for coroutines. https://rules.sonarsource.com/kotlin/tag/coroutines. Accessed 18 May 2022

22. Sústrik, M.: Blog post detailing structured concurrency. http://250bpm.com/blog:71. Accessed 18 May 2022

23. Vella, M., Colombo, C.: Spotcheck: On-device anomaly detection for Android. In: Örs, S.B., Elçi, A. (eds.) SIN 2020: 13th International Conference on Security of Information and Networks, Virtual Event / Istanbul, Turkey, 4–6 November 2020, pp. 20:1-20:6. ACM (2020)

# Short and Tool Papers

# AspectSol: A Solidity Aspect-Oriented Programming Tool with Applications in Runtime Verification

Shaun Azzopardi[2] , Joshua Ellul[1] , Ryan Falzon[3] ,
and Gordon J. Pace[1(✉)] 

[1] University of Malta, Msida, Malta
joshua.ellul@um.edu.mt, gordon.pace@um.edu.mt
[2] University of Gothenburg, Gothenburg, Sweden
shaun.azzopardi@gu.se
[3] Hash Data, George Town, Cayman Islands
ryan@hashdata.co

**Abstract.** Aspect-oriented programming tools aim to provide increased code modularity by enabling programming of cross-cutting concerns separate from the main body of code. Since the inception of runtime verification, aspect-oriented programming has regularly been touted as a perfect accompanying tool, by allowing for non-invasive monitoring instrumentation techniques. In this paper we present, AspectSol, which enables aspect-oriented programming for smart contracts written in Solidity, and then discuss the design space for pointcuts and aspects in this context. We present and evaluate practical runtime verification uses and applications of the tool.

**Keywords:** Aspect-oriented programming · Smart contracts · Runtime verification

## 1 Introduction

Blockchain [11] and other distributed ledger technologies (DLTs) have enabled the management of digital assets without the need for a central authority, and with strong guarantees regarding immutability of transactions. Smart contracts residing on a blockchain, go a step further in that they handle the execution

This research has received funding from the ERC consolidator grant D-SynMA (No. 772459) and the University of Malta Research Awards project *"Systematising Smart Contracts within Classical Contract Law Theory"*, and the European Agricultural Fund for Rural Development project *"VinoVeritas: An Authority to Consumer Wine Audit Solution"*.

T. Dang and V. Stolz (Eds.): RV 2022, LNCS 13498, pp. 243–252, 2022.
https://doi.org/10.1007/978-3-031-17196-3_13

of logic on such a decentralised platform, thus ensuring faithful execution and enabling trustless operationalisation of protocols of behaviour between parties.

By being deployed on a platform with decentralised control, a blockchain or a variant thereof, these smart contracts come with the benefit of immutability—once written, the protocol cannot be modified unless in a manner that was originally planned and built into the protocol itself. This autonomous and guaranteed computation platform provides a guarantee not granted by traditional centralised systems. Benefits rarely come without a related cost though, and in this case the cost emanates similarly from immutability.

Smart contracts are nothing more than executable code (running on a DLT platform), for which an unavoidable feature (as with any other software) is the presence of bugs. Immutable code may be the selling point of smart contracts, but immutable bugs are the cost. Add to this the fact that smart contracts typically deal with digital assets, making their correctness critical.

Although smart contracts are typically small programs, modularisation of code is a key measure to reduce potential errors. However, the way smart contracts call each other on platforms like Ethereum [13] is unlike that found in traditional systems, due to overheads, such as gas[1] costs, which can be prohibitive.

Beyond modularisation within the same smart contract, one would also desire to have the tools to encode features and transformations commonly in use across different smart contracts. One technique that has been used for such cross-cutting modularisation is that of aspect-oriented programming (AOP) [10]. In this paper we present an AOP tool for Solidity [6], one of the most commonly used smart contract programming languages. The tool is publicly available at https://github.com/ryanfalzon/aspectSol.

AOP has frequently been used as a tool for instrumentation of runtime monitoring and verification code, e.g. [4,7,12]. We show how our tool, ASPECTSOL, can be effective in both instrumenting verification code for specifications, and injecting new features modularly, in a monitoring-oriented programming [2] style.

## 2   Aspect-Oriented Programming

The main idea behind AOP is to allow for the writing of cross-cutting features separate from the main system. Such an approach allows for the specification of *joinpoints* (points during the execution of the underlying system) where specified *advice* (specific instructions or code) will be weaved in. Joinpoints are typically specified using *pointcuts*, essentially specifying a set of joinpoints to be matched. Such an aspect-oriented specification can then be used to weave in the advice onto the existing system. Different joinpoint types are supported by different languages. For instance, for imperative languages, one allows hooking onto points

---

[1] The notion of *gas* as a resource to be paid for to execute code is the most common way thorough which public blockchains motivate miners (the nodes in the decentralised network which process transactions and record them on the blockchain) to execute and record execution of smart contract code.

such as the start and end of a function call, on an exception being raised, and updates of state.

## 3    Smart Contract AOP: Design Considerations

The design of an AOP tool must necessarily take into consideration the nature of the programming language it is to be used for.

**Joinpoints.** In particular, the choice of joinpoints, the candidate points in a program's execution where an aspect can trigger, is a crucial decision. Solidity is essentially an imperative language, and any AOP tool for the language will certainly borrow much from other tools for this class of languages, e.g. ASPECTC [3] and AspectJ [9]. Function entry and exit points are such joinpoints, which we adopt in ASPECTSOL, allowing us to write aspects such as `before call-to Wallet.addFunds()` (just before the `addFunds()` function in the smart contract Wallet is called, on the caller's side) or `after call-to Wallet.withdrawFunds()` (at the end of the execution of the `withdrawFunds()` function in the smart contract Wallet, on the caller's side). In order to match on the callee's side, one would simply replace `execution-of` by `call-to`.

Given the imperative nature of Solidity, computation revolves around the notion of state and the points where the contract state is read or written— indicating relevant joinpoints in this context. In ASPECTSOL we provide automated instrumentation of such points, e.g. `before set uint count` and `after get bool is_paid`. It is worth noting that read pointcuts only trigger when variables are read from within the smart contract being instrumented. This is unavoidable on public blockchains, where state can be read by external entities without having to explicitly call a smart contract.

Solidity's notion of computation failure through the use of reverted execution is unlike that of traditional exceptions. Rather than returning control to the current execution context with an exception flag, `revert` aborts all computation and returns the state of the contract to that which it was before computation started. This makes the use of such exceptions as joinpoints difficult (and expensive in terms of gas) to handle, and therefore not handled in ASPECTSOL.

ASPECTSOL allows the use of the wildcard symbol * throughout (for contract names, function names, parameter names, and types), but provides a means of capturing the matched name in order to allow references to it by using double square brackets, e.g. `set [[typevar]] [[varname]]` acts just like `set * *` (triggering whenever a variable is set) but provides access to `typevar` and `varname`, for instance to enable declaring an auxiliary variable of the same type and to access the variable's value in the advice.

**Smart Contract and Language-Specific Considerations.** ASPECTSOL's salient features are particular to smart contracts in general and to Solidity in particular. Since smart contracts essentially encode a protocol between parties, the notion of such parties as active actors of transactions is at its very core. In order to facilitate aspects that use such notions, ASPECTSOL provides a pointcut filter, `originating-from`, to trigger only when the call is made by a particular party, from a particular contract, or from a particular function. For instance, the following pointcut triggers at the start of calls to `depositMoney()` in the `Wallet` smart contract with `msg.sender` being `owners[0]`:

```
before
    execution-of Wallet.depositMoney()
    originating-from owners[0]
```

Another such feature is native cryptocurrency transfer for which it could be useful to implement pointcuts. In Solidity, sending funds is achieved through calling the `send` or `transfer` functions targeting the recipient's address, meaning that we can already capture such pointcuts as function calls, e.g. `before call-to [[recipient_address]].transfer()`. Receiving funds is, however, different in that functions can be tagged as `payable`, meaning that funds can be transferred to the smart contract whenever such a function is called. ASPECTSOL allows for pointcut filtering based on such function tags, thus allowing us to capture calls to functions which transfer funds, e.g.:

```
after execution-of Wallet.*(*) tagged-with payable
```

Solidity modifiers allow functions to be tagged, which would result in changing their behaviour, e.g. to execute certain code before or after the function body. We treat modifiers similar to the `payable` tag, allowing aspects to capture functions which use (or do not use) certain modifiers. We similarly treat visibility annotations such as `public` and `internal` in the same manner.

**Advice and Aspects.** Pointcuts are associated with executable advice by appending a subsequent executable block of code. Consider writing an aspect to make sure that no more than 100 deposits are performed to a wallet without a reconciliation process taking place. This can be achieved by keeping track of the number of deposits and checking that they have not exceeded 100 whenever a deposit takes place. In addition, we would need to declare the new variable which will be used to keep track of this number. This can be written as an aspect as follows:

```
aspect LimitDeposits {
    add-to-declaration Wallet {
        uint private number_of_deposits = 0;
    }

    before execution-of Wallet.addDeposit() {
        require (number_of_deposits < 100);
        number_of_deposits++;
    }
    before execution-of Wallet.reconciliation() {
        number_of_deposits = 0;
    }
}
```

Another mechanism particular to ASPECTSOL is that of adding or removing tags by using pointcuts referring to a function and using `add-tag` or `remove-tag` to update the definition. For instance, if we want to make all public fields private, we can write the following:

```
update-definition Wallet.* tagged-with public {
    remove-tag public;
    add-tag private;
}
```

This approach can be used, for instance, to make a field private and add an appropriate getter and setter to the smart contract.

**Weaving Considerations.** We now move on to weaving considerations, for which different AOP tools take different strategies. For instance, AspectJ performs weaving at the byte-code level, but provides three points in time when it can be applied: compile time, pre-load time, or load time. ASPECTSOL takes a source-code level weaving approach, thus transpiling from the original Solidity source code to produce updated Solidity code which takes the aspects into account. This simplifies testing the updated version of the smart contract more straightforward. The process flow of ASPECTSOL is shown below:

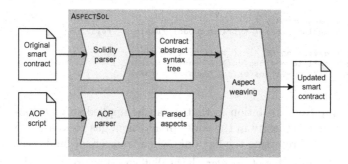

# 4 Runtime Verification Using ASPECTSOL

In order to show the use of ASPECTSOL, in particular for runtime verification instrumentation, and enable a qualitative assessment of the utility of the tool, we present three small case studies of smart contracts. For all three, we present verification code for runtime verification of desirable properties using ASPECTSOL. All three examples can be found in the ASPECTSOL repository.

**Guarding Against Reentrancy Attacks.** Since a transaction invoking a smart contract executes in one go, with no interaction or interference from other blockchain transactions, as a programmer one sees smart contract functions as atomic. This eliminates having to consider concurrency issues, making design and implementation easier. Unless a function explicitly calls another function, no other function code will be executed before the termination of the current call. For example, consider a smart contract which implements a wallet in which owners may deposit funds and send them out to other users. In addition, one may have further functionality such as placing an amount of money in escrow for another user. Atomicity means that when the function placeInEscrow(..) is called, the programmer need not be concerned that there may be a concurrent call to withdraw funds, thus sufficing to check that there are enough funds available at the beginning of the call to placeInEscrow(..).

However, reality is not so simple. If `placeInEscrow(..)` makes a call to another smart contract, that smart contract may call back and withdraw funds. The atomicity assumption thus breaks down. To make things worse, on Ethereum the mechanism for a smart contract to send funds to another, is to invoke a special function `transfer` (or `send`) on the receiving smart contract. This is an opportunity for the receiver to call the original contract back, once again breaking the assumption of the atomicity of function calls. Such reentrancy was the source of bugs which led to the loss of the equivalent of millions of dollars.

One way in which reentrancy can be ruled out altogether is to use a Boolean flag to ensure such code is executed only once until a transaction is complete. Some developers do this manually where and when needed, whilst others advocate the use of a function modifier which uses a blanket rule to check that a running flag is false and set it to true upon entry to every function and reset it upon exit. Using ASPECTSOL, we can refine the latter to be used only if and when control is yielded through a call to transfer funds as shown below:[2]

```
aspect SafeReenentrancy {
    add-to-declarations * { private bool running = false; }

    before execution-of *.* { require (!running); }
    before call-to *.transfer() { running = true; }
    after call-to *.transfer() { running = false; }
}
```

This is a universal solution in that it can be applied to *any* smart contract, without adding complexity in the code. In addition, gas costs are kept to a minimum, setting and resetting the flag only when transfers of funds are attempted.

**Enforcing Properties.** Consider the wallet smart contract, with a property that states: *No more than 1000 outgoing payments, or 100 ether[3] may be sent from the wallet, unless the smart contract is first verified by a trusted regulator.* If `sendFunds()` is the function provided by the smart contract to send funds to third parties, and `verifyWallet()` is the function used by the regulator to verify the owner of the wallet, we can encode runtime checks to ensure adherence to the specification using the following aspect:

```
aspect WalletVerification {
    add-to-declarations Wallet {
        private bool is_verified = false;
        private uint number_of_payments = 0;
        private uint sum_of_payments = 0;
    }

    before execution-of Wallet.sendFunds(payable address dst, uint amount) {
        if (!is_verified) {
            require (number_of_payments < 1000);
            require (sum_of_payments + amount <= 100 ether);
            number_of_payments ++;
            sum_of_payments += amount;
        }
    }
    after execution-of Wallet.verifyWallet() {
```

---

[2] In practice, we would also need to do this for the `send` function.
[3] Ether is the native cryptocurrency used in Ethereum.

```
        is_verified = true;
    }
}
```

Note that `require` stops and reverts the computation altogether if the condition fails. In this manner, any attempt to send funds beyond the set limits is aborted, effectively enforcing the property.

**Adherence to a Business Process Flow.** Finally, we show how AspectSol can be used to runtime verify that a smart contract can only be used as intended. Consider a casino smart contract which allows the casino to open bets on a coin toss, enabling a player to place a guess, and then resolve the bet. The expected business process flow of the smart contract is shown below:

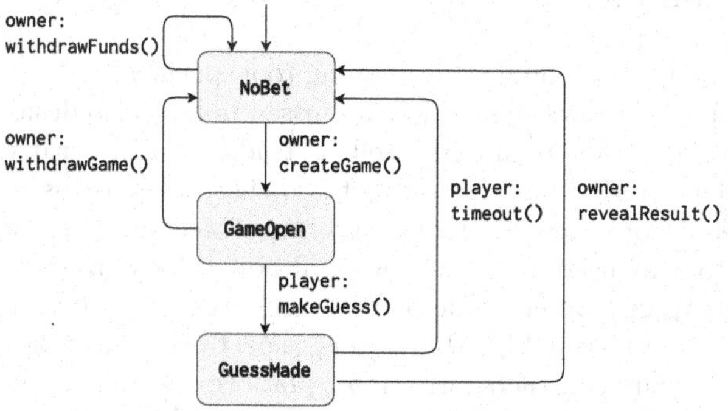


Transitions are tagged by a pair `party:function`, denoting that the transition is taken when the identified party calls the named function. Furthermore, we take the semantics of the notation to indicate that invoking a function when in a state with no outgoing transition tagged with that function (and calling party) should fail. For instance, the function `withdrawFunds()` should only succeed when in mode `NoBet` and called by the `owner` of the casino, thus disallowing the owner from taking funds to leave the player without their winnings after they guessed correctly. We can encode such a business process flow to ensure that the implementation does not diverge from the expected behaviour using aspects as follows:[4]

```
aspect CasinoBusinessProcessFlow {
    add-to-declarations Casino {
        enum Mode { NoBet, GameOpen, GuessMade }
        private Mode mode = Mode.NoBet;
    }

    before execution-of Casino.createGame() {
        require (mode == Mode.NoBet);
        require (msg.sender == owner);
    }
    after execution-of Casino.createGame() {
        mode = Mode.GameOpen;
    }
    ...
}
```

[4] The full code of the example can be found in the tool repository.

It is worth noting that such AspectSol code would typically be generated by a runtime verification tool from the graph-based specification. In practice, we can make the specification notation richer by, for instance, allowing conditions on the transitions to specify properties such as allowing `createGame()` only if there are sufficient funds in the smart contract. Similarly, we can deal with failure in a manner other than simply by disallowing violating calls, e.g. rewarding the player with a win if the casino attempts a disallowed action after the player has placed a bet. The fact that the specification is made independent of the code (which we do not even show here) is the strength of using aspect-oriented programming to specify such properties.

## 5   Discussion and Conclusions

The only other aspect-oriented programming tool specifically designed for smart contracts which we are aware of is that discussed in [8]—also designed for Solidity but adopts the same pointcuts used in traditional imperative and object oriented language AOP tools. In contrast, we chose to reassess relevant pointcuts in the context of smart contracts. In terms of weaving approach, it appears to be similar to that used in AspectSol, although they make more extensive use of modifiers to instrument code. Direct comparison is, however, not possible since their tool is not available. Many other aspect-oriented programming tools can be used for smart contracts written for platforms which support traditional languages, but these approaches do not specifically address concepts specific to smart contracts. In particular for runtime verification, having native notions of digital asset transfers, parties, and access to modifiers and other tags can be particularly useful.

One valid question is whether one really needs aspect-oriented programming in Solidity, given it provides modifiers, which allow for tagging functions whose behaviour will be changed accordingly, e.g. by adding code before or after the main body of the function. Indeed, some simple use of aspect-oriented programming, e.g. injecting advice at the start or the end of a function can be done using modifiers. However, this has severe limitations in that one cannot inject code on the caller's side, or around specific calls to external functions—functionality which AspectSol provides. Similarly, tag-based filtering and manipulation is a powerful tool which cannot be replicated using modifiers. Finally, modifiers reside within a particular smart contract, and thus lose advantages of separation-of-concerns between the business logic and the cross-cutting aspects, and of reuse. Despite modifiers being a powerful programming construct, they do not replace the role an aspect-oriented tool can provide.

We have presented AspectSol, an aspect-oriented programming tool for Solidity, designed specifically for smart contracts and going beyond traditionally used aspects, pointcuts, and advice for imperative and object-oriented languages.

Although Solidity is an imperative language, smart contract notions of value flow, and interacting parties provide an opportunity for more domain specific aspect-oriented programming. In particular, we have argued and showed how the tool is particularly suited to instrument runtime monitoring and verification code into smart contacts, and we are currently in the process of redesigning ContractLarva [1,5] to use ASPECTSOL for instrumentation.

# References

1. Azzopardi, S., Ellul, J., Pace, G.J.: Monitoring smart contracts: ContractLarva and open challenges beyond. In: Colombo, C., Leucker, M. (eds.) Runtime Verification. LNCS, vol. 11237, pp. 113–137. Springer, Cham (2018). https://doi.org/10.1007/978-3-030-03769-7_8
2. Chen, F., Roşu, G.: Java-MOP: a monitoring oriented programming environment for Java. In: Halbwachs, N., Zuck, L.D. (eds.) TACAS 2005. LNCS, vol. 3440, pp. 546–550. Springer, Heidelberg (2005). https://doi.org/10.1007/978-3-540-31980-1_36
3. Coady, Y., Kiczales, G., Feeley, M.J., Smolyn, G.: Using aspectC to improve the modularity of path-specific customization in operating system code. In: Tjoa, A.M., Gruhn, V. (eds.) Proceedings of the 8th European Software Engineering Conference held jointly with 9th ACM SIGSOFT International Symposium on Foundations of Software Engineering 2001, Vienna, Austria, 10–14 September 2001, pp. 88–98. ACM (2001). https://doi.org/10.1145/503209.503223
4. Colombo, C., Pace, G.J., Schneider, G.: Dynamic event-based runtime monitoring of real-time and contextual properties. In: Cofer, D., Fantechi, A. (eds.) FMICS 2008. LNCS, vol. 5596, pp. 135–149. Springer, Heidelberg (2009). https://doi.org/10.1007/978-3-642-03240-0_13
5. Ellul, J., Pace, G.J.: Runtime verification of Ethereum smart contracts. In: 14th European Dependable Computing Conference, EDCC 2018, Iaşi, Romania, 10–14 September 2018, pp. 158–163. IEEE Computer Society (2018). https://doi.org/10.1109/EDCC.2018.00036
6. Ethereum: Solidity. Online Documentation (2016). http://solidity.readthedocs.io/en/develop/introduction-to-smart-contracts.html
7. Havelund, K.: Runtime verification of C programs. In: Suzuki, K., Higashino, T., Ulrich, A., Hasegawa, T. (eds.) FATES/TestCom -2008. LNCS, vol. 5047, pp. 7–22. Springer, Heidelberg (2008). https://doi.org/10.1007/978-3-540-68524-1_3
8. Hung, C., Chen, K., Liao, C.: Modularizing cross-cutting concerns with aspect-oriented extensions for Solidity. In: IEEE International Conference on Decentralized Applications and Infrastructures, DAPPCON 2019, Newark, CA, USA, 4–9 April 2019, pp. 176–181. IEEE (2019). https://doi.org/10.1109/DAPPCON.2019.00033
9. Kiczales, G., Hilsdale, E., Hugunin, J., Kersten, M., Palm, J., Griswold, W.G.: An overview of AspectJ. In: Knudsen, J.L. (ed.) ECOOP 2001. LNCS, vol. 2072, pp. 327–354. Springer, Heidelberg (2001). https://doi.org/10.1007/3-540-45337-7_18
10. Kiczales, G., et al.: Aspect-oriented programming. In: Akşit, M., Matsuoka, S. (eds.) ECOOP 1997. LNCS, vol. 1241, pp. 220–242. Springer, Heidelberg (1997). https://doi.org/10.1007/BFb0053381
11. Nofer, M., Gomber, P., Hinz, O., Schiereck, D.: Blockchain. Bus. Inf. Syst. Eng. **59**(3), 183–187 (2017)

12. Shin, H., Endoh, Y., Kataoka, Y.: ARVE: aspect-oriented runtime verification environment. In: Sokolsky, O., Taşıran, S. (eds.) RV 2007. LNCS, vol. 4839, pp. 87–96. Springer, Heidelberg (2007). https://doi.org/10.1007/978-3-540-77395-5_8
13. Wood, G., et al.: Ethereum: a secure decentralised generalised transaction ledger. Ethereum Project Yellow Paper **151**(2014), 1–32 (2014)

# Towards Specificationless Monitoring
# of Provenance-Emitting Systems

Martin Stoffers$^{(\boxtimes)}$ and Alexander Weinert$^{(\boxtimes)}$

German Aerospace Center (DLR), Institute for Software Technology, Cologne,
Germany
`{martin.stoffers,alexander.weinert}@dlr.de`

**Abstract.** Monitoring often requires insight into the monitored system
as well as concrete specifications of expected behavior. More and more
systems, however, provide information about their inner procedures by
emitting provenance information in a W3C-standardized graph format.
In this work, we present an approach to monitor such provenance data
for anomalous behavior by performing spectral graph analysis on slices
of the constructed provenance graph and by comparing the characteristics of each slice with those of a sliding window over recently seen
slices. We argue that this approach not only simplifies the monitoring of
heterogeneous distributed systems, but also enables applying a host of
well-studied techniques to monitor such systems.

**Keywords:** W3C Provenance · Runtime monitoring · Spectral graph
analysis

## 1 Introduction

In current research on monitoring complex systems, the system is often
abstracted to a set of streams of values [12]. Even when monitoring distributed
systems, the problem of transporting the distributed data streams to the monitor is assumed to be solved by the monitored system [35]. In modern real-world
systems, in contrast, it is a non-trivial effort to engineer a central component
that efficiently consolidates data for monitoring in a heavily distributed system.

Moreover, these streams may be annotated with metadata, e.g., information
about their creation times [38], whether an agent is a natural person or a software
agent, or whether some input data was required or optional for the execution
of a process. However, these metadata typically do not include information on
their relation. Consider, e.g., a scenario in which a system provides a value $x$
as an output to the user and also uses $x$ as input for further computations.
This monitored information typically does not indicate whether the two values
coincide by design or by accident. Although this relation might be recovered

T. Dang and V. Stolz (Eds.): RV 2022, LNCS 13498, pp. 253–263, 2022.
https://doi.org/10.1007/978-3-031-17196-3_14

from the logging stream, doing so is typically incomplete and error-prone. The metadata and relations of data produced by a system are known as provenance data [51].

Monitoring the provenance data of a system addresses both issues identified above: Provenance data describes, among other information, the relation between individual data points emitted by the system. Thus, it is typically consolidated by the system itself and made available for inspection or monitoring. Moreover, it contains more information on the inner workings of the system than the functional data. Hence, monitoring both provenance data and the functional data may lead to earlier detection of undesired system states.

In practice, monitoring approaches may take metadata of functional data into account. These metadata, however, are usually domain-specific. In contrast, provenance data are non-domain-specific, yet provide information about the structure of the monitored data as well as meta-data.

One major challenge when monitoring provenance data, however, is that users typically lack intuition about the relation between data they expect from the system. Thus, formulating specifications for monitoring provenance data is harder for users than formulating specifications for classical monitoring.

To alleviate this shortcoming, in this work we instead focus on anomaly detection, thus using previously seen data as specification. We believe monitoring of provenance data to be an interesting problem. The explicit graphs of provenance data allow for the application of well-known graph analyses to monitoring.

We present an approach for monitoring provenance data for anomalies without requiring explicit specifications. To this end, we proceed as follows: After discussing related work in Sect. 2, we formally define provenance data as provenance graphs in Sect. 3 before subsequently describing the monitoring of provenance-emitting systems in Sect. 4. Afterwards we outline how to use spectral graph theory to detect anomalous provenance data in Sect. 5. Finally, in Sect. 6 we summarize our work and give an outlook on future work.

## 2    Related Work

*Provenance.* Early works highlight the importance of provenance to enable audits of automated workflow systems [17,29]. Moreau identified the building blocks for standardized provenance recording and proposes the Open Provenance Model (OPM) [36], which was later superseded by the W3C PROV standard [37,51]. Provenance data is either extracted from software systems after [43] or during their operation [24,27,47]. There is active work towards recording provenance information without instrumenting the system or process [3,5,18,39].

*System Monitoring.* Runtime verification (or system monitoring) is an established building block for ensuring system correctness [4,28]. Existing approaches to monitoring often take a specification of "good" or "bad" patterns and efficiently detect them in the output data of the system. This specification is typically given in temporal logics [6,13,14,26,32,40] or in higher-level languages [7,11,15].

*Anomaly Detection in Provenance Graphs.* Since provenance data give structured information about the relation between data points emitted by the system, there has been work towards identifying anomalies in provenance data. However, such work explicitly focuses on the detection of attacks on the system [8], uses bespoke projections from graphs to vector spaces [20,21] or only analyzes individual characteristics of the computation process [41]. Other approaches aim to compare provenance graphs by "summarizing" via clustering [2,31].

# 3   Provenance Graphs

The W3C defines provenance information as "information about entities, activities, and people involved in producing a piece of data or thing, which can be used to form assessments about its quality, reliability or trustworthiness." [51]

The PROV standard prescribes a non-domain-specific graph-based ontology of such information. Each vertex in such a graph denotes either an *entity*, i.e., some piece of data, an *activity*, i.e., a process or action, or an *agent*, i.e., a person, machine or software responsible for a process. The edges between these vertices denote the relationships between entities, activities, and agents.

We illustrate the possible relationships in Fig. 1. We draw entities as yellow rounded boxes, activities as blue rectangular boxes, and agents as red pentagons. In Fig. 1, we write ATTR, DERIV, USE, GEN, and ASSOC to abbreviate "was attributed to", "was derived from", "used", "was generated by", and "was associated with", respectively. The full standard admits additional vertices and edges. We restrict ourselves to the edges shown in Fig. 1 for conciseness.

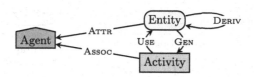

**Fig. 1.** The core provenance meta-model. Reproduced after and adapted from the Prov Primer [50].

Intuitively, the provenance of a software system is a record of a) the data that was generated or used, b) the process that generated and used these data, and c) the responsible entities (both human and software) for these processes.

Formally, a provenance graph $G = (V_{\text{AGT}}, V_{\text{ENT}}, V_{\text{ACT}}, E)$ consists of finite sets of agent vertices $V_{\text{AGT}}$, entity vertices $V_{\text{ENT}}$, and activity vertices $V_{\text{ACT}}$, all of which are pairwise disjoint, and a set of edges $E \subseteq (V_{\text{ENT}} \times (V_{\text{AGT}} \cup V_{\text{ENT}} \cup V_{\text{ACT}})) \cup (V_{\text{ACT}} \times (V_{\text{AGT}} \cup V_{\text{ENT}}))$. We call $V_{\text{AGT}} \cup V_{\text{ENT}} \cup V_{\text{ACT}}$ the *vertex set* of $G$.

In practice, a provenance-emitting system does not provide its complete provenance at the end of its computation. Instead, whenever an activity has terminated, the system provides a "partial" provenance graph that contains the respective activity as well as the entities that this activity used and generated.

We also call these provenance graphs emitted during execution of the system *provenance updates* to differentiate them from the complete graph that the system constructs during its execution. To obtain a less local view of the provenance of the complete system execution, we construct the union over provenance via the component-wise union of the constituent elements of a provenance graph.

In this work, a *provenance-emitting system* is a software or hardware system that constructs a provenance graph that contains vertices representing the data points it generated, the processes that used and generated these data points, and makes this provenance graph accessible to external systems. In the following section, we provide greater detail and a more formal description of such systems. We moreover describe a process for monitoring provenance-emitting systems.

Having given a brief introduction to the W3C Provenance standard, we now illustrate how provenance data is collected from distributed provenance-emitting systems and made available for monitoring in the following section.

## 4   Monitoring Provenance-Emitting Systems

Intuitively, a provenance-emitting system emits information about its execution by making its provenance graph available for monitoring and inspection. To do so, it emits provenance updates at certain points in time, i.e., sub-graphs of the complete provenance graph of its execution. A monitor can observe these updates and monitor them for anomalies. In Fig. 2 we illustrate a lightweight architecture for recording provenance, initially outlined in [47].

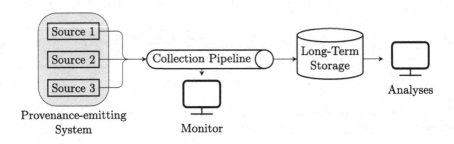

**Fig. 2.** A lightweight architecture for capturing provenance information from a complex distributed system. (Taken from [47] and simplified.)

Formally, we say that an *execution* of a provenance-emitting system is an infinite sequence $G_1 G_2 G_3 \cdots$. The graphs are not necessarily temporally ordered. As an example, $G_3$ may only contain activities that started at time $t$, while $G_4$ only contains activities that ended at time $t' < t$.

In this section we present a method to monitor an execution of provenance-emitting systems for anomalies. The complete provenance graph constructed by the system is unbounded and may be infinite for non-terminating systems. It is the task of the long-term Storage (cf. Fig. 2) to provide sufficient storage capacity for this complete graph as required for post-hoc analyses. The monitor, in contrast, should not require unbounded memory, but instead work with restricted resources to function as lightweight as possible.

Let $\varphi = G_1 G_2 G_3 \cdots$ be the execution of a provenance-emitting system. In each time step the monitor obtains the earliest $G$ from $\varphi$ that it has not yet obtained. The monitor shall produce a sequence $b_1 b_2 b_3 \cdots$ where $b_i$ is one of $\checkmark, ✗, ?$. The value $\checkmark$ (✗) denotes that the monitor has not (has) detected an anomaly in the last time step, respectively, while $?$ denotes that the monitor does not have sufficient information to make a decision. Moreover, the monitor shall not require unbounded memory.

In this problem formulation, we explicitly omit a definition of "anomalies". Recall that the PROV meta model only imposes very limited structure on provenance graphs. Thus, whether a provenance graph describes expected or unexpected behavior is strongly application-dependent. Analogously, it is not expedient to formally define anomalies independent of the monitored application.

Consider, e.g., a provenance-emitting system in which all activities so far take two entities as inputs and produce one entity as output. Assume there arrives a provenance update in which an activity takes four inputs and produces one output. Whether or not the latter update is anomalous depends on the purpose of the system. If the system processes temperature readings since the last step, then the occurrence of fewer temperature readings than previously indicates, e.g., faulty sensors. In contrast, if a system processes observations made by an optical telescope [16,48], then the system may process more information due to improved weather conditions. This would not be considered anomalous.

This example illustrates that there can be no "turnkey" solution for monitoring provenance-emitting systems: Either the user provides an explicit specification of expected or unexpected provenance patterns, or the monitor requires knowledge about the purpose of the system to infer anomalous graphs itself. Thus, we aim to construct a parametrized monitor that measures the "anomaly" of a provenance update against those updates witnessed previously. Due to space constraints, this monitor cannot store all previously witnessed provenance graphs explicitly. Instead, it retains only a window of previously witnessed partial provenance graphs. We illustrate our monitoring architecture in Fig. 3.

The main purpose of the windowing is to construct a sequence of classical graphs that it then passes to anomaly detection. By retiring vertices representing entities that have not been used by the system, windowing ensures that the graphs passed to anomaly detection do not exceed a given size. We call this size the *window size*. This allows the anomaly detection to focus on comparing an incoming graph to the one previously obtained and to raise an alarm to the user if these two graphs differ significantly. To give the anomaly detection enough data to reliably identify structural anomalies, the windowing step reports $?$ until it has collected sufficient provenance updates to fill a predetermined window size.

When converting provenance graphs into classical directed graphs, structural information about the "kinds" of vertices is lost, as a classical graph does not differentiate between, e.g., vertices representing processes and vertices representing

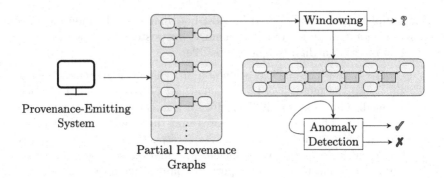

**Fig. 3.** An overview over our monitoring architecture.

entities. Moreover, similar information about the kinds of edges is lost as well. This information can be reconstructed in the fragment of provenance graphs used in this work. Such a reconstruction is, however, not necessarily possible when using the full expressive power of W3C Provenance.

To retain this information, it may be encoded as vertex- or edge-weights. How weights should be assigned is again strongly application-specific and strongly influences the subsequent anomaly detection. One could, e.g., assign a high weight to all edges adjacent to activity-vertices. This would lead to the anomaly detection being highly sensitive to anomalous patterns in the vicinity of activity-vertices and less sensitive to the vicinity of other vertices. In the next section we describe possible approaches to detecting anomalies via spectral graph theory.

## 5    Anomaly Detection with Spectral Graph Theory

To identify structural anomalies of graphs, we need to quantify their topological properties, e.g., patterns of connectivity. We propose using spectral graph theory [45] to this end. This theory relies on studying the Eigenvalues and Eigenvectors of matrices associated with graphs, e.g., the adjacency matrix, the degree matrix, or the Laplace matrix. Intuitively, these values capture the topological properties of the investigated graphs [45]. Spectral graph theory has been successfully applied in some fields [44,46]. In particular, Gera, Alonso, Crawford, et al. have used spectral graph theory to determine whether incoming observations of a graph significantly deviate from previous observations [19].

We illustrate our general approach in Fig. 4. Let $G$ be an incoming graph obtained by anomaly detection and let $n$ be the window size determined when constructing or configuring the windowing. By computing Eigenvalues and Eigenvectors of matrices associated with $G$ we can obtain vectors $\nu_1, \ldots, \nu_n$, where $\nu_i \in \mathbb{C}^m$ for all $\nu_i$ and some $m \leq n$. These vectors may, e.g., comprise the Eigenvalues of the used matrix or its Eigenvectors. In the former case, we have $m = 1$, in the latter $m = n$. Intuitively, if the investigated matrix is well-chosen, this set of vectors quantifies the structure of the graph. We call this

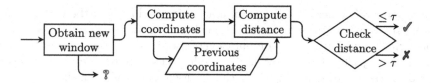

**Fig. 4.** Our framework for anomaly detection.

set of vectors the *coordinates* of the graph. Having obtained the coordinates of both the current and the previous provenance graph, we can then compute the distance between these two coordinates and use this distance as a measure of the structural differences between the two graphs. We discuss possibilities and challenges for both steps, obtaining coordinates and computing their distance in the following sections. Moreover, we report on the results of a preliminary evaluation in Sect. 5.3.

### 5.1 Compute Coordinates

To obtain coordinates, we compute Eigenvalues and Eigenvectors of matrices associated with the graph. Typically, one uses the adjacency matrix or the Laplacian matrix of the graph [45]. Multiple works have shown that some graph properties can be determined based on the multiplicity, size or position of the Eigenvalues and corresponding Eigenvectors [9,22,30,33,34]. In graph drawing, Eigenvectors are selected based on their Eigenvalues and used as source for coordinates to visually reveal structural properties of graphs [25].

Most applications of spectral graph theory, however, assume the graph to be undirected. In that case, the adjacency matrix and the Laplacian matrix are real symmetric matrices, thus their Eigenvalues are integers. Provenance graphs, however, are directed. Thus, to apply standard methods of spectral graph analysis to them, we have to transform them into undirected graphs [42], which loses structural information. Another approach would be to use bespoke spectral graph analysis methods that handle directed graphs [10,49]. These methods are, however, not as well-investigated as those for undirected graphs.

### 5.2 Compute Distance

To identify anomalous updates we need to compare the current and the previous coordinate vectors. To this end, we aim to compute a normalized distance measure. Recall that coordinates are sets of vectors. Thus, a common method is to first calculate the pairwise distances for sets of vectors separately using different metrics, such as the euclidean distances, cosine similarity or correlation. By taking the average over the resulting vector of distance measurements we can obtain a distance between coordinates.

Directly computing the difference between two sets of vertices is rather sensitive to "noisy" coordinates: Minor differences between individual vectors may lead to large differences. We can counteract this via clustering the vectors comprising the coordinates prior to distance calculation. In this case, the complete monitoring pipeline up to the computation of coordinates is tantamount to spectral clustering [30] of the provenance graph. Via clustering we obtain cluster centroids, the coordinates of which can be used to calculate a distance measurement as outlined before. Having obtained a distance measure, we can check the distance against a provided threshold. If the distance exceeds this threshold, anomaly detection alerts the user to anomalous system behavior.

### 5.3   Proof of Concept

We implemented our method using the Eigenvalues of the Laplacian matrix as coordinates and the distance between the centroids of the Eigenvalues as the distance metric. We evaluated this implementation on a synthetic example as well as a realistic one. In the synthetic example, in each time step the system adds two numbers during normal operation. We have injected anomalies into the provenance data representing the addition of ten numbers in one time step. In the realistic example, in each time step a robot executes some actions based on some plan [23]. There are anomalies where no such plan is present.

Our prototypical implementation was able to successfully differentiate between the nominal and anomalous updates. This illustrates that our proposed method can indeed determine anomalies at least in these two use cases.

## 6   Conclusion and Future Work

In contrast to streams solely comprising the output data of a system, provenance data allows far greater insight into the inner workings of such a system. Thus, we believe that monitoring provenance data in addition to output data allows for earlier detection of system failures. We have outlined an approach to monitor these provenance data that reduces the problem of monitoring provenance data to that of determining anomalies in graphs. This greatly reduces the parameter space that has to be explored when constructing a real-world monitor to determining useful well-studied approaches for detecting anomalies in graphs [1]. Moreover, we illustrated that this approach can serve as a framework for detecting anomalies in provenance data via a prototypical proof of concept.

As a next step, we aim to identify real-life use cases in which we can apply and evaluate our approach. This use case will allow us to compare different definitions of coordinates and distances between coordinates. Moreover, we will be able to evaluate our proposed approach against other approaches to anomaly detection in graphs [1]. In addition, we aim to quantify the structure of graphs by additional properties, e.g., their diameter or depth. Finally, we are looking to compare our approach based on spectral graph analysis against existing machine learning approaches to anomaly detection.

**Acknowledgements.** We gratefully acknowledge suggestions by anonymous reviewers, which have significantly improved this work.

# References

1. Akoglu, L., Tong, H., Koutra, D.: Graph based anomaly detection and description: a survey. Data Min. Knowl. Disc. **29**(3), 626–688 (2014). https://doi.org/10.1007/s10618-014-0365-y
2. Alawini, A., Chen, L., Davidson, S., Fisher, S., Kim, J.: Discovering similar workflows via provenance clustering: a case study. In: Belhajjame, K., Gehani, A., Alper, P. (eds.) IPAW 2018. LNCS, vol. 11017, pp. 115–127. Springer, Cham (2018). https://doi.org/10.1007/978-3-319-98379-0_9
3. Alter, G.C., et al.: Capturing data provenance from statistical software. Int. J. Dig. Curat. **16**(1), 14 (2022). https://doi.org/10.2218/ijdc.v16i1.763
4. Bartocci, E., Falcone, Y., Francalanza, A., Reger, G.: Introduction to runtime verification. In: Bartocci, E., Falcone, Y. (eds.) Lectures on Runtime Verification. LNCS, vol. 10457, pp. 1–33. Springer, Cham (2018). https://doi.org/10.1007/978-3-319-75632-5_1
5. Bates, A., Tian, D., Butler, K.R.B., Moyer, T.: Trustworthy whole-system provenance for the Linux kernel. In: Jung, J., Holz, T. (eds.) USENIX Security Symposium 2015, pp. 319–334. USENIX (2015). https://www.usenix.org/conference/usenixsecurity15/technical-sessions/presentation/bates
6. Bauer, A., Leucker, M., Schallhart, C.: Runtime verification for LTL and TLTL. ACM Trans. Softw. Eng. Methodol. **20**(4), 1–64 (2011). https://doi.org/10.1145/2000799.2000800
7. Baumeister, J., Finkbeiner, B., Schirmer, S., Schwenger, M., Torens, C.: RTLola cleared for take-off: monitoring autonomous aircraft. In: Lahiri, S.K., Wang, C. (eds.) CAV 2020. LNCS, vol. 12225, pp. 28–39. Springer, Cham (2020). https://doi.org/10.1007/978-3-030-53291-8_3
8. Berrada, G., Cheney, J.: Aggregating unsupervised provenance anomaly detectors. In: TaPP 2019. USENIX (2019). https://www.usenix.org/conference/tapp2019/presentation/berrada
9. Biyikoğu, T., Leydold, J., Stadler, P.F.: Laplacian Eigenvectors of Graphs. Springer, Cham (2007). https://doi.org/10.1007/978-3-540-73510-6
10. Chung, F.: Laplacians and the cheeger inequality for directed graphs. Ann. Combinator. **9**(1), 1–19 (2005). https://doi.org/10.1007/s00026-005-0237-z
11. D'Angelo, B., et al.: LOLA: Runtime monitoring of synchronous systems. In: TIME 2005. IEEE (2005). https://doi.org/10.1109/time.2005.26
12. Dauer, J.C., Finkbeiner, B., Schirmer, S.: Monitoring with verified guarantees. In: Feng, L., Fisman, D. (eds.) RV 2021. LNCS, vol. 12974, pp. 62–80. Springer, Cham (2021). https://doi.org/10.1007/978-3-030-88494-9_4
13. Dawes, J.H., Bianculli, D.: Specifying properties over inter-procedural, source code level behaviour of programs. In: Feng, L., Fisman, D. (eds.) RV 2021. LNCS, vol. 12974, pp. 23–41. Springer, Cham (2021). https://doi.org/10.1007/978-3-030-88494-9_2
14. Dawes, J.H., Reger, G.: Specification of temporal properties of functions for runtime verification. In: SAC 2019. ACM (2019). https://doi.org/10.1145/3297280.3297497
15. Faymonville, P., et al.: StreamLAB: stream-based monitoring of cyber-physical systems. In: Dillig, I., Tasiran, S. (eds.) CAV 2019. LNCS, vol. 11561, pp. 421–431. Springer, Cham (2019). https://doi.org/10.1007/978-3-030-25540-4_24
16. Fiedler, H., Herzog, J., Prohaska, M., Schildknecht, T., Weigel, M.: SMARTnet(TM)-Status and Statistics. In: IAC 2017 (2017). https://elib.dlr.de/115884/

17. Foster, I., Vockler, J., Wilde, M., Zhao, Y.: Chimera: A Virtual Data System for Representing, Querying, and Automating Data Derivation. In: SSDBM 2002, pp. 37–46 (2002). https://doi.org/10.1109/SSDM.2002.1029704

18. Gehani, A., Tariq, D.: SPADE: support for provenance auditing in distributed environments. In: Narasimhan, P., Triantafillou, P. (eds.) Middleware 2012. LNCS, vol. 7662, pp. 101–120. Springer, Heidelberg (2012). https://doi.org/10.1007/978-3-642-35170-9_6

19. Gera, R., et al.: Identifying network structure similarity using spectral graph theory. Appl. Network Sci. **3**(1), 1–15 (2017). https://doi.org/10.1007/s41109-017-0042-3

20. Han, X., Pasquier, T., Ranjan, T., Goldstein, M., Seltzer, M.: FRAPpuccino: fault-detection through runtime analysis of provenance. In: HotCloud 2017. USENIX. https://www.usenix.org/conference/hotcloud17/program/presentation/han

21. Han, X., Pasquier, T., Seltzer, M.: Provenance-based intrusion detection: opportunities and challenges. In: TaPP 2018. USENIX, London. https://www.usenix.org/conference/tapp2018/presentation/han

22. Hong, Y.: Bounds of eigenvalues of graphs. Discret. Math. **123**(1), 65–74 (1993). https://doi.org/10.1016/0012-365X(93)90007-G

23. Huynh, D.: c50b1f3a-89c2-11ec-a4ca-24418cc781d9 (2022). https://openprovenance.org/store/documents/5427

24. Johnson, M.A.C., et al.: Astronomical pipeline provenance: a use case evaluation. In: TaPP 2021. USENIX (2021). https://www.usenix.org/conference/tapp2021/presentation/johnson

25. Koren, Y.: Drawing graphs by eigenvectors: theory and practice. Comput. Math. Appl. **49**(11), 1867–1888 (2005). https://doi.org/10.1016/j.camwa.2004.08.015

26. Koymans, R.: Specifying real-time properties with metric temporal logic. Real-Time Syst. **2**(4), 255–299 (1990). https://doi.org/10.1007/bf01995674

27. Kühnert, J., Göddeke, D., Herschel, M.: Provenance-integrated parameter selection and optimization in numerical simulations. In: TaPP 2021. USENIX (2021). https://www.usenix.org/conference/tapp2021/presentation/kühnert

28. Leucker, M., Schallhart, C.: A brief account of runtime verification. J. Log. Algebraic Methods Program. **78**(5), 293–303 (2009). https://doi.org/10.1016/j.jlap.2008.08.004

29. Ludäscher, B., Altintas, I., Berkley, C., Higgins, D., Jaeger, E., Jones, M., Lee, E.A., Tao, J., Zhao, Y.: Scientific workflow management and the Kepler system. Concurr. Comput. Pract. Exp. **18**(10), 1039–1065 (2006). https://doi.org/10.1002/cpe.994

30. von Luxburg, U.: A tutorial on spectral clustering. Stat. Comput. **17**(4), 395–416 (2007). https://doi.org/10.1007/s11222-007-9033-z

31. Macko, P., Margo, D., Seltzer, M.: Local clustering in provenance graphs. In: CIKM 2013, pp. 835–840. ACM (2013). https://doi.org/10.1145/2505515.2505624

32. Maler, O., Ničković, D.: Monitoring properties of analog and mixed-signal circuits. Int. J. Softw. Tools Technol. Transf. **15**(3), 247–268 (2012). https://doi.org/10.1007/s10009-012-0247-9

33. Merris, R.: Laplacian matrices of graphs: a survey. Lin. Alg. App. **197–198**, 143–176 (1994). https://doi.org/10.1016/0024-3795(94)90486-3

34. Mohar, B.: Laplace eigenvalues of graphs-a survey. Discret. Math. **109**(1), 171–183 (1992). https://doi.org/10.1016/0012-365X(92)90288-Q

35. Momtaz, A., Basnet, N., Abbas, H., Bonakdarpour, B.: Predicate monitoring in distributed cyber-physical systems. In: Feng, L., Fisman, D. (eds.) RV 2021. LNCS,

vol. 12974, pp. 3–22. Springer, Cham (2021). https://doi.org/10.1007/978-3-030-88494-9_1

36. Moreau, L.: The Foundations for Provenance on the Web. Found. Trends Web Sci. **2**(2–3), 99–241 (2010). https://doi.org/10.1561/1800000010
37. Moreau, L., Groth, P., Cheney, J., Lebo, T., Miles, S.: The rationale of PROV. J. Web Semant. **35**, 235–257 (2015). https://doi.org/10.1016/j.websem.2015.04.001
38. Nenzi, L., Bortolussi, L., Ciancia, V., Loreti, M., Massink, M.: Qualitative and quantitative monitoring of spatio-temporal properties. In: Bartocci, E., Majumdar, R. (eds.) RV 2015. LNCS, vol. 9333, pp. 21–37. Springer, Cham (2015). https://doi.org/10.1007/978-3-319-23820-3_2
39. Pasquier, T., et al.: Practical whole-system provenance capture. In: SoCC 2017. ACM (2017). https://doi.org/10.1145/3127479.3129249
40. Pnueli, A.: The temporal logic of programs. In: SFCS 1977. IEEE (1977). https://doi.org/10.1109/sfcs.1977.32
41. Pouchard, L., et al.: Prescriptive provenance for streaming analysis of workflows at scale. In: NYSDS 2018. IEEE (2018). https://doi.org/10.1109/nysds.2018.8538951
42. Satuluri, V., Parthasarathy, S.: Symmetrizations for clustering directed graphs. In: EDBT 2011. ACM (2011). https://doi.org/10.1145/1951365.1951407
43. Schreiber, A., de Boer, C., von Kurnatowski, L.: GitLab2PROV—provenance of software projects hosted on GitLab. In: TaPP 2021. USENIX (2021). https://www.usenix.org/conference/tapp2021/presentation/schreiber
44. Shi, J., Malik, J.: Normalized cuts and image segmentation. In: CVPR 1997, pp. 731–737 (1997). https://doi.org/10.1109/CVPR.1997.609407
45. Spielman, D.: Combinatorial Scientific Computing, chap. Spectral Graph Theory, p. 30. Chapman and Hall/CRC (2011)
46. Spielman, D.A.: Spectral graph theory and its applications. In: FOCS 2007, pp. 29–38 (2007). https://doi.org/10.1109/FOCS.2007.56
47. Stoffers, M., Meinel, M., Hofmann, B., Schreiber, A.: Integrating provenance-awareness into the space debris processing system BACARDI. In: IEEE Aerospace Conference 2022 (2022, to appear)
48. Stoffers, M., et al.: BACARDI: a system to track space debris. In: ESA NEO and Debris Detection Conference. https://elib.dlr.de/126572/
49. Van Lierde, H.: Spectral clustering algorithms for directed graphs. Master's thesis, Université catholique de Louvain (2015)
50. W3C Working Group: PROV Model Primer (2013). https://www.w3.org/TR/2013/NOTE-prov-primer-20130430/. Accessed 28 Apr 2022
51. W3C Working Group: PROV-Overview. An Overview of the PROV Family of Documents (2013). https://www.w3.org/TR/2013/NOTE-prov-overview-20130430/. Accessed 28 Apr 2022

# A Python Library for Trace Analysis

Dennis Dams[1(✉)], Klaus Havelund[2(✉)], and Sean Kauffman[3(✉)]

[1] ESI (TNO), Eindhoven, The Netherlands
dennis.dams@tno.nl
[2] Jet Propulsion Laboratory, California Institute of Technology, Pasadena, USA
klaus.havelund@jpl.nasa.gov
[3] Aalborg University, Aalborg, Denmark
seank@cs.aau.dk

**Abstract.** We present a Python library for trace analysis named
PyContract. PyContract is a shallow internal DSL, in contrast to many
trace analysis tools that implement external or deep internal DSLs. The
library has been used in a project for analysis of logs from NASA's
Europa Clipper mission. We describe our design choices, explain the API
via examples, and present an experiment comparing PyContract against
other state-of-the-art tools from the research and industrial communities.

## 1 Introduction

Runtime Verification (RV) is an approach to checking that a system under execution does the right thing, complementary to testing and static verification.
Numerous RV systems have been developed over time. Many of these systems
offer so-called *external* domain-specific languages (DSLs) [1,2,4,5,7,9,11,18,19,
22]. These parse a specification and synthesize a runtime monitor from the specification. *Internal* (or embedded) DSLs, on the other hand, extend an existing
host programming language, usually as a library.

There are two kinds of internal DSLs: deep and shallow [14]. In a *deep* internal
DSL, data structures in the host language are used to represent DSL constructs
in an explicit manner, e.g., as an Abstract Syntax Tree (AST), which can then
be processed by writing either an interpreter or a compiler for execution. Some
examples are [15,26]. A *shallow* internal DSL includes the constructs of the
host language as part of the DSL, using the host language's native runtime
system to execute them. This is how most programming language libraries are
implemented. Shallow Scala-internal DSLs developed by the authors, and their
use, are described in [3,16,17,20].

In this work we present a shallow Python-internal DSL for RV. Our motivation stems from our experiences in infusing monitoring technology into practice.
The main reason for implementing a monitoring library in Python is the language's popularity [28]. The most recent version of Python provides pattern

T. Dang and V. Stolz (Eds.): RV 2022, LNCS 13498, pp. 264–273, 2022.
https://doi.org/10.1007/978-3-031-17196-3_15

matching, which we demonstrate is useful for writing monitors. We believe that an internal DSL increases *adoption*. For example, in our experience with applying the CommaSuite tool [8] in industrial contexts, we have observed that having to learn a new specification language is sometimes experienced by potential users as a barrier to using the tool. An internal DSL is "just" another library in a familiar language, and modern programmers commonly use many libraries [24]. They can continue to use their favorite development tools (such as IDEs) and other libraries for the host language. The chance of adoption is furthermore increased due to the fact that shallow internal DSLs offer full *expressiveness*, since the host language can be leveraged for complex calculations. This is an essential design point to expand PyContract's possible uses. This has been demonstrated by its application in the analysis of telemetry logs from testing the Europa Clipper mission [12] flight computer.

Furthermore, *design and implementation* are much easier for internal DSLs than fosr external DSLs, because the syntax and semantics of the host language are used. A noteworthy aspect of our solution is its small implementation. For the same reason, *maintenance* requires less effort. The effort to respond to feature requests can be reduced due to the availability of language constructs in the host language. E.g., the development of the external CommaSuite DSL has involved regularly occurring user requests for more "richness" in the language such as dictionaries (hash maps) as an additional data type and a notation for namespaces. In an external DSL, adding such features is made more challenging by the need to handle all aspects of the language interpretation. A potential disadvantage of shallow internal DSLs (when compared to external DSLs and deep internal DSLs) is *analyzability*. However, Python supports powerful meta-programming features allowing a program to inspect its own AST.

We support monitoring of events that carry data, allowing specification of the relationship between data in events arriving at different time points (i.e. we support first-order temporal properties). PyContract implements a form of *slicing (indexing)* [22,26] for optimizing monitoring events with data, limiting the search when an event is submitted to the monitor. We use an *automaton* flavored language rather than temporal logic for the specification of monitors as we find automata to be more flexible. Our DSL resembles a cross between Extended Finite State Machines (EFSMs) [6], such as Quantified Event Automata (QEA) [26], and rule-based programming, such as RuleR [4]. It most closely resembles the Scala DSL Daut [10,16].

We support *two flavors of states*. In *next*-states, the next event must match a transition. This allows the definition of state machines as found in standard textbooks on finite automata [27]. In *skip*-states, events may be skipped until a transition matches. This can be used for state machines in the style of SysML [29] and UML [31]. We support *skip*-states as the default and treat all states as implicitly accepting unless marked as rejecting. In our experience, this provides a flexible way to write concise monitors.

We support *visualization* of monitors to improve user comprehension. Visualization is an efficient way to communicate the meaning of a specification [30]. We use a format based on standard EFSM displays that leverages user familiarity with such diagrams.

## 2   The PyContract Library

PyContract is an internal Python DSL for writing event monitors. It is inspired by rule-based programming [4,17] in that the memory of a monitor is a set of facts, where a fact is a named data record. Furthermore, facts, like states in state machines, can have transitions which, upon triggering, can generate other facts. As in EFSMs one can also define variables, local to a monitor, to which the transitions can refer in conditions and in actions. Finally, since the DSL is a Python library, one can write arbitrary Python code as part of the monitors. PyContract is inspired by the Scala DSL Daut [10,16] and is developed for Python 3.10 that supports pattern matching [25]. We use pattern matching extensively for defining transition functions. The general approach is to define a monitor as a sub-class of the `Monitor` class, create an instance of it, and then feed it with events. Events are fed, one by one, using the `evaluate(event: Event)` method and, in the case of a finite sequence of observations, a call of the `end()` method signals the monitor that the sequence has ended, at which point any outstanding obligations that have not been satisfied (expected events that did not occur) will be reported as errors. PyContract is available under the Apache 2.0 open-source license at [23]. In the following we shall illustrate how to write monitors with two examples.

### 2.1   Example 1

Consider a sequence of events, where each event indicates the acquisition or the release of a lock by a thread. PyContract can monitor events of any kind: numbers, strings, dictionaries (maps), objects of user defined classes, etc. We shall here assume the definition of two such event classes `Acquire` and `Release` defined as data classes[1], each taking a thread and a lock as argument, allowing the construction of objects such as `Acquire(thread, lock)` and `Release(thread, lock)`, and performing pattern matching over these.

The monitor we shall present is a "kitchen sink" example of features, and implements property $P_1$, consisting of five sub-properties:

$P_{1.1}$ A thread acquiring a lock must eventually release it.
$P_{1.2}$ While a lock is acquired by a thread it cannot be acquired by any thread.
$P_{1.3}$ A thread can only release a lock if it has acquired and not yet released it.
$P_{1.4}$ A maximum of $N$ locks can be acquired at any point in time, where $N$ is a monitor parameter.
$P_{1.5}$ An acquired lock should never later be freed as memory.

---

[1] A data class is a class decorated with `@dataclass`, which allows to perform pattern matching over objects of the class, including their parameters.

The monitor is shown in Fig. 1, and is defined as the class M1 extending the Monitor class. The monitor is parameterized with the maximal number of locks, limit (line 2) that can be acquired at any point in time. A variable, count (line 4), is introduced to count the number of active acquisitions. The body of M1 defines a transition function (lines 7–20), and two states: DoRelease (lines 22–33), parameterized with a thread id and a lock id; and DoNotFree (lines 35–42), parameterized with a lock id. The PyContract @data decorator implies @dataclass and introduces a hash-function to store states in hash sets. These two states themselves each contain a transition function. A transition function takes as argument an event and returns a list of states (or None if not applicable).

The outermost transition function (lines 7–20) is *always* enabled, and can be perceived as representing the temporal logic box operator □. This outermost transition function, when applied to an event, will match it against two patterns: Acquire(thread, lock) and Release(thread, lock), where thread and lock will be bound to the actual values of the incoming event. The transition corresponding to an acquisition (lines 9–17) is conditioned on the non-existence of a DoRelease-state with the same lock (lines 10–11), representing the fact that the lock has already been acquired by some thread (it does not matter which). If the number of active monitors is less than the limit, count is bumped up and a list of two states (lines 14–15) is returned, each of which is then added to the memory of the monitor. The transition corresponding to a release (lines 18–20) returns an error if no DoRelease(thread, lock) exists with the same thread and lock (line 19). Note how we can use a fact as a Boolean expression if all arguments are known, in contrast to the more verbose call of the exists predicate in lines 10–11.

An event that does not match any of the **case** entries is considered to not match any transition. How this is treated depends on the kind of state. Since PyContract's default is to use skip-states (in contrast to next-states), in this case it means that the event is skipped and the state stays active in memory.

The DoRelease state is a HotState, meaning that at the end of a run, an error is reported if such a state is active. In case of an acquisition, a match occurs if the second lock argument is the same as self.lock (the underscore '_' pattern matches any value). In general, any dotted name in a pattern indicates that the incoming value has to match this exact value. In case of a match, two states are returned (line 30): an error state, and the self state, keeping it active in the monitor. In case of a release by the thread that holds the lock, the counter is decreased and the state ok is returned, corresponding to removing the DoRelease state. The DoNotFree state is a normal State (line 36), effectively a skip state that forever monitors that the lock is not freed with a Free event.

## 2.2   Example 2

Consider the property $P_2$ consisting of just the first three sub-properties $P_{1.1}$, $P_{1.2}$, and $P_{1.3}$ of $P_1$. A consequence of this property is that acquisitions and releases of a lock must strictly alternate. The monitor M2 in Fig. 2 monitors this property. In monitor M1, Fig. 1, line 19, we used a memory query to check that

```
1  class M1(Monitor):
2      def __init__(self, limit: int):
3          super().__init__()
4          self.count: int = 0
5          self.limit = limit
6
7      def transition(self, event):
8          match event:
9              case Acquire(thread, lock)
10                 if not self.exists(lambda s:
11                     isinstance(s, M1.DoRelease) and s.lock==lock):
12                     if self.monitor.count < self.limit:
13                         self.monitor.count += 1
14                         return [M1.DoRelease(thread, lock),
15                                 M1.DoNotFree(lock)]
16                     else:
17                         return error(f'limit_reached')
18             case Release(thread, lock)
19                 if not M1.DoRelease(thread, lock):
20                     return error(f'releasing_un-acquired_lock')
21
22     @data
23     class DoRelease(HotState):
24         thread: str
25         lock: int
26
27         def transition(self, event):
28             match event:
29                 case Acquire(_, self.lock):
30                     return [error('already_acquired'), self]
31                 case Release(self.thread, self.lock):
32                     self.monitor.count -= 1
33                     return ok
34
35     @data
36     class DoNotFree(State):
37         lock: int
38
39         def transition(self, event):
40             match event:
41                 case Free(self.lock):
42                     return error(f'Lock_freed')
```

**Fig. 1.** The monitor M1

a lock is only released by the thread that acquired it. In monitor M2 we instead use indexing (slicing) and next-states, which results in a more efficient and more succinct monitor. We shall slice on locks, meaning that for each lock encountered in the trace, PyContract will, in a hash map, map it to a monitor memory (set of states) for only that lock. All events concerning that lock are sent to only

the states in that lock-specific memory. This yields two advantages: first, we do
not need to search all states when an event arrives, we can just look up and
search the states for the relevant lock, and second, since only events concerning
that lock are sent to that lock-specific memory, we can write our monitor more
succinctly using next-states. The `Monitor` class defines a method:

```
def key(self, event) -> Optional[object]:
    return None
```

which is called on each event to return its slicing index (`None` is the default,
meaning no slicing is performed). The user can override this method to indicate
which events should be sliced upon. Figure 2 (lines 2–5) shows such an overriding
of this method, defining the lock to be the slicing index (key) for `Acquire` and
`Release` events. The second step is to define our states as next-states (lines 8
and 15). The semantics of these is that it is an error if the next observed event
(sent to that state) does not match any of its transitions. A `NextState` is an
acceptance state while a `HotNextState` is not.

```
1  class M2(Monitor):
2      def key(self, event) -> Optional[object]:
3          match event:
4              case Acquire(_, lock) | Release(_, lock):
5                  return lock
6
7      @initial
8      class Idle(NextState):
9          def transition(self, event):
10             match event:
11                 case Acquire(thread, lock):
12                     return M2.DoRelease(thread, lock)
13
14     @data
15     class DoRelease(HotNextState):
16         thread: str
17         lock: int
18
19         def transition(self, event):
20             match event:
21                 case Release(self.thread, self.lock):
22                     return M2.Idle()
```

**Fig. 2.** The monitor M2

Slicing is used in efficient runtime verification tools such as MOP [22] and
QEA [26]. In PyContract the slicing criterion is, as just shown, user defined (by
overriding method `key`), which allows for a more expressive form of indexing
than in e.g. MOP where all data parameters are used for indexing. QEA allows

for more flexible slicing criteria. Slicing is used in MOP and QEA to express past
time properties, as in this example (a release must be preceded by an acquisition).

## 3    Comparison with Other Frameworks

Using M2 from Fig. 2, we compared PyContract against three other tools: the
research tools Daut [16] and QEA [26], and the industrial tool CommaSuite [8,
21], inspired by the RV tool RuleR [21]. At [13], the implementations of M2 in
those other tools are available. We encourage the reader to compare these to the
PyContract code from Fig. 2.

We compared the performance of PyContract monitoring with the other tools
to investigate whether it is fast enough for practical use. We ran three experiments with the four tools, using the monitors for M2. The first experiment simu-
lates one thread acquiring and then immediately releasing one lock, many times.
In the second experiment, one thread acquires many locks at once before releasing them. The third experiment is the same as the second except that each lock
is acquired and released by a different thread. For each experiment, we recorded
the processing times for traces with 500,000; 1,000,000; 2,000,000; and 4,000,000
events.

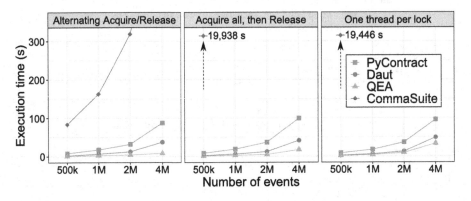

**Fig. 3.** Benchmark results comparing PyContract with three other tools.

Figure 3 shows the results running the experiment on an Intel Xeon E5-2680
frequency-locked to 2.40 GHz. We ran PyContract 1.0.1 on Python 3.10.4 and
QEA 1.0, Daut 0.1, and CommaSuite 1.1.0 on the Oracle JVM 11.0.12 running
on 64-bit Linux 4.15. The graph shows the number of events in the trace (x-axis)
against the time the tool took to complete offline analysis. Each point represents
the mean of at least six runs. PyContract, Daut, and CommaSuite read events
from JSONL files while QEA read them from a special kind of CSV file that this
tool supports. The experiments and raw results are available at [13].

In the experiment, it is clear that QEA and Daut are the fastest tools, but
PyContract remains usable with processing times under 100 s for four million

events. Additionally, PyContract has similar results for all three experiments while QEA and CommaSuite are noticeably slower when many locks are acquired at once. For example, QEA with 4M events completes in about 8 s when only one lock is acquired at once but takes about 33 s when 2M locks are acquired at once by 2M separate threads. One possible explanation of the superior performance of Daut over PyContract, in spite of their similar implementation, may be the superiority of the JVM and its just-in-time compilation compared to Python's runtime system.

In the cases where no CommaSuite results are reported it is because the tests took more than 320 s. The CommaSuite developers pointed out several potential reasons for the observed performance. Most importantly, performance has never been a main requirement[2]. CommaSuite models may be nondeterministic, which requires additional bookkeeping during monitoring. This feature cannot be disabled. Additional data is also collected to provide e.g. coverage information after monitoring; again this is not optional.

# 4   Conclusion

We have presented a shallow internal DSL (library) for trace analysis in Python, and argued that such DSLs have important advantages. These advantages include ease of infusion into projects due to a flattened learning curve, taking advantage of development tools (such as IDEs) and libraries for the programming language, expressiveness, and fast development and reduced maintenance making it easier to adapt to feature requests. Since Python is one of the most popular programming languages, we believe that a Python library for monitoring is valuable. We compared the performance of PyContract to two research tools and one industrial tool for RV, all three JVM-based. PyContract performed reasonably well compared to the two research tools, considering that the JVM is a high performance platform compared to Python's runtime system, and PyContract convincingly outperformed the industrial tool. The longer term objective of the library is to support activities that normally are associated with monitoring, providing a "Swiss pocket knife" for monitoring. This includes, as already mentioned, various forms of visualization, but also trace mining. Since PyContract is embedded in Python, allowing a mix of monitoring DSL and free style Python code, the door is open to experiment with the connection between runtime verification and data analysis. This line of work has already been pursued on the application to the Europa Clipper project, and we intend to pursue it further.

**Acknowledgments.** Part of the research was funded by the ERC Advanced Grant LASSO, the Villum Investigator Grant S4OS, and DIREC, Digital Research Center Denmark. Part of the research was performed at Jet Propulsion Laboratory, California Institute of Technology, under a contract with the National Aeronautics and Space Administration. Part of the research was carried out as part of the Accelerando program

---

[2] CommaSuite has been designed to be used to monitor the logs from automated tests in nightly builds, where "the traces are short enough, and the nights long enough".

272    D. Dams et al.

under the responsibility of ESI (TNO) with Philips as the carrying industrial partner. The Accelerando research is supported by the Netherlands Organisation for Applied Scientific Research TNO.

# References

1. Ancona, D., Franceschini, L., Ferrando, A., Mascardi, V.: RML: theory and practice of a domain specific language for runtime verification. Sci. Compute. Programm. **205**, 102610 (2021)
2. Barringer, H., Goldberg, A., Havelund, K., Sen, K.: Rule-based runtime verification. In: Steffen, B., Levi, G. (eds.) VMCAI 2004. LNCS, vol. 2937, pp. 44–57. Springer, Heidelberg (2004). https://doi.org/10.1007/978-3-540-24622-0_5
3. Barringer, H., Havelund, K.: TraceContract: A Scala DSL for Trace Analysis. In: Butler, M., Schulte, W. (eds.) FM 2011. LNCS, vol. 6664, pp. 57–72. Springer, Heidelberg (2011). https://doi.org/10.1007/978-3-642-21437-0_7
4. Barringer, H., Rydeheard, D., Havelund, K.: Rule systems for run-time monitoring: from EAGLE to RULER. In: Sokolsky, O., Taşıran, S. (eds.) RV 2007. LNCS, vol. 4839, pp. 111–125. Springer, Heidelberg (2007). https://doi.org/10.1007/978-3-540-77395-5_10
5. Basin, D.A., Klaedtke, F., Marinovic, S., Zălinescu, E.: Monitoring of temporal first-order properties with aggregations. Formal Methods Syst. Des. **46**(3), 262–285 (2015)
6. Cheng, K.-T., Krishnakumar, A.: Automatic functional test generation using the extended finite state machine model. In: 30th ACM/IEEE Design Automation Conference, pp. 86–91 (1993)
7. Colombo, C., Pace, G.J., Schneider, G.: LARVA – safer monitoring of real-time Java programs (tool paper). In: Proceedings of the 2009 Seventh IEEE International Conference on Software Engineering and Formal Methods, SEFM 2009, pp. 33–37. IEEE Computer Society, Washington, DC (2009)
8. CommaSuite. https://projects.eclipse.org/projects/technology.comma
9. D'Angelo, B., et al.: LOLA: runtime monitoring of synchronous systems. In: Proceedings of TIME 2005: the 12th International Symposium on Temporal Representation and Reasoning, pp. 166–174. IEEE (2005)
10. Daut. https://github.com/havelund/daut
11. Decker, N., Leucker, M., Thoma, D.: Monitoring modulo theories. Softw. Tools Technol. Transf. (STTT), **18**(2), 205–225 (2016)
12. Europa Clipper mission. https://europa.nasa.gov
13. Experiments Repository. https://bitbucket.org/seanmk/rv-bench
14. Gibbons, J., Wu, N.: Folding domain-specific languages: deep and shallow embeddings (functional pearl). In: Proceedings of the 19th ACM SIGPLAN International Conference on Functional Programming, ICFP 2014, pp. 339–347. Association for Computing Machinery, New York (2014)
15. Hallé, S., Villemaire, R.: Runtime enforcement of web service message contracts with data. IEEE Trans. Serv. Comput. **5**(2), 192–206 (2012)
16. Havelund, K.: Data automata in Scala. In: 2014 Theoretical Aspects of Software Engineering Conference, TASE 2014, Changsha, China, 1–3 September, 2014, pp. 1–9. IEEE Computer Society (2014)
17. Havelund, K.: Rule-based runtime verification revisited. Softw. Tools Technol. Transf. (STTT) **17**(2), 143–170 (2015)

18. Kauffman, S., Havelund, K., Joshi, R.: nfer – a notation and system for inferring event stream abstractions. In: Falcone, Y., Sánchez, C. (eds.) RV 2016. LNCS, vol. 10012, pp. 235–250. Springer, Cham (2016). https://doi.org/10.1007/978-3-319-46982-9_15

19. Kim, M., Kannan, S., Lee, I., Sokolsky, O.: Java-MaC: a run-time assurance tool for Java. In: Proceedings of the 1st International Workshop on Runtime Verification (RV'01). Electronic Notes in Theoretical Computer Science, vol. 55(2). Elsevier (2001)

20. Kurklu, E., Havelund, K.: A flight rule checker for the LADEE Lunar spacecraft. In: 17th International Colloquium on Theoretical Aspects of Computing (ICTAC'20), vol. TBD of LNCS (2020)

21. Kurtev, I., Schuts, M., Hooman, J., Swagerman, D.-J.: Integrating interface modeling and analysis in an industrial setting. In: Proceedings of the 5th International Conference on Model-Driven Engineering and Software Development (MODELSWARD 2017), pp. 345–352. SciTePress, February 2017

22. Meredith, P.O., Jin, D., Griffith, D., Chen, F., Roşu, G.: An overview of the MOP runtime verification framework. Int. J. Softw. Tech. Technol. Transf., 249–289 (2011). https://doi.org/10.1007/s10009-011-0198-6

23. PyContract. https://github.com/pyrv/pycontract

24. PyPi Stats Website. https://pypistats.org

25. Python pattern matching. https://peps.python.org/pep-0636

26. Reger, G., Cruz, H.C., Rydeheard, D.: MarQ: monitoring at runtime with QEA. In: Baier, C., Tinelli, C. (eds.) TACAS 2015. LNCS, vol. 9035, pp. 596–610. Springer, Heidelberg (2015). https://doi.org/10.1007/978-3-662-46681-0_55

27. Sipser, M.: Introduction to the Theory of Computation, 3rd edn. MA, Course Technology, Boston (2013)

28. StackOverflow Developer Survey (2021). https://insights.stackoverflow.com/survey/2021

29. OMG Systems Modeling Language (SysML). http://www.omgsysml.org

30. Tufte, E.R., Goeler, N.H., Benson, R.: Envisioning information, vol. 126. Graphics press Cheshire, CT (1990)

31. OMG Unified Modeling Language (UML). http://www.omg.org/spec/UML

# Lock Contention Performance Classification for Java Intrinsic Locks

Nahid Hasan Khan[1], Joseph Robertson[1], Ramiro Liscano[1(✉)], Akramul Azim[1], Vijay Sundaresan[2], and Yee-Kang Chang[2]

[1] Ontario Tech University, L1G 0C5 Oshawa, ON, Canada
{hasan.khan,joseph.robertson}@ontariotechu.net,
{ramiro.liscano,akramul.azim}@ontariotechu.ca
[2] IBM Canada, Toronto, ON, Canada
{vijaysun,yeekangc}@ca.ibm.com

**Abstract.** Improper management of locks and threads can lead to contention and can cause performance degradation and prevent software applications from further scaling. Nowadays, performance engineers use legacy tools and their experience to determine causes of lock contention. In this paper, a clustering-based approach is presented to help identify the type of lock contention fault to facilitate the procedure that performance engineers follow, intending to eventually support developers with less experience. The classifier is based on the premise that if lock contention exists it is reflected as either threads spending too much time inside the critical section and/or high frequency access requests to the locked resources. Our results show that a KMeans classifier is able to identify three classes of lock contention from run-time data where one of these classes is clearly caused by high hold times. The other two classes are more challenging to label but one appears to be caused by high frequency requests to the locked resource.

**Keywords:** Lock contention · Concurrency · Run-time faults · Classification · Software engineering

## 1 Introduction

Synchronization is essential in multi-threaded applications and introduces some level of thread contention when applied. When this contention is significant it results in performance degradation and is typically known as a lock contention fault or performance bottleneck due to contention.

It is difficult to write concurrent programs and developers usually come back to refactor the portion of the code where the concurrency feature resides to make their concurrent code more efficient. A recent study reports that more than 25%

of all critical sections are changed at some point by the developers, both to fix correctness bugs and to enhance performance [7,14].

Lock contention bottlenecks have been investigated in the software community for a while but they are still difficult to detect [11,12] and analyze and usually it is a job performed by an experienced performance engineer. Typically application developers do not have the skill set that a performance engineer has to detect contention bottlenecks. The long term motivation of our work is to develop a recommendation system for software developers that encounter lock contention faults. We are proposing a combined approach that leverages a classification of the contention bottle neck based on those defined by Goetz [6] with the eventual goal of matching these contention types with patterns in the code. This paper focuses on preliminary work in the classification of lock contentions based on run-time performance metrics of the application.

In Goetz's book titled "Java Concurrency in Practice" he identifies the following 2 potential causes for contention faults:

- Type 1 - Threads spending too much time inside the critical sections.
- Type 2 - High frequency access requests by multiple threads to the locked resources.

The reason why these types are important to identify is that recommendations to alleviate the lock contention differs for types 1 and 2 [1]. In Type 1 the focus in on reducing the hold time on the lock while for Type 2 the solutions focus mostly on reducing the scope of the lock.

The paper is organized as follows. We introduce some related works in Sect. 2. The paper's main methodology is presented in Sect. 3. Section 4 describes the analysis of the clustering results. Some of the limitations of our approach and concluding remarks are presented in Sect. 5.

## 2    Related Works

Lock contention performance bottlenecks have been well investigated in the past few years with most works focusing on detecting and locating the root cause of the lock contention but very few papers have attempted to categorize the lock contention with the goal to suggest recommendations to alleviate the contention.

One of the few papers that tries to distinguish between type 1 and 2 lock contentions for categorizing and diagnosing synchronization performance faults is the work on SyncPerf by Mejbah ul Alam et al. [1]. In their work they reviewed several papers and categorized them in a quadrant based on the level of contention rate vs. lock acquisition frequency and concluded that there were no publications that addressed the detection of lock contention type 2 but focused primarily on the detection of locks of type 1.

Nathan R. Tallent et al. [13] details three approaches to gaining insight into performance losses due to lock contention. Their first two approaches use call stack profiling and prove that this profiling does not yield insight into lock contention. The final approach used an associated lock contention attribute called thread spinning that helps provide insight into lock contention.

Florian David et al. proposed a profiler named "free-lunch" that measures critical section pressure (CSP) and the progress of the threads that impede the performance [3]. This paper stated that they failed to determine a correlation among the metrics extracted from the IBM Java Lock Analyzer (JLA) while we have been able to observe some relations between the performance metrics and the lock contention. This paper also lacks a description of the metrics related to different contention fault types.

## 3    Methodology

Our approach uses run-time logs from several performance analyzers such as Linux *perf* [10], and JLM [9], then analyzes them utilizing a popular clustering technique (KMeans) to determine the existence of different types of contention faults. This analysis is a form of unsupervised classification and it was chosen over supervised classification because performance engineers do not label the types of lock contention faults.

A high-level workflow of our methodology is shown in Fig. 1. The approach can be divided into two main parts; the dataset creation and the feature engineering and classification. The principal processes in the dataset creation stage are the run-time performance data analysis and the data filtering. The run-time performance data analysis process consists of a compiled Java program that reflects a multi-threaded concurrent example integrated with a benchmark tool such as IBM Performance Inspector. The main process in the feature engineering and classification part of the workflow is the contention classification process that extracts from the performance data a set of clusters.

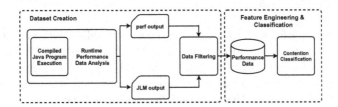

**Fig. 1.** High level workflow of our methodology where the steps are divided into two main parts, the Dataset creation and, the Feature engineering and classification.

### 3.1    Dataset Creation

Our methodology requires the generation of a dataset of lock contention performance metrics and currently no such dataset exist so the creation of such a dataset is an important part of this work. This code is shown in Listing 1.1 and is executed in a controlled environment. The code is compiled before running, and necessary command-line arguments are provided prior to execution. The command-line arguments are the number of threads and the execution time of the critical section (emulated by putting the thread to sleep and shown in line 8 of the code.) The number of threads is set in the main program that executes this code. The code is executed multiple times to reduce the effects of outliers in the metrics, and we usually skip the first 10s of the execution to avoid the JVM's code optimization and warm-up period.

**Listing 1.1.** A Java example class "SyncTask" that is being used to emulate different types of faults in our controlled environment

```
1   class SyncTask {
2       public ArrayList<Integer> arrList;
3       public int sleep_t,
4
5       public synchronized void taskOne(Integer value){
6           try {
7               arrList.put(value);
8               Thread.sleep(sleep_t);
9           } catch(Exception e) {
10              e.printStackTrace();
11          }
12      }
13  }
```

There were two configurations that we used to generate the dataset: the first was 10, 100, 500, and 1000 threads with sleeptimes from 1 to 20000ns in 100ns increments, the second was 10, 50, 100, 200, 300, 400, 500, and 1000 threads with sleeptimes from 1 to 20000ns in 100ns increments.

The two configurations were created for convenience and to break up the total time it takes to create the dataset. One single run takes 40 to 45 s to complete and creates a single row in the dataset. As an example, configuration 1 takes about 9.4 h on average to generate the dataset. The output of the two configurations are combined to create the final dataset.

Once the Java code bench marking is completed, the *perf* and JLM performance analyzers are executed to collect the necessary run-time performance profile data. It is best to ensure that a high-performance machine with a bare-metal operating system is installed to execute the concurrent code and collect performance data. We installed these tools on a high-performance Linux machine with a 24 core processor (3800 MHz MHz) and 32 GB of RAM. For the Java environment, we use Openj9 JVM because it is compatible with JLM [4].

JLM provides quite a few metrics related to Java inflated monitors and a brief description of the most important of those metrics is helpful to the readers to understand how they relate to lock contention faults.

- GETS: Total number of successful acquires. GETS = NONREC + REC.
- TIER2: The number of inner loops to obtain locks.

- TIER3: The number of cycles in the outer layer to obtain the lock.
- %UTIL: Monitor hold time divided by total JLM recording time.
- AVER-HTM: Average amount of time the monitor was held.

When lock contention occurs, JLM lists the Java monitors under the "JLM Inflated Monitors" along with the specific values for each metric as defined above.

The *perf* tool is capable of capturing the symbols from system memory. These symbols are mainly method names, variables, or class names usually used in the OS itself, the kernel, or in the Java application. The reference of how the *perf* tool works can be found here [10]. With the help of a script, we managed to extract a human-readable log containing the following 3 columns of values; the sample count, the percentage of the sample count relative to the total sample counts, and the symbol name.

## 3.2    Feature Engineering and Classification

Feature engineering enhances the performance of the model and is essential for enhancing the results of the clustering algorithm [8]. In order to achieve this, the following initial data pre-processing is done prior to applying clustering techniques:

1. Merge the *perf* and JLM data files into one file and Python data frame.
2. Remove features that contain string values (e.g., the monitor name in JLM).
3. Remove features that contain a value of zero.
4. Scale the data. Scaling is applied to all the features utilizing the Python library StandardScaler from sklearn.preprocessing.
5. Remove correlated features from the dataset.

After performing the steps listed above the final dataset consisted then of the following twelve metrics: The metrics %MISS, GETS, NONREC, SLOW, TIER2, TIER3, REC, %UTIL and AVER_HTM are collected from JLM and the metrics "_raw_spin_lock", "ctx_sched_in" and "delay_mwaitx" are collected from the *perf* tool.

**Determining Ideal Number of Clusters.** The KMeans clustering algorithm requires that the number of clusters be specified prior to determining the clusters from a dataset. This value is known as the KMeans "k" value. In our research we determined the "ideal" number of clusters by calculating the Silhouette Coefficient [15] or silhouette score of the clusters.

Results of the silhouette scores, determined by leveraging the Python library silhouette_score from sci-kit learn sklearn.metrics, are shown in Fig. 2. The figure illustrates that a cluster number of 3 achieves the highest silhouette score against other cluster numbers so it can be considered as the "ideal" number of clusters. We have also validated that a cluster number of 3 is ideal using other methods such as the Elbow Method [5] and NbClust [2] package.

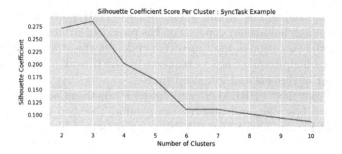

**Fig. 2.** The Silhouette Coefficient score for cluster number 3 is the highest. This indicates the optimal number of clusters is 3 that can be found within the dataset. Based on this verification, argument k = 3 is set to KMeans algorithm.

The KMeans algorithm of the Python library `KMeans` from `sklearn.cluster` was utilized to cluster the data set. The parameters "expected number of clusters" is set to three, "maximum number of iterations" is set to 600, and "minimum iterations" is set to 10. The extracted clusters are shown in Fig. 3.

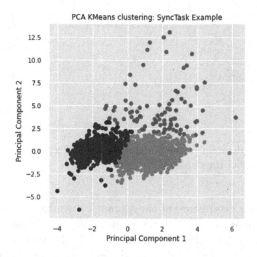

**Fig. 3.** Identified clusters from the lock-contention performance dataset using KMeans with a value of k = 3.

## 4  Cluster Analysis

In our data set 3 clusters were discovered and are numbered 0 to 2 but it is not clear if any of these clusters represent the lock contention types defined by Goetz [6]. For this simple example on can determine this by considering the distribution of the sleep time and number of threads in the clusters. Hypothetically, fault type 1 (fault due to high hold-time) depends on the provided variable parameter sleep times during the execution of the concurrent code. On the other hand, fault type 2 (fault due to high frequent access requests by the threads) should depend on a high number of threads and low sleep times.

Hence we plot the "THREADS" and "SLEEP" distribution against the clusters utilizing a box plot and observe the results. The two graphs are shown in Fig. 4a and Fig. 4b. CLUSTER_TYPE = 0 possesses a higher range of sleep times, indicating that more likely it represents fault type 1. On the other hand for the other 2 clusters it is challenging to label one of these as fault type 2. The figures illustrate that CLUSTER_TYPE = 2 contains a high number of threads compared to the other 2 clusters but the sleep time is slightly higher than CLUSTER_TYPE = 1. With this knowledge we believe that CLUSTER_TYPE = 2 can be labelled as fault type 2 while CLUSTER_TYPE = 1 is a form of low contention.

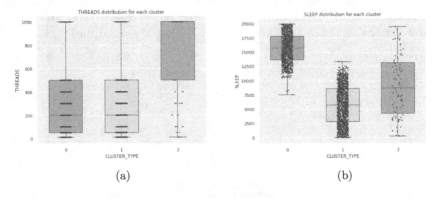

(a)                                (b)

**Fig. 4.** Box plot visualization of the Threads (a) and Sleep (b) parameters related to the clusters to help label the clusters.

In order to get a better sense of the semantic meaning of the clusters it helps to observe the dominant features in the clusters. Figures 5 show 4 box plots of the JLM metrics AVG_HTM, GETS, TIER2, and TIER3 relative to the 3 clusters. The AVG_HTM and GETS metrics are typically negatively correlated and one can observe this in CLUSTER_TYPES 0 and 1. This is not that obvious for CLUSTER_TYPE 2 as statistically these 2 values are indistinguishable.

The AVER_HTM value is a significant feature and from Fig. 5a one can see that the AVER_HTM value is higher for fault type 1 (CLUSTER_TYPE 0) than the other clusters. Moreover, the figure also illustrates that CLUSTER_TYPE 1 has a lower value than that of CLUSTER_TYPE 2 but the difference is not significant. This could imply that CLUSTER_TYPE 1 represents fault type 2 better than CLUSTER_TYPE 2 though when one looks at the threads distribution it is on par to those for CLUSTER_TYPE 0 and lower than those for CLUSTER_TYPE 2.

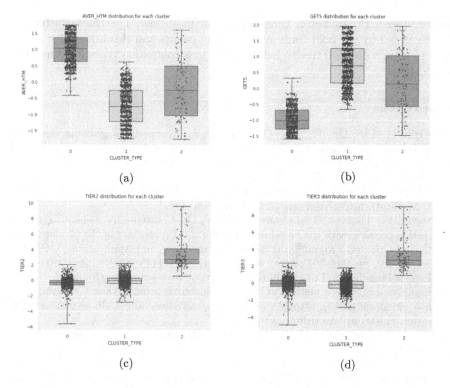

**Fig. 5.** Box plot visualization of the dominant features for each of the clusters. The AVER_HTM feature (a), the GETS feature (b), the TIER2 feature (c), and the TIER 3 feature (d).

Our expectation for the features related to spin counts (TIER2 and TIER3) are that they should experience high numbers for high lock request rates (fault type 2). The results in Fig. 5c and Fig. 5d show that CLUSTER_TYPE 2 has higher spin counts values than the other 2 clusters and presents more evidence that CLUSTER_TYPE 2 represents fault type 2.

After this analysis we conclude the following: (1) "Contention Fault 1" has high hold times, (2) "Contention Fault 2" has low in hold times and high spinning counts, (3) CLUSTER_TYPE 1 is more likely a form of "Low Contention", and (4) CLUSTER_TYPE 1 is more likely a form of "Low Contention" since it contains low spinning counts as well as low hold times.

## 5   Conclusions

In this paper, we demonstrate that Java intrinsic locks could be classified into the two types and we used a unsupervised KMeans classifier to investigate the types using run-time performance metrics. We find lock-contention faults do appear to classify into three distinct clusters rather than two based on run-time performance metrics where fault type 1 can be clearly identified due to the high hold times while fault type 2 is more challenging to identify as there is no cluster with a clear high number of threads and low hold time. The three clusters are differentiated by the hold times and spinning counts and this knowledge can be used to train a decision tree to help identify lock contention types for other Java applications.

# References

1. Alam, M.M.U., Liu, T., Zeng, G., Muzahid, A.: Syncperf: categorizing, detecting, and diagnosing synchronization performance bugs. In: Proceedings of the Twelfth European Conference on Computer Systems, pp. 298–313 (2017)
2. Charrad, M., Ghazzali, N., Boiteau, V., Niknafs, A.: Nbclust: an R package for determining the relevant number of clusters in a data set. J. Stat. Softw. **61**(6), 1–36 (2014). https://doi.org/10.18637/jss.v061.i06
3. David, F., Thomas, G., Lawall, J., Muller, G.: Continuously measuring critical section pressure with the Free-Lunch profiler. In: Proceedings of the Conference on Object-Oriented Programming Systems, Languages, and Applications, OOPSLA, vol. 49(10), pp. 291–307 (2014). https://doi.org/10.1145/2660193.2660210
4. Eclipse Foundation, I.: OpenJ9 (2017). https://www.eclipse.org/openj9/
5. Franklin, J.S.: Elbow method of K-means clustering using Python - Analytics Vidhya - Medium (2019). https://medium.com/analytics-vidhya/elbow-method-of-k-means-clustering-algorithm-a0c916adc540
6. Göetz, B., Professional, A.W.: Java concurrency in practice. Building **39**(11), 384 (2006)
7. Gu, R., Jin, G., Song, L., Zhu, L., Lu, S.: What change history tells us about thread synchronization. In: 2015 10th Joint Meeting of the European Software Engineering Conference and the ACM SIGSOFT Symposium on the Foundations of Software Engineering, ESEC/FSE 2015 - Proceedings, pp. 426–438 (2015). https://doi.org/10.1145/2786805.2786815
8. Hale, J.: Scale, Standardize, or Normalize with Scikit-Learn (2019). https://towardsdatascience.com/scale-standardize-or-normalize-with-scikit-learn-6ccc7d176a02
9. IBM: Java Lock Monitor (1999). http://perfinsp.sourceforge.net/examples.html#jlm
10. Kernel.org: Linux kernel profiling with perf (2015). https://perf.wiki.kernel.org/index.php/Tutorial
11. Kohler, M.: A Simple Way to Analyze Thread Contention Problems in Java (2006). https://blogs.sap.com/2006/10/18/a-simple-way-to-analyze-thread-contention-problems-in-java/
12. Salnikov-Tarnovski, N.: Improving Lock Performance (2015). https://dzone.com/articles/improving-lock-performance
13. Tallent, N.R., Mellor-Crummey, J.M., Porterfield, A.: Analyzing lock contention in multithreaded applications. ACM SIGPLAN Notices **45**(5), 269–279 (2010). https://doi.org/10.1145/1837853.1693489
14. Yu, T., Pradel, M.: Pinpointing and repairing performance bottlenecks in concurrent programs. Empir. Softw. Eng. **23**(5), 3034–3071 (2017). https://doi.org/10.1007/s10664-017-9578-1
15. Zhou, H.B., Gao, J.T.: Automatic method for determining cluster number based on silhouette coefficient. In: Advanced Materials Research. Advanced Materials Research, vol. 951, pp. 227–230. Trans Tech Publications Ltd, Switzerland (2014). https://doi.org/10.4028/www.scientific.net/AMR.951.227

# TestSelector: Automatic Test Suite Selection for Student Projects

Filipe Marques[1,2(✉)], António Morgado[1], José Fragoso Santos[1,2], and Mikoláš Janota[3]

[1] INESC-ID, Lisboa, Portugal
[2] Instituto Superior Técnico, University of Lisbon, Lisboa, Portugal
filipe.s.marque@tecnico.ulisboa
[3] Czech Technical University in Prague, Prague, Czechia

**Abstract.** Computer Science course instructors routinely have to create comprehensive test suites to assess programming assignments. The creation of such test suites is typically not trivial as it involves selecting a limited number of tests from a set of (semi-)randomly generated ones. Manual strategies for test selection do not scale when considering large testing inputs needed, for instance, for the assessment of algorithms exercises. To facilitate this process, we present TestSelector, a new framework for automatic selection of optimal test suites for student projects. The key advantage of TestSelector over existing approaches is that it is easily extensible with arbitrarily complex code coverage measures, not requiring these measures to be encoded into the logic of an exact constraint solver. We demonstrate the flexibility of TestSelector by extending it with support for a range of classical code coverage measures and using it to select test suites for a number of real-world algorithms projects, further showing that the selected test suites outperform randomly selected ones in finding bugs in students' code.

**Keywords:** Constraint-based test suite selection · Runtime monitoring · Code coverage measures

## 1 Introduction

Computer science course instructors routinely have to create comprehensive test suites to automatically assess programming assignments. It is not uncommon for these test suites to have to be created before students actually submit their solutions. This is, for instance, the case when students are allowed to submit their solutions multiple times with the selected tests being run each time and feedback given to the student. In typical algorithms courses, testing inputs must be large enough to ensure that the students' solutions have the required asymptotic

© The Author(s), under exclusive license to Springer Nature Switzerland AG 2022
T. Dang and V. Stolz (Eds.): RV 2022, LNCS 13498, pp. 283–292, 2022.
https://doi.org/10.1007/978-3-031-17196-3_17

complexity. In such scenarios, course instructors usually resort to semi-random test generation, selecting only a small number of the generated tests due to the limited computational resources of testing platforms. Hence, the included tests must be judiciously chosen. Manual strategies for test selection, however, do not scale for large testing inputs.

This paper presents TESTSELECTOR, a new framework for optimal test selection for student projects. With our framework, the instructor provides a canonical implementation of the project assignment, a set of generated tests $T$, and the number $n$ of tests to be selected, and TESTSELECTOR determines a subset $T' \subseteq T$ of size $n$ that maximises a given code coverage measure. By maximising coverage of the canonical solution, TESTSELECTOR provides relative assurances that most of the corner case behaviours of the expected solution are covered by the selected test suite. Naturally, the better the coverage measure, the better those assurances. Importantly, the best coverage measure is often project-specific, there being no silver bullet.

The main advantage of TESTSELECTOR over existing approaches [1, 11, 14, 25] is that it is easily extensible with arbitrarily complex code coverage measures specifically designed for the project at hand. Unlike previous approaches, TEST-SELECTOR does not require the targeted coverage measures to be encoded into the logic of an exact constraint solver. We achieve this by using as our optimisation algorithm, a specialised version of the recent SEESAW algorithm [12] for exploring the Pareto optimal frontier of a pair of functions. We demonstrate the flexibility of TESTSELECTOR by extending it with support for a range of classical code coverage measures and using it to select test suites for a number of real-world algorithms projects, further showing that the selected test suites outperform randomly selected ones in finding bugs in students' code.

The paper starts with Sect. 2 that overviews the TESTSELECTOR framework presenting its main modules and how they interact. Section 3 presents an experimental evaluation of the framework. Section 4 overviews related work and concludes the paper. An extended version of the paper can be found in [16].

## 2    TestSelector Overview

We give an overview of our approach for selecting optimal test suites for student projects. As illustrated in Fig. 1, the TESTSELECTOR framework receives three inputs: **(1)** the instructor's implementation for the project, which we refer to as the *canonical solution*; **(2)** a JSON configuration file with a description of the coverage measure to be used for test selection as well as the number of tests to be selected; and **(3)** an initial set of input tests, $T$. Given these inputs, TESTSELECTOR computes an optimal subset of tests, $T' \subseteq T$, that maximises the selected coverage measure for the chosen number of tests, $n$ ($|T'| = n$). Due to the combinatorial nature of the problem and the sheer size of the search space, it is often the case that TESTSELECTOR is not able to find the optimal solution within the given time constraints. In such cases, it returns the best solution found so far. Our experimental evaluation indicates that this solution is typically not far from the optimal one.

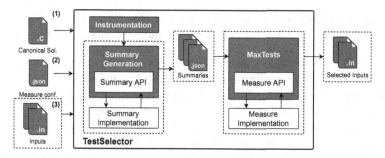

**Fig. 1.** TESTSELECTOR high-level architecture.

The TESTSELECTOR framework consists of two main building blocks:

– *Summary Generation Module:* The summary generation module automatically instruments the code of the canonical solution in order for its execution to additionally produce a *coverage summary* of each given input test. Different coverage measures require different summaries. For instance, a *block coverage summary* simply includes the identifiers of the code blocks that were executed during the running of the canonical solution.
– MAXTESTS *Module:* The MAXTESTS module receives as input the coverage measure to be used, the number $n$ of tests to be selected, and a set of summaries, and selects the subset of size $n$ of the given summaries that maximises the coverage measure. For instance, for the *block coverage measure*, MAXTESTS selects the summaries corresponding to the testing inputs that maximise the overall number of executed code blocks.

At the core of MAXTESTS is an adapted implementation of the SEESAW algorithm [12], a novel algorithm for exploring the Pareto optimal frontier of two given functions using the well-known implicit hitting set paradigm [3, 4]. The key innovation of SEESAW is that it allows one to treat one of the two functions to optimise in a black-box manner. In our case, this black-box function corresponds to the targeted coverage function, meaning that we are able to select optimal test suites without encoding the targeted coverage functions into the logic of an exact constraint solver.

*Supporting New Coverage Measures.* The key advantage of TESTSELECTOR when compared to existing approaches for constraint-base test suite selection in the general setting [1,11,14,23,25] is that it is trivial to extend TESTSELECTOR with support for new, arbitrarily complex coverage measures. In contrast, existing approaches require users to encode the targeted coverage measures into the logic of an exact constraint solver, typically SMT [5] or Integer Linear Programming (ILP) solvers [10]. The manual construction of such encodings has two main inconveniences when compared to our approach. First, it requires expert knowledge of logic and inner workings of the targeted solver. Even simple encodings must be carefully engineered so that they can be efficiently solved. Second, there might be a mismatch between the expressivity of the existing solvers and the nature of the measure to be encoded. In contrast, with TESTSELECTOR, if one wants to add support for a new coverage measure, one simply has to:

1. Implement a *Coverage Summary API* that dynamically constructs a coverage summary during the execution of the canonical solution;
2. Implement a *Coverage Evaluation Function* that maps a given set of coverage summaries to a numeric coverage score. Importantly, in order for TESTSELECTOR to work properly, the coverage evaluation function must be *monotone*; meaning that for any two sets of summaries $S_1$ and $S_2$, it must hold that: $S_1 \subseteq S_2 \implies f(S_1) \leq f(S_2)$. Monotonicity is a natural requirement for coverage scoring functions.

*Natively Supported Coverage Measures.* Even though our main goal is to allow for users to easily implement their own coverage measures, TESTSELECTOR comes with built-in support for various standard code coverage measures. In particular, it implements: **(1)** *Block Coverage (BC)*—counts the number of executed code blocks; **(2)** *Array Coverage (AC)*—counts the number of programmatic interactions with distinct array indexes; **(3)** *Loop Coverage (LC)*—counts the number of loop executions with a distinct number of iterations; **(4)** *Decision Coverage (DC)*—counts the number of conditional guards that evaluate both to **true** and to **false**; **(5)** *Condition Coverage (CC)*—counts the number of conditional guards for which all subexpressions evaluate both to **true** and to **false**. We refer the reader to [22] for a detailed account of standard coverage measures in the software engineering literature.

*Linear Combination of Coverage Measures.* In addition to the coverage measures described above, TESTSELECTOR allows the user to specify a linear combination of coverage measures. Observe that, as the linear combination of two monotone functions is also monotone, the user is free to combine any monotone coverage measures without compromising the correct behaviour of MAXTESTS.

## 3    Evaluation

We evaluate TESTSELECTOR with respect to three research questions:

- **RQ1: How easy is it to extend TestSelector with new code coverage measures?** We show that the currently supported coverage measures are implemented with a small number of lines of code, demonstrating the practicality of our approach.
- **RQ2: Do classical code coverage measures improve test suite selection for bug finding in student projects?** We show that the test suites selected by TESTSELECTOR outperform randomly selected ones in finding bugs in students' code.
- **RQ3: Do linear combinations of code coverage measures further improve test suite selection for bug finding?** We show that by combining the best code coverage measures, we can find more bugs in students' code.

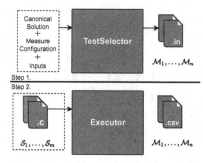

**Fig. 2.** Evaluation diagram.

**Table 1.** Benchmark characterisation.

| Project | $C_{\mathrm{LoC}}$ | $n_{proj}$ | $T_{\mathrm{LoC}}$ | $Avg_{\mathrm{LoC}}$ | $n_{inpts}$ |
|---|---|---|---|---|---|
| P1 | 256 | 398 | 140,349 | 352.64 | 1,002 |
| P2 | 529 | 349 | 176,547 | 505.86 | 600 |
| P3 | 416 | 193 | 26,890 | 139.32 | 1,000 |
| P4 | 208 | 166 | 34,512 | 207.90 | 1,000 |
| P5 | 304 | 172 | 21,114 | 122.76 | 1,000 |
| P6 | 204 | 185 | 24,091 | 130.22 | 800 |
| P7 | 108 | 174 | 24,035 | 138.13 | 1,000 |
| Total | 2,125 | 1,637 | 447,538 | 273.39 | 6,402 |

*Experimental Procedure.* The experimental procedure is a two-step process, as illustrated in Fig. 2. In the first step, TESTSELECTOR selects the test suites for a given canonical solution, set of inputs, and configuration file specifying the coverage measures and the size of the computed test suites. This step generates a set of test suites, each corresponding to one of the specified measures. In the second step, an executor will run every student's project against the selected test suites. In the end, the executor creates a report detailing the passing/failing rate for every student's project on each selected test suite.

All the experiments were performed on a server with a 12-core Intel Xeon E5–2620 CPU and 32GB of RAM running Ubuntu 20.04.2 LTS. For the ILP solver we used the Gurobi Optimizer v9.1.2. For each execution of MAXTESTS we set a time limit of 30 min.

*Benchmarks.* We curated a benchmark suite comprising students' projects from seven editions of two programming courses organised by the authors. Table 1 presents the benchmark suite characterisation. For each project, we show the number of lines of code of the canonical solution ($C_{\mathrm{LoC}}$), the number of student projects ($n_{proj}$), the total number of lines of code of the student projects ($T_{\mathrm{LoC}}$), the average number of lines of code per student project ($Avg_{\mathrm{LoC}}$), and the number of available input tests ($n_{inpts}$). In summary, we tested 1,637 projects, which totalled 447K lines of code ($\approx$ 273 LoC/project).

### 3.1 RQ1: TESTSELECTOR Extensibility

The table below presents the number of lines of code of the implementation of each coverage measure: *Loop Coverage* (LC), *Array Coverage* (AC), *Block Coverage* (BC), *Condition Coverage* (CC), and *Decision Coverage* (DC). For each measure, we give the number of lines of code of both its implementation of the coverage summary API and evaluation function.

| Module | LC | AC | BC | CC | DC |
|---|---|---|---|---|---|
| Coverage Summary API | 90 | 60 | 42 | 120 | 120 |
| Measure Evaluation Function | 54 | 58 | 48 | 74 | 64 |

**Table 2.** Results for each measure with linear search (LS) and progression search (PS).

| Project | Search | LC | AC | BC | Size | CC | DC | Rnd |
|---|---|---|---|---|---|---|---|---|
| P1 | LS | **14.67** | 14.48 | 13.69 | 0.20 | 13.95 | 14.41 | 4.81 |
|  | PS | 14.53 | 14.34 | 13.56 | 0.19 | 13.82 | 14.27 |  |
| P2 | LS | 18.07 | 17.15 | **19.47** | 6.14 | 15.60 | 14.35 | 5.60 |
|  | PS | 18.07 | 17.20 | **19.47** | 6.14 | 15.60 | 14.35 |  |
| P3 | LS | 16.39 | 20.38 | 7.49 | 28.07 | 7.49 | 7.49 | 7.56 |
|  | PS | 16.77 | 20.70 | 7.95 | **28.31** | 7.95 | 7.95 |  |
| P4 | LS | **23.68** | 22.78 | 11.99 | 23.59 | 17.95 | 17.93 | 13.52 |
|  | PS | **23.68** | 22.82 | 11.99 | 23.59 | 17.93 | 17.93 |  |
| P5 | LS | **3.76** | 3.23 | 3.56 | 3.74 | 3.56 | 3.56 | 3.09 |
|  | PS | **3.76** | 3.25 | 3.56 | 3.74 | 3.56 | 3.56 |  |
| P6 | LS | 6.91 | 8.22 | 8.01 | **8.39** | 4.72 | 4.68 | 6.61 |
|  | PS | 6.91 | 8.22 | 8.01 | **8.39** | 4.72 | 4.66 |  |
| P7 | LS | **10.46** | 6.08 | 6.71 | 6.39 | 7.17 | 7.17 | 6.28 |
|  | PS | **10.46** | 6.08 | 6.71 | 6.39 | 7.17 | 7.17 |  |
| Average | LS | 13.42 | 13.19 | 10.13 | 10.93 | 10.06 | 9.94 | 6.78 |
|  | PS | **13.45** | 13.23 | 10.18 | 10.96 | 10.11 | 9.98 |  |

When it comes to the implementation of the coverage summary API, we observe that the simpler coverage measures, such as LC, AC, and BC require fewer than 100 lines of code to implement and the more complex coverage measures, such as CC and DC, require 120 lines of code. As expected, the measure evaluation function is simpler to implement than the coverage summary API, requiring even fewer lines of code (between 48–74 LoC).

## 3.2    RQ2: Classical Code Coverage Selection

We investigate the effectiveness of TESTSELECTOR when used to select test suites for finding bugs in students' code. In particular, we compare the number of bugs found by the test suites selected by TESTSELECTOR against those found by test suites obtained through random selection. In all experiments, we ask for test suites of size 30 out of 900 available randomly generated tests (the number of tests used to assess the students in the corresponding courses was 30). We consider the five coverage measures described in Sect. 2 and an additional measure corresponding to the size of the testing input. Furthermore, we run the SEESAW algorithm with two complementary search strategies: linear search (LS) and progression search (PS). Details can be found in [12,16].

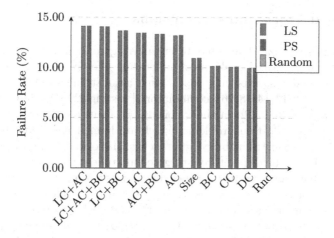

**Fig. 3.** Failure rate (%) for each measure, comparing linear search (LS) with progression search (PS).

*Results.* Table 2 presents the results of the experiment. For each project, the table shows the resulting failure rates for the measures *Loop Coverage* (LC), *Array Coverage* (AC), *Block Coverage* (BC), *Size, Condition Coverage* (CC), and *Decision Coverage* (DC). We observe that the best measure is project-dependent, with LC being the best measure in four projects, BC in one, and Size in two. Importantly, we also observe that the more sophisticated measures, such as CC and DC, have lower failure rates than simpler measures, such as LC and AC. This may be explained by the fact that the students' most common programming errors are often encoded in loops and array accesses. All coverage measures consistently perform better than the random test suite selection.

### 3.3    RQ3: Linear Combinations of Coverage Measures

To investigate whether using linear combinations of code coverage measures can further improve the bug finding results, we replay the experiment described in Sect. 3.2 with the following combinations of coverage measures: **(1)** AC+LC; **(2)** BC+LC; **(3)** AC+BC; and **(4)** AC+BC+LC.

*Results.* Figure 3 presents the obtained results for the four linear combinations[1] and the five individual code coverage measures presented in Table 2. For each measure, we give a blue and a red bar, each corresponding to one of the search strategies supported by the SEESAW algorithm. It is easy to observe that the majority of the combinations, i.e., LC+AC, LC+AC+BC, and LC+BC, are able to find more bugs in the students' code than the overall best-performing single measure (LC), with only AC+BC obtaining worse results.

---

[1] LC+AC, LC+BC, AC+BC, and LC+AC+BC.

290 F. Marques et al.

## 4 Related Work and Conclusions

*Test Suit Construction.* The software engineering community has dedicated a considerable effort to the problem of generating effective test suites for complex software systems, exploring topics such as: test suite reduction and test case selection [1,2,13,14,18,26], combinatorial testing [23–25], and a variety of fuzzying strategies [6–9,19]. In the following, we focus on the test suite reduction and test case selection problems, which are immediately close to our own goal, highlighting constraint-based approaches. Importantly, we are not aware on any works in this field specifically targeted at student projects. The testing of such projects has, however, its own specificities when compared to the testing of large-scale industrial software systems. In particular, the time constraints on the test generation process are less severe and the code being tested less complex.

The *test suite reduction problem* [1,2,17,21,26] aims at reducing the size of a given test suite while satisfying a given test criterion. Typical criteria are the so-called coverage-based criteria, which ensure that the coverage of the reduced test suite is above a certain minimal threshold. The *test case selection problem* [1,2,17,21,26] is the dual problem, in that it tries to determine the minimal number of tests to be added to a given test suite so that a given test criterion is attained. As most of these algorithms target industrial settings, they assume severe time constraints on the test selection process. Hence, the vast majority of the proposed approaches for test suite reduction and selection are approximate, such as similarity-based algorithms [2,17], which are not guaranteed to find the optimal test suite even when given enough resources. In order to achieve a compromise between precision and scalability, the authors of [1] proposed a combination of standard ILP encodings and heuristic approaches. Finally, the authors of [14] proposed a SAT-based encoding for selecting optimal test suites according to the modified condition decision coverage criterion [13,22]. They argue that, as this criterion is enforced by safety standards in both the automative and the avionics industries, one is obliged to resort to exact approaches.

*Conclusions and Future Work.* We have presented TESTSELECTOR, a new framework for the automatic selection of optimal test suites for student projects. The key innovation of TESTSELECTOR is its extensibility to support new code coverage measures without these measures being encoded into the logic of an exact constraint solver. We evaluate TESTSELECTOR against a benchmark comprised of 1,637 real-world student projects, demonstrating that: (1) it is trivial to extend TESTSELECTOR with support for new coverage measures and (2) the selected test suites outperform randomly selected ones in finding bugs in students' code.

In the future, we plan to conduct a more thorough investigation on the relation between the characteristics of a project and the code coverage measures that are appropriate for it. We also plan to integrate TESTSELECTOR with an existing testing platform for student projects, such as Mooshak [15] or Pandora [20].

**Acknowledgements.** The authors were supported by Portuguese national funds through Fundação para a Ciência e a Tecnologia (UIDB/50021/2020, INESC-ID multi-annual funding program) and projects INFOCOS (PTDC/CCI-COM/32378/2017) and DIVINA (CMU/TIC/0053/2021). The results were also supported by the MEYS within the dedicated program ERC CZ under the project *POSTMAN* no. LL1902, and it is part of the *RICAIP* project that has received funding from the European Union's Horizon 2020 under grant agreement No 857306.

# References

1. Chen, Z., Zhang, X., Xu, B.: A degraded ILP approach for test suite reduction. In: Proceedings of the Twentieth International Conference on Software Engineering & Knowledge Engineering (SEKE), pp. 494–499. Knowledge Systems Institute Graduate School (2008)
2. Cruciani, E., Miranda, B., Verdecchia, R., Bertolino, A.: Scalable approaches for test suite reduction. In: Proceedings of the 41st International Conference on Software Engineering, ICSE, pp. 419–429. IEEE / ACM (2019)
3. Davies, J., Bacchus, F.: Solving MaxSAT by solving a sequence of simpler SAT instances. In: Principles and Practice of Constraint Programming (2011)
4. Davies, J., Bacchus, F.: Exploiting the power of MIP solvers in MaxSAT. In: Theory and Applications of Satisfiability Testing (2013)
5. De Moura, L., Bjørner, N.: Z3: An Efficient SMT Solver. In: Tools and Algorithms for the Construction and Analysis of Systems (2008)
6. Godefroid, P.: Compositional dynamic test generation. In: POPL, vol. 42, pp. 47–54 (2007)
7. Godefroid, P., Klarlund, N., Sen, K.: Dart: Directed automated random testing. In: ACM Sigplan Notices (2005)
8. Godefroid, P., Levin, M.Y., Molnar, D.A.: Automated whitebox fuzz testing. In: NDSS (2008)
9. Godefroid, P., Nori, A.V., Rajamani, S.K., Tetali, S.: Compositional may-must program analysis: Unleashing the power of alternation. In: POPL (2010)
10. Gurobi Optimization, LLC: Gurobi Optimizer Reference Manual (2022). https://www.gurobi.com
11. Hnich, B., Prestwich, S.D., Selensky, E., Smith, B.M.: Constraint models for the covering test problem. Constraints An Int. J. **11**(2–3), 199–219 (2006)
12. Janota, M., Morgado, A., Fragoso Santos, J., Manquinho, V.: The Seesaw Algorithm: Function Optimization Using Implicit Hitting Sets. In: Principles and Practice of Constraint Programming (2021)
13. Jones, J.A., Harrold, M.J.: Test-suite reduction and prioritization for modified condition/decision coverage. IEEE Trans. Software Eng. **29**(3), 195–209 (2003)
14. Kitamura, T., Maissonneuve, Q., Choi, E.-H., Artho, C., Gargantini, A.: Optimal test suite generation for modified condition decision coverage using SAT solving. In: Gallina, B., Skavhaug, A., Bitsch, F. (eds.) SAFECOMP 2018. LNCS, vol. 11093, pp. 123–138. Springer, Cham (2018). https://doi.org/10.1007/978-3-319-99130-6_9
15. Leal, J.P., Paiva, J.C., Correia, H.: Mooshak (2022). https://mooshak2.dcc.fc.up.pt
16. Marques, F., Morgado, A., Santos, J.F., Janota, M.: TestSelector: automatic test suite selection for student projects - extended version (2022). https://doi.org/10.48550/ARXIV.2207.09509. https://arxiv.org/abs/2207.09509

17. Miranda, B., Cruciani, E., Verdecchia, R., Bertolino, A.: FAST approaches to scalable similarity-based test case prioritization. In: Proceedings of the 40th International Conference on Software Engineering, ICSE, pp. 222–232. ACM (2018)

18. Rojas, J.M., Campos, J., Vivanti, M., Fraser, G., Arcuri, A.: Combining multiple coverage criteria in search-based unit test generation. In: Barros, M., Labiche, Y. (eds.) SSBSE 2015. LNCS, vol. 9275, pp. 93–108. Springer, Cham (2015). https://doi.org/10.1007/978-3-319-22183-0_7

19. Sen, K., Agha, G.: Cute and jcute: Concolic unit testing and explicit path model-checking tools. In: CAV, pp. 419–423 (2006)

20. Serra, P.: Pandora: Automatic Assessment Tool (AAT) (2022). https://saturn.ulusofona.pt

21. Shi, A., Yung, T., Gyori, A., Marinov, D.: Comparing and combining test-suite reduction and regression test selection. In: Proceedings of the 2015 10th Joint Meeting on Foundations of Software Engineering, ESEC/FSE, pp. 237–247. ACM (2015)

22. Szűgyi, Z., Porkoláb, Z.: Comparison of DC and MC/DC code coverages. Research report, Acta Electrotechnica et Informatica (2013)

23. Wu, H., Nie, C., Petke, J., Jia, Y., Harman, M.: A survey of constrained combinatorial testing. CoRR abs/1908.02480 (2019)

24. Yamada, A., Biere, A., Artho, C., Kitamura, T., Choi, E.: Greedy combinatorial test case generation using unsatisfiable cores. In: Proceedings of the 31st IEEE/ACM International Conference on Automated Software Engineering, ASE, pp. 614–624. ACM (2016)

25. Yamada, A., Kitamura, T., Artho, C., Choi, E., Oiwa, Y., Biere, A.: Optimization of combinatorial testing by incremental SAT solving. In: 8th IEEE International Conference on Software Testing, Verification and Validation, ICST, pp. 1–10. IEEE Computer Society (2015)

26. Yoo, S., Harman, M.: Pareto efficient multi-objective test case selection. In: Proceedings of the ACM/SIGSOFT International Symposium on Software Testing and Analysis, ISSTA, pp. 140–150. ACM (2007)

# DECENT: A Benchmark for Decentralized Enforcement

Florian Gallay$^{(\boxtimes)}$ and Yliès Falcone

Univ. Grenoble Alpes, CNRS, Grenoble INP, Inria, LIG, 38000 Grenoble, France
florian.gallay1@etu.univ-grenoble-alpes.fr

**Abstract.** DECENT is a benchmark for evaluating decentralized enforcement. It implements two enforcement algorithms that differ in their strategy for correcting the execution: the first one explores all alternatives to perform a globally optimal correction, while the second follows an incremental strategy based on locally optimal choices. Decent allows comparing these algorithms with a centralized enforcement algorithm in terms of computational metrics and metrics for decentralized monitoring such as the number and size of messages or the required computation on each component. Our experiments show that (i) the number of messages sent and the internal memory usage is much smaller with decentralized algorithms (ii) the locally optimal algorithm performs closely to the globally optimal one.

## 1 Introduction

*Runtime enforcement* consists in preventing the violation of a specification by using the so-called enforcers, which alter the execution whenever necessary. Conceptually the execution is typically abstracted as a trace, that is a sequence of system states. An enforcer takes as input such trace, modifies it *if needs be* to comply with the specification and then produces it as output. Existing enforcement frameworks are defined in the so-called centralized setting where there is a single enforcer acting on a global observation and control point.

As systems become increasingly decentralized (e.g. finance, vehicles, drone swarms), it is desirable to be able to ensure their critical properties while preserving their decentralization. In decentralized enforcement, a system consists of several components with one enforcer attached to each component. Since every enforcer can only observe what is happening locally, they need to communicate to gather information on the whole system and collaborate to modify the current execution.

In [13], we introduced two algorithms for the decentralized enforcement of properties specified using Linear-time Temporal Logic (LTL) [19]. Both of these algorithms are online algorithms that modify the current event if by appending this event to the trace output so far, this would violate the property. These algorithms differ by how they compute the corrected event. In the so-called *global* algorithm, all the possible alternatives for the emitted event are explored so that we are guaranteed to find the most *optimal* correction, whereas, in the so-called *local-incremental* algorithm, safe choices are made on each component in an incremental manner, without backtracking. However, these algorithms were not implemented nor evaluated.

© The Author(s), under exclusive license to Springer Nature Switzerland AG 2022
T. Dang and V. Stolz (Eds.): RV 2022, LNCS 13498, pp. 293–303, 2022.
https://doi.org/10.1007/978-3-031-17196-3_18

This paper introduces DECENT, a simulation environment that implements the two decentralized enforcement algorithms to benchmark them against randomly generated formulas and patterns or using a specific formula. In DECENT, enforcement is performed offline on randomly generated traces as the goal is to get results on the performance of the algorithms independently of a system. In practice, however, our algorithms also work for online enforcement by reading the execution as it is produced by the system under scrutiny. The paper is structured as follows. Sect. 2 recalls the main principles of the approaches we presented previously. In Sect. 3, we overview the tool, and in Sect. 4 we discuss how we evaluated the algorithms, and we present the results. In Sect. 5, we discuss related work. Finally, we conclude in Sect. 6.

## 2    Principles of Decentralized Enforcement

We briefly overview the decentralized enforcement algorithms and refer to [13] for a formal definition. In the decentralized setting, multiple enforcers communicate to gather information. Whenever they observe an event, the enforcers use their internal memory to compute alternatives to the observed event in case of a violation. Common to the two enforcement algorithms are the following steps. The enforcers maintain a formula to enforce at any time, which is rewritten using *progression* [1] to separate the present from the future obligations. Then, in turn, the enforcers partially evaluate the formula using every possible assignment of their local atomic propositions while keeping track of the number of modifications compared to the original observed event. If one of the assignments leads to the partially evaluated formula being simplified to $\bot$, then the corresponding event is a violation and is removed from the memory of the enforcer.

The algorithms differ in their strategy to modify their local observation. In the global algorithm, once an enforcer is done evaluating the formula, it sends its memory to the next enforcer. Once the present obligations of the formula are entirely evaluated, the last enforcer applies a decision rule to pick which event to emit and communicates its decision to all the others. In the local-incremental algorithm, once an enforcer has evaluated the formula, it applies a local decision to send a single partial event (that may already be different from the observed event) to the next enforcer instead of the whole memory (which contains multiples events and the associated partially evaluated formulas). When the last enforcer is done, it applies the local decision rule to determine the event to emit. In this case, the last enforcer communicates the next formula to enforce as the other enforcers have already decided which event to emit locally.

We proved that the algorithms guarantee classical properties in enforcement: they are *sound*, meaning that the global output sequence of the enforcers does not violate the specification, and *transparent*, meaning that the global event is only modified if it does not comply with the specification. Additionally, the global algorithm is also *optimal* because the number of modifications to atomic propositions is minimal.

## 3    DECENT Overview

DECENT[1] implements the algorithms mentioned above using the functional programming language OCaml (in about 2200 LLOC). We reused some modules implemented

---

[1] https://gitlab.inria.fr/monitoring/decent.

in DECENTMON [2,3], mainly the implementation of LTL, events, traces and the associated generators. We implemented a few additional modules for the centralized and decentralized enforcement algorithms. The other functionalities of DECENTMON are left as is to allow monitoring or enforcement of formulas.

With DECENT, we can either parse specific formulas given in a file or randomly generate them. In both cases, formulas are enforced against a randomly generated trace using the decentralized algorithms as well as a "centralized" orchestration-based enforcement algorithm to compare them. When generating random formulas, it is possible to either specify a (maximum) size or to choose the specification patterns (defined in [6]) as templates to generate properties. Moreover, formula generation can be "biased" to place using more atomic propositions on a component. The underlying system is represented by an alphabet expressing how the atomic propositions are spread over the components. The alphabet is given as a command line argument, but it is also possible to use multiple different alphabets given in a file (to vary the distribution of the atomic propositions over the components or to add extra components/atomic propositions, for example). When generating traces (i.e. lists of events), each atomic proposition of the alphabet has a fixed probability of being included in each event (flip coin distribution), and it is possible to choose a different probability distribution such as Bernoulli, exponential or beta. Finally, DECENT offers two enforcement modes: *optimistic* or *pessimistic*. In the former, possible alternative local events are computed only when the observed event leads to a violation (i.e. after performing a round of verification first), while in the latter, local alternatives are always computed (i.e. at the same time as the verification). By default, the *pessimistic* mode is used.

# 4    Evaluating the Algorithms

We define the evaluation metrics in Sect. 4.1 and present the experiments to compare the algorithms in Sect. 4.2.

## 4.1    Metrics

The metrics we consider for this benchmark are mainly related to messages and the internal memory of the enforcers. We explain how measuring these metrics helps to understand the intricate behavior of enforcement algorithms.

*Number of Modifications of the Events.*    As mentioned in Sect. 2, the local algorithm does not guarantee *optimality*. This metric allows us to observe how far is the local algorithm from optimality. It is worth noting that *optimality* is defined for each event individually when compared to the observed event, not for the whole trace. More specifically, it is possible (although quite rare from our experiments) for the total number of modifications in the enforced trace produced with the local algorithm to be lower than it would have been using the global algorithm (on the same trace and formula). As the local algorithm relies on local information to decide the event to send to the next enforcer, it is impossible to guarantee that the two algorithms emit the same event. Consequently, the algorithms can end up with a different formula to enforce at some point (since the formula depends on the emitted event). Therefore, getting a stricter formula in the global version is possible in which the next observed event is a violation (forcing the enforcers to modify it). However, it is not in the local version. The number of modifications should, however, be identical between the global version and the centralized one because they both explore every alternative and should therefore be able to pick the same verdict every time. To see whether these differences are common, we also measured the number of differing events and the number of events with a different number of modifications between the enforced traces. Result tables show the average number of modifications in column **#mod**.

*Number and Size of Messages.* To measure the intensity of the communication required between monitors, we also measure the number (**#msg**) and the size of messages in the number of bytes used to encode them (**|msg|**). We only count the messages sent during the main evaluation process and not the ones sent after the final decision as their size depends on an implementation choice, that is, whether we send only the enforced event (which means the enforcers have to re-compute the next formula to enforce) or both the event and the next formula. In both cases, the last enforcer has to send a message to all the others, which causes the same number of extra messages as in the centralized version (the central enforcer also has to notify the local enforcers of the verdict). If we only send the event, the extra messages contain the same information as in the centralized version (so their size would be close if not identical). Otherwise, the final messages are larger in the decentralized version as they contain the next formula to enforce.

*Size of the Temporal Correction Log.* We also measure the size of the tcl (in bytes, given in |tcl|), i.e. the main internal structure used by the enforcers to compute the alternatives to compare the usage of the internal memory.

## 4.2  Experiments

For each experiment, we compare the performances of three algorithms (centralized "orchestration-based" [4], decentralized "global" and decentralized "local") using the same randomly generated traces and formulas (with some added constraints on the generation depending on the experiment). In all of them, we generate 1000 formulas and traces of size 100 (the size of a trace is the number of events composing it). We did not use larger traces because 1) it made the execution time of the experiments much longer while not changing much in the results but mainly, 2) it made the pathological cases much worse. We will talk about the latter in more detail with the first experiment. Also, we did not measure the execution time or the delays that would be caused by the algorithms because the results would not be realistic as we do not take into account the cost of communication between the enforcers and because interacting with the system in a real application may have a significant impact on the overhead. We detail the two experiments in the following (an additional one can be found in Appendix A).

*Varying Formula Size.* Here, the generated formulas are of different sizes (from 1 to 6) to assess the scalability of our approach. As in DECENTMON, we use the maximum nesting of operator as a measure of size because it reflects well the difficulty to evaluate a formula. For example, $\mathbf{G}(a \vee b)$ has a size of 2 and $\mathbf{G}b \vee \mathbf{F}\neg a$ has a size of 3. Also, it is worth noting that we consider the size before we apply a simplification on the formula (so the simplified one could be smaller). We used the alphabet $\{a1, a2|b1, b2|c1, c2\}$, that is, there are 3 components in the system that can observe 2 atomic proposition each (for instance, the first component can observe $a1$ and $a2$).

Table 1. Results of the first experiment: varying formula size.

| Algorithm | $|\varphi|$ | #mod | #msg | lmsgl | ltcll | $|\varphi|$ | #mod | #msg | lmsgl | ltcll |
|---|---|---|---|---|---|---|---|---|---|---|
| Cent. |  | 0.434 | 3. | 4.494 | 33.535 |  | 0.256 | 3. | 4.496 | 284.037 |
| Global | 1 | 0.434 | 0.33 | 9.305 | 35.261 | 4 | 0.256 | 0.597 | 114.253 | 290.589 |
| Local |  | 0.429 | 0.258 | 4.087 | 27.845 |  | 0.252 | 0.448 | 40.996 | 151.169 |
| Cent. |  | 0.354 | 3. | 4.496 | 57.655 |  | 0.242 | 3. | 4.496 | 614.369 |
| Global | 2 | 0.354 | 0.403 | 23.296 | 60.801 | 5 | 0.242 | 0.609 | 196.24 | 630.496 |
| Local |  | 0.348 | 0.304 | 9.958 | 43.168 |  | 0.237 | 0.469 | 71.083 | 335.887 |
| Cent. |  | 0.313 | 3. | 4.496 | 111.421 |  | 0.214 | 3. | 4.493 | 2145.78 |
| Global | 3 | 0.313 | 0.463 | 48.572 | 117.324 | 6 | 0.214 | 0.777 | 386.229 | 2124.98 |
| Local |  | 0.311 | 0.357 | 20.256 | 76.424 |  | 0.211 | 0.618 | 108.125 | 635.299 |

Table 2. Differences between the enforced traces in the first experiment.

| Variables | Average number of different events | | | Average number of events with a different #mod | | |
|---|---|---|---|---|---|---|
| $|\varphi|$ | Cent. $\leftrightarrow$ Glob. | Cent. $\leftrightarrow$ Loc. | Glob. $\leftrightarrow$ Loc. | Cent. $\leftrightarrow$ Glob. | Cent. $\leftrightarrow$ Loc. | Glob. $\leftrightarrow$ Loc. |
| 1 | 0. | 0.059 | 0.059 | 0. | 0. | 0. |
| 2 | 0. | 0.634 | 0.634 | 0. | 0. | 0. |
| 3 | 0. | 0.758 | 0.758 | 0. | 0.026 | 0.026 |
| 4 | 0. | 1.174 | 1.174 | 0. | 0.057 | 0.057 |
| 5 | 0. | 0.99 | 0.99 | 0. | 0.022 | 0.022 |
| 6 | 0. | 1.302 | 1.301 | 0. | 0.075 | 0.075 |

Table 1 and 2 show the results of the first experiment. Here, the average number of modifications between the three version is almost identical. Although it is an average over the whole trace, it at least means that, in practice, the local algorithm is very close to the other versions (even though it does not guarantee *optimality*). It is worth noting that #mod sometimes has a lower value for the local algorithm. This could be caused either by what we mentioned in the previous section or because, in some cases, we can reach a state where the next formula to enforce is $\top$ (at which point we stop the enforcement). As we cannot guarantee that the local algorithm outputs the same trace as the others, it may miss this state and enforce a few more events before reaching it. Because of this, as we do the average of #mod on the whole trace, if the trace given by the local version is larger, it skews the average by a little bit. Aside from this, the cost in terms of local memory usage (|tcl|) is greatly reduced by the local algorithm (upwards of almost 3 times smaller with formulas of size 6) and the number of messages (#msg) is much smaller with the decentralized algorithms. There are fewer messages because the enforced formulas do not necessarily contain every atomic proposition of the alphabet, and therefore, some enforcers may not need to do any work. However, the size of messages (|msg|) is much larger than in the centralized algorithm because they contain more information (alternatives and the associated partially evaluated formulas vs only the local observations in the centralized version). It is worth noting that messages with the local version are much smaller than with the global one (about 2 to 4 times depending on the size of the formula). Moreover, the traces produced by the centralized and the global algorithm are identical. The traces given by the local version are almost identical, with about one event different from the other two. This supports our claim that the local version is very close to being *optimal* despite not guaranteeing it.

An issue of this experiment is that some formulas are particularly bad for these methods because the rewriting to separate their present and future obligations cause an explosion of their size. As we generate some random formulas, we may get one of these pathological cases for only one size and not the others, which would majorly impact the results for this size. Typically, pathological cases are formulas with many Until (**U**) and Globally (**G**) operators interleaved so they are quite uncommon for smaller formulas and we have not seen any using specification patterns (i.e. the next experiment). As we mentioned earlier, these formulas are one of the reasons why we chose to use traces of this size (with larger traces, the execution would take way too much time to complete as the formula size tends to increase after each event in these cases).

*Using Realistic Specifications.* In this experiment with realistic specifications, we used formulas generated with the LTL specification patterns [6] (we omitted universality response chain because of size constraint, the complete tables are available on the tool repository). Here, we also compare the two enforcement modes *optimistic* and *pessimistic* (on the same formulas/traces by setting a seed). We used the same alphabet as in the previous experiment (Table 4).

Results of the second experiment: using specification patterns

**Table 3.** Pessimistic algorithm

| Algorithm | Pattern | #mod | #msg | lmsgl | ltcll |
|---|---|---|---|---|---|
| Cent. | | 0.37 | 3. | 4.502 | 180.414 |
| Global | abs | 0.37 | 0.629 | 79.477 | 181.993 |
| Local | | 0.372 | 0.472 | 39.586 | 116.784 |
| Cent. | | 0.162 | 3. | 4.503 | 201.799 |
| Global | exist | 0.162 | 0.684 | 77.222 | 199.828 |
| Local | | 0.162 | 0.463 | 40.489 | 119.418 |
| Cent. | | 0.242 | 3. | 4.502 | 743.064 |
| Global | bexist | 0.242 | 0.586 | 389.644 | 809.429 |
| Local | | 0.242 | 0.392 | 211.063 | 732.576 |
| Cent. | | 0.149 | 3. | 4.502 | 347.696 |
| Global | prec | 0.149 | 1.087 | 136.227 | 350.039 |
| Local | | 0.14 | 0.63 | 55.954 | 164.459 |
| Cent. | | 0.039 | 3. | 4.501 | 637.256 |
| Global | resp | 0.039 | 1.084 | 252.875 | 618.055 |
| Local | | 0.039 | 0.729 | 100.551 | 337.767 |
| Cent. | | 0.191 | 3. | 4.503 | 640.231 |
| Global | pchain | 0.191 | 1.037 | 218.258 | 634.57 |
| Local | | 0.19 | 0.656 | 90.923 | 334.564 |
| Cent. | | 0.193 | 3. | 4.504 | 1441.1 |
| Global | cchain | 0.193 | 1.255 | 491.208 | 1362.17 |
| Local | | 0.204 | 0.955 | 163.378 | 623.357 |

**Table 4.** Optimistic algorithm

| Algorithm | Pattern | #mod | #msg | lmsgl | ltcll |
|---|---|---|---|---|---|
| Cent. | | 0.37 | 3. | 4.502 | 158.365 |
| Global | abs | 0.37 | 0.586 | 51.782 | 165.268 |
| Local | | 0.372 | 0.583 | 43.809 | 117.334 |
| Cent. | | 0.162 | 3. | 4.503 | 188.028 |
| Global | exist | 0.162 | 0.532 | 49.569 | 198.448 |
| Local | | 0.162 | 0.529 | 45.389 | 152.229 |
| Cent. | | 0.242 | 3. | 4.502 | 243.993 |
| Global | bexist | 0.242 | 0.418 | 281.677 | 307.038 |
| Local | | 0.242 | 0.417 | 272.871 | 293.366 |
| Cent. | | 0.149 | 3. | 4.502 | 433.583 |
| Global | prec | 0.149 | 0.74 | 72.624 | 443.767 |
| Local | | 0.14 | 0.706 | 65.051 | 198.991 |
| Cent. | | 0.039 | 3. | 4.501 | 945.261 |
| Global | resp | 0.039 | 0.759 | 129.307 | 1026.3 |
| Local | | 0.039 | 0.753 | 121.769 | 630.653 |
| Cent. | | 0.191 | 3. | 4.503 | 709.02 |
| Global | pchain | 0.191 | 0.777 | 122.98 | 722.777 |
| Local | | 0.19 | 0.758 | 108.346 | 392.53 |
| Cent. | | 0.193 | 3. | 4.504 | 1706.91 |
| Global | cchain | 0.193 | 1.114 | 244.29 | 1691.65 |
| Local | | 0.204 | 1.115 | 197.499 | 755.796 |

**Table 5.** Differences between the enforced traces in the second experiment.

| Variables | Average number of differing events | | | Average number of event with a different #mod | | |
|---|---|---|---|---|---|---|
| Pattern | Cent. ↔ Global | Cent. ↔ Local | Global ↔ Local | Cent. ↔ Global | Cent. ↔ Local | Global ↔ Local |
| abs | 0. | 1.805 | 1.805 | 0. | 0.005 | 0.005 |
| exist | 0. | 0.276 | 0.276 | 0. | 0. | 0. |
| bexist | 0. | 0.009 | 0.009 | 0. | 0.001 | 0.001 |
| prec | 0. | 0.946 | 0.946 | 0. | 0.005 | 0.005 |
| resp | 0. | 0.257 | 0.257 | 0. | 0.001 | 0.001 |
| pchain | 0. | 0.655 | 0.655 | 0. | 0.01 | 0.01 |
| cchain | 0. | 3.974 | 3.974 | 0. | 0.274 | 0.274 |

Tables 3 to 5 give the results of this experiment. There is still an improvement in memory usage (ltcll) using the local algorithm. However, it is not as large as in the previous experiment (about two times smaller at most instead of three previously, and the same observation applies to the message sizes). A notable difference with the *pessimistic* mode is that, for some patterns, there seems to be a large difference in the number of messages between both decentralized algorithms: for instance, with the *precedence* pattern, there were almost twice as many messages sent in the global version on average. Using the *optimistic* mode, the memory usage is improved for some patterns (e.g. *bounded existence*) but it is also worse for others (e.g. *response*). It seems that this mode is better for certain types of formulas although it is hard to tell exactly because our metrics are not well suited to compare both. For example, with |tcl|, we only include in the average the results of runs where enforcement was required. Otherwise, it would skew the result and make it seem like *optimistic* is significantly better, which is untrue as the (enforcement) cost is identical to the other mode when enforcement is required (and null when it is not). However, this metric largely depends on the enforced formula and has consequently a large variance over the different runs. Therefore, if the runs that required enforcement are the ones where |tcl| was large, then the average will be worse (or at best similar) than what we get with the *pessimistic* mode, even though we might have gained a lot overall in computation time by not doing useless enforcement steps. The main drawback of this mode is that the overhead is larger when enforcement is required because of the initial verification phase. Table 5 shows that, for some patterns, the local algorithm produces traces that have more differences compared to the other two versions than with random formulas (mainly constrained chain where we measured 4 different on average). We have not included a table showing the difference between the enforced traces with the *optimistic* mode because the values are identical (i.e. the exact same traces are produced).

## 5   Related Work

There are many approaches to tackling the problem of *decentralized monitoring* (see [12] for an overview). The closest approaches to ours are the ones using formula rewriting on LTL [2,3,22]. Other methods use different formalisms to express the specifications like finite-state automata [9] or Stream Runtime Verification (SRVs) [5] or have different assumptions on the system like in monitoring decentralized specifications [7], that is having an independent specification for each component instead of one for the whole system. The aforementioned approaches have been implemented in various tools such as DECENTMON [2,3,9], using Maude [22], dLola [5] or THEMIS [7,8]. All these approaches only perform verification: they report violations or satisfaction of a property and do not consider enforcement.

   On the topic of *runtime enforcement*, most of the work has been done for centralized systems with varying assumptions about the underlying system: specification expressed with discrete-time formalisms [10,11], timed properties [17] or with uncontrollable events in the system [16,20]. We note that fewer methods have been actually implemented for centralized enforcement, see TiPEX [18] or GREP [21] for instance. Although there are a few approaches [14,15] considering decentralized enforcement in decentralized systems, these are tailored to specific systems and our work is the first generic approach able to enforce any property expressed in linear-temporal logic.

## 6   Conclusions

DECENT allows the evaluation of two decentralized enforcement algorithms introduced in [13]. Our experiments demonstrate that, although the messages are much larger with the decentralized algorithms, we need less of them. The internal memory usage is significantly reduced with the local-incremental algorithm. Also, even though the latter algorithm does not guarantee the *optimality*, it is very close to it in practice.

We plan to implement our algorithms into a larger tool (THEMIS, for instance) which would allow us to use these algorithms in real systems. We also plan to improve the algorithms as they suffer from a few limitations, mainly the dependence on a powerful simplification function (to not miss any verdict) and the exponential blowup of the formulas in some rare cases. As both of these limitations come from LTL and rewriting, we plan to use different specifications formalism such as finite-state automata or even a more expressive one like timed properties or streams. Finally, we also plan to study in greater detail the *optimistic* and *pessimistic* modes to try and find settings in which one method is better than the other using more suited metrics.

## A    Third experiment

We observe how the performance evolves when we add more components to the system and/or add atomic propositions to the alphabet. Here, the generated formulas are of fixed size (6, chosen arbitrarily). We study six different systems where components can observe either 1, 2 or 3 atomic proposition(s) each and with 3 or 5 components. The number of observable atomic propositions is indicated by $|\Sigma_i|$ and the number of components by $|\Sigma|$.

Table 7 and 6 show the results of this experiment. The difference in size of the messages between both decentralized versions seems to get larger when the system gets larger (in particular when adding more atomic propositions to each component). This makes sense as the global version explores every possible alternative and a larger system has more of them. The local version is not affected as much because a local decision is applied before an enforcer communicates with the next one to limit the growth of the internal memory (we can also observe this when looking at |tcl|) which,

**Table 6.** Differences between the enforced traces in the third experiment

| Algorithm | $|\Sigma_i|$ | $|\Sigma|$ | #mod | #msg | Imsgl | Itcll | $|\Sigma_i|$ | $|\Sigma|$ | #mod | #msg | Imsgl | Itcll |
|---|---|---|---|---|---|---|---|---|---|---|---|---|
| Cent. | | | 0.2 | 3. | 3.5 | 608.58 | | | 0.183 | 5. | 3.5 | 2441.84 |
| Global | 1 | 3 | 0.2 | 0.771 | 236.249 | 636.719 | 1 | 5 | 0.183 | 1.093 | 537.952 | 2503.89 |
| Local | | | 0.196 | 0.609 | 108.197 | 401.75 | | | 0.177 | 0.838 | 168.346 | 739.348 |
| Cent. | | | 0.202 | 3. | 4.501 | 8765.14 | | | 0.221 | 5. | 4.502 | 2941.78 |
| Global | 2 | 3 | 0.202 | 0.759 | 1250.89 | 8967.43 | 2 | 5 | 0.221 | 1.098 | 534.934 | 2952.26 |
| Local | | | 0.198 | 0.58 | 322.203 | 2703.01 | | | 0.219 | 0.839 | 115.972 | 580.382 |
| Cent. | | | 0.205 | 3. | 5.754 | 3707.75 | | | 0.177 | 5. | 5.757 | 11485. |
| Global | 3 | 3 | 0.205 | 0.76 | 614.68 | 3705.48 | 3 | 5 | 0.177 | 1.091 | 1133.39 | 11466. |
| Local | | | 0.203 | 0.609 | 124.239 | 859.064 | | | 0.172 | 0.837 | 236.039 | 1396.81 |

**Table 7.** Results of the third experiment: varying system size

| Variables | | Average number of different event | | | Average number of event with a different #mod | | |
|---|---|---|---|---|---|---|---|
| $|\Sigma_i|$ | $|\Sigma|$ | Cent. $\leftrightarrow$ Global | Cent. $\leftrightarrow$ Local | Global $\leftrightarrow$ Local | Cent. $\leftrightarrow$ Global | Cent. $\leftrightarrow$ Local | Global $\leftrightarrow$ Local |
| 1 | 3 | 0. | 1.264 | 1.264 | 0. | 0.015 | 0.015 |
| 1 | 5 | 0. | 1.147 | 1.147 | 0. | 0.05 | 0.05 |
| 2 | 3 | 0. | 1.16 | 1.16 | 0. | 0.059 | 0.059 |
| 2 | 5 | 0. | 1.459 | 1.459 | 0. | 0.065 | 0.065 |
| 3 | 3 | 0. | 0.951 | 0.951 | 0. | 0.029 | 0.029 |
| 3 | 5 | 0. | 1.377 | 1.377 | 0. | 0.084 | 0.084 |

in turn, limits the growth of the messages as they contain the internal memory. Adding components to the system seems to increase the average memory usage in the global and centralized versions which makes sense as there are more alternatives to consider in this case as well. Table 6 suggests that the system size does not have a major impact on the differences between the traces produced by the algorithms.

# References

1. Bacchus, F., Kabanza, F.: Planning for temporally extended goals. Ann. Math. Artif. Intell. **22**(1–2), 5–27 (1998)
2. Bauer, A., Falcone, Y.: Decentralized LTL Monitoring. Technical report, March 2012. 31 pages
3. Colombo, C., Falcone, Y.: Organising LTL monitors over distributed systems with a global clock. In 14th International Conference on Runtime Verification, Toronto, Canada, September 2014
4. Colombo, C., Falcone, Y.: Organising LTL monitors over distributed systems with a global clock. Formal Methods Syst. Des. **49**(1), 109–158 (2016)
5. Danielsson, L.M., Sánchez, C.: Decentralized stream runtime verification. In: Finkbeiner, B., Mariani, L. (eds.) RV 2019. LNCS, vol. 11757, pp. 185–201. Springer, Cham (2019). https://doi.org/10.1007/978-3-030-32079-9_11
6. Dwyer, M.B., Avrunin, G.S., Corbett, J.C.: Patterns in property specifications for finite-state verification. In Proceedings of the 1999 International Conference on Software Engineering (IEEE Cat. No.99CB37002), pp. 411–420 (1999)
7. El-Hokayem, A., Falcone, Y.: Monitoring decentralized specifications. In: Bultan, T., Sen, K. (eds.) Proceedings of the 26th ACM SIGSOFT International Symposium on Software Testing and Analysis, Santa Barbara, CA, USA, 10–14 July, 2017, pp. 125–135. ACM (2017)
8. El-Hokayem, A., Falcone, Y.: THEMIS: a tool for decentralized monitoring algorithms. In: ISSTA 2017. Proceedings of the 26th ACM SIGSOFT International Symposium on Software Testing and Analysis, pp. 125–135. Santa Barbara, United States (2017)
9. Falcone, Y., Cornebize, T., Fernandez, J.-C.: Efficient and generalized decentralized monitoring of regular languages. In: Ábrahám, E., Palamidessi, C. (eds.) FORTE 2014. LNCS, vol. 8461, pp. 66–83. Springer, Heidelberg (2014). https://doi.org/10.1007/978-3-662-43613-4_5
10. Falcone, Y., Fernandez, J.-C., Mounier, L.: What can you verify and enforce at runtime? Int. J. Softw. Tools Technol. Transf. **14**(3), 349–382 (2012)

11. Falcone, Y., Mounier, L., Fernandez, J.-C., Richier, J.-L.: Runtime enforcement monitors: composition, synthesis, and enforcement abilities. Formal Methods Syst. Des. **38**(3), 223–262 (2011)

12. Francalanza, A., Pérez, J.A., Sánchez, C.: Runtime verification for decentralised and distributed systems. In: Bartocci, E., Falcone, Y. (eds.) Lectures on Runtime Verification. LNCS, vol. 10457, pp. 176–210. Springer, Cham (2018). https://doi.org/10.1007/978-3-319-75632-5_6

13. Gallay, F., Falcone, Y.: Decentralized LTL enforcement. In: GandALF 2021–12th International Symposium on Games. Automata, Logics, and Formal Verification, pp. 1–18. Padua, France (2021)

14. Hallé, S., Khoury, R., Betti, Q., El-Hokayem, A., Falcone, Y.: Decentralized enforcement of document lifecycle constraints. Inf. Syst. **74**(Part), 117–135 (2018)

15. Hu, C., Dong, W., Yang, Y., Shi, H., Deng, F.: Decentralized runtime enforcement for robotic swarms. Front. Inf. Technol. Electron. Eng. **21**(11), 1591–1606 (2020). https://doi.org/10.1631/FITEE.2000203

16. Khoury, R., Hallé, S.: Runtime enforcement with partial control. In: Garcia-Alfaro, J., Kranakis, E., Bonfante, G. (eds.) FPS 2015. LNCS, vol. 9482, pp. 102–116. Springer, Cham (2016). https://doi.org/10.1007/978-3-319-30303-1_7

17. Pinisetty, S.: Runtime enforcement of timed properties revisited. Formal Methods Syst. Des. **45**(3), 381–422 (2014). https://doi.org/10.1007/s10703-014-0215-y

18. Pinisetty, S., Falcone, Y., Jéron, T., Marchand, H., Rollet, A., Nguena Timo, O.: Runtime enforcement of timed properties revisited. Formal Methods Syst. Des. **45**(3), 381–422 (2014). https://doi.org/10.1007/s10703-014-0215-y

19. Pnueli, A.: The temporal logic of programs. In 18th Annual Symposium on Foundations of Computer Science, Providence, Rhode Island, USA, 31 October - 1 November 1977, pp. 46–57. IEEE Computer Society, 1977

20. Renard, M., Falcone, Y., Rollet, A., Jéron, T., Marchand, H.: Optimal enforcement of (timed) properties with uncontrollable events. Math. Struct. Comput. Sci. **29**(1), 169–214 (2019)

21. Renard, M., Rollet, A., Falcone, Y.: GREP: games for the runtime enforcement of properties. In: Yevtushenko, N., Cavalli, A.R., Yenigün, H. (eds.) ICTSS 2017. LNCS, vol. 10533, pp. 259–275. Springer, Cham (2017). https://doi.org/10.1007/978-3-319-67549-7_16

22. Rosu, G., Havelund, K.: Rewriting-based techniques for runtime verification. Autom. Softw. Eng. **12**(2), 151–197 (2005)

# Runtime Verification for FMI-Based Co-simulation

Anastasios Temperekidis, Nikolaos Kekatos, and Panagiotis Katsaros[✉]

Aristotle University of Thessaloniki, 54124 Thessaloniki, Greece
{anastemp,nkekatos,katsaros}@csd.auth.gr

**Abstract.** Co-simulation allows modelling and simulation of heterogeneous systems: the analysis of a system is achieved through the joint simulation of coupled stand-alone sub-simulators for its individual parts, using a standardized interface (e.g. Functional Mock-up Interface - FMI). Runtime verification can be employed to validate the evolution of co-simulation runs, but currently this is feasible only within the scope of individual simulators that may support very diverse monitoring functionalities. This work introduces a technical approach for the runtime verification of properties for the entire co-simulated system. We present the integration of the DejaVU monitor synthesis tool at the master algorithm level of FMI-based co-simulation, such that predicates and events from all constituents of a simulated system can be monitored. Communication between the master and the individual Functional Mock-Up Units (FMUs) is bidirectional, whereas the FMI master does not need to change for monitoring the property of interest. Since FMUs are synchronized by the master algorithm, runtime monitors can be used also as a means to control the co-simulation run. We provide results from co-simulation experiments to give insight into the runtime overhead.

**Keywords:** Co-simulation · Runtime verification · First-order LTL

## 1 Introduction

Today's systems are heterogeneous, since they often combine computation with physical processes. For their design and verification, several different tools are usually used, to develop semantically diverse models. Discrete modeling is more appropriate for the computing elements, whereas continuous modeling is usually preferred for the physical components. When focusing on the verification and validation of the system as a whole, then the problem is how to combine and analyse a set of diverse models for the system under design.

Co-simulation [18] is a technology aiming to address the aforementioned problem. It is based on a coordinating component responsible for the passage of time and the data sharing between the diverse simulators running the models of the system's parts. Co-simulation plays an important role in hardware-in-the-loop and software-in-the-loop simulation-based validation [10]. For the

---

Supported by the european project Horizon 2020 research and innovation programme under grant agreement No. 956123.

T. Dang and V. Stolz (Eds.): RV 2022, LNCS 13498, pp. 304–313, 2022.
https://doi.org/10.1007/978-3-031-17196-3_19

design of cyber-physical systems, co-simulation is the means to validate their behaviour [11], since they are specified using a variety of languages and tools.

FMI (Functional Mockup Interface) [6] is an interoperability standard, which allows to import and co-simulate model components that have been designed with different modeling formalisms, languages, and tools [19]. FMI defines an API and the format of the co-simulated components, known as FMUs (Functional Mockup Units). FMUs by themselves are passive objects (*slaves*), since they do not execute; they can be seen as black boxes that implement the methods of the FMI API. Some of these methods are optional, whereas others are compulsory and must be implemented by all FMUs. A set of FMUs that are coupled together, are executed through the mediation of a *master algorithm* (MA), which is not defined by the standard. The network of FMUs forms the overall system model and the FMUs its sub-models. A simulation run generates a simulation trace by applying the MA to the system model.

Runtime verification [3] relies on continuously monitoring the behaviour of the simulated system, with the aim to detect if it is consistent with a given high-level specification. Results are provided in the form of a verdict for the property(-ies) specified using a temporal logic language. The property specification(s) is/are the basis for the automated synthesis of the runtime monitor(s) with appropriate tools.

In system design, runtime verification can be used to make the verification and validation process more systematic and rigorous, while remaining scalable. It allows the early stopping of possibly costly simulations upon the detection of a property violation, whereas the verification outcomes can guide the test generation in search-based testing. Moreover, online verification of simulation traces is also particularly useful, as a means to control the simulation run, detect anomalies, and trigger runtime recovery or enforcement mechanisms [2,17].

Runtime verification tools have been integrated into various simulators (e.g. in [1,20]), but we are not aware of related works on the integration of runtime verification into FMI-based co-simulation. While it is straightforward to use the runtime monitoring/verification capabilities of individual FMUs, if any, our work concerns with how to integrate runtime monitors at the MA level of FMI-based co-simulations, to allow verifying properties for the overall system model.

We use the DejaVU monitor synthesis tool [14] that allows for parametric specifications in First-order Linear Temporal Logic (LTL); such specifications give rise to runtime monitors for events that carry data, to which the properties can refer. This level of language expressiveness fits well into the need for specifying properties based on a set of semantically diverse FMUs, since the properties can refer to relations or predicates over different domains. However, there are still important challenges to be addressed, such as the monitoring overhead, which depends on the monitor integration approach into the FMI MA. The concrete contributions of this work are the following.

- An approach for online runtime verification of any FMU network, in which:
  • The control flow of the MA does not depend on the property specified and the particular needs for data sharing between the co-simulated FMUs.

- Co-simulation can be controlled by the MA based on the monitor verdict.
- An alternative approach for the integration of runtime monitoring in the form of an additional FMU.
- Experimental results on the online verification of a co-simulated system that provides insights and allows comparing the overhead of the two solutions.

The rest of the paper is structured as follows. Section 2 provides background information on FMI-based co-simulation and runtime monitoring of First-order LTL with the DejaVU tool. Section 3 presents the technical approach for online verification of FMU networks, along with the alternative of runtime monitoring through an additional FMU. In Sect. 4, we provide experimental results that allow comparing the solutions proposed with respect to the overhead for various properties expressed in the past-time fragment of First-order LTL. The paper concludes with a summary of our contributions and the future research prospects.

## 2   Background

### 2.1   Co-simulation

Comprehensive surveys on co-simulation can be found in [11,12]. For FMI-based co-simulation, it suffices to refer to essential technical details concerning the MA. An FMU can be formulated as a (timed) state machine with a set of input variables (or ports), a set of output variables, and a set of internal states [8]. The state machine interacts with its environment via a set of interface methods complying with the FMI standard. The MA performs step-wise co-simulation of a network of FMUs from the *tStart* time till *tStop*. The time step is chosen by the MA and it can be fixed or variable. Time advances locally on FMUs that are simulated independently between two discrete communication points $t_i$ and $t_{i+1}$ with a step size $h = t_{i+1} - t_i > 0$; the MA waits for all FMUs to simulate up to the communication point before advancing the time. At these communication points, the MA collects the outputs $y(t_i)$ and sets the inputs $u(t_i)$ for all FMUs.

### 2.2   Runtime Verification for First-Order LTL

For the runtime verification of co-simulated systems, we are interested in building monitors for events carrying data, which may be denoted by one or more relations or predicates over different domains. This representation is adopted in the (past-time fragment of) first-order LTL in [5,13] that is suitable for runtime monitoring. If $a_i$ is a constant for a value in some domain $\mathcal{D}$, and $x_i$ a variable over the same domain, the syntax of this formalism is defined as follows:

$$\varphi :: = true \mid false \mid p(x_1,\ldots,x_n) \mid (\varphi \vee \varphi) \mid (\varphi \wedge \varphi) \mid$$
$$\neg\varphi \mid (\varphi \, S \, \psi) \mid \ominus\varphi \mid \exists x \, \varphi \mid \forall x \, \varphi \mid e \sim e$$

with $p$ a *predicate/relation* over domains $\mathcal{D}_1, \ldots, \mathcal{D}_n$, $\sim \in \{<, \leq, >, \geq, =, \neq\}$ and

$$e :: = x \mid a \mid e + e \mid e - e \mid e \times e \mid e \, / \, e.$$

*Since* operator, for e.g. $\varphi \, S \, \psi$ means that "$\psi$ was true in the past, and since then, including that point in time, $\phi$ has been true". $\ominus \varphi$ specifies that "in the previous state $\varphi$ was true". The following also hold: $false = \neg true$, $\forall x \, \varphi = \neg \exists x \, \neg \varphi$, and $\varphi \vee \psi = \neg(\neg \varphi \wedge \neg \psi)$. Some additional operators that are useful in property specifications are: $P\varphi = true \, S \, \varphi$ (for "previously"), $\varphi \, R \, \psi = \neg(\neg \varphi \, S \, \neg \psi)$ (the dual of the Since operator), and $H\varphi = (false \, R \, \varphi)$ (for "always in the past").

DejaVU is a runtime verification tool for traces of events with data that synthesizes runtime monitors based on past-time First-order LTL formulas. When a trace is fed into the monitor, a Boolean value (verdict) is returned, for each event. Upon having completed the verification of a trace, a file is created containing the number of events, which violate the property.

DejaVU monitors allow evaluating property specifications over sets of data observed, with values that may be unbounded or not provided in advance. The efficiency of these monitors at runtime is therefore of fundamental importance within the context of FMI-based co-simulations, especially when the event traces are originated from multiple heterogenous FMUs.

# 3   Online Runtime Verification of FMI-Based Co-simulation

Two alternatives are proposed for the integration of DejaVU runtime monitors in FMI-based co-simulations. First, we present an FMI MA for the runtime verification of any FMU network and then an FMU acting as DejaVU runtime monitor. For the latter approach, there is no need to modify the FMI MA used.

## 3.1   FMI Master Algorithm for Runtime Verification

The FMI standard for co-simulation aims to support a general class of MAs. The MA orchestrates the entire simulation and its main functionalities include i) the instantiation (fmiInstantiate function call) and initialization (fmiEnterIniti-alizationMode, fmiExitIntializationMode function calls) of the FMUs, ii) the computation and propagation of variable values among FMUs (fmiSetXXX and fmiGetXXX function calls where XXX refers to the data type, in order to set or respectively retrieve values to/from FMU input/output variables), iii) the step-wise simulation of the FMUs in an order (fmiDoStep function call which advances the simulation of each FMU by the simulation step), iv) the termination of the simulation. We assume that the MA guarantees deterministic execution, it is free from algebraic loops and ensures determinacy and termination [7,9,16].

A high-level overview of an FMI MA with an integrated runtime monitor is shown in Fig. 1. The workflow for the runtime verification of a co-simulated system using the DejaVU tool is as follows (Fig. 2a).

1. Property specification in first-order LTL.
2. Synthesis of the runtime monitor in Scala.
3. For the property specified in Step 1, a suitably formatted file is provided with all event names (predicates) and their value references (FMU variables) that determine how each event is evaluated.

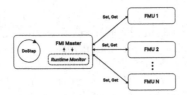

**Fig. 1.** An FMI MA for runtime verification

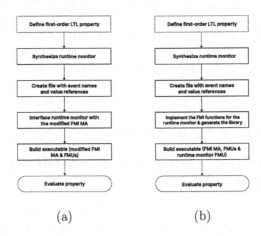

(a)                              (b)

**Fig. 2.** Workflows for using (a) the FMI MA, (b) an FMU for runtime verification

4. The runtime monitor from Step 2 is interfaced with the FMI MA. This involves a slight modification to the Scala code (the `eval` function is called by the FMI MA) and then converting it into a .jar file that is interfaced with the FMI MA through JNI (Java Native Interface).
5. The FMI MA is compiled along with the FMUs.

The workflow can be fully automated. The pseudocode for the FMI MA is shown in Algorithm 1. Function calls in blue are for integrating the runtime monitor, whereas the rest are standard calls of a typical MA. The `monitorInitialization()` call instantiates and loads the runtime monitor, along with the function `eval()`. The file from workflow Step 3 is then read with `monitorMapping()`. With `synthesizeEvent()`, the FMU variables for the predicates of the property are extracted and formatted, according to how a `DejaVU` monitor expects them. Finally, the monitoring function is called for the event at the current time step.

### 3.2   FMU for Runtime Verification

Figure 3 depicts the integration of a runtime monitor in FMI-based co-simulation, in the form of an additional FMU. The runtime monitoring FMU implements the necessary methods required by FMI and the MA contains only

---

**Algorithm 1:** FMI master algorithm for runtime monitoring

---

```
/* Co-simulation parameters */
tCurrent: current simulation time
tStart: start time
tStop: stop time
h: simulation step


/* Instantiate and initialize FMUs in set C */
foreach FMU c ∈ C do
    fmiInstantiate();
    fmiEnterInitializationMode();
    fmiSetupExperiments(tStart, tStop);
    fmiSetXXX(v)          /* where XXX is Real, Integer, Boolean, String */
    fmiExitInitializationMode();


/* Initialize Runtime Monitor */
monitorInitialization();              /* instantiates runtime monitor */
monitorMapping();            /* defines property variables and ordering */


/* Step-wise simulation */
while tCurrent<tStop do
    foreach connection between an input u and an output y do
        v=fmiGetXXX(y);
        fmiSetXXX(u,v);
        fmiDoStep(h);
    event=synthesizeEvent();          /* constructs event from values */
    monitorEval(event);               /* property evaluation */
    tCurrent=tCurrent+h;


/* Termination */
foreach FMU c ∈ C do
    fmiTerminate();
```

---

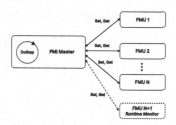

**Fig. 3.** An FMU for runtime verification

standard FMI function calls. The workflow for the runtime verification of a co-simulated system using the runtime monitoring FMU is as follows (Fig. 2b).

1. Property specification in First-order LTL.
2. Synthesis of the runtime monitor in Scala.
3. For the property specified in Step 1, a suitably formatted file is provided.
4. A shared object file for the runtime monitoring FMU is created and a model description file (XML) with all definitions of exposed variables are packaged all together into a `.zip` file.
5. The FMI MA is compiled along with all FMUs.

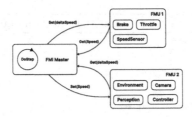

**Fig. 4.** FMU connection graph for the traffic sign recognition case study

## 4   Experimental Results

Our case study is a closed-loop system of an autonomous vehicle that performs traffic sign recognition and speed regulation [15], designed using the BIP modeling language [4]. The system model consists of five components: environment, camera, perception, controller, and plant. It has been broken into two parts corresponding to separate FMUs. $FMU_1$ enables the braking or throttling system according to delta speed and adjusts the vehicle's speed. $FMU_2$ consists of four *atoms* and is responsible for traffic sign detection and delta speed computation. The FMU connection graph is shown in Fig. 4. The controller needs the vehicle speed (input) in order to compute the deviation from the recognized speed limit. The synchronization between the two FMUs is achieved via the FMI MA, which retrieves and communicates the corresponding values. We apply the two runtime monitoring approaches of Sect. 3 to evaluate the property:

*"The vehicle speed should always be less than or equal to the current speed limit."*

In first-order LTL, the aforementioned property can be written as

$$\phi_1 := vehicleSpeed \leq speedLimit$$

or if a single speed limit violation is enough to invalidate the property, as

$$\phi_2 := H \ vehicleSpeed \leq speedLimit$$

We simulated the system using 453 image frames with various traffic signs, which produced simulation traces of length 3000 steps. Runtime verification of properties $\phi_1$ and $\phi_2$ took place using both approaches of Sect. 3 and the induced computational overhead was estimated through comparison with the computational time taken for co-simulation without runtime monitoring. For $\phi_1$, six property violations were found and all of them happened at time instants in which a lower speed limit has been detected - three time units are required to apply the new limit to the SpeedSensor. For $\phi_2$, as expected, once the property was violated, it continued to be violated for the rest of the simulation trace.

Our simulation time measurements, initially showed imperceptible monitoring overhead, due to the computation time for traffic sign perception (neural network) that was orders of magnitude larger than the time spent in each simulation step, for all other tasks ($\sim 0.2 - 0.5$ ms). Thus, we report the computation times and the relative increase from the co-simulation without runtime monitoring, by excluding the times spent for the perception task and monitor initialization, in the beginning of the co-simulation. The results in Table 1 show a very high overhead, when the computation time for each simulation step is in the range of $\sim 0.2 - 0.5$ ms. The overhead is even higher, when the $H$ operator is used. Finally, no conclusive results are drawn for potential efficiency differences between the two runtime monitoring alternatives proposed in Sect. 3.

**Table 1.** Runtime monitoring and overhead for properties $\phi_1$ and $\phi_2$ of the traffic sign recognition and speed regulation case study.

| Id | Property | Approach 1 (Sec. 3.1) | | | Approach 2 (Sec. 3.2) | | |
|----|----------|------|-----------|----------|------|-----------|----------|
|    |          | #ev  | Time [ms] | overhead | #ev  | Time [ms] | overhead |
| 1  | none     | 3000 | 137.6728  | -        | 3000 | 137.6728  | -        |
| 2  | $\phi_1$ | 3000 | 315.3487  | 129 %    | 3000 | 328.35    | 138.5 %  |
| 3  | $\phi_2$ | 3000 | 762.478   | 453.8 %  | 3000 | 661.30    | 380.3 %  |

## 5 Conclusion

In this work, two runtime verification alternatives were presented for FMI-based co-simulation, which enable the verification of requirements for a co-simulated system. Both solutions have been applied to co-simulations of fixed time steps and can be fully automated to completely eliminate any manual manipulation of intermediate artifacts.

For the runtime monitors, we opted the DejaVU monitor synthesis tool that allows specifying properties in the past-time portion of a first-order extension of LTL. We believe that this level of expressiveness fits into the needs for expressing properties based on a set of semantically diverse simulation components (FMUs) that emit events with data.

The efficiency of the two solutions was studied through experimentation with a case study, namely an autonomous system co-simulation. For the monitored properties, we observed a significant overhead compared to the co-simulation without monitoring, when the computation time for each simulation step is in the range of $\sim 0.2 - 0.5$ ms. When the simulation step included a computationally intensive task, the monitoring overhead was imperceptible. The code for the runtime monitoring solutions applied to our case study is available online[1].

Of course, the induced overhead depends predominantly on the monitored property and the operators used. However, as a future research prospect, we are interested to adapt the FMI master algorithm, so that the runtime monitor will be selectively called under specific conditions, instead of every time step.

---

[1] https://depend.csd.auth.gr:8443/anastast/fmu_monitoring_rv22.

# References

1. Balakrishnan, A., Deshmukh, J., Hoxha, B., Yamaguchi, T., Fainekos, G.: Perce-Mon: online monitoring for perception systems. In: Feng, L., Fisman, D. (eds.) RV 2021. LNCS, vol. 12974, pp. 297–308. Springer, Cham (2021). https://doi.org/10.1007/978-3-030-88494-9_18
2. Bartocci, E., et al.: Specification-based monitoring of cyber-physical systems: a survey on theory, tools and applications. In: Bartocci, E., Falcone, Y. (eds.) Lectures on Runtime Verification. LNCS, vol. 10457, pp. 135–175. Springer, Cham (2018). https://doi.org/10.1007/978-3-319-75632-5_5
3. Bartocci, E., Falcone, Y., Francalanza, A., Reger, G.: Introduction to runtime verification. In: Bartocci, E., Falcone, Y. (eds.) Lectures on Runtime Verification. LNCS, vol. 10457, pp. 1–33. Springer, Cham (2018). https://doi.org/10.1007/978-3-319-75632-5_1
4. Basu, A., Bensalem, S., Bozga, M., Bourgos, P., Sifakis, J.: Rigorous system design: the BIP approach. In: Kotásek, Z., Bouda, J., Černá, I., Sekanina, L., Vojnar, T., Antoš, D. (eds.) MEMICS 2011. LNCS, vol. 7119, pp. 1–19. Springer, Heidelberg (2012). https://doi.org/10.1007/978-3-642-25929-6_1
5. Bensalem, S., et al.: Formal specification for learning-enabled autonomous systems. EasyChair Preprint No. 8564, EasyChair (2022)
6. Blochwitz, T., et al.: Functional mockup interface 2.0: the standard for tool independent exchange of simulation models. In Proceedings of the 9th International Modelica Conference, pp. 173–184. The Modelica Association (2012)
7. Bogomolov, S., et al.: Co-simulation of hybrid systems with SpaceEx and Uppaal. In 11th International Modelica Conference, pp. 159–169. Linköping University Electronic Press (2015)
8. Broman, D., et al.: Determinate composition of FMUs for co-simulation. In: 2013 Proceedings of the International Conference on Embedded Software (EMSOFT), pp. 1–12. IEEE (2013)
9. Cremona, F., et al.: Hybrid co-simulation: it's about time. Soft. Syst. Model. 18(3), 1655–1679 (2019). https://doi.org/10.1007/s10270-017-0633-6
10. Düser, T.: X-in-the-Loop - an integrated validation framework for vehicle development using powertrain functions and driver assistance systems, Ph.D. thesis (2010)
11. Gomes, C., Thule, C., Broman, D., Larsen, P.G., Vangheluwe, H.: Co-simulation: state of the art. arXiv preprint arXiv:1702.00686 (2017)
12. Gomes, C., Thule, C., Broman, D., Larsen, P.G., Vangheluwe, H.: Co-simulation: a survey. ACM Comput. Surv. (CSUR) 51(3), 1–33 (2018)
13. Havelund, K., Peled, D., Ulus, D.: First order temporal logic monitoring with BDDs. In: Formal Methods in Computer Aided Design, FMCAD, pp. 116–123. IEEE (2017)
14. Havelund, K., Peled, D., Ulus, D.: First-order temporal logic monitoring with BDDs. Formal Methods Syst. Des. 56(1), 1–21 (2020)
15. He, W.: Modeling and simulation for AI-based systems, master thesis (2021)
16. Liboni, G.: Complex systems co-simulation with the CoSim20 framework: for efficient and accurate distributed co-simulations, Ph.D. thesis, Université Côte d'Azur (2021)
17. Maler, O.: Some thoughts on runtime verification. In: Falcone, Y., Sánchez, C. (eds.) RV 2016. LNCS, vol. 10012, pp. 3–14. Springer, Cham (2016). https://doi.org/10.1007/978-3-319-46982-9_1

18. Thule, C., Lausdahl, K., Gomes, C., Meisl, G., Larsen, P.G.: Maestro: the INTO-CPS co-simulation framework. Simul. Model. Pract. Theory **92**, 45–61 (2019)
19. Tripakis, S.: Bridging the semantic gap between heterogeneous modeling formalisms and FMI. In: 2015 International Conference on Embedded Computer Systems: Architectures, Modeling, and Simulation (SAMOS), pp. 60–69. IEEE (2015)
20. Zapridou, E., Bartocci, E., Katsaros, P.: Runtime verification of autonomous driving systems in CARLA. In: Runtime Verification - 20th International Conference, RV 2020, Los Angeles, CA, USA, 6–9 October 2020, pp. 172–183. Proceedings (2020)

# TeSSLa – An Ecosystem for Runtime Verification

Hannes Kallwies[1]([✉]), Martin Leucker[1], Malte Schmitz[1], Albert Schulz[2], Daniel Thoma[1], and Alexander Weiss[2]

[1] Institute for Software Engineering and Programming Languages, University of Lübeck, Lübeck, Germany
{kallwies,leucker,schmitz,thoma}@isp.uni-luebeck.de
[2] Accemic Technologies GmbH, Kiefersfelden, Germany
{aschulz,aweiss}@accemic.com

**Abstract.** Runtime verification deals with checking correctness properties on the runs of a system under scrutiny. To achieve this, it addresses a variety of sub-problems related to monitoring of systems: These range from the appropriate design of a specification language over efficient monitor generation as hardware and software monitors to solutions for instrumenting the monitored system, preferably in a non-intrusive way. Further aspects play a role for the usability of a runtime verification toolchain, e.g. availability, sufficient documentation and the existence of a developer community. In this paper we present the TeSSLa ecosystem, a runtime verification framework built around the stream runtime verification language TeSSLa: It provides a rich toolchain of mostly freely available compilers for monitor generation on different hardware and software backends, as well as instrumentation mechanisms for various runtime verification requirements. Additionally, we highlight how the online resources and supporting tools of the community-driven project enable the productive usage of stream runtime verification.

## 1 Introduction

*Runtime verification* is the discipline of computer science that develops methods for verifying whether a system behavior adheres to its specification. To this extent the given specification in some specification language is typically translated into a *monitor* that analyzes the behavior in question. The analysis may be performed *online*, while the system is executing, or it may be analyzed *offline* when for example the trace is pre-recorded [1].

While the heart of a runtime verification framework consequently consists of the specification language itself and its synthesizers deriving monitors from given specifications, a practically viable tool suite has to support in many further aspects. One of the main challenges is how to get the observation of the system

T. Dang and V. Stolz (Eds.): RV 2022, LNCS 13498, pp. 314–324, 2022.
https://doi.org/10.1007/978-3-031-17196-3_20

under consideration. Most often, observing a system may slow it down or, more generally, may affect its timing. Even more, the monitor may affect the timing of the overall system. This may lead to both false positive and false negative verdicts which should of course be avoided.

Another aspect is the concrete application scenario. Runtime verification may be used as a form of debugging, for finding errors in a given system, or for showing (statistically) that the system is indeed correct. Depending on the application scenario, supporting tools either have to provide a quick turnaround time (i.e. the time to observing a new execution of the system once the specification has changed), or, have to be extremely efficient to support long-term observations. Finally, runtime verification may also be used for life-long supervision of the underlying system (and enforcing correctness of the system) such that the whole runtime verification machinery becomes a part of the system which, again, requires different properties to be fulfilled. An overview of the general stream runtime verification architecture with the required components and involved configuration documents, which are subject to these considerations is shown in Fig. 1.

However for practical applications, it is not only important to get the system right but likewise to get the specifications right. As such, supporting tools for writing meaningful specifications are helpful. Last but not least, a vivid community and open-source tools are a further plus when using runtime verification in industrial settings.

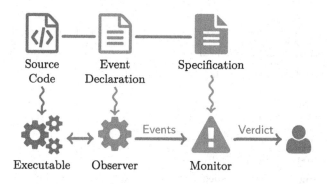

**Fig. 1.** General architecture of stream runtime verification.

Altogether we see that from a theoretical point of view runtime verification is often simplified to synthesizing monitors for your specification formalism, while a practically viable runtime verification framework has to meet a variety of different requirements and needs a variety of supporting tools.

In the following we focus on stream runtime verification (SRV) which has been pioneered by the specification language LOLA [2]. Later on RTLola [3], Striver [4] and TeSSLa [5,6] emerged. In this paper we will present TeSSLa's different compiler backends and supporting tools to meet the various requirements of the runtime verification process discussed above. While the TeSSLa language itself [5,6] and some of its synthesizers [7,8] have been described before, this paper describes mainly the TeSSLa tool suite as a whole, which aims supporting software engineers and testers to achieve efficient and powerful verification.

This paper is organized as follows: In Sect. 2 we briefly recall the TeSSLa language by providing a specification that can be used for monitor synthesis. In Sect. 3 we give a broad overview of the backends such monitors may be compiled to. Section 4 presents the different instrumentation approaches that are compatible with the TeSSLa framework. In Sect. 5 we finally give an overview about additional tools and aspects connected to the TeSSLa ecosystem. We conclude the paper in Sect. 6.

## 2    The TeSSLa Specification Language

This section presents the TeSSLa language on the basis of an example to give a rough impression of the language features supported there: The specification in Listing 1.1, used as running example throughout the paper, checks that the time that passes between the activation of brakes of an automotive system and the reading of the brake sensors (which are used to supervise the braking process) is less than or equal to 4 ms.

```
# Inputs
@InstFunctionCall("read_brake_sensor")
in read_brake_sensor: Events[Unit]
@InstFunctionCall("activate_brakes")
in activate_brakes: Events[Unit]

# Trace Processing
def latency = measureLatency(read_brake_sensor, activate_brakes)
def error = latency > 4ms
def high = filter(latency, error) − 4ms
def is_critical = count(high) > 10
def critical = filter(high, is_critical)

# Output
@VisDots out high
@VisEvents out critical

# Macro
def measureLatency[A, B](a: Events[A], b: Events[B]) =
   time(b) − last(time(a), b)
```

**Listing 1.1.** TeSSLa specification for the *Brake Sensor* example.

The specification does so by defining two input streams read_brake_sensor and activate_brakes. The type of the events carried by these streams is Unit, i.e. they have no value, as they only represent calls to functions. The input streams are preceded by @InstFunctionCall annotations. During the following monitoring process, these annotations are extracted from the stream specification and passed to connected tools of the tool chain. In this specific case these annotations are meant for the instrumenter who is instructed to raise an event on the input streams, always when in the supervised system a call of the functions read_brake_sensor and activate_brakes happens. In the following lines five further streams are defined. The first one latency is defined as a call of the macro measureLatency. This macro receives two streams a and b of generic types A, B and produces a new stream of events. It is defined at the end of the specification using two operators: time(x) provides access to the timestamps of the events on stream x and last(y, z) provides the last event on $y$ for every event on $z$. The expression time(b) - last(time(a), b) calculates the difference between the timestamp of the current event on stream b and the timestamp of the last event on stream a. As a consequence the stream latency in our example always carries the latency between a call of activate_brakes and the subsequent call of read_brake_sensor. The other streams are defined based on this latency and via macros from the TeSSLa standard library. The stream error is *true* if the measured latency is higher than 4ms. If error is *true* then high contains the value by which amount the 4ms are surpassed. Stream is_critical counts the number of events on stream high, i.e. the number of breaches of the property and gets *true* if this number exceeds 10. critical finally filters the events of high if critical is true. In the third part the specification eventually defines which streams shall be printed out by the monitor (high and critical). Again these streams contain annotations which are passed to subsequent tools. In this case @VisDots and @VisEvents which indicate the graphical representation of the streams in a monitor GUI.

Note that the TeSSLa language, from a theoretical point of view, as presented in [6], only consists of six core operators. In practice, however, it provides several additional features, like annotations, macro definitions and access to macros from a standard library, which do not make the language more expressive, but are necessary for a comfortable usage of the tool chain and the language itself.

## 3 TeSSLa Compilers and Backends

The TeSSLa tool suite addresses different compilation targets for TeSSLa specifications. It comes with an interpreter that evaluates a TeSSLa specification on the JVM without compilation, compilers that synthesize the specification into software monitors that can be executed on different target platform, and a compiler for specialized event processing hardware.

The interpreter is written in Scala and available as a runnable Jar archive. It follows a straightforward evaluation strategy and serves as a reference implementation for TeSSLa, but is significantly slower than other backends (see measurements in Fig. 3). Still, it is a ready-to-use tool for simple experiments, e.g. when exploring the TeSSLa language. The interpreter provides results without compilation overhead, while the other software compilers translate TeSSLa to imperative languages first, which are then further compiled to binaries. The interpreter's direct evaluation supports the interactive process of writing new specifications and checking them on sample inputs. It also provides an API that can be used to integrate it with custom tools and trace sources.

The software compilers generate Scala or Rust code. The Scala code is compiled into a Jar which can be executed platform-independent on any JVM. Complex data structures like maps, sets and lists are implemented using the immutable data structures provided by the Scala standard library. Additional Scala and Java data structures and functions can be used via native externs: They allow the declaration and utilization of TeSSLa functions that are implemented natively in the target language of the compilation. The Rust code is compiled into a native binary for all targets supported by the LLVM project. Complex data structures are implemented using immutable data structures for Rust provided by the library rust-im[1] and additional data structures and native externs are supported, too. Both software compilers generate a monitoring library and an exemplary command line application.

The TeSSLa framework also supports a specialized event processing hardware, Accemic's embedded processing units (EPUs) [8–13]. EPUs are implemented on an FPGAand allow data flow processing while maintaining short reconfiguration cycles: The EPUs are programmed by writing special commands into their memory. They can be reconfigured entirely without the need for a new FPGA synthesis. The TeSSLa EPU compiler generates such an EPU configuration which can be directly uploaded to EPU hardware. The maximal processing speed of the EPUs is 100 MEvent/s (million events per second).

The TeSSLa language is designed to be modular such that the requirements of different target platforms can be considered. For example, the EPUs do not support complex data structures to the same extent as the software compilers. The interpreter, the software compilers and the EPU compiler rely on the same compiler frontend, which compiles a TeSSLa specification into so-called TeSSLa Core. TeSSLa Core is a special form of a TeSSLa specification, representing the data flow graph of the TeSSLa specification. In TeSSLa Core every stream and every function has type annotations, and all macros are expanded. The compiler frontend can either print TeSSLa Core using the syntax for TeSSLa specifications, or provide the object graph as a data structure to compiler backends so that they do not need to parse it again.

The compiler frontend consists of an ANTLR-based parser, a type checker and a constant folder, which operates on macros and functions on statically known values and simplifies the translation for the further backends. The frontend is written in Scala and available as a library packaged as a Jar archive that the backends can use, for example as a Maven dependency. This makes it possible to extend the tool suite with further specialized synthesizer backends.

## 4    Observation and Instrumentation

The TeSSLa tool suite provides utilities for the entire runtime verification workflow: The previous section introduced several monitoring syntheses; this section discusses approaches to observe events from the system under test (SUT).

As already pointed out in the introduction, the requirements for the mechanism to do this are diverse and depend on the specific application scenario. While for some settings a powerful and highly customizable software instrumentation is

---

[1] https://docs.rs/im/latest/im/.

the desired mechanism, other scenarios may require a fully non-intrusive observation generation strategy, which has no interference with the SUT. Depending on the monitoring target (hardware or software) the TeSSLa tool chain is compatible with/offers different instrumentation utilities.

The software monitors can be used for online and offline monitoring. They can process trace data from text-based or binary files recorded earlier. In combination with instrumentation tools like AspectJ [14,15] they can be used for online monitoring, too: The instrumented executable sends a stream of events to the compiled monitor running as a separate process in order to reduce the influence of the monitoring on the SUT. The upper part of Fig. 2 shows this approach.

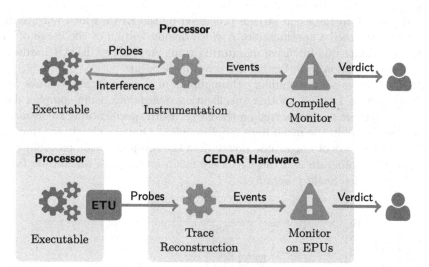

**Fig. 2.** Architecture of runtime verification with instrumented binary and compiled monitor (top) in comparison with dedicated CEDAR hardware for non-intrusive monitoring with the embedded tracing unit (ETU) of the processor (bottom).

The TeSSLa tool suite also comes with its own instrumentation tool for C code using the clang compiler tool chain. Instrumenting source code instead of binaries has the advantage that the instrumented source code is still human-readable and can manually be customized after the instrumentation by the user according to his needs and then be compiled with the existing compilation tool chain.

The C-Code instrumenter is available as a native binary that is integrated into the TeSSLa Jar package. It uses the information about the specification's input streams and annotations (e.g. @InstFunctionCall in Listing 1.1) to add dedicated calls to a logging library into the source code of the SUT. The logging library is also part of the TeSSLa tool suite. It uses multi-producer multi-consumer channels for message passing to allow multiple threads of the SUT to send messages to the monitor without any locking.

In contrast to the intrusive software monitoring approach, the TeSSLa tool suite also supports non-intrusive monitoring using Accemic's CEDAR hardware [8,11–13,16,17]. The lower part of Fig. 2 shows how non-intrusive monitoring utilises the processor's embedded tracing unit (ETU). The unmodified executable runs on the processor and the ETU provides a debugging trace. This trace contains information about the program counter, i.e. which instructions are currently executed by the processor. The ETU's trace is encoded: From time to time it contains absolute program counter addresses, but most of the time it only indicates if a conditional jump was taken or not. The trace reconstruction of the CEDAR hardware decodes the current program counter address online from the ETU's trace. Again, annotations in the TeSSLa specification are used to declare points of interest. If the program reaches such a point, the trace reconstruction adds an event into the event stream processed by the EPUs which were configured with the TeSSLa specification. A video demonstration of the usage of the TeSSLa tool suite non-intrusive monitoring using Accemic's CEDAR hardware with the specification from Listing 1.1 is available online.[2]

Figure 3 shows some exemplary throughputs of the specification *Brake Sensor* from Listing 1.1 and another specification *Scheduling* using complex data structures that are not supported on the EPUs. Both specifications are available in the playground in the menu item *RV Examples*.[3] One can clearly see that the interpreter is orders of magnitude slower than the compiled Scala program. The compiled Rust program and the EPUs are again an order of magnitude faster than the compiled Scala program.

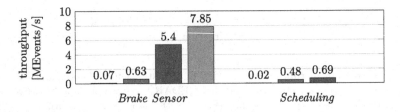

**Fig. 3.** Exemplary throughput of ■ the interpreter, ■ the compiled Scala monitor, ■ the compiled Rust monitor, and ■ the EPUs. (Color figure online)

## 5   The TeSSLa Ecosystem

The TeSSLa tool suite provides the necessary components for online and offline runtime verification: Instrumentation, logging, and monitor synthesis. However, the TeSSLa ecosystem goes beyond these software tools and covers further aspects that supports the practical application of runtime verification:

---

[2] www.youtube.com/watch?v=3AYVWK-X9nw.

[3] https://play.tessla.io/.

*Playground.* The TeSSLa website[4] contains an interactive playground (see Footnote 3) intended for a first exploration of the TeSSLa language and the runtime verification tools. TeSSLa specifications can be interpreted and C code can be instrumented and executed in a sand-boxed environment. Further, the stream visualizer provides a graphical intuition for TeSSLa streams. It helps to recognize event patterns and assists users with the interactive process of writing and testing TeSSLa specifications. The playground is shown in Fig. 4: Note how the annotations @VisDots and @VisEvents on the output stream declarations in Listing 1.1 determine the representation of the streams in the visualizer.

*Documentation.* Further, the TeSSLa website contains material on the formal semantics of the language, introductions and tutorials on writing TeSSLa specifications and using the instrumentation for runtime verification. The language specification precisely describes the syntax and semantics of the language. We developed TeSSLadoc to support documentation of TeSSLa specifications. The tool is inspired by Javadoc and used e.g. for the documentation of the standard library. The documentation includes examples which are graphically represented using the stream visualizer.

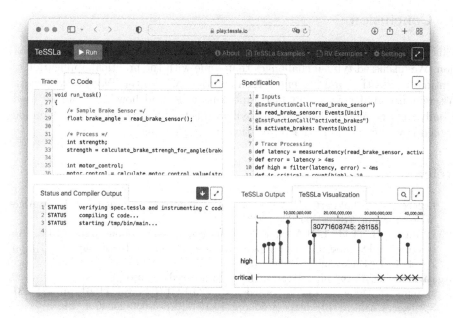

**Fig. 4.** The TeSSLa playground is a web-based IDE that can interpret TeSSLa specifications on instrumented C code or manually entered input traces. Output traces can be graphically visualized in the interactive stream visualizer.

---

[4] www.tessla.io.

*Libraries.* TeSSLa's macro system supports modular extensions for special application domains. There are currently libraries for AUTOSAR Timex [18,19], past-time LTL and timed dyadic deontic logic [20]. These documented user libraries are available for download on the TeSSLa website[5] and are contributed and maintained by the community.

*Scientific Publications.* TeSSLa itself is presented, analyzed and discussed in several publications [5,6,8,12,13,21–23] and used to implement and analyze advanced concepts for stream runtime verification like for example monitoring streams with partial information using ideas of abstraction [24] and new approaches to the aggregate update problem for multi-clocked data flow languages [7]. The application of TeSSLa for race detection is described in [25].

*Community.* The TeSSLa language, the language specification, the compiler frontend and several backends are available under a free license. TeSSLa is maintained and developed further by the TeSSLa community. It is used in several projects and the open source licensing allows all TeSSLa users to share their contributions with the growing community.

## 6    Conclusion

This paper provided an overview of the TeSSLa tool suite for runtime verification. We discussed typical challenges that come with the practical application of runtime verification and presented their solutions within the TeSSLa framework. We demonstrated how the main components work and how they can be used. Finally we sketched further accompanying aspects of the TeSSLa ecosystem and argued how they support the verification process further.

## References

1. Leucker, M., Schallhart, C.: A brief account of runtime verification. J. Logic Algebraic Program. **78**(5), 293–303 (2009)
2. D'Angelo, B., et al.: LOLA: runtime monitoring of synchronous systems. In: 12th International Symposium on Temporal Representation and Reasoning (TIME), pp. 166–174. IEEE Computer Society (2005)
3. Faymonville, P., et al.: StreamLAB: stream-based monitoring of cyber-physical systems. In: Dillig, I., Tasiran, S. (eds.) CAV 2019. LNCS, vol. 11561, pp. 421–431. Springer, Cham (2019). https://doi.org/10.1007/978-3-030-25540-4_24
4. Gorostiaga, F., Sánchez, C.: Striver: stream runtime verification for real-time event-streams. In: Colombo, C., Leucker, M. (eds.) RV 2018. LNCS, vol. 11237, pp. 282–298. Springer, Cham (2018). https://doi.org/10.1007/978-3-030-03769-7_16
5. Leucker, M., Sánchez, C., Scheffel, T., Schmitz, M., Schramm, A.: Tessla: runtime verification of non-synchronized real-time streams. In: SAC, ACM, pp. 1925–1933 (2018)

---

[5] www.tessla.io/usrLibs/overview/.

6. Convent, L., Hungerecker, S., Leucker, M., Scheffel, T., Schmitz, M., Thoma, D.: TeSSLa: temporal stream-based specification language. In: Massoni, T., Mousavi, M.R. (eds.) SBMF 2018. LNCS, vol. 11254, pp. 144–162. Springer, Cham (2018). https://doi.org/10.1007/978-3-030-03044-5_10

7. Kallwies, H., Leucker, M., Scheffel, T., Schmitz, M., Thoma, D.: Aggregate update problem for multi-clocked dataflow languages. In: Symposium on Code Generation and Optimization (CGO), pp. 79–91. IEEE (2022)

8. Decker, N., et al.: Rapidly adjustable non-intrusive online monitoring for multi-core systems. In: Cavalheiro, S., Fiadeiro, J. (eds.) SBMF 2017. LNCS, vol. 10623, pp. 179–196. Springer, Cham (2017). https://doi.org/10.1007/978-3-319-70848-5_12

9. Weiss, A.: Event Processing US 2021081145 A1, March 18 (2021)

10. Weiss, A.: Event Processing EP 3792767 A1, March 17 (2021)

11. Weiss, A., et al.: Understanding and fixing complex faults in embedded cyberphysical systems. Computer **54**(1), 49–60 (2021)

12. Decker, N., et al.: Online analysis of debug trace data for embedded systems. In: DATE, pp. 851–856. IEEE (2018)

13. Convent, L., Hungerecker, S., Scheffel, T., Schmitz, M., Thoma, D., Weiss, A.: Hardware-based runtime verification with embedded tracing units and stream processing. In: Colombo, C., Leucker, M. (eds.) RV 2018. LNCS, vol. 11237, pp. 43–63. Springer, Cham (2018). https://doi.org/10.1007/978-3-030-03769-7_5

14. Hilsdale, E., Hugunin, J., Kersten, M., Kiczales, G., Lopes, C.V., Palm, J.: AspectJ: the language and support tools. In: OOPSLA Addendum, ACM, p.163 (2000)

15. Kiczales, G., Hilsdale, E., Hugunin, J., Kersten, M., Palm, J., Griswold, W.G.: An overview of AspectJ. In: Knudsen, J. (ed.) ECOOP 2001. LNCS, vol. 2072, pp. 327–354. Springer, Heidelberg (2001). https://doi.org/10.1007/3-540-45337-7_18

16. Weiss, A., Lange, A.: Trace-Data Processing and Profiling Device EP 2873983 A1, May 20 (2015)

17. Weiss, A., Lange, A.: Trace-Data Processing and Profiling Device US 9286186 B2, March 15 (2016)

18. Friese, M.J., Kallwies, H., Leucker, M., Sachenbacher, M., Streichhahn, H., Thoma, D.: Runtime verification of AUTOSAR timing extensions. In: International Conference on Real-Time Networks and Systems (RTNS), ACM, pp. 173–183 (2022)

19. Partnership, A.D.: Specification of timing extensions, version 1.0.0, release 4.0.1

20. Kharraz, K.Y., Leucker, M., Schneider, G.: Timed dyadic deontic logic. In: JURIX, Volume 346 of Frontiers in Artificial Intelligence and Applications, pp. 197–204. IOS Press (2021)

21. Leucker, M., Sánchez, C., Scheffel, T., Schmitz, M., Schramm, A.: Runtime verification of real-time event streams under non-synchronized arrival. Software Qual. J. **28**(2), 745–787 (2020). https://doi.org/10.1007/s11219-019-09493-y

22. Kallwies, H., Leucker, M., Prilop, M., Schmitz, M.: Optimizing trans-compilers in runtime verification makes sense - sometimes. In: Ameur, Y. et al. (eds.) Theoretical Aspects of Software Engineering. TASE 2022. LNCS, vol. 13299, pp. 197–204. Springer, Cham (2022). https://doi.org/10.1007/978-3-031-10363-6_14

23. Kauffman, S.: nfer – a tool for event stream abstraction. In: Calinescu, R., Păsăreanu, C.S. (eds.) SEFM 2021. LNCS, vol. 13085, pp. 103–109. Springer, Cham (2021). https://doi.org/10.1007/978-3-030-92124-8_6

24. Leucker, M., Sánchez, C., Scheffel, T., Schmitz, M., Thoma, D.: Runtime verification for timed event streams with partial information. In: Finkbeiner, B., Mariani, L. (eds.) RV 2019. LNCS, vol. 11757, pp. 273–291. Springer, Cham (2019). https://doi.org/10.1007/978-3-030-32079-9_16

25. Ahishakiye, F., Jarabo, J.L.R., Pun, V., Stolz, V.: Hardware-assisted online data race detection. In: Bartocci, E., Falcone, Y., Leucker, M. (eds.) Formal Methods in Outer Space. LNCS, vol. 13065, pp. 108–126. Springer, Cham (2021). https:// doi.org/10.1007/978-3-030-87348-6_6

# Real-Time Visualization of Stream-Based Monitoring Data

Jan Baumeister[1]([✉])(iD), Bernd Finkbeiner[1](iD), Stefan Gumhold[2],
and Malte Schledjewski[1](iD)

[1] CISPA Helmholtz Center for Information Security, 66123 Saarbrücken, Germany
{jan.baumeister,finkbeiner,malte.schledjewski}@cispa.de
[2] Technische Universität Dresden, 01069 Dresden, Germany
stefan.gumhold@tu-dresden.de

**Abstract.** Stream-based runtime monitors are used in safety-critical applications such as Unmanned Aerial Systems (UAS) to compute comprehensive statistics and logical assessments of system health that provide the human operator with critical information in hand-over situations. In such applications, a visual display of the monitoring data can be much more helpful than the textual alerts provided by a more traditional user interface. This visualization requires extensive real-time data processing, which includes the synchronization of data from different streams, filtering and aggregation, and priorization and management of user attention. We present a visualization approach for the RTLOLA monitoring framework. Our approach is based on the principle that the necessary data processing is the responsibility of the monitor itself, rather than the responsibility of some external visualization tool. We show how the various aspects of the data transformation can be described as RTLOLA stream equations and linked to the visualization component through a bidirectional synchronous interface. In our experience, this approach leads to highly informative visualizations as well as to understandable and easily maintainable monitoring code.

**Keywords:** Runtime verification · Stream-based monitoring · Data visualization

## 1 Introduction

Over the past decades, the scope of runtime verification has grown from an essentially boolean check, indicating whether or not a program execution satisfies a given formal specification, towards the real-time computation of more and

This work was partially supported by the German Research Foundation (DFG) as part of the Collaborative Research Center Foundations of Perspicuous Software Systems (TRR 248, 389792660).

T. Dang and V. Stolz (Eds.): RV 2022, LNCS 13498, pp. 325–335, 2022.
https://doi.org/10.1007/978-3-031-17196-3_21

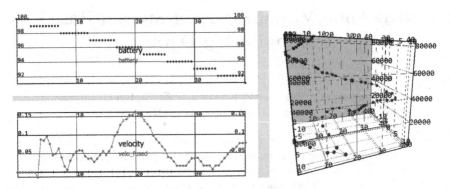

**Fig. 1.** Screenshot of a visualization displaying the battery status, velocity, and GPS coordinates of a UAS.

more expressive statistical data. A typical example are Unmanned Aerial Systems (UAS), where the monitor continuously collects and aggregates inputs from sensors and on-board components to provide the human operator with critical information in hand-over situations [1,3,26].

Traditionally, the interaction between runtime verification tools and their users has largely been based on textual interfaces, such as "alert" messages that are issued in case of a violation of the specification. In applications like UAS, however, such a simple user interface is often no longer sufficient. In addition to understanding that the monitor has detected a problem, the human operator must quickly grasp the situation and decide on potentially time-critical corrective action. A well-designed *visual* presentation of the available data is therefore of critical importance for the safe operation of the system.

Generating useful visualizations is far from trivial. First and foremost, the visualization must ensure that important or dangerous information is clearly visible to the user; because of the abundance of available data, data must be prioritized, and less important data must be hidden in favor of more important data. Similarly, the frequency of data points must be adjusted to provide meaningful information avoiding overlaps and adjusting for discrepancies in the availability of the raw data. All these computations have to be adjusted in response to actions by the user, who may look at multidimensional data from different angles or zoom into data areas of particular interest.

In this paper, we report on our recent effort in extending the RTLoLA monitoring framework with real-time visualization capabilities. RTLoLA [4,11] is a stream-based monitoring framework for cyber-physical systems and networks. RTLoLA processes, evaluates, and aggregates streams of input data, such as sensor readings, and provides a real-time analysis in the form of comprehensive statistics and logical assessments of the system's health. An RTLoLA monitor is generated from a formal description given in the RTLoLA specification language. The specifications consist of stream equations that translate input streams into output streams. RTLOLA specifications are statically analyzed to determine the required memory and are then either directly executed by the RTLOLA interpreter, or compiled onto an FPGA.

The fundamental insight of our approach is that the data processing needed to generate the visualization should be the responsibility of the monitor itself, rather than that of some external visualization tool. The monitor has access to all information and is therefore in the best position to determine the relevancy of individual data points. Because of the expressive power of the monitoring language, the monitor also has the computational means to interpolate and aggregate the raw data as required. Finally, keeping all data manipulations in one place reduces redundancy and avoids errors and misinterpretations.

We organize the RTLOLA specification of the data processing for the visualization into three functional areas: **1. Data Synchronization:** This part of the specification guarantees *synchronous* data updates for the visualization. This is important because the visualization combines data from different streams into a single entry in the plot: for example, a point indicating the position of a drone might be annotated with the speed of the drone. If different attributes have different timing, for example because of the variations in the frequency of the sensors, the monitor interpolates the missing data. **2. Filtering and Aggregation:** This part of the specification avoids overlapping markers in the visualization, which are caused if readings arrive at a high rate. The monitor smoothes the input signal and adjusts the rate according to the current visualization. **3. Priorization and Attention Management:** This part of the specification determines the criticality of the available information and ensures that the human operator does not miss important information.

The monitor and the visualization component are connected via a synchronous interface. The responsibility of the visualization component is to create the graphical display and to react to user requests. Since this user interaction may affect the visibility of plots or change the scaling, a backchannel provides this information to the monitor in the form of additional input streams. Fig. 1 shows a screenshot of our prototype implementation, which is based on the monitoring framework RTLOLA and the visualization framework cgv [16]. The monitor interacts with configurable 2D and 3D plots that support time-series plots, scatter plots, trajectory plots and multi-variate visualization through a flexible mapping of data attributes to the visual attributes color, opacity and size. We have applied our approach to the real-time visualization of UAS and other cyber-physical systems, based on existing RTLOLA case studies; our experience suggests that adding the visualization specification inside the monitor leads to highly informative visualizations as well as to understandable and easily maintainable monitoring code.

## 1.1  Related Work

This paper connects two traditionally separate areas of research: runtime monitoring and visualization. Somewhat surprisingly, visualization has not played a major role in monitoring research before. Despite a wide range of monitoring approaches, from formal logic [9,12,17,25] to stream-based specification languages [6,7,10,15], most tools have in common that they rely on textual, rather than visual, methods for data presentation. This paper shows that stream-based monitoring languages like RTLOLA are very well suited to carry out the needed data processing for useful visualizations. Our focus on RTLOLA is motivated by recent work on RTLola-based monitoring for UAS [2,3] and other cyber-physical systems [4,5,11]. However, the approach of the paper is clearly transferrable to other monitoring tools for CPS [22–24].

In the area of visualization, research on streaming visualization is also still in an early stage. A notable result are streaming processing models for data [28] and techniques for kernel density estimation in aggregated views over 2D maps [19]. There has been a systematic discussion of the suitability and problems of traditional visual analysis techniques [8,18,27]. Additionally, visualization frameworks [14] and visualization techniques that allow the user to better cope with changes over time have been developed, such as zoomable navigation [21], paged views [13], and transformation-based smooth transitions [20]. These approaches differ substantially from the approach taken in this paper, in that these are independent visualization tools, which prepare the data for the visualization independently of the monitor. By contrast, our setup tightly integrates the monitor with the visualization, keeping all data manipulations in one place.

## 2   RTLola

RTLOLA is a stream-based monitoring framework for cyber-physical systems and networks. An RTLOLA monitor is generated from a formal specification description given in the RTLOLA specification language. The specification consists of stream equations that describe the transformation of incoming data streams into output streams, and a set of trigger conditions that result in notifications to the user. The RTLOLA framework includes automatic static analysis methods that ensure the predictability of the monitor with respect to memory consumption and other relevant properties. We illustrate the RTLOLA specification language with a small example; for more details, we refer the reader to [4,11].

```
input gps: (Float64, Float64), charge: Float64, time: Float64
output charge_time @charge := time.hold(or: 0.0)
output filtered_gps filter gps != (0.0,0.0) := gps
trigger δ(charge) / δ(charge_time) > 2.0
trigger filtered_gps.0 > 6.0 ∧ filtered_gps.1 > 6.0
```

The specification declares three input streams: The first stream gps represents readings received by the GNSS (global navigation satellite system) module, the second stream charge shows the battery charge status, and the third one time contains the current time. Next, the specification declares the charge_time output stream, which filters the time stream to timestamps of newly received battery readings. For this, it binds the timing of the charge_time stream to the timing of charge, indicated by the @charge annotation. In RTLOLA, such a filter is called a static filter. As time might have a different timing, the value is

```
input charge: Float64, gps: (Float64, Float64)
input pixel_scale: (Float64, Float64), visible: Bool
output xLim: (Float64, Float64) @gps
:=(min(gps.0, xLim.0.offset(by:-1, or:gps.0)), max(gps.0, xLim.1.offset(by:-1, or:gps.0)))
output yLim: (Float64, Float64) @gps :=...
output δx @gps∨charge
:= (gps.hold(or:gps_s).0 - marker.offset(by:-1, or:marker_s).0) /
    (xLim.hold(or:1.0).1-xLim.hold(or:1.0).0) * pixel_scale.hold(or:pixel_scale_s)
output δy @gps∨charge := ...
output δc @gps∨charge := charge.hold(or:charge_s) - marker.offset(by:-1, or:marker_s).2
output send @gps∨charge := sqrt(δx**2.0 + δy**2.0) > τ_gps ∨ δc > τ_charge
output marker: (Float64, Float64, Float64) @gps ∨ charge
  filter send ∧ visible.hold(or: false)
  := (gps.hold(or:gps_s).0, gps.hold(or:gps_s).1,charge.hold(or:charge_s))
```

**Fig. 2.** RTLOLA specification demonstrating the interplay.

accessed via a 0-order hold interpolation. The next stream `filtered_gps` uses a dynamic filtering to exclude noisy sensor readings. In our example, the GNSS sends $(0.0, 0.0)$ coordinates during initialization that the specification can discard. The last two lines contain triggers checking if there is an unusual drop in the battery status and if the coordinates do not exceed some thresholds.

In RTLOLA, the static and dynamic filters are combined into a *pacing type*, which defines the timing of each stream. This type is either inferred or explicitly annotated. RTLOLA's type checker verifies the timing of the streams and RTLOLA provides different operators to interpolate data if the timing constraints cannot be guaranteed in the stream expression.

# 3   Generating Visualization Data

We now describe in more detail the generation of visualization data with RTLOLA stream equations. For the communication from the monitor to the visualization component, the specification contains output streams that are mapped to plot coordinates and visual attributes such as size and color. It also contains an output stream per axis, setting its displayed range. For the backchannel, the specification has input streams that receive the data from the visualization reflecting the interaction of the visualization component with the user. For each 2D-plot, we include one input stream to transfer the current scale factors; for each 3D-plot we include two input streams, representing the projection matrix and window size. Additionally, the specification has an input stream for each plot indicating which plot is visible.

We structure the generation of the visualization data into three areas: *Data Synchronization and Interpolation*, *Filtering and Aggregation*, and *Prioritization*. For each area, we shortly describe the problem, then describe the mechanism of how RTLOLA solves the task and explain the solution in more detail with our running example shown in Fig. 2. We display the coordinates of a GNSS in a 2-dimensional plot, and the remaining battery charge is mapped onto the color

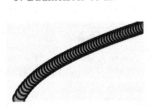 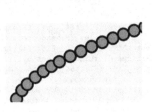

**Fig. 3.** Screenshot of the prototype with different monitors. On the left side, we use a monitor forwarding all data, whereas the right monitor filters the data using the specification in Fig. 2.

of the marker. The input streams `charge` and `gps` represent the sensor readings followed by the streams `pixel_scale` and `visible` implementing the backchannel. The output streams `xLim` and `yLim` compute the upper and lower bound per axis which is in our case the global minimum and maximum. Alternatively, our plot could represent with the following stream expression the data over a time-period $\sigma$:

```
output x_limits: (Float64, Float64) @1Hz
   := (gps.0.aggregate(over: σ, using: min), gps.0.aggregate(over: σ, using: max))
```

The next streams are helper streams to filter the data and the last output stream `marker` contains all information needed for a new marker in the plot.

### 3.1 Data Synchronization and Interpolation

For drawing a marker, the visualization needs to know all its visual attributes which might be based on sensors with different frequencies. We use RTLOLA's type system to guarantee that the monitor sends synchronized updates per plot. For this task, we use the concept of pacing types as introduced in Sect. 2. We define a pacing for each plot and annotate the streams for this plot with the desired pacing. Then, we use RTLOLA's type checker to verify that the data is available. In our example, we want to create a marker whenever at least one sensor sends an update and therefore use the disjunction of the two input streams as the pacing type. This pacing type `@gps∨charge` is annotated to the stream `marker`. Similarly, we want to update the axis limits, represented by the streams `xLim` and `yLim`, whenever we get a new GPS sensor reading.

We cannot directly access the current value of each stream because they may have different timings. Instead, we specify how missing data is interpolated. RTLOLA offers different approaches for this task, e.g., by using data aggregations, zero-order hold operations, or even different forms of data interpolations. In our example, we use a zero-order hold on the missing data.

### 3.2 Data Filtering and Aggregation

This section shows how a monitor prepares data to provide more understandable updates to the user. Figure 3 shows two plots from the same execution. On the

**Fig. 4.** On the left side, one marker with irrelevant information covers a critical marker, whereas the monitor on the right encodes a form of priority.

left side, the monitor forwards all data to the visualization resulting in over-lapping markers. These overlapping markers overload the plot with unrequired information and even overlap some information, as in our example, the color illustrating the battery status. On the right side, the monitor tailors the data for visualization and transfers the prepared data, so we do not have this problem.

The monitor on the right uses RTLOLA's dynamic filtering mechanism to prepare the data. With this filtering approach, the monitor can dynamically adapt the throughput to the visualization. Dependent on the scenario, different filters are helpful: For example, a filter forwards the GPS data dependent on the current velocity or increasing the sample rate if the system violates a property could be easily expressed in RTLOLA. In our running example, we forward the markers only if the difference between the new marker and the previous marker exceeds a threshold and if the plot is visible. For this, the output stream `marker` has two such filters connected by a disjunction. Both filters use the information provided by the visualization to describe the current state of the plot – visibility and scaling. With the second disjunct, we ensure that a marker is transmitted only if the plot is visible. The other filter is encoded by the stream `send`. In this stream, we decide whether the difference to the previously transmitted marker is sufficient to warrant a new marker. For this, we first compute the distance between the pixel coordinates of the candidate marker and the last marker based on the current bounds and scaling, and compare it with a defined threshold that prevents overlapping. We also check whether the difference in the charging level warrants a new marker. A similar approach also applies to 3D plots. Instead of the `pixel_scale`, we use the projecting matrix that encodes besides the scaling, the viewing rotation, and perspective.

Depending on the scenario and the size of the plot, it can be useful to aggregate values (such as by computing the average, minimum, and maximum of the data since the last marker) instead of dropping values. In RTLOLA, this can easily be done using the corresponding aggregation functions.

### 3.3 Attention Management

In Sect. 3.2, we have already discussed how the monitor can filter data points if they do not contain relevant information. Often, however, this is not sufficient, and we need to *prioritize* information: Fig. 4 shows two plots containing a critical state that the operator should recognize, illustrated by the red marker. This marker is partially covered on the left by plotting a new marker that does not contain this information anymore. The operator can easily miss this information, so the monitor on the right prioritizes them and thus does not send the candidate marker to the visualization tool.

Again, we use RTLOLA's dynamic filtering mechanism to prevent the coverage of higher prioritized information. We also introduce new streams encoding the priority of information and checking the coverage of markers. In our running example, we need to change the stream expression of **send** and add the following streams to the specification:

```
output critical: Bool @gps∨charge := ...
output marker_lc @gps∨charge
:= if send ∧ critical then marker else marker_lc.offset(by:-1, or:marker_s)
output δxc @gps∨charge
:= (gps.hold(or:gps_s).0 - marker_lc.offset(by:-1, or:marker_s).0) /
    (xLim.hold(or:1.0).1-xLim.hold(or:1.0).0) * pixel_scale.hold(or:pixel_scale_s)
output δyc @gps∨charge := ...
output send @gps ∨ charge
:= (sqrt(δx**2.0 + δy**2.0) > τ_gps ∨ δc > τ_charge) ∧ ((sqrt(δxc**2.0 + δyc**2.0) > τ_c ∨
    critical)
```

The stream **critical** encodes the priority of a marker and the next stream **marker_lc** stores the values of the last critical marker. The changed stream **send** now also determines if a potential new marker would overlap the last critical marker by computing the distance between the markers with the help of δxc and δyc and then checking if this distance is sufficient.

Preventing covering markers with less relevant information is only one example of how we can encode the priority of information. Another example occurs when the specification aggregates data points to make the plots more readable: With aggregations, we lose information about the system. In general, this behavior is intended because the human supervisor cannot process all information from every sensor. In critical situations, however, the operator usually is focused on the part that misbehaves. In these situations, the monitor can switch to transferring each data point instead of aggregating them, or it might reduce the required difference for new markers, so the supervisor gets all the required information. Such a property can be expressed in RTLOLA by adapting the timing of a stream or by using different aggregation functions.

## 4    Conclusions

In this paper, we have introduced a principled approach to the real-time visualization of stream-based monitoring data. The key contributions are the novel design principle, which shifts the responsibility for the data preparation from the visualization component to the monitor; the organization of the approach into three major functional areas; and the solution of the visualization challenges with the mechanisms of a stream-based monitoring language.

Our practical experience with the approach of the paper has been very positive. We have used the approach to visualize stream-based monitoring data from recent case studies that use RTLOLA for UAS [2,3] and other cyber-physical systems [4,5,11]. The visual tools provided by cgv have proven very useful for the type of data produced by our monitors. For example, we have visualized the failure of the GPS module in a drone, which was recognized by the system health check in the existing monitor specification, by adding a halo to the markers of the estimated position and by increasing the marker frequency. While clearly more research is needed in order to determine the best visualizations, our experience already indicates that this type of visualization is very helpful in quickly understanding complicated situations.

We hope that this paper will inspire other developers of runtime verification tools to invest in real-time visualization as well. We believe that our "monitoring-oriented" visualization approach provides a significant step towards meaningful visualizations that exploit the wealth of information available within the monitor. In future work, it might even be possible to integrate explicit visualization operators into monitoring languages like RTLoLA, and thus largely automate the visualization process presented in this paper.

# References

1. Adolf, F., Faymonville, P., Finkbeiner, B., Schirmer, S., Torens, C.: Stream runtime monitoring on UAS. In: Lahiri, S.K., Reger, G. (eds.) RV 2017. LNCS, vol. 10548, pp. 33–49. Springer (2017). https://doi.org/10.1007/978-3-319-67531-2_3
2. Adolf, F.M., Faymonville, P., Finkbeiner, B., Schirmer, S., Torens, C.: Stream runtime monitoring on UAS. In: Lahiri, S., Reger, G. (eds.) Runtime Verification, pp. 33–49. Springer International Publishing, Cham (2017). https://doi.org/10.1007/978-3-319-67531-2_3
3. Baumeister, J., Finkbeiner, B., Schirmer, S., Schwenger, M., Torens, C.: RTLola cleared for take-off: monitoring autonomous aircraft. In: Lahiri, S.K., Wang, C. (eds.) CAV 2020. LNCS, vol. 12225, pp. 28–39. Springer, Cham (2020). https://doi.org/10.1007/978-3-030-53291-8_3
4. Baumeister, J., Finkbeiner, B., Schwenger, M., Torfah, H.: FPGA stream-monitoring of real-time properties. ACM Trans. Embedded Comput. Syst. **18**(5s), 1–24 (2019). https://doi.org/10.1145/3358220
5. Biewer, S., Finkbeiner, B., Hermanns, H., Köhl, M.A., Schnitzer, Y., Schwenger, M.: RTLola on board: testing real driving emissions on your phone. In: TACAS 2021. LNCS, vol. 12652, pp. 365–372. Springer, Cham (2021). https://doi.org/10.1007/978-3-030-72013-1_20
6. Convent, L., Hungerecker, S., Leucker, M., Scheffel, T., Schmitz, M., Thoma, D.: TeSSLa: temporal stream-based specification language. In: Massoni, T., Mousavi, M.R. (eds.) SBMF 2018. LNCS, vol. 11254, pp. 144–162. Springer, Cham (2018). https://doi.org/10.1007/978-3-030-03044-5_10
7. D'Angelo, B., et al.: Lola: Runtime monitoring of synchronous systems. In: 12th International Symposium on Temporal Representation and Reasoning (TIME2005), pp. 166-174. IEEE Computer Society Press (2005)
8. Dasgupta, A., Arendt, D.L., Franklin, L.R., Wong, P.C., Cook, K.A.: Human factors in streaming data analysis: challenges and opportunities for informtion visualization. Comput. Graph. Forum **37**(1), 254–272 (2018). https://doi.org/10.1111/cgf.13264
9. Donzé, A., Ferrère, T., Maler, O.: Efficient robust monitoring for STL. In: Sharygina, N., Veith, H. (eds.) CAV 2013. LNCS, vol. 8044, pp. 264–279. Springer, Heidelberg (2013). https://doi.org/10.1007/978-3-642-39799-8_19

10. Faymonville, P., Finkbeiner, B., Schirmer, S., Torfah, H.: A stream-based specification language for network monitoring. In: Falcone, Y., Sánchez, C. (eds.) RV 2016. LNCS, vol. 10012, pp. 152–168. Springer, Cham (2016). https://doi.org/10.1007/978-3-319-46982-9_10

11. Faymonville, P., et al.: StreamLAB: stream-based monitoring of cyber-physical systems. In: Dillig, I., Tasiran, S. (eds.) CAV 2019. LNCS, vol. 11561, pp. 421–431. Springer, Cham (2019). https://doi.org/10.1007/978-3-030-25540-4_24

12. Finkbeiner, B., Sipma, H.: Checking finite traces using alternating automata. Formal Methods Syst. Des. **24**(2), 101–127 (2004). https://doi.org/10.1023/B:FORM.0000017718.28096.48

13. Fischer, F., Keim, D.A.: NStreamAware: real-time visual analytics for data streams to enhance situational awareness. In: Proceedings of the Eleventh Workshop on Visualization for Cyber Security, pp. 65–72. VizSec 2014, Association for Computing Machinery, New York, NY, USA (2014). https://doi.org/10.1145/2671491.2671495

14. Fischer, F., Mansmann, F., Keim, D.A.: Real-time visual analytics for event data streams. In: Proceedings of the 27th Annual ACM Symposium on Applied Computing, pp. 801–806. SAC 2012, Association for Computing Machinery, New York, NY, USA (2012). https://doi.org/10.1145/2245276.2245432

15. Gorostiaga, F., Sánchez, C.: Striver: stream runtime verification for real-time event-streams. In: Colombo, C., Leucker, M. (eds.) RV 2018. LNCS, vol. 11237, pp. 282–298. Springer, Cham (2018). https://doi.org/10.1007/978-3-030-03769-7_16

16. Gumhold, S.: CGV. https://github.com/sgumhold/cgv (2022)

17. Havelund, K., Roşu, G.: Synthesizing monitors for safety properties. In: Katoen, J.-P., Stevens, P. (eds.) TACAS 2002. LNCS, vol. 2280, pp. 342–356. Springer, Heidelberg (2002). https://doi.org/10.1007/3-540-46002-0_24

18. Krstajic, M., Keim, D.A.: Visualization of streaming data: Observing change and context in information visualization techniques. In: 2013 IEEE International Conference on Big Data, Silicon Valley, CA, USA, pp. 41–47. IEEE (2013). https://doi.org/10.1109/BigData.2013.6691713

19. Lampe, O.D., Hauser, H.: Interactive visualization of streaming data with kernel density estimation. In: 2011 IEEE Pacific visualization symposium, pp. 171–178. IEEE (2011)

20. Li, C., Baciu, G., Han, Y.: StreamMap: smooth dynamic visualization of high-density streaming points. IEEE Trans. Visual. Comput. Graph. **24**(3), 1381–1393 (2018). https://doi.org/10.1109/TVCG.2017.2668409

21. Li, C., Baciu, G., Han, Y.: Interactive visualization of high density streaming points with heat-map. In: 2014 International Conference on Smart Computing, pp. 145–149 (2014). https://doi.org/10.1109/SMARTCOMP.2014.7043852

22. Luppen, Z., et al.: Elucidation and analysis of specification patterns in aerospace system telemetry. In: Deshmukh, J.V., Havelund, K., Perez, I. (eds.) NFM 2022. LNCS, vol. 13260. Springer, Cham (2022). https://doi.org/10.1007/978-3-031-06773-0_28

23. Moosbrugger, P., Rozier, K.Y., Schumann, J.: R2U2: monitoring and diagnosis of security threats for unmanned aerial systems. Formal Methods Syst. Des. **51**(1), 31–61 (2017). https://doi.org/10.1007/s10703-017-0275-x

24. Pike, L., Goodloe, A., Morisset, R., Niller, S.: Copilot: a hard real-time runtime monitor. In: Barringer, H., et al. (eds.) RV 2010. LNCS, vol. 6418, pp. 345–359. Springer, Heidelberg (2010). https://doi.org/10.1007/978-3-642-16612-9_26

25. Raskin, J.-F., Schobbens, P.-Y.: Real-time logics: fictitious clock as an abstraction of dense time. In: Brinksma, E. (ed.) TACAS 1997. LNCS, vol. 1217, pp. 165–182. Springer, Heidelberg (1997). https://doi.org/10.1007/BFb0035387
26. Schumann, J., Moosbrugger, P., Rozier, K.Y.: R2U2: monitoring and diagnosis of security threats for unmanned aerial systems. In: Bartocci, E., Majumdar, R. (eds.) RV 2015. LNCS, vol. 9333, pp. 233–249. Springer, Cham (2015). https://doi.org/10.1007/978-3-319-23820-3_15
27. Smestad, G.: Interactive visual analysis of streaming data, master's thesis, Universitetet i Bergen (UiB) (2014)
28. Szewczyk, W.: Streaming data. Wiley Interdisc. Rev. Comput. Stat. 3(1), 22–29 (2011). Publisher: Wiley Online Library

# Automating Numerical Parameters Along the Evolution of a Nonlinear System

Luca Geretti[1]([⊠]), Pieter Collins[2], Davide Bresolin[3], and Tiziano Villa[1]

[1] Università di Verona, Verona, Italy
{luca.geretti,tiziano.villa}@univr.it
[2] Maastricht University, Maastricht, The Netherlands
pieter.collins@maastrichtuniversity.nl
[3] Università di Padova, Padova, Italy
davide.bresolin@unipd.it

**Abstract.** When analysing cyber-physical systems for runtime verification purposes, reachability analysis can be used to identify whether the set of reached points stays within given safe bounds. If the system dynamics exhibits nonlinearity, approximate numerical techniques (with rigorous numerics) are often necessary when dealing with system evolution. Since the error involved in numerical approximation should be kept low to perform verification successfully, the associated processing and memory costs become relevant especially when runtime verification is considered. Given a reachability analysis tool, the issue of controlling its numerical accuracy is not trivial from the user's perspective, due to the complex interaction between the configuration parameters of the tool. As a result, user intervention in the tuning of a specific problem is always required. This paper explores the problem of automatically choosing numerical parameters that drive the computation of the finite-time reachable set, when the configuration parameters of the tool are specified within bounds or lists of values. In particular, it is designed to be performed along evolution, in order to adapt to local properties of the dynamics and to reduce the setup overhead, essential for runtime verification.

## 1 Introduction

In the verification of a generic cyber-physical system, modeling nonlinearity is important in order to accurately capture the interaction of the digital control with the continuous environment. In fact, studying the full interaction between controller and environment, where continuous variables evolve in a possibly nonlinear way, represents a significantly harder problem compared to the analysis of a digital controller in partial isolation. However, the formal methods community in recent years has shown that the approach is feasible and applied it to different systems especially in the field of robotics (such as [2,7,13]).

© The Author(s), under exclusive license to Springer Nature Switzerland AG 2022
T. Dang and V. Stolz (Eds.): RV 2022, LNCS 13498, pp. 336–345, 2022.
https://doi.org/10.1007/978-3-031-17196-3_22

The formalism of *hybrid automata* is commonly used to define the composition of controller and environment along with the semantics for its behavior (see [3,6]). *Reachability analysis* in particular is concerned with the computation of the *reachable set*, i.e., the set of points reached from an initial set that evolves under the system's dynamics. Given a dynamical system, obtaining its reachable set allows to reason about its behavior, where a safety specification is represented as geometric constraints on the reached points.

For linear hybrid systems, tools like HyPro [17] and SpaceEx [11] allow an efficient representation of the evolution of the system. For nonlinear systems, computing the reachable set is more problematic. To solve this issue, different solutions are proposed in the literature, using either a numerical or symbolic approach: see the tools Ariadne [4], CORA [1], Flow* [8], HSolver [15], JuliaReach [5] and KeYmaera X [12] for some examples. In this paper we focus on a numerical approach based on computing over-approximations of the reachable set.

Regardless of the preferred tool, it is apparent that automation plays a very important role when approximate representations of the reachable set are involved. Typically, the user needs to provide sensible values for *configuration parameters* such as the integration step size or the polynomial order of a set representation. These parameters usually affect the quality of numerical approximation or enable/disable specific features, but in general they control the over-approximation error. The problem is that the optimal values of the parameters are difficult to know before the system under analysis is properly understood. As a result, the user ends up refining configuration parameter values iteratively until an acceptable result is obtained. This operation, usually done manually with a trial-and-error approach, can become very time-consuming. This is especially important for systems exhibiting nonlinear dynamics, where symbolic approaches are more difficult to pursue and where evaluating the reachable set can be computationally intensive. In any case, the overhead due to user interaction with the tool is non-negligible, in the worst case requiring to spend hours observing the behavior of the system and repeatedly trying with different configurations, for lack of an intuition on the complex interaction among all configuration parameters. It is apparent that such approach does not work very well for runtime verification, where real time constraints are incompatible with manual tuning.

Hence, in this paper we propose a methodology for automated choice of the values of configuration parameters. Differently from approaches that compute a sequence of converging approximations to the exact result, the methodology aims to solve the problem within a single run of execution in order to be compatible with runtime verification. The approach exploits concurrency by executing a single step of evolution on multiple configurations. The user is required to supply only a reasonable range of values for each configuration parameter of interest, hence its active role in optimising the reachable set calculation is greatly reduced. In particular, safety specifications drive optimisation by generating geometric constraints to hold along evolution. The distance to the specification is the metric that allows to rank the various configurations and consequently use the most effective parameter values required. This approach has the advantage that the chosen parameter values have *local* validity, i.e., they are selected at each integration step, and thus they adapt across reachability problems and also across different integration steps of the same problem, since different subspaces usually have different dynamical responses.

This approach should be considered a heuristic compared to, say, the generation of invariants from a formal analysis of the dynamics [16]. In fact, rigorously guaranteeing bounds on the numerical over-approximation error would mean to rely on worst-case formulae for error. Those in turn would yield overly-conservative values for numerical configuration parameters, resulting in excessive accuracy (e.g., a smaller integration step size than what is actually necessary). By pursuing a heuristic approach instead we privilege performance.

The methodology proposed is generic enough to be adopted by any tool that performs approximate reachability by integration of nonlinear vector field dynamics from an initial set. The actual implementation and the corresponding experimental evaluation comes from a general framework for configuration tuning available in the ARIADNElibrary. ARIADNEdiffers from existing packages since it is based on the theory of computable analysis and on a rigorous *function calculus* to achieve provable approximation bounds on the computations [9,10].

In this work we describe the methodology for the continuous behavior, while the extension to hybrid systems will be the subject of a future publication. We remark that the actual challenge lies in the continuous aspects of evolution, so we deem the continuous benchmark in the reported experiments sufficient to confirm the validity of the approach.

To the best of our knowledge, this is the first work that addresses automation in such a general way, in particular for nonlinear dynamics where numerical approaches are preferred. Current tools seem to focus specifically on automated refinement of the integration step size or possibly the polynomial order (which were already accounted for in our tool before). A recent work [19] proposed a solution for nonlinear systems, which tunes values of parameters introduced in their reachability algorithm performing linearization. In this solution however parameters are hard-coded, being related to the specific algorithm. On the contrary, our approach is generic in two aspects: 1) the parameters are not defined a priori, meaning that any subset of parameters involved in any reachability algorithm can be chosen for tuning, and 2) no assumptions on the impact of a given parameter are made.

In the following, in Sect. 2 we explain the general methodology involved, also describing the details of dealing with a set of configuration values and ranking the results obtained from them. Section 3 briefly comments on some preliminary results obtained by using the methodology in our tool. Finally, Sect. 4 draws the conclusions of the paper.

## 2   Methodology

The proposed methodology is based on the following assumption:

**Error Control Assumption.** *Given a system whose finite-time reachable set is within a safe set, it is possible to obtain an over-approximation of the reachable set within the same safe set by controlling the growth of the approximation error.*

In practice this is the assumption on which Computable Analysis [18] relies, stating that the over-approximated output converges to the exact output when the approximated input converges to the exact input, where the initial set and configuration parameter values are the input, and the reachable set $R$ is the output. The objective is not to repeat evolution of the system with progressively finer configuration parameter values, until the over-approximation of the reachable set lies within the safe set. Such approach would be easy from the point of view of tuning configuration parameters: once a reasonable initial configuration is chosen, safety would be ultimately verified by progressively changing configuration parameters to increase the accuracy of computation. Instead, in this paper we aim to identify a strategy that achieves the desired result in a *single* run of evolution by adjusting configuration parameter values along evolution steps.

In order to achieve this result while being as general as possible with respect to the system dynamics, we need to control at each time step $k$ the growth of the corresponding *evolve set* $E_k$, i.e., the section of the flow tube of evolution. If we control the evolve set, then the *reach set* $R_k$, i.e., the flow tube between steps $k-1$ and $k$, is controlled as well according to the integration scheme described later in the paper. In fact, if we focus on rigorous numerical integration, the value of the over-approximation error is bounded by a remainder term whose addition to an under-approximation of the flow tube guarantees the enclosure of the exact flow tube. Additionally, the so-called *reconditioning* operations on an evolve set $E_k$ transform the error into additional parameters in the set representation: this causes a loss of information on the error component of the set along evolution. Finally, based on the local contractive or expansive character of the dynamics, the evolve set may even be reduced for a given evolution step (and the error with it, if reconditioning is used).

### 2.1   General Approach

Due to the previous considerations, a global strategy for control of the growth of the evolve set is difficult to devise. Conversely, an adaptive control relying on the growth of the evolve set within a single integration step is more feasible. Nevertheless, in order to drive configuration tuning based on safety objectives it is necessary to set some global targets in terms of the growth of the evolve set. To identify these targets we rely on fixed-step *simulation* of the system, as opposed to rigorous evolution. Simulation returns a sequence of approximate points, but its computation cost is mostly negligible with respect to rigorous evolution and consequently can be performed as a pre-analysis phase that gathers valuable information on the expected reachable set.

Once pre-analysis has identified the constraints for error control, rigorous evolution can be performed while tuning configuration parameter values according to their ability to satisfy the constraints. Due to the complex interaction of these numerical parameters with the actual value of the error, we don't pursue an analytical approach based on, e.g., a gradient descent algorithm optimising a cost function. Instead, we rather *rank* the results obtained from running each integration step concurrently on a multitude of configuration values. In order to explore a finite amount of configuration values, we rely on an automated discretisation of the configuration parameters.

Summarising, the approach proposed is divided into the following main phases:

1. Simulate the system in a non-rigorous way, returning a set of timed approximate points
2. Identify the points whose distance from the unsafe set has a (local) minimum and construct a list of timed distances called *targets* $\{\tau_i\}$
3. From each $\tau_i$ construct a ranking parameter related to the rate of growth of the evolve set $E_k$, which will drive the optimisation for rigorous evolution
4. From the safety specification construct additional ranking parameters, which will check if a given reachable subset $R_k$ is possibly unsafe
5. Evolve the system rigorously, where for each evolution step $k$:
   (a) Select a set of points in the configuration search space
   (b) For each point, concurrently, compute $E_k$ and $R_k$
   (c) Rank the results using the ranking parameters
   (d) Take the best result as the actual $E_k$ and $R_k$ and generate the next set of search points

Termination happens as soon as the evolution time is hit, or if any safety objective is missed for all points. In the following two Subsections, we provide the necessary details related to the search space and ranking respectively.

## 2.2   Constructing and Exploring the Search Space

The search space for configuration parameter values is defined as a space over the integers. For parameters defined in the boolean domain or as an enumeration, the conversion onto integer values is trivial by using the index in the enumeration (i.e., between 0 and $n-1$ for an enumeration of size $n$). For values defined in an interval we need to define a conversion policy. Most commonly, values for continuous parameters are discretised in their use: e.g., if a value ranges between $10^{-2}$ to $10^{-8}$ typically, we are driven to change the value by multiplication/division by ten. Given this consideration, we shall define parameters along with the conversion rule they are expected to adopt, for example:

- linear: rounds to the nearest integer;
- $log_2$, $log_{10}$: takes the logarithm and rounds to the nearest integer.

By supplying the rule and a conversion back and forth, we can map values for continuous (or relatively dense) parameters into a bounded integer space.

Finally, we must decide how to explore such space. For that purpose, we assume that the search space is also *bounded*. The space is necessarily bounded for enumeration parameters, like e.g. the choice between different integration schemes. For parameters defined within intervals, such as the integration step size, an unbounded approach is feasible and offers more freedom to the user but it has some drawbacks. First, it does not allow to assess the size of the search space, which would be useful to drive the exploration. Second, it does not allow to choose a random initial point in the search space at the beginning of evolution.

For parameters defined as enumerations, any value is acceptable and we shall try all values with equal probability. For parameters defined in intervals instead, it is reasonable to assume that adjacent values return similar results, or equivalently that results obtained by varying the value of the parameter have some regular behavior such as monotonicity or concavity.

The distance between values of an enumeration parameter is taken as 1, i.e., all values are adjacent. In summary, exploration of the search space is made by adjacency, in the case of interval parameters meaning that we either choose one of the two adjacent values randomly, or we choose the only adjacent value of the upper/lower bound of the interval. Given a concurrency level $\gamma$, the procedure to evolve a set of $\gamma$ points in the search space is the following:

1. At the beginning of evolution, construct a random initial point $\hat{P}_0$ in the space of integer representations of parameters, and add it to the set of initial points $\Pi$;
2. Choose a random point $p$ from $\Pi$ and construct a random adjacent point $\hat{p}$; add $\hat{p}$ to $\Pi$; repeat 2. until $\|\Pi\| = \gamma$;
3. For each point in $\Pi$, convert it into the space of the parameters values and execute the integration step;
4. Outputs from all points are ranked, yielding an ordering of the points in $\Pi$;
5. Choose the output from the highest ranked point of $\Pi$ as the effective output for the step;
6. Exit if the evolution time is hit;
7. Otherwise discard the lowest ranked half of the points and return to 2.

Here the update strategy for $\Pi$ is very simple but it can be improved upon in any way, for example to discourage the addition of points that have been ranked particularly low in the past.

Note that the concurrent approach also introduces failure tolerance as a byproduct: if one or more integration steps are not successful (e.g., by failing to construct the flow function, a likely occurrence when an evolve set becomes particularly large), we can simply discard the failing configuration points and regenerate $\Pi$ up to $\gamma$ using the remaining points.

## 2.3   Ranking the Search Points

In order to select the best configuration point, it is first necessary to identify ranking parameters (where we use the term *parameter* again, not to be confused with a configuration parameter, for lack of a better term) dependent on the safety specification. We distinguish between *safety* ranking parameters and *optimisation* ranking parameters: the former come directly from the constraints that define the safe set, while the latter are associated to some error growth rate targets (which again depend on the constraints). Both kinds of ranking parameters identify a score when applied to one evolution step.

Safety parameters are the simplest, each associated to a safety constraint function $c(S)$, where if $c(R_k) > 0$ then the reach subset $R_k$ is safe. The score for the ranking parameter is represented by $c(R_k)$ and the threshold for the score is zero. If the threshold is crossed, we say that there is a *hard failure* with respect to the specific ranking parameter.

An optimisation ranking parameter is more complicated, since it uses a target to compare *set growth rates*. The growth rate $\rho_k$ for an integration step $k$, with starting evolve set $E_{k-1}$ and finishing evolve set $E_k$, is defined as

$$\rho_k = \frac{|E_k| - |E_{k-1}|}{T_k - T_{k-1}} \tag{1}$$

where $|E_k|$ is a measure of the radius of the set, i.e., $\rho_k$ is the increase of radius in units of evolution time and $T_k$ is the initial time at step $k$.

In particular, from a constraint we can construct a target $\tau = (W^\tau, T^\tau)$, made of a radius $W^\tau$ at a time $T^\tau$, which represents (an approximation of) the maximum flow tube radius that does not intersect the boundary of the safe set. This identifies a target growth rate $\rho_k^\tau$:

$$\rho_k^\tau = \frac{W^\tau - |E_{k-1}|}{T^\tau - T_{k-1}} \tag{2}$$

Here we notice that $\rho_k^\tau$ is a value projected from the current step and consequently it adapts to variations of $|E_k|$ along evolution. In particular, it allows to compensate for any positive or negative $\rho - \rho^\tau$ deviation on the successive steps.

The score is given by $\rho_k$, where $\rho_k^\tau$ represents the threshold; when $\rho_k > \rho_k^\tau$ we say that there is a *soft failure* with respect to the ranking parameter. When $T_{k-1} > T^\tau$ instead we say that the target *expired* and the corresponding ranking parameter correspondingly expires, i.e., it is not used for ranking.

Summarising, the $i$-th ranking parameter yields an individual score $\sigma_i$ and possibly a soft or hard failure. In order to compare the scores on an equal basis, each score must be normalised based on the best and worst values across all search points. Consequently, the normalised score $\hat{\sigma}_i$ becomes

$$\hat{\sigma}_i = \frac{\sigma_i - \sigma_i^m}{\sigma_i^M - \sigma_i^m} \tag{3}$$

with $m$ and $M$ the minimum and maximum values respectively, where clearly $0 \le \hat{\sigma}_i \le 1$ holds. The score function for a search point $P$ then becomes

$$\sigma(P) = \sum_i \hat{\sigma}_i(P) \tag{4}$$

To each score $\sigma$ we also associate the number of soft failures $n_s$ and hard failures $n_h$.

In order to establish which of two search points $P_1$ and $P_2$ rank higher, we compare score, soft failures and hard failures:

- $n_h(P_1) > n_h(P_2) \implies P_1 < P_2$
- $n_h(P_1) = n_h(P_2) \wedge n_s(P_1) > n_s(P_2) \implies P_1 < P_2$
- $n_h(P_1) = n_h(P_2) \wedge n_s(P_1) = n_s(P_2) \wedge \sigma(P_1) < \sigma(P_2) \implies P_1 < P_2$

where $P_1 < P_2$ means that $P_2$ is ranked higher, i.e., it is more likely to be chosen as the winning point for the evolution step, as well as being kept as a point for the next step.

In particular, if all the points used for computing the $k$-th step have at least 1 hard failure, then safety verification necessarily fails and evolution is stopped. Conversely, progress is not prevented by all the points having soft failures: it simply means that it was not possible to satisfy one or more of the target growth rates on the $k$-th step, but that could be amended in the following steps with the updated target growth rates.

## 3   Preliminary Experimental Results

In this Section we briefly provide some preliminary results applied to the well-known van der Pol oscillator, often used in the verification community as a benchmark for nonlinear dynamics [14]. Due to space reasons, we only provide summary information on the setup. The number of evolution parameters chosen was 4, with 4–4–4–3 possible discretised values each, yielding 192 points in the search space. We performed evolution with increasing concurrency $\gamma = \{1, ..., 5\}$, where $\gamma = 1$ means that no search is performed and $\gamma = 5$ means that 5 threads are used to evaluate 5 different points. Results were averaged over 1000 tries for each value of $\gamma$. For $\gamma = 1$, failure in completing evolution was $\%f = 62.9$, with an average execution time $t_x = 5.2$ seconds. With $\gamma = 2$, we got $\%f = 0.7$ and $t_x = 7.6$, up to $\gamma = 5$ yielding $\%f = 0.0$ and $t_x = 10.8$. Summarising, searching using our approach gave a dramatic decrease in average failures even for minimal concurrency, with a contained increase in execution time, and showed practically no failures with only 5 threads used.

## 4   Conclusions

In this paper we described a methodology to perform safety verification of a nonlinear system with a significant reduction in the time spent by the user on tuning the tool configuration. The approach leverages concurrent execution of the integration step, where configuration values are explored to optimise their choice. Our preliminary results on a benchmark system show that it is possible to succeed at the task practically 100% of the times within a single run with minimum concurrency used. Conversely, manual tuning using the same config-uration space would yield below 40% success. While the framework has been validated in the continuous case, a future publication will cover the extension to the hybrid case in detail. Additionally, different search strategies can be envisioned and implemented. The research activity on tuning is still in its infancy, with no comparable papers at this level of generality in the literature as far as we are aware. From our preliminary hands-on experience using ARIADNE, we can already state that the leap in tool usability introduced by this approach is very significant. In particular, by leveraging the corresponding improvement in the ratio between evolution time and processing time, more sophisticated runtime verification routines can be envisioned.

# References

1. Althoff, M.: An introduction to CORA 2015. In: Frehse, G., Althoff, M. (eds.) ARCH14-15. 1st and 2nd International Workshop on Applied Verification for Continuous and Hybrid Systems, volume 34 of EPiC Series in Computing, pp. 120–151. EasyChair (2015)
2. Althoff, M., Dolan, J.M.: Online verification of automated road vehicles using reachability analysis. IEEE Trans. Rob. **30**(4), 903–918 (2014)
3. Alur, R., Courcoubetis, C., Henzinger, T.A., Ho, P.-H.: Hybrid automata: an algorithmic approach to the specification and verification of hybrid systems. In: Grossman, R.L., Nerode, A., Ravn, A.P., Rischel, H. (eds.) HS 1991-1992. LNCS, vol. 736, pp. 209–229. Springer, Heidelberg (1993). https://doi.org/10.1007/3-540-57318-6_30
4. Benvenuti, L., Bresolin, D., Collins, P., Ferrari, A., Geretti, L., Villa, T.: Assume-guarantee verification of nonlinear hybrid systems with Ariadne. Int. J. Robust Nonlinear Control **24**(4), 699–724 (2014)
5. Bogomolov, S., Forets, M., Frehse, G., Potomkin, K., Schilling, C.: JuliaReach: a toolbox for set-based reachability. In: HSCC 2019 - Proceedings of the 2019 22nd ACM International Conference on Hybrid Systems: Computation and Control, pp. 39–44 (2019)
6. Bresolin, D., Collins, P., Geretti, L., Segala, R., Villa, T., Zivanovic, S.: A computable and compositional semantics for hybrid automata. In: Proceedings of the 23rd International Conference on Hybrid Systems: Computation and Control, pp. 1–11 (2020)
7. Bresolin, D., Geretti, L., Muradore, R., Fiorini, P., Villa, T.: Formal verification applied to robotic surgery. In: van Schuppen, J.H., Villa, T. (eds.) Coordination Control of Distributed Systems. LNCIS, vol. 456, pp. 347–355. Springer, Cham (2015). https://doi.org/10.1007/978-3-319-10407-2_40
8. Chen, X., Ábrahám, E., Sankaranarayanan, S.: Flow*: an analyzer for non-linear hybrid systems. In: Sharygina, N., Veith, H. (eds.) CAV 2013. LNCS, vol. 8044, pp. 258–263. Springer, Heidelberg (2013). https://doi.org/10.1007/978-3-642-39799-8_18
9. Collins, P.: Semantics and computability of the evolution of hybrid systems. SIAM J. Control. Optim. **49**, 890–925 (2011)
10. Collins, P., Bresolin, D., Geretti, L., Villa, T.: Computing the evolution of hybrid systems using rigorous function calculus. In: Proceedings of the 4th IFAC Conference on Analysis and Design of Hybrid Systems (ADHS12), Eindhoven, The Netherlands, pp. 284–290 (2012)

11. Frehse, G., et al.: SpaceEx: scalable verification of hybrid systems. In: Gopalakrishnan, G., Qadeer, S. (eds.) CAV 2011. LNCS, vol. 6806, pp. 379–395. Springer, Heidelberg (2011). https://doi.org/10.1007/978-3-642-22110-1_30
12. Fulton, N., Mitsch, S., Quesel, J.-D., Völp, M., Platzer, A.: KeYmaera X: an axiomatic tactical theorem prover for hybrid systems. In: Felty, A.P., Middeldorp, A. (eds.) CADE 2015. LNCS (LNAI), vol. 9195, pp. 527–538. Springer, Cham (2015). https://doi.org/10.1007/978-3-319-21401-6_36
13. Geretti, L., Muradore, R., Bresolin, D., Fiorini, P., Villa, T.: Parametric formal verification: the robotic paint spraying case study. In: Proceedings of the 20th IFAC World Congress, pp. 9248–9253 (2017)
14. Immler, F., et al.: Arch-comp19 category report: Continuous and hybrid systems with nonlinear dynamics. In: Frehs, G., Althoff, M. (eds.) 6th International Workshop on Applied Verification of Continuous and Hybrid Systems (ARCH19), volume 61 of EPiC Series in Computing, pp. 41–61. EasyChair (2019)
15. Ratschan, S., She, Z.: Safety verification of hybrid systems by constraint propagation based abstraction refinement. In: Morari, M., Thiele, L. (eds.) HSCC 2005. LNCS, vol. 3414, pp. 573–589. Springer, Heidelberg (2005). https://doi.org/10.1007/978-3-540-31954-2_37
16. Sankaranarayanan, S.: Automatic invariant generation for hybrid systems using ideal fixed points. In: Proceedings of the 13th ACM International Conference on Hybrid Systems: Computation and Control, HSCC 2010, New York, NY, USA, pp. 221–230. Association for Computing Machinery (2010)
17. Schupp, S., Ábrahám, E., Makhlouf, I.B., Kowalewski, S.: HyPro: A C++ library of state set representations for hybrid systems reachability analysis. In: Barrett, C., Davies, M., Kahsai, T. (eds.) NFM 2017. LNCS, vol. 10227, pp. 288–294. Springer, Cham (2017). https://doi.org/10.1007/978-3-319-57288-8_20
18. Weihrauch, K.: Computable Analysis - An Introduction. Texts in Theoretical Computer Science, 1st edn. Springer-Verlag, Heidelberg (2000). https://doi.org/10.1007/978-3-642-56999-9
19. Wetzlinger, M., Kulmburg, A., Althoff, M.: Adaptive parameter tuning for reachability analysis of nonlinear systems. In: HSCC 2021 - Proceedings of the 24th International Conference on Hybrid Systems: Computation and Control (part of CPS-IoT Week) (2021)

# Correction to: Rule-Based Runtime Mitigation Against Poison Attacks on Neural Networks

Muhammad Usman, Divya Gopinath, Youcheng Sun,
and Corina S. Păsăreanu

**Correction to:**
**Chapter "Rule-Based Runtime Mitigation Against Poison
Attacks on Neural Networks" in: T. Dang and V. Stolz (Eds.):**
*Runtime Verification*, **LNCS 13498,**
**https://doi.org/10.1007/978-3-031-17196-3_4**

In an older version of this paper, there was error in the figure 3, (e) and (f) was incorrect. This has been corrected.

---

The updated original version of this chapter can be found at
https://doi.org/10.1007/978-3-031-17196-3_4

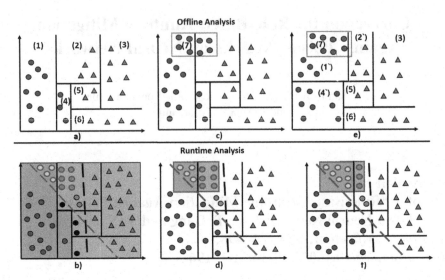

**Fig. 3.** Rule-based detection and correction of poison attacks. Rule(1) $=N1<A_1$. Rule(2) $=(N_1\geq A_1)\wedge(N_1<A_3)\wedge(N_0\geq B_2)$. Rule(3) $=(N_1\geq A_3)\wedge(N_0\geq B_1)$. Rule(4) $=(N_1\geq A_1)\wedge(N_1<A_2)\wedge(N_0<B_2)$. Rule(5) $=(N_1\geq A_2)\wedge(N_1<A_3)\wedge(N_0\geq B_1)\wedge(N_0<B_2)$. Rule(6) $=(N_1\geq A_2)\wedge(N_0<B_1)$. Rule(7) $=(N_1\geq A_5)\wedge(N_1<A_6)\wedge(N_0\geq B_5)\wedge(N_0<B_6)$. Rule(1') $=N1<A_1'\wedge(N_0\geq B_2)$. Rule(2') $=(N_1\geq A_1')\wedge(N_1<A_3)\wedge(N_0\geq B_2)$. Rule(4') $=(N_1<A_2)\wedge(N_0<B_2)$. $A_i$ and $B_i$ are threshold values for $N_0$ and $N_1$ respy. (Color figure online)

# Author Index

Printed in the United States
by Baker & Taylor Publisher Services